The World's Navies

The World's NAVIES

General Editor **Chris Chant**

David & Charles Newton Abbot London

© Talos Publishing Ltd 1979
4 Chillingworth Road, London, N7 8QJ

British Library Cataloguing in Publication Data

The world's navies.
  1. Navies – Dictionaries
  359'.003   VA40

  ISBN 0–7153–7689–6

Typeset and printed in Great Britain
by Redwood Burn Limited, Trowbridge and Esher
for David & Charles (Publishers) Limited
Brunel House   Newton Abbot   Devon

Contents

Introduction

The World's Navies is intended as a manageable but nonetheless comprehensive guide to the navies of the world at the beginning of 1979, and it is hoped that periodic editions of the book will enable the information to be updated in the light of developments. Unfortunately, it is in the very nature of such works that they are inherently 'out-of-date', perhaps by only a few months, as continued procurement of new equipment, the phasing out of older equipment, and attrition ('natural' in the event of disasters such as collision at sea or running aground, and 'operational' in the event of hostilities) alter the situation. At the same time, political and economic fluctuations alter the number and types of ships and other weapons on order (a case in point being Iran in the aftermath of the Shah's downfall at the beginning of 1979: the interim government headed by Mr Bakhtiar cut Iran's order for US 'Spruance' class guided-missile destroyers from four to two, and the current Islamic government, beset by internal problems associated with left-wing guerrillas and a determination to move out of the free West's sphere of influence, is likely to cut the remaining orders still further). More changes in naval strengths have resulted from the overrunning of Kampuchea by Vietnam and other small-scale conflicts, while economic considerations have made difficult the forecasting of future naval equipment orders. In general, however, the naval strengths and types quoted in the present work are up-to-date as far as the beginning of 1979.

For a variety of reasons it has been impossible to cover every type of ship and weapon currently operated by the world's navies, and an editorial selection of the types covered has therefore been inevitable. The types covered, accordingly, are basically the following:

    (i) aircraft-carriers (attack and anti-submarine warfare)
    (ii) anti-submarine cruisers
    (iii) cruisers (over 10,000 tons/10,160 tonnes)
    (iv) light cruisers (between 5,000 tons/5,080 tonnes and 10,000 tons/ 10,160 tonnes)
    (v) destroyers (between 3,000 tons/3,048 tonnes and 5,000 tons/5,080 tonnes)
    (vi) frigates (between 1,100 tons/1,118 tonnes and 3,000 tons/3,048 tonnes)
    (vii) submarines
    (viii) corvettes (between 500 tons/508 tonnes and 1,100 tons/1,118 tonnes)
    (ix) fast attack craft (missile), capable of more than 25 knots
    (x) fast attack craft (gun), capable of more than 25 knots
    (xi) fast attack craft (torpedo), capable of more than 25 knots
    (xii) fast attack craft (patrol), capable of more than 25 knots
    (xiii) large patrol craft (between 100 tons/101.6 tonnes and 500 tons/508 tonnes)
    (xiv) coastal patrol craft (under 100 tons/101.6 tonnes)
    (xv) assault ships
    (xvi) minelayers
    (xvii) ocean minesweepers
    (xviii) minehunters
    (xix) coastal minesweepers.

All ships in categories (i) to (v) and (vii) are covered, and representative examples of each class, plus a few important or interesting additional ships or craft, of categories (vi) and (viii) to (xix) are described. With the aid of the index, therefore, the reader can look up the main entry for an ex-US 'Auk' class corvette, and relate these details to the vessels operated by another country. It must be emphasised, however, that substantially different armament may be fitted to the same basic hull design by various users. It should also be noted, moreover, that the classification above (derived from *Jane's Fighting Ships*), is an ideal one, and that some of the distinctions are blurred by the use to which a vessel is put, and the armament carried: this is particularly true of the borderlines between light cruiser/destroyer, frigate/corvette and fast attack craft (patrol)/large patrol craft/coastal patrol craft. The reader should therefore not be surprised to find the occasional anomaly.

Apart from ships, the other main weapons covered in this work are:

(i) missiles (shipborne surface-to-air, surface-to-surface and underwater-to-surface)
(ii) torpedoes.

The tabular sections give the numbers and types of aircraft operated by the various countries' naval air arms, and these can be found in the companion volume, *The World's Air Forces*.

The volume is arranged alphabetically by country, and consists of two main 'strands':

(a) the tabular sections detailing the numbers and types of ships, craft and aircraft operated by each country's navy, together with an organisational break-down of the more important navies
(b) the technical sections giving details of the ships, craft, torpedoes and missiles; these have in general been arranged in the order of the categories (i) to (xix) above, though exceptions have been made where a particular type of vessel plays an especially important part in the nation's maritime defence planning (this aspect is most apparent in the sections dealing with the Union of Soviet Socialist Republics, the United Kingdom and the United States of America, and to a lesser extent in those sections dealing with China and France – all countries which have or soon will have submarines capable of launching ballistic thermonuclear missiles).

A third, occasional strand is provided by brief examinations of the nature and capabilities of the world's most important (not necessarily largest) navies.

Each technical entry has been designed to provide an easily assimilable, but relatively complete, quantity of data, to allow the reader to assess the capabilities of the ship, together with brief notes designed to elucidate the ship's or missile's history, design and variants.

Within each technical entry for ships there are 12 sub-headings:

(i) *Class* indicates the class of ship to which the vessel belongs, thus allowing the reader to compare the ship with others of the same class used by different nations
(ii) *Displacement* indicates the 'weight' of the vessel, in four different categories:
  (a) light: actual minimum displacement in seagoing condition
  (b) standard: weight of vessel fully manned and equipped, with stores and ammunition, but without reserve feed-water or fuel (also known as the Washington Treaty tonnange)
  (c) normal
  (d) full load: as (b) but with reserve feed-water and fuel
  (for submarines, the two usual displacement figures are surfaced and dived tonnages, which are self explanatory.)
(iii) *Dimensions* indicate the overall length, maximum beam and maximum draught of the vessel unless otherwise specified
(iv) *Armament* indicates the vessel's weapons in five categories:
  (a) guns (excluding saluting guns), with the number of weapons in each calibre, and generally their mountings
  (b) missiles, with their launchers, functions and reserve rounds
  (c) A/S weapons, designed for operations against submarines: these are mostly small-calibre torpedo tubes (sometimes listed under torpedo tubes), depth-charge racks, depth-charge throwers (DCTs), rocket-launchers and various types of pattern-bomb throwers
  (d) torpedo tubes, usually for anti-ship work, and listed by calibre and number of tubes in a mounting
  (e) aircraft
(v) *Radar and electronics* indicate the types and functions of the radar and other electronic combat aids carried by the ship
(vi) *Sonar* indicates the type of sonar (asdic) carried
(vii) *Powerplant* indicates the type and power of the ship's engines, and the number of shafts driven
(viii) *Speed* indicates the vessel's speed in knots
(ix) *Range* indicates the vessel's range at a given speed or speeds
(x) *Crew* indicates the vessel's complement: where the sign (+) is used, the

figure before the sign shows the number of officers carried, that after
the sign the number of other ranks carried

(xi) *Used* indicates the countries which use that class of vessel

(xii) *Notes* give further information about alterations, sister-ships, and key
dates.

The sub-headings for torpedoes are fully self-explanatory, but those for missiles
may need some amplification:

(i) *Type* indicates the function of the missile

(ii) *Guidance* indicates the principle and method by which the missile is
guided in flight

(iii) *Dimensions* are self-explanatory

(iv) *Booster* indicates the method by which the missile is accelerated at
launch towards cruising speed

(v) *Sustainer* indicates the method by which the missile is maintained at
cruising speed

(vi) *Warhead* indicates the nature and weight of the warhead

(vii) *Weights* are self-explanatory

(viii) *Performance* indicates the missile's speed, range and (where relevant)
the circular error probable (CEP) or the radius of the circle within
which half the missiles fired at the same target might be expected to fall

(ix) *Used* indicates user nations

(x) *Notes* give a brief summary of the missile's history and variant, where
applicable.

All measurements are given in Imperial and metric equivalents, the following
conversion factors having been used:

ton to tonne: multiply by 1.016
inch to centimetre: multiply by 2.54
inch to millimetre: multiply by 25.4
foot to metre: divide by 3.2808
mile to kilometre: multiply by 1.6094
pound to kilogramme: divide by 2.2046
(NB: 1 knot = 1.1515 mph = 1.85 kph)

Where the compiler of the technical sections has been unable to find an exact
figure, or where sources conflict, he has left the sub-heading blank, so that the
reader may fill in the space for himself should he be able to find a figure which
satisfies him. In this context, the publishers would be most grateful for any
comments on the book and for any further information that readers may be able
to supply.

Albania

3,000 men (1,000 conscripts)

SS:
3 Whiskey

Corvettes:
4 Kronshtadt

Light Forces:
4 Hoku FAC(M)
32 Hu Chwan FAH(T)
6 Shanghai II FAC(G)
6 P-4 FAC(T)

Mine Warfare Forces:
2 T-43
6 T-301
10 PO 2

Auxiliaries:
4 tankers
c 20 others

'Kronshtadt' class corvette (4)

Class: 4 ex-Russian ships
Displacement: 310 tons (315 tonnes) standard; 380 tons (386 tonnes) full load
Dimensions: Length 170 ft 7 in (52.0 m)
Beam 21 ft 6 in (6.5 m)
Draught 9 ft (2.7 m)
Armament:
Guns 1 85-mm (3.5-in)
2 37-mm
6 12.7-mm machine-guns (twin mounts)
Missile systems
none
A/S weapons
2 DC projectors; 2 DC rails; 2 5-tube rocket-launchers
Torpedo tubes
none
Aircraft
none
Radar and electronics: 'Ball Gun' surface search, 'Neptun' navigation and 'High Pole' IFF radars
Sonar: 'Tamir'
Powerplant: 3 diesels, delivering 3,300 bhp to three shafts
Speed: 24 knots
Range: 1,500 miles (2,414 km) at 12 knots
Crew: 65
Used also by: China, Cuba, Indonesia, Romania
Notes: All four ships transferred from the USSR in 1958. Two were returned for updating in 1960, and the other two in 1961. The ships are fitted for minelaying with two rails and about eight mines.

'Hu Chwan' class fast attack hydrofoil (torpedo) (32)

Class: 32 ex-Chinese craft
Displacement: 45 tons (45.7 tonnes)
Dimensions: Length 71 ft (21.8 m)
Beam 14 ft 6 in (4.5 m)
Draught 3 ft 1 in (0.9 m)
Armament:
Guns 2 14.5-mm machine-guns in a twin mounting
Missile systems
none
A/S weapons
none
Torpedo tubes
2 533-mm (21-in)
Aircraft
none
Radar and electronics: 'Skinhead' target acquisition radar
Sonar:
Powerplant: 3 M50 diesels, delivering 3,600 hp to two shafts
Speed: 55 knots
Range:
Crew:
Used also by: China, Pakistan, Romania, Tanzania
Notes: These craft ride on foils forward while the stern planes. Known transfers were as follows: 6 in 1968, 15 in 1969, 2 in 1970, 7 in 1971 and 2 in 1974.

'Shanghai II' class fast attack craft (6)

Class: 6 ex-Chinese craft
Displacement: 120 tons (121.9 tonnes) standard; 155 tons (157.5 tonnes) full load
Dimensions: Length 128 ft (39.0 m)
Beam 18 ft (5.5 m)
Draught 5 ft 7 in (1.7 m)
Armament:
Guns 4 37-mm in twin mountings
4 25-mm in twin mountings
Missile systems
none
A/S weapons
8 DCs
Torpedo tubes
none
Aircraft
none
Radar and electronics: 'Skinhead' target acquisition radar
Sonar:
Powerplant: 4 diesels, delivering 4,800 hp
Speed: 30 knots
Range:
Crew: 25
Used also by: Cameroon, China, Pakistan, Sierra Leone, Sri Lanka
Notes: The first four craft were transferred in the middle of 1974, the last two following in 1975.

Algeria

3,800 men

Light Forces:
6 SO I PC
6 Komar FAC(M)
3 Osa I FAC(M)
3 Osa II FAC(M)
10 P-6 FAC(T)
10 Baglietto type FAC(G)

Aircraft:
(3 F 28)

Mine Warfare Forces:
2 T-43

Auxiliaries:
5 others

'Komar' class fast attack craft (missile) (6)

Class: 6 ex-Russian craft (*671–676*)
Displacement: 70 tons (71.12 tonnes) standard; 80 tons (81.3 tonnes) full load
Dimensions: Length 84 ft 2 in (25.7 m)
Beam 21 ft 1 in (6.4 m)
Draught 5 ft (1.5 m)
Armament:
Guns 2 25-mm in a twin mounting

Missile systems
2 SS-N-2 'Styx'
A/S weapons
none
Torpedo tubes
none
Aircraft
none
Radar and electronics: 'Square Tie', 'High Pole' and 'Dead Duck'
Sonar:
Powerplant: 4 diesels, delivering 4,800 bhp to four shafts
Speed: 40 knots
Range: 400 miles (644 km) at 30 knots
Crew: 20
Used also by: China, Cuba, Egypt, Indonesia, Syria, Vietnam
Notes: Handed over in 1967.

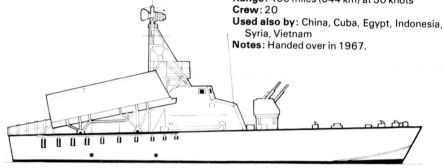

'Osa I and II' class fast attack craft (missile) (6)

Class: 3 ex-Russian craft (*R167, R267, R367*) and 3 others (Osa II)
Displacement: 165 tons (167.65 tonnes) standard; 200 tons (203.2 tonnes) full load
Dimensions: Length 128 ft 8 in (39.3 m)
Beam 25 ft 1 in (7.7 m)
Draught 5 ft 11 in (1.8 m)
Armament:
Guns 4 30-mm in twin mountings
Missile systems
4 SS-N-2 'Styx'

A/S weapons
none
Torpedo tubes
none
Aircraft
none
Radar and electronics: 'Square Tie', 'Drum Tilt', 'High Pole' and 'Square Head'
Sonar:
Powerplant: 3 diesels, delivering 13,000 bhp
Speed: 32 knots
Range: 800 miles (1,288 km) at 25 knots
Crew: 25
Used also by: Bulgaria, Cuba, East Germany, Egypt, India, Iraq, North Korea, Syria, USSR
Notes: All three Osa Is were handed over in 1967, and the three Osa IIs in 1976–77.

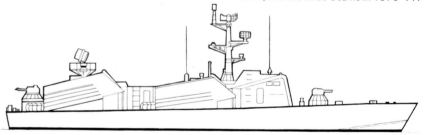

Angola

1,500 men

Light Forces:
4 Argos PC
2 Jupiter PC
4 Bellatrix PC
1 Zhuk PC

Auxiliaries:
2 Alfange LCT
5 LCU (Russian)

'Argos' class large patrol craft (4)

Class: ex-*Lira* (P361); ex-*Pegaso* (P362); ex-*Escorpiao* (P375); ex-*Centauro* (P1130), all ex-Portuguese craft
Displacement: 180 tons (182.9 tonnes) standard; 210 tons (213.4 tonnes) full load
Dimensions: Length 136 ft 10 in (41.6 m)
Beam 20 ft 6 in (6.2 m)
Draught 7 ft (2.2 m)

Armament:
Guns 2 40-mm
Missile systems
none
A/S weapons
none
Torpedo tubes
none
Aircraft
none
Radar and electronics:
Sonar:
Powerplant: 2 Maybach MTU diesels, delivering 1,200 bhp

Speed: 17 knots
Range:
Crew: 24
Used only by: Angola
Notes: The first two were built by Arsenal do Alfeite, Lisbon, and the second pair by Estaleiros Navais de Viano do Castelo. Commissioned into Portuguese service between 1963 and 1965. It is reported that *Argos, Dragao* and *Orion* of the same type have been handed over to Angola for cannibalization.

Anguilla

(Royal St Christopher, Nevis and Anguilla Police Force)

Light Forces:
1 Fairey Huntsman PC

Argentina

32,900 men (12,000 conscripts) including air arm and marine force

CV:
1 Colossus

Cruisers:
2 Brooklyn (CL)

Destroyers:
1 Type 42 (+1)
3 Fletcher
3 Allen M. Sumner
1 Gearing FRAM II

Corvettes:
2 King
4 ATA type
2 ATF type
1 Bouchard

SS:
2 Salta (Type 209) (+2)
2 Guppy 1A and II

Amphibious Forces:
1 LSD
1 LST
3 LST type
1 LCT type
27 LCVP

Light Forces:
2 Type 148 FAC(M) (+1)
2 Type TNC 45 FAC(G)
3 Lynch PC
3 patrol craft
2 Higgins FAC(T)

Mine Warfare Forces:
6 Ton

Naval Air Force (4,000):
1 FB sqn with 15 A-4Q.
1 MR sqn with 6 S-2A/E, 10 SP-2H, 3 HU-16B, ? PBY-5A
18 transports
17 utility
21 (+3) helicopters
29 (+12) trainers

Marine Force (7,000):
5 bns
1 cdo bn
1 fd arty bn
1 AD regiment
Support forces

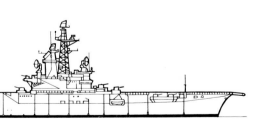

'Colossus' class aircraft-carrier (1)

Class: *Veinticinco de Mayo* (V2), ex-Dutch *Karel Doorman*, ex-British *Venerable*
Displacement: 15,892 tons (16,147 tonnes) standard; 19,896 tons (20.216 tonnes) full load
Dimensions: Length 693 ft 2 in (211.3 m)
Beam 80 ft (24.4 m), Width 121 ft 4 in (37.0 m)
Draught 25 ft (7.6 m)
Armament:
Guns 9 40-mm Bofors L70
Missile systems
none
A/S weapons
none
Torpedo tubes
none
Aircraft
21
Radar and electronics: HSA LW-01 and -08 warning radars, plus DA-08 tactical and ZW navigation radars; Ferranti CAAIS with Plessey Super-CAAIS display electronics
Sonar:
Powerplant: 4 3-drum boilers supplying steam to Parsons geared turbines, delivering 40,000 shp to two shafts
Speed: 24¼ knots
Range: 12,000 miles (19,313 km) at 14 knots; 6,200 miles (9,978 km) at 23 knots
Crew: 1,500
Used also by: Brazil
Notes: Built by Cammell Laird at Birkenhead and commissioned into British service in 1945. Sold to Argentina by the Netherlands in 1968. Appearance altered considerably by raked funnel, lattice mast and modified 'island'.

'Brooklyn' class cruiser (2)

Class: *General Belgrano* (C4), ex-*17 de Octubre*, ex-*Phoenix* (CL46); *Nueve de Julio* (C5), ex-*Boise* (CL47)
Displacement: 10,800 tons (10,973 tonnes) standard and 13,645 tons (13,864 tonnes) full load for *General Belgrano*; 10,500 tons (10,668 tonnes) standard and 13,645 tons (13,684 tonnes) full load for *Nueve de Julio*
Dimensions: Length 608 ft 4 in (185.4 m)
Beam 69 ft (21.0 m)
Draught 24 ft (7.3 m)
Armament:
Guns 15 6-in (152-mm) in triple mountings
8 5-in (127-mm); 6 5-in in *Nueve de Julio*
2 40-mm twins; 4 40-mm twins in *Nueve de Julio*
Missile systems
2 quadruple Sea Cat launchers (*General Belgrano* only)

A/S weapons
none
Torpedo tubes
none
Aircraft
2 helicopters
Radar and electronics: Signaal LWO and DA search radars, and gunnery radars
Sonar:
Powerplant: 8 Babcock & Wilcox Express boilers supplying steam to Parsons geared turbines, delivering 100,000 shp to four shafts

Speed: 32½ knots (when new)
Range: 7,600 miles (12,231 km) at 15 knots
Crew: 1,200
Used also by: Chile
Notes: Built respectively by New York and Newport News Ship-Building companies, and commissioned into US service in 1939. Bought by Argentina in 1951. Armour as follows: belt 1½–4 in (38–102 mm); decks 2–3 in (51–76 mm); turrets 3–5 in (76–127 mm); conning tower 8 in (203 mm).

Type 42 destroyer (2)

Class: *Hercules* (D28), *Santissima Trinidad* (D29)
Displacement: 3,150 tons (3,201 tonnes) standard; 3,500 tons (3,556 tonnes) full load
Dimensions: Length 410 ft (125.0 m)
Beam 48 ft (14.6 m)
Draught 17 ft (5.2 m)
Armament:
Guns 1 4.5-in (114.3-mm) automatic
2 20-mm Oerlikon
Missile systems
1 twin Sea Dart launcher
A/S weapons
see below

Torpedo tubes
2 triple 12.75-in (324-mm) Mark 32
Aircraft
1 Lynx helicopter
Radar and electronics: Type 965 primary search, Type 992Q general-purpose, two Type 909 trackers and illuminators for the Sea Dart; Type 1006 high-definition surface warning, navigation and helicopter control radars; Plessey-Ferranti ADAWS-4 for information co-ordination
Sonar: Type 184 hull-mounted and Type 162 classification
Powerplant: Rolls-Royce Olympus gas turbines for full power and Rolls-Royce Tyne gas turbines for cruising, delivering 50,000 shp to two shafts

Speed: 30 knots
Range: 4,000 miles (6,438 km) at 18 knots
Crew: 300
Used also by: UK
Notes: *Hercules* was built by Vickers at Barrow-in-Furness, and *Santissima Trinidad* by AFNE in Rio Santiago. The first was commissioned in the middle of 1976, but the completion date of the latter remains uncertain. The electronics provide computer-to-computer data links with *Veinticinco de Mayo*.

14

'Fletcher' class destroyer (3)

Class: *Rosales* (D22), ex-*Stembel*; *Almirante Domecq Garcia* (D23), ex-*Braine*; *Almirante Storni* (D24), ex-*Cowell*
Displacement: 2,100 tons (2,134 tonnes) standard; 3,050 tons (3,099 tonnes) full load
Dimensions: Length 376 ft 6 in (114.8 m)
Beam 39 ft 6 in (12.0 m)
Draught 18 ft (5.5 m)

Armament:
Guns 4 5-in (127-mm)
6 3-in (76-mm)
2 40-mm in D20–22 only
Missile systems
none
A/S weapons
2 Hedgehogs, 1 Mk 3 DC rack; 2 side-launching torpedo racks (D 20–22 only)
Torpedo tubes
1 quadruple 21-in (533-mm) in D20–22; 2 triple 12.75-in (324-mm) Mark 32
Aircraft
none

Radar and electronics: SPS 6 search, SPS 10 tactical, and Mk 25 (with Mk 37 director), Mk 35 (Mk 56), Mk 34 (Mk 63) gunnery radars
Sonar: SQS 4
Powerplant: 4 Babcock & Wilcox boilers supplying steam to 2 GE or AC geared turbines, delivering 60,000 shp to two shafts
Speed: 35 knots
Range: 6,000 miles (9,656 km) at 15 knots
Crew: 300
Used also by: Brazil, Chile, Greece, Italy, Mexico, Peru, South Korea, Spain, Taiwan, Turkey, West Germany
Notes: All commissioned into US service in 1943. The first two were transferred in 1961, the last two in 1971.

'Allen M. Sumner' class destroyer (3)

Class: *Segui* (D25), ex-*Hank*; *Bouchard* (D26), ex-*Borie*; *Buena Piedra* (D29), ex-*Collett*
Displacement: 2,200 tons (2,235 tonnes) standard; 3,320 tons (3,373 tonnes) full load
Dimensions: Length 376 ft 6 in (114.8 m)
Beam 40 ft 11 in (12.5 m)
Draught 19 ft (5.8 m)
Armament:
Guns 6 5-in (127-mm) in twin mountings
4 3-in (76-mm) in *Segui* only

Missile systems
MM38 Exocet to be fitted
A/S weapons
2 Hedgehogs
Torpedo tubes
2 triple 12.75-in (324-mm) Mark 32
Aircraft
provision for 1 small A/S helicopter (on *Bouchard* only)
Radar and electronics: SPS 6 search, SPS 10 tactical; Mk 25 (with Mk 37 director) and Mk 35 (Mk 56 director) radars (the last on *Segui* only)
Sonar: SQS 30 and SQA 10 (VDS) on *Bouchard*; SQS 30 on *Segui*

Powerplant: 4 boilers supplying steam to 2 General Electric geared turbines, delivering 60,000 shp to two shafts
Speed: 34 knots
Range: 3,865 miles (6,220 km) at 11 knots, 990 miles (1,593 km) at 31 knots
Crew: 291 on *Bouchard*, 331 on *Segui*
Used also by: Brazil, Colombia, Greece, Taiwan, Venezuela
Notes: Commissioned into US service in 1944 and transferred to Argentina in 1972. Two other ships of the same class, *Mansfield* and *Collett*, were transferred in 1974 for cannibalization, *Collett* being commissioned as *Buena Piedra*.

'Gearing FRAM II' class destroyer (1)

Class: *Py* (D27), ex-*Perkins*
Displacement: 2,425 tons (2,464 tonnes) standard; approximately 3,500 tons (3,556 tonnes) full load
Dimensions: Length 390 ft 6 in (119.0 m)
Beam 40 ft 11 in (12.4 m)
Draught 19 ft (5.8 m)
Armament:
Guns 6 5-in (127-mm) in twin mountings
Missile systems
MM38 Exocet to be fitted
A/S weapons
2 Hedgehogs
Torpedo tubes
2 triple 12.75-in (324-mm) Mark 32

Aircraft
provision for a small A/S helicopter
Radar and electronics: SPS 37 air search radar
Sonar: SQS 29
Powerplant: 4 Babcock & Wilcox boilers supplying 2 Westinghouse turbines, delivering 60,000 shp to two shafts
Speed: 31½ knots
Range: 6,150 miles (9,898 km) at 11 knots, 1,475 miles (2,374 km) at 30 knots

Crew: 275
Used also by: Greece, South Korea, Taiwan, Turkey
Notes: Commissioned into US service in 1945 from the Consolidated Steel Corporation's yard. Sold to Argentina in 1973 after Fleet Rehabilitation and Modernization Stage II (FRAM II) conversion.

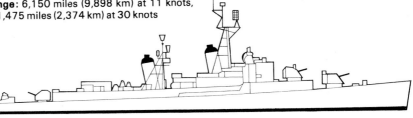

'King' class corvette (2)

Class: *Murature* (P20), *King* (P21)
Displacement: 913 tons (928 tonnes) standard; 1,032 tons (1,049 tonnes) full load
Dimensions: Length 252 ft 8 in (77.0 m)
　　　　　　Beam 29 ft (8.8 m)
　　　　　　Draught 7 ft 6 in (2.3 m)
Armament:
Guns 3 105-mm (4.1-in)
　4 40-mm Bofors L70
5 machine-guns
Missile systems
　none
A/S weapons
　4 DCTs
Torpedo tubes
　none
Aircraft
　none
Radar and electronics:
Sonar:
Powerplant: 2 Werkspoor diesels, delivering 2,500 bhp to two shafts
Speed: 18 knots
Range: 6,000 miles (9,656 km) at 12 knots
Crew: 130
Used only by: Argentina
Notes: Built by Astillero Nav. of Rio Santiago and commissioned in 1946.

'Salta' class (Type 209) submarine (2)

Class: *Salta* (S31), *San Luis* (S32)
Displacement: 980 tons (996 tonnes) surfaced; 1,230 tons (1,250 tonnes) dived
Dimensions: Length 183 ft 5 in (55.9 m)
　　　　　　Beam 20 ft 6 in (6.25 m)
　　　　　　Draught 17 ft 11 in (5.4 m)
Armament:
Guns none
Missile systems
　none
A/S weapons
　none
Torpedo tubes
　8 533-mm (21-in) with reloads
Aircraft
　none
Radar and electronics:
Sonar:
Powerplant: MTU diesels and 4 generators, delivering 5,000 hp to one shaft
Speed: 10 knots surfaced; 22 knots dived
Range:
Crew: 32
Used also by: Colombia, Ecuador, Iran, Peru, Turkey, Uruguay, Venezuela
Notes: Highly successful type of boat, built in sections by Howaldtswerke of Kiel to the Ingenieurkontor of Lübeck IKL 68 design. The sections were assembled in Argentina by Tandanor in Buenos Aires. Two more examples are projected.

'Guppy 1A and II' class submarine (2)

Class: *Santa Fe* (S21), ex-*Catfish*; *Santiago del Estero* (S22), ex-*Chivo*
Displacement: 1,870 tons (1,900 tonnes) surfaced; *Santa Fe* 2,420 tons (2,459 tonnes) and *Santiago* 2,540 tons (2,581 tonnes) dived
Dimensions: Length 307 ft 6 in (93.8 m)
　　　　　　Beam 27 ft 2 in (8.3 m)
　　　　　　Draught 18 ft (5.5 m) for *Santa Fe*, 17 ft (5.2 m) for *Santiago*
Armament:
Guns none
Missile systems
　none
A/S weapons
　none
Torpedo tubes
　10 21-in (533-mm)
Aircraft
　none
Radar and electronics:
Sonar:
Powerplant: 3 diesels, delivering 4,800 shp, and 2 electric motors, delivering 5,400 shp to two shafts
Speed: 18 knots surfaced; 15 knots dived
Range: 12,000 miles (19,313 km) at 10 knots
Crew: 82–84
Used also by: Brazil, Peru, Taiwan, Turkey, Venezuela
Notes: Both built by the Electric Boat Company and commissioned into US service in 1945. *Catfish* was modernised in the 1948–50 Guppy II programme, and *Chivo* under the 1951 Guppy 1A programme. Both boats were sold to Argentina in 1971.

Type TNC 45 class fast attack craft (gun) (2)

Class: *Intrepida* (P85), *Indomita* (P86)
Displacement: 268 tons (272.3 tonnes)
Dimensions: Length 148 ft 11½ in (45.4 m)
　　　　　　Beam 24 ft 3⅓ in (7.4 m)
　　　　　　Draught 7 ft 6½ in (2.3 m)
Armament:
Guns 1 76-mm (3-in) OTO Melara
　2 40-mm Bofors
Missile systems
　1 twin 81-mm Oerlikon launcher
A/S weapons
　none
Torpedo tubes
　2 533-mm (21-in) for wire-guided torpedoes
Aircraft
　none
Radar and electronics: Hollandse Signaal WM20 fire-control radar
Sonar:
Powerplant: 4 diesels, delivering 12,000 hp to four shafts
Speed: 40 knots
Range:
Crew: 35
Used only by: Argentina
Notes: The two craft were ordered in 1970 and built by Lürssen of Vegesack. Commissioned in the second half of 1974.

'Lynch' class large patrol craft (3)

Class: *Lynch* (GC21), *Toll* (GC22), *Erezcano* (GC23)
Displacement: 100 tons (101.61 tonnes) normal; 117 tons (118.9 tonnes) full load
Dimensions: Length 90 ft (27.5 m)
　　　　　　Beam 19 ft (5.8 m)
　　　　　　Draught 6 ft (1.8 m)
Armament:
Guns 1 20-mm
Missile systems
　none
A/S weapons
　none
Torpedo tubes
　none
Aircraft
　none
Radar and electronics:
Sonar:
Powerplant: 2 Maybach diesels, delivering 2,700 hp
Speed: 22 knots
Range:
Crew: 16
Used only by: Argentina
Notes: Built by AFNE at Rio Santiago, and commissioned between 1964 and 1967. Used by the *Prefectura Naval Argentina*.

Australia

The Royal Australian Navy

Australia has a very long coastline, many island dependencies, and two major sets of treaty obligations. Considering these factors, the Royal Australian Navy seems small in numbers and reserves, but relatively high in quality and general flexibility. This is particularly important in view of Australia's need to extend naval assistance to Christmas Island, the Cocos (Keeling) Islands, the Coral Sea Islands, Norfolk Island, Papua-New Guinea, Malaysia and Singapore (under the Five-Power defence arrangement of 1971), and to American and New Zealand territories in the Pacific (under the ANZUS tripartite treaty of 1951).

Military service in the Royal Australian Navy is voluntary, and its 16,342 men constitute 23.3 per cent of the manpower strength of Australia's armed forces (regulars only). Considering the extent of Australia's maritime interests, the provision of only 12 large patrol craft ('Attack' class) seems quite small. However, given that the total defence budget is only 2.64 per cent of the gross national product, it is perhaps inevitable that Australia should concentrate her naval resources in a flexible offensive force, centred round the somewhat elderly, but extensively updated, carrier *Melbourne*, which embarks eight A-4 attack aircraft, six S-2 ASW aircraft, and 10 helicopters with SAR/ASW

capability. *Melbourne* is partnered by the three 'Perth' class ASW destroyers, which have Ikara A/S weapons and Tartar SAM missiles for fleet defence. This combination is as powerful as any force the Royal Australian Navy is likely to encounter in the foreseeable future. The A/S forces also include the six 'River' class frigates, soon to be joined by three 'FFG7' (or 'Oliver Hazard Perry') class frigates, the latter being very flexible in their tactical capabilities. This leaves, for patrol and attack on surface targets, two 'Daring' class destroyers and six 'Oberon' class submarines, supported by the eight attack aircraft embarked on *Melbourne*.

Australia therefore has a limited, but perhaps adequate, navy. What it lacks, however, is the reserve to ensure that the navy can operate in war, sustain losses, and still maintain its role. There are only 925 reservists with training obligations, and no aircraft or ship reserves worthy of note. The burden on the patrol forces should be eased soon by the addition of 15 more patrol craft.

16,342 men including air arm

CV:
1 Majestic

Destroyers:
3 Perth
2 Daring

Frigates:
(3 Oliver Hazard Perry)
6 River

SS:
6 Oxley (Oberon)

Mine Warfare Forces
3 Modified Ton

Light Forces:
12 Attack PC
(15 PC)

Auxiliaries:
1 Daring DD training ship
1 oiler
1 DD tender
6 LCH
(1 heavy lift ship)
4 survey ships (+1)
others

Fleet Air Arm:
1 FB sqn with 8 A-4G
2 ASW sqns with 3 S-2E, 11 S-2G
1 ASW/SAR sqn with 7 Sea King, 2 Wessex
1 helicopter sqn with 5 UH-1H, 2 Bell 206B, 4 Wessex
1 training sqn with 8 MB 326H, 3 TA-4G, 5 A-4G
2 HS748 FCM trainers

'Modified Majestic' class aircraft-carrier (1)

Class: *Melbourne* (21), ex-British *Majestic*
Displacement: 16,000 tons (16,257 tonnes) standard; 19,966 tons (20,287 tonnes) full load
Dimensions: Length 701 ft 6 in (213.8 m)
Beam 80 ft 2 in (24.5 m), flight-deck width 126 ft (38.4 m)
Draught 25 ft 6 in (7.8 m)
Armament:
Guns 12 40-mm Bofors (4 twin and 4 single)
Missile systems
none

A/S weapons
none
Torpedo tubes
none
Aircraft
about 17
Radar and electronics: HSA LW-02 early warning for aircraft direction, Type 293 target indicator and surface warning, and carrier-controlled approach radars; Plessey tactical displays and electronic warfare and intelligence systems
Sonar:
Powerplant: 4 Admiralty 3-drum boilers supplying steam to Parsons single-

reduction geared turbines, delivering 42,000 shp to two shafts
Speed: 23 knots
Range: 12,000 miles (19,313 km) at 14 knots; 6,200 miles (9,978 km) at 23 knots
Crew: 1,335 as a carrier; 75 + 995 as flagship
Used only by: Australia
Notes: Built by Vickers Armstrong at Barrow-in-Furness and commissioned into Australian service in 1955. The balance of the various types of aircraft carried can be varied according to tactical requirements.

'Perth' class guided missile destroyer (3)

Class: *Perth* (38), *Hobart* (39), *Brisbane* (41)
Displacement: 3,370 tons (3,424 tonnes) standard; 4,618 tons (4,692 tonnes) full load
Dimensions: Length 437 ft (132.2 m)
Beam 47 ft 1 in (14.3 m)
Draught 20 ft 1 in (6.1 m)
Armament:
Guns 2 5-in (127-mm)
Missile systems
1 Tartar launcher
A/S weapons
2 Ikara launchers

Torpedo tubes
2 triple 12.75-in (324-mm) Mark 32
Aircraft
none
Radar and electronics: SPS 52 three-dimensional, SPS 40 air search and SPS 10 surface search radars; Naval Combat Data System in *Perth* (to be fitted to others during current modernization programme)

Sonar: SQS 23F, AN/UQC 1D/E and Type 189
Powerplant: 4 Foster Wheeler 'D' type boilers supplying steam to 2 General Electric double-reduction geared turbines, delivering 70,000 shp to two shafts
Speed: 35 knots

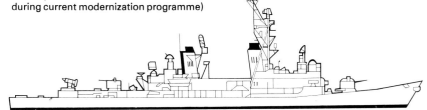

Range: 4,500 miles (7,242 km) at 15 knots;
2,000 miles (3,219 km) at 30 knots
Crew: 21+312
Used only by: Australia
Notes: Generally similar to the US 'Charles F. Adams' class and built by the Defoe Shipbuilding company at Bay City, Michigan, between 1962 and 1966. The first two ships were commissioned into Australian service in 1965 and the last in 1967. The superstructure is made of aluminium.

'Daring' class destroyer (2)

Class: Vendetta (08), Vampire (11)
Displacement: 2,800 tons (2,845 tonnes) standard; 3,600 tons (3,658 tonnes) full load
Dimensions: Length 388 ft 6 in (118.4 m)
Beam 43 ft (13.1 m)
Draught 12 ft 10 in (3.9 m)
Armament:
Guns 6 4.5-in (115-mm) in twin mountings
6 40-mm
Missile systems
none
A/S weapons
1 3-barrelled Limbo mortar
Torpedo tubes
none

Aircraft
none
Radar and electronics: HSA LW-02 early warning, 8GR301 and M22 fire-control radars
Sonar: Type 162, 170, 174, 185
Powerplant: 2 Foster Wheeler boilers supplying steam to English Electric geared turbines, delivering 54,000 shp to two shafts
Speed: 30½ knots

Range: 3,700 miles (5,955 km) at 20 knots
Crew: 14+306
Used also by: Peru
Notes: Similar design to the British 'Darings', but built in Australia between 1949 and 1959. Sistership Voyager was sunk in collision in 1964.

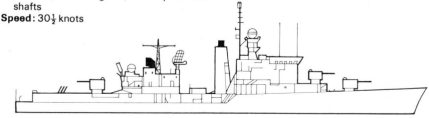

18

'Oliver Hazard Perry' (FFG 7) class guided missile frigate (3)

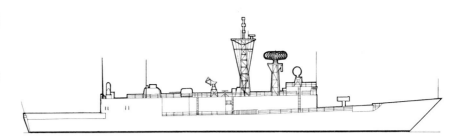

Class: three ships, as yet unnamed
Displacement: 3,605 tons (3,663 tonnes) full load
Dimensions: Length 445 ft (135.6 m)
Beam 45 ft (13.7 m)
Draught 24 ft 6 in (7.5 m)
Armament:
Guns 1 76-mm OTO Melara
Missile systems
1 Mark 13 Model 4 launcher for Standard/Harpoon missiles
A/S weapons
2 triple 12.75-in (324-mm) Mark 32 tubes
Torpedo tubes
as above
Aircraft
2 ASW helicopters

Radar and electronics: AN/SPS 49 long-range search and early warning, AN/SPS 55 search and navigation radars, plus Mark 92/STIR fire-control system for guns and missiles
Sonar: SQS 56
Powerplant: 2 General Electric LM 2500 gas turbines, delivering 40,000 shp to one shaft

Speed: 28+ knots
Range: 4,500 miles (7,242 km) at 20 knots
Crew: 185–190
Used only by: Australia
Notes: Two ships have been ordered from the USA, for delivery in 1981, and the purchase of a third vessel has been confirmed. The ships are of the basic 'Oliver Hazard Perry' type.

'River' class frigate (6)

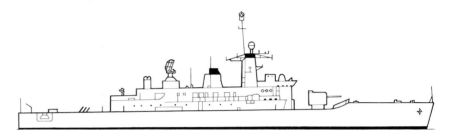

Class: *Yarra* (45), *Parramatta* (46), *Stuart* (48), *Derwent* (49), *Swan* (50), *Torrens* (53)
Displacement: 2,100 tons (2,134 tonnes) standard; 2,700 tons (2,743 tonnes) full load)
Dimensions: Length 370 ft (112.8 m)
Beam 41 ft (12.5 m)
Draught 17 ft 3 in (5.3 m)
Armament:
Guns 2 4.5-in (115-mm)
Missile systems
1 quadruple Sea Cat launcher
A/S weapons
1 Ikara launcher
1 3-barrelled Limbo launcher (not *Yarra*)
Torpedo tubes
none
Aircraft
none

Radar and electronics: HSA LW-02 early-warning, Type 293 air/surface warning (*Swan* and *Torrens* have 8GR-301 warning radar) and MRS or HSA fire-control systems
Sonar: Type 162, 170, 177m, 185, 189 in *Swan* and *Torrens*
Powerplant: 2 Babock & Wilcox boilers supplying steam to 2 double-reduction geared turbines, delivering 30,000 shp to two shafts
Speed: 30 knots

Range: 3,400 miles (5,472 km) at 12 knots
Crew: 13+234 in *Swan* and *Torrens*; 13+237 in others
Used also by: Burma, Dominican Republic, Sri Lanka
Notes: Built by Williamstown Naval Dockyard in Melbourne, and by Cockatoo Island Dockyard in Sydney between 1957 and 1971. The first four are basically the same as the British Type 12 frigates, and the last pair to the Leander class frigates. The class is in the process of modernization.

'Oxley' class submarine (6)

Class: *Oxley* (57), *Otway* (59), *Onslow* (60), *Orion* (61), *Otama* (62), *Ovens* (70)
Displacement: 2,196 tons (2,231 tonnes) surfaced; 2,417 tons (2,456 tonnes) dived
Dimensions: Length 295 ft 6 in (90.1 m)
Beam 26 ft 6 in (8.1 m)
Draught 18 ft (5.5 m)
Armament:
Guns none
Missile systems
none
A/S weapons
none
Torpedo tubes
8 21-in (533-mm)
Aircraft
none
Radar and electronics: Type 1006 high-definition navigation radar
Sonar: Type 187C attack, Type 197 interception, Type 719 torpedo warning and Type 2007 long-range passive search
Powerplant: 2 Admiralty Standard Range diesels, delivering 3,600 bhp, and 2 electric motors, delivering 6,000 shp to two shafts
Speed: 16 knots surfaced; 18 knots dived
Range: 12,000 miles (19,313 km) at 10 knots
Crew: 7+55
Used also by: Brazil, Canada, Chile, UK

Notes: Built by Scotts' Shipbuilding & Engineering company at Greenock between 1965 and 1977 to the British 'Oberon' class design. All the boats are to be modernized with advanced radar, sonar and torpedoes.

Modified 'Ton' class minesweeper and minehunter (3)

Class: *Snipe* (1102), ex-*Alcaston*; *Curlew* (1121), ex-*Chediston*; *Ibis* (1183), ex-*Singleton*
Displacement: 375 tons (381 tonnes) standard; 445 tons (452 tonnes) full load
Dimensions: Length 152 ft (46.3 m)
Beam 28 ft 10 in (8.8 m)
Draught 8 ft 2 in (2.5 m)
Armament:
Guns 2 40-mm (*Ibis*)
1 40-mm (*Snipe* and *Curlew*)
Missile systems
none
A/S weapons
none
Torpedo tubes
none
Aircraft
none
Radar and electronics: Type 975 surface warning radar
Sonar: Type 163 (except *Ibis*)
Powerplant: 2 Napier Celtic diesels, delivering 3,000 bhp to two shafts
Speed: 16 knots
Range: 2,300 miles (3,702 km) at 13 knots; 3,500 miles (5,633 km) at 8 knots
Crew: 4+30 (*Ibis*); 3+35 (others)
Used also by: UK

Notes: Built between 1952 and 1954 and sold to Australia in 1961. *Curlew* and *Snipe* were turned into minehunters in 1967–8 and 1969–70 respectively.

'Attack' class large patrol craft (12)

Class: *Acute* (81), *Adroit* (82), *Advance* (83), *Ardent* (87), *Assail* (89), *Attack* (89), *Aware* (91), *Barbette* (97), *Barricade* (98), *Bombard* (99), *Buccaneer* (100), *Bayonet* (101)
Displacement: 146 tons (148.3 tonnes) full load
Dimensions: Length 107 ft 6 in (32.8 m)
Beam 20 ft (6.1 m)
Draught 7 ft 4 in (2.2 m)

Armament:
Guns 1 40-mm
2 machine-guns
(*Aware* is unarmed)
Missile systems
none
A/S weapons
none
Torpedo tubes
none
Aircraft

Radar and electronics: Type 975 surface warning radar (to be replaced soon by RM916)

Sonar:

Powerplant: 2 Paxman 16 YJCM diesels, delivering 3,500 hp to two shafts

Speed: 24 knots

Range: 1,220 miles (1,963 km) at 13 knots

Crew: 3+16

Used also by: Indonesia

Notes: *Arrow* was lost in a cyclone in 1974. The class was built between 1967 and 1969 by Evans Deakin Ltd and Walkers Ltd. Mostly used for fishery patrol and rescue work off northern Australia.

Ikara

Type: guided missile carrying a homing torpedo (Mark 44 typical)

Guidance: radio command by computer with aid of sonar and radar information

Launch method: ramp

Dimensions: Length about 10 ft 2 in (3.1 m)
Span about 4 ft 11 in (1.5 m)

Weight:

Engine: dual-thrust rocket motor

Speed:

Range:

Warhead: as for torpedo carried

Used also by: Brazil, UK

Notes: Highly effective method of dispatching a torpedo to the optimum position over the target area, where it descends to the water by parachute and then homes on the submarine using its own terminal homing system. Information on the submarine's movements are fed to the shipboard computer continuously, and this latter steers the missile in flight. The launch ship's computer can also operate from information supplied by other ships and by helicopters.

Austria

27 men (under army control)

Riverine Forces:
2 river patrol craft, 10 M3 patrol craft

Bahamas

(under police control)

Patrol Craft:
2 Vosper 31.4-m type
4 Keith Nelson 18.9-m type (+3)

Bahrain

About 150 men (under coastguard control)

Patrol Craft:
1 Fairey Tracker
2 Fairey Spear
1 Cheverton 15.25-m type
3 Cheverton 8.2-m type
2 PC
1 Cheverton Loadmaster amphibian

Bangladesh

3,500 men

Frigates:
1 Type 61 Salisbury
1 Type 41 Leopard

Patrol Craft:
2 Kraljevica PC
2 Akshay class
5 Pabna riverine PC

Auxiliaries:
1 training ship

'Salisbury' class (Type 61) frigate (1)

Class: *Umar Farooq* (F16), ex-*Llandaff*

Displacement: 2,170 tons (2,205 tonnes) standard; 2,408 tons (2,447 tonnes) full load

Dimensions: Length 339 ft 10 in (103.6 m)
Beam 40 ft (12.2 m)
Draught 15 ft 6 in (4.7 m)

Armament:
Guns 2 4.5-in (114-mm) in twin mounting
2 40-mm
Missile systems
none
A/S weapons
1 3-barrelled Squid DC mortar

Radar and electronics: Type 965 long-range surveillance, Type 993 air/surface warning, Type 977Q height-finding, Type 982 target indicator, Type 975 fire-control and navigation radars

Sonar: Type 174 and 170B

Powerplant: 8 ASR diesels, delivering 14,400 bhp to two shafts

Speed: 24 knots

Range: 7,500 miles (12,071 km) at 16 knots; 2,300 miles (3,702 km) at 24 knots

Crew: 14+223

Used also by: UK

Notes: Built by Hawthorn Leslie Ltd at Hebburn-on-Tyne and commissioned into British service in 1958. Transferred to Bangladesh in 1976.

'Leopard' class frigate (1)

Class: *Ali Hyder,* ex-British *Jaguar*
Displacement: 2,300 tons (2,337 tonnes) standard; 2,520 tons (2,560 tonnes) full load
Dimensions: Length 339 ft 9 in (103.6 m)
Beam 40 ft (12.2 m)
Draught 16 ft (4.9 m)
Armament:
Guns 4 4.5-in (114-mm) in twin turrets
1 40-mm
Missile systems
none
A/S weapons
13-barrel Squid mortar
Torpedo tubes
none
Aircraft
none
Radar and electronics: Type 965 air search, Type 275 fire-control, and Type 975 navigation radars
Sonar: Types 174 and 164
Powerplant: 8 Admiralty Standard Range diesels, delivering 14,400 bhp to two shafts
Speed: 24 knots
Range: 7,500 miles (12,070 km) at 16 knots
Crew: 15+220
Used also by: India, UK
Notes: *Jaguar* was built by William Denny & Brothers at Dumbarton between 1953 and 1957, being commissioned into British service in 1959. She was sold to Bangladesh in 1977.

Barbados

61 men (under coastguard control)

Patrol Craft:
1 Guardian 20-m
3 Guardian 12-m

Belgium

The Royal Belgian Navy
Belgium has only a relatively small navy, made up for the most part of minor warships, but this reflects the short length of her coastline, lack of ocean areas in which she has interests, and the fact that her commitments internationally are only to NATO, and those within northern Europe.

The 4,300 men of the Royal Belgian Navy (including 800 conscripts) constitute only 4.94 per cent of the manpower strength of the Belgian armed forces, which receive some 2.48 per cent of the gross national product as a defence budget. With the exception of the four new 'E-71' class general-purpose frigates, most of the navy's budget usually goes to the maintenance and improvement of its mine warfare forces. This is the navy's primary task, for the Belgian ports, together with those of the Netherlands, are the prime ports of entry for US military support for Europe in time of war. Only from these ports can the swift arrival of *matériel* on the North German plain be ensured. In the confined waters at the eastern end of the English Channel, therefore, Belgium's seven MSO Type 498 ocean minehunters, six MSC Type 60 coastal minesweepers and minehunters, and 14 'Herstal' class inshore minesweepers, play a decisive part in NATO's defence plans. To supplement these forces, and to contribute to NATO's general naval strength, Belgium has built four new general-purpose frigates, fitted with sophisticated electronic equipment, and armed with specialist A/S weapons, long-range surface-to-surface missiles, and short-range SAM defences.

Within the limitations of budget and requirements, therefore, Belgium possesses a small but adequate naval force. Naval airpower is limited to five helicopters, but this is not necessarily a hindrance: the Belgian navy is intended for operations in inshore and coastal waters, where land-based airpower can provide more than adequate air cover.

4,300 (800 conscripts)

Frigates:
4 E-71

Mine Warfare Forces:
7 MSO (ex-AM) Type 498
6 MSC (ex-AMS) Type 60
14 Herstal

Patrol Craft:
6 riverine PC

Auxiliaries:
2 support ships
2 research ships
12 others

Aircraft:
3 Alouette III
1 Sikorsky S-58

'E-71' class frigate (4)

Class: *Wielingen* (F910), *Westdiep* (F911), *Wandelaar* (F912), *Westhinder* (F913)
Displacement: 1,880 tons (1,910 tonnes) light; 2,283 tons (2,320 tonnes) deep load
Dimensions: Length 347 ft 9 in (106.0 m)
Beam 40 ft 4 in (12.3 m)
Draught 18 ft 10 in (5.6 m)
Armament:
Guns 1 100-mm (3.9-in)
1 Close-In Weapon System
Missile systems
1 octuple NATO RIM-7H-2 Sea Sparrow SAM launcher
4 MM38 Exocet SSM launcher
A/S weapons
1 sextuple 375-mm (14.76-in) launcher
Torpedo racks
2 533-mm (21-in) for L-5 torpedoes
Aircraft
none
Radar and electronics: air/surface warning, target indicator and navigation radars; HSA (SEWACO 4) integrated weapons control electronics with ECM capability
Sonar: Westinghouse SQS 505A
Powerplant: (CODOG) 1 Rolls-Royce Olympus TM3 gas turbine, delivering 28,000 bhp, and 2 Cockerill CO-240 diesels, delivering 6,000 bhp to two shafts
Speed: 28 knots (18 knots on diesels)
Range: 4,500 miles (7,242 km) at 18 knots
Crew: 14+146
Used only by: Belgium
Notes: Built by Boelwerf of Temse and Cockerill of Hoboken. All four were in service by the end of 1979.

'MSO (ex-AM) Type 498' minehunter (7)

Class: *Van Haverbeke* (M902), ex-*MSO 522*; *A.F. Dufour* (M903), ex-*Lagen*; *De Brouwer* (M904), ex-*Nansen*; *Breydel* (M906), ex-*MSO 504*; *Artevelde* (M907), ex-*MSO 503*; *G. Truffaut* (M908), ex-*MSO 515*; *F. Bovesse* (M909), ex-*MSO 516*
Displacement: 720 tons (732 tonnes) standard; 780 tons (793 tonnes) full load
Dimensions: Length 172 ft 6 in (52.6 m)
Beam 35 ft (10.7 m)
Draught 11 ft (3.4 m)

Armament:
Guns 1 40-mm (only *Artevelde*)
Missile systems
  none
A/S weapons
  none
Torpedo tubes
  none
Aircraft
  none
Radar and electronics:
Sonar: General Electric SQQ 14 (except *Artevelde*)
Powerplant: 2 General Motors diesels, delivering 1,600 bhp to two shafts

Speed: 14 knots
Range: 300 miles (483 km) at 10 knots
Crew: 5+67
Used only by: Belgium
Notes: Built in the US between 1953 and 1960. *De Brouwer* and *A.F. Dufour* were transferred from Norway in 1966, the others from the US between 1956 and 1960. Built of wood and non-magnetic metal, they are capable of sweeping all types of mine. *Artevelde* now used as a diving vessel, though retaining minehunting capacity.

Belize

50 men

Patrol Craft:
2 PC

Bolivia

1,500 men, including marine force

Patrol Craft:
16 PC

Auxiliaries:
1 transport

Brazil

49,000 (3,000 conscripts), including naval air force, marine force and auxiliary corps

CV:
1 Colossus

Destroyers:
6 Niteroi
7 Fletcher
1 Allen M. Sumner
4 Allen M. Sumner FRAM II
2 Gearing FRAM I

SS:
3 Oberon
2 Guppy III
5 Guppy II

Amphibious Forces:
1 LST 511-1152
1 De Soto County LST
7 EDVP
4 LCU
28 LCVP

Patrol Craft:
10 Imperial Marinheiro
2 Pedro Teixeira riverine PC
1 Thornycroft river monitor
3 Roraima river PC

Light Forces:
6 Piratini PC
6 Anchova PC
4 riverine PC

Mine Warfare Forces:
6 Schütze

Auxiliaries:
8 survey ships
1 submarine rescue ship
1 support ship
3 tankers
15 transports
3 floating docks
others

Air Arm:
1 ASW sqn with 5 SH-3D
1 utility helicopter sqn with 5 Whirlwind, 6 Wasp, 1 FH 1110, 2 Bell 47, 18 AB 206B, 2 Lynx
1 training sqn with 10 Hughes 269/ 300
(7 Lynx)

'Colossus' class aircraft-carrier (1)

Class: *Minas Gerais* (A11), ex-British *Vengeance*
Displacement: 15,890 tons (16,145 tonnes) standard; 19,890 tons (20,209 tonnes) full load
Dimensions: Length 695 ft (211.8 m)
  Beam 80 ft (24.4 m), flight-deck width 121 ft (37.0 m)
  Draught 24 ft 6 in (7.5 m)
Armament:
Guns 10 40-mm in 2 quadruple and 1 twin mounting
  2 47-mm saluting
Missile systems
  none
A/S weapons
  none
Torpedo tubes
  none
Aircraft
  20
Radar and electronics: SPS 12 air-surveillance, SPS 4 surface-search, SPS 8B fighter-direction, SPS 8A air-control, SPG 34 gunfire-control, MP 1402 navigation radars
Sonar:
Powerplant: 4 Admiralty boilers supplying steam to Parsons geared turbines, delivering 40,000 shp to two shafts
Speed: 25½ knots
Range: 12,000 miles (19,313 km) at 14 knots; 6,200 miles (9,978 km) at 23 knots
Crew: 1,000 (ship) + 300 (air group)
Used also by: Argentina

Notes: Laid down in November 1942 at Swan, Hunter & Wigham Richardson of Wallsend on Tyne, launched in February 1944 and commissioned into British service in January 1945. Sold to Brazil in December 1956 and refitted in Rotterdam. Commissioned into Brazilian service in December 1960, and since used mostly for A/S duties with fixed- and rotary-winged aircraft.

'Niteroi' class destroyer (6)

Class: *Niteroi* (F40), *Defensora* (F41), *Constituiçao* (F42), *União* (F43), *Independencia* (F44), *Liberal* (F45)

Displacement: 3,200 tons (3,251 tonnes) standard; 3,800 tons (3,861 tonnes) full load

Dimensions: Length 424 ft (129.2 m)
Beam 44 ft 3½ in (13.5 m)
Draught 18 ft (5.5 m)

Armament:
Guns 2 4.5-in (114-mm) Mark 8 in general-purpose version
1 4.5-in (114-mm) Mark 8 in A/S version
2 40 mm
Missile systems
2 twin MM38 Exocet launchers in general-purpose version
1 Ikara launcher in A/S version
2 triple Sea Cat launchers in both versions
A/S weapons
1 375-mm (14.76-in) Bofors twin-tube rocket-launcher and 1 DC rail
Torpedo tubes
2 triple 12.75-in (324-mm) Mark 32
Aircraft
1 WG13 Lynx helicopter

Radar and electronics: Plessey AWS-12 air-warning, Signal ZW-O-6 surface-warning, 2 Selenia RTN-10X weapon-control and tracking, with an Ikara tracking radar in A/S versions; Ferranti CAAIS and Decca ECM fit

Sonar: medium-range EDO 610E and variable-depth EDO 700E (in A/S versions)

Powerplant: (CODOG) 2 Rolls-Royce Olympus gas turbines, delivering 56,000 bhp, and 4 MTU diesels, delivering 18,000 shp

Speed: 30 knots on gas turbines; 22 knots on diesels

Range: 4,200 miles (6,759 km) on 4 diesels; 1,300 miles (2,092 km) on gas turbines

Crew: 200

Used only by: Brazil

Notes: F40, F41, F44, F45 were built by the designers, Vosper Thornycroft, and the last two by Arsenal de Marinho, Rio de Janeiro. *Niteroi* was laid down in June 1972, *Liberal* in May 1975. *Niteroi* was commissioned in November 1976, and *União* was commissioned in October 1978. These Vosper Mark 10 ships are very economical in manpower.

'Fletcher' class destroyer (7)

Class: *Para* (D27), ex-US *Guest* (DD472); *Paraiba* (D28), ex-US *Bennett* (DD473); *Paraña* (D29), ex-US *Cushing* (DD797); *Pernambuco* (D30), ex-US *Hailey* (DD556); *Piaui* (D31), ex-US *Lewis Hancock* (DD675); *Santa Catarina* (D32), ex-US *Irwin* (DD794); *Maranhão* (D33), ex-US *Shields* (DD596)
Displacement: 2,050 tons (2,083 tonnes) standard; 3,050 tons (3,099 tonnes) full load
Dimensions: Length 376 ft 6 in (114.8 m)
Beam 39 ft 3½ in (12.0 m)
Draught 18 ft (5.5 m)
Armament:
Guns 5 5-in (127-mm) in single mountings (*Pernambuco*: 4 5-in)
4 5-in (127-mm) in twin mountings (*Pernambuco* only)
10 40-mm in 2 quadruple and 1 twin mounting (*Para*: 6 40-mm in 3 twin mountings)
Missile systems
1 quadruple Sea Cat (*Maranhão* only)
A/S weapons
2 Hedgehog, 1 DC rack, 2 side-launching torpedo racks (except *Maranhão*) and 2 triple 12.75-in (324-mm) Mark 32 tubes
Torpedo tubes
5 21-in (533-mm) except in *Maranhão*
Aircraft
none
Radar and electronics: SPS 6 search, SPS 10 tactical and I-band fire-control radars
Sonar:
Powerplant: 4 Babcock & Wilcox boilers supplying steam to 2 General Electric geared turbines, delivering 60,000 shp to two shafts
Speed: 35 knots
Range: 5,000 miles (8,047 km) at 15 knots
Crew: 260
Used also by: Argentina, Chile, Greece, Italy, Mexico, Peru, South Korea, Spain, Taiwan, Turkey, West Germany
Notes: The ships were transferred between 1959 and 1968, and bought by Brazil in 1972 and 1973.

'Allen M. Sumner' and 'Allen M. Sumner FRAM II' destroyer (5)

Class: *Mato Grosso* (D34), *Sergipe* (D35), *Alagoas* (D36), *Rio Grande do Norte* (D37) and *Espirito Santo* (D38), ex-US *Compton* (DD705), *James C. Owens* (DD776), *Buck* (DD761), *Strong* (DD758) and *Lowry* (DD770)
Displacement: 2,200 tons (2,235 tonnes) standard; 3,320 tons (3,373 tonnes) full load
Dimensions: Length 376 ft 6 in (114.8 m)
Beam 40 ft 11 in (12.5 m)
Draught 19 ft (5.8 m)
Armament:
Guns 6 5-in (127-mm) in twin mountings
Missile systems
Sea Cat (*Mato Grosso* only)
A/S weapons
2 Hedgehog ahead-firers; DCs (*Mato Grosso* only)
Torpedo tubes
2 triple 12.75-in (324-mm) Mark 32
Aircraft
small helicopter (FRAM II ships only)
Radar and electronics: SPS 6, SPS 10 and Mark 20 director (*Mato Grosso*); SPS 10 and SPS 37 (*Espiritu Santo*); SPS 10 and SPS 40 (rest)
Sonar: SQS 31 (*Mato Grosso*); SQA 10 and SQS 40 (rest)
Powerplant: 4 boilers supplying steam to 2 geared turbines, delivering 60,000 shp to two shafts
Speed: 34 knots
Range: 4,600 miles (7,403 km) at 15 knots; 1,260 miles (2,028 km) at 30 knots
Crew: 274
Used also by: Chile, Colombia, Iran, South Korea, Turkey, Venezuela
Notes: *Mato Grosso* was built by Federal Shipbuilding and commissioned into US service in 1944; the others were built by Bethlehem at San Francisco and San Pedro, commissioning between 1944 and 1946. *Mato Grosso* is a basic Sumner class ship, but the others are FRAM II conversions. All were transferred to Brazil in the early 1970s.

'Gearing FRAM I' destroyer(2)

Class: *Marcilio Dias* (D25) and *Mariz E. Barros* (D26), ex-US *Henry W. Tucker* (DD875) and *Brinkley Bass* (DD887)
Displacement: 2,425 tons (2,464 tonnes) standard; 3,500 tons (3,556 tonnes) full load
Dimensions: Length 390 ft 6 in (119.0 m)
Beam 40 ft 11 in (12.5 m)
Draught 19 ft (5.8 m)
Armament:
Guns 4 5-in (127-mm) in twin mountings
Missile systems
none
A/S weapons
1 octuple ASROC launcher
Torpedo tubes
2 triple 12.75-in (324-mm) Mark 32
Aircraft
facilities for small helicopter
Radar and electronics: SPS 10 surface-search and SPS 40 air-search/surveillance radars
Sonar: SQS 23
Powerplant: 4 Babcock & Wilcox boilers supplying steam to 2 General Electric geared turbines, delivering 60,000 shp to two shafts
Speed: 34 knots
Range: 5,800 miles (9,335 km) at 15 knots
Crew: 14+260

Used also by: Greece, Pakistan, South Korea, Spain, Taiwan, Turkey, USA
Notes: Both ships were built by Consolidated Steel between 1944 and 1945, and commissioned into US service in 1945. Both were transferred to Brazil in December 1973. FRAM = Fleet Rehabilitation And Modernization, I = basic scheme for improved A/S capabilities and provision of helicopter facilities.

'Oberon' class submarine(3)

Class: *Humaita* (S20), *Tonelero* (S21), *Riachuelo* (S22)
Displacement: 1,610 tons (1,636 tonnes) standard; 2,030 tons (2,062 tonnes) surfaced; 2,410 tons (2,449 tonnes) dived
Dimensions: Length 295 ft 6 in (90.1 m)
Beam 26 ft 6 in (8.1 m)
Draught 18 ft (5.5 m)

Armament:
Guns none
Missile systems
none
A/S weapons
none
Torpedo tubes
8 21-in (533-mm)
Aircraft
none
Radar and electronics:

Sonar:
Powerplant: 2 Admiralty Standard diesels, delivering 3,680 shp, and two AEI-English Electric electric motors, delivering 6,000 shp to two shafts
Speed: 12 knots (surfaced); 17 knots (dived)
Range:
Crew: 6+64
Used also by: Australia, Canada, Chile, UK
Notes: All three boats were built between 1970 and 1977 by Vickers at Barrow.

'Guppy III' patrol submarine (2)

Class: *Goiàz* (S15) and *Amazonas* (S16), ex-US *Trumpetfish* (SS425) and *Greenfish* (SS351)
Displacement: 1,975 tons (2,007 tonnes) standard; 2,450 tons (2,489 tonnes) dived
Dimensions: Length 326 ft 6 in (99.4 m)
Beam 27 ft (8.2 m)
Draught 17 ft (5.2 m)

Armament:
Guns none
Missile systems
none
A/S weapons
none
Torpedo tubes
10 21-in (533-mm)
Aircraft
none
Radar and electronics:
Sonar: BQR 2 array and BQR 4 fire-control

Powerplant: 4 diesels, delivering 6,400 hp; 2 electric motors, delivering 5,400 hp to two shafts
Speed: 20 knots surfaced; 15 knots dived
Range:
Crew: 85
Used also by: Greece, Italy, Turkey
Notes: Built by Cramp Shipbuilding and Electric Boat between 1943 and 1945; commissioned into US service in 1946. Both boats were updated in 1960–2, and sold to Brazil in October 1973.

'Guppy II' class submarine (5)

Class: *Guanabara* (S10), ex-US *Dogfish* (SS350); *Rio Grande do Sul* (S11), ex-US *Grampus* (SS523); *Bahia* (S12), ex-US *Sea Leopard* (SS483); *Rio de Janeiro* (S13), ex-*Guanabara*, ex-US *Odax* (SS484); *Ceara* (S13), ex-US *Amberjack* (SS522)
Displacement: 1,870 tons (1,900 tonnes) standard; 2,420 tons (2,459 tonnes) dived
Dimensions: Length 307 ft 6 in (93.8 m)
　　　　　　　Beam 27 ft 2½ in (8.3 m)
　　　　　　　Draught 18 ft (5.5 m)
Armament:
Guns none
Missile systems
　none
A/S weapons
　none
Torpedo tubes
　10 21-in (533-mm)
Aircraft
　none
Radar and electronics:
Sonar:
Powerplant: 3 diesels, delivering 4,800 shp, and 2 electric motors, delivering 5,400 shp to two shafts
Speed: 18 knots (surfaced); 15 knots (dived)
Range: 12,000 miles (19,313 km) at 10 knots surfaced
Crew: 82
Used also by: Argentina, Taiwan, Venezuela
Notes: The five boats were built by Electric Boat, Boston Navy Yard, Portsmouth Navy Yard (2), and Boston Navy Yard respectively between 1944 and 1945, being commissioned into US service in 1945 and 1946. All except *Rio de Janeiro* were modernised to Guppy II standard between 1948 and 1950, with *Rio de Janeiro* being modernised first to Guppy I and then to Guppy II standard. All were transferred to Brazil in 1972 and 1973.

'Piratini' class large patrol craft (6)

Class: *Piratini* (P10), *Piraja* (P11), *Pampeiro* (P12), *Parati* (P13), *Penedo* (P14), *Poti* (P15)
Displacement: 105 tons (106.7 tonnes) standard
Dimensions: Length 95 ft (30.5 m)
　　　　　　　Beam 19 ft (6.1 m)
　　　　　　　Draught 6 ft 6 in (1.9 m)

Armament:
Guns 3 0.5-in (12.7-mm) machine-guns
　1 81-mm mortar
Missile systems
　none
A/S weapons
　none
Torpedo tubes
　none
Aircraft
　none

Radar and electronics:
Sonar: none
Powerplant: 4 diesels, delivering 1,100 bhp
Speed: 17 knots
Range: 1,700 miles (2,736 km) at 12 knots
Crew: 15
Used only by: Brazil
Notes: All were built by Arsenal de Marinha at Rio de Janeiro, being commissioned in 1970 and 1971.

Brunei

292 men (under command of Royal Brunei Regiment)

Light Forces:
3 Perwira
3 Raja Isteri
3 riverine PC

Amphibious Forces:
2 Cheverton Loadmaster
24 fast assault craft

'Pahlawan' class fast attack craft (missile) (1)

Class: *Pahlawan* (PO1)
Displacement: 95 tons (96.5 tonnes) standard; 114 tons (115.8 tonnes) full load
Dimensions: Length 99 ft (30 3 m)
　　　　　　　Beam 24 ft (7.3 m)
　　　　　　　Draught 7 ft (2.2 m)
Armament:
Guns 1 40-mm
　2 20-mm
Missile systems
　2 quadruple SS12 launchers
A/S weapons
　none
Torpedo tubes
　none
Aircraft
　none
Radar and electronics: Decca TM616
Sonar: none
Powerplant: 3 Bristol Siddeley Proteus gas turbines, delivering 12,750 bhp to three shafts, plus 2 diesels for cruising and manoeuvring
Speed: 57 knots
Range: 2,300 miles (3,702 km) at 10 knots; 450 miles (724 km) at 57 knots
Crew: 20
Used only by: Brunei
Notes: Built by Vosper Thornycroft in 1966. Missiles were added in 1972.

Bulgaria

10,000 men (6,000 conscripts) and
15,000 reservists

Frigates:
2 Riga

SS:
2 Romeo

Corvettes:
3 Poti

Light Forces:
6 S0 I coastal escort
4 Osa I FAC(M)
6 Shershen FAC(T)
4 P4 FAC(T)

Mine Warfare Forces:
2 T-43
4 Vanya
12 PO 2

Amphibious Forces:
10 Vydra LCU
10 MFP

Auxiliaries:
2 Varna survey ships
3 tankers
19 others

Aircraft:
2 Mi-1
6 Mi-6 ASW

'Riga' class frigate (2)

Class: *Druzki* (31), *Smeli* (32)
Displacement: 1,200 tons (1,219 tonnes)
    standard; 1,600 tons (1,626 tonnes) full
    load
Dimensions: Length 298 ft 7 in (91.0 m)
        Beam 33 ft 6 in (10.2 m)
        Draught 11 ft (3.4 m)
Armament:
Guns 3 3.9-in (100-mm) in single mountings
    4 37-mm
Missile systems
    none
A/S weapons
    4 quintuple MBU 1800 launcher and 4
    DCTs
Torpedo tubes
    3 21-in (533-mm)
Aircraft
    none
Radar and electronics: 'Slim Net' search,
    'Neptune' navigation, 'Highpole A' IFF,
    'Wasphead' and 'Sunvisor A' fire-control
    radars
Sonar: 'Tamir' or 'Hercules'
Powerplant: ? boilers supplying steam to
    geared turbines, delivering 25,000 shp to
    two shafts
Speed: 28 knots
Range: 2,500 miles (4,024 km) at 15 knots
Crew: 150
Used also by: China, East Germany, Finland,
    Indonesia, USSR
Notes: Transferred from the USSR in 1957
    and 1958.

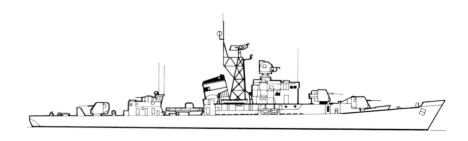

'Romeo' class patrol submarine (2)

Class: *Pobeda, Slava*
Displacement: 1,000 tons (1,016 tonnes)
    surfaced; 1,600 tons (1,626 tonnes) dived
Dimensions: Length 249 ft 4 in (76.0 m)
        Beam 24 ft (7.3 m)
        Draught 14 ft 6 in (4.4 m)
Armament:
Guns none
Missile systems
    none
A/S weapons
    none
Torpedo tubes
    8 21-in (533-mm)
Aircraft
    none
Radar and electronics: 'Snoop Plate' sub-
    marine surveillance radar
Sonar:
Powerplant: 2 diesels, delivering 4,000 hp,
    and 2 electric motors, delivering 4,000
    hp to two shafts
Speed: 17 knots surfaced; 14 knots dived
Range: 8,060 miles (12,975 km)
Crew: 65
Used also by: China, Egypt, North Korea,
    USSR
Notes: Transferred to Bulgaria in 1972–3 as
    replacements for a pair of 'Whiskey' class
    boats.

'Poti' class corvette (3)

Class: Nos *33, 34, 35*
Displacement: 550 tons (558.8 tonnes)
    standard; 600 tons (609.6 tonnes) full load
Dimensions: Length 193 ft 6 in (59.0 m)
        Beam 26 ft 3 in (8.0 m)
        Draught 9 ft 2 in (2.8 m)
Armament:
Guns 2 57-mm in twin mounting
Missile systems
    none
A/S weapons
    2 MBU 2500A launchers
Torpedo tubes
    4 16-in (406-mm) for A/S torpedoes
Aircraft
    none
Radar and electronics: 'Strut Curve' search,
    'Muff Cob' fire-control and 'Don' naviga-
    tion radars
Sonar: 'Hercules'
Powerplant: 2 gas turbines and 2 diesels,
    delivering a total of 20,000 shp to four
    shafts
Speed: 28 knots
Range:
Crew:
Used also by: Romania, USSR
Notes: Built in the USSR between 1961 and
    1968; transferred to Bulgaria in late 1975.

'Shershen' class fast attack craft (torpedo) (6)

Class: Nos *27, 28, 29, 30* and two others
Displacement: 150 tons (152.4 tonnes) standard; 160 tons (162.6 tonnes) full load
Dimensions: Length 115 ft 6 in (35.2 m)
Beam 23 ft 3½ in (7.1 m)
Draught 5 ft (1.5 m)
Armament:
Guns 4 30-mm in twin mountings
Missile systems
none
A/S weapons
12 DCs
Torpedo tubes
4 21-in (533-mm)
Aircraft
none

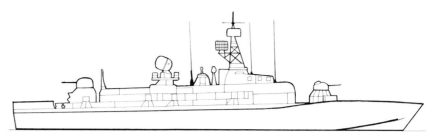

Radar and electronics: 'Pot Drum' surface-search, 'Drum Tilt' fire-control and 'High Pole A' IFF radars
Sonar: none
Powerplant: 3 diesels, delivering 13,000 bhp to three shafts

Speed: 41 knots
Range: 700 miles (1,127 km) at 20 knots
Crew: 25
Used also by: East Germany, Egypt, North Korea, USSR, Yugoslavia
Notes: Transferred from USSR in 1970.

Burma

9,000 men (800 marines)

Frigates:
1 British River
1 Algerine

Corvettes:
1 PCE 827
1 Admirable
2 Nawarat

Light Forces:
10 River PC
25 Yugoslav river PC
3 LCG(M) type gunboats
10 Y301 gunboats
2 Improved Y301 gunboats
8 gunboats (ex-transports)
6 PGM type gunboats
7 CGC type gunboats

Auxiliaries:
2 survey ships
1 support ship
1 LCU transport
8 LCM 3 transports

British 'River' class frigate (1)

Class: *Mayu*, ex-British *Fal*
Displacement: 1,460 tons (1,483 tonnes) standard; 2,170 tons (2,205 tonnes) full load
Dimensions: Length 301 ft 4 in (91.8 m)
Beam 36 ft 8 in (11.3 m)
Draught 12 ft (3.7 m)
Armament:
Guns 1 4-in (102-mm)
4 40-mm
Missile systems
none
A/S weapons
none
Torpedo tubes
none
Aircraft
none
Radar and electronics: Type 974 radar
Sonar: none
Powerplant: 2 boilers supplying steam to reciprocating engines, delivering 5,500 ihp to two shafts
Speed: 19 knots
Range: 4,200 miles (6,759 km) at 12 knots
Crew: 140
Used also by: Australia, Dominican Republic, Sri Lanka
Notes: Laid down at Smiths Dock in May 1942, launched in November 1942 and commissioned into British service in July 1943. Acquired by Burma in March 1948.

'Algerine' class frigate (1)

Class: *Yan Myo Aung*, ex-British *Mariner*, ex-Canadian *Kincardine*
Displacement: 1,040 tons (1,057 tonnes) standard; 1,335 tons (1,356 tonnes) full load
Dimensions: Length 235 ft (71.6 m)
Beam 35 ft 6 in (19.8 m)
Draught 11 ft 6 in (3.5 m)
Armament:
Guns 1 4-in (102-mm)
4 40-mm
Missile systems
none
A/S weapons
none
Torpedo tubes
none
Aircraft
none

Radar and electronics: Decca Type 202 navigational and tactical radar
Sonar: Type 144
Powerplant: 2 boilers supplying steam to reciprocating engines, delivering 2,000 ihp to two shafts
Speed: 16½ knots
Range: 4,000 miles (6,438 km) at 12 knots
Crew: 140
Used also by: Greece, Thailand
Notes: Laid down in August 1943 at Port Arthur Shipyards, Canada, as an ocean minesweeper. Launched in May 1944 and commissioned into Canadian service in May 1945. Used as an escort. Handed over to Burma in April 1958 and refitted as a minelayer for up to 16 mines.

'PCE 827' class corvette (1)

Class: *Yan Taing Aung* (PCE41), ex-US *Farmington* (PCE894)
Displacement: 640 tons (650 tonnes) standard; 903 tons (917 tonnes) full load
Dimensions: Length 184 ft (56.1 m)
Beam 33 ft (10.1 m)
Draught 9 ft 6 in (2.9 m)
Armament:
Guns 1 3-in (76-mm) dual-purpose
2 40-mm in twin mounting
8 20-mm in twin mountings
Missile systems
none
A/S weapons
1 Hedgehog, 2 DCTs and 2 DC racks
Torpedo tubes
none
Aircraft
none
Radar and electronics:
Sonar:
Powerplant: General Motors diesels, delivering 1,800 hp to two shafts
Speed: 15 knots
Range:
Crew:
Used also by: Philippines, South Korea
Notes: Laid down in December 1942 at Willamette Iron & Steel, Oregon; launched in May 1943 and commissioned into US service as a patrol escort in August 1943. Transferred to Burma in June 1965.

'Admirable' class corvette (1)

Class: *Yan Gyi Aung* (PCE42), ex-US *Creddock* (MSF356)
Displacement: 650 tons (660 tonnes) standard; 945 tons (960 tonnes) full load
Dimensions: Length 184 ft 6 in (56.2 m)
Beam 33 ft (10.1 m)
Draught 9 ft 9 in (2.8 m)
Armament:
Guns 1 3-in (76-mm)
4 40-mm in twin mountings
4 20-mm in twin mountings
Missile systems
none
A/S weapons
1 Hedgehog, 2 DCTs and 2 DC racks
Torpedo tubes
none
Aircraft
none
Radar and electronics:
Sonar:

Powerplant: diesels, delivering 1,710 shp to two shafts
Speed: 14¾ knots
Range: 4,300 miles (6,920 km) at 10 knots
Crew:
Used also by: Dominican Republic, Mexico, Philippines
Notes: Laid down in November 1943 at the Willamette Iron & Steel yards in Oregon as a minesweeper; launched in July 1944 and commissioned into US service in 1944. Transferred to Burma in March 1967.

'Narawat' class corvette (2)

Class: *Nawarat, Nagakyay*
Displacement: 400 tons (406 tonnes) standard; 450 tons (457 tonnes) full load
Dimensions: Length 163 ft (49.7 m)
Beam 26 ft 10 in (8.2 m)
Draught 5 ft 10 in (1.8 m)

Armament:
Guns 2 25-pounders
2 40-mm
Missile systems
none
A/S weapons
none
Torpedo tubes
none
Aircraft
none
Radar and electronics:
Sonar:
Powerplant: 2 Paxman-Ricardo diesels, delivering 1,160 bhp to two shafts
Speed: 12 knots
Range:
Crew: 43
Used only by: Burma
Notes: Built by the Government Dockyard, Rangoon, and commissioned in April and December 1960 respectively.

Cameroon

300 men

Light Forces:
2 Shanghai FAC(G)
1 PR 48 type PC
4 large PC
3 coastal PC (+3)

Auxiliaries:
1 LCM
5 LCVP
7 others

Canada

The Canadian Armed Forces (Maritime)
The armed forces of Canada were unified in 1968, with subordinate commands for land, sea and air forces within the overall structure. Canada has two very long coastlines, to the west and the east of the country, that require naval protection, and one even longer one, in the north of the country, that has the natural protection of semi-permanent ice stretching down from the polar ice cap. Apart from local defence considerations, Canada also plays a vital part in NATO planning for Atlantic operations, especially in the escort of convoys from North America to Europe, and in the suppression of Russian seapower in the Atlantic in time of war.

Service in the Canadian Armed Forces is voluntary, and the navy has some 17.75 per cent of the manpower total. The defence budget is about 1.84 per cent of the gross national product. The naval forces have a manpower strength of some 14,200, about 9,000 of them directly controlled by the Maritime Command. The navy has responsibilities on both coasts, as reflected in the disposition of ships: all three submarines, 13 surface vessels (one in reserve), and two support ships in the Atlantic; and 10 surface vessels

(two in reserve) and one support ship in the Pacific. Operationally, the balance is about 2:1 in favour of the Atlantic. Canada's coastline is felt fairly secure, as proved by the fact that coastal patrol is entrusted primarily to the six coastal patrol/training ships of the 'Bay' class, supported by the one 'Fort' and five 'Porte' class vessels. For offensive purposes in ocean areas this leaves the three 'Oberon' class submarines in the Atlantic, four helicopter destroyers of the 'Tribal' class, two helicopter frigates of the 'Annapolis' class, six helicopter frigates of the 'St Laurent' class, and 11 conventional frigates of the 'Mackenzie', Improved 'Restigouche' and 'Restigouche' classes. Operating in conjunction with the Maritime Group of the Air Command, which comes under the operational control of Maritime Command, this provides Canada with a powerful A/S capability, fixed wing aircraft helping to locate submarines, which can then be attacked by shipborne helicopters (CHSS-2 Sea King) and the ships themselves. All Canadian surface warships are well provided with A/S weapons (torpedoes, Limbo launchers and ASROC), so perhaps the main criticism that can be made of them is lack of surface-to-surface armament other than guns. It

must be added, though, that many of Canada's ships are close to the end of their useful lives, and that no adequate replacement programme has been set in motion.

14,200 men

Destroyers:
4 Tribal

Frigates:
2 Annapolis
4 Mackenzie
3 Restigouche
4 Improved Restigouche
6 St Laurent

SS:
3 Oberon

Auxiliaries:
3 replenishment ships
2 tankers
1 maintenance ship
5 research ships
1 A/S hydrofoil
6 Bay (ex-MSC) training ships
1 Fort training ship
5 Porte training ships
10 diving support ships
17 others

Patrol Craft:
6 PC

'Tribal' class destroyer (4)

Class: *Iroquois* (280), *Huron* (281), *Athabaskan* (282), *Algonquin* (283)
Displacement: 4,200 tons (4,267 tonnes) full load
Dimensions: Length 426 ft (129.8 m)
Beam 50 ft (15.2 m)
Draught 14 ft 6 in (4.4 m)
Armament:
Guns 1 5-in (127-mm) OTO-Melara
Missile systems
2 quadruple Raytheon GMLS Sea Sparrow launchers
A/S weapons
1 Mark 10 Limbo
Torpedo tubes
2 triple 12.75-in (324-mm) Mark 32
Aircraft
2 CHSS-2 Sea King A/S helicopters
Radar and electronics: SPQ 2D surface-warning and navigation, SPS 501 (SPS 12) long-range warning and M 22

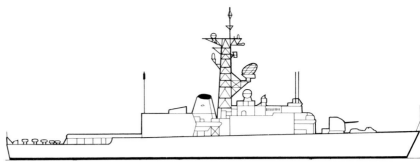

fire-control radars; Hollandse Signaal Mark 22 weapon-control system
Sonar: hull-mounted SQS 505, variable-depth 18 ft (5.5 m) towed body, and SQS 501 bottomed target identification
Powerplant: 2 Pratt & Whitney FT4A2 gas turbines, delivering 50,000 shp; 2 Pratt & Whitney FT12AH3 gas turbines for cruising, delivering 7,400 shp to two shafts
Speed: 29+ knots

Range: 4,500 miles (7,242 km) at 20 knots
Crew: 20+225 (plus 7+33 in air unit)
Used only by: Canada
Notes: First two built by Marine Industries of Sorel, the second pair by Davies Shipbuilding of Lauzon. All laid down in 1969, launched in 1970 and 1971, and commissioned in 1972 and 1973. They are designed as A/S vessels. Also known as 'DD280' class.

'Annapolis' class frigate (2)

Class: *Annapolis* (265), *Nipigon* (266)
Displacement: 2,400 tons (2,439 tonnes) standard; 3,000 tons (3,048 tonnes) full load
Dimensions: Length 371 ft (113.1 m)
Beam 42 ft (12.8 m)
Draught 14 ft 5 in (4.4 m)
Armament:
Guns 2 3-in (76-mm) in twin mounting
Missile systems
none
A/S weapons
1 Mark 10 Limbo
Torpedo tubes
2 triple 12.75-in (324-mm) Mark 32
Aircraft
1 CHSS-2 Sea King A/S helicopter
Radar and electronics: SPS 12 search, SPS 10 tactical, and I-band fire-control
Sonar: Types 501, 502, 503, 504 and SQS 10/11
Powerplant: 2 boilers supplying steam to geared turbines, delivering 30,000 shp to two shafts
Speed: 28 knots

Range: 4,570 miles (7,355 km) at 14 knots
Crew: 11+199
Used only by: Canada
Notes: Laid down in July and April 1960 at Halifax Shipyards and Marine Industries of Sorel, and launched in April 1963 and December 1961 respectively, for commissioning in December 1964 and May 1964. Designed for A/S operations.

'Mackenzie' class frigate (4)

Class: *Mackenzie* (261), *Saskatchewan* (262), *Yukon* (263), *Qu'Appelle* (264)
Displacement: 2,380 tons (2,418 tonnes) standard; 2,880 tons (2,926 tonnes) full load
Dimensions: Length 366 ft (111.5 m)
Beam 42 ft (12.8 m)
Draught 13 ft 6 in (4.1 m)
Armament:
Guns 4 3-in (76-mm) in two twin turrets
2 3-in (76-mm) 50 cal (*Qu'Appelle* only)
Missile systems
none
A/S weapons
2 Mark 10 Limbos
Torpedo tubes
side launchers for Mark 43 torpedoes
Aircraft
none

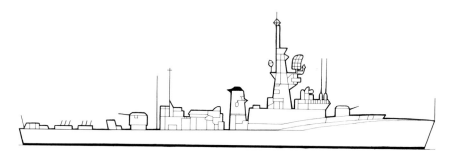

Radar and electronics: SPS 12 search, SPS 10 tactical and I-band fire-control radars
Sonar: Types 501, 502, 503 and SQS 10/11
Powerplant: 2 boilers supplying steam to geared turbines, delivering 30,000 shp to two shafts
Speed: 28 knots
Range: 4,750 miles (7,645 km) at 14 knots
Crew: 11+199
Used only by: Canada
Notes: Laid down in four yards between 1958 and 1960, launched in 1961 and 1962, and commissioned in 1962 and 1963. Designed as A/S vessels, but officially designated DDE.

'Restigouche' class frigate (3)

Class: *Chaudière* (235), *Saint Croix* (256), *Columbia* (260)
Displacement: 2,370 tons (2,408 tonnes) standard; 2,880 tons (2,926 tonnes) full load
Dimensions: Length 366 ft (111.5 m)
Beam 42 ft (12.8 m)
Draught 13 ft 6 in (4.1 m)
Armament:
Guns 4 3-in (76-mm) in twin mountings
Missile systems
none
A/S weapons
2 Mark 10 Limbos
Torpedo tubes
side launchers for Mark 43 torpedoes
Aircraft
none
Radar and electronics: SPS 12 search, SPS 10 tactical and SPG 48 fire-control radars
Sonar: Types 501, 502, 503 and SQS10/11
Powerplant: 2 boilers supplying steam to geared turbines, delivering 30,000 shp to two shafts
Speed: 28 knots
Range: 4,750 miles (7,645 km) at 14 knots
Crew: 12+236
Used only by: Canada
Notes: Laid down in 1953 and 1954, launched in 1956 and 1957, and commissioned in 1958 and 1959, these three ships are now in reserve.

'Improved Restigouche' class frigate (4)

Class: *Gatineau* (236), *Restigouche* (257), *Kootenay* (258), *Terra Nova* (259)
Displacement: 2,390 tons (2,428 tonnes) standard; 2,900 tons (2,947 tonnes) full load
Dimensions: Length 371 ft (113.1 m)
Beam 42 ft (12.8 m)
Draught 14 ft 1 in (4.3 m)
Armament:
Guns 2 3-in (76-mm) in twin mounting
Missile systems
none
A/S weapons
1 ASROC and 1 Mark 10 Limbo
Torpedo tubes
none
Aircraft
none

Radar and electronics: SPS 12 search, SPS 10 tactical, SPG 48 fire-control and Sperry Mark II navigation radars
Sonar: hull-mounted Types 501 and 505, and variable depth Type 505
Powerplant: 2 boilers supplying steam to geared turbines, delivering 30,000 shp to two shafts
Speed: 28+ knots
Range: 4,750 miles (7,645 km) at 14 knots
Crew: 13+201
Used only by: Canada

Notes: Laid down in 1952 and 1953, launched in 1954 to 1957, commissioned in 1958 and 1959. The aft 3-in (76-mm) gun was removed to make room for the ASROC and Limbo mountings.

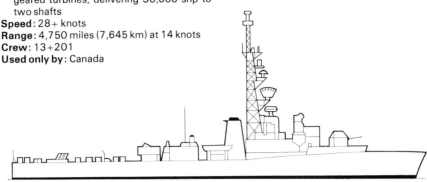

'Saint Laurent' class frigate (6)

Class: *Saguenay* (206), *Skeena* (207), *Ottawa* (229), *Margaree* (230), *Fraser* (233), *Assiniboine* (234)
Displacement: 2,260 tons (2,296 tonnes) standard; 2,858 tons (2,904 tonnes) full load
Dimensions: Length 366 ft (111.5 m)
Beam 42 ft (12.8 m)
Draught 13 ft 2 in (4.0 m)
Armament:
Guns 2 3-in (76-mm) in twin mounting
Missile systems
none
A/S weapons
1 Mark 10 Limbo
Torpedo tubes
2 triple 12.75-in (324-mm) Mark 32
Aircraft
1 CHSS-2 Sea King A/S helicopter
Radar and electronics: SPS 12 search, SPS 10 tactical, SPG 48 fire-control and Sperry Mark II navigation radars
Sonar: Types 501, 502, 503, 504 and SQS 502
Powerplant: 2 boilers supplying steam to English Electric geared turbines, delivering 30,000 shp to two shafts
Speed: 28½ knots
Range: 4,570 miles (7,355 km) at 14 knots
Crew: 11+197 (plus 7+13 for air unit)
Used only by: Canada

Notes: Laid down in 1951 and 1952, launched between 1952 and 1954, commissioned in 1956 and 1957. Original armament was 4 3-in (76-mm), 2 40-mm and 2 Limbos.

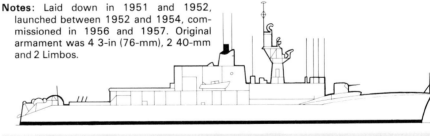

33

'Oberon' class submarine (3)

Class: *Ojibwa* (72), *Onondaga* (73), *Okanagan* (74)
Displacement: 2,200 tons (2,235 tonnes) normal surfaced; 2,420 tons (2,459 tonnes) dived
Dimensions: Length 294 ft 2½ in (90.0 m)
Beam 26 ft 6 in (8.1 m)
Draught 18 ft (5.5 m)
Armament:
Guns none
Missile systems
none
A/S weapons
none
Torpedo tubes
8 21-in (533-mm)
Aircraft
none
Radar and electronics: Type 1006 radar
Sonar: Type 187 attack, Type 197 intercept, Type 719 torpedo warning and Type 2007 long-range passive search
Powerplant: 2 Admiralty Standard diesels, delivering 3,680 bhp; 2 AEI-English Electric electric motors, delivering 6,000 shp to two shafts
Speed: 12 knots (surfaced); 17 knots (dived)
Range:
Crew: 7+58
Used also by: Australia, Brazil, Chile, UK
Notes: All three boats were built by HM Dockyard, Chatham, between 1962 and 1966, being commissioned in 1965, 1967 and 1968. *Ojibwa* had been laid down as the RN *Onyx*.

Chile

24,000 men (1,600 conscripts) including naval air arm and marines

Cruisers:
1 Göta Lejon
1 Brooklyn (CL)

Destroyers:
2 Almirante
2 Fletcher
2 Allen M. Sumner FRAM II

Frigates:
2 Leander
3 Charles Lawrence

SS:
2 Oberon
1 Balao

Patrol Craft:
2 Sotomoyo
1 Cherokee
1 PC 1638
2 large PC
2 coastal PC

Light Forces:
4 Lürssen type FAC(T)

Amphibious Forces:
3 LST
1 LCM
2 LCU
6 LCVP

Auxiliaries:
1 Cherokee survey ship
1 training ship (sail)
4 transports
3 tankers (+1)
2 ARD floating docks
9 others

Air Arm (500 men):
1 ASW/SAR sqn with 6 EMB-111, 2 PBY-5A, 3 PBY-6A, 4 SP-2E, 5 Beech D18S, 1 Piper Navajo, 1 F27,

4 UH-19, 2 UH-1D
12 Bell 47 helicopters
6 Alouette III
5 T-34 trainers
(5 EMB-111N)
4 C-47 transports
6 EMB-110C transports
4 AB 206 helicopters
3 UH-19
2 UH-1D

'Göta Lejon' class cruiser (1)

Class: *Latorre* (04), ex-Swedish *Göta Lejon*
Displacement: 8,200 tons (8,332 tonnes) standard; 9,200 tons (9,348 tonnes) full load
Dimensions: Length 597 ft 1 in (182.0 m)
Beam 54 ft 2 in (16.5 m)
Draught 21 ft 6 in (6.6 m)
Armament:
Guns 7 5.9-in (150-mm)
4 57-mm
11 40-mm
Missile systems
none
A/S weapons
none
Torpedo tubes
6 21-in (533-mm)
Aircraft
none
Radar and electronics: LW-03 and Type 227 search, Type 293 tactical, and I-band fire-control radars
Sonar:
Powerplant: 4 boilers supplying steam to 2 sets of Laval geared turbines, delivering 100,000 shp to two shafts
Speed: 33 knots
Range:
Crew: 610
Used only by: Chile
Notes: Laid down in September 1943 at the yards of Eriksberg Mekaniska Verkstad in Göteborg, launched in November 1945 and commissioned into Swedish service in

December 1947. Bought by Chile in July 1971. She has a capacity of 120 mines. The main armament (2 twin and 1 triple mounting) are automatically loaded and have an elevation of 70° for AA use. Armour is from 3 in to 5 in (75 mm to 125 mm).

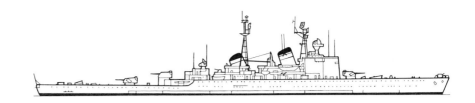

'Brooklyn' class cruiser (1)

Class: *Prat* (03), ex-US *Nashville* (CL43)
Displacement: 10,000 tons (10,161 tonnes) standard; 13,500 tons (13,717 tonnes) full load
Dimensions: Length 608 ft 3 in (185.4 m)
Beam 69 ft (21.0 m)
Draught 24 ft (7.3 m)
Armament:
Guns 6-in (152-mm) in triple mountings
8 5-in (127-mm) in single mountings
28 40-mm
24 20-mm
Missile systems
none
A/S weapons
none
Torpedo tubes
none
Aircraft
1 Bell helicopter
Radar and electronics: SPS 12 search and SPS 10 tactical radars
Sonar:
Powerplant: 8 Babcock & Wilcox Express boilers supplying steam to Parsons geared turbines, delivering 100,000 shp to four shafts

Speed: 32½ knots
Range: 14,500 miles (23,336 km) at 15 knots
Crew: 888–975 (in peace)
Used also by: Argentina
Notes: Laid down in January 1935 at New York Shipbuilding, launched in October 1937 and commissioned into US service in November 1938. Sold to Chile in 1951. Her sistership *Brooklyn* (CL40) was bought as *O'Higgins*, but is now used as an accommodation vessel and is non-operational. Armour varies from 1½ in to 5 in (38 mm to 127 mm).

'Almirante' class destroyer (2)

Class: *Almirante Riveros* (18), *Almirante Williams* (19)
Displacement: 2,730 tons (2,774 tonnes) standard; 3,300 tons (3,353 tonnes) full load
Dimensions: Length 402 ft (122.5 m)
Beam 43 ft (13.1 m)
Draught 13 ft 4 in (4.0 m)
Armament:
Guns 4 4-in (102-mm) in single mountings
4 40-mm in single mountings
Missile systems
4 MM38 Exocet launchers
2 quadruple Sea Cat launchers
A/S weapons
2 triple Squid DC mortars
Torpedo tubes
2 triple 12.75-in (324-mm) Mark 32
Aircraft
none
Radar and electronics: Plessey AWS-1 and target indication radars are being fitted
Sonar:
Powerplant: 2 Babcock & Wilcox boilers supplying steam to Parsons Pametrada geared turbines, delivering 54,000 shp to two shafts
Speed: 34½ knots
Range: 6,000 miles (9,656 km) at 16 knots
Crew: 266
Used only by: Chile
Notes: Laid down at Vickers-Armstrong's Barrow yards in April 1957 and June 1956, these two vessels were launched in December and May 1958, and commissioned in December and March 1960 respectively. Sea Cat and Exocet fitted later.

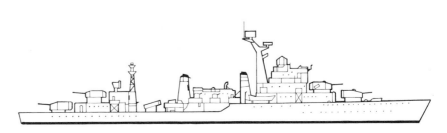

'Fletcher' class destroyer (2)

Class: *Blanco Encalada* (14), ex-US *Wadleigh* (DD689); *Cochrane* (15), ex-US *Rooks* (DD804)
Displacement: 2,100 tons (2,134 tonnes) standard; 2,750 tons (2,794 tonnes) full load
Dimensions: Length 376 ft 6 in (110.5 m)
Beam 39 ft 6 in (12.0 m)
Draught 18 ft (5.5 m)
Armament:
Guns 4 5-in (127-mm) in single mountings
6 3-in (76-mm) in single mountings
Missile systems
none
A/S weapons
2 Hedgehog
1 DC rack
6 'K' DCTs
2 side-launching torpedo racks
Torpedo tubes
1 quintuple 21-in (533-mm)
Aircraft
none

Radar and electronics: SPS 6 search, SPS 10 tactical and I-band fire-control radars
Sonar:
Powerplant: 4 Babcock & Wilcox boilers supplying steam to 2 Westinghouse geared turbines, delivering 60,000 shp to two shafts
Speed: 35 knots
Range: 5,000 miles (8,047 km) at 15 knots

Crew: 14+236
Used also by: Argentina, Brazil, Greece, Italy, Mexico, Peru, South Korea, Spain, Taiwan, Turkey, West Germany
Notes: The two vessels were built in 1943 and 1944 respectively by Bath Iron Works and Todd Pacific Shipyards, and commissioned into US service in 1943 and 1944. Both were transferred to Chile in 1963.

'Allen M. Sumner FRAM II' class destroyer (2)

Class: *Ministro Zenteno* (16), ex-US *Charles S. Sperry* (DD697); *Ministro Portales* (17), ex-US *Douglas H. Fox* (DD779)
Displacement: 2,200 tons (2,235 tonnes) standard; 3,320 tons (3,373 tonnes) full load
Dimensions: Length 376 ft 6 in (114.8 m)
Beam 40 ft 11 in (12.4 m)
Draught 19 ft (5.8 m)
Armament:
Guns 6 5-in (127-mm) in twin mountings
Missile systems
none
A/S weapons
2 Hedgehog
2 triple 12.75-in (324-mm) Mark 32 tubes
Torpedo tubes
1 quintuple 21-in (533-mm)
Aircraft
facilities for 1 small helicopter

Radar and electronics: SPS 37 (*Ministro Zenteno*) and SPS 40 (*Ministro Portales*) search, and SPS 10 tactical radars
Sonar: SQS 40
Powerplant: 4 Babcock & Wilcox boilers supplying steam to 2 geared turbines, delivering 60,000 shp to two shafts
Speed: 34 knots
Range: 4,600 miles (7,403 km) at 15 knots

Crew: 274
Used also by: Brazil, Colombia, Iran, South Korea, Turkey, Venezuela
Notes: The two vessels were built in 1944 and 1943 respectively by Todd Pacific Shipyards and Federal Shipbuilding Dry Dock, and commissioned into US service in 1944. Both were transferred to Chile in 1974.

'Leander' class frigate (2)

Class: *Condell* (06), *Almirante Lynch* (07)
Displacement: 2,500 tons (2,540 tonnes) standard; 2,962 tons (3,010 tonnes) full load
Dimensions: Length 372 ft (113.4 m)
Beam 43 ft (13.1 m)
Draught 18 ft (5.5 m)
Armament:
Guns 2 4.5-in (114-mm) in twin mounting
2 20-mm
Missile systems
4 MM38 Exocet launchers
1 quadruple Sea Cat launcher
A/S weapons
see below
Torpedo tubes
2 triple 12.75-in (324-mm) Mark 32
Aircraft
1 light helicopter
Radar and electronics: Type 922Q surveillance and target indication, Type 965 air-search, Type 975 navigation, GWS 22/ MRS3 gun- and missile-control
Sonar: Types 162, 170, 177
Powerplant: 2 boilers supplying steam to 2

geared turbines, delivering 30,000 shp to two shafts
Speed: 30 knots
Range: 4,500 miles (7,242 km) at 12 knots
Crew: 263
Used also by: India, New Zealand, UK
Notes: Laid down in June and December

1971 at Yarrow's Scotstoun yards, launched in June and December 1972 and commissioned in December 1973 and May 1974. The foremasts are slightly higher than British ones, and the Exocets are located on the quarterdeck.

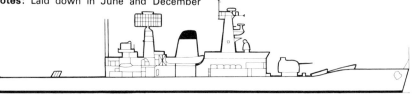

'Charles Lawrence' class frigate (3)

Class: *Serrano* (26), ex US-*Odum* (APD71); *Orella* (27), ex-US *Jack C. Robinson* (APD72); *Uribe*, ex-US *Daniel Griffin* (APD38)
Displacement: 1,400 tons (1,422 tonnes) standard; 2,130 tons (2,164 tonnes) full load
Dimensions: Length 306 ft (93.3 m)
Beam 37 ft (11.3 m)
Draught 12 ft 7 in (3.8 m)
Armament:
Guns 1 5-in (127-mm)
6 40-mm
Missile systems
none
A/S weapons
2 Hedgehogs and 2 DC racks
Torpedo tubes
none
Aircraft
none

Radar and electronics: AN/SPS 4 search and commercial navigation radars
Sonar:
Powerplant: 2 Foster Wheeler 'D' boilers supplying steam to General Electric turbo-electric engines, delivering 12,000 shp to two shafts
Speed: 23½ knots
Range: 5,000 miles (8,047 km) at 15 knots

Crew: 209
Used also by: Ecuador, Mexico, South Korea
Notes: Built between 1942 and 1944, these former high-speed transports were commissioned into US service in 1943 and 1945. They were bought by Chile in 1966. *Riquelme* was bought at the same time, but cannibalized for spare parts.

'Oberon' class submarine (2)

Class: *O'Brien* (22); *Hyatt*, ex-*Condell* (23)
Displacement: 1,610 tons (1,634 tonnes) standard; 2,030 tons (2,062 tonnes) surfaced; 2,410 tons (2,449 tonnes) dived
Dimensions: Length 295 ft 2½ in (90.0 m)
Beam 26 ft 6 in (8.1 m)
Draught 18 ft 1¼ in (5.5 m)
Armament:
Guns none
Missile systems
none
A/S weapons
none
Torpedo tubes
8 21-in (533-mm)
Aircraft
none

Radar and electronics:
Sonar:
Powerplant: 2 Admiralty Standard diesels, delivering 3,680 shp, and 2 AEI-English Electric electric motors, delivering 6,000 shp to two shafts
Speed: 12 knots (surfaced); 17 knots (dived)

Range:
Crew:
Used also by: Australia, Brazil, Canada, UK
Notes: Both boats were built by Scott-Lithgow between 1971 and 1973, being commissioned into Chilean service in 1976.

'Balao' class submarine (1)

Class: *Simpson* (SS21), ex-US *Spot* (SS413)
Displacement: 1,816 tons (1,845 tonnes) surfaced; 2,425 tons (2,464 tonnes) dived
Dimensions: Length 311 ft 7 in (95.0 m)
Beam 27 ft (8.2 m)
Draught 17 ft (5.2 m)
Armament:
Guns none
Missile systems
none
A/S weapons
none
Torpedo tubes
10 21-in (533-mm)

Aircraft
none
Radar and electronics:
Sonar:
Powerplant: 4 General Motors Corporation diesels, delivering 6,500 hp, and 2 electric motors, delivering 4,610 bhp to two shafts
Speed: 20 knots (surfaced); 10 knots (dived)

Range:
Crew: 80
Used also by: Greece, Italy, Turkey, Venezuela
Notes: *Simpson* was built by Mare Island Navy Yard between 1943 and 1944, and commissioned into US service in 1944. She was sold to Chile in 1961.

'Sotoyomo' class corvette (2)

Class: *Lientur* (60), ex-US *ATA 177*; *Lautaro* (62), ex-US *ATA 122*
Displacement: 534 tons (543 tonnes) standard; 835 tons (848 tonnes) full load
Dimensions: Length 143 ft (43.6 m)
Beam 33 ft (10.1 m)
Draught 13 ft 2½ in (4.0 m)
Armament:
Guns 1 3-in (76-mm)
2 20-mm
Missile systems
none
A/S weapons
none

Torpedo tubes
none
Aircraft
none
Radar and electronics:
Sonar:
Powerplant: General Motors Corporation diesel-electric drive, delivering 1,500 shp
Speed: 12½ knots
Range:
Crew: 33
Used also by: Dominican Republic, Peru, South Korea, Taiwan, USA
Notes: Both vessels were built by Levingstone Shipbuilding, and commissioned into US service as ocean rescue tugs 1943–4.

'PC-1638' class large patrol craft (1)

Class: *Papudo* (37), ex-US *PC 1646*
Displacement: 450 tons (457 tonnes) full
    load
Dimensions: Length 173 ft (52.8 m)
           Beam 23 ft (7.0 m)
           Draught 10 ft 2 in (3.1 m)
Armament:
Guns 1 40-mm
  2 20-mm in twin mounting
Missile systems
  none
A/S weapons
  1 Mark 15 Hedgehog
  2 DCTs
  4 DC racks
Torpedo tubes
  none
Aircraft
  none
Radar and electronics:
Sonar:
Powerplant: 2 diesels, delivering 2,800 bhp
    to two shafts

Speed: 19 knots
Range:
Crew: 4+65
Used only by: Chile
Notes: Built by Asmar at Talcahuano and
    commissioned in November 1971. The
    design is similar to that of the Turkish
    'Hisar' class.

'Lürssen' type fast attack craft (torpedo) (4)

Class: *Guacolda* (80), *Fresia* (81), *Quidora*
  (82), *Tequalda* (83)
Displacement: 134 tons (136 tonnes)
Dimensions: Length 118 ft 1 in (36.0 m)
           Beam 18 ft 4½ in (5.6 m)
           Draught 7 ft 2½ in (2.2 m)
Armament:
Guns 2 40-mm

Missile systems
  none
A/S weapons
  none
Torpedo tubes
  4 21-in (533-mm)
Aircraft
  none
Radar and electronics:
Sonar:

Powerplant: diesels delivering 4,800 bhp to
    two shafts
Speed: 32 knots
Range: 1,500 miles (2,414 km) at 15 knots
Crew: 20
Used only by: Chile
Notes: All four craft were built by Bazan of
    Cadiz to the designs of Lürssen of Vege-
    sack. The first pair were commissioned in
    1965, the second pair in 1966.

China

The Chinese Navy

Communist China has only recently begun to build up a modern navy with ocean-going ships, such developments having been considered unnecessary during the period up to the end of the 1960s, when Chinese politico-military thought centred on the desirability and inevitability of 'people's war'. In this, the mass of the Chinese people, without sophisticated equipment or weapons for the most part, would inevitably prevail – or so it was decreed. However, in the last years of Chairman Mao Tse-tung's life, a switch in Chinese military thought became evident, with the larger-scale development of modern weapons, and increasing efforts to buy western military technology (as such or in the form of weapons), which is some twenty years more advanced than Chinese technology. Yet even today the Chinese armed forces are marked by relatively simple equipment and large numbers of personnel. The Chinese Navy has about 300,000 men, about 6.9 per cent of China's total armed forces' manpower, but only 23 major surface warships. Total defence spending is about 7 per cent of gross national product, it is believed.

The bulk of China's navy consists of large numbers of patrol craft and FAC types, there being about 395 FAC(G) boats of the 'Shanghai', 'Swatow' and 'Whampoa' classes, and about 160 FAC(M) boats of the 'Osa' and 'Komar/Hoku' classes, armed with SS-N-2 surface-to-surface missiles. Other than these, there are some 70 'P-6' and 30 'P-4' FAC(T) craft, and rapidly diminishing numbers of obsolete and obsolescent craft.

Support and auxiliary ships are few in number, but China inherited from the Nationalist Chinese in 1949 a fair number of American landing craft, giving the navy a useful amphibious capability. The most important of these amphibious craft are 15 of the LST 511-1152 type, 13 LSM types, 15 LSIL types, and 17 modified LCT types. The Chinese have built some 300 landing craft of the 'Yunnan' class, and have inherited some 150 British and American LCMs to supplement some 450 or more locally built craft.

Chinese submarine development is very retarded, and the bulk of Chinese boats are of the Russian 'Romeo' (51 boats) and 'Whiskey' (21 boats) classes. 'Romeo' class boats are still being built in Chinese yards, despite the obsolescence of the type. The only Chinese-designed boats are the two 'Ming' class and one 'Han' class, the latter being nuclear-powered. The fact that this was completed in 1974 but has not been followed by any other such boats probably indicates trouble with the nuclear powerplant. However, once this has been solved, the combination of

nuclear power and Chinese developments in the field of solid propellants may allow SLBM-equipped submarines to be built in the 1980s. At the moment, China has just one missile-capable boat, a modified 'Golf' class built in China. It is doubtful if the boat is operational, however. It will probably be used for testing Chinese SLBMs when these reach the hardware stage.

Chinese ocean-going surface vessels are few in number, the most modern being the missile-equipped 'Luta' class, of which five have been built so far. Also fitted with launchers for the SS-N-2 or Chinese equivalent are four ex-Russian 'Gordy' class destroyers of venerable age. Other major Chinese surface vessels are the 'Kiang Hu' and 'Kiangtung' missile-armed frigate classes, the conventional 'Kiangnan' class frigates, and the four 'Riga' class frigates built in China in the late 1950s.

The Chinese Navy also possesses an air arm of some size, with 30,000 men and some 700 combat aircraft. The naval fighters are integrated into the overall Chinese air defence system, but the bombers and torpedo-bombers would be of considerable use in operations in Chinese coastal waters. So far, no Chinese warship has been able to operate a helicopter.

Deployment is into three major fleets. The South Sea Fleet has some 300 vessels, and operates from the Vietnamese frontier north to Tangshan, with bases at Yulin, Huangpu and Chanchiang; the East Sea Fleet has some 450 vessels, and operates northwards from Tangshan to a point south of Lienyunkang, with bases at Ta Hsiehtao, Shanghai and Chou Shan; and the North Sea Fleet has some 300 vessels, and operates from south of Lienyunkang north to the Yalu River, with bases at Tsingtao, Luta and Lushun.

300,000 men, including naval air force (30,000) and marines (38,000)

Destroyers:
5 Luta (+ others building)
4 Gordy

Frigates:
3 Kiang Hu (+2)
1 Kiang Tung (+2?)
5 Kiang Nan
4 Riga

SSN:
1 Han

SSB:
1 Golf

SS:
51 Romeo
21 Whiskey
1 S-1
2 Ming

Escorts:
15 ships of foreign construction

Light Forces:
20 Kronshtadt submarine chasers
23 Hainan class submarine chasers
1 US 170-ft type
2 (?) Hai Dau (+?) FAC(M)
80 Osa FAC(M)
4 Komar FAC(M)
76 Hoku FAC(M)
25 Shanghai I FAC(G)
340 Shanghai II FAC(G)
6 Hai Kou FAC(G)
30 Swatow FAC(G)
120 Hu Chwan FAC(T)
70 P-6 FAC(T)
30 P-4 FAC(T)

25 Whampoa FAC(G)
2 Shantung FAH(G)
1 Fukien FAC(G)
? Yu Lin coastal PC
? Ying Kou coastal PC
4 Tai Shan coastal PC
30 Wu Hsi/Pei Hai coastal PC

Mine Warfare Forces:
18 T-43

Amphibious Forces:
15 LST 511-1152
13 LSM
15 LSIL
17 LCT
1 Yu Ling LSM
300 Yunnan
450+ LCM/LCU
c 150 LCM

Auxiliaries:
1 submarine support ship
1 repair ship
2 Shih Jian research ships
1 Yen Hsi research ship
3+ research ships
9 survey ships
13 supply ships
20+ tankers
3 icebreakers
Others

Naval Air Force:
700 combat aircraft in four bombers and five fighters divisions. Aircraft include: 130 Il-28 torpedo-bombers, Tu-2 and Tu-16 light bombers, MiG-17, MiG-19/F-6 and F-9 fighters, Be-6 MR aircraft
50 Mi-4 helicopters

'Luta' class guided-missile destroyer (7)

Class: Nos 240, 241, 242, 243, 244, 245, 246
Displacement: 3,250 tons (3,302 tonnes) standard; 3,750 tons (3,810 tonnes) full load
Dimensions: Length 450 ft (137.3 m)
Beam 45 ft (13.7 m)
Draught 15 ft (4.6 m)
Armament:
Guns 4 130-mm (5.1-in) in twin mountings
8 37- or 57-mm
8 25-mm
Missile systems
2 triple SS-N-2 type
A/S weapons
2 A/S rocket-launchers
Torpedo tubes
none
Aircraft
none
Radar and electronics: 'Cross Slot' air-search, 'Wasphead' and 'Postlamp' gun-fire-control, 'Square Tie' missile-control and 'Neptune' navigation radars
Sonar:
Powerplant: ? boilers supplying steam to geared turbines, delivering 60,000 shp
Speed: 32 + knots
Range: 4,000 miles (6,438 km) at 15 knots (estimate)
Crew: 300 (estimate)
Used only by: China
Notes: These are the first such Chinese destroyers, five so far commissioned from the Dairen (Luta) yards, with another two building.

'Gordy' class guided-missile destroyer (4)

Class: Anshan, Chang Chun, Chi Lin, Fu Chun (ex-Russian ships)
Displacement: 1,657 tons (1,684 tonnes) standard; 2,040 tons (2,073 tonnes) full load
Dimensions: Length 370 ft 1 in (112.8 m)
Beam 33 ft 6 in (10.2 m)
Draught 13 ft (4.0 m)
Armament:
Guns 4 130-mm (5.1-in) in single mountings
8 37-mm in twin mountings
Missile systems
2 twin SS-N-2 type launchers
A/S weapons
2 DC racks
Torpedo tubes
none
Aircraft
none
Radar and electronics: 'Cross Bird' air-search, 'Square Tie' fire-control, 'Neptune' navigation and 'Ski Pole' IFF radars
Sonar:
Powerplant: ? boilers supplying steam to Tosi geared turbines, delivering 48,000 shp to two shafts
Speed: 36 knots
Range: 2,600 miles (4,184 km) at 19 knots; 800 miles (1,288 km) at 36 knots
Crew: 250
Used only by: China
Notes: Built in Russia between 1936 and 1941, and commissioned into Russian service between 1939 and 1943. The design is Italian. One pair of ships was transferred to China in December 1954 and the other pair in July 1955. Between 1971 and 1974 they were converted, the torpedo tubes being replaced by missile launchers. The class is now known as the 'Anshan' class.

'Kiang Hu' class guided-missile frigate (3)

Class: Nos 521, 525 and one other
Displacement: approximately 1,800 tons (1,829 tonnes)
Dimensions: Length about 347 ft 9 in (106.0 m)
Beam about 39 ft 4 in (12.0)
Draught
Armament:
Guns 4 100-mm (3.9-in) in twin mountings
8 or 12 37-mm
Missile systems
2 twin SS-N-2 type launchers
A/S weapons
unknown
Torpedo tubes
unknown
Aircraft
none
Radar and electronics:
Sonar:
Powerplant:
Speed:
Range:
Crew:
Used only by: China
Notes: Two ships were launched in 1975 and commissioned in 1976, with the third unit being launched in 1976 and commissioned in 1977. The class appears to be a modification of the 'Kiang Tung' design.

'Kiang Tung' class guided-missile frigate (1)

Class: Chung Tung
Displacement: 1,800 tons (1,829 tonnes) standard
Dimensions: Length about 347 ft 9 in (106.0 m)
Beam about 39 ft 4 in (12.0 m)
Draught
Armament:
Guns 4 100-mm (3.9-in) in twin mountings
12 37-mm in twin mountings
Missile systems
2 twin SAM launchers
A/S weapons
2 MBU 1800 rocket-launchers
2 DCTs
Torpedo tubes
none
Aircraft
none
Radar and electronics:
Sonar:
Powerplant: diesels
Speed: about 28 knots
Range:
Crew:
Used only by: China
Notes: Laid down at the Hutang yards in Shanghai in 1971, launched in 1973 and commissioned in 1977. There are indications that Chung Tung is not operational because of problems with the SAM system, and that severe problems with Chinese heavy shipbuilding have resulted in the dropping of plans to build more than a sistership launched in 1974, and possibly not yet commissioned.

'Kiang Nan' class frigate (5)

Class: Nos 209, 214, 231, 232, 233
Displacement: 1,350 tons (1,372 tonnes) standard; 1,600 tons (1,697 tonnes) full load
Dimensions: Length 297 ft 10 in (90.8 m)
Beam 33 ft 6 in (10.2 m)
Draught 11 ft (3.4 m)
Armament:
Guns 3 100-mm (3.9-in) in single mountings
6 37-mm in twin mountings
4 12.7-mm in twin mountings
Missile systems
none
A/S weapons
2 MBU 1800 rocket-launchers
4 DCTs
2 DC racks
Torpedo tubes
none
Aircraft
none
Radar and electronics: 'Ball Gun' surface warning, 'Wok Won' fire-control and 'Neptun' navigation radars
Sonar:
Powerplant: diesels, delivering 24,000 shp
Speed: 28 knots
Range:
Crew: 175
Used only by: China
Notes: Built at Canton and Shanghai from 1965 and commissioned between 1967 and 1969. These were the first ships of the new building programme initiated in 1965.

'Golf' class ballistic missile submarine (1)

Class: one boat
Displacement: 2,350 tons (2,388 tonnes) surfaced; 2,800 tons (2,845 tonnes) dived
Dimensions: Length 320 ft (97.5 m)
　　　　　Beam 25 ft 1 in (7.6 m)
　　　　　Draught 22 ft (6.7 m)

Armament:
Guns none
Missile systems
　3 vertical tubes
A/S weapons
　none
Torpedo tubes
　10 21-in (533-mm)
Aircraft
　none
Radar and electronics:
Sonar:

Powerplant: 3 diesels delivering 6,000 shp and 3 electric motors, delivering 6,000 hp to three shafts
Speed: 20 knots surfaced; 20 knots dived
Range: 22,700 miles (36,533 km) surfaced
Crew: 1+74
Used only by: China
Notes: Built at Dairen in 1964 to the Russian 'Golf' design. The three missile tubes are located in the long 'sail', but there may be no missiles as yet.

'Romeo' class submarine (51)

Class: 51 Chinese and ex-Russian boats
Displacement: 1,100 tons (1,118 tonnes) surfaced; 1,600 tons (1,626 tonnes) dived
Dimensions: Length 246 ft (75.0 m)
　　　　　Beam 24 ft (7.3 m)
　　　　　Draught 14 ft 6 in (4.4 m)
Armament:
Guns none
Missile systems
　none
A/S weapons
　none
Torpedo tubes
　6 21-in (533-mm) with 18 torpedoes

Radar and electronics: 'Snoop Plate' surface-search radar
Sonar: 'Hercules' and 'Feniks'
Powerplant: 2 diesels, delivering 4,000 hp, and 2 electric motors, delivering 4,000 hp to two shafts
Speed: 17 knots (surfaced); 14 knots (dived)
Range: 8,060 miles (12,975 km) at 5 knots surfaced
Crew: 65
Used also by: Bulgaria, Egypt, North Korea, USSR

Notes: China probably received four Russian boats (to which the technical specification above applies), and is building her own version at the rate of about six boats per year. These are probably somewhat larger, with a surfaced/dived displacement of 1,400/1,800 tons (1,422/1,829 tonnes), a length of 252 ft (76.8 m), an armament of 8 21-in (533-mm) tubes, and the capability of carrying 36 mines in place of torpedoes.

'Whiskey' class submarine (21)

Class: 21 ex-Russian boats
Displacement: 1,030 tons (1,046 tonnes) surfaced; 1,180 tons (1,199 tonnes) dived
Dimensions: Length 240 ft (73.2 m)
　　　　　Beam 22 ft (6.7 m)
　　　　　Draught 15 ft (4.6 m)
Armament:
Guns 2 25-mm in a twin mounting in some boats
Missile systems
　none

A/S weapons
　none
Torpedo tubes
　6 21-in (533-mm) with 20 torpedoes or 40 mines
Aircraft
　none
Radar and electronics: 'Snoop Plate' surface-search radar
Sonar: 'Tamir'
Powerplant: diesels delivering 4,000 hp and electric engines delivering 2,500 hp to two shafts

Speed: 17 knots (surfaced); 15 knots (dived)
Range: 13,000 miles (20,922 km) at 8 knots surfaced
Crew: 60
Used also by: Albania, Bulgaria, Egypt, Indonesia, North Korea, Poland, USSR
Notes: These boats were assembled in Chinese yards from 'kits' supplied by the Russians between 1956 and 1964. They are fitted with schnorkels.

'Ming' class submarine (2)

Class: 2 boats
Displacement: possibly 1,500 tons (1,524 tonnes)
Dimensions: Length about 250 ft (76.2 m)
Beam
Draught
Armament:
Guns none
Missile systems
none
A/S weapons
none
Torpedo tubes
probably 6 21-in (533-mm)
Aircraft
none
Radar and electronics:
Sonar:
Powerplant: probably diesels and electric motors
Speed:
Range:
Crew:
Used only by: China
Notes: These two boats, of which very few details are available, were laid down in 1971 and 1972, and probably entered service in 1974 and 1975.

'Hainan' class fast attack craft (gun) (23)

Class: Nos 267 to 285 and four others
Displacement: 360 tons (366 tonnes) standard; 400 tons (406 tonnes) full load
Dimensions: Length 196 ft 10 in (60.0 m)
Beam 24 ft 3 in (7.4 m)
Draught 6 ft 10 in (2.1 m)
Armament:
Guns 2 3-in (76-mm) in single mountings
4 25-mm in twin mountings
Missile systems
none
A/S weapons
4 MBU 1800 rocket-launchers
2 DCTs
2 DC racks
Torpedo tubes
none
Aircraft
none
Radar and electronics: 'Pothead' surface-search radar in most craft; 'Skinhead' surface-search radar in others
Sonar:
Powerplant: diesels, delivering 8,000 shp
Speed: 28 knots
Range: 1,000 miles (1,609 km) at 10 knots (estimate)
Crew: 60 (estimate)
Used also by: Pakistan
Notes: Built from 1963 at the rate of about four craft per year.

'Shanghai' class Type I fast attack craft (gun) (25)

Class: 25 Chinese-built craft
Displacement: 100 tons (101.6 tonnes) full load
Dimensions: Length 115 ft 2 in (35.1 m)
Beam 18 ft (5.5 m)
Draught 5 ft 6 in (1.7 m)
Armament:
Guns 1 57-mm
2 37-mm in twin mounting
Missile systems
none
A/S weapons
8 DCs
Torpedo tubes
2 18-in (457-mm), mostly removed
Aircraft
none
Radar and electronics: 'Skinhead' surface-search radar
Sonar: none
Powerplant: 4 diesels, delivering 4,800 bhp
Speed: 28 knots
Range:
Crew: 25
Used only by: China
Notes: First appeared in 1959.

'Shanghai' class Type II fast attack craft (gun) (340)

Class: 340 Chinese-built craft
Displacement: 120 tons (122 tonnes) standard; 155 tons (157 tonnes) full load
Dimensions: Length 128 ft (39.0 m)
Beam 18 ft (5.5 m)
Draught 5 ft 7 in (1.7 m)
Armament:
Guns 4 37-mm in twin mountings
4 25-mm in twin mountings
1 twin 75-mm recoilless rifle in some craft
Missile systems
none
A/S weapons
8 DCs

Torpedo tubes
none
Aircraft
none
Radar and electronics: 'Skinhead' surface-search radar
Sonar: none
Powerplant: 4 diesels, delivering 4,800 bhp

Speed: 30 knots
Range:
Crew: 25
Used also by: Albania, Cameroon, Pakistan, Sierra Leone, Sri Lanka
Notes: Being built at the rate of about 10 craft per year.

'Hai Kou' class fast attack craft (gun) (6)

Class: 6 Chinese-built craft
Displacement: 160 tons (162.6 tonnes) standard; 175 tons (177.8 tonnes) full load
Dimensions: Length about 149 ft 3 in (45.5 m)
Beam about 18 ft (5.5 m)
Draught about 6 ft 10 in (2.1 m)
Armament:
Guns 4 37-mm in twin mountings
4 25-mm in twin mountings
Missile systems
none
A/S weapons
none
Torpedo tubes
none
Aircraft
none
Radar and electronics:
Sonar: none
Powerplant: diesels
Speed: 30 knots (estimate)

Range: 850 miles (1,368 km) at 20 knots (estimate)
Crew:
Used only by: China
Notes: Believed to be an enlarged 'Shanghai' type built during the 1960s.

'Swatow' class fast attack craft (gun) (30)

Class: 30 Chinese-built craft
Displacement: 80 tons (81.3 tonnes) full load
Dimensions: Length 83 ft 8 in (25.5 m)
Beam 19 ft (5.8 m)
Draught 6 ft 7 in (2.0 m)
Armament:
Guns 4 37-mm in twin mountings
2 12.7-mm machine guns
1 twin 75-mm recoilless rifle in some craft
Missile systems
none
A/S weapons
8 DCs

Torpedo tubes
none
Aircraft
none
Radar and electronics:
Sonar: none
Powerplant: 4 diesels, delivering 3,000 bhp
Speed: 28 knots
Range: 500 miles (805 km) at 28 knots
Crew: 17
Used also by: North Korea, Vietnam
Notes: Built at Canton, Dairen and Shanghai after 1958. Now being deleted.

'Whampoa' class fast attack craft (gun) (25)

Class: 25 craft
Displacement: 42 tons (42.7 tonnes) standard; 50 tons (50.8 tonnes) full load
Dimensions: Length 75 ft 6 in (23.0 m)
Beam 13 ft (4.0 m)
Draught 5 ft (1.5 m)
Armament:
Guns 2 37-mm in single mountings

2 machine-guns in single mountings
Missile systems
  none
A/S weapons
  none
Torpedo tubes
  none
Aircraft
  none
Radar and electronics:
Sonar:
Powerplant: 2 diesels, delivering 600 hp
Speed: 12 knots
Range: 400 miles (644 km) at 9 knots
Crew: 25
Used only by: China

Notes: These craft were built in Canton and Shanghai during the first half of the 1950s, and are used only for coastal and riverine duties as they are slow and have only low freeboards.

'Shantung' class fast attack hydrofoil (gun) (2)

Class: 2 craft
Displacement: about 85 tons (86.4 tonnes)
Dimensions: Length 80 ft (24.4 m)
      Beam 16 ft (4.9 m)
      Draught 6 ft (1.9 m)
Armament:
Guns 4 37-mm in twin mountings

Missile systems
  none
A/S weapons
  none
Torpedo tubes
  none
Aircraft
  none
Radar and electronics:
Sonar:
Powerplant:
Speed: 40 knots
Range:
Crew:
Used only by: China
Notes: This attack hydrofoil proved only slightly useful in service and is now being phased out.

Colombia

9,800 men, including marines

Destroyers:
2 Modified Halland
1 Allen M. Sumner FRAM II

Frigates:
1 APD type
1 Courtney

SS:
2 Type 209
4 Type SX-506

Light Forces:
7 PC
3 Arauca gunboats
1 Barranquilla gunboat
10 gunboats

Auxiliaries:
3 survey vessels
1 Patapsco tanker
4 transports
1 training ship (sail)
14 others

Marine Force (2,800 men):
2 bns

Modified 'Halland' class destroyer (2)

Class: *Veinte de Julio* (D05), *Siete de Agosto* (D06)
Displacement: 2,650 tons (2,693 tonnes) standard; 3,300 tons (3,353 tonnes) full load
Dimensions: Length 397 ft 4 in (121.1 m)
      Beam 40 ft 8 in (12.4 m)
      Draught 15 ft 5 in (4.7 m)
Armament:
Guns 6 4.7-in (120-mm) in twin mountings
  4 40-mm
Missile systems
  none
A/S weapons
  1 375-mm (14.76-in) Bofors rocket-launcher
Torpedo tubes
  4 21-in (533-mm)
Aircraft
  none

Radar and electronics: LW-03/SGR 114 search, DA-02/SGR 105 tactical and M20 (probably) fire-control radars, all built by Hollandse Signaalapparaten
Sonar:
Powerplant: 2 Penhöet, Motala Verkstad boilers supplying steam to De Laval double-reduction geared turbines, delivering 55,000 shp to two shafts
Speed: 25 knots
Range: 445 miles (716 km) at 25 knots
Crew: 20+240
Used also by: Sweden
Notes: Built between 1955 and 1956 by Kockums Mek Verkstads of Malmo and Götaverken of Göteborg; commissioned into Colombian service in June and October 1958. They differ from the Swedish 'Halland' class in having six main guns instead of four, no 57-mm guns, four instead of eight torpedo tubes, and different accommodation.

'Allen M. Sumner FRAM II' class destroyer (1)

Class: *Santander* (D03), ex-US *Waldron* (DD699)

Displacement: 2,200 tons (2,235 tonnes) standard; 3,320 tons (3,373 tonnes) full load
Dimensions: Length 376 ft (114.8 m)
      Beam 40 ft 11 in (12.4 m)
      Draught 19 ft (5.8 m)

Armament:
Guns 6 5-in (127-mm) in twin mountings
Missile systems
  none
A/S weapons
  2 Hedgehog
  2 triple 12.75-in (324-mm) Mark 32 tubes
  facilities for 1 small helicopter (in *Santander* only)
Torpedo tubes
  none

Aircraft
  facilities for 1 small helicopter
Radar and electronics: SPS 10 search and SPS 10 Mark 25 fire-control radars
Sonar:
Powerplant: 4 boilers supplying steam to 2 geared turbines, delivering 60,000 shp to two shafts
Speed: 34 knots
Range: 4,800 miles (7,725 km) at 15 knots

Crew: 274
Used also by: Brazil, Chile, Iran, South Korea, Turkey, Venezuela
Notes: The ship was launched from Federal Shipbuilding in 1944 and commissioned into US service in the same year. She was sold to Colombia in 1973.

'APD' type frigate (1)

Class: *Cordoba* (DT15), ex-US *Ruchamkin* (LPR89)
Displacement: 1,400 tons (1,422 tonnes) standard; 2,130 tons (2,164 tonnes) full load
Dimensions: Length 306 ft (93.3 m)
            Beam 37 ft (11.3 m)
            Draught 12 ft 7 in (3.8 m)

Armament:
Guns 1 5-in (127-mm)
  4 40-mm
Missile systems
  none
A/S weapons
  see below
Torpedo tubes
  2 12.75-in (324-mm) Mark 32
Aircraft
  none
Radar and electronics:
Sonar:

Powerplant: 2 'D' Express boilers supplying steam to General Electric turbines with electric drive, delivering 12,000 shp to two shafts
Speed: 23 knots
Range: 5,500 miles (8,852 km) at 15 knots
Crew: 204 (+ optional 162 troops)
Used only by: Colombia
Notes: Built by Philadelphia Navy Yard between 1943 and 1944; commissioned into US service in 1945. Transferred to Colombia in 1969. *Cordoba* has been modernized to FRAM II standards.

'Courtney' class frigate (1)

Class: *Boyaca* (DE16), ex-US *Hartley* (DE1029)
Displacement: 1,450 tons (1,473 tonnes) standard; 1,914 tons (1,945 tonnes) full load
Dimensions: Length 314 ft 6 in (95.9 m)
            Beam 36 ft 10 in (11.2 m)
            Draught 13 ft 7 in (4.1 m)

Armament:
Guns 2 3-in (76-mm) in twin mounting
Missile systems
  none
A/S weapons
  1 DC rack
Torpedo tubes
  2 triple 12.75-in (324-mm) Mark 32
Aircraft
  provision for 1 small helicopter
Radar and electronics: SPS 6 air-search and SPS 10 surface-search radars

Sonar:
Powerplant: 2 Foster Wheeler boilers supplying steam to 1 Laval geared turbine, delivering 20,000 shp to one shaft
Speed: 25 knots
Range:
Crew: 165
Used only by: Colombia
Notes: Built by New York Shipbuilding and commissioned into US service in 1957. Sold to Colombia in July 1972.

Type 209 patrol submarine (2)

Class: *Pijao* (SS28), *Tayrona* (SS29)
Displacement: 1,000 tons (1,016 tonnes) surfaced; 1,290 tons (1,311 tonnes) dived
Dimensions: Length 183 ft 5 in (55.9 m)
            Beam 20 ft 6 in (6.25 m)
            Draught
Armament:
  Guns none
Missile systems
  none

A/S weapons
  none
Torpedo tubes
  8 21-in (533-mm)
Aircraft
  none
Radar and electronics:
Sonar:
Powerplant: (diesel-electric) 4 MTU diesels and 1 Siemens electric motor, delivering 5,000 shp to one shaft
Speed: 10 knots surfaced; 22 knots dived

Range: 50 days endurance
Crew: 31
Used also by: Argentina, Ecuador, Iran, Peru, Turkey, Uruguay, Venezuela
Notes: Examples of the highly successful Type 209 designed by Ingenieurkontor of Lübeck and built by Howaldtswerke of Kiel. Commissioned into Colombian service in April and July 1975.

Type SX-506 submarine (4)

Class: *Intrepido* (SS20), *Indomable* (SS21), *Roncador* (SS23), *Quita Sueno* (SS24)
Displacement: 58 tons (58.9 tonnes) surfaced; 70 tons (71.1 tonnes) dived
Dimensions: Length 75 ft 5½ in (23.0 m)
 Beam 6 ft 7 in (2.0 m)
 Draught 13 ft 1 in (4.0 m)
Armament:
Guns none
Missile systems
 none

A/S weapons
 none
Torpedo tubes
 none
Aircraft
 none
Radar and electronics:
Sonar:
Powerplant: diesel-electric, delivering 300 bhp to one shaft
Speed: 8 knots surfaced; 7 knots snorting; 6 knots dived
Range: 1,200 miles (1,931 km) at 7 knots

Crew: 5
Used only by: Colombia
Notes: Built by Cosmos, of Livorno, and delivered in sections for assembly at Cartagena. First pair commissioned in 1972 and second pair in 1974. Can carry 8 attack swimmers with 2 tons of explosive, plus two swimmer delivery vehicles. Diving depth 328 ft (100 m).

Congo

200 men

Patrol Craft:
3 Shanghai
4 river PC
12(?) small river PC

Costa Rica

50 men

Patrol Craft:
3 coastal PC

Cuba

9,000 men

Light Forces:
12 SO I submarine chasers
6 Kronshtadt submarine chasers
18 Komar FAC(M)
5 Osa I FAC(M)
3 Osa II FAC(M)
12 P-6 FAC(T)
12 P-4 FAC(T)

Patrol Forces:
8 Zhuk FAC(P)
12 coastal PC

Amphibious Forces:
7 T-4 LCM

Auxiliaries:
6 Nyryat I survey vessels
1 training ship
7 others

'SO-I' class patrol craft (12)

Class: 12 ex-Russian craft
Displacement: 215 tons (218.4 tonnes) standard; 250 tons (254 tonnes) full load
Dimensions: Length 137 ft 9½ in (42.0 m)
 Beam 21 ft 4 in (6.5 m)
 Draught 9 ft 2 in (2.8 m)
Armament:
Guns 4 25-mm in twin mountings
Missile systems
 none
A/S weapons
 2 DC racks
 4 quintuple MBU-4800 rocket-launchers
Torpedo tubes
 none
Aircraft

Radar and electronics: 'Pot Head' short-range surface search, 'High Pole' IFF, and 'Dead Duck' IFF radars
Sonar: 'Tamir'
Powerplant: 3 diesels, delivering 6,000 hp to three shafts
Speed: 29 knots
Range: 1,100 miles (1,770 km) at 13 knots
Crew: 30
Used also by: Algeria, Bulgaria, East Germany, Egypt, Iraq, North Korea, South Yemen, USSR, Vietnam
Notes: Six of these craft were transferred from Russia in 1964, the other six in 1967.

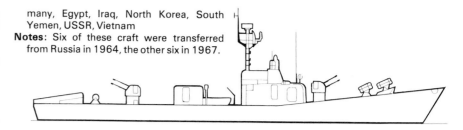

Cyprus

50 men

Patrol Craft:
2 R (?)

Denmark

6,100 men (1,900 conscripts)

Frigates:
2 Peder Skram
4 Hvidbjørnen
1 Modified Hvidbjørnen
(3 Niels Juel)

Corvettes:
3 Triton

SS:
2 Narhvalen
4 Delfinen

Light Forces:
10 Willemoes FAC(M)
6 Søløven FAC(T)

Patrol Forces:
9 Daphne PC
2 Agdleq PC
9 Barsø PC
2 Maagen PC
1 Tejsten PC
2 Botved type coastal PC
3 small Botved type coastal PC
3 Y type coastal PC
6 MHV 90 coastal PC
6 MHV 80 coastal PC
3 MHV 70 coastal PC

Mine Warfare Forces:
3 Falster minelayers
2 Lindormen minelayers
1 Langeland minelayer
8 Sund coastal minesweepers

Auxiliaries:
2 tankers
3 icebreakers
2 others

Aircraft:
8 Alouette III
(? Lynx)

'Peder Skram' class frigate (2)

Class: *Peder Skram* (F352), *Herluf Trolle* (F353)
Displacement: 2,030 tons (2,063 tonnes) standard; 2,720 tons (2,764 tonnes) full load
Dimensions: Length 396 ft 6 in (112.6 m)
Beam 39 ft 6 in (12.0 m)
Draught 11 ft 10 in (3.6 m)
Armament:
Guns 2 5-in (127-mm) in twin mountings
4 40-mm
Missile systems
1 4-cell Sea Sparrow
2 quadruple Harpoon launchers
A/S weapons
DCs
Torpedo tubes
4 21-in (533-mm) for wire-guided torpedoes
Aircraft
none

Radar and electronics: two CWS 3 combined warning, three CGS 1 fire-control, NWS 1 tactical and NWS 2 navigation radars
Sonar: PMS 26
Powerplant: (CODOG) 2 General Motors 16-567D diesels, delivering 4,800 bhp and 2 Pratt & Whitney PWA GG 4A-3 gas turbines, with a total output of 44,000 shp to two shafts
Speed: 30 knots
Range:
Crew: 190
Used only by: Denmark
Notes: Both built to Danish designs by Helsingörs J & M between 1964 and 1965; commissioned into Danish service in June 1966 and April 1967 respectively. The Harpoon launcher has replaced B turret (see drawing and photograph).

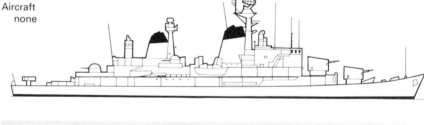

'Hvidbjørnen' class frigate (4)

Class: *Hvidbjørnen* (F348), *Vaedderen* (F349), *Ingolf* (F350), *Fylla* (F351)
Displacement: 1,345 tons (1,367 tonnes) standard; 1,650 tons (1,656 tonnes) full load

Dimensions: Length 238 ft 2 in (72.6 m)
Beam 38 ft (11.6 m)
Draught 16 ft (4.9 m)
Armament:
Guns 1 3-in (76-mm)
Missile systems

A/S weapons
  none
Torpedo tubes
  none
Aircraft
  1 Alouette III helicopter
Radar and electronics: AWS 1/CWS 2 search and NWS 1 tactical radars

Sonar: PMS 26
Powerplant: 4 General Motors 16-567C diesels, delivering 6,400 bhp to one shaft
Speed: 18 knots
Range: 6,000 miles (9,656 km) at 13 knots
Crew: 75
Used only by: Denmark

Notes: The first was built by Aarhus Flydedok, the second and fourth by Aarlborg Vaerft and the third by Svendborg Vaerft in 1961 and 1962, for commissioning in 1962 and 1963. They are fishery protection and survey vessels for operation in northern waters.

'Modified Hvidbjørnen' class frigate (1)

Class: *Beskytteren* (F340)
Displacement: 1,970 tons (2,002 tonnes) full load
Dimensions: Length 244 ft (74.4 m)
  Beam 39 ft (11.8 m)
  Draught 15 ft (4.5 m)
Armament:
Guns 1 76-mm (3-in) OTO Melara

Missile systems
  none
A/S weapons
  none
Torpedo tubes
  none
Aircraft
  1 Alouette III helicopter
Radar and electronics: AWS 1/CWS 2 search, NWS 1 tactical and NWS 2 navigation radars
Sonar: PMS 26

Powerplant: 3 BW Alpha diesels, delivering 7,440 bhp to one shaft
Speed: 18 knots
Range: 6,000 miles (9,656 km) at 13 knots on one engine
Crew: 60
Used only by: Denmark
Notes: Built by Aarborg Vaerft between 1974 and 1975, for commissioning in February 1976. Designed as a fishery protection and survey vessel for northern waters, strengthened for operations in ice.

'Niels Juel' class frigate (3)

Class: *'Niels Juel'* (F354), Olfert *Fischer* (F355), *Peter Tordenskjold* (F356)
Displacement: 1,320 tons (1,341 tonnes) full load
Dimensions: Length 275 ft (84.0 m)
  Beam 33 ft 10 in (10.3 m)
  Draught 10 ft 1 in (3.1 m)
Armament:
Guns 1 76-mm (3-in) OTO Melara
Missile systems
  1 octuple Sea Sparrow
  2 quadruple Harpoon
A/S weapons
  unfixed as yet
Torpedo tubes
  none
Aircraft
  none

Radar and electronics: Plessey AWS 5 search radar
Sonar:
Powerplant: (CODOG) 1 Rolls-Royce Olympus gas turbine, delivering 25,400 hp, and 2 MTU 20V-956 diesels, delivering 6,000 hp to two shafts

Speed: 28 knots
Range:
Crew: 90
Used only by: Denmark
Notes: First keel laid early in 1977 for a class intended finally to number six.

'Triton' class corvette (3)

Class: *Bellona* (F344), *Flora* (F346), *Triton* (F347)
Displacement: 760 tons (772 tonnes) standard; 873 tons (887 tonnes) full load
Dimensions: Length 250 ft 4 in (76.3 m)
  Beam 31 ft 6 in (9.6 m)
  Draught 9 ft (2.7 m)
Armament:
Guns 2 76-mm (3-in) in single mountings
  1 40-mm
Missile systems
  none

A/S weapons
  1 Hedgehog
  4 DCTs
Torpedo tubes
  none
Aircraft
  none
Radar and electronics: Plessey AWS 1 search and E-band navigation radars
Sonar: QCU-2
Powerplant: 2 Ansaldo Fiat 409T diesels, delivering 4,400 bhp to two shafts

Speed: 20 knots
Range: 3,000 miles (4,828 km) at 18 knots
Crew: 110
Used only by: Denmark
Notes: Built between 1953 and 1955 by Naval Meccanica of Castellammare, Cantiere del Tirreno of Riva Trigosa and Cantiere Navali di Taranto, as sisters to the Italian 'Albatros' class. The three ships were commissioned in 1957, 1956 and 1955 respectively. A fourth 'Triton', *Diana* (F345), was deleted in 1974.

'Narhvalen' class submarine (2)

Class: *Narhvalen* (S320), *Nordkaperen* (S321)
Displacement: 370 tons (376 tonnes) surfaced; 450 tons (457 tonnes) dived
Dimensions: Length 144 ft 5 in (44.3 m)
Beam 15 ft (4.6 m)
Draught 12 ft 6 in (3.8 m)
Armament:
Guns none
Missile systems
none
A/S weapons
none
Torpedo tubes
8 21-in (533-mm)
Aircraft
none
Radar and electronics:
Sonar: active and passive
Powerplant: 2 MB diesels, delivering 1,500 bhp, and 2 electric motors, delivering 1,500 bhp
Speed: 12 knots surfaced; 17 knots dived
Range:
Crew: 22
Used only by: Denmark
Notes: Built under licence by the Royal Dockyard at Copenhagen to the Improved Type 205 design of Ingenieurkontor of Lübeck. S320 laid down in February 1965, launched in September 1968 and commissioned in February 1970; S321 in January 1966, December 1969 and December 1970.

'Delfinen' class submarine (4)

Class: *Delfinen* (S326), *Spaekhuggeren* (S327), *Tumleren* (S328), *Springeren* (S329)
Displacement: 595 tons (604.5 tonnes) surfaced; 643 tons (653.3 tonnes) dived
Dimensions: Length 117 ft 2 in (54.0 m)
Beam 15 ft 5 in (4.7 m)
Draught 13 ft 1 in (4.0 m)
Armament:
Guns none
Missile systems
none
A/S weapons
none
Torpedo tubes
4 21-in (533-mm)
Aircraft
none
Radar and electronics:
Sonar: active and passive
Powerplant: 2 Burmeister & Wain diesels, delivering 1,200 bhp, and electric motors, delivering 1,200 hp
Speed: 15 knots surfaced and dived
Range: 4,000 miles (6,438 km) at 8 knots
Crew: 33
Used only by: Denmark
Notes: All built by the Royal Dockyard in Copenhagen. The first three were laid down between July 1954 and May 1956, launched between May 1956 and May 1958, and commissioned between September 1958 and January 1960. S329 was laid down in January 1961, launched in April 1963 and commissioned in October 1964.

'Willemoes' class fast attack craft (missile) (10)

Class: *Bille* (P540), *Bredal* (P541), *Hammer* (P542), *Huitfelde* (P543), *Krieger* (P544), *Norby* (P545), *Rodsteen* (P546), *Sehested* (P547), *Suenson* (P548), *Willemoes* (P549)
Displacement: 240 tons (243.8 tonnes) full load
Dimensions: Length 150 ft 11 in (46.0 m)
Beam 24 ft (7.4 m)
Draught 8 ft (2.4 m)
Armament:
Guns 1 76-mm (3-in) OTO Melara
Missile systems
4 or 8 Harpoon missiles (in place of aft torpedo tubes)
A/S weapons
none
Torpedo tubes
2 or 4 21-in (533-mm) (see notes)
Aircraft
none
Radar and electronics: combined warning, fire-control and NWS 3 navigation radars
Sonar:
Powerplant: (CODAG) 3 Rolls-Royce Proteus gas turbines, delivering 12,000 hp, and diesels for cruising, delivering 8,000 hp
Speed: 40 knots; 12 knots on diesels
Range:
Crew: 6+18
Used only by: Denmark
Notes: Designed by Lürssen, and similar to the Swedish 'Spica II' class. Built by Frederikshavn V & F. *Willemoes* was put in commission in October 1975, with *Bille*, *Bredal* and *Hammer* following in 1976. *Willemoes* was tested with four tubes and no missiles. A class of 24 craft is planned.

'Søløven' class fast attack craft (torpedo) (6)

Class: *Søløven* (P510), *Søridderen* (P511), *Søbjornen* (P512), *Søhesten* (P513), *Søhunden* (P514), *Søulven* (P515)
Displacement: 95 tons (96.5 tonnes) standard; 114 tons (115.8 tonnes) full load
Dimensions: Length 99 ft (30.3 m)
Beam 25 ft 6 in (7.3 m)
Draught 7 ft (2.2 m)
Armament:
Guns 2 40-mm Bofors in single mountings
Missile systems
none
A/S weapons
none
Torpedo tubes
4 21-in (533-mm)
Aircraft
none
Radar and electronics: NWS 1 tactical radar
Sonar:
Powerplant: 3 Bristol Siddeley Proteus gas turbines, delivering 12,750 bhp, and General Motors diesels for cruising
Speed: 54 knots; 10 knots on diesels
Range: 400 miles (644 km) at 46 knots
Crew: 29
Used only by: Denmark
Notes: First two built by Vosper and commissioned in February 1965. The rest were built by the Royal Dockyard at Copenhagen, commissioning between September 1965 and March 1967. The type combines the 'Brave' class hull with 'Ferocity' class construction.

'Falken' class fast attack craft (torpedo) (4)

Class: *Falken* (P506), *Glenten* (P507), *Gribben* (P508), *Høgen* (P509)
Displacement: 119 tons (120.9 tonnes)
Dimensions: Length 118 ft (35.9 m)
Beam 17 ft 10 in (5.4 m)
Draught 6 ft (1.8 m)
Armament:
Guns 1 40-mm
1 20-mm
Missile systems
none
A/S weapons
none
Torpedo tubes
4 21-in (533-mm)
Aircraft
none
Radar and electronics: NWS 1 tactical radar
Sonar:
Powerplant: 3 MTU diesels, delivering 9,000 bhp to three shafts
Speed: 40 knots
Range:
Crew: 23
Used only by: Denmark
Notes: All built by the Royal Dockyard at Copenhagen with US finance, and commissioned in October and December 1962, and April and June 1963. Now deleted.

'Daphne' class large patrol craft (9)

Class: *Daphne* (P530), *Dryaden* (P531), *Havmanden* (P532), *Havfruen* (P533), *Najaden* (P534), *Nymfen* (P535), *Neptun* (P536), *Ran* (P537), *Rota* (P538)
Displacement: 170 tons (172.7 tonnes)
Dimensions: Length 121 ft 4 in (38.0 m)
Beam 20 ft (6.8 m)
Draught 6 ft 6 in (2.0 m)
Armament:
Guns 1 40-mm
2 51-mm flare-launchers
Missile systems
none
A/S weapons
DCs
Torpedo tubes
none
Aircraft
none
Radar and electronics: NWS 3 navigation radar
Sonar:
Powerplant: 2 Foden FD6 diesels, delivering 2,600 bhp, and 1 cruising diesel, delivering 100 bhp, to two shafts
Speed: 20 knots
Range:
Crew: 23
Used only by: Denmark
Notes: All built by the Royal Dockyard at Copenhagen, and commissioned between December 1961 and January 1965. Built with US finance, and some craft have now been disarmed.

'Falster' class minelayer (3)

Class: *Falster* (N80), *Fyen* (N81), *Moen* (N82)
Displacement: 1,900 tons (1,930 tonnes) full load
Dimensions: Length 252 ft 7 in (77.0 m)
　　　　　　Beam 41 ft (12.5 m)
　　　　　　Draught 9 ft 10 in (3.0 m)
Armament:
Guns 4 3-in (76-mm) in twin mountings
Missile systems
　Sea Sparrow
Mines
　400
A/S weapons
　none
Torpedo tubes
　none
Aircraft
　none
Radar and electronics: CWS 2 combined warning, CGS 1 fire-control, NWS 1 tactical and NWS 2 navigation radars
Sonar:
Powerplant: 2 General Motors 567D3 diesels, delivering 4,800 shp to two shafts
Speed: 17 knots
Range:
Crew: 120
Used only by: Denmark
Notes: The first was built by Nakskov Skibsvaerft, and the second pair by Frederikshavn Vaerft, the first two commissioning in 1963 and the third in 1964. A sistership, *Sjaelland* (N83) was converted to a FAC and submarine depot ship in 1976. The hulls are strengthened for ice navigation.

'Lindormen' class minelayer (2)

Class: *Lindormen* (N43), *Lossen* (N44)
Displacement: 570 tons (579 tonnes)
Dimensions: Length 147 ft 7 in (45.0 m)
　　　　　　Beam 29 ft 6 in (9.0 m)
　　　　　　Draught 8 ft 10 in (2.7 m)
Armament:
Guns 2 20-mm
Missile systems
　none
A/S weapons
　none
Torpedo tubes
　none
Aircraft
　none
Radar and electronics:
Sonar:
Powerplant: diesels, delivering 1,600 hp
Speed: 14 knots
Range:
Crew: 27
Used only by: Denmark
Notes: Both built by Svendborg Vaerft and commissioned in 1978.

Dominican Republic

4,050 men

Frigates:
2 Tacoma
1 Canadian River

Corvettes:
2 Canadian Flower
2 Admirable
3 Cohoes

Patrol Forces:
3 Argo
1 PGM PC
1 large PC
12 coastal PC

Amphibious Forces:
1 LCT
1 LCM

Auxiliaries:
5 survey vessels
2 tankers
10 others

'Tacoma' class frigate (2)

Class: *Gregorio Luperon* (452), ex-US *Pueblo* (PF13); *Capitano General Pedro Santana* (453), ex-US *Knoxville* (PF64)
Displacement: 1,430 tons (1,453 tonnes) standard; 2,415 tons (2,454 tonnes) full load
Dimensions: Length 304 ft (92.7 m)
　　　　　　Beam 37 ft 6 in (11.4 m)
　　　　　　Draught 13 ft 8 in (4.2 m)
Armament:
Guns 3 3-in (76-mm) in single mountings
　4 40-mm in twin mountings
　6 20-mm
　4 0.5-in (12.7-mm) machine-guns
Missile systems
　none
A/S weapons
　none
Torpedo tubes
　none
Aircraft
　none
Radar and electronics:
Sonar:
Powerplant: 2 boilers supplying steam to triple-expansion reciprocating engines, delivering 5,500 ihp to two shafts
Speed: 19 knots
Range: 9,500 miles (15,289 km) at 12 knots
Crew: 140
Used also by: Thailand
Notes: Built by Leatham D. Smith Ship Building and Kaiser Ship Yards respectively between April 1943 and January 1944; commissioned into US service in April and May 1944. They were transferred to the Dominican Republic in September 1947 and July 1946 respectively, with the names *Presidente Troncoso* and *Presidente Peynado* until 1962. Now in reserve.

Canadian 'Flower' class corvette (2)

Class: *Cristobal Colon* (401), ex-Canadian *Lachute*; *Juan Alejandro Acosta* (402), ex-Canadian *Louisburg*
Displacement: 1,060 tons (1,077 tonnes) standard; 1,350 tons (1,372 tonnes) full load
Dimensions: Length 208 ft (63.4 m)
　　　　　　Beam 33 ft (10.0 m)
　　　　　　Draught 13 ft 4 in (4.0 m)
Armament:
Guns 1 4-in (102-mm)
　2 40-mm, 6 20-mm and 4 0.5-in in *Colon*
　1 40-mm, 6 20-mm and 2 0.5-in in *Acosta*
Missile systems
　none
A/S weapons
　none
Torpedo tubes
　none
Aircraft
　none
Radar and electronics:
Sonar:
Powerplant: 2 boilers supplying steam to triple expansion reciprocating engines, delivering 2,750 ihp
Speed: 16 knots
Range: 2,900 miles (4,667 km) at 15 knots
Crew: 53
Used only by: Dominican Republic
Notes: Both built by Morton Ltd of Quebec City, they were launched in June 1944 and July 1943 respectively, and commissioned into Canadian service in October 1944 and December 1943. Five of these ships were transferred to the Dominican Republic during 1947.

PGM Type large patrol craft (1)

Class: *Betelgeuse* (GC102), ex-US *PGM 71*
Displacement: 145.5 tons (147.8 tonnes)
Dimensions: Length 101 ft 6 in (30.9 m)
　　　　　　Beam 21 ft (6.4 m)
　　　　　　Draught 5 ft (1.5 m)
Armament:
Guns 1 40-mm
　4 20-mm in twin mountings
　2 0.5-in (12.7-mm) machine-guns
Missile systems
　none
A/S weapons
　none
Torpedo tubes
　none
Aircraft
　none
Radar and electronics:
Sonar:
Powerplant: 8 General Motors 6-71 diesels, delivering 2,200 bhp to two shafts
Speed: 21 knots
Range: 1,500 miles (2,414 km) at 10 knots
Crew: 20
Used also by: Burma, Ethiopia, Philippines, Turkey
Notes: Built in the US by Peterson, and commissioned into US service in 1966 before transfer to the Dominican Republic later in the year.

East Germany

16,000 men (10,000 conscripts)

Frigates:
1 Riga

Light Forces:
12 Osa I FAC(M)
3 Osa II FAC(M)
18 Shershen FAC(T)
7 Libelle FAC(T)
40 Iltis FAC(T)

Patrol Forces:
4 SO-I large PC
14 Hai large PC
4 P-6 FAC(P)
18 KB 123 coastal PC

Amphibious Forces:
5 Frösch LST
10 Robbe LST
12 Labo LCT

Mine Warfare Forces:
52 Kondor I and II

Auxiliaries:
2 Kondor intelligence ships
4 survey ships
10 training ships
3 icebreakers
34 others

Aircraft:
1 sqn with 8 Mi-4, 5 Mi-8

'Hai' class large patrol craft (14)

Class: *Bad Doberan, Bützow, Grevesmühlen, Gadebusch, Lübz, Ludwigslust, Parchim, Perleberg, Ribnitz-Damgarten, Sternberg, Teterow, Wismar* and two others
Displacement: 300 tons (304.8 tonnes) standard; 370 tons (375.9 tonnes) full load
Dimensions: Length 187 ft (57.0 m)
　　　　　　Beam 19 ft (5.8 m)
　　　　　　Draught 10 ft (3.1 m)
Armament:
Guns 4 30-mm in twin mountings
Missile systems
　none
A/S weapons
　4 quintuple RBU 1800 launchers
　2 DC racks
Torpedo tubes
　none
Aircraft
　none
Radar and electronics:
Sonar:
Powerplant: 2 gas turbines, and diesels, delivering 8,000 bhp
Speed: 25 knots
Range:
Crew: 45
Used only by: East Germany
Notes: Built between 1962 and 1969 by Peenewerft of Wolgast.

Ecuador

3,800 men (700 marines)

Destroyers:
1 Gearing FRAM I

Frigates:
1 Charles Lawrence
2 Hunt Type 1
(1 Lupo)

Corvettes:
2 PCE type
(4 ?)

SS:
2 Type 209

Light Forces:
3 Lürssen type FAC(M)
3 Manta FAC(T)

Patrol Forces:
2 PGM 71 PC
5 coastal PC

Amphibious Forces:
1 LST 511-1152
2 LSM-1

Auxiliaries:
1 Aloe survey ship
4 tugs
1 training ship
6 others

Aircraft:
3 Arava transports
2 T-37 trainers
2 T-41 trainers
1 Cessna 320
1 Cessna 177
2 Alouette III

'Hunt' Type 1 class frigate (2)

Class: *Presidente Alfaro* (D02), ex-British *Quantock*; *Presidente Velasco Ibarra* (D03), ex-British *Meynell*
Displacement: 1,000 tons (1,016 tonnes) standard; 1,490 tons (1,514 tonnes) full load
Dimensions: Length 280 ft (85.4 m)
Beam 29 ft (8.8 m)
Draught 14 ft (4.3 m)
Armament:
Guns 4 4-in (102-mm) in twin mountings
2 40-mm in twin mounting
2 20-mm
Missile systems
none
A/S weapons
DCTs and DC racks

Torpedo tubes
none
Aircraft
none
Radar and electronics:
Sonar:
Powerplant: 2 Admiralty type boilers supplying steam to Parsons geared turbines, delivering 19,000 shp to two shafts
Speed: 23 knots
Range: 2,000 miles (3,218 km) at 12 knots
Crew: 146
Used also by: Egypt, India, UK
Notes: Built in 1939 and 1940 by Scotts Ship Building of Greenock and Swan Hunter of Wallsend, and commissioned into British service in February 1941 and December 1940 respectively. Both ships were bought by Ecuador in 1954 and handed over after refits in 1955. They are now due for deletion.

Type 209 submarine (2)

Class: *Shyri* (SS11), *Huancavilca* (SS12)
Displacement: 980 tons (995.7 tonnes) surfaced; 1,356 tons (1,378 tonnes) dived
Dimensions: Length 183 ft 5 in (55.9 m)
Beam 20 ft 8 in (6.3 m)
Draught 17 ft 8½ in (5.4 m)
Armament:
Guns none
Missile systems
none
A/S weapons
none
Torpedo tubes
8 21-in (533-mm)

Aircraft
none
Radar and electronics:
Sonar:
Powerplant: MTU diesels, and 4 electric motors, delivering 5,000 shp to one shaft
Speed: 10 knots (surfaced); 22 knots (dived)
Range:
Crew: 32
Used also by: Argentina, Colombia, Iran, Peru, Turkey, Uruguay, Venezuela
Notes: Built by Howaldtswerke of Kiel, these two boats were laid down in 1975 and commissioned in 1977. Two more boats of the same class are reportedly on order.

Egypt

20,000 men (15,000 reservists)

Destroyers:
4 Skory
1 Z

Frigates:
1 Black Swan
1 British River
1 British Hunt
(2 Lupo)

SS:
6 Romeo
6 Whiskey

Light Forces:
6 Osa I FAC(M)
10 Komar FAC(M)
6 Shershen FAC(T) and FAC(G)
20 P-6 FAC(T)
4 P-4 FAC(T)
(6 Vosper Ramadan FAC(G))

Patrol Forces:
12 SO I PC
3 Nisr PC
20 Bertram type coastal PC

Amphibious Forces:
3 Polnocny LCT
10 Vydra LCU
4 SMB1 LCU
10 LCM

Mine Warfare Forces:
6 T-43 ocean minesweepers
4 Yurka ocean minesweepers
2 T-301 inshore minesweepers
2 K-8 inshore minesweepers

Auxiliaries:
3 SRN-6 hovercraft (+3)
3 training ships
2 tugs

Aircraft:
6 Sea King ASW helicopters

'Skory' class destroyer (4)

Class: *Al Zaffer*; *Damiette*; *6 October*, (ex-*Al Nasser*); *Suez*
Displacement: 2,600 tons (2,642 tonnes) standard; 3,500 tons (3,556 tonnes) full load
Dimensions: Length 395 ft 4 in (120.5 m)
Beam 38 ft 8 in (11.8 m)
Draught 15 ft 1 in (4.6 m)
Armament:
Guns 4 5.1-in (130-mm)
2 3.4-in (88-mm)
8 37-mm and 4 25-mm in twin mountings (unmodified ships)
4 57-mm in quadruple mounting, 4 37-mm and 4 25-mm in twin mountings (modified ships)
A/S weapons
2 DCTs and 2 DC racks (unmodified ships)
2 12-barrel RBU 2500 launchers, 2 DCTs and 2 DC racks (modified ships)

Torpedo tubes
2 quintuple 21-in (533-mm)
Aircraft
none
Radar and electronics: E/F-band (probably) search, G-band (probably) tactical and 'Hawk Screech' fire-control radars
Sonar:
Powerplant: 3 boilers supplying steam to geared turbines, delivering 60,000 shp to two shafts
Speed: 35 knots
Range: 4,000 miles (6,438 km) at 15 knots
Crew: 260
Used also by: USSR
Notes: Built in Russia and launched in 1951. Egypt received the original *Al Nasser* and *Al Zaffer* in 1956, and *Damiette* and *Suez* in 1962. During April 1967 *Al Nasser* and *Damiette* were exchanged for modified vessels which took the same names.

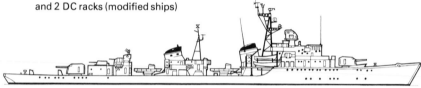

'Z' class destroyer (1)

Class: *El Fateh*, ex-British *Zenith*
Displacement: 1,730 tons (1,758 tonnes) standard; 2,575 tons (2,616 tonnes) full load
Dimensions: Length 362 ft 9 in (110.6 m)
Beam 35 ft 9 in (10.9 m)
Draught 17 ft 1 in (5.2 m)
Armament:
Guns 4 4.5-in (114-mm) in single mountings
6 40-mm
Missile systems
none
A/S weapons
4 DCTs
Torpedo tubes
none
Aircraft
none

Radar and electronics: Type 960 search, Type 293 tactical and I-band fire-control
Sonar:
Powerplant: 2 Admiralty boilers supplying steam to Parsons geared turbines, delivering 40,000 shp to two shafts
Speed: 31 knots
Range: 2,800 miles (4,506 km) at 20 knots
Crew: 250
Used only by: Egypt
Notes: Built by William Denny & Brothers at Dumbarton between 1942 and 1944, and commissioned into British service in December 1944. She was bought by Egypt in 1956, refitted and handed over in 1956.

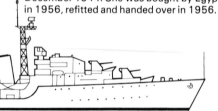

'Black Swan' class frigate (1)

Class: *Tariq* (555), ex-*Malek Farouq* (42), ex-British *Whimbrel*
Displacement: 1,925 tons (1,956 tonnes)
Dimensions: Length 299 ft 6 in (91.3 m)
Beam 38 ft 6 in (11.7 m)
Draught 14 ft (4.3 m)
Armament:
Guns 6 4-in (102-mm) in twin mountings
4 40-mm

2 20-mm
Missile systems
none
A/S weapons
4 DCTs
DC racks
Torpedo tubes
none
Aircraft
none
Radar and electronics:
Sonar:

Powerplant: 2 boilers supplying steam to geared turbines, 4,300 shp to two shafts
Speed: 19¾ knots
Range: 4,500 miles (7,242 km) at 12 knots
Crew: 180
Used also by: India
Notes: Built by Yarrow at Glasgow between October 1941 and August 1942, and commissioned into British service in January 1943. Transferred to Egypt in November 1949.

'Romeo' class submarine (6)

Class: Nos *744, 745, 765, 766* and two others
Displacement: 1,000 tons (1,016 tonnes) surfaced; 1,600 tons (1,626 tonnes) dived
Dimensions: Length 249 ft 4 in (76.0 m)
Beam 23 ft 11½ in (7.3 m)
Draught 14 ft 5 in (4.4 m)
Armament:
Guns none
Missile systems
none

A/S weapons
none
Torpedo tubes
8 21-in (533-mm), with 18 torpedoes or 36 mines
Aircraft
none
Radar and electronics: 'Snoop Plate' surveillance radar and 'Stop Light' ECM
Sonar: 'Herkules' and 'Feniks'
Powerplant: 2 diesel engines delivering 4,000 hp, and 2 electric motors, delivering 4,000 hp to two shafts

Speed: 17 knots (surfaced); 14 knots (dived)
Range: 8,078 miles (13,000 km) at 5 knots surfaced
Crew: 65
Used also by: Bulgaria, China, North Korea, USSR
Notes: The six Egyptian 'Romeo' class attack submarines were transferred from Russia in the period 1966–9. Their construction probably took place in Leningrad, starting in 1961.

'Whiskey' class submarine (6)

Class: Nos *415, 418, 421, 455* and two others
Displacement: 1,030 tons (1,046 tonnes) surfaced; 1,350 tons (1,372 tonnes) dived
Dimensions: Length 249 ft 4 in (76.0 m)
Beam 22 ft (6.7 m)
Draught 15 ft 1 in (4.6 m)
Armament:
Guns none
Missile systems
none
A/S weapons
none
Torpedo tubes
6 21-in (533-mm) with 18 torpedoes or 24 mines
Aircraft
none

Radar and electronics: 'Snoop Plate' surface search radar and 'Stop Light' ECM
Sonar: 'Tamir'
Powerplant: 2 diesels, delivering 4,000 hp, and 2 electric motors, delivering 2,500 hp to two shafts
Speed: 17 knots (surfaced); 15 knots (dived)
Range: 13,000 miles (20,922 km) at 8 knots surfaced

Crew: 60
Used also by: Albania, Bulgaria, China, Indonesia, North Korea, Poland, USSR
Notes: Four 'Whiskey' class boats were transferred to Egypt in 1957, another three in 1958, and an eighth in 1962. In 1966 two of the boats were replaced by 'Romeo' class boats. The 'Whiskey' class is designed for torpedo attack.

Eire

600 men

Corvettes:
2 Deidre (+1)

Mine Warfare Forces:
3 Ton coastal minesweepers

Auxiliaries:
1 training ship
1 tender

'Deidre' class patrol vessel (2)

Class: *Deidre* (P20), *Emer* (P21)
Displacement: 972 tons (988 tonnes)
Dimensions: Length 184 ft 4 in (56.2 m)
Beam 34 ft 1 in (10.4 m)
Draught 14 ft 5 in (4.4 m)
Armament:
Guns 1 40-mm Bofors
Missile systems
none
A/S weapons
none
Torpedo tubes
none

Aircraft
none
Radar and electronics:
Sonar:
Powerplant: 2 British Polar diesels, delivering 4,200 bhp to one shaft
Speed: 18 knots
Range: 5,000 miles (8,047 km) at 12 knots
Crew: 5+41
Used only by: Eire
Notes: Both vessels were built by Verolme of Cork, *Deidre* being commissioned in 1972. *Emer*, commissioned in 1978, is 6ft 7 in (2.0 m) longer, and has SEMT Pielstick diesels, improving speed by 2 knots. She displaces 1,020 tons (1,037 tonnes).

El Salvador

130 men

Patrol Craft:
4 PC

Equatorial Guinea

Light Forces:
1 P-6 FAC(T)

Patrol Forces:
1 Poluchat PC

Ethiopia

1,500 men

Patrol Craft:
4 PGM type PC
1 Kraljevica PC
4 Sewart large PC
4 Sewart coastal PC
4 Swift PC (?)

Light Forces:
2 Osa II FAC(M)
Mine Warfare Forces:
1 Wildervank coastal minesweeper

Auxiliaries:
1 Barnegat training ship
2 LCM
2 LCVP

Fiji

159 men (under command of Royal Fiji
Military Forces)

Mine Warfare Forces:
3 Redwing coastal minesweepers

Auxiliaries:
1 survey vessel

Finland

2,500 men

Frigates:
2 Riga

Corvettes:
2 Turunmaa

Light Forces:
4 Tuima FAC(M) (+5)
1 experimental FAC(M)
13 Nuoli FAC(G)
1 Vasama FAC(G)

Patrol Forces:
3 Ruissalo PC
2 Rihtniemi PC

Mine Warfare Forces:
1 Improved Ruotsinsalmi minelayer
6 Kuha inshore minesweepers
(1 ? minelayer)

Auxiliaries:
2 HQ ships
6 Kala LCU transports
5 Kave LCU transports
3 Pukkio support ships
9 icebreakers

The Coastguard has 600 men, and
operates five large patrol craft and
eight coastal patrol craft, plus large
numbers of inshore patrol boats, one
training ship and one supply ship.

'Turunmaa' class corvette (2)

Class: *Karjala, Turunmaa*
Displacement: 660 tons (671 tonnes) stan-
    dard; 770 tons (782 tonnes) full load
Dimensions: Length 243 ft 1 in (74.1 m)
    Beam 25 ft 7 in (7.8 m)
    Draught 7 ft 10 in (2.4 m)
Armament:
Guns 1 4.7-in (120-mm) Bofors
    2 40-mm
    2 30-mm (twin)
Missile systems
    none
A/S weapons
    2 DCTs and 2 DC racks
Torpedo tubes
    none

Aircraft
    none
Radar and electronics: search and tactical
    radar by Hollandse Signaal
Sonar:
Powerplant: (CODOG) 3 Mercedes-Benz
    MTU diesels, 3,000 bhp and 1 Rolls-Royce
    Olympus gas turbine, 22,000 hp
Speed: 35 knots (17 knots on diesels)
Range:
Crew: 70
Used only by: Finland
Notes: Laid down in March 1967, launched
    later that year and commissioned in the
    second half of 1968. Fitted with Vosper
    Thornycroft stabilizers.

'Tuima' class fast attack craft (missile) (4)

Class: *Tuima, Tuuli, Tuisku, Tyrsky*
Displacement: 165 tons (167.6 tonnes)
    standard; 200 tons (203.2 tonnes) full load
Dimensions: Length 128 ft 8 in (39.3 m)
    Beam 25 ft 1 in (7.7 m)
    Draught 5 ft 11 in (1.8 in)
Armament:
Guns 4 30-mm in twin mountings

Missile systems
    4 SS-N-2 launchers
A/S weapons
    none
Torpedo tubes
    none
Aircraft
    none
Radar and electronics: Finnish search and
    fire-control radars
Sonar:
Powerplant: 3 diesels, delivering 13,000 hp

Speed: 36 knots
Range: 800 miles (1,288 km) at 25 knots
Crew: 25
Used only by: Finland
Notes: Built in the USSR as 'Osa' class craft, but fitted with Finnish electronics. Five more are planned

Experimental missile craft (1)

Class: *Isku*
Displacement: 140 tons (142.25 tonnes) full load
Dimensions: Length 86 ft 6 in (26.0 m)
Beam 28 ft 7 in (8.7 m)
Draught 5 ft 11 in (1.8 m)
Armament:
Guns 2 30-mm in twin mounting
Missile systems
4 SS-N-2 launchers
A/S weapons
none
Torpedo tubes
none
Aircraft
none
Radar and electronics:
Sonar:
Powerplant: 4 Russian M50 diesels, delivering 3,600 bhp
Speed: 15 knots
Range:
Crew: 25
Used only by: Finland
Notes: Commissioned in 1970 from the Reposaaron yard at Konepaja as an experimental and training craft. It is basically a combination of missile-craft superstructure and armament with a landing-craft hull.

'Ruissalo' class large patrol craft (3)

Class: *Ruissalo* (3) *Raisio* (4), *Röytta* (5)
Displacement: 110 tons (111.8 tonnes) standard; 130 tons (132.1 tonnes) full load
Dimensions: Length 111 ft 6 in (33.0 m)
Beam 19 ft 10 in (6.0 m)
Draught 5 ft 11 in (1.8 m)
Armament:
Guns 1 40-mm
1 20-mm
2 machine-guns
Missile systems
none
A/S weapons
1 Squid mortar
Torpedo tubes
none
Aircraft
none
Radar and electronics: Decca
Sonar: one (hull-mounted)

Powerplant: 2 Mercedes-Benz MTU diesels, 2,500 bhp
Speed: 18 knots
Range:
Crew: 20

Used only by: Finland
Notes: Built by Laivatteollisuus at Turku in 1958 and 1959. All three boats were commissioned in the second half of 1959.

'Rihtniemi' class large patrol craft (2)

Class: *Rihtniemi* (1), *Rymättlyä* (2)
Displacement: 90 tons (91.45 tonnes) standard; 110 tons (111.8 tonnes) full load
Dimensions: Length 101 ft 8 in (31.0 m)
　　　　　　　Beam 18 ft 8 in (5.6 m)
　　　　　　　Draught 5 ft 11 in (1.8 m)
Armament:
Guns 1 40-mm
　　　1 20-mm
　　　2 machine-guns
Missile systems
　　　none
A/S weapons
　　　2 DC racks
Torpedo tubes
　　　none
Aircraft
　　　none
Radar and electronics:
Sonar:

Powerplant: 2 Mercedes-Benz MTU diesels, 1,400 bhp
Speed: 15 knots
Range:
Crew: 20
Used only by: Finland
Notes: Built by Rauma-Repola at Rauma in 1955 and 1956, and commissioned in the first half of 1957. Both craft can lay mines.

'Improved Ruotsinsalmi' class minelayer (1)

Class: *Keihassalmi*
Displacement: 360 tons (365.8 tonnes)
Dimensions: Length 168 ft (52.0 m)
　　　　　　　Beam 23 ft (7.0 m)
　　　　　　　Draught 6 ft (1.9 m)
Armament:
Guns 4 30-mm in twin mountings
　　　2 20-mm
Missile systems
　　　none
Mines
　　　100 capacity
A/S weapons
　　　none
Torpedo tubes
　　　none
Aircraft
　　　none
Radar and electronics: search and tactical radar; Decca navigation
Sonar:
Powerplant: 2 Wärtsilä diesels, 2,000 bhp to two shafts

Speed: 15 knots
Range:
Crew: 60
Used only by: Finland

Notes: Ordered in 1955, launched in 1957 from the Helsinki yard of Valmet and commissioned towards the end of the year. The armament was updated in 1972.

France

The French Navy
The French Navy is faced with the prospect of maritime war on three fronts – coastal operations in the north along the English Channel coast, and ocean as well as coastal operations along the Atlantic and Mediterranean 'fronts'. France is no longer a member of the integrated military organisation of NATO, but her forces are clearly designed to operate with NATO's forces in time of war, and are thus to be considered in the *de facto* if not *de iure* light of NATO's overall military strategy. Accordingly, France has a large and well-balanced fleet commensurate with her European and international obligations and interests. The French Navy has some 68,300 men, including 17,400 conscripts, about 13.56 per cent of the total armed forces' personnel. The defence budget is about 4.67 per cent of the gross national budget.

France, as a nuclear power, has opted for a triple delivery capability, with submarine- and silo-launched missiles, and air-dropped bombs. The SLBMs are under the control of the navy, which has four special nuclear-powered ballistic missile-launching submarines, plus one building and a sixth (of a new type) ordered in 1978. France has also embarked on a programme of nuclear attack submarine construction, the first boat being laid down in 1976 for commissioning in 1981. It is expected that these boats, which will incorporate many of the systems used in the 'Agosta' class of conventional submarines, will eventually comprise two squadrons (eight boats), one squadron based at Brest for Atlantic operations, and the other at Toulon for Mediterranean operations. France also has 23 conventional attack submarines, four of them of the excellent 'Agosta'

and nine of them of the redoubtable 'Daphné' classes.
France's major surface ships are a well balanced mix of A/S ships and surface strike vessels. The A/S force is centred on the new PA75 type nuclear-powered helicopter carrier to be laid down in 1980 or 1981, the three new Type C70 dual-purpose destroyers, the three Type F67 destroyers, the five Type T47ASW destroyers, several other 'one off' destroyers, and the 12 (plus two building) Type A69 frigates. Eventually the force will be joined by three A/S versions of the Type C70 destroyer, and other new construction vessels. For the strike role, France has two attack carriers of the 'Clemenceau' class, provided with SAM defence and the radar control of their air strikes by the cruiser *Colbert*, and supported by the guided-missile destroyers of the 'Suffren' class. *Colbert* and the two 'Suffren' class ships are to be retrofitted

with Exocet surface-to-surface missiles to improve their attack capabilities. Further missile support is provided by the four destroyers of the Type T47 DDG SAM class, and the nine frigates of the 'Commandant Rivière' SSM missile class. Other ships are fitted with SAM, SSM or surface-to-underwater missile systems, making the French Navy extremely strong in this aspect of modern naval war. France also has five FAC(M) fitted with the older SS.11 and SS.12 surface-to-surface missiles, and another six large FAC(M), probably armed with Exocet, are to be built by 1982.

These missile boats are designed for coastal operations, in which they are joined by 31 large patrol craft and a number of coastal patrol craft. Also intended for operations in these waters are 26 coastal minesweepers, supported in ocean waters by the five minehunters of the 'Circé' class and 13 minehunters/minesweepers of the 'Aggressive' and 'MSO498' classes.

Until recently, the possibility of major amphibious operations has featured prominently in France's naval thinking, and this has left the country with two landing ships (dock), two light transports, five landing ships (tank) and a number of other amphibious warfare vessels.

Although it has only 123 combat aircraft, the French Navy's air arm, the *Aéronavale*, is of high quality in men and *matériel*, well able to fulfil the tasks envisaged for it. Particularly important are the two Etendard IVM attack squadrons, the two Alizé ASW squadrons, the three shore-based helicopter ASW squadrons, and the four shore-based maritime reconnaissance squadrons equipped with Atlantic and Neptune aircraft.

The French Navy has good manpower reserves, a fairly modern and carefully thought out support force, and a forward-looking building programme, all of which should ensure that France maintains her present efficient navy.

68,300 men (17,400 conscripts) including naval air arm (about 50,000 reservists)

SSNB:
4 Le Redoutable (+1)
(1 ?)
SSN:
(1 + 4 SNA 72)

SS:
4 Agosta
9 Daphné
4 Aréthuse
6 Narval
1 experimental SS

CV:
2 Clemenceau
(1 PA75 nuclear-powered)

Cruisers:
1 La Résolue (CAH)
1 Colbert

Destroyers:
3 Type C70 (+3)
2 Suffren
3 Type F67 (C67A)
1 Type T56
1 Modified Type T53 ASW
2 Type T53
4 Type T47 DDG
5 Type T47 ASW
1 Type C65

Frigates:
9 Commandant Rivière
10 Type E52
1 Type E50
12 Type A69 (+4)

Amphibious Forces:
2 TCD LSD
2 Batral type transports
5 BDC LST
12 EDIC LCT
16 CTM LCM
20 LCM (miscellaneous)

Light Forces:
4 Trident FAC(M)
1 La Combattante I FAC(M)

Patrol Forces:
10 Sirius PC
3 Le Fougueux PC
6 La Dunkerquoise PC
5 Ham PC
1 Fairmile ML type PC
4 Tecimar coastal PC
2 coastal PC

Mine Warfare Forces:
5 Circé minehunters
13 Aggressive and MSO498 ocean mine-hunters and ocean minesweepers
6 Sirius coastal minesweepers
15 Adjutant coastal minesweepers
1 Type DB1 coastal minesweeper
(1 + 14 Modified Circe minehunters)

Auxiliaries:
9 survey vessels
10 tankers
5 depot ships
4 maintenance ships
5 stores ships
6 trials ships
others

Naval Air Arm (*Aéronavale*) (13,000 men):
24 Etendard IVM (2 attack sqns)
20 F-8E (2 interceptor sqns)
24 Alizé (2 ASW sqns)
(4 MR sqns) 25 Atlantic, 10 SP-2H
8 Etendard IVP (1 recce sqn)
(2 OCUs) 12 Etendard IVM 14 Magister, 4 Nord 262
(3 ASW sqns) 12 Super Frelon, 12 SH-34 J, 8 Alouette III
12 SH-34 J (1 assault helicopter sqn)
20 Alouette II/III (2 SAR sqns)
(1 GP helicopter sqn) 4 Alouette II, 7 Super Frelon, 18 Lynx
(9 communications sqns) DC-6, C-47, Alouette, Super Frelon
(4 training/liaison sqns) Nord 262, C-47, Falcon/Mystère 20, Paris, Alizé, Rallye
(29 Super Etendard)
(8 Lynx)

'Le Redoutable' class nuclear ballistic missile submarine (5+1)

Class: *Le Foudroyant* (S610), *Le Redoutable* (S611), *Le Terrible* (S612), *L'Indomptable* (S613), *Le Tonnant* (S614), and possibly *L'Inflexible* (Q260)
Displacement: 7,500 tons (7,620 tonnes) surfaced; 9,000 tons (9,144 tonnes) dived
Dimensions: Length 420 ft (128.0 m)
  Beam 34 ft 9 in (10.6 m)
  Draught 32 ft 10 in (10.0 m)
Armament:
Guns none
Missile systems
  16 launcher tubes for MSBS
A/S weapons
  none

Torpedo tubes
  4 21.7-in (550-mm) with 18 torpedoes
Aircraft
  none
Radar and electronics: Calypso navigation and attack radar; passive ECM and DF systems

Sonar:
Powerplant: 1 pressurized water-cooled reactor; 1 2,670-hp auxiliary diesel
Speed: 20 knots surfaced; 25 knots dived
Range:
Crew: 15+120 (two alternating crews)
Used only by: France

Notes: Diving depth over 700 ft (213 m). All five current boats built by Cherbourg Naval Dockyard: *Le Redoutable* launched in March 1967 and *Le Tonnant* in 1975.

L'Inflexible may be laid down in 1982 as the lead boat of a new class. All boats will eventually carry M-4 missiles.

'Agosta' class patrol submarine (4)

Class: *Agosta* (S620), *Bévéziers* (S621), *La Praya* (S622), *Ouessant* (S623)
Displacement: 1,450 tons (1,473 tonnes) surfaced; 1,725 tons (1,753 tonnes) dived
Dimensions: Length 221 ft 9 in (67.6 m)
Beam 22 ft 4 in (6.8 m)
Draught 17 ft 1 in (5.2 m)
Armament:
Guns none
Missile systems
none
A/S weapons
none
Torpedo tubes
4 21.7-in (550-mm) tubes with 24 torpedoes
Aircraft
none

Radar and electronics: possibly Calypso TH D 1030 or TH D 1031 search and navigation radar
Sonar: DUUA 2 active and DSUV passive
Powerplant: (diesel electric) 2 SEMT Pielstick 16 PA4 diesels delivering 3,600 hp; 1

3,500 kW electric motor delivering 4,600 hp to one shaft
Speed: 12 knots surfaced; 20 knots dived
Range: 8,500 miles (13,680 km) at 9 knots (snorting); 350 miles (563 km) at 3½ knots (dived)
Crew: 7+43

Used by: France; to be built for Spain at Cartagena; and 2 ordered for South Africa
Notes: All built by Cherbourg Naval Dockyard. All were laid down 1972–4 and launched between October 1974 and January 1976. They are very quiet boats, and have an endurance of 45 days.

'Daphné' class patrol submarine (9)

Class: *Daphné* (S641), *Diane* (S642), *Doris* (S643), *Flore* (S645), *Galatée* (S646), *Junon* (S648), *Venus* (S649), *Psyché* (S650), *Sirène* (S651)
Displacement: 869 tons (883 tonnes) surfaced; 1,043 tons (1,060 tonnes) dived
Dimensions: Length 189 ft 8 in (57.8 m)
Beam 22 ft 4 in (6.8 m)
Draught 15 ft 1 in (4.6 m)
Armament:
Guns none
Missile systems
none
A/S weapons
none
Torpedo tubes
12 21.7-in (550-mm)
Aircraft
none
Radar and electronics: Calypso II search and navigation

Sonar: DUUA 2 active; passive ranging; interception set
Powerplant: (diesel electric) SEMT-Pielstick motors delivering 1,300 bhp surfaced and 1,600 bhp dived to two shafts
Speed: 13½ knots (surfaced); 16 knots (dived)
Range: 2,700 miles (4,345 km) at 12½ knots (surfaced); 4,500 miles 7,242 km) at 5 knots (snorting); 3,000 miles (4,828 km) at 7 knots (snorting)
Crew: 6+39

Used also by: Libya, Pakistan, Portugal, South Africa, Spain
Notes: Basically improved Aréthuse class boats with a diving depth of 984 ft (300 m). The first two were built by Dubigeon, the next five by Cherbourg Naval Dockyard, and the last two by Brest Naval Dockyard. The nine French boats were built between 1958 and 1967, the last commissioning in March 1970.

'Aréthuse' class patrol submarine (4)

Class: *Aréthuse* (S635), *Argonaute* (S636), *Amazone* (S639), *Ariane* (S640)
Displacement: 543 tons (552 tonnes) surfaced; 669 tons (680 tonnes) dived
Dimensions: Length 162 ft 9 in (49.6 m)
Beam 19 ft (5.8 m)
Draught 13 ft 1 in (4.0 m)
Armament:
Guns none
Missile systems
none
A/S weapons
none
Torpedo tubes
4 21.7-in (550-mm) with 8 torpedoes
Aircraft
none
Radar and electronics:

Sonar: DUUA 2 active
Powerplant: SEMT-Pielstick diesel electric, delivering 1,060 bhp (surfaced); electric motors delivering 1,300 hp (dived) to one shaft
Speed: 12½ knots (surfaced); 16 knots (dived)

Range:
Crew: 6+34
Used only by: France
Notes: All built by Cherbourg Naval Dockyard between 1955 and 1958, they are excellent boats. Diving depth about 656 ft (200 m).

'Narval' class patrol submarine (6)

Class: *Narval* (S631), *Marsouin* (S632), *Dauphin* (S633), *Requin* (S634), *Espadon* (S636), *Morse* (S638)
Displacement: 1,635 tons (1,661 tonnes) surfaced; 1,910 tons (1,941 tonnes) dived
Dimensions: Length 254 ft 7 in (77.6 m)
Beam 25 ft 7 in (7.8 m)
Draught 17 ft 9 in (5.4 m)
Armament:
Guns none
Missile systems
 none
A/S weapons
 none
Torpedo tubes
 6 21.7-in (550-mm) with 20 torpedoes
Aircraft
 none
Radar and electronics:
Sonar: DUUA 1
Powerplant: (diesel electric) 3 SEMT-

Pielstick diesels and 2 electric motors, delivering 4,800 hp to two shafts
Speed: 15 knots (surfaced); 18 knots (dived)
Range: 15,000 miles (24,141 km) at 8 knots (snorting)
Crew: 7+56
Used only by: France
Notes: Improved German Type XXI boats. Built between 1951 and 1958, the first

four by Cherbourg Naval Dockyard, the fifth by Normand, and the sixth by Seine Maritime.

'Clemenceau' class aircraft-carrier (2)

Class: *Clemenceau* (R98), *Foch* (R99)
Displacement: 27,307 tons (27,745 tonnes) standard; 32,780 tons (33,306 tonnes) full load
Dimensions: Length 869 ft 5 in (265.0 m)
Beam 104 ft (31.7 m) over bulges
Draught 28 ft 3 in (8.6 m)
Armament:
Guns 8 3.9-in (100-mm) automatic in single mountings
Missile systems
 none
A/S weapons
 none
Torpedo tubes
 none
Aircraft
 40
Radar and electronics: DRBV 20C long-range search, DRBV 23B air-search and surveillance, 2 DRBI 10 height-finder, DRBV 50 search and DRBC 31 gunfire-control radars; SENIT 4 tactical data system; DF and ECM fits
Sonar: SQS 505
Powerplant: 6 boilers supplying steam to 2 Parsons geared turbines, delivering 126,000 shp to two shafts
Speed: 32 knots

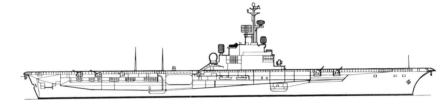

Range: 7,500 miles (12,070 km) at 18 knots; 3,500 miles (5,633 km) at 32 knots
Crew: 65+1,163
Used only by: France
Notes: First specially designed French aircraft-carriers. *Clemenceau* was built by

Brest Dockyard between November 1955 and December 1957; *Foch* by Chantiers de l'Atlantique between February 1957 and July 1960. The two ships commissioned in November 1961 and July 1963 respectively.

'La Résolue' class guided missile cruiser (1)

Class: *Jeanne d'Arc* (R97)
Displacement: 10,000 tons (10,161 tonnes) standard: 12,365 tons (12,563 tonnes) full load
Dimensions: Length 597 ft 1 in (182.0 m)
Beam 78 ft 9 in (24.0 m)
Draught 23 ft 11 in (7.3 m)
Armament:
Guns 4 3.9-in (100-mm) in single mounts
Missile systems
 6 MM38 Exocet
 Crotale to be fitted
A/S weapons
 none
Torpedo tubes
 none
Aircraft
 heavy A/S helicopters (4 in peace, 8 in war)
Radar and electronics: DRBV 22D search, DRBV 50 search, DRBN 32 air-surveillance and DRBI 10 height-finder radars
Sonar: SQS 503
Powerplant: 4 boilers supplying steam to Rateau-Bretagne geared turbines, delivering 40,000 shp to two shafts
Speed: 26½ knots
Range: 6,000 miles (9,656 km) at 15 knots
Crew: 30+587, and 192 cadets in peace
Used only by: France

Notes: Built between July 1960 and September 1961 as *La Résolue* by Brest Dockyard. Commissioned in July 1963 and became *Jeanne d'Arc* on the decommissioning of the previous ship of that name. Used as a cadet ship in peace, in war would be converted into commando carrier, troop transport or anti-submarine helicopter carrier.

'Colbert' class guided missile cruiser (1)

Class: *Colbert* (C611)
Displacement: 8,500 tons (8,636 tonnes) standard; 11,300 tons (11,481 tonnes) full load
Dimensions: Length 593 ft 2 in (180. m)
Beam 66 ft 3 in (20.2 m)
Draught 25 ft 3 in (7.7 m)
Armament:
Guns 2 3.9-in (100-mm) in single mounts
12 57-mm in twin mountings
Missile systems
1 twin Masurca SAM launcher with 48 Masurcas
MM38 Exocet to be fitted
A/S weapons
none
Torpedo tubes
none
Aircraft
none
Radar and electronics: Decca RM416 navigation, DRBV 50 surveillance, DRBV 23C air-surveillance, DRBV 20 warning, two DRBR 51 fire-control, DRBR 32C fire-control, two DRBC 31 fire-control and DRBI 10 height-finder radars; SENIT data automation system
Sonar: hull-mounted
Powerplant: 4 Indret boilers supplying steam to 2 sets of CEM-Parsons geared turbines,

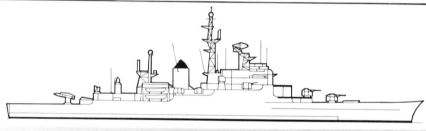

delivering 86,000 shp to two shafts
Speed: 31½ knots
Range: 4,000 miles (6,438 km) at 25 knots
Crew: 24+536
Used only by: France
Notes: Built by Brest Dockyard between December 1953 and March 1956, commissioned in May 1959. Original armament was 16 5-in (127-mm) guns, and armour is 50- 80-mm belt and 50-mm deck. Now equipped as command ship and for radar control of air strikes.

Type C70 guided missile destroyer (3)

Class: *Georges Leygues* (D640), *Dupleix* (D641), *Montcalm* (D642)
Displacement: 3,800 tons (3,861 tonnes) standard; 4,100 tons (4,166 tonnes) full load
Dimensions: Length 456 ft (139.0 m)
Beam 45 ft 11 in (14.0 m)
Draught 18 ft 8 in (5.7 m)
Armament:
Guns 1 3.9-in (100-mm) in A/S version; 2 3.9-in (100-mm) in AA version
2 20-mm
Missile systems
4 MM38 Exocet launchers
1 Crotale launcher

AA version to carry Standard/Tartar SM1 system
A/S weapons
none
Torpedo tubes
2 quintuple 21-in (533-mm) for L5 torpedoes
Aircraft
2 WG13 Lynx A/S helicopters

Radar and electronics: DRBV 26 search, DRBV 51 fire-control, DRBV 32E and Decca 1226 radars (AA versions will carry DRBV 26, DRBJ 11 and two SPG 51C); SENIT data automation system
Sonar: hull-mounted DUBV 23 and variable-depth DUBV 43 (DUBV 25 or 26 in AA version)

Powerplant: (CODOG) 2 Rolls-Royce Olympus gas turbines delivering 42,000 shp and 2 SEMT-Pielstick 16PA6 diesels delivering 10,000 shp to two shafts
Speed: 29¾ knots (19½ knots on diesels)
Range: 9,000 miles (14,485 km) at 18 knots on diesels
Crew: 19+223
Used only by: France
Notes: These three vessels, all built by Brest Dockyard, are the precursors of a class to number 24 by 1985. Eighteen are to be A/S versions like *Georges Leygues* and the other six AA versions. *George Leygues* was laid down in September 1974, launched in December 1976 and commissioned in 1978. *Dupleix* and *Montcalm* were laid down in October and December 1975 respectively.

'Suffren' class guided missile destroyer (2)

Class: *Suffren* (D602), *Duquesne* (D603)
Displacement: 5,090 tons (5,172 tonnes) standard; 6,090 tons (6,188 tonnes) full load
Dimensions: Length 517 ft (157.6 m)
Beam 50 ft 10 in (15.5 m)
Draught 20 ft (6.1 m)
Armament:
Guns 1 3.9-in (100-mm) automatic in single mounting
Missile systems
2 Masurca launchers with 48 Masurcas
4 MM38 Exocet launchers
A/S weapons
1 Malafon launcher with 13 missiles
Torpedo tubes
2 double 21-in (533-mm) for L5 torpedoes
Aircraft
none
Radar and electronics: DRBN 32 navigation, DRBI 23 air-surveillance and target designator (in dome), DRBV 50 surface-surveillance, DRBR 51 Masurca fire-control and DRBC 32A gunfire-control radars; SENIT I data automation system and twin Syllex
Sonar: hull-mounted DUBV 23 and variable-depth DUBV 43

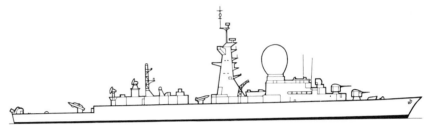

Powerplant: 4 boilers supplying steam to Rateau double-reduction geared turbines, delivering 72,500 shp to two shafts
Speed: 34 knots
Range: 5,100 miles (8,208 km) at 18 knots; 2,400 miles (3,863 km) at 29 knots
Crew: 23+332
Used only by: France

Notes: *Suffren* was laid down at Lorient Dockyard in December 1962, launched in May 1965 and commissioned in July 1967; *Duquesne* was laid down at Brest Dockyard in November 1964, launched in February 1966 and commissioned in April 1970.

Type F67 (ex C67A) guided missile destroyer (3)

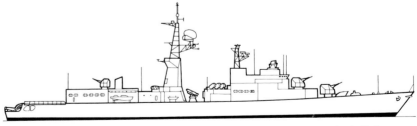

Class: *Tourville* (D610), *Duguay Trouin* (D611), *De Grasse* (D612)
Displacement: 4,580 tons (4,654 tonnes) standard; 5,745 tons (5,837 tonnes) full load
Dimensions: Length 501 ft 4 in (152.8 m)
Beam 50 ft 2 in (15.3 m)
Draught 18 ft 8 in (5.7 m)
Armament:
Guns 2 3.9-in (100-mm)
Missile systems
6 MM38 Exocet launchers
1 octuple Crotale launcher

A/S weapons
1 Malafon launcher with 13 missiles
Torpedo tubes
2 21-in (533-mm) tubes for L5 torpedoes
Aircraft
2 WG13 Lynx A/S helicopters
Radar and electronics: DRBV 51 surface- and air-surveillance, DRBC 32D fire-control, twin Decca 1226 navigation and DRBV 26 air-search radars; SENIT data

automation system and twin Syllex
Sonar: hull-mounted DUBV 23 and variable-depth DUBV 43
Powerplant: 4 boilers supplying steam to Rateau geared turbines, delivering 54,400 shp to two shafts
Speed: 31 knots
Range: 5,000 miles (8,047 km) at 18 knots
Crew: 25+278
Used only by: France

Notes: Developed from the Type C65 design, and originally designated corvettes; now frigates, although with destroyer pennant numbers. All three were built at Lorient Naval Dockyard, *Tourville* being laid down in March 1970, launched in May 1972 and commissioned in June 1974; *Duguay Trouin* in February 1971, June 1973 and September 1975; and *De Grasse* in 1972, November 1974 and July 1976.

Type T56 guided missile destroyer (1)

Class: *La Galissonnière* (D638)
Displacement: 2,750 tons (2,794 tonnes) standard; 3,740 tons (3,800 tonnes) full load
Dimensions: Length 435 ft 8 in (132.8 m)
Beam 41 ft 8 in (12.7 m)
Draught 20 ft 8 in (6.3 m)
Armament:
Guns 2 3.9-in (100-mm) automatic in single mountings
Missile systems
none
A/S weapons
1 Malafon launcher
Torpedo tubes
2 triple 21.7-in (550-mm) for K2 and L3 torpedoes
Aircraft
1 A/S helicopter
Radar and electronics: DRBV 50 surface- and air-surveillance, DRBN 32 navigation, DRBV 22 air-search and DRBC 32A gun-fire-control radars; TACAN beacon; full DF and ECM fits

Sonar: hull-mounted DUBV 23 and variable-depth DUBV 43
Powerplant: 4 Indret boilers supplying steam to 2 Rateau geared turbines, delivering 63,000 shp to two shafts
Speed: 32 knots
Range: 5,000 miles (8,047 km) at 18 knots
Crew: 15+255
Used only by: France

Notes: Laid down at Lorient Naval Dockyard in November 1958, launched in March 1960 and commissioned in July 1962, *La Galissonnière* was France's first operational guided-missile vessel.

Type T53 (Modified ASW) guided missile destroyer (1)

Class: *Duperré* (D633)
Displacement: 2,800 tons (2,845 tonnes) standard; 3,900 tons (3,963 tonnes) full load
Dimensions: Length 435 ft 8 in (132.8 m)
Beam 41 ft 8 in (12.7 m)
Draught 20 ft (6.1 m)
Armament:
Guns 1 3.9-in (100-mm)
Missile systems
4 MM38 Exocet
A/S weapons
none
Torpedo tubes
1 octuple 21-in (533-mm) for L5 torpedoes
Aircraft
1 WG13 Lynx A/S helicopter
Radar and electronics: DRBV 22A air-search, Decca navigation and helicopter, DRBC 32E fire-control and DRBV 51 surface- and air-surveillance radars; SENIT data automation system and twin Syllex
Sonar: hull-mounted DUBV 23 and variable-depth DUBV 43

Powerplant: 4 Indret boilers supplying steam to 2 sets of Rateau geared turbines, delivering 63,000 shp to two shafts
Speed: 32 knots
Range: 5,000 miles (8,047 km) at 18 knots
Crew: 15+257
Used only by: France

Notes: Laid down at Lorient Naval Dockyard in November 1954, launched in June 1955 and commissioned in October 1957 with an armament of 6 5-in (127-mm) guns. Served as a trials ship 1967–71, and then refitted to her present condition, commissioning in May 1974.

Type T53 destroyer (2)

Class: *Forbin* (D635), *Tartu* (D636)
Displacement: 2,750 tons (2,794 tonnes) standard; 3,740 tons (3,800 tonnes) full load
Dimensions: Length 421 ft 11 in (128.6 m)
Beam 41 ft 8 in (12.7 m)
Draught 20 ft (6.1 m)
Armament:
Guns 6 5-in (127-mm) in twin mountings except *Forbin*: 4 5-in
6 57-mm in twin mountings
2 20-mm
Missile systems
none

A/S weapons
1 375-mm (14.76-in) Mark 54 projector
Torpedo tubes
2 triple 21.7-in (550-mm) for K2 or L3 torpedoes
Aircraft
none
Radar and electronics: DRBI 10A 3D air-search, DRBV 22A air-search and DRBV 31 navigation; SENIT data automation system and TACAN beacon
Sonar: DUBA 1 and DUBV 24
Powerplant: 4 Indret boilers supplying steam to 2 geared turbines, delivering 63,000 shp to two shafts
Speed: 32 knots

Range: 5,000 miles (8,047 km) at 18 knots
Crew: 15+261
Used only by: France
Notes: Built by Brest Naval Dockyard, Chantiers de Bretagne and Gironde respectively: *Forbin* laid down August 1954, launched October 1955 and commissioned February 1958; *Tartu* November 1954, December 1955 and February 1958; now used as air-direction vessels. *Forbin* has a helicopter platform aft.

Type T47 guided missile destroyer (4)

Class: *Kersaint* (D622), *Bouvet* (D624), *Dupetit Thouars* (D625), *Du Chayla* (D630)
Displacement: 2,750 tons (2,794 tonnes) standard; 3,740 tons (3,800 tonnes) full load
Dimensions: Length 421 ft 11 in (128.6 m)
Beam 41 ft 8 in (12.7 m)
Draught 20 ft 8 in (6.3 m)
Armament:
Guns 6 57-mm in twin mountings
Missile systems
1 Mark 13 Tartar launcher with 40 missiles
A/S weapons
1 375-mm (14.76-in) Mark 54 projector
Torpedo tubes
2 triple 21.7-in (550-mm) for K2 or L3 torpedoes
Aircraft
none
Radar and electronics: DRBV 20A air-search, SPS 39 3D search for Tartar, two SPG 51B Tartar control and DRBV 31 navigation radars; SENIT data automation system

Sonar: DUBA 1 and DUBV 24
Powerplant: 4 Indret boilers supplying steam to 2 geared turbines, delivering 63,000 shp to two shafts
Speed: 32 knots
Range: 5,000 miles (8,047 km) at 18 knots
Crew: 17+260
Used only by: France

Notes: First two built by Lorient Naval Dockyard between 1951 and 1953, being commissioned in March and May 1956; second pair built by Brest Naval Dockyard between 1952 and 1954, being commissioned in September 1956 and June 1957. Built as gun destroyers with 6 5-in (127-mm) guns, and converted into AA destroyers between 1961 and 1965.

Type T47 (ASW) destroyer (5)

Class: *Maille Brézé* (D627), *Vauquelin* (D628), *D'Estrées* (D629), *Casabianca* (D631), *Guépratte* (D632)
Displacement: 2,750 tons (2,794 tonnes) standard; 3,900 tons (3,963 tonnes) full load
Dimensions: Length 434 ft 8 in (132.5 m)
Beam 41 ft 8 in (12.7 m)
Draught 20 ft 8 in (6.3 m)
Armament:
Guns 2 3.9-in (100-mm) in single mountings
2 20-mm
Missile systems
none
A/S weapons
1 Malafon launcher
1 375-mm (14.76-in) Mark 54 projector
Torpedo tubes
2 triple 21.7-in (550-mm) for K2 or L3 torpedoes
Aircraft
none
Radar and electronics: DRBN 32 navigation, DRBV 22A air-surveillance, DRBV 50 air- and surface-search, and two DRBC 32A gunfire-control radars; SENIT data automation system
Sonar: hull-mounted DUBV 23 and variable-depth DUBV 43
Powerplant: 4 Indret boilers supplying steam to 2 geared turbines, delivering 63,000 shp to two shafts
Speed: 32 knots

Range: 5,000 miles (8,047 km) at 18 knots
Crew: 15+245
Used only by: France
Notes: First two built by Lorient Naval Dockyard, the last three by Brest Naval Dockyard, Gironde and Bretagne respectively. All were laid down in 1953 and launched in 1954. They were commissioned as gun destroyers with 6 5-in (127-mm) guns in May 1957, November 1956, March 1957, May 1957 and June 1957 respectively. The class was converted to ASW between 1968 and 1971.

Type C65 destroyer (1)

Class: *Aconit* (D609, ex F703)
Displacement: 3,500 tons (3,556 tonnes) standard; 3,900 tons (3,963 tonnes) full load
Dimensions: Length 416 ft 8 in (127.0 m)
Beam 44 ft (13.4 m)
Draught 19 ft (5.8 m)
Armament:
Guns 2 3.9-in (100-mm)
Missile systems
MM38 Exocet to be fitted
A/S weapons
1 Malafon launcher
1 quadruple 305-mm (12-in) mortar
Torpedo tubes
2 21-in (533-mm) for L5 torpedoes
Aircraft
none
Radar and electronics: pulse doppler surveil-lance, DRBC 32B gunfire-control, DRBN 32 navigation, and DRBV 22A air-surveillance radars; centralized data analysis and twin Syllex
Sonar: hull-mounted DUBV 23 and variable-depth DUBV 43
Powerplant: 2 boilers supplying steam to 1 Rateau geared turbine, delivering 28,650 shp to one shaft
Speed: 27 knots
Range: 5,000 miles (8,047 km) at 18 knots
Crew: 15+213
Used only by: France
Notes: Laid down at Lorient Naval Dockyard in January 1966, launched in March 1970 and commissioned in March 1973. This is a one-off prototype of the F67 type.

'Commandant Rivière' class frigate (9)

Class: *Victor Schoelcher* (F725), *Commandant Bory* (F726), *Amiral Charner* (F727), *Doudart de Lagrée* (F728), *Balny* (F729), *Commandant Rivière* (F733), *Commandant Bourdais* (F740), *Protet* (F748), *Enseigne de Vaisseau Henry* (F749)
Displacement: 1,750 tons (1,778 tonnes) standard; 2,250 tons (2,286 tonnes) full load (*Balny* 1,650/1,676; 1,950/1,981 tons/tonnes)
Dimensions: Length 340 ft 3 in (103.7 m)
Beam 38 ft 5 in (11.7 m)
Draught 15 ft 9 in (4.8 m)
Armament:
Guns 2 3.9-in (100-mm) automatic in single mountings
2 30-mm
Missile systems
4 MM38 Exocet (except *Balny*)
A/S weapons
1 quadruple 305-mm (12-in) mortar
Torpedo tubes
2 triple 21-in (533-mm) for K2 or L3 torpedoes
Aircraft
provision for a helicopter aft
Radar and electronics: DRBN 32 navigation, DRBC 32A fire control, DRBV 22A air-search, DRBV 50 surface- and air-search, DRBC 32C Exocet radars
Sonar: DUBA 3 and SQS 17
Powerplant: 4 SEMT-Pielstick diesels delivering 16,000 shp to two shafts (*Balny* has an experimental CODAG arrangement of two diesels and one Turbomeca M38 gas turbine, powering one shaft)
Speed: 25 knots
Range: 7,500 miles (12,070 km) at 15 knots, except *Balny*, 8,000 miles (12,875 km) at 12 knots
Crew: 10+157
Used only by: France
Notes: All built by Lorient Naval Dockyard. The class was laid down between April 1957 and September 1962, launched between October 1958 and December 1963, and commissioned between December 1962 and February 1971. The class are capable of worldwide operations, and can carry a senior officer and his staff, plus 80 troops and two landing craft.

Type E52 frigate (10)

Class: *Le Normand* (F765), *Le Picard* (F766), *Le Gascon* (F767), *Le Savoyard* (F771), *Le Basque* (F773), *L'Agenais* (F774), *Le Béarnais* (F775), *L'Alsacien* (F776), *Le Provençal* (F777), *Le Vendéen* (F778)
Displacement: 1,250 tons (1,270 tonnes) standard; 1,702 tons (1,729 tonnes) full load
Dimensions: Length 327 ft 5 in (99.8 m)
Beam 33 ft 10 in (10.3 m)
Draught 13 ft 5 in (4.1 m)
Armament:
Guns 6 57-mm in twin mountings, except 4 57-mm in F771, F772, F773
Missile systems
none
A/S weapons
1 sextuple Bofors ASM mortar, except F776, F777, F778
1 quadruple 305-mm (12-in) mortar in F776, F777, F778
2 DC mortars and 1 DC rack
Torpedo tubes
4 triple 21-in (533-mm) for K2 or L3 torpedoes
Aircraft
none
Radar and electronics: DRBV 31 navigation, DRBV 22A air-search and DRBC 31 fire-control radars
Sonar: DUBV 24 and DUBA 1, except F771, F772, F773 which have DUBV 1 and DUBA 1
Powerplant: 2 Indret boilers supplying steam to Parsons or Rateau geared turbines, delivering 20,000 shp to two shafts
Speed: 27 knots
Range: 4,500 miles (7,242 miles) at 15 knots
Crew: 12+192
Used only by: France
Notes: Built between 1953 and 1957 by Lorient Naval Dockyard, Penhoet, Loire, and Chantiers de la Mediterranée, being commissioned between 1956 and 1960. *Le Lorrain* and *Le Champenois* were disarmed in 1975, and *Le Breton* and *Le Bourguignon* placed in reserve during 1976. *Le Picard*, *Le Gascon* and *L'Agenais* went into reserve in 1977.

Type A69 frigate (12)

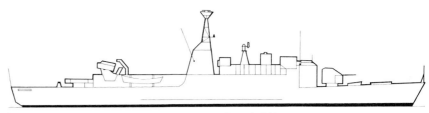

Class: *D'Estienne d'Orves* (F781), *Amyot d'Indville* (F782), *Drogou* (F783), *Détroyat* (F784), *Jean Moulin* (F785), *Quartier Maître Anquetil* (F786), *Commandant de Pimodan* (F787), *Second Maître Le Bihan* (F788), *Lieutenant de Vaisseau Lavallée* (F790), *Premier Maître L'Her* (F792), *Commandant Blaison* (F793), *Enseigne de Vaisseau Jacoubet* (F794)
Displacement: 950 tons (965 tonnes) standard; 1,170 tons (1,189 tonnes) full load
Dimensions: Length 262 ft 6 in (80.0 m)
Beam 33 ft 10 in (10.3 m)
Draught 9 ft 10 in (3.0 m)
Armament:
Guns 1 3.9-in (100-mm)
2 20-mm
Missile systems
2 MM38 Exocet in F781, F783, F787

A/S weapons
1 375-mm (14.76-in) Mark 54 rocket-launcher
Torpedo tubes
4 21.7-in (550-mm) for L3 and L5 torpedoes
Aircraft
none
Radar and electronics: Decca 202 navigation, DRBN 32 navigation, DRBV 51 air- and surface-search, DRBC 32E fire-control
Sonar: hull-mounted DUBA 25
Powerplant: 2 SEMT-Pielstick PC2V diesels, delivering 11,000 bhp to two shafts

Speed: 24 knots
Range: 4,500 miles (7,242 km) at 15 knots
Crew: 64 (+optional 29)
Used also by: South Africa possibly
Notes: Built by Lorient Naval Dockyard from September 1972. F794 has not yet been laid down for financial reasons, and another two are to be built to replace *Lieutenant de Vaisseau Le Henaff* (F789) and *Commandant l'Herminier* (F791), sold to South Africa while still building, but still in France after a UN embargo on arms sales to South Africa. Designed for coastal A/S operations, these vessels have an endurance of 15 days.

'Trident' class fast attack craft (missile) (4)

Class: *Trident* (P670), *Glaive* (P671), *Epée* (P672), *Pertuisine* (P673)
Displacement: 115 tons (116.8 tonnes) standard; 130 tons (132 tonnes) full load
Dimensions: Length 121 ft 5 in (37.0 m)
Beam 18 ft (5.5 m)
Draught 5 ft 3 in (1.6 m)

Armament:
Guns 1 40-mm
Missile systems
6 SS12
A/S weapons
none
Torpedo tubes
none
Aircraft
none
Radar and electronics:
Sonar:
Powerplant: 2 AGO diesels, delivering 4,000 hp to two shafts

Speed: 26 knots
Range: 1,500 miles (2,414 km) at 25 knots
Crew: 1+17
Used only by: France
Notes: First two built by Auroux of Arcachon between December 1974 and August 1975; the second pair by CMN, Cherbourg, between April 1975 and June 1976. The four boats were commissioned in June, November, August and October 1976 respectively, and were intended as the lead craft for a class of 30, 16 of them for overseas service.

'La Combattante I' class fast attack craft (missile) (1)

Class: *La Combattante* (P730)
Displacement: 180 tons (182.9 tonnes) standard; 202 tons (205.25 tonnes) full load
Dimensions: Length 147 ft 8 in (45.0 m)
Beam 24 ft 3 in (7.4 m)
Draught 6 ft 7 in (2.5 m)

Armament:
Guns 2 40-mm
Missile systems
1 quadruple SS11 launcher
A/S weapons
none
Torpedo tubes
none
Aircraft
none
Radar and electronics:
Sonar:

Powerplant: 2 SEMT-Pielstick diesels, delivering 3,200 bhp to two shafts
Speed: 23 knots
Range: 2,000 miles (3,219 km) at 12 knots
Crew: 3+22
Used only by: France
Notes: Built by CM de Normandie between April 1962 and June 1963, and commissioned in March 1963. Can carry an 80-man raiding force over very short ranges.

'Le Fougueux' class large patrol craft (3)

Class: L'Ardent (P635), Le Fringant (P640), L'Adroit (P644)
Displacement: 325 tons (330.2 tonnes) standard; 400 tons (406.4 tonnes) full load
Dimensions: Length 173 ft 11 in (53.0 m)
　　　　　　　Beam 23 ft 11 in (7.3 m)
　　　　　　　Draught 10 ft 2 in (3.1 m)
Armament:
Guns 2 40-mm Bofors

Missile systems
　none
A/S weapons
　1 120-mm (4.7-in) A/S mortar
　2 DC mortars
　2 DC racks
Torpedo tubes
　none
Aircraft
　none
Radar and electronics: Decca radar
Sonar: QCU 2

Powerplant: 4 SEMT-Pielstick diesels, delivering 3,240 bhp to two shafts
Speed: 18½ knots
Range: 3,000 miles (4,828 km) at 12 knots
Crew: 4+42
Used also by: Tunisia, Yugoslavia
Notes: Fourteen of these craft were built between 1956 and 1959, and the first three were deleted in 1975. L'Attentif, L'Enjoué, L'Étourdi and L'Intrépide were placed in reserve in 1976; L'Alerte, L'Effronté, Le Frondeur and Le Hardi were placed in reserve in 1977.

'La Dunkerquoise' class large patrol craft (4)

Class: La Lorientaise (P652), ex-Canadian Miramichi; La Dunkerquoise (P653), ex-Canadian Fundy; La Dieppoise (P655), ex-Canadian Chaleur; La Paimpolaise (P657), ex-Canadian Thunder
Displacement: 370 tons (375.9 tonnes) standard; 470 tons (477.5 tonnes) full load
Dimensions: Length 152 ft (46.3 m)
　　　　　　　Beam 28 ft (8.5 m)
　　　　　　　Draught 8 ft 8 in (2.7 m)
Armament:
Guns 1 40-mm

Missile systems
  none
A/S weapons
  none
Torpedo tubes
  none
Aircraft
  none
Radar and electronics:
Sonar:

Powerplant: General Motors diesels, delivering 2,500 bhp to two shafts
Speed: 15 knots
Range: 4,500 miles (7,242 km) at 11 knots
Crew: 4+31
Used only by: France
Notes: All built in Canada between 1951 and 1954 to the 'Bay' class design for minesweepers, and transferred to France as patrol craft in 1973. *La Malouine* and *La Bayonnaise*, two other ex-Canadian craft, are in reserve.

'Circé' class minehunter (5)

Class: *Cybèle* (M712), *Calliope* (M713), *Clio* (M714), *Circé* (M715), *Ceres* (M716)
Displacement: 460 tons (467.4 tonnes) standard; 510 tons (518.2 tonnes) full load
Dimensions: Length 167 ft (50.9 m)
  Beam 29 ft 2 in (8.9 m)
  Draught 11 ft 2 in (3.4 m)
Armament:
Guns 1 20-mm

Missile systems
  none
A/S weapons
  none
Torpedo tubes
  none
Aircraft
  none
Radar and electronics:
Sonar: DUBM 20
Powerplant: 1 MTU diesel, delivering 1,800 bhp to one shaft

Speed: 18 knots
Range: 3,000 miles (4,828 km) at 12 knots
Crew: 4+44
Used only by: France
Notes: All built by CM de Normandie and commissioned in 1972 and 1973. No normal minesweeping gear is carried, the ships finding mines with the aid of sonar and TV in a remotely controlled PAP. The mine is then detonated by a 220-lb (100-kg) charge laid by the PAP.

'Aggressive' and 'MSO 498' class ocean minesweeper and minehunter (13)

Class: *Narvik* (M609), ex-US *MSO 512*; *Ouistrehem* (M610), ex-US *MSO 513*; *Alencon* (M612), ex-US *MSO 453*; *Berneval* (M613), ex-US *MSO 450*; *Cantho* (M615), ex-US *MSO 476*; *Dompaire* (M616), ex-US *MSO 454*; *Garigliano* (M617), ex-US *MSO 452*; *Mytho* (M618), ex-US *MSO 475*; *Vinh Long* (M619), ex-US *MSO 477*; *Berlaimont* (M620), ex-US *MSO 500*; *Autun* (M622), ex-US *MSO 502*; *Baccarat* (M623), ex-US *MSO 505*; *Colmar* (M624), ex-US *MSO 514*
Displacement: 700 tons (711.2 tonnes) standard; 780 tons (792.5 tonnes) full load
Dimensions: Length 171 ft (52.1 m)
  Beam 35 ft (10.66 m)
  Draught 10 ft 4 in (3.15 m)
Armament:
Guns 1 40-mm
Missile systems
  none
A/S weapons
  none
Torpedo tubes
  none
Aircraft
  none

Radar and electronics:
Sonar:
Powerplant: 2 General Motors diesels, delivering 1,600 shp to two shafts
Speed: 13½ knots
Range: 3,000 miles (4,828 km) at 10 knots
Crew: 5+53
Used also by: Spain, Uruguay, USA
Notes: Transferred in three batches during 1953. *Bir Hacheim* (M614), ex-US *MSO 451*, was returned in 1970 and subsequently transferred to Uruguay as *Maldonado*. *Origny* converted to survey vessel in 1960. *Cantho*, *Dompaire*, *Garigliano*, *Mytho* and *Vinh Long* were converted to minehunters between 1975 and 1977; *Autun*, *Baccarat*, *Berlaimont*, *Colmar* and *Ouistrehem* were converted from 1977 to 1979.

Aérospatiale MM38 Exocet

Type: naval surface-to-surface missile
Guidance: inertial plus active radar terminal
homing
Dimensions: Span 39¾ in (100.4 cm)
Body diameter 13⅘ in (35.0 cm)
Length 17 ft 1 in (5.21 m)
Booster: solid-propellant rocket
Sustainer: solid-propellant rocket
Warhead: 364 lb (165 kg) high explosive
Weights: Launch 1,620 lb (735 kg)
Burnt out
Performance: speed Mach 0.93; range 26
miles (42 km)
Used also by: various nations
Notes: A powerful anti-ship system, the
MM38 Exocet is launched by the parent
ship's fire-control computer, then flies at
very low level at high subsonic speed in the
predetermined direction of the target,
before homing in the terminal phases of the
flight under the guidance of the active radar
head. There are two variants of the MM38
Exocet:

1. AM39 Exocet air-launched anti-ship
   missile, with a length of 15 ft 4⅔ in
   (4.69 m), a weight of 1,433 lb (650
   kg), and a range of up to 31 miles (50
   km)
2. MM40 Exocet, a version with
   improved range (up to 43½ miles/70
   km), a length of 18 ft 6⅖ in (5.65 m),
   and a weight of 1,819 lb (825 kg).

DTCN Crotale Navale

Type: naval surface-to-air tactical guided
weapon system
Guidance: radio command based on radar
and infra-red tracking
Dimensions: Span 21¼ in (54.0 cm)
Body diameter 5⁹⁄₁₀ in (15.0 cm)
Length 9 ft 5⅘ in (2.89 m)
Booster: single-stage solid-propellant rocket
Sustainer: see above
Warhead: 33-lb (15-kg) high explosive
Weights: Launch about 176 lb (80 kg)
Burnt out
Performance: speed Mach 2.3; range about
5¼ miles (8.5 km)
Used also by: other nations
Notes: The missile used in the system is the
Crotale land-mobile all-weather missile, in-
stalled for deployment in French vessels in
an octuple launcher containing its own
tracking radar and infra-red system. The

weight of the entire launcher with 8 rounds is 6.5 tons, and further equipment below deck weighs another 3.5 tons. The Crotale system needs its own single-man fire-control room, whose activities are supervised from the ship's central operations room. The specifications for the missile in its container are weight 331 lb (150 kg), diameter 20 in (51.5 cm) and length 10 ft 6 in (3.2 m).

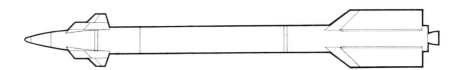

DTCN Masurca

Type: naval surface-to-air tactical guided missile system
Guidance: semi-active radar terminal homing
Dimensions: Span 4 ft 11 in (1.5 m)
Body diameter $16\frac{1}{10}$ in (41.0 cm)
Length (with booster) 28 ft $2\frac{3}{8}$ in (8.6 m); (without booster 17 ft $4\frac{1}{4}$ in (5.29 m)
Booster: solid-propellant rocket
Sustainer: solid-propellant rocket
Warhead: 110-lb (50-kg) high explosive
Weights: Launch (with booster) 4,079 lb (1,850 kg); (without booster) 1,852 lb (840 kg)
Burnt out
Performance: range more than 25 miles (40 km); speed Mach 2.5
Used only by: France
Notes: The Masurca system arms the French vessels *Colbert, Duquesne* and *Suffren,* to provide long-range anti-aircraft protection. The version in service is the Mark 2 Model

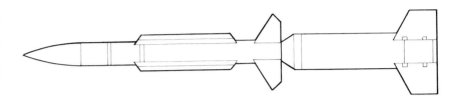

3, the earlier Mark 2 Model 2 having had radio command guidance. Masurca is fired from a twin launcher, and is used in conjunction with DRBR 51 tracking radar, which follows the target and controls the illuminating radar.

Latecoère Malafon

Type: surface to underwater missile system: winged missile carrying an acoustic torpedo
Guidance: radio command
Launch method: ramp
Dimensions: Length 20 ft 2 in (6.15 m)
Span 10 ft 10 in (3.3 m)
Weight: 3,307 lb (1,500 kg)
Engine: 2 solid-fuel boosters
Speed: 520 mph (837 kph)
Range: about 8 miles (13 km)
Warhead: as for torpedo carried
Used only by: France
Notes: After computer-controlled launch, the missile cruises under the control of a radio altimeter in a flat trajectory until it reaches a distance some 875 yards (800 m) from the target submarine or ship, where a parachute drogue slows the missile and so ejects the torpedo from the nose. The torpedo falls into the water and homes normally.

MSBS M-2/M-20

Type: submarine-launched medium-range ballistic missile
Guidance: inertial
Dimensions: Body diameter 4 ft $11\frac{1}{10}$ in (1.5 m)
Length 34 ft $1\frac{1}{2}$ in (10.4 m)
Booster (1st stage): SEP Type 904 rocket with 9.842 tons (10 tonnes) of solid fuel, delivering 99,207-lb (45,000-kg) thrust for 50 secs
Sustainer (2nd stage) SEP RITA II rocket with 5.91 tons (6 tonnes) of solid fuel, delivering 70,547-lb (32,000-kg) thrust for 52 secs
Warhead: M-2 nuclear, 500 kilotons
M-20 thermonuclear, 1 megaton

Weights: Launch approximately 19.684 tons
(20 tonnes)
Burnt out
Performance: range 1,864 miles (3,000 km)
Used only by: France
Notes: The M-2 is an upgraded model of the
M-1, with the superior RITA II replacing the
RITA I 2nd stage. The M-20 features the
same vehicle as the M-2, but has a more
powerful warhead with improved pen-
etration aids and hardening against high-
altitude ABM nuclear detonations. (MSBS
= *Mer-Sol Balistique Stratégique* or Sea-
to-Surface Strategic Ballistic Missile).

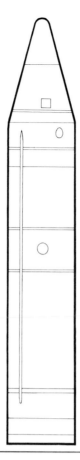

E14

Type: submarine-launched anti-ship (and
anti-submarine) acoustic torpedo
Guidance: passive acoustic homing
Launch method: tube
Dimensions: Length 14 ft 0¾ in (4.291 m)
Diameter 21⅝ in (550 mm)
Weight: 1,984 lb (900 kg)
Engine: 40 kW electric
Speed: 25 knots
Range: 6,015 yards (5,500 m)
Warhead: 441 lb (200 kg) high explosive
Used only by: France
Notes: Can be set to operate between 20 and
59 ft (6 and 18 m). Primary targets are sur-
face vessels, although submarines close to
the surface can also be engaged. The fuses
are contact and magnetic.

E15

Type: submarine-launched anti-ship (and
anti-submarine) acoustic torpedo
Guidance: passive acoustic homing
Launch method: tube
Dimensions: Length 19 ft 8¼ in (6.0 m)
Diameter 21⅔ in (550 mm)
Weight: 2,976 lb (1,350 kg)
Engine: 50 kW electric
Speed: 25 knots
Range: 13,123 yards (12,000 m)
Warhead: 661 lb (300 kg) high explosive
Used only by: France
Notes: Can be set to operate between 20 and
59 ft (6 and 18 m), against surface vessels
moving at speeds of up to 20 knots and
against submarines close to the surface.
The fuses are contact and magnetic.

L3

Type: ship- or submarine-carried anti-
submarine acoustic torpedo
Guidance: AS-3 active acoustic homing
Launch method: tube
Dimensions: Length 14 ft 1 in (4.3 m)
Diameter 21⅔ in (550 mm)
Weight: 2,006 lb (910 kg)
Engine: 40 kW electric
Speed: 25 knots
Range: 6,015 yards (5,500 m)
Warhead: 441 lb (200 kg) high explosive
Used only by: France
Notes: Capable of operating to depths of 984
ft (300 m), and against targets moving
at up to 20 knots. There is also a 21-in
(533-mm) version, although this is not in
production. The fuses are contact and
proximity (acoustic).

L4

Type: aircraft-launched anti-submarine
acoustic torpedo
Guidance: active acoustic homing
Launch method: air-dropped from aircraft or
Malafon
Dimensions: Length 10 ft 3 in (3.13 m) with
parachute stabiliser
Diameter 21 in (533 mm)
Weight: 1,190 lb (540 kg)
Engine: electric
Speed: 30 knots
Range:
Warhead: high explosive
Used only by: France
Notes: After landing in the water, the torpedo
circles until its homing system picks up the
sound of the submarine. If the latter is
moving at under 20 knots the torpedo
homes, detonating by either its contact or
acoustic proximity fuses.

L5

Type: ship- (Modèle 1) or submarine-
(Modèle 3) launched torpedo
Guidance: Thomson-CSF active/passive
homing
Launch method: tube
Dimensions: Length
Diameter 21 in (533 mm)
Weight: Modèle 1: 2,205 lb (1,000 kg);
Modèle 2: 2,866 lb (1,300 kg)
Engine: electric
Speed: 35 knots
Range:
Warhead: high explosive
Used only by: France
Notes: These two torpedoes have four
methods of operation: active direct attack,
active programmed search, passive direct
attack and passive programmed search.

Z16

Type: submarine-launched anti-ship torpedo
Guidance: preset plus pattern
Launch method: tube
Dimensions: Length 23 ft 7½ in (7.2 m)
Diameter 21⅔ in (550 mm)
Weight: 3,748 lb (1,700 kg)
Engine: electric
Speed: 30 knots
Range: 6.2 miles (10 km)
Warhead: 661 lb (300 kg)
Used only by: France
Notes: Probably obsolescent. This is a free-
running torpedo, preset for a certain angle,
depth (up to 59 ft/18 m) and distance. If no
target is met, the torpedo switches to a pro-
grammed zig-zag pattern. The fuses are
contact and magnetic proximity.

Gabon

100 men

Light Forces:
1 FAC(M)
3 FAC(G)

Patrol Forces:
3 large PC

There is also a coastguard service with
6 Arcoa coastal PB and 1 Arcoa 960
PC.

Gambia

Patrol Forces:
2 coastal PC

Ghana

1,300 men

Corvettes:
2 Vosper Mark 1

Light Forces:
(2 Type 45 FAC(M))
(2 PB 57 type FAC(M))

Patrol Forces:
2 Ford PC
2 large PC

Mine Warfare Forces:
1 Ton coastal minesweeper

Auxiliaries:
1 service craft
1 training ship (LCT)

'Kromantse' class (Vosper Mark 1) corvette (2)

Class: *Kromantse* (F17), *Keta* (F18)
Displacement: 440 tons (447 tonnes) standard; 500 tons (508 tonnes) full load
Dimensions: Length 177 ft (54.0 m)
Beam 28 ft 6 in (8.7 m)
Draught 13 ft (4.0 m)
Armament:
Guns 1 4-in (102-mm)
1 40-mm
Missile systems
none
A/S weapons
1 triple Squid A/S mortar
Torpedo tubes
none

Aircraft
none
Radar and electronics: Plessey AWS 1 search radar
Sonar: hull-mounted
Powerplant: 2 Bristol Siddeley Maybach diesels, delivering 7,100 bhp to two shafts
Speed: 20 knots
Range: 2,900 miles (4,667 km) at 14 knots
Crew: 9+45
Used only by: Ghana
Notes: Joint Vosper and Vickers Armstrong venture, the former building *Kromantse* and the latter *Keta*. The two were launched in 1963 and 1965 respectively, and commissioned in July 1964 and May 1965. Intended principally as anti-submarine vessels.

'Ford' class large patrol craft (2)

Class: *Elmina* (P13), *Romenda* (P14)
Displacement: 120 tons (121.9 tonnes) standard; (144.3 tonnes) full load
Dimensions: Length 117 ft 6 in (35.8 m)
Beam 20 ft (6.1 m)
Draught 7 ft (2.1 m)
Armament:
Guns 1 40-mm Bofors L60
Missile systems
none
A/S weapons
DCTs
Torpedo tubes
none
Aircraft
none
Radar and electronics:
Sonar:
Powerplant: 2 MTU MD16 V53 87 B90 diesels, delivering 3,000 hp to two shafts
Speed: 30 knots
Range: 1,000 miles (1,609 km) at 30 knots
Crew: 3+29
Used also by: Nigeria, Singapore, South Africa, UK
Notes: Commissioned in the early 1960s.

'Ruthof' type large patrol craft (2)

Class: *Diela* (P24), *Sahene* (P25)
Displacement: 160 tons (162.6 tonnes)
Dimensions: Length 115 ft 6 in (35.2 m)
Beam 21 ft 4 in (6.5 m)
Draught 7 ft (2.1 m)
Armament:
Guns 2 40-mm
Missile systems
none
A/S weapons
none
Torpedo tubes
none
Aircraft
none
Radar and electronics:
Sonar:
Powerplant:
Speed:
Range:
Crew:
Used only by: Ghana
Notes: Both craft were commissioned in 1974 after building at the yards of Ruthof Werft, Mainz. Six were planned, but the other four were not built because the yard went bankrupt.

Greece

17,500 men (11,000 conscripts)

Destroyers:
1 Gearing FRAM II
4 Gearing FRAM I
1 Allen M. Sumner
6 Fletcher

Frigates:
4 Cannon

SS:
4 Glavkos (Type 209) (+4)
1 Guppy III
1 Guppy IIA
1 Balao

Light Forces:
4 La Combattante III FAC(M)
4 La Combattante II FAC(M) (+6)
2 FAC(M)
5 Nasty FAC(T)
7 Jaguar FAC(T)
1 Brave FAC(T)

Patrol Forces:
(10? FAC(P)
2 PGM-9 PC
3 coastal PC (+?)
2 KW coastal PC

Amphibious Forces:
1 Cabildo LSD
2 Terrebonne Parish LST
2 LST 511-1152
5 LST1-510
5 LSM1
6 LCT6
13 LCM
34 LCVP
(14 LCP)

Mine Warfare Forces:
2 coastal minelayers
10 Falcon coastal minesweepers
5 Adjutant coastal minesweepers

Auxiliaries:
4 surveying craft
(1 training ship)
1 depot ship
2 Patapsco tankers
1 ammunition ship
6 Larbour tankers
31 others

Aircraft:
4 Alouette III (1 sqn)

'Gearing FRAM I' and 'Gearing FRAM II' class destroyer (5)

Class: *Themistokles* (210), ex-US *Frank Knox* (DD742); *Kanaris* (212), ex-US *Stickell* (DD888); *Kontouriotis* (213), ex-US *Rupertus* (DD851); *Sachtouris* (214), ex-US *Arnold J. Isbell* (DD869); *Tombasiz* (215), ex-US *Gurke* (DD783)
Displacement: 2,425 tons (2,464 tonnes) standard; 3,500 tons (3,556 tonnes) full load
Dimensions: Length 390 ft 6 in (119.0 m)
Beam 40 ft 10 in (12.4 m)
Draught 19 ft (5.8 m)
Armament:
Guns 4 5-in (127-mm) in twin mountings, except *Themistokles* 2 76-mm (3-in) OTO-Melara Compact
Missile systems
1 octuple Albatros BPDM launcher to be fitted
MM38 Exocet to be fitted
A/S weapons
2 fixed Hedgehogs in *Themistokles*
1 octuple ASROC launcher in others
Torpedo tubes
2 triple 12.75-in (324-mm) Mark 32
Aircraft
facilities for small helicopter in all except *Themistokles*
Radar and electronics: SPS 10 surface-search and SPS 37/40 air-search radars
Sonar: variable-depth to be fitted
Powerplant: 4 Babcock & Wilcox boilers supplying steam to 2 Westinghouse geared turbines, delivering 60,000 shp to two shafts
Speed: 34 knots
Range: 4,800 miles (7,725 km) at 15 knots
Crew: 16+253
Used also by: (FRAM I) Brazil, Pakistan, South Korea, Spain, Taiwan, Turkey, USA; (FRAM II) Argentina, South Korea, Taiwan, Turkey

Notes: Built in the last two years of World War II, and commissioned into US service between 1944 and 1946. The vessels were transferred in 1971, 1972, 1973, 1974 and 1977 respectively. All are to undergo an extensive modernisation by Cantieri Navali Riuniti. *Themistokles* was a FRAM II radar-picket conversion, the others FRAM I destroyer conversions. *Sachtouris* and *Kanaris* have one 76-mm forward and one 40-mm aft.

'Allen M. Sumner' class destroyer (1)

Class: *Miaoulis* (211), ex-US *Ingraham* (DD694)
Displacement: 2,200 tons (2,235 tonnes) standard; 3,320 tons (3,373 tonnes) full load
Dimensions: Length 376 ft 6 in (114.8 m)
Beam 40 ft 10 in (12.4 m)
Draught 19 ft (5.8 m)

Armament:
Guns 6 5-in (127-mm) in twin mountings
Missile systems
none
A/S weapons
2 Hedgehogs
Torpedo tubes
2 triple 12.75-in (324-mm) Mark 32
Aircraft
none
Radar and electronics: SPS 6 search and SPS 10 tactical radars
Sonar: SQS 30

Powerplant: 4 boilers supplying steam to 2 geared turbines, delivering 60,000 shp to two shafts
Speed: 34 knots
Range: 4,600 miles (7,403 km) at 15 knots
Crew: 16+253
Used also by: Argentina, Brazil, Colombia, Taiwan, Venezuela
Notes: Built by Federal Shipbuilding & Dry Dock between 1943 and 1944, and commissioned into US service in March 1944. Transferred in July 1971. Has been modernised to FRAM II standards.

'Fletcher' class destroyer (6)

Class: *Aspis* (06), ex-US *Conner* (DD582); *Velos* (16), ex-US *Charette* (DD581); *Thyella* (28), ex-US *Bradford* (DD545); *Lonkhi* (56), ex-US *Hall* (DD583); *Navarinon* (63), ex-US *Brown* (DD546); *Sfendoni* (85), ex-US *Aulick* (DD569)
Displacement: 2,100 tons (2,134 tonnes) standard; 3,050 tons (3,099 tonnes) full load
Dimensions: Length 376 ft 6 in (114.7 m)
Beam 39 ft 6 in (12.0 m)
Draught 18 ft (5.5 m)
Armament:
Guns 4 5-in (127-mm) in *Aspis, Velos, Lonkhi, Sfendoni*
5 5-in (127-mm) in *Thyella, Navarinon*
6 3-in (76-mm) in twin mountings in *Aspis, Velos, Lonkhi, Sfendoni*
10 40-mm in 2 quadruple and 1 twin mounting in *Thyella, Navarinon*

Missile systems
none
A/S weapons
Hedgehogs and DCs
Torpedo tubes
1 quintuple 21-in (533-mm) in all but *Thyella* and *Navarinon*
side-launching racks for A/S torpedoes
Aircraft
none

Radar and electronics: SPS 6 search, SPS 10 search, GFC 56 fire-control and GFC 56 fire-control radars
Sonar:
Powerplant: 4 Babcock & Wilcox boilers supplying steam to 2 General Electric geared turbines, delivering 60,000 shp to two shafts
Speed: 32 knots
Range: 6,000 miles (9,656 km) at 15 knots

Crew: 250
Used also by: Argentina, Brazil, Chile, Italy, Mexico, Peru, South Korea, Spain, Taiwan, Turkey, West Germany
Notes: Built between 1941 and 1943, and commissioned into US service in 1942 and 1943. *Aspis, Velos* and *Sfendoni* were transferred in 1959, *Lonkhi* in 1960, and *Thyella* and *Navarinon* in 1962. Greece bought the vessels in 1976.

'Cannon' class frigate (4)

Class: *Aetos* (01), ex-US *Slater* (DE766); *Ierax* (31), ex-US *Elbert* (DE768); *Leon* (54), ex-US *Eldridge* (DE173); *Panthir* (67), ex-US *Garfield Thomas* (DE193)
Displacement: 1,240 tons (1,260 tonnes) standard; 1,900 tons (1,930 tonnes) full load
Dimensions: Length 306 ft (93.3 m)
Beam 36 ft 8 in (11.2 m)
Draught 14 ft (4.3 m)
Armament:
Guns 3 3-in (76-mm) in single mountings
6 40-mm in twin mountings
14 20-mm in twin mountings

Missile systems
none
A/S weapons
1 Hedgehog
8 DCTs
1 DC rack
Torpedo racks
side-launching for A/S torpedoes
Aircraft
none
Radar and electronics:
Sonar:
Powerplant: 4 General Motors diesel-electric, delivering 6,000 bhp to two shafts
Speed: 19¼ knots

Range: 9,000 miles (14,485 km) at 12 knots
Crew: 220
Used also by: Peru, Philippines, South Korea, Thailand, Uruguay
Notes: The first two were built by Tampa Shipbuilding between 1943 and 1944, and commissioned into US service in May and July 1944; the second pair by Federal Shipbuilding & Dry Dock in 1943, and were commissioned into US service in August 1943 and January 1944. The first pair were transferred in March 1951, the second pair in January 1951. The triple 21-in (533-mm) tubes were removed.

'Glavkos' class (Type 209) submarine (4)

Class: *Glavkos* (S110), *Nereus* (S111), *Triton* (S112), *Proteus* (S113)
Displacement: 990 tons (1,006 tonnes) surfaced; 1,290 tons (1,311 tonnes) dived
Dimensions: Length 177 ft 1 in (54.0 m)
Beam 20 ft 4 in (6.2 m)
Draught 18 ft 0½ in (5.5 m)
Armament:
Guns none
Missile systems
none
A/S weapons
none
Torpedo tubes
8 21-in (533-mm)
Aircraft
none
Radar and electronics:
Sonar:

Powerplant: 4 MTU diesels, Siemens diesel-generators and 1 Siemens electric motor, powering one shaft
Speed: 10 knots surfaced; 22 knots dived
Range: 50 days endurance
Crew: 31

Used also by: Colombia, Indonesia, Peru, Turkey, Venezuela
Notes: All built by Howaldtswerke of Kiel, launched in 1971 and commissioned one in 1971 and three in 1972. Four more boats are on order, three having been ordered in November 1975 and the fourth in September 1976, for 1978 launch.

'Guppy III' class submarine (1)

Class: *Katsonis* (S115), ex-US *Remora* (SS487)
Displacement: 1,975 tons (2,007 tonnes) standard; 2,450 tons (2,489 tonnes) dived
Dimensions: Length 326 ft (99.4 m)
Beam 27 ft (8.2 m)
Draught 17 ft (5.2 m)
Armament:
Guns none

Missile systems
none
A/S weapons
none
Torpedo tubes
10 21-in (533-mm)
Aircraft
none
Radar and electronics:
Sonar: BQG-4 and BQR-2

Powerplant: 4 diesels, delivering 6,400 hp, and 2 electric motors, delivering 5,400 shp to two shafts
Speed: 20 knots surfaced; 15 knots dived
Range: 12,000 miles (19,313 km) at 10 knots surfaced
Crew: 85
Used also by: Brazil, Italy, Turkey
Notes: Built in 1945 by Portsmouth Navy Yard as a 'Tench' class boat. Later modified to 'Guppy II' and 'Guppy III' standards; transferred to Greece in October 1973.

'Guppy IIA' class submarine (1)

Class: *Papanikolis* (S114), ex-US *Hardhead* (SS365)
Displacement: 1,840 tons (1,870 tonnes) standard; 2,445 tons (2,484 tonnes) dived
Dimensions: Length 306 ft (93.2 m)
Beam 27 ft (8.3 m)
Draught 17 ft (5.2 m)
Armament:
Guns none
Missile systems
none
A/S weapons
none
Torpedo tubes
10 21-in (533-mm)
Aircraft
none
Radar and electronics:
Sonar:
Powerplant: 3 diesels, delivering 4,800 shp, and 2 electric motors, delivering 5,400 shp to two shafts
Speed: 17 knots surfaced; 15 knots dived
Range: 12,000 miles (19,313 km) at 10 knots surfaced

Crew: 84
Used also by: Spain, Turkey
Notes: Built in 1943 by Manitowoc Shipbuilding, and commissioned into US service in April 1944. Transferred to Greece in July 1972.

'Balao' class submarine (1)

Class: *Triaina* (S86), ex-US *Scabbardfish* (SS397)
Displacement: 1,816 tons (1,845 tonnes) surfaced; 2,425 tons (2,464 tonnes) dived
Dimensions: Length 311 ft 6 in (94.9 m)
Beam 27 ft (8.2 m)
Draught 17 ft (5.2 m)
Armament:
Guns none
Missile systems
none

A/S weapons
  none
Torpedo tubes
  10 21-in (533-mm)
Aircraft
  none
Radar and electronics:

Sonar:
Powerplant: Fairbanks Morse diesels, delivering 6,500 bhp, and Elliot Motors electric
  motors, delivering 4,610 bhp to two shafts
Speed: 20 knots surfaced; 10 knots dived
Range: 12,000 miles (19,313 km) at 10
  knots surfaced

Crew: 85
Used also by: Chile, Italy, Turkey, Venezuela
Notes: Built by Portsmouth Navy Yard in
  1943 and 1944, and commissioned into
  US service in April 1944. Later fitted with a
  streamlined conning tower. Transferred to
  Greece in February 1965.

'La Combattante III' class fast attack craft (missile) (4)

Class: *Antiploiarhos Laskos* (P50), *Plotarhis
  Blessas* (P51), *Ipoploiarhos Troupakis*
  (P52), *Ipoploiarhos Mikonios* (P53)
Displacement: 385 tons (391.2 tonnes)
  standard; 425 tons (431.8 tonnes) full load
Dimensions: Length 184 ft (56.2 m)
  Beam 26 ft (8.0 m)
  Draught 7 ft (2.1 m)
Armament:
Guns 2 76-mm (3-in) OTO Melara
  4 30-mm Emerlec in twin mountings

Missile systems
  4 MM38 Exocet
A/S weapons
  none
Torpedo tubes
  2 21-in (533-mm)
Aircraft
  none
Radar and electronics: Triton navigation and
  surveillance, I-band fire-control radars
Sonar:
Powerplant: 4 MTU diesels, delivering
  18,000 bhp to four shafts
Speed: 35¾ knots

Range: 2,000 miles (3,219 km) at 15 knots
Crew: 42
Used only by: Greece
Notes: All built by Constructions Mécaniques
  de Normandie at Cherbourg to an order
  placed in September 1974. The first craft
  was commissioned in October 1976, and
  the other three in 1977.

'La Combattante II' class fast attack craft (missile) (4)

Class: *Ipoploiarhos Batsis* (P54), *Ipoploiarhos
  Arliotis* (P55), *Ipoploiarhos Anninos* (P56),
  Ipoploiarhos Konidis (P57)
Displacement: 234 tons (237.75 tonnes)
  standard; 255 tons (259.1 tonnes) full load
Dimensions: Length 154 ft 2 in (47.0 m)
  Beam 23 ft 4 in (7.1 m)
  Draught 8 ft 2 in (2.5 m)
Armament:
Guns 4 35-mm in twin mountings
Missile systems
  4 MM38 Exocet
A/S weapons
  none
Torpedo tubes
  2 wire-guided torpedoes
Aircraft
  none
Radar and electronics: Triton navigation and
  surveillance, Plessey Mark 10 IFF radars
Sonar:
Powerplant: 4 MTU diesels, delivering
  12,000 bhp to four shafts

Speed: 36½ knots
Range: 850 miles (1,370 km) at 25 knots
Crew: 4+36
Used only by: Greece
Notes: All built by Constructions Mécaniques

de Normandie at Cherbourg to an order
placed in 1969. P54 was commissioned in
December 1971, the other three craft in
1972. In December 1976 another six were
ordered, two to be built in France and the
other four in Greece.

Fast Attack Craft (missile) (2)

Class: *Kelefstis Stamou* (P28), *Diopos Antoniou* (P29)
Displacement: 80 tons (81.3 tonnes)
Dimensions: Length 105 ft (32.0 m)
Beam 21 ft (6.4 m)
Draught 5 ft 3 in (1.6 m)
Armament:
Guns 2 20-mm
Missile systems
4 SS.12
A/S weapons
none
Torpedo tubes
none
Aircraft
none
Radar and electronics:
Sonar:
Powerplant: 2 MTU 12V 331 TC81 diesels, delivering 2,700 hp
Speed: 30 knots
Range: 1,500 miles (2,414 km) at 15 knots

Crew: 17
Used only by: Greece
Notes: These two craft were built by Chantiers Navales de l'Esterel to a Cypriot order. They were later transferred to Greece, and commissioned in 1975 and 1976 respectively.

'Jaguar' class fast attack craft (torpedo) (7)

Class: *Hesperos* (P196), ex-German *Seeadler* (P6068); *Kataigis* (P197), ex-German *Falke* (P6072); *Kentauros* (P198), ex-German *Habicht* (P6075); *Kyklon* (P199), ex-German *Greif* (P6071); *Lelaps* (P228), ex-German *Kondor* (P6070); *Scorpios* (P229), ex-German *Kormoran* (P6077); *Tyfon* (P230), ex-German *Geier* (P6073)
Displacement: 160 tons (163 tonnes) standard; 190 tons (193 tonnes) full load
Dimensions: Length 139 ft 5 in (42.5 m)
Beam 23 ft 7½ in (6.2 m)
Draught 7 ft 10½ in (2.4 m)
Armament:
Guns 2 40-mm Bofors L/70 in single mountings
Missile systems
none
A/S weapons
none
Torpedo tubes
4 21-in (533-mm)
Aircraft
none
Radar and electronics:
Sonar:
Powerplant: 4 diesels, delivering 12,000 bhp to four shafts

Speed: 42 knots
Range:
Crew: 39
Used also by: Saudi Arabia, Turkey

Notes: These vessels were built by Lürssen or Kroger, and commissioned into German service in 1958. The first three were transferred in 1976, the rest in 1977. Greece also has ex-*Albatros*, ex-*Bussard* and ex-*Sperber* for spares.

'Brave' class fast attack craft (torpedo) (1)

Class: *Astrapi* (P20), ex-German *Strahl* (P6194)
Displacement: 95 tons (96.5 tonnes) standard; 110 tons (111.8 tonnes) full load
Dimensions: Length 99 ft (30.2 m)
Beam 25 ft (7.6 m)
Draught 7 ft (2.1 m)
Armament:
Guns 2 40-mm Bofors in single mountings
Missile systems
none
A/S weapons
none
Torpedo chutes
4 21-in (533-mm) side-launching
Aircraft
none
Radar and electronics:
Sonar:

Powerplant: 3 Bristol Siddeley Marine Proteus gas turbines, delivering 12,750 bhp to three shafts
Speed: 55½ knots
Range:
Crew:
Used only by: Greece
Notes: Built by Vosper Thornycroft of Portsmouth, this craft was launched in 1962 and commissioned into German service at the end of that year. Transferred to Greece in 1967.

'PGM-9' class large patrol craft (2)

Class: *Ploiarhos Arslanoglou* (P14), ex-US *PGM 25*, ex-US *PC 1565*; *Antiploiarhos Pezopoulos* (P70), ex-US *PGM 21*, ex-US *PC 1552*
Displacement: 335 tons (340 tonnes) standard; 439 tons (446 tonnes) full load
Dimensions: Length 174 ft 8 in (53.3 m)
　　　　　　　Beam 23 ft (7.0 m)
　　　　　　　Draught 10 ft 10 in (3.3 m)

Armament:
Guns 1 3-in (76-mm)
　　6 20-mm
Missile systems
　　none
A/S weapons
　　1 Hedgehog
　　DC racks
　　side-launching torpedo racks
Torpedo tubes
　　none
Aircraft
　　none

Radar and electronics:
Sonar:
Powerplant: 2 General Motors Corporation diesels, delivering 3,600 bhp to two shafts
Speed: 19 knots
Range:
Crew:
Used only by: Greece
Notes: The three craft were built in 1943–4, and bought from the US in 1947. In 1963 the two 40-mm guns were removed, and a Hedgehog was fitted.

Grenada

Patrol Forces:
1 coastal PC

Guatemala

400 men (including 200 marines)

Patrol Forces:
16 coastal PC

Auxiliaries:
1 LCM6
1 repair barge
1 tug

'Broadsword' class patrol craft (3)

Class: *P1051, P1052, P1053*
Displacement: 90.5 tons (91.95 tonnes)
Dimensions: Length 105 ft (32.0 m)
　　　　　　　Beam 20 ft 6 in (6.3 m)
　　　　　　　Draught 6 ft 4 in (1.9 m)

Armament:
Guns 1 75-mm recoilless rifle
　　1 81-mm mortar
　　5 0.5-in (12.7-mm) machine-guns
Missile systems

A/S weapons
  none
Torpedo tubes
  none
Aircraft
  none
Radar and electronics:
Sonar:

Powerplant: 2 General Motors Corporation diesels
Speed: 32 knots
Range:
Crew: 19
Used only by: Guatemala
Notes: The craft are built by Halter Marine (Halmar) of Louisiana, the first two being delivered in 1976, and the last in 1977.

Guinea-Bissau

100 men

Patrol Forces:
1 P-6 FAC(T)
? riverine PC
?LCU

Guyana

Patrol Forces:
1 Vosper 31.4-m type PC
3 Vosper 12.2-m type coastal PC

Auxiliaries:
1 lighter

Haiti

300 men

Patrol Craft:
2 Cape class coastal PC
5 coastal PC

Honduras

50 men

Patrol Forces:
5 coastal PC

Auxiliaries:
1 survey launch

Hong Kong

1,292 men of the Marine District of the Royal Hong Kong Police Force

Patrol Forces:
29 patrol craft

Auxiliaries:
2 command vessels
2 logistic craft
11 launches

Hungary

500 men of the Maritime Wing of the Hungarian Army

Patrol Forces:
10 river PC

Mine Warfare Forces:
? river mine countermeasures craft

Auxiliaries:
? troop transports
5 LCU
? tugs
? icebreakers
? barges

Iceland

170 men of the Coast Guard Service

Patrol Craft:
6 fishery protection ships

Aircraft:
1 Fokker Friendship
2 Bell helicopters
1 Hughes helicopter

India

46,000 men including Naval Air Force

CV:
1 Majestic

Cruiser:
1 Fiji

Destroyers:
(2 Kashin)

Frigates:
4 Leander (+2)
12 Petya II
2 Whitby
3 Leopard
2 Blackwood
1 British Hunt Type II
2 Black Swan
1 British River

Corvettes:
4 Nanuchka (+2?)

SS:
8 Foxtrot (+2?)

Light Forces:
16 Osa I and II FAC(M)

Patrol Forces:
4 Improved Abhay (+4)
1 Abhay PC
5 Poluchat coastal PC
2 Sharada coastal PC

Amphibious Forces:
1 LST(3)
6 Polnocny LCT
(3 ?)

Mine Warfare Forces:
4 Ton coastal minesweepers
4 Ham inshore minesweepers

Auxiliaries:
3 survey ships
1 Ugra submarine tender
1 Modified T-58 submarine rescue ship
1 repair ship
4 tankers
others

Naval Air Force:
25 Sea Hawk (1 attack sqn)
12 Alizé (1MR sqn)
3 MR sqns with 5 Super Constellation, 3 Il-38, 5 Defender, 2 Devon.
1 SAR helicopter sqn 10 Alouette III
3 ASW sqns with 12 Sea King, 10 Alouette III
Training units:
Kiran, Vampire, Sea Hawk, Hughes 360

'Majestic' class aircraft-carrier (1)

Class: *Vikrant* (R11), ex-British *Hercules*
Displacement: 16,000 tons (16,256 tonnes) standard; 19,500 tons (19,812 tonnes) full load
Dimensions: Length 700 ft (213.4 m)
Beam (hull) 80 ft (24.4 m)
Draught 24 ft (7.4 m)
Armament:
Guns 15 40-mm Bofors in 4 twin and 7 single mountings
Missile systems
none
A/S weapons
none
Torpedo tubes
none
Aircraft
22
Radar and electronics: Types 277 and 960 search, Type 293 tactical, and Type 963 carrier approach radars
Sonar:
Powerplant: 4 Admiralty boilers supplying steam to Parsons geared turbines, delivering 40,000 shp to two shafts
Speed: 24½ knots
Range: 12,000 miles (19,313 km) at 14 knots; 6,200 miles (9,978 km) at 23 knots
Crew: 1,075 in peace; 1,345 in war
Used only by: India
Notes: *Hercules* was built by Vickers-Armstrong between 1943 and 1945, but never commissioned into British service. She was bought by India in 1957 and completed by Harland & Wolff. Commissioned into Indian service in 1961. The flight deck is 128 ft (39.0 m) wide.

'Fiji' class cruiser (1)

Class: *Mysore* (C 60), ex-British *Nigeria*
Displacement: 8,700 tons (8,839 tonnes) standard; 11,040 tons (11,217 tonnes) full load
Dimensions: Length 555 ft 6 in (169.3 m)
Beam 62 ft (18.9 m)
Draught 21 ft (6.4 m)
Armament:
Guns 9 6-in (152-mm) in triple turrets
8 4-in (102-mm) in twin turrets
12 40-mm Bofors in 2 single and 5 twin mountings
Missile systems
none
A/S weapons
none
Torpedo tubes
none
Aircraft
none
Radar and electronics: Types 277 and 960 search, Type 293 tactical and I-band fire-control radars
Sonar:
Powerplant: 4 Admiralty boilers supplying steam to Parsons geared turbines, delivering 72,500 shp to four shafts
Speed: 31½ knots
Range:
Crew: 800
Used only by: India
Notes: *Nigeria* was built between 1938 and 1939 by Vickers-Armstrong, and commissioned into British service in 1940. She was bought by India in 1954, and extensively modernized before her commissioning in 1957. Main armour thicknesses are sides 4½ in (114 mm), deck 2 in (51 mm), conning tower 4 in (102 mm) and turrets 2 in (51 mm).

'Leander' class frigate (6)

Class: *Nilgiri* (F32), *Himgiri* (F33), *Dunagiri* (F34), *Udaygiri* (F35), *Taragiri* (F36), *Vindhyagiri* (F38)
Displacement: 2,450 tons (2,489 tonnes) standard; 2,800 tons (2,845 tonnes) full load
Dimensions: Length 372 ft (113.4 m)
Beam 43 ft (13.1 m)
Draught 18 ft (5.5 m)
Armament:
Guns 2 4.5-in (114-mm) in a twin mounting
2 20-mm
Missile systems
2 quadruple Seacat launchers (except *Nilgiri*: 1 quadruple Seacat launcher)
A/S weapons
1 triple Limbo DC mortar
Torpedo tubes
none
Aircraft
1 Alouette III helicopter

Radar and electronics: Hollandse Signaalapparat radars
Sonar:
Powerplant: 2 boilers supplying steam to 2 geared turbines, delivering 30,000 shp to two shafts
Speed: 30 knots
Range: 4,500 miles (7,242 km) at 12 knots

Crew: 263
Used also by: Chile, New Zealand, UK
Notes: These six examples of broad-beamed 'Leander' class frigates were the first large warships built in Indian yards, all being built in Mazagon Docks of Bombay. Work on the first began in 1966, and *Nilgiri* was commissioned in 1972.

'Petya II' class frigate (12)

Class: *Arnala* (P68), *Androth* (P69), *Anjadip* (P73), *Andaman* (P74), *Amini* (P75), *Kamorta* (P77), *Kadmath* (P78), *Kiltan* (P79), *Kavaratti* (P80), *Katchal* (P81), *Kanjar* (P82), *Amindivi* (P83) all ex-Russian vessels
Displacement: 950 tons (965 tonnes) standard; 1,150 tons (1,168 tonnes) full load
Dimensions: Length 270 ft (82.3 m)
Beam 29 ft 10 in (9.1 m)
Draught 10 ft 6 in (3.2 m)
Armament:
Guns 4 76-mm in twin mountings
Missile systems
none
A/S weapons
4 MBU 2500 16-barrel rocket-launchers
2 DC racks

Torpedo tubes
3 533-mm (21-in)
Aircraft
none
Radar and electronics: 'Slim Net' surface search, 'Neptune' navigation, 'Hawk Screech' fire-control, 'High Pole' IFF, 'Square Head' IFF, 'Watch Dog' ECM radars and systems
Sonar: 'Hercules'
Powerplant: 2 gas turbines, delivering

30,000 hp, and 2 diesels, delivering 6,000 hp, to two shafts
Speed: 30 knots
Range: 5,190 miles (8,350 km) at 20 knots
Crew: 100
Used also by: USSR
Notes: All vessels of the 'Petya' class are built at Nikolayev and at Kaliningrad, the first unit being laid down in 1960 and completed in 1963. The first of the type transferred to India arrived in 1969.

'Whitby' class frigate (2)

Class: *Talwar* (F40), *Trishul* (F43)
Displacement: 2,144 tons (2,178 tonnes) standard; 2,545 tons (2,586 tonnes) and 2,557 tons (2,598 tonnes) full load respectively
Dimensions: Length 369 ft 10 in (112.7 m)
Beam 41 ft (12.5 m)
Draught 17 ft 10 in (5.4 m)
Armament:
Guns 2 4.5-in (114-mm) in a twin turret (*Trishul* only)
4 40-mm Bofors in one twin and two single mountings

Missile systems
3 SS-N-2 'Styx' launchers (*Talwar* only)
A/S weapons
2 Limbo 3-barrel DC mortars
Torpedo tubes
none
Aircraft
none
Radar and electronics: Types 277 and 293 tactical, I-band fire-control, and (*Talwar* only) 'Square Tie' SS-N-2 missile control radars
Sonar:

Powerplant: 2 Babcock & Wilcox boilers supplying steam to 2 geared turbines, delivering 30,000 shp to two shafts
Speed: 30 knots
Range: 4,500 miles (7,243 km) at 12 knots
Crew: 11+220
Used also by: New Zealand, UK
Notes: The two vessels were built between 1957 and 1959 by Cammell Laird of Birkenhead and Harland & Wolff of Belfast, and commissioned into Indian service in 1960. *Talwar* had her 4.5-in (114-mm) gun turret replaced by three SS-N-2 launchers in 1975.

'Leopard' class frigate (3)

Class: *Brahmaputra*, ex-*Panther* (F31); *Beas* (F137); *Betwa* (F139)
Displacement: 2,251 tons (2,287 tonnes) standard; 2,515 tons (2,555 tonnes) full load
Dimensions: Length 339 ft 10 in (103.6 m)
Beam 40 ft (12.2 m)
Draught 16 ft (4.9 m)
Armament:
Guns 4 4.5-in (114-mm) in twin turrets
2 40-mm Bofors
Missile systems
none
A/S weapons
1 Squid 3-barrel DC mortar

Torpedo tubes
none
Aircraft
none
Radar and electronics: Type 960 search, Type 293 tactical and I-band fire-control
Sonar:

Powerplant: Admiralty Standard diesels, delivering 12,380 bhp to two shafts
Speed: 25 knots
Range: 7,500 miles (12,070 km) at 16 knots
Crew: 210
Used also by: Bangladesh, UK

Notes: The *Brahmaputra* was ordered from John Brown Ltd as the British *Panther,* laid down in 1956, launched in 1957 and commissioned into Indian service in 1958. The other two were built by Vickers-Armstrong between 1957 and 1959, and commissioned into Indian service in 1960.

'Blackwood' class frigate (2)

Class: *Kirpan* (F144), *Kuthar* (F146)
Displacement: 1,180 tons (1,199 tonnes) standard; 1,456 tons (1,479 tonnes) full load
Dimensions: Length 310 ft (64.5 m)
Beam 33 ft (10.0 m)
Draught 15 ft 6 in (4.7 m)
Armament:
Guns 3 40-mm Bofors in single mountings
Missile systems
none
A/S weapons
2 Limbo 3-barrel DC mortars
Torpedo tubes
none
Aircraft
none

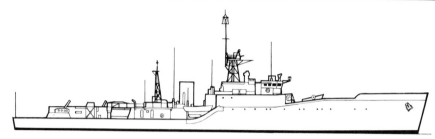

Radar and electronics: E-band air and surface surveillance radar
Sonar:
Powerplant: Babcock & Wilcox boilers supplying steam to 1 geared turbine, delivering 15,000 shp to one shaft
Speed: 27¾ knots
Range: 4,000 miles (6,438 km) at 12 knots
Crew: 150

Used also by: UK
Notes: The two ships were laid down in 1957, launched in 1958 and commissioned in 1959. The builders were Alex Stephen & Sons of Govan, and J. Samuel White of Cowes respectively. The sistership *Khukri* was sunk in the 1971 Indo-Pakistani War. Now used by Indian Coastguard.

'Foxtrot' class submarine (8)

Class: *Kursura* (S20), *Karanj* (S21), *Kanderi* (S22), *Kalvari* (S23), *Vela* (S40), *Vagir* (S41), *Vagli* (S42), *Vagsheer* (S43) all ex-Russian boats
Displacement: 2,000 tons (2,032 tonnes) surfaced; 2,300 tons (2,337 tonnes) dived
Dimensions: Length 296 ft 11 in (90.5 m)
Beam 23 ft 11 in (7.3 m)
Draught 19 ft (5.8 m)
Armament:
Guns none
Missile systems
none
A/S weapons
none

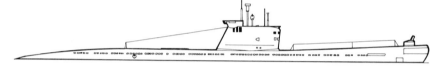

Torpedo tubes
10 533-mm (21-in) forward and 4 400-mm (15.75-in) aft, with 22 torpedoes or 44 mines
Radar and electronics: 'Snoop Plate' surface search radar and 'Stop Light' passive ECM
Sonar: 'Hercules' and 'Feniks'
Powerplant: 3 diesels, delivering 6,000 bhp, and 3 electric motors, delivering 6,000 hp to three shafts
Speed: 20 knots (surfaced); 15 knots (dived)

Range: 13,825 miles (22,250 km) at 5 knots surfaced
Crew: 70
Used also by: Libya, USSR
Notes: The boats of the 'Foxtrot' class are designed as torpedo attack submarines, and entered production at Leningrad in 1958. The first Indian boat was handed over in 1968 and the last in 1975, although there are reports that India may be getting another pair.

'Abhay' class large patrol craft (1)

Class: *Abhay* (P3135)
Displacement: 120 tons (121.9 tonnes) standard; 151 tons (153.4 tonnes) full load
Dimensions: Length 117 ft 1½ in (35.7 m)
Beam 20 ft (6.1 m)
Draught 5 ft (1.5 m)

Armament:
Guns 1 40-mm Bofors
Missile systems
none
A/S weapons
none
Torpedo tubes
none
Aircraft
none

Radar and electronics: none
Sonar: none
Powerplant: 2 diesels
Speed: 18 knots
Range:
Crew:
Used also by: Bangladesh, Mauritius
Notes: Six of the class were originally built by the Hooghly Docking & Engineering Co of Calcutta, in the late 1950s and early 1960s.

Indonesia

39,000 including 1,000 naval air arm and 12,000 marines

Frigates:
4 Claud Jones
3 Riga
2 Surapati
2 Pattimura
(3 ?)

SS:
3 Whiskey
(2 Type 209)

Light Forces:
4 PSSM Mark 5 FAC(M)
9 Komar FAC(M)
4 Lürssen TNC-45 FAC(T)

Patrol Forces:
6 Kronshtadt PC
3 PC 461 PC
3 PGM 39 PC
2 Attack PC
5 Kraljevica PC
3 Kelabang
2 Fairey Spear coastal PC
6 Australian de Havilland type coastal PC

Amphibious Forces:
6 LST 511-1152
2 LST 1-511
1 Japanese LST
3 LCU
3 LCM (+10)
25+ LCM type
20+ LCVP type

Mine Warfare Forces:
5 T-43 ocean minesweepers
2 R coastal minesweepers

Auxiliaries:
4 survey ships
2 submarine tenders
1 destroyer depot ship
1 repair ship
8 tankers
1 training ship
1 cable ship
3 tugs

Naval Air Arm:
5 HU-16
6 C-47
6 Nomad MR (+6)
4 Bell 47G
6 Alouette II/III

The customs service operates a large number of coastal patrol craft. The army operates 14 large transports, 2 LSTs and 5 cargo ships. The air force operates six cargo ships.

'Claud Jones' class frigate (4)

Class: *Samadikun* (341), ex-US *John R. Perry* (DE1034); *Martadinata* (342), ex-US *Charles Berry* (DE1035); *Mongisidi* (343), ex-US *Claud Jones* (DE1033); *Ngurah Rai* (344), ex-US *McMorris* (DE1036)
Displacement: 1,450 tons (1,473 tonnes) standard; 1,750 tons (1,778 tonnes) full load
Dimensions: Length 310 ft (94.5 m)
Beam 37 ft (11.3 m)
Draught 18 ft (5.5 m)
Armament:
Guns 1 3-in (76-mm) (341 and 342)
2 37-mm in a twin mounting (341 and 342)
2 25-mm in a twin mounting (341 and 342)
2 3-in (76-mm) in single mountings (343 and 344)
2 25-mm in a twin mounting (343 and 344)
Missile systems
none

A/S weapons
2 Hedgehogs
2 triple 12.75-in (324-mm) Mark 32 tubes
Torpedo tubes
none
Aircraft
none
Radar and electronics: SPS 6 search and SPS 10 tactical radars
Sonar: SQS 29 to 32 series
Powerplant: 4 diesels, delivering 9,200 hp to one shaft
Speed: 22 knots
Range:
Crew: 175
Used only by: Indonesia
Notes: The four ships were built between 1957 and 1959 by Avondale Marine Ways and American Shipbuilding. They were commissioned into US service in 1959 and 1960. The first unit was transferred to Indonesia in 1973, the remaining three in 1974. The secondary armament is Russian.

'Surapati' class frigate (2)

Class: *Iman Bondjol* (355), *Surapati* (356)
Displacement: 1,150 tons (1,168 tonnes) standard; 1,500 tons (1,524 tonnes) full load
Dimensions: Length 324 ft 9½ in (99.0 m)
Beam 36 ft 1 in (11.0 m)
Draught 8 ft 6½ in (2.6 m)
Armament:
Guns 4 4-in (102-mm) in twin mountings
6 30-mm in twin mountings
6 20-mm in twin mountings
Missile systems
none
A/S weapons
2 Hedgehogs
4 DCTs

Torpedo tubes
3 21-in (533-mm)
Aircraft
none
Radar and electronics:
Sonar:
Powerplant: 2 Foster Wheeler boilers supplying steam to 2 Parsons geared turbines, delivering 24,000 shp to two shafts
Speed: 32
Range: 2,800 miles (4,500 km) at 22 knots
Crew: 200
Used only by: Indonesia
Notes: Built by Ansaldo at Genoa in 1956, these two near-sisters to the Venezuelan 'Almirante Clemente' class were commissioned into Indonesian service in 1958. Both are now in reserve.

'Pattimura' class frigate (2)

Class: *Pattimura* (801), *Sultan Hasanudin* (802)
Displacement: 950 tons (965 tonnes) standard; 1,200 tons (1,219 tonnes) full load

Dimensions: Length 270 ft 3 in (82.4 m)
Beam 34 ft 1½ in (10.4 m)
Draught 8 ft 10 in (2.7 m)
Armament:
Guns 2 3-in (76-mm) in single mountings
2 30-mm in a twin mounting
Missile systems

A/S weapons
2 Hedgehogs
4 DCTs
Torpedo tubes
none
Aircraft
none

Radar and electronics:
Sonar:
Powerplant: 3 Ansaldo-Fiat diesels, delivering 6,900 shp to three shafts
Speed: 22 knots
Range: 2,400 miles (3,863 km) at 18 knots
Crew: 110

Used only by: Indonesia
Notes: These two vessels, basically similar to the Italian 'Albatros' class, were built by Ansaldo at Livorna, the first in 1956 and the second in 1957. Both vessels were commissioned into Indonesian service in 1958. 802 is now in reserve.

'Whiskey' class submarine (3)

Class: *Nagga Banda* (403), *Pasopati* (410), *Bramastra* (412), all ex-Russian boats
Displacement: 1,030 tons (1,046 tonnes) surfaced; 1,350 tons (1,372 tonnes) dived
Dimensions: Length 249 ft 4 in (76.0 m)
Beam 22 ft (6.7 m)
Draught 15 ft 1 in (4.6 m)
Armament:
Guns 2 25-mm in a twin mounting (in 403)
Missile systems
none
A/S weapons
none
Torpedo tubes
6 21-in (533-mm) with 18 torpedoes or 40 mines
Aircraft
none
Radar and electronics: 'Snoop Plate' surface search radar and 'Stop Light' passive ECM
Sonar: 'Tamir'
Powerplant: 2 diesels, delivering 4,000 hp, and 2 electric motors, delivering 2,500 hp to two shafts
Speed: 17 knots (surfaced); 15 knots (dived)
Range: 13,000 miles (20,900 km) at 8 knots surfaced

Crew: 60
Used also by: Albania, Bulgaria, China, Egypt, North Korea, Poland, USSR
Notes: The arrival of four 'Whiskey' class torpedo attack submarines in Indonesia in 1962 brought the total delivered to that

country to 14, though only three are operational. Nine others are in reserve, and two are being cannibalised for spares. The 'Whiskey' class entered production in 1950, the first boat being completed in 1951.

PSSM Mark 5 fast attack craft (missile) (4)

Class: four craft
Displacement: 250 tons (254 tonnes) full load
Dimensions: Length 165 ft (50.3 m)
Beam 24 ft (7.3 m)
Draught 6 ft 7 in (2.0 m)
Armament:

Guns 1 3-in (76-mm)
2 40-mm Bofors
2 0.5-in (12.7-mm) machine-guns
Missile systems
4 Harpoon SSM launchers
A/S weapons
none
Torpedo tubes
none
Aircraft
none
Radar and electronics:

Sonar:
Powerplant: 1 General Electric LM 2500 gas turbine and 2 MTU diesels, delivering power to two shafts
Speed: 45 knots (gas);
17 knots (diesel)
Range:
Crew: 32
Used also by: Taiwan
Notes: Ordered from Tacoma Boatbuilding, these four craft have been built by a South Korean yard.

'Lürssen TNC-45' class fast attack craft (torpedo) (4)

Class: *Beruang* (652), *Matjan Kumbang* (653), *Harimau* (654), *Anoa* (655)
Displacement: 160 tons (162.6 tonnes) standard; 190 tons (193 tonnes) full load
Dimensions: Length 140 ft 9 in (42.9 m)
Beam 22 ft (6.7 m)
Draught 7 ft 6½ in (2.3 m)

Armament:
Guns 2 40-mm Bofors in single mountings
Missile systems
none
A/S weapons
none
Torpedo tubes
4 21-in (533-mm)
Aircraft
none

Radar and electronics:
Sonar:
Powerplant: 4 MTU diesels, delivering 12,000 bhp to four shafts
Speed: 42 knots
Range:
Crew: 39
Used only by: Indonesia
Notes: Basically similar to the German 'Jaguar' class, the 'TNC-45' class were built in a Singapore yard, the first and last being commissioned in 1959, and the middle pair in 1960.

'PGM 39' class large patrol craft (3)

Class: *Bentang Kalungkang* (570), ex-US *PGM 57*; *Bentang Waltatire* (571), ex-US *PGM 56*; *Bentang Silungkang* (572), ex-US *PGM 55*
Displacement: 122 tons (124 tonnes) full load
Dimensions: Length 100 ft (30.5 m)
Beam 21 ft (6.4 m)
Draught 8 ft 6 in (2.6 m)

Armament:
Guns 2 20-mm
2 machine-guns
Missile systems
none
A/S weapons
none
Torpedo tubes
none
Aircraft
none

Radar and electronics:
Sonar:
Powerplant: 2 Mercedes-Benz MB 820 dB diesels, delivering power to two shafts
Speed: 17 knots
Range:
Crew:
Used only by: Indonesia
Notes: Designed as amphibious control craft, the three craft of the 'PGM 39' class were transferred from the US in 1962, and are now used as patrol craft.

Iran

28,000 men

Destroyers:
(2 Spruance)
1 Battle
2 Allen M. Sumner FRAM II

Frigates:
4 Saam
(6 Lupo)

Corvettes:
4 PF 103

SS:
3 Tang
(6 Type 209)

Light Forces:
6 Kaman FAC(M) (+6)

Patrol Forces:
3 Improved PGM 71 PC
4 Cape PC
6 BH.7 hovercraft
8 SR.N6 hovercraft

Mine Warfare Forces:
3 MSC292 and 268 coastal minesweepers
2 MSI inshore minesweepers

Auxiliaries:
2 LCU
1 tanker
2 landing ships logistic
2 supply ships (+4)
1 repair ship
9 others

Naval Air Arm:
6 P-3F (1 MR sqn)
12 SH-3D (1 ASW sqn)
1 transport sqn with 6 Shrike Commander, 4 F-27.
5 AB205A
7 AB212
6 RH-53D
10 SH-3D
(39 P-3C MR)
(15 SH-3D)

Marine Force:
3 bns

'Battle' class guided missile destroyer (1)

Class: *Artemiz* (51), ex-British *Sluys* (D60)
Displacement: 2,325 tons (2,362 tonnes) standard; 3,360 tons (3,414 tonnes) full load
Dimensions: Length 379 ft (115.5 m)
  Beam 40 ft 6 in (12.3 m)
  Draught 17 ft 6 in (5.2 m)
Armament:
Guns 4 4.5-in (114-mm) in twin turrets
  4 40-mm Bofors in single mountings
Missile systems
  4 Standard SSM launchers with 8 missiles
  1 quadruple Seacat launcher
A/S weapons
  1 Squid 3-barrel A/S mortar
Torpedo tubes
  none
Aircraft
  none
Radar and electronics: Plessey AWS 1 search, Contraves Sea Hunter fire-control and Decca RDL 1 interception radars
Sonar:
Powerplant: 2 Admiralty boilers supplying steam to Parsons geared turbines, delivering 50,000 shp to two shafts
Speed: 35½ knots
Range: 3,000 miles (4,828 km) at 20 knots
Crew: 270
Used also by: Pakistan
Notes: *Sluys* was built by Cammell Laird at Birkenhead between 1943 and 1945, and commissioned into British service in 1946. Transferred to Iran in 1967 as *Artemiz*.

'Allen M. Sumner FRAM II' class guided missile destroyer (2)

Class: *Babr* (61), ex-US *Zellers* (DD777); *Palang* (62), ex-US *Stormes* (DD780)
Displacement: 2,200 tons (2,235 tonnes) standard; 3,320 tons (3,373 tonnes) full load
Dimensions: Length 376 ft 6 in (114.8 m)
  Beam 40 ft 10 in (12.4 m)
  Draught 19 ft (5.8 m)
Armament:
Guns 4 5-in (127-mm) in twin turrets
Missile systems
  4 Standard SSM launchers with 8 missiles
A/S weapons
  2 Hedgehogs
  2 triple 12.75-in (324-mm) Mark 32 tubes
Torpedo tubes
  none
Aircraft
  1 ASW helicopter
Radar and electronics: SPS 10 search, SPS 37 air surveillance and IFF, Mark 37 fire-control with Mark 25 radar, and navigational radars; ULQ/6 ECM arrays
Sonar: SQS 29 series, plus variable-depth sonar on *Babr*
Powerplant: 4 boilers supplying steam to 2 geared turbines, delivering 60,000 shp to two shafts
Speed: 34 knots
Range:
Crew: 14+260
Used also by: Brazil, Chile, Colombia, South Korea, Turkey, Venezuela
Notes: Both vessels were built by Todd Pacific Shipyards, and commissioned into US service in 1944 and 1945 respectively. The two units were extensively modernised and altered before sailing for Iran in 1972. Iran has ex-*Kenneth D. Bailey* (DD713) of the 'Gearing' class for spares.

'Saam' class guided missile frigate (4)

Class: *Saam* (71), *Zaal* (72), *Rostam* (73), *Faramarz* (74)
Displacement: 1,110 tons (1,128 tonnes) standard; 1,290 tons (1,311 tonnes) full load
Dimensions: Length 310 ft (94.4 m)
  Beam 34 ft (10.4 m)
  Draught 11 ft 2 in (3.4 m)

Armament:
Guns 1 4.5-in (114-mm)
  2 35-mm Oerlikon in a twin mounting
Missile systems
  1 quintuple Sea Killer launcher
  1 triple Seacat launcher
A/S weapons
  1 Limbo 3-barrel A/S mortar
Torpedo tubes
  none
Aircraft
  none
Radar and electronics: Plessey AWS 1 air
surveillance and IFF, Contraves Sea Hunter
fire-control and Decca RDL 1 interception
radars
Sonar:

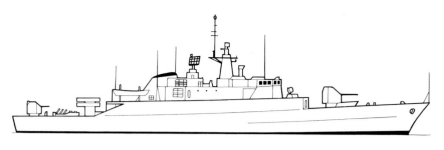

Powerplant: 2 Rolls-Royce Olympus gas tur-
bines, delivering 46,000 shp, and 2
Paxman diesels, delivering 3,800 shp to
two shafts
Speed: 40 knots
Range:
Crew: 125
Used only by: Iran

Notes: The first and last ships were built by
Vosper Thornycroft at Woolston, and the
middle pair by Vickers at Newcastle and
Barrow. Laid down in 1967 and 1968, the
vessels were launched in 1968 and 1969,
being commissioned into Iranian service in
1971 and 1972.

'PF 103' class corvette (4)

Class: *Bayandor* (81), ex-US *PF 103*; *Haghdi*
(82), ex-US *PF 104*; *Milanian* (83), ex-US
PF 105; *Kahnamuie* (84), ex-US *PF 106*
Displacement: 900 tons (914.4 tonnes)
standard; 1,135 tons (1,153 tonnes) full
load
Dimensions: Length 275 ft (83.8 m)
          Beam 33 ft (10.0 m)
          Draught 10 ft 2 in (3.1 m)
Armament:
Guns 2 3-in (76-mm) in single mountings
  2 40-mm Bofors in a twin mounting
  2 23-mm in a twin mounting

Missile systems
  none
A/S weapons
  4 DCTs
  2 DC racks
Torpedo tubes
  none
Aircraft
  none
Radar and electronics: SPS 6 search, Raytheon navigation and AN/SPG 34 fire-
control radars
Sonar:

Powerplant: F-M diesels, delivering 6,000
bhp to two shafts
Speed: 20
Range:
Crew: 140
Used also by: Thailand
Notes: All four ships were built by Levingstone Shipbuilding, the first pair being laid
down in 1962, launched in 1963 and commissioned into US service in 1964, the
equivalent dates for the second pair being
1967, 1968 and 1969. The two pairs were
transferred to Iran in 1964 and 1969, im-
mediately after commissioning.

'Tang' class submarine (3)

Class: *Kusseh* (101), ex-US *Trout* (SS566);
Nahang (102), ex-US *Wahoo* (SS565);
Dolfin (103), ex-US *Tang* (SS563)
Displacement: 2,100 tons (2,134 tonnes)
surfaced; 2,700 tons (2,743 tonnes) dived
Dimensions: Length 287 ft (87.4 m)
          Beam 27 ft 4 in (8.3 m)
          Draught 19 ft (6.2 m)
Armament:
Guns none
Missile systems
  none
A/S weapons
  none

Torpedo tubes
  8 21-in (533-mm)
Aircraft
  none
Radar and electronics:
Sonar:
Powerplant: 3 diesels, delivering 4,500 bhp,
and 2 electric motors, delivering 5,600 shp
to two shafts

Speed: 16 knots (surfaced and dived)
Range:
Crew: 8+79
Used also by: Italy, USA
Notes: The three boats were built between
1949 and 1951, and commissioned into
US service in 1952. Designed as patrol
boats, the submarines are being transferred
to Iran in 1978, 1979 and 1980 unless the
political situation in Iran dictates otherwise.

'Kaman' class fast attack craft (missile) (12)

Class: *Kaman* (P221), *Zoubin* (P222), *Kha-
dang* (P223), *Peykan* (P224), *Joshan*
(P225), *Falakhon* (P226), *Shamshir*
(P227), *Gorz* (P228), *Gardouneh* (P229),
Khanjar (P230), *Neyzeh* (P231), *Tabarzin*
(P232)
Displacement: 249 tons (253 tonnes) stan-
dard; 275 tons (279.4 tonnes) full load
Dimensions: Length 154 ft 2½ in (47.0 m)
          Beam 23 ft 3½ in (7.1 m)
          Draught 6 ft 3 in (1.9 m)

Armament:
Guns 1 76-mm OTO Melara
  1 40-mm Bofors
Missile systems
  2 twin Harpoon launchers
A/S weapons
  none
Torpedo tubes
  none
Aircraft
  none

Radar and electronics: Hollandse Signaalap-
paraten WM 28 tactical and fire-control
radar
Sonar: none
Powerplant: 4 MTU diesels, delivering
14,400 bhp to four shafts
Speed: 36 knots
Range: 700 miles (1,125 km) at more than
30 knots
Crew: 30
Used only by: Iran
Notes: Of the 'La Combattante II' class, these
12 craft were ordered from Construction de
Mecanique, Normandie, in 1974, to be
completed by spring 1979.

Improved 'PGM 71' class large patrol craft (3)

Class: *Parvin* (211), ex-US *PGM 103*; *Bahraam* (212), ex-US *PGM 112*; *Nahid* (213), ex-US *PGM 122*
Displacement: 105 tons (106.7 tonnes) standard; 146 tons (148.3 tonnes) full load
Dimensions: Length 100 ft (30.5 m)
Beam 22 ft (6.7 m)
Draught 10 ft (3.1 m)

Armament:
Guns 1 40-mm Bofors
2 0.5-in (12.7-mm) machine-guns
Missile systems
none
A/S weapons
none
Torpedo tubes
none
Aircraft
none
Radar and electronics:
Sonar:

Powerplant: 8 General Motors Corporation diesels, delivering 2,000 bhp
Speed: 15 knots
Range:
Crew:
Used also by: Liberia
Notes: The first craft was built by Peterson Builders, the other two by Tacoma Boatbuilding, being commissioned into US service (for disposal overseas) in 1970, 1967 and 1968.

'Cape' class large patrol craft (4)

Class: *Kayvan* (201), *Tiran* (202), *Mehran* (203), *Mahan* (204)
Displacement: 85 tons (86.4 tonnes) standard; 107 tons (108.7 tonnes) full load
Dimensions: Length 95 ft (28.9 m)
Beam 20 ft 2 in (6.2 m)
Draught 6 ft 10 in (2.1 m)

Armament:
Guns 1 40-mm Bofors
Missile systems
none
A/S weapons
1 7.2-in (183-mm) 8-barrel projector
8 DCs
Torpedo tubes
none
Aircraft
none

Radar and electronics:
Sonar:
Powerplant: 4 Cummins diesels, delivering 2,200 bhp to two shafts
Speed: 20 knots
Range: 1,500 miles (2,415 km)
Crew: 15
Used also by: South Korea, Thailand
Notes: All built to a US Coast Guard design in the late 1950s, the four Iranian units of the 'Cape' class are used for coastal patrol.

Iraq

4,000 men

Light Forces:
3 SO I submarine chasers
6 Osa I FAC(M)
8 Osa II FAC(M)
10 P-6 FAC(T)

Patrol Forces:
2 Poluchat I PC
4 Nyryat II coastal PC
4 Zhuk coastal PC
2 PO 2 coastal PC
8 Thornycroft 36-ft coastal PC
4 Thornycroft 21-ft coastal PC

Mine Warfare Forces:
2 T-43 ocean minesweepers
3 Yevgenya inshore minesweepers

Amphibious Forces:
3 Polnocny LCT

'Poluchat I' class large patrol craft (2)

Class: 2 ex-Russian craft
Displacement: 100 tons (101.6 tonnes) standard
Dimensions: Length 98 ft 5 in (30.0 m)
Beam 19 ft (5.8 m)
Draught 5 ft 11 in (1.8 m)
Armament:
Guns 2 25-mm in a twin mounting
Missile systems
none
A/S weapons
none
Torpedo tubes
none
Aircraft
none

Radar and electronics:
Sonar: none
Powerplant: 2 diesels, delivering 2,400 hp to two shafts
Speed: 20 knots
Range:
Crew: 15
Used also by: Albania, Algeria, Egypt, Equatorial Guinea, India, Mozambique, North Yemen, Somali Republic, South Yemen, Tanzania, USSR
Notes: 'Poluchat' class craft have been built in Russia since the early 1960s for use as patrol craft and torpedo recovery vessels. Two were transferred to Iraq in the late 1960s. An alternative armament installation uses two 14.5-mm AA machine-guns on a twin mounting.

Israel

5,000 men (1,000 conscripts), and 3,000 reservists

SS:
3 Type 206

Corvettes:
(2 Qu-9-35 type)

Light Forces:
6 Reshef FAC(M) (+6)
12 Saar FAC(M)
(2 Flagstaff FAH(G))
2 Dvora FAC(M) (+?)

Patrol Forces:
35 Dabur coastal PC
3 PBR coastal PC
3 Firefish Model III coastal PC

Amphibious Forces:
3 LSM 1
3 Ash LCT
3 LC LCT
3 LCM

Auxiliaries:
1 support ship
2 transports
others

Naval Air Arm:
3 IAI 1124 Westwind MR (+3)

Type 206 submarine (3)

Class: *Gal, Gur, Rahav*
Displacement: 420 tons (426.7 tonnes) surfaced; 600 tons (609.6 tonnes) dived
Dimensions: Length 147 ft 7½ in (45.0 m)
Beam 15 ft 5 in (4.7 m)
Draught 12 ft 1½ in (3.7 m)
Armament:
Guns none
Missile systems
SLAM launcher for Blowpipe SAM in sail
A/S weapons
none
Torpedo tubes
8 21-in (533-mm)
Aircraft
none
Radar and electronics:
Sonar:

Powerplant: diesels, delivering 2,000 hp, and 1 electric motor, delivering 1,800 hp to one shaft
Speed: 11 knots (surfaced); 17 knots (dived)
Range:
Crew: 22

Used also by: West Germany
Notes: Type 206 is a design by Ingenieur-kontor of Lübeck, built by Vickers at Barrow. The first two boats were built between 1975 and 1976, and commissioned into Israeli service in 1977. A third unit was commissioned in 1978.

'T' class submarine (1)

Class: *Dolphin* (77), ex-British *Truncheon*
Displacement: 1,310 tons (1,331 tonnes) standard; 1,535 tons (1,560 tonnes) surfaced; 1,740 tons (1,768 tonnes) dived
Dimensions: Length 293 ft 6 in (89.5 m)
Beam 26 ft 6 in (8.1 m)
Draught 14 ft 9 in (4.5 m)
Armament:
Guns none
Missile systems
none
A/S weapons
none
Torpedo tubes
6 21-in (533-mm)
Aircraft
none
Radar and electronics:
Sonar:
Powerplant: diesels, delivering 2,500 bhp, and electric motors, delivering 2,900 hp, to two shafts
Speed: 15¼ knots (surfaced); 15 knots (dived)
Range:

Crew: 65
Used only by: Israel
Notes: *Truncheon* was built by HM Dockyard at Devonport between 1942 and 1944, and commissioned into British service in

1945. After sale to Israel, she was lengthened by some 20 ft (6.1 m). *Dolphin*'s sister submarine *Dakar*, ex-British *Totem*, was lost in 1968. Now deleted.

'Reshef' class fast attack craft (missile) (12)

Class: *Reshef, Keshet, Romah, Kidon, Tarshish, Yaffo* and six others
Displacement: 415 tons (421.6 tonnes) standard
Dimensions: Length 190 ft 3½ in (58.0 m)
Beam 25 ft 7 in (7.8 m)
Draught 7 ft 10½ in (2.4 m)
Armament:
Guns 2 76-mm OTO Melara in single mountings
2 20-mm Oerlikons
Missile systems
6 Gabriel and 4 Harpoon SSM launchers
A/S weapons
none
Torpedo tubes
none
Aircraft
none
Radar and electronics: EL/M-2207 search radar

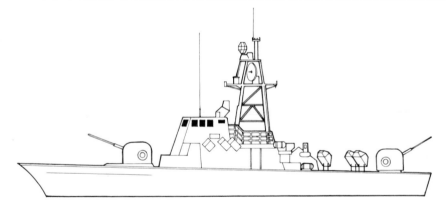

Sonar: ELAC fitted to craft in the Red Sea
Powerplant: 4 MTU diesels, delivering 10,680 hp to two shafts
Speed: 32 knots
Range: about 1,500 miles (2,415 km) at 30 knots
Crew: 45
Used also by: South Africa

Notes: All Israeli craft are built by Haifa Shipyard. The first six 'Reshef' class craft were commissioned between 1973 and 1975, and the first of the second group of six in 1977. The second group is slightly larger, with a length of 202 ft 5 in (61.7 m).

'Saar' class fast attack craft (missile) (12)

Class: *Mivtach* (311), *Miznach* (312), *Misgav* (313), *Eilat* (321), *Haifa* (322), *Acco* (323), all of Group A; *Saar* (331), *Soufa* (332), *Gaash* (333), *Herev* (341), *Hanit* (342), *Hetz* (343), all of Group B
Displacement: 220 tons (223.5 tonnes) standard; 250 tons (254 tonnes) full load
Dimensions: Length 147 ft 7½ in (47.0 m)
Beam 23 ft (7.0 m)
Draught 8 ft 2½ in (2.5 m)
Armament:
Guns 76-mm OTO Melara or 40-mm Bofors (see Notes)

Missile systems
  Gabriel SSM launchers (see Notes)
A/S weapons
  none
Torpedo tubes
  none
Aircraft
  none
Radar and electronics: EL/M-2207 search radar
Sonar: ELAC in Group A craft

Powerplant: 4 MTU diesels, delivering 13,500 bhp to four shafts
Speed: 40+ knots
Range: 2,500 miles (4,025 km) at 15 knots; 1,000 miles (1,609 km) at 30 knots
Crew: 35 to 40
Used only by: Israel
Notes: All 12 craft were built by Chantiers de Normandie, the first group being commissioned in 1968 and the second group in 1969. Originally, the craft of Group A

had 3 40-mm Bofors AA guns and 4 Mark 32 tubes, while the craft of Group B had 76-mm OTO Melara guns. Gabriel SSM launchers have been added in Israel, with Group A craft now capable of accepting 1 40-mm gun and 8 Gabriel launchers, and Group B craft 1 76-mm gun and 2 triple Gabriel launchers.

Israeli Aircraft Industries Gabriel

Type: naval surface-to-surface missile
Guidance: radar control, plus (probable) active radar terminal homing
Dimensions: Span 23¾ in (60.0 cm) for tail; 54⅓ in (138.0 cm) for wings
Body diameter 12⅘ in (32.5 cm)
Length 11 ft (3.35 m)
Booster: solid-propellant rocket, developing 7,937-lb (3,600-kg) thrust for 3 seconds
Sustainer: solid-propellant rocket, developing 170-lb (77-kg) thrust for 100 seconds in the short-range version
Warhead: 397 lb (180 kg) of high explosive
Weights: Launch 882 lb (400 kg)
Burnt out
Performance: speed Mach 0.7; range 1¼ to 13⅔ miles (2 to 22 km)
Used also by: Argentina, Malaysia, Singapore, South Africa
Notes: The Gabriel anti-ship missile is fired from a fixed container/launcher. With its course controlled by the launch vessel's sensors and fire-control computer, the Gabriel cruises at about 246 ft (75 m) and then at 32 ft (10 m), finally descending to just above the sea for the terminal homing phase under the guidance of its active (the Israelis claim semi-active) homing head. The Gabriel Mark II has a larger engine, giving a range of some 25½ miles (42 km). Weight is about 1,102 lb (500 kg).

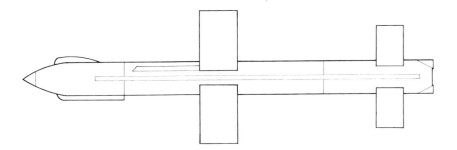

Italy

The Italian Navy
The Italian Navy is designed for operations in the 'landlocked' Mediterranean, within easy reach of land-based airpower, a factor that has greatly influenced the latest trends in Italian naval design and construction, as has the need to provide surface warships with the latest in anti-submarine weapons and techniques. The manpower strength of the Italian Navy is 42,000, some 11.6 per cent of the total strength of the armed forces, whose budget amounts to 2.6 per cent of the gross national product.

The need to combine air and underwater protection has led the Italian Navy to the forefront of helicopter cruiser development and service, with three such ships in existence, and another to enter service in the mid-1980s. The latest ship is *Andrea Doria*, which can operate nine A/S helicopters, but also has two triple A/S torpedo tube mountings, and a combined twin launcher for ASROC A/S

weapons and Terrier SAMs. She also has a useful gun armament, making her an excellent all-round vessel whose only major disadvantage appears to be her size, which is something of a liability. The two other helicopter cruisers of the 'Andrea Doria' class are smaller, and can handle only four A/S helicopters. The gun armament is the same, and the combined ASROC/Terrier launcher is not fitted, these earlier ships having a twin launcher for Terrier SAMs alone, A/S armament being restricted to two triple torpedo tube mountings. All three ships can make over 30 knots, and are quite manoeuvrable.

The importance of SAMs in Italian naval thinking is emphasised by the four ships of the 'Audace' and 'Impavido' classes, each of which has a single Tartar SAM launcher. Anti-submarine torpedo tubes are fitted, and an A/S helicopter (two in the case of the 'Audace' class) are carried. Two of an Improved 'Audace' class are to be built for service in the 1980s. The three other

Italian destroyers are of a conventional nature, although CODAG machinery was pioneered in *San Giorgio*.

The Italians make extensive use of CODOG-powered frigates, their speed, acceleration and manoeuvrability being ideal for Mediterranean conditions. Six 'Maestrale' (basically improved 'Lupo') class are to be built in the 1980s, but for the moment Italy has four 'Lupo' class, with two A/S helicopters, Otomat SSMs and a Selenia Albatros SAM system, two 'Alpino' class with two A/S helicopters, four 'Bergamini' class with one helicopter, and four 'Centauro' class with no helicopter. The 'Bergamini' and 'Centauro' classes are steam powered.

Italy has 13 corvettes, none of them particularly distinguished, and five of them fairly old and now used for a variety of secondary roles.

Submarines can be useful in Mediterranean conditions, and Italy has six modern submarines of the

'Sauro' and 'Toti' classes, with another two building. There are also six ex-American boats, only two of which are of any real operational importance.

For coastal operations, Italy has surprisingly few attack craft, with only one 'Sparviero' class missile hydrofoil (with another six building), and four convertible fast attack craft with gun or torpedo armament. Amphibious forces are limited to two 'De Soto County' LSTs, one 'Kenneth Whiting' transport, and landing craft. Mine warfare forces are better provided for, however, with 10 minehunters/ minesweepers to be built in the 1980s, four 'Agile' class ocean minesweepers, 14 'Bluebird' class coastal minesweepers, 17 'Agave' class coastal minesweepers, and 10 'Aragosta' class inshore minesweepers.

The support and replenishment of Italian warships is well catered for, leaving the Italian Navy with the shortage of small missile-armed craft as its one major weakness. The utility of such craft in a major war has yet to be proved, so perhaps the Italians are not running much risk. However, there does seem to be a role for such craft, and relatively large numbers of them can be built quite cheaply.

As the areas in which it is to operate are all within easy reach of land-based aircraft, the naval air arm of the Italian Navy has been kept small, with only five ASW helicopter squadrons using 71 helicopters. Another 24 ASW helicopters are on order.

42,000 men (24,000 conscripts) including 750 naval air arm, 1,700 marines, and 115,800 reservists

Helicopter Cruisers:
(1 ?)
1 Vittorio Veneto
2 Andrea Doria

Destroyers (DDG):
2 Audace
2 Impavido

Destroyers (DD):
1 San Giorgio
2 Impetuoso

Frigates (FFG):
(6 Maestrale)
4 Lupo

Frigates (FF):
2 Alpino
4 Bergamini
4 Centauro

Corvettes:
4 De Cristofaro
4 Albatros
4 Ape

SS:
2 Sauro (+ 2)
4 Toti
2 Tang
2 Guppy III

Light Forces:
1 Sparviero FAH(M) (+6)
2 Freccia FAC(G/T)
2 Lampo FAC(G/T)
3 Higgins FAC(P)
2 FAC(T)

Amphibious Forces:
2 De Soto County LST
1 Kenneth Whiting transport
57 landing craft

Mine Warfare Forces:
(10 ? minehunters)
4 Agile ocean minesweepers
13 Adjutant coastal minesweepers
17 Agave coastal minesweepers
10 Aragosta inshore minesweepers

Auxiliaries:
4 survey vessels
2 replenishment tankers
1 Barnegat support ship
10 coastal transports
2 training ships (sail)
others

Naval Air Arm:
5 ASW helicopter sqns with 3 SH-34, 24 SH-3D, 32 AB 204AS, 12 AB 212
(15 AB 212)
(9 SH-3D)

'Vittorio Veneto' class helicopter cruiser (1)

Class: *Vittorio Veneto* (C550)
Displacement: 7,500 tons (7,620 tonnes) standard; 8,850 tons (8,992 tonnes) full load
Dimensions: Length 589 ft 3 in (179.6 m)
Beam 63 ft 8 in (19.4 m)
Draught 19 ft 8 in (6.0 m)
Armament:
Guns 8 76-mm in single mountings
Missile systems
1 twin Terrier/ASROC launcher
A/S weapons
2 triple 12.75-in (324-mm) Mark 32 tubes
Torpedo tubes
none
Aircraft
9 ASW helicopters

Radar and electronics: SPS 52 3D air search and target designator, SPS 40 long-range search, SMA/SPQ-2 search and navigation, SPG 55B Terrier fire-control and Orion (Argo/Elsag NA9 system) gun fire-control; TACAN AN/URN-20
Sonar: SQS 23
Powerplant: 4 Foster Wheeler boilers supplying steam to 2 Tosi double-reduction geared turbines, delivering 73,000 hp to two shafts
Speed: 32 knots
Range: 6,000 miles (9,650 km) at 20 knots
Crew: 60+500
Used only by: Italy
Notes: *Vittorio Veneto* is based on the 'Andrea Doria' class, but with vastly improved helicopter and A/S facilities. She was built by Navalmeccanica at Castellammare di Stabia between 1965 and 1967, and commissioned into Italian service in 1969.

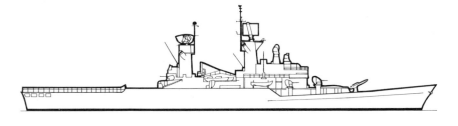

'Andrea Doria' class escort cruiser (2)

Class: *Andrea Doria* (C553), *Caio Duilio* (C554)

Displacement: 5,000 tons (5,080 tonnes) standard; 6,500 tons (6,604 tonnes) full load

Dimensions: Length 489 ft 10 in (149.3 m)
Beam 56 ft 5 in (17.2 m)
Draught 16 ft 5 in (5.0 m)

Armament:
Guns 8 76-mm in single mountings
Missile systems
1 twin Terrier launcher
A/S weapons
2 triple 12.75-in (324-mm) Mark 32 tubes
Torpedo tubes
none
Aircraft
4 ASW helicopter

Radar and electronics: SPS 39 (SPS 76B on C553) 3D target designator and air surveillance, SPS 40 long-range search, SPG 55A (SPG 55C on C553) Terrier fire-control, and Orion (Argo/Elsag NA9 system) gun fire-control; TACAN AN/URN-20

Sonar: SQS 23

Powerplant: 4 Foster-Wheeler boilers supplying steam to 2 double-reduction geared turbines, delivering 60,000 shp to two shafts

Speed: 31 knots

Range: 6,000 miles (9,655 km) at 20 knots

Crew: 45+440

Used only by: Italy

Notes: *Andrea Doria* was built by Cantieri del Tirreno between 1958 and 1963, and commissioned in 1964; *Caio Duilio* by Navalmeccanico di Stabia between 1958 and 1962, and commissioned in 1964.

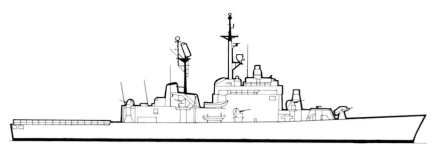

'Audace' class guided missile destroyer (2)

Class: *Ardito* (D550), *Audace* (D551)

Displacement: 3,600 tons (3,658 tonnes) standard; 4,400 tons (4,470 tonnes) full load

Dimensions: Length 448 ft 2 in (136.6 m)
Beam 47 ft 7 in (14.5 m)
Draught 15 ft 1 in (4.6 m)

Armament:
Guns 2 5-in (127-mm) in single mountings
4 76-mm in single mountings
Missile systems
1 Tartar launcher
A/S weapons
2 triple 12.75-in (324-mm) Mark 32 tubes
Torpedo tubes
4 533-mm (21-in)
Aircraft
2 ASW helicopters

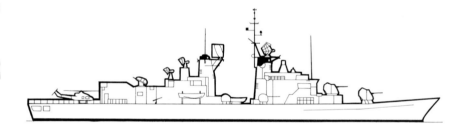

Radar and electronics: SPS 52 3D air surveillance, SPG 51 tracking and missile guidance, SPS 12 surface search, Orion RTN 10X (Argo 10/Elsag NA 10 system) radars

Sonar: CWE 610

Powerplant: 4 Foster Wheeler boilers supplying steam to 2 geared turbines, delivering 73,000 shp to two shafts

Speed: 33 knots

Range:

Crew: 30+350

Used only by: Italy

Notes: The vessels were built by Navalmeccanica at Castellammare and Cantieri del Tirreno at Riva Trigosa between 1968 and 1971, and commissioned in 1973 and 1972 respectively. The design is an improved version of that of the 'Impavido' class.

'Impavido' class guided missile destroyer (2)

Class: *Impavido* (D570), *Intrepido* (D571)
Displacement: 3,201 tons (3,252 tonnes) standard; 3,851 tons (3,913 tonnes) full load
Dimensions: Length 430 ft 9 in (131.3 m)
Beam 44 ft 7½ in (13.6 m)
Draught 14 ft 9 in (4.5 m)
Armament:
Guns 2 5-in (127-mm) in a twin turret
4 76-mm in single turrets
Missile systems
1 Tartar launcher
A/S weapons
2 triple 12.75-in (324-mm) Mark 32 tubes
Torpedo tubes
none
Aircraft
1 helicopter
Radar and electronics: SPS 39 3D search, SPS 12 search, SPG 51 Tartar fire-control, and Argo 10/Elsag NA 10 gun fire-control radars
Sonar: SQS 23
Powerplant: 4 Foster Wheeler boilers supplying steam to 2 double-reduction geared turbines, delivering 70,000 shp to two shafts
Speed: 34 knots
Range: 3,300 miles (5,310 km) at 20 knots; 2,900 miles (4,667 km) at 25 knots
Crew: 23+312
Used only by: Italy

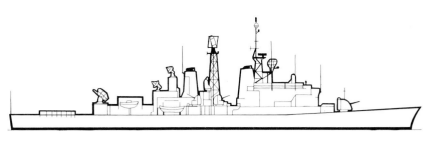

Notes: *Impavido* was built by Cantieri del Tirreno at Riva Trigosa between 1957 and 1962, and commissioned in 1963; *Intrepido* was built by Ansaldo at Livorno between 1959 and 1962, and commissioned in 1964.

'San Giorgio' class destroyer (1)

Class: *San Giorgio* (D562)
Displacement: 3,950 tons (4,013 tonnes) standard; 4,350 tons (4,420 tonnes) full load
Dimensions: Length 466 ft 10 in (142.3 m)
Beam 47 ft 3 in (14.4 m)
Draught 14 ft 9 in (4.5 m)
Armament:
Guns 4 5-in (127-mm) in twin turrets
3 76-mm in one twin and one single mounting
Missile systems
none

A/S weapons
1 MENON 3-barrel A/S mortar
2 triple 12.75-in (324-mm) Mark 32 tubes
Torpedo tubes
none
Aircraft
none
Radar and electronics: SPS-6 search and I-band fire-control radars
Sonar: SQS 11
Powerplant: 2 Tosi Metrovick gas turbines, delivering 15,000 bhp, and 4 Fiat diesels, delivering 16,000 hp, to two shafts

Speed: 28 knots on gas turbines and diesels; 20 knots on diesels
Range: 4,800 miles (7,725 km) at 20 knots
Crew: 15+280+130 cadets
Used only by: Italy
Notes: *San Giorgio* was built by Cantieri Navali Riuniti of Ancona between 1939 and 1941, and commissioned into Italian service in 1943 as *Pompeo Magno*. She was converted into a fleet destroyer in 1951, and into a cadet training vessel/destroyer between 1963 and 1965. It was during this modernisation that the gas turbine/diesel propulsion arrangement was installed.

'Impetuoso' class destroyer (2)

Class: *Impetuoso* (D558), *Indomito* (D559)
Displacement: 2,755 tons (2,799 tonnes) standard; 3,800 tons (3,861 tonnes) full load
Dimensions: Length 418 ft 7½ in (127.6 m)
Beam 43 ft 7½ in (13.3 m)
Draught 14 ft 9 in (4.5 m)
Armament:
Guns 4 5-in (127-mm) in twin turrets
16 40-mm Bofors in twin mountings

Missile systems
none
A/S weapons
1 three-barrel A/S mortar
4 DCTs and 1 DC rack
2 triple 12.75-in (324-mm) Mark 32 tubes
Torpedo tubes
none
Aircraft
none
Radar and electronics: SPS 6 and SPQ 2 search and Mark 25 (Mark 37 FCS) and SPG 34 (Mark 63 FCS) fire-control radars
Sonar: SQS 11

Powerplant: 4 Foster Wheeler boilers supplying steam to 2 double-reduction geared turbines, delivering 65,000 shp to two shafts
Speed: 35 knots
Range: 3,400 miles (5,475 km) at 20 knots
Crew: 15+300
Used only by: Italy
Notes: Both ships were built between 1952 and 1956, for commissioning in 1958, by Cantieri del Tirreno of Riva Trigosa and Ansaldo of Livorno. They were the first destroyers built in Italy since World War II.

'Fletcher' class destroyer (2)

Class: *Geniere* (D555), ex-US *Pritchett* (DD561); *Fante* (D561), ex-US *Walker* (DD517)
Displacement: 2,080 tons (2,113 tonnes) standard; 2,940 tons (2,987 tonnes) full load
Dimensions: Length 376 ft 6 in (114.8 m)
Beam 39 ft 6 in (12.0 m)
Draught 18 ft (5.5 m)
Armament:
Guns 2 5-in (127-mm) in single mountings
4 3-in (76-mm) in twin mountings

Missile systems
none
A/S weapons
2 Hedgehog
1 DC rack
2 triple 12.75-in (324-mm) Mark 32 tubes
Torpedo tubes
none
Aircraft
none
Radar and electronics: SPS-6 and SPS-10 search radars
Sonar: SQS-4

Powerplant: 4 Babcock & Wilcox boilers supplying steam to General Electric geared turbines, delivering 60,000 shp to two shafts
Speed: 35 knots
Range: 6,000 miles (9,655 km) at 20 knots
Crew: 10+240
Used also by: Argentina, Brazil, Chile, Greece, Mexico, Peru, South Korea, Spain, Taiwan, Turkey, West Germany
Notes: The two ships were built by Seattle-Tacoma Shipbuilding and Bath Iron Works between 1942 and 1943, and were commissioned into US service in 1944 and 1943 respectively. *Fante* was transferred in 1969, and *Geniere* in 1970. Now deleted.

'Lupo' class guided missile frigate (4)

Class: *Lupo* (D564), *Sagittario* (F565), *Perseo* (F566), *Orsa* (F567)
Displacement: 2,208 tons (2,243 tonnes) standard; 2,500 tons (2,540 tonnes) full load
Dimensions: Length 355 ft 7½ in (108.4 m)
Beam 37 ft 1 in (11.3 m)
Draught 12 ft 1½ in (3.7 m)
Armament:
Guns 1 127-mm OTO Melara Compact
4 40-mm Breda in twin Dardo systems
Missile systems
1 octuple Otomat SSM launcher
1 octuple NATO Seasparrow SAM launcher system
2 SCLAR system launchers
A/S weapons
2 triple 12.75-in (324-mm) Mark 32 tubes
Torpedo tubes
none
Aircraft
2 ASW helicopters

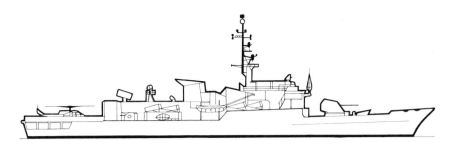

Radar and electronics: MM/SPS 774 air search, Selenia RAN 11L/X system combined search and Orion (Argo 10/Elsag NA10 system) gun fire-control radars; Selenia IPN 10 automatic command and control system; Elletronica ECM system
Sonar: Raytheon DE 1160B hull-mounted
Powerplant: CODOG arrangement, with 2 Fiat LM 2500 gas turbines, delivering 50,000 shp, and 2 GMT diesels, delivering 7,800 hp, to two shafts
Speed: 35 knots on gas turbines; 21 knots on diesels

Range: 4,400 miles (7,080 km) at 16 knots on diesel power
Crew: 16+169
Used also by: Ecuador, Egypt, Iran, Peru, Venezuela
Notes: All four vessels will be built by Cantieri Navali Riuniti of Riva Trigosa. *Lupo* was laid down in 1974, launched in 1976 and commissioned in 1977. *Sagittario* was commissioned in May 1978, and *Perseo* and *Orsa* are due for commissioning in February and August 1979.

'Alpino' class frigate (2)

Class: *Alpino* (F580), ex-*Circe*; *Carabiniere* (F581), ex-*Climene*
Displacement: 2,700 tons (2,743 tonnes) full load
Dimensions: Length 371 ft 8½ in (113.3 m)
Beam 43 ft 7½ in (13.3 m)
Draught 12 ft 9½ in (3.0 m)
Armament:
Guns 3 76-mm in single mountings
Missile systems
none
A/S weapons
1 DC mortar
2 triple 12.75-in (324-mm) Mark 32 tubes
Torpedo tubes
none
Aircraft
2 helicopters
Radar and electronics: SPS 12 combined search, SPQ 2 air/surface search and navigation, Orion (Elsag/Argo 'O' system) fire-control and MM/SPR A interception radars

Sonar: hull-mounted SQS 29; SQA 10 variable-depth
Powerplant: 4 Tosi diesels, delivering 16,800 hp, and 2 Tosi Metrovick gas turbines, delivering 15,000 hp, to two shafts

Speed: 29 knots on diesels and gas turbines; 22 knots on diesels
Range: 4,200 miles (6,760 km) at 18 knots
Crew: 20+233
Used only by: Italy

Notes: Both vessels were built by Cantieri Navali del Tirreno of Riva Trigosa between 1963 and 1967, and 1965 and 1967, for commissioning in 1968. The design is derived from that of the 'Centauro' class frigates, with features of the 'Bergamini' class frigates.

'Bergamini' class frigate (4)

Class: *Carlo Bergamini* (F593), *Virginio Fasan* (F594), *Carlo Margotinni* (F595), *Luigi Rizzo* (F596)
Displacement: 1,650 tons (1,676 tonnes) full load
Dimensions: Length 311 ft 8 in (95.0 m)
Beam 37 ft 5 in (11.4 m)
Draught 10 ft 6 in (3.2 m)
Armament:
Guns 2 76-mm in single mountings
Missile systems
none
A/S weapons
1 DC mortar
2 triple 12.75-in (324-mm) Mark 32 tubes
Torpedo tubes
none
Aircraft
1 helicopter
Radar and electronics: SPS 12 combined search, SPQ 2 air/surface search and navigation, Orion (Elsag/Argo system) fire-control, and MM/SPR A interception radars
Sonar: SQS 40
Powerplant: 4 diesels (Fiat in 594 and 595, Tosi in 593 and 596), delivering 15,000 bhp to two shafts

Speed: 24½ knots
Range: 4,000 miles (6,440 km) at 18 knots
Crew: 19+139
Used only by: Italy

Notes: The lead ship was built by the San Marco yard of Trieste, and the other three ships by Navalmeccanica of Castellammare, between 1957 and 1960; the first to be commissioned was *Luigi Rizzo* in 1961, the other three following in 1962.

'Centauro' class frigate (4)

Class: *Canopo* (F551), ex-*D570*; *Castore* (F553), ex-*D573*; *Centauro* (F554), ex-*D571*; *Cigno* (F555), ex-*D572*
Displacement: 1,807 tons (1,836 tonnes) standard; 2,250 tons (2,286 tonnes) full load
Dimensions: Length 338 ft 3 in (103.1 m)
Beam 39 ft 4½ in (12.0 m)
Draught 12 ft 5½ in (3.8 m)
Armament:
Guns 3 76-mm in single mountings
Missile systems
none
A/S weapons
1 three-barrel DC mortar
2 triple 12.75-in (324-mm) Mark 32 tubes
Torpedo tubes
none
Aircraft
none
Radar and electronics: SPS 6 search, SMA/SPQ 2 combined search and navigation, I-band fire-control, and MM/SPR A interception radar
Sonar: SQS 11 and SQS 36
Powerplant: 2 Foster Wheeler boilers supplying steam to 2 double-reduction geared turbines, delivering 22,000 shp to two shafts

Speed: 25 knots
Range: 3,660 miles (5,890 km) at 20 knots
Crew: 16+209
Used only by: Italy

Notes: *Centauro* was built between 1952 and 1954 by Ansaldo at Livorno, and commissioned in 1957. The other three ships were built by Cantieri Navali of Taranto between 1952 and 1956, and were commissioned in 1957 and 1958.

'De Cristofaro' class corvette (4)

Class: *Pietro de Cristofaro* (F540), *Umberto Grosso* (F541), *Licio Visintini* (F546), *Salvatore Todaro* (F550)
Displacement: 850 tons (863.6 tonnes) standard; 1,020 tons (1,036 tonnes) full load

Dimensions: Length 263 ft 1½ in (80.2 m)
Beam 33 ft 9½ in (10.3 m)
Draught 8 ft 10 in (2.7 m)
Armament:
Guns 2 76-mm in single mountings
Missile systems
none
A/S weapons
1 single-barrel DC mortar
2 triple 12.75-in (324-mm) Mark 32 tubes

Torpedo tubes
none
Aircraft
none
Radar and electronics: SMA/SPQ 2 combined search and Orion 3 (OG3 FCS) fire-control radars
Sonar: SQS 36 hull-mounted and variable-depth, with Elsag DLB-1 fire-control system

Powerplant: 2 diesels, delivering 8,400 bhp
to two shafts
Speed: 23½ knots
Range: 4,000 miles (6,440 km) at 18 knots
Crew: 8+123

Used only by: Italy
Notes: *Visintini* was built between 1963 and
1965 by CRDA at Monfalcone, *de Cristofaro* between 1963 and 1965 by Cantiere
Navali del Tirreno at Riva Trigosa, and the

other two by Cantiere Ansaldo at Livorno
between 1962 and 1964. The four ships
were commissioned in 1965 and 1966.
Design was based on that of the 'Albatros'
class corvettes.

'Albatros' class corvette (4)

Class: *Aquila* (F542), *Albatros* (F543),
Alcione (F544), *Airone* (F545)
Displacement: 800 tons (812.8 tonnes)
standard; 950 tons (965.2 tonnes) full load
Dimensions: Length 250 ft 4 in (76.3 m)
Beam 31 ft 6 in (9.6 m)
Draught 9 ft 10½ in (2.8 m)
Armament:
Guns 4 40-mm Bofors
Missile systems
none
A/S weapons
2 Hedgehog Mark II
2 DCTs
1 DC rack
2 triple 12.75-in (324-mm) Mark 32 tubes
Torpedo tubes
none
Aircraft
none
Radar and electronics: SMA/SPQ 2 com-
bined search and navigation, and fire-
control radar as part of the Elsag NA 2 fire-
control system
Sonar: QCU 2
Powerplant: 2 Fiat diesels, delivering 5,200
bhp to two shafts
Speed: 19 knots
Range: 3,000 miles (4,830 km) at 18 knots
Crew: 109

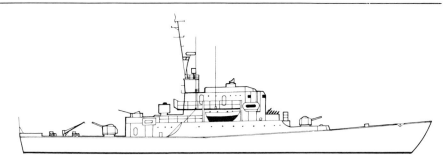

Used only by: Italy
Notes: The first unit was built by Breda
Marghera in Venice, between 1953 and
1954, and commissioned in 1956. The
other three units were built by Navalmeccanica at Castellammare di Stabia, during

the same period. The 'Albatros' class was
financed by the US, and originally com-
prised one ship (*Aquila*) for the Netherlands, four for Denmark and three for Italy.
Aquila was transferred to Italy in 1961.

'Sauro' class submarine (4)

Class: *Nazario Sauro* (S518), *Fecia di Cossato*
(S519), *Leonardo da Vinci* (S520), *Gug-
lielmo Marconi* (S521)
Displacement: 1,456 tons (1,480 tonnes)
surfaced; 1,631 tons (1,657 tonnes) dived
Dimensions: Length 209 ft 7¾ in (63.9 m)
Beam 22 ft 3½ in (6.8 m)
Draught 18 ft 8½ in (5.7 m)
Armament:
Guns none
Missile systems
none
A/S weapons
none
Torpedo tubes
6 533-mm (21-in) with 12 torpedoes
Aircraft
none
Radar and electronics: search radar, and
ECM fit
Sonar: active and passive

Powerplant: 3 diesels, delivering 3,210 bhp,
and 1 electric motor, delivering 3,650 hp to
one shaft
Speed: 11 knots (surfaced); 20 knots (dived)
Range: 7,000 miles (11,265 km) surfaced;
12,500 miles (20,120 km) at 4 knots
snorting; 400 miles (645 km) at 4 knots
dived; 20 miles (32 km) at 20 knots dived

Crew: 45
Used only by: Italy
Notes: Both current boats were built by
Italcantieri at Monfalcone, *Sauro* being commissioned in 1977 and *Cossato* in 1978. The
boats have an endurance of 45 days, and a
diving depth of 984+ ft (300+ m). Two more
of the class are on order.

'Toti' class submarine (4)

Class: *Attilio Bagnolini* (S505), *Enrico Toti* (S506), *Enrico Dandolo* (S513), *Lazzaro Mocenigo* (S514)
Displacement: 460 tons (467.4 tonnes) standard; 524 tons (532.4 tonnes) surfaced; 582 tons (591.3 tonnes) dived
Dimensions: Length 151 ft 7 in (46.2 m)
　　　　　　　Beam 15 ft 5 in (4.7 m)
　　　　　　　Draught 13 ft 1½ in (4.0 m)
Armament:
Guns none
Missile systems
　none
A/S weapons
　none
Torpedo tubes
　4 533-mm (21-in)
Aircraft
　none
Radar and electronics: search and navigation radar; ECM fit
Sonar: active and passive
Powerplant: 2 Fiat MB 820 N/I diesels and 1 electric motor, for a diesel-electric drive delivering 2,200 hp to one shaft
Speed: 14 knots (surfaced); 15 knots (dived)
Range: 3,000 miles (4,830 km) at 5 knots surfaced
Crew: 4+22
Used only by: Italy
Notes: All four boats were built by Italcantieri at Monfalcone, the first pair between 1965 and 1967, for commissioning in 1968, and the second pair between 1967 and 1968, for commissioning in 1968 and 1969. The boats can dive to a depth of 590 ft (180 m).

'Tang' class submarine (2)

Class: *Livio Piomarta* (S515), ex-US *Trigger* (SS564); *Romeo Romei* (S516), ex-US *Harder* (SS568)
Displacement: 2,100 tons (2,134 tonnes) surfaced; 2,700 tons (2,743 tonnes) dived
Dimensions: Length 287 ft (87.5 m)
　　　　　　　Beam 27 ft 4 in (8.33 m)
　　　　　　　Draught 19 ft (5.8 m)
Armament:
Guns none
Missile systems
　none
A/S weapons
　none
Torpedo tubes
　8 21-in (533-mm)
Aircraft
　none
Radar and electronics: PPS-12
Sonar:
Powerplant: 3 diesels, delivering 4,500 shp, and 2 electric motors, delivering 5,600 hp to two shafts
Speed: 20 knots (surfaced); 18 knots (dived)
Range: 11,000 miles (17,703 km) at 11 knots
Crew: 7 + 68
Used also by: Iran, USA
Notes: Both boats were built by the Electric Boat Division of General Dynamics between 1949 and 1951, and were com-

missioned into US service in 1952. The boats were transferred to Italy in 1973 and 1974.

'Guppy III' class submarine (2)

Class: *Primo Longobardo* (S501), ex-US *Volador* (SS 490); *Gianfranco Gazzana Priaroggia* (S502), ex-US *Pickerel* (SS524)
Displacement: 1,975 tons (2,007 tonnes) standard; 2,450 tons (2,489 tonnes) dived
Dimensions: Length 326 ft 6 in (99.5 m)
　　　　　　　Beam 27 ft (8.23 m)
　　　　　　　Draught 17 ft (5.2 m)
Armament:
Guns none
Missile systems
　none
A/S weapons
　none
Torpedo tubes
　10 21-in (533-mm)
Aircraft
　none
Radar and electronics:

Sonar:
Powerplant: 4 diesels, delivering 6,400 bhp, and 2 electric motors, delivering 5,400 shp to two shafts
Speed: 20 knots (surfaced); 15 knots (dived)
Range: 12,000 miles (19,313 km) at 10 knots surfaced
Crew: 10+75
Used also by: Brazil, Greece, Turkey
Notes: *Pickerel* was built by Boston Navy Yard in 1944, and commissioned into US service in 1949. *Volador* was built by Portsmouth Navy Yard between 1945 and 1946, for commissioning in 1948. Both boats were transferred to Italy in 1972.

'Balao' class submarine (2)

Class: *Alfredo Cappellini* (S507), ex-US *Capitaine* (SS336); *Evangelista Torricelli* (S512), ex-US *Lizardfish* (SS373)
Displacement: 1,600 tons (1,626 tonnes) standard; 1,855 tons (1,885 tonnes) surfaced; 2,455 tons (2,494 tonnes) dived
Dimensions: Length 311 ft 6 in (94.95 m)
Beam 27 ft (8.2 m)
Draught 17 ft (5.2 m)
Armament:
Guns none

Missile systems
none
A/S weapons
none
Torpedo tubes
10 21-in (533-mm)
Aircraft
none
Radar and electronics:
Sonar:
Powerplant: 4 General Motors Corporation 16/278 diesels, delivering 6,000 hp, and 4 electric motors, delivering 2,750 hp to two shafts

Speed: 18 knots (surfaced); 10 knots (dived)
Range: 14,000 miles (22,532 km) at 10 knots surfaced
Crew: 7+68
Used also by: Chile, Greece, Turkey, Venezuela
Notes: Both boats were built during 1944, the first by the Electric Boat Division of General Dynamics for commissioning in 1945, the second by Manitowoc Shipbuilding for commissioning in 1944. The two boats were transferred to Italy in 1966. Both now deleted.

'Sparviero' class hydrofoil (missile) (1)

Class: *Sparviero* (P420)
Displacement: 62½ tons (63.5 tonnes)
Dimensions: Length 80 ft 8½ in (24.6 m) with foils extended
Beam 39 ft 8¼ in (12.1 m) with foils extended
Draught 14 ft 5¼ in (4.4 m) hull-borne
Armament:
Guns 1 76-mm OTO Melara
Missile systems
2 Otomat SSM launchers
A/S weapons
none
Torpedo tubes
none
Aircraft
none

Radar and electronics: Orion RTN-10X radar as part of the Elsag NA 10 fire-control system
Sonar: none
Powerplant: 1 Bristol Siddeley Proteus gas turbine, delivering 4,500 bhp to the water-jet pump, and 1 diesel for propeller drive

Speed: 50 knots
Range: 400 miles (645 km) at 40 knots; 1,200 miles (1,930 km) at 8 knots
Crew: 2+8
Used only by: Italy
Notes: *Sparviero* was commissioned in 1974 after building at the La Spezia yards of Alinavi. Another six craft are planned.

'Freccia' class fast attack craft (2)

Class: *Freccia* (P493), ex-*MC590*; *Saetta* (P494), ex-*MC591*
Displacement: 188 tons (191 tonnes) standard; 205 tons (208.3 tonnes) full load
Dimensions: Length 150 ft 3 in (45.8 m)
Beam 23 ft 11½ in (7.3 m)
Draught 5 ft 7 in (1.7 m)
Armament:
Guns (as gunboat) 2 or 3 40-mm
(as fast minelayer) 1 40-mm
(as torpedo craft) 2 40-mm
Missile systems
1 quintuple Sea Killer Mark 1 SSM launcher (*Saetta* only)
A/S weapons
none
Torpedo tubes
(as torpedo boat) 2 533-mm (21-in)
Aircraft
none
Radar and electronics: E-band navigation and tactical radar (*Freccia*); Contraves fire-control system (*Saetta*)
Sonar:
Powerplant: 2 diesels, delivering 7,600 bhp, and 1 Bristol Siddeley Proteus gas turbine, delivering 4,250 shp
Speed: 40 knots
Range:
Crew: 4+33
Used only by: Italy
Notes: *Freccia* was built by Cantiere del Tirreno at Riva Trigosa for commissioning in 1965; *Saetta* by CRDA at Monfalcone for commissioning in 1966. The two craft can be altered within 24 hours to act as gunboats, fast minelayers (with eight mines), torpedo boats and finally as a missile craft (*Saetta*), although this last is still experimental.

'Lampo' class fast attack craft (2)

Class: *Lampo* (P491), ex-*MC491*; *Baleno* (P492), ex-*MC492*
Displacement: 170 tons (172.7 tonnes) standard; 196 tons (199.1 tonnes) full load
Dimensions: Length 131 ft 6¾ in (40.1 m)
Beam 21 ft (6.4 m)
Draught 4 ft 11 in (1.5 m)
Armament:
Guns (as gunboat) 2 or 3 40-mm
(as torpedo boat) 2 40-mm
Missile systems
none
A/S weapons
none
Torpedo tubes
(as torpedo boat) 2 533-mm (21-in)
Aircraft
none
Radar and electronics: 3 ST 7-250 radar
Sonar:

Powerplant: 2 Fiat diesels and 1 Metrovick gas turbine, delivering a total of 11,700 hp to three shafts
Speed: 39 knots
Range:
Crew: 5+28
Used only by: Italy
Notes: Both craft were built by Arsenale MM of Taranto, the first being commissioned in 1963 and the second in 1965. Both craft can be used as gunboats or torpedo boats.

'Agile' class ocean minesweeper (4)

Class: *Salmone* (M5430), ex-US *MSO507*; *Storione* (M5431), ex-US *MSO506*; *Sgombro* (M5432), ex-US *MSO517*; *Squalo* (M5433), ex-US *MSO518*
Displacement: 665 tons (675.6 tonnes) standard; 750 tons (762 tonnes) full load
Dimensions: Length 173 ft (52.7 m)
Beam 35 ft (10.67 m)
Draught 13 ft 7 in (4.14 m)
Armament:
Guns 1 40-mm
Missile systems
none
A/S weapons
none
Torpedo tubes
none
Aircraft
none
Radar and electronics:

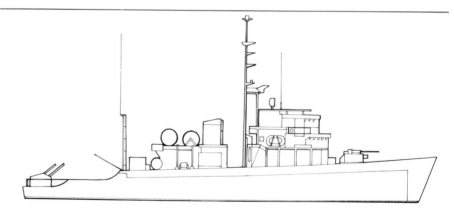

Sonar:
Powerplant: 2 diesels, delivering 1,600 bhp to two shafts
Speed: 14 knots
Range: 3,000 miles (4,830 km) at 10 knots
Crew: 7+44
Used also by: USA
Notes: These vessels have wooden hulls and stainless steel engines to make them non-magnetic. The first pair were commissioned in 1956, the second pair in 1957.

Selenia/Elsag Albatros Naval Defence System

Type: naval surface-to-air tactical guided missile and gun weapon system
Guidance: semi-active radar homing
Dimensions: Span 31½ in (80.0 cm)
Body diameter 8 in (20.3 cm)
Length 12 ft 1⅔ in (3.7 m)
Booster: solid-propellant rocket
Sustainer: none
Warhead: high explosive
Weights: Launch 485 lb (220 kg)
Burnt out
Performance: speed more than Mach 2.5
Used only by: Italy
Notes: The Albatros weapon system is designed to give Italian ships an all-weather defence against air attack by the use of an integrated missile and gun system. The missile used is the *Aspide*, to which the technical details above apply. The system has four major components:
1. one or two missile and gun fire-control systems
2. up to three groups of guns with two ballistic characteristics
3. one missile-launching system
4. *Aspide* missiles.

The *Aspide* launcher is an octuple unit.

Sistel Sea Killer Mark 1

Type: naval surface-to-surface tactical guided missile
Guidance: beam-riding/command/radio altimeter, or optical radio command/radio altimeter
Dimensions: Span 33½ in (85.0 cm)
Body diameter 7⁹⁄₁₀ in (20.0 cm)
Length 12 ft 3 in (3.73 m)
Booster: solid-propellant rocket, rated at 4,410-lb (2,000-kg) static thrust
Sustainer: as above
Warhead: 77 lb (35 kg) high explosive fragmentation type

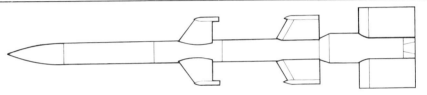

Weights: Launch 370 lb (168 kg)
Burnt out 260 lb (118 kg)
Performance: speed Mach 1.9; range 6¼ miles (10 km)
Used only by: Italy
Notes: The Sea Killer Mark 1 was developed as a short-range attack missile for use on patrol boats. The guidance system, with two alternative forms of control, allows use of the missile in all weathers. The Sea Killer Mark 1 is also being used for the development of the *Marte* weapons system for helicopters.

OTO Melara/Matra Otomat

Type: naval surface-to-surface missile
Guidance: inertial, with active radar terminal homing
Dimensions: Span 4 ft 5¼ in (1.35 m)
Body diameter 18¹⁄₁₀ in (46.0 cm)
Length 14 ft 7⅜ in (4.46 m)
Booster: two solid-fuel jettisonable boosters
Sustainer: Turboméca turbojet
Warhead: 132 lb (60 kg) of high explosive
Weights: Launch 1,698 lb (770 kg)
Burnt out
Performance: speed Mach 0.9; range 37¼ miles (60 km) effective, and 112 miles (180 km) maximum
Used also by: Ecuador, Egypt, Libya, Peru, Venezuela
Notes: The Otomat is fired from a fixed container/launcher on board the parent ship on a course predetermined by the ship's fire-control computer. In the terminal homing phase of the flight, the missile seeks its target with the aid of its active radar head, climbs sharply and then dives into the target. The Otomat Mark II has an effective range of about 62 miles (100 km), and a

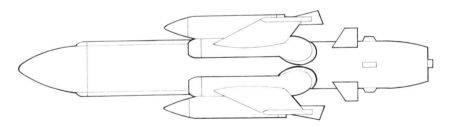

Mark III, to be designated Teseo, is a 124-mile (200-km) range coastal defence missile currently under development.

Sistel Sea Killer Mark 2

Type: naval surface-to-surface and air-to-surface tactical guided missile
Guidance: beam-riding/command/radio altimeter, or optical radio command/radio altimeter
Dimensions: Span 39$\frac{4}{8}$ in (1.0 m)
Body diameter 7$\frac{9}{16}$ in (20.0 cm)
Length 15 ft 5 in (4.7 m)
Booster: SEP 299 solid-propellant rocket, rated at 9,702-lb (4,400-kg) static thrust for 1.6 seconds
Sustainer: SEP 300 solid-propellant rocket, rated at 220$\frac{1}{2}$-lb (100-kg) static thrust for 73 seconds
Warhead: 154 lb (70 kg) high explosive semi-armour piercing
Weights: Launch 661 lb (300 kg)
Burnt out
Performance: cruising speed Mach 0.74; range 15$\frac{1}{2}$ miles (25 km)
Used also by: Iran
Notes: Essentially a Sea Killer Mark 1 with a more powerful warhead, and with a booster stage to increase range, the Sea Killer Mark 2 is in service with Iran as part of her frigates' armament, and is also being used in the development of the *Marte* anti-shipping weapon system for helicopter use.

A184

Type: ship- and submarine-launched torpedo
Guidance: wire-guidance from launch vessel, plus active/passive sonar homing
Launch method: tube
Dimensions: Length 19 ft 8$\frac{1}{4}$ in (6.0 m)
Diameter 21 in (533 mm)
Weight:
Engine: electric
Speed:
Range:
Warhead: high explosive
Used only by: Italy
Notes: capable of use against both surface and submarine targets.

A244

Type: aircraft- and ship-launched lightweight torpedo
Guidance: acoustic homing
Launch method: air-drop or tube
Dimensions: Length 8 ft 10 in (2.7 m)
Diameter 12.75 in (324 mm)
Weight:
Engine: electric
Speed:
Range:
Warhead: high explosive
Used by: Italy
Notes: A development of the US Mark 44 with improved electronics, especially in the acoustic homing head (the A244/S has even better homing characteristics).

G6E 'Kangaroo'

Type: submarine-launched torpedo
Guidance: wire-guidance from the launch boat, plus active acoustic homing
Launch method: tube
Dimensions: Length 20 ft 4 in (6.2 m)
Diameter 21 in (533 mm)
Weight:
Engine: electric
Speed:
Range:
Warhead: high explosive
Used only by: Italy
Notes: This weapon system comprises the obsolete G6E torpedo modified to carry a Mark 44 lightweight torpedo instead of its conventional warhead. After launch, the G6E parent torpedo moves under wire guidance towards the target, ejecting the Mark 44 torpedo at the end of its run.

Ivory Coast

250 men

Light Forces:
2 Franco-Belge type missile craft

Patrol Forces:
(1 Patra type PC)
1 VC type PC
5 river PC

Amphibious Forces:
1 Batral type transport
2 LCVP

Auxiliaries:
1 transport

Franco-Belge type missile craft (2)

Class: *Vigilant, Le Valeureux*
Displacement: 235 tons (238.8 tonnes) standard for *Vigilant*; 250 tons (254 tonnes) standard for *Le Valeureux*
Dimensions: Length 155 ft 10 in (47.5 m) for *Vigilant*; 157 ft 6 in (48.0 m) for *Le Valeureux*
Beam 22 ft 11$\frac{1}{2}$ in (7.0 m)
Draught 8 ft 6$\frac{1}{2}$ in (2.6 m)
Armament:
Guns 2 40-mm
Missile systems
8 SS.12 SSM launchers
A/S weapons
none
Torpedo tubes
none
Aircraft
none
Radar and electronics:
Sonar:
Powerplant: 2 AGO diesels, delivering 4,220 hp to two shafts
Speed: 18$\frac{1}{2}$ knots (*Vigilant*); 22 knots (*Le Valeureux*)
Range: 2,000 miles (3,220 km) at 15 knots
Crew: 3+22
Used only by: Ivory Coast
Notes: Both craft were built by SFCN, *Vigilant* being commissioned in 1968, and the improved *Le Valeureux* in 1976. Similar craft used by Cameroon, Malagasy Republic, Senegal and Tunisia.

Jamaica

133 men of the Coast Guard, the Maritime Arm of the Defence Force

Patrol Forces:
1 Sewart 31.5-m PC
3 Sewart 25.9-m coastal PC
2 coastal PC

Patrol craft (1)

Class: *Fort Charles* (P7)
Displacement: 103 tons (104.6 tonnes)
Dimensions: Length 105 ft (32.0 m)
Beam 22 ft (6.7 m)
Draught 7 ft (2.13 m)
Armament:
Guns 1 20-mm
2 0.5-in (12.7-mm) machine-guns
Missile systems
none
A/S weapons
none
Torpedo tubes
none
Aircraft
none
Radar and electronics:
Sonar:
Powerplant: 2 MBU 16V 538 TB90 diesels, delivering 7,000 shp
Speed: 32 knots
Range: 1,200 miles (1,931km) at 18 knots
Crew: 16
Used by: Jamaica
Notes: *Fort Charles* was built by Teledyne Sewart Seacraft of Berwick, Louisiana, and commissioned in 1974. She has accommodation for 24 troops or 24 hospital beds.

Japan

The Japanese Navy
With the long coastlines of five major islands, as well as vital sealanes, to defend, Japan needs and has a strong navy, inferior in the Pacific only to those of the United States and the Union of Soviet Socialist Republics. The latter is seen as Japan's only likely opponent in war during the immediate future, and the former is bound to Japan by a bilateral defence treaty. Manpower is 41,000, some 17.1 per cent of Japan's military manpower, which is supported by 1.27 per cent of the gross national product.

With the whole range of Russian warships as likely opponents, Japan has been forced to build a large number of versatile warships to meet the threat, and aims to have, in 1982, some 60 destroyers, 16 submarines, 40 to 45 mine warfare ships, 25 to 30 other warships, 15 supply ships and LSTs, and 220 aircraft. With American aid, Japan can thus hope to meet the threat posed by the Russian Pacific Fleet based at Vladivostok.

The latest Japanese ship is *Tachikaze*, the second unit of whose class is due for commissioning in 1979. She has a Tartar launcher for the Standard missile, anti-submarine torpedo tube mountings, and an octuple ASROC mounting. This last is clear evidence of the threat posed by Russian submarines and appreciated by the planners of the Japanese Navy. Surprisingly, no provision has been made for a helicopter in the 'Tachikaze' class design. Three A/S helicopters are carried in the two units of the 'Haruna' class, as they will be in the two ships of the Improved 'Haruna' class scheduled for commissioning in 1981 and 1982. These also have provision for Sea Sparrow short-range SAM defence. The four ships of the 'Takatsuki' class each carry two A/S helicopters as well as an octuple ASROC launcher. The slightly older 'Yamagumo' class ships, six in number, are more limited, being slower and having no helicopter, and only a single ASROC launcher. The same applies to the basically similar 'Minegumo' class of three ships. Other Japanese destroyers are less well equipped, and it is notable that with the exception of the 'Tachikaze' class ships and the one unit of the 'Amatsukaze' class, Japanese destroyers are not fitted for missiles. It is possible, though, that up to eight new destroyers will be built by 1981, and their design allows for a helicopter, Harpoon SSMs and Sea Sparrow SAMs.

Japanese frigates are similar to Japanese destroyers in their heavy anti-submarine armaments, the 11 ships of the 'Chikugo' class having octuple ASROC launchers and two triple torpedo tube mountings. Up to eight

ships of a new frigate class are planned, however, and these may have only a single ASROC launcher and several Harpoon SSM launchers. Japanese corvettes also have a fairly powerful A/S armament, but are clearly designed more for coastal operations, with their low freeboards and limited ranges.

So far as submarines are concerned, the Japanese have shown considerable skill in the design and production of the Improved 'Uzushio', 'Uzushio', 'Ooshio', 'Hayashio' and 'Natsushio' classes, totalling 15 boats in commission and one building. All are fast, well armed, deep diving and safe boats, with a fair measure of the manoeuvrability so essential in underwater craft. Surprisingly, though, the Japanese have virtually ignored the FAC type with the exception of five torpedo boats. Patrol of the home islands has been left in the hands of the Maritime Safety Agency, the Japanese coastguard service, which uses 10 large patrol ships, 57 medium patrol ships, 24 small patrol ships, and 209 coastal patrol craft.

The amphibious forces have six LSTs, and the mine warfare forces, as always where the Russians are a likely enemy, are strong: two support ships, 33 coastal minesweepers, with two more under construction, and six minesweeping boats. The Japanese Navy is intended, as its official title of Maritime Self-Defence Force suggests, to operate solely in defence of Japan, and so there is little need for support and service forces of more than a minor type, as the ships operate from Japan's five main bases and a number of smaller ones scattered through the home islands.

In the great expanses of the Pacific, the Japanese clearly appreciate that maritime airpower is vital, especially in the ASW and reconnaissance roles. The main strength of the naval air arm, with 12,000 personnel, is thus 11 maritime reconnaissance squadrons with US- and Japanese-built P-2 Neptune aircraft, S2F aircraft, and PS-1 flying-boats, plus seven helicopter squadrons with KV-107 and HSS-2 helicopters, as well as a number of SAR flights.

Japan's Maritime Self-Defence Force is thus in good shape with personnel and ships. However, in the future it will have to concentrate on more versatile ships, with SSMs and SAMs in addition to A/S weapons, and possibly the introduction of FAC types.

41,000 men, including 12,000 naval air arm, plus 600 reservists

Destroyers (DDG):
1 Tachikaze (+1)
(3 ?)

Destroyers (DD):
2 Haruna
(2 Improved Haruna)
4 Takatsuki
6 Yamagumo
3 Minegumo
1 Amatsukaze
2 Akizuki
3 Murasame
7 Ayanami
2 Harukaze

Frigates:
(6–8 ?)
11 Chikugo
4 Isuzu

Corvettes:
8 Mizutori
4 Umitaka

SS:
7 Uzushio
(1 Improved Uzushio)
5 Ooshio
3 Hayashio and Natsushio

Light Forces:
5 FAC(T)

Patrol Forces:
10 coastal PC

Amphibious Forces:
3 Miura LST
3 Atsumi LST

Mine Warfare Forces:
1 Souya minesweeper support ship
1 Hayase minesweeper support ship
1 MSC 649 type coastal minesweeper (+2)
13 Kasado coastal minesweepers
19 Takami coastal minesweepers
1 Kouzu mine countermeasures support ship
6 Nana-Go minesweeping boats

Auxiliaries:
2 training support ships
2 submarine rescue ships
7 survey ships
15 tenders
1 icebreaker
others

Naval Air Arm:
11 MR sqns with 110 P-2, S2F, 18 PS1
7 helicopter sqns with 7 KV-107, 61 HSS-2
1 transport sqn with 4 YS-11, 1 S2F
c 100 trainers
(19 P-2 MR)
(18 KM-2)
(14 HSS-2)
(5 PS-1)
(2 US-1)
(4 SH-3)

The Maritime Safety Agency (coast-guard) has 11,200 men, and operates 91 patrol vessels.

'Tachikaze' class guided missile destroyer (2)

Class: *Tachikaze* (DD168), *Asakaze* (DD169) (DD169)
Displacement: 3,900 tons (3,962 tonnes)
Dimensions: Length 469 ft 2 in (143.0 m)
  Beam 46 ft 11 in (14.3 m)
  Draught 15 ft 1 in (4.3 m)
Armament:
Guns 2 127-mm in single mountings
Missile systems
  1 Mark 13 Model 3 Tartar D
  launcher for Standard SAMs
A/S weapons
  1 octuple ASROC launcher
  2 triple 12.75-in (324-mm) Mark 32 tubes
Torpedo tubes
  none
Aircraft
  none
Radar and electronics: SPS-52 3D search, OPS 17 tactical and SPG 51 missile-control radars
Sonar: SQS-35(J) variable-depth
Powerplant: 2 turbines, delivering 60,000 shp to two shafts
Speed: 33 knots
Range:
Crew: 260
Used only by: Japan
Notes: Both ships were built by Mitsubishi Heavy Industries, *Tachikaze* between 1973 and 1974 for commissioning in 1976, and *Asakaze* between 1976 and 1977 for commissioning in 1979.

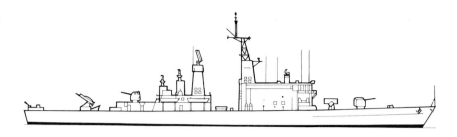

'Haruna' class destroyer (2)

Class: *Haruna* (DD141), *Hiei* (DD142)
Displacement: 4,700 tons (4,775 tonnes)
Dimensions: Length 501 ft 11½ in (153.0 m)
  Beam 57 ft 5 in (17.5 m)
  Draught 16 ft 8¾ in (5.1 m)
Armament:
Guns 2 127-mm in single mountings
Missile systems
  none
A/S weapons
  1 octuple ASROC launcher
  2 triple 12.75-in (324-mm) Mark 32 tubes
Torpedo tubes
  none
Aircraft
  3 ASW helicopters
Radar and electronics: OPS-11 and OPS-17 air- and surface-search radars
Sonar: OQS-3
Powerplant: 2 turbines, delivering 70,000 shp to two shafts
Speed: 32 knots
Range:
Crew: 364
Used only by: Japan
Notes: *Haruna* was built by Mitsubishi Heavy Industries at Nagasaki between 1970 and 1972, for commissioning in 1973; *Hiei* was built by Ishikawajima at Tokyo between 1972 and 1973 for commissioning in 1974.

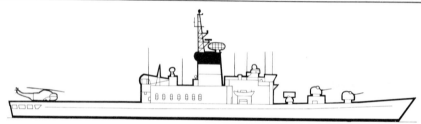

Improved 'Haruna' class guided missile destroyer (2)

Class: two unnamed vessels (DD143 and DD144)
Displacement: 5,200 tons (5,283 tonnes)
Dimensions: Length 521 ft (158.8 m)
  Beam 57 ft 5 in (17.5 m)
  Draught 17 ft 4½ in (5.3 m)

Armament:
Guns 2 127-mm in single mountings
  2 35-mm
Missile systems
  1 Sea Sparrow Basic Point Defence
  Missile System
A/S weapons
  1 octuple ASROC launcher
  2 triple 12.75-in (324-mm) Mark 32 tubes

Torpedo tubes
  none
Aircraft
  3 ASW helicopters
Radar and electronics: OPS-12 and OPS-28
  radars
Sonar: OQS-101 hull-mounted and
  SQS-35(J) variable-depth
Powerplant: 2 turbines, delivering 75,000
  shp to two shafts

Speed: 32 knots
Range:
Crew: 370
Used by: building for Japan
Notes: DD143 is building in the Tokyo yards
  of Ishikawajima Heavy Industries for
  launch in late 1978 and commissioning in
  1980. DD144 is scheduled for launching
  in 1979.

'Takatsuki' class destroyer (4)

Class: *Takatsuki* (DD164), *Kikuzuki* (DD165),
  Mochizuki (DD166), *Nagatsuki* (DD167)
Displacement: 3,100 tons (3,150 tonnes)
Dimensions: Length 446 ft 2 in (136.0 m)
  Beam 44 ft (13.4 m)
  Draught 14 ft 5¼ in (4.4 m)
Armament:
Guns 2 127-mm in single mountings
Missile systems
  none
A/S weapons
  1 octuple ASROC launcher
  1 four-barrel rocket-launcher
  2 triple 12.75-in (324-mm) Mark 32 tubes
Torpedo tubes
  none
Aircraft
  2 ASW helicopters

Radar and electronics: OPS-11 search,
  OPS-17 tactical and Mark 35 (GFCS 56
  system) fire-control radars
Sonar: hull-mounted SQS-23 in D164 and
  D165; OQS-3 in DD166 and DD167;
  SQS-35(J) variable-depth in DD164 and
  DD165
Powerplant: 2 Mitsubishi CE boilers supply-
  ing steam to 2 Mitsubishi WH geared tur-
  bines, delivering 60,000 shp to two shafts

Speed: 32 knots
Range: 7,000 miles (11,265 km) at 20 knots
Crew: 270
Used only by: Japan
Notes: The four ships were built in alternating
  pairs by Ishikawajima and Mitsubishi
  Heavy Industries at their Tokyo and Naga-
  saki yards between 1964 and 1969. The
  four ships were commissioned in 1967,
  1968, 1969 and 1970.

'Yamagumo' class destroyer (6)

Class: *Yamagumo* (DD113), *Makigumo*
  (DD114), *Asagumo* (DD115), *Aokumo*
  (DD119), *Akigumo* (DD120), *Yuugumo*
  (DD121)
Displacement: 2,100 tons (2,134 tonnes)
Dimensions: Length 377 ft 3½ in (115.0 m)
  Beam 38 ft 8½ in (11.8 m)
  Draught 13 ft 1½ in (4.0 m)
Armament:
Guns 4 76-mm in twin turrets
  none
A/S weapons
  1 ASROC launcher
  1 four-barrel rocket-launcher
  2 triple 12.75-in (324-mm) Mark 32 tubes
Torpedo tubes
  none

Aircraft
  none
Radar and electronics: OPS-11 search,
  OPS-17 tactical and Mark 35 (GFCS 56
  system) fire-control radars
Sonar: hull-mounted SQS-23 in DD113,
  DD114, DD115, but OQS-3 in DD119,
  DD120 and DD121; variable-depth
  SQS-35(J) in DD113, DD114, DD115
Powerplant: 6 diesels, delivering 26,500 bhp
  to two shafts
Speed: 27 knots
Range: 7,000 miles (11,265 km) at 20 knots
Crew: 210
Used only by: Japan
Notes: The original five units of this class
  were built between 1964 and 1973, being
  commissioned between 1966 and 1974.

The new member of the class, *Yuugumo*,
built by Sumitomo Heavy Industries for
commissioning in 1978, was to have been
the leader of an improved sub-class, of
slightly greater dimensions and with a
CODOG machinery arrangement giving
speeds of up to 32 knots.

'Minegumo' class destroyer (3)

Class: *Minegumo* (DD116), *Natsugumo*
  (DD117), *Murakumo* (DD118)
Displacement: 2,100 tons (2,134 tonnes)
Dimensions: Length 377 ft 3½ in (115.0 m)
  Beam 38 ft 8½ in (11.8 m)
  Draught 13 ft 1½ in (4.0 m)
Armament:
Guns 4 76-mm in twin turrets
Missile systems
  none
A/S weapons
  1 ASROC launcher
  1 four-barrel rocket-launcher
  2 triple 12.75-in (324-mm) Mark 32 tubes
Torpedo tubes
  none
Aircraft
  none
Radar and electronics: OPS-11 search,
  OPS-17 tactical and Mark 35 (GFCS 56
  system) fire-control radars
Sonar: OQS-3 hull-mounted; SQS-35(J) vari-
  able-depth in DD118
Powerplant: 6 diesels, delivering 26,500 bhp
  to two shafts

Speed: 27 knots
Range: 7,000 miles (11,265 km) at 20 knots
Crew: 210
Used only by: Japan
Notes: Very similar to the ships of the 'Yama-
  gumo' class, the units of the 'Minegumo'
  class differ mainly in the arrangements of

the upper works. So far as equipment was
concerned, the only original difference between the two classes was that the 'Minegumo' class had two Dash helicopters in
place of the ASROC launcher, which was
retrofitted in 1977-79. The three ships were
built between 1967 and 1969, commissioning in 1968, 1969 and 1970.

'Amatsukaze' class guided missile destroyer (1)

Class: *Amatsukaze* (DD163)
Displacement: 3,050 tons (3,099 tonnes)
  standard; 4,000 tons (4,064 tonnes) full
  load
Dimensions: Length 429 ft 9½ in (131.0 m)
  Beam 43 ft 11½ in (13.4 m)
  Draught 13 ft 9½ in (4.2 m)
Armament:
Guns 4 76-mm in twin turrets
Missile systems
  1 Tartar SAM launcher
A/S weapons
  1 octuple ASROC launcher
  2 Hedgehogs
  2 triple 12.75-in (324-mm) Mark 32 tubes
Torpedo tubes
  none
Aircraft
  1 ASW helicopter
Radar and electronics: SPS-52 3D search,
  SPS-29 air-search, OPS-16 surface-search,
  SPS-51 Tartar fire-control, and I-band gun
  fire-control radars
Sonar: SQS-23
Powerplant: 2 Ishikawajima/Foster Wheeler
  boilers supplying steam to 2 Ishikawajima/
  General Electric geared turbines, delivering
  60,000 shp to two shafts
Speed: 33 knots
Range: 7,000 miles (11,265 km) at 18 knots

Crew: 290
Used only by: Japan
Notes: *Amatsukaze* was built between 1962
  and 1963 and commissioned in 1965.

'Akizuki' class destroyer (2)

Class: *Akizuki* (DD161), *Teruzuki* (DD162)
Displacement: 2,350 tons (2,388 tonnes) standard; 2,890 tons (2,936 tonnes) full load
Dimensions: Length 387 ft 1½ in (118.0 m)
Beam 39 ft 4½ in (12.0 m)
Draught 13 ft 1½ in (4.0 m)
Armament:
Guns 3 127-mm in single turrets
4 76-mm in twin turrets
Missile systems
none
A/S weapons
1 4-barrel 14.75-in (375-mm) Bofors rocket-launcher
2 triple 12.75-in (324-mm) Mark 32 tubes
Torpedo tubes
1 quadruple 533-mm (21-in)
Aircraft
none
Radar and electronics: OPS-1 air-search, OPS-15 surface-search and Mark 34 (Mark 57 and 63 GFCS) radars

Sonar: SQS-29 hull-mounted; OQA-1 variable-depth
Powerplant: 2 Mitsubishi CE boilers supplying steam to 2 geared turbines (Mitsubishi Escher-Weiss in DD161, Westinghouse in DD162), delivering 45,000 shp to two shafts
Speed: 32 knots

Range:
Crew: 330
Used only by: Japan
Notes: DD161 was built by Mitsubishi Zoosen at Nagasaki between 1958 and 1959, and commissioned in 1960; DD162 was built by Shin Mitsubishi Jyuko at Kobe between 1958 and 1959, and commissioned in 1960.

'Murasame' class destroyer (3)

Class: *Murasame* (DD107), *Yudachi* (DD108), *Harusame* (DD109)
Displacement: 1,800 tons (1,829 tonnes) standard; 2,500 tons (2,540 tonnes) full load
Dimensions: Length 354 ft 4 in (108.0 m)
Beam 36 ft 1 in (11.0 m)
Draught 12 ft 1½ in (3.7 m)
Armament:
Guns 3 127-mm in single turrets
4 76-mm in twin turrets
Missile systems
none
A/S weapons
2 12.75-in (324-mm) Mark 32 tubes
1 Hedgehog
1 DC rack
1 Y-gun (replaced in *Murasame* by 2 triple 12.75-in (324-mm) Mark 32 tubes)
Torpedo tubes
none
Aircraft
none

Radar and electronics: OPS-1 air-search, OPS-15 surface-search and Mark 34 (Mark 57 and 63 GFCS) radars
Sonar: SQS-29 hull-mounted; OQA-1 variable-depth in *Harusame*
Powerplant: 2 boilers (Mitsubishi CE in DD107, and Ishikawajima FW-D in DD108 and DD109) supplying steam to 2 geared turbines (Mitsubishi Jyuko in DD107, and Ishikawajima Harima Jyuko in DD108 and DD109), delivering 30,000 shp to two shafts
Speed: 30 knots
Range: 6,000 miles (9,655 km) at 18 knots
Crew: 250
Used only by: Japan
Notes: The three ships were built between 1957 and 1959, and were commissioned in 1959. The builders were Mitsubishi Zoosen at Nagasaki, Ishikawajima Jyuko at Tokyo, and Uraga Dock.

'Ayanami' class destroyer (7)

Class: *Ayanami* (DD103), *Isonami* (DD104), *Uranami* (DD105), *Shikinami* (DD106), *Takanami* (DD110), *Oonami* (DD111), *Makinami* (DD112)
Displacement: 1,700 tons (1,727 tonnes) standard; 2,500 tons (2,540 tonnes) full load
Dimensions: Length 257 ft 7¼ in (109.0 m)
Beam 35 ft 1¼ in (10.7 m)
Draught 12 ft 1½ in (3.7 m)
Armament:
Guns 6 76-mm in twin turrets
Missile systems
none
A/S weapons
2 US Mark 15 Hedgehogs
2 triple 12.75-in (324-mm) Mark 32 tubes (in DDs 103, 104, 105, 106, 112)
2 12.75-in (324-mm) Mark 32 tubes
Torpedo tubes
1 quadruple 533-mm (21-in)

Aircraft
none
Radar and electronics: OPS-1 or -2 air-search, OPS-15 or -16 surface-search, and Mark 34 (Mark 57 and 63 GFCS) fire-control radars
Sonar: hull-mounted OQS-12; variable-depth OQA-1 in DDs 103, 104, 110
Powerplant: 2 boilers (Mitsubishi CE in Ayanami, Isonami and Uranami; Hitachi/Babcock & Wilcox in Oonami, Shikinami and Takanami; Kawasaki Jyuko BD in Makinami) supplying steam to 2 Mitsubishi/Escher-Weiss geared turbines, delivering 35,000 shp to two shafts
Speed: 32 knots
Range: 6,000 miles (9,655 km) at 18 knots
Crew: 230

Used only by: Japan
Notes: The seven ships of the class were built by six yards during the period between 1956 and 1960, with commissioning dates between 1958 and 1960. Isonami and Shikinami have been converted into training ships, with their 533-mm torpedo tubes removed and replaced by teaching facilities.

'Harukaze' class destroyer (2)

Class: Harukaze (DD101), Yukikaze (DD102)
Displacement: 1,700 tons (1,727 tonnes) standard; 2,340 tons (2,377 tonnes) full load
Dimensions: Length 358 ft 6 in (109.3 m)
Beam 34 ft 6 in (10.5 m)
Draught 12 ft (3.7 m)
Armament:
Guns 3 127-mm in single turrets
8 40-mm in quadruple mountings
Missile systems
none

A/S weapons
2 12.75-in (324-mm) Mark 32 tubes
2 Hedgehogs
4 K-guns
1 DC rack
Torpedo tubes
none
Aircraft
none
Radar and electronics: SPS-6 air-search, OPS-37 surface-search and Mark 26 and 34 fire-control radars
Sonar: SQS-29
Powerplant: 2 boilers (Hitachi/Babcock in Harukaze; Combustion Engineering in Yukikaze) supplying steam to 2 geared turbines (Mitsubishi/Escher Weiss in Harukaze; Westinghouse in Yukikaze), delivering 30,000 shp to two shafts
Speed: 30 knots
Range: 6,000 miles (9,655 km) at 18 knots
Crew: 240
Used only by: Japan
Notes: Both ships were built in 1954 and 1955, and commissioned in 1956. Harukaze was built by Mitsubishi Zoosen at Nagasaki; Yukikaze by Shin Mitsubishi Jyuko at Kobe. These were the first two proper destroyers built in Japan after World War II.

'Chikugo' class frigate (11)

Class: Chikugo (DE215), Ayase (DE216), Mikuma (DE217), Tokachi (DE218), Iwase (DE219), Chitose (DE220), Niyodo (DE221), Teshio (DE222), Yoshino (DE223), Kumano (DE224), Noshiro (DE225)
Displacement: 1,470 tons (1,494 tonnes) for DEs 216, 217, 218, 219, 221; 1,480 tons (1,504 tonnes) for DEs 215, 220; 1,500 tons (1,524 tonnes) for DEs 222, 223, 224, 225
Dimensions: Length 305 ft 6 in (93.0 m)
Beam 35 ft 6 in (10.8 m)
Draught 11 ft 6 in (3.5 m)
Armament:
Guns 2 76-mm in a twin turret
2 40-mm in a twin mounting
Missile systems
none
A/S weapons
1 octuple ASROC launcher
2 triple 12.75-in (324-mm) Mark 32 tubes
Torpedo tubes
none
Aircraft
none
Radar and electronics: OPS-14 air-search, OPS-17 surface-search and I-band (GFCS Mark 1 system) fire-control
Sonar: hull-mounted OQS-3; SPS-35(J) variable-depth
Powerplant: 4 diesels (Mitsui B & W in DEs 215, 217, 218, 219, 221, 223, 225; Mitsubishi UEV 30/40N in DEs 216, 220, 222, 224), delivering 16,000 shp to two shafts

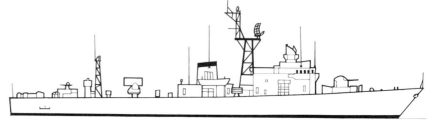

Speed: 25 knots
Range:
Crew: 165
Used only by: Japan

Notes: The 11 ships were built between 1969 and 1976, and commissioned from 1970 to 1977. Seven of the class were built by Mitsui Zoosen at Tamano, three by Hitachi Zoosen at Maizuru, and the lead ship by Ishikawajima Harima Jyuko at Tokyo.

'Isuzu' class frigate (4)

Class: Isuzu (DE211), Mogami (DE212), Kitakami (DE213), Ooi (DE214)
Displacement: 1,490 tons (1,514 tonnes) standard; 1,700 tons (1,727 tonnes) full load
Dimensions: Length 309 ft 6 in (94.3 m)
Beam 34 ft 2½ in (10.4 m)
Draught 11 ft 6 in (3.5 m)
Armament:
Guns 4 76-mm in twin turrets
Missile systems
none

A/S weapons
1 four-barrel Bofors A/S rocket-launcher
2 triple 12.75-in (324-mm) Mark 32 tubes
1 Y-gun; 1 DC rack (211 and 214)
Torpedo tubes
1 quadruple 533-mm (21-in)
Aircraft
none

Radar and electronics: OPS-1 air-search, OPS-16 surface-search and Mark 34 (Mark 63 GFCS) fire-control radars
Sonar: hull-mounted SQS-29; variable-depth OQA-1 in *Mogami* and *Kitakami*
Powerplant: 4 diesels (Mitsui in *Isuzu* and *Ooi*; Mitsubishi in *Mogami* and *Kitakami*), delivering 16,000 hp to two shafts
Speed: 25 knots
Range:
Crew: 180

Used only by: Japan
Notes: The ships were built in two pairs, the first between 1960 and 1961, commissioning in 1961; and the second between 1962 and 1963, commissioning in 1964. In 1966 the Y-gun and DC racks were removed from *Mogami* and *Kitakami* to make room for the variable-depth sonar; and in 1974 the latest Bofors A/S launcher was added in *Isuzu* and *Mogami*.

'Mizutori' class large patrol craft (8)

Class: *Mizutori* (311), *Yamadori* (312), *Otori* (313), *Kasasagi* (314), *Hatsukari* (315), *Umidori* (316), *Shiratori* (319), *Hiyodori* (320)
Displacement: between 420 tons (426.7 tonnes) and 440 tons (447 tonnes) standard
Dimensions: Length 197 ft (60.1 m)
Beam 23 ft 3½ in (7.1 m)
Draught 8 ft (2.4 m)
Armament:
Guns 2 40-mm in a twin mounting
Missile systems
none
A/S weapons
1 Hedgehog
1 DC rack
2 triple Short A/S torpedo tubes (316, 319, 320); 2 Short A/S torpedo launchers (rest)
Torpedo tubes
none
Aircraft
none
Radar and electronics: OPS-35 (311, 312), OPS-36 (313, 314, 315, 316), or OPS-16 (319, 320)

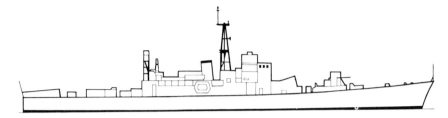

Sonar: SQS-11A
Powerplant: 2 MAN diesels, delivering 3,800 bhp to two shafts
Speed: 20 knots
Range: 2,000 miles (3,220 km) at 12 knots

Crew: 80
Used only by: Japan
Notes: These eight vessels were built by four yards in the period between 1959 and 1965, for commissioning between 1960 and 1966.

'Umitaka' class large patrol craft (4)

Class: *Umitaka* (309), *Otaka* (310), *Wakataka* (317), *Kumataka* (318)
Displacement: between 440 tons (447 tonnes) and 460 tons (467.4 tonnes) standard
Dimensions: Length 197 ft (60.1 m)
Beam 23 ft 3½ in (7.1 m)
Draught 8 ft (2.4 m)
Armament:
Guns 2 40-mm in a twin mounting

Missile systems
none
A/S weapons
1 Hedgehog
1 DC rack
2 triple 12.75-in (324-mm) Mark 32 tubes (317, 318)
2 12.75-in (324-mm) Mark 32 tubes (309, 310)
Torpedo tubes
none
Aircraft
none

Radar and electronics: OPS-35 (309, 310), OPS-36 (317), or OPS-16 (318) radars
Sonar: SQS-11A
Powerplant: 2 B & W diesels, delivering 4,000 bhp to two shafts
Speed: 20 knots
Range: 3,000 miles (4,830 km) at 12 knots
Crew: 80
Used only by: Japan
Notes: The four ships were built by three yards in two pairs, the first in 1959 for commissioning in 1959 and 1960, and the second in 1962 and 1963, for commissioning in 1963 and 1964.

'Uzushio' and Improved 'Uzushio' class submarine (8)

Class: *Uzushio* (SS566), *Makishio* (SS567), *Isoshio* (SS568), *Narushio* (SS569), *Kuroshio* (SS570), *Takashio* (SS571), *Yaeshio* (SS572) and one unnamed boat (SS573)
Displacement: 1,850 tons (1,880 tonnes) standard
Dimensions: Length 236 ft 2½ in (72.0 m)
Beam 29 ft 6 in (9.0 m)
Draught 24 ft 7 in (7.5 m)
Armament:
Guns none
Missile systems
none
A/S weapons
none
Torpedo tubes
6 533-mm (21-in)
Aircraft
none

Radar and electronics:
Sonar:
Powerplant: 2 Kawasaki/MAN diesels, delivering 3,400 bhp, and 1 electric motor, delivering 7,200 hp, to one shaft
Speed: 12 knots (surfaced); 20 knots (dived)
Range:

Crew: 80
Used only by: Japan
Notes: The boats of this class are built alternately by Kawasaki Jyuko at Kobe and by Mitsubishi Jyuko, also at Kobe. The boats were laid down between 1968 and 1976, launched between 1970 and 1978, and commissioned between 1971 and 1979. SS573 is the lead boat of the Improved 'Uzushio' class, with a displacement of 2,200 tons (2,235 tonnes), dimensions of 249 ft 4 in (76.0 m) by 32 ft 6 in (9.9 m) by 24 ft 7 in (7.5 m), and increased diving depth.

'Ooshio' class submarine (5)

Class: Ooshio (SS561), Asashio (SS562), Harushio (SS563), Michishio (SS564), Arashio (SS565)
Displacement: 1,650 tons (1,676 tonnes) standard except Ooshio 1,600 tons (1,626 tonnes)
Dimensions: Length 288 ft 8½ in (88.0 m)
Beam 26 ft 11 in (8.2 m)
Draught 16 ft 2½ in (4.9 m), except Ooshio 15 ft 5 in (4.7 m)
Armament:
Guns none
Missile systems
none
A/S weapons
2 A/S torpedoes in swim-out tubes
Torpedo tubes
6 533-mm (21-in)
Aircraft
none

Radar and electronics:
Sonar:
Powerplant: 2 diesels, delivering 2,900 bhp, and 2 electric motors, delivering 6,300 hp to two shafts
Speed: 14 knots (surfaced); 18 knots (dived)

Range:
Crew: 80
Used only by: Japan
Notes: The boats were built alternately by Mitsubishi Jyuko and Kawasaki Jyuko, both at Kobe, between 1963 and 1968, and commissioned between 1965 and 1969.

'Hayashio' and 'Natsushio' class submarine (3)

Class: Wakashio (SS522), Natsushio (SS523), Fuyushio (SS524)
Displacement: 750 tons (762 tonnes) standard for Wakashio; 790 tons (802.6 tonnes) standard for Natsushio and Fuyushio
Dimensions: Length 193 ft 6¾ in (93.0 m) for Wakashio; 200 ft 1½ in (61.0 m) for SS 523 and 524
Beam 21 ft 3½ in (6.5 m)
Draught 13 ft 6 in (4.1 m)

Armament:
Guns none
Missile systems
none
A/S weapons
none
Torpedo tubes
3 533-mm (21-in)
Aircraft
none
Radar and electronics:
Sonar:
Powerplant: 2 diesels, delivering 900 hp, and 2 electric motors, delivering 2,300 hp, to two shafts

Speed: 11 knots (surfaced); 15 knots (dived) for Natsushio and Fuyushio, 14 knots (dived) for Wakashio
Range:
Crew: 40
Used only by: Japan
Notes: The boats were built at Kobe by Kawasaki Jyuko and Mitsubishi Jyuko between 1960 and 1962, for commissioning between 1962 and 1963. The first boat of the class (Hayashio/SS521) was decommissioned in 1977. Natsushio and Fuyushio comprise the 'Natsushio' class.

Fast Attack Craft (torpedo) (5)

Class: PT 11 (811), PT 12 (812), PT 13 (813), PT 14 (814), PT 15 (815)
Displacement: 100 tons (101.6 tonnes)
Dimensions: Length 116 ft 5½ in (35.5 m)
Beam 30 ft 2½ in (9.2 m)
Draught 3 ft 11 in (1.2 m)
Armament:
Guns 2 40-mm in single mountings
Missile systems
none
A/S weapons
none
Torpedo tubes
4 533-mm (21-in)
Aircraft
none
Radar and electronics: OPS-13 radar
Sonar:
Powerplant: CODAG arrangement, with 2 Mitsubishi diesels and 2 Ishikawajima Heavy Industries gas turbines, delivering a total of 11,000 hp to three shafts
Speed: 40 knots
Range:
Crew: 26 to 28
Used only by: Japan
Notes: All five craft were built by Mitsubishi at Shimonoseki, and commissioned between 1971 and 1975.

Jordan

300 men

Patrol Forces:
10 coastal PC

Kampuchea

Patrol Forces:
c 88 small PC

Amphibious Forces:
7 landing craft

Kenya

400 men

Patrol Forces:
3 Brooke 37.5-m PC
1 Brooke 32.6-m PC
3 Vosper 31-m PC

Brooke Marine 37.5-m type large patrol craft (3)

Class: *Madaraka* (P3121), *Jamhuri* (P3122), *Harambee* (P3123)
Displacement: 125 tons (127 tonnes) standard; 160 tons (162.6 tonnes) full load
Dimensions: Length 123 ft (37.5 m)
Beam 22 ft 6 in (6.9 m)
Draught 5 ft 2½ in (1.6 m)
Armament:
Guns 2 40-mm Bofors in single mountings
Missile systems
none
A/S weapons
none

Torpedo tubes
none
Aircraft
none
Radar and electronics:
Sonar:
Powerplant: 2 Ruston diesels, delivering 4,000 hp to two shafts
Speed: 25 knots
Range: 3,300 miles (5,310 km) at 13 knots
Crew: 3+22
Used also by: Oman
Notes: Built by Brooke Marine at Lowestoft.

Brooke Marine 32.6-m type large patrol craft (1)

Class: *Mamba* (P3100)
Displacement: 120 tons (121.9 tonnes) standard; 145 tons (147.3 tonnes) full load
Dimensions: Length 107 ft (30.6 m)
Beam 20 ft (6.1 m)
Draught 5 ft 7 in (1.7 m)

Armament:
Guns 2 40-mm Bofors in single mountings
Missile systems
none
A/S weapons
none
Torpedo tubes
none
Aircraft
none

Radar and electronics:
Sonar:
Powerplant: 2 Ruston-Paxman Valenta diesels, delivering 5,400 bhp to two shafts
Speed: 25½ knots
Range: 2,500 miles (4,025 km) at 12 knots
Crew: 3+18
Used also by: Nigeria
Notes: Built by Brooke Marine at Lowestoft.

Vosper 31-m type large patrol craft (3)

Class: *Simba* (P3110), *Chui* (P3112), *Ndovu* (P3117)
Displacement: 96 tons (97.5 tonnes) standard; 109 tons (110.7 tonnes) full load
Dimensions: Length 103 ft (31.4 m)
Beam 19 ft 10 in (6.0 m)
Draught 5 ft 10 in (1.8 m)
Armament:
Guns 2 40-mm Bofors in single mountings
Missile systems
none
A/S weapons
none
Torpedo tubes
none
Aircraft
none

Radar and electronics:
Sonar:
Powerplant: 2 Paxman Valenta diesels, delivering 2,800 bhp to two shafts
Speed: 24 knots

Range: 1,500 miles (2,415 km) at 16 knots
Crew: 3+20
Used only by: Kenya
Notes: All three craft were built by Vosper at Portsmouth, and commissioned in 1966.

Kuwait

500 men of the Coastguard

Patrol Forces:
10 Thornycroft 23.8-m coastal PC
2 Vosper Thornycroft 17.8-m coastal PC
7 Thornycroft 15.25-mm coastal PC
1 Vosper Thornycroft 14-m coastal PC
8 Vosper Thornycroft 10.3-m coastal PC

Amphibious Forces:
3 Vosper Thornycroft 27-m landing craft

Laos

About 550 men

Patrol Forces:
c 20 river patrol craft

Amphibious Forces:
14 landing craft

Lebanon

300 men

Patrol Forces:
1 large PC
3 coastal PC
1 LCU

Liberia

About 200 men

Patrol Forces:
1 PGM71 gunboat
3 coastal PC

Auxiliaries:
1 yacht

Libya

2,000 men

Frigate:
1 Vosper Thornycroft Mark 7

SS:
2 Foxtrot (+4?)

Corvettes:
4 550-ton
1 Tobruk

Light Forces:
(10 La Combattante II G FAC(M))
5 Osa II FAC(M) (+?)
3 Susa FAC(M)

Patrol Forces:
4 Garian PC
6 Thornycroft 30.5-m PC
1 Thornycroft 23.8-m coastal PC

Amphibious Forces:
2 LSD type support ships
2 PS700 LST

Auxiliaries:
1 maintenance craft

Vosper Thornycroft Mark 7 frigate (1)

Class: *Dat Assawari* (F01)
Displacement: 1,325 tons (1,346 tonnes) standard; 1,625 tons (1,651 tonnes) full load
Dimensions: Length 330 ft (100.6 m)
Beam 36 ft (11.0 m)
Draught 11 ft 3 in (3.4 m)

Armament:
Guns 1 4.5-in (114-mm)
2 40-mm Bofors in single mountings
2 35-mm in a twin mounting
Missile systems
2 triple Seacat SAM launchers
A/S weapons
1 Mark 10 A/S mortar
Torpedo tubes
none
Aircraft
none

Radar and electronics: AWS-1 air surveillance, RDL-1 radar direction finding, and fire-control radars
Sonar:
Powerplant: CODOG arrangement, with 2 Rolls-Royce Olympus gas turbines, delivering 23,200 shp, and 2 Paxman diesels, delivering 3,500 bhp, to two shafts
Speed: 37½ knots (gas turbines); 17 knots (diesels)
Range: 5,700 miles (9,175 km) at 17 knots
Crew:

Used only by: Libya
Notes: The ship was built by Vosper Thornycroft between 1968 and 1969, and commissioned in 1973. She is similar to the two Iranian Mark 5 frigates, but larger and with a heavier armament.

'Daphné' class submarine (4)

Class: four boats building
Displacement: 869 tons (882.9 tonnes) surfaced; 1,043 tons (1,060 tonnes) dived
Dimensions: Length 189 ft 7½ in (57.8 m)
Beam 22 ft 3¾ in (6.8 m)
Draught 15 ft 1 in (4.6 m)
Armament:
Guns none

Missile systems
none
A/S weapons
none
Torpedo tubes
12 550-mm (21.7-in)
Aircraft
none
Radar and electronics:
Sonar:
Powerplant: SEMT-Pielstick diesel-electric,

delivering 1,600 hp to two shafts
Speed: 13½ knots (surfaced); 16 knots (dived)
Range: 2,700 miles (4,345 km) at 12½ knots surfaced; 3,000 miles (4,830 km) at 7 knots snorting
Crew: 52
Used also by: France, Pakistan, Portugal, South Africa, Spain
Notes: The four boats are building in the Cartagena yards of Bazan for delivery in 1981. Order now cancelled.

'Foxtrot' class submarine (2)

Class: Babr and one other
Displacement: 2,100 tons (2,134 tonnes) surfaced; 2,400 tons (2,438 tonnes) dived
Dimensions: Length 292 ft (89.0 m)
Beam 27 ft 2¾ in (8.3 m)
Draught 15 ft 9 in (4.8 m)
Armament:
Guns none
Missile systems
none
A/S weapons
none

Torpedo tubes
10 533-mm (21-in) with 22 torpedoes or
Aircraft
none
Radar and electronics: 'Snoop Plate' search radar and 'Stop Light' ECM
Sonar: 'Hercules' and 'Feniks'
Powerplant: 3 diesels, delivering 6,000 bhp, and 3 electric motors, delivering 5,000 hp to three shafts
Speed: 18 knots (surfaced); 17 knots (dived)
Range: 20,000 miles (32,188 km) surfaced
Crew: 70
Used also by: India, USSR
Notes: Babr and her sisterships (another four units as possible additions to the unit already delivered) are built in a reopened line at the Sudomekh yard in Leningrad.

Babr was delivered in December 1976 and her first sistership in 1977. The other four units await the training of Libyan crews in the USSR.

Missile corvette (4)

Class: four vessels
Displacement: 547 tons (555.8 tonnes) full load
Dimensions: Length 202 ft 5 in (61.7 m)
Beam 30 ft 6 in (9.3 m)
Draught 16 ft 3 in (5.0 m)
Armament:
Guns 1 76-mm OTO Melara
2 40-mm Breda in a twin turret
Missile systems
4 Otomat SSM launchers
A/S weapons
2 triple 12.75-in (324-mm) Mark 32 tubes
Torpedo tubes
none
Aircraft
none
Radar and electronics: Selenia RAN 11 LX air/surface search, Decca TM 1226 navigation, and Elsag NA 10 fire-control radars; ECM fit
Sonar: Thomson-CSF Diodon

Powerplant: 4 MTU MA 16V 956 TB91 diesels, delivering 1,800 hp to four shafts
Speed: 31 knots
Range:
Crew: 54
Used only by: Libya
Notes: Four vessels are building at the yards of Cantieri Navali del Tirreno e Riuniti, probably for delivery in 1978 or 1979.

'Tobruk' class corvette (1)

Class: Tobruk (C01)
Displacement: 440 tons (447 tonnes) standard; 500 tons (508 tonnes) full load
Dimensions: Length 177 ft (54.0 m)
Beam 28 ft 6 in (8.7 m)
Draught 13 ft (4.0 m)
Armament:
Guns 1 4-in (102-mm)
4 40-mm Bofors in single mountings
Missile systems
none
A/S weapons
none

Torpedo tubes
none
Aircraft
none
Radar and electronics: surface warning radar
Sonar:
Powerplant: 2 Paxman Ventura diesels, delivering 3,800 bhp to two shafts
Speed: 18 knots
Range: 2,900 miles (4,665 km) at 14 knots
Crew: 5+58
Used only by: Libya
Notes: Tobruk was built by Vosper and Vickers between 1965 and 1966, and commissioned in 1966.

'La Combattante IIG' class fast attack craft (missile) (10)

Class: 10 craft building
Displacement: 311 tons (316 tonnes)
Dimensions: Length 160 ft 9 in (49.0 m)
Beam 24 ft 11 in (7.6 m)
Draught 7 ft 10½ in (2.4 m)
Armament:
Guns 1 76-mm OTO Melara
2 40-mm Breda in a twin mounting
Missile systems
4 MM38 Exocet SSM launchers
A/S weapons
none
Torpedo tubes
none
Aircraft
none

Radar and electronics: Thomson-CSF Triton surface-search and Castor target-tracking radars (Veja system)
Sonar:
Powerplant: 4 diesels, delivering 20,000 bhp to four shafts
Speed: 40 knots
Range: 1,600 miles (2,575 km) at 15 knots
Crew: 31
Used only by: Libya
Notes: The 10 craft are building at the Cherbourg yards of CMN for delivery 1978–80.

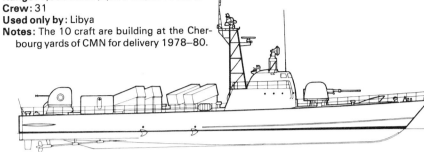

'Susa' class fast attack craft (missile) (3)

Class: *Susa* (PO1), *Sirte* (PO2), *Sebha*, ex-*Sokna* (PO3)
Displacement: 95 tons (96.5 tonnes) standard; 114 tons (115.8 tonnes) full load
Dimensions: Length 100 ft (30.5 m)
Beam 25 ft 6 in (7.8 m)
Draught 7 ft (2.1 m)

Armament:
Guns 2 40-mm Bofors in single mountings
Missile systems
8 SS.12 SSM launchers
A/S weapons
none
Torpedo tubes
none
Aircraft
none
Radar and electronics:
Sonar:

Powerplant: 3 Bristol Siddeley Proteus gas turbines, delivering 12,750 bhp to three shafts
Speed: 54 knots
Range:
Crew: 20
Used only by: Libya
Notes: Advanced craft with a sighting turret for the SS.12 missiles, the 'Susa' class were built by Vosper at Portsmouth, and commissioned in 1969. The craft are similar to the Danish 'Søløven' class boats.

'Garian' class large patrol craft (4)

Class: *Garian, Khawlan, Merawa, Sabratha*
Displacement: 120 tons (121.9 tonnes) standard; 159 tons (161.5 tonnes) full load
Dimensions: Length 106 ft (32.3 m)
Beam 21 ft 3 in (6.5 m)
Draught 5 ft 6 in (1.7 m)
Armament:
Guns 1 40-mm Bofors
1 20-mm
Missile systems
none
A/S weapons
none
Torpedo tubes
none

Aircraft
none
Radar and electronics:
Sonar:
Powerplant: 2 Paxman diesels, delivering 2,200 bhp to two shafts
Speed: 24 knots

Range: 1,500 miles (2,415 km) at 12 knots
Crew: 15 to 22
Used only by: Libya
Notes: All four craft were built by Brooke Marine at Lowestoft, the first pair being commissioned in 1969, and the second pair in 1970.

Thornycroft type large patrol craft (6)

Class: *Akrama, Ar Rakib, Benina, Farwa, Homs, Misurata*
Displacement: 100 tons (101.6 tonnes)
Dimensions: Length 100 ft (30.5 m)
　　　　　　Beam 21 ft (6.4 m)
　　　　　　Draught 5 ft 6 in (1.7 m)
Armament:
Guns 1 20-mm
Missile systems
　none
A/S weapons
　none
Torpedo tubes
　none
Aircraft
　none
Radar and electronics:

Sonar:
Powerplant: 3 Rolls-Royce DV8TLM diesels, delivering 1,740 bhp to two shafts
Speed: 18 knots
Range: 1,800 miles (2,895 km) at 14 knots
Crew:

Used also by: Kuwait
Notes: Four of the craft were built by Vosper Thornycroft, the other two by John I. Thornycroft at Woolston. Two craft were commissioned in each of 1967, 1968 and 1969.

Malagasy Republic

600 men

Patrol Forces:
1 large PC
5 coastal PC

Auxiliaries:
1 landing ship (transport)
1 training ship
1 tender

Malawi

Patrol Forces:
4 lake PC

Malaysia

6,000 men

Frigates:
1 Yarrow 93.9-m type
1 Yarrow 103.5-m type

Light Forces:
6 Jerong FAC(G)
(4 Spica-M FAC(M))
4 Perdana FAC(M)

Patrol Forces:
4 Kedah PC
4 Sabah PC
14 Kris PC

Amphibious Forces:
3 LST511-1152

Mine Warfare Forces:
5 Ton coastal minesweepers

Auxiliaries:
1 survey vessel
1 diving tender

The Royal Malaysian Police operate 27 coastal PC

Yarrow type frigate (1)

Class: *Rahmat*, ex-*Hang Jebat* (F24)
Displacement: 1,250 tons (1,270 tonnes) standard; 1,600 tons (1,626 tonnes) full load
Dimensions: Length 308 ft (93.9 m)
　　　　　　Beam 34 ft 1 in (10.4 m)
　　　　　　Draught 14 ft 10 in (4.5 m)
Armament:
Guns 1 4.5-in (114-mm)
　2 40-mm Bofors in single mountings
Missile systems
　1 quadruple Seacat SAM launcher
A/S weapons
　1 Limbo 3-barrel mortar
Torpedo tubes
　none
Aircraft
　facilities for 1 small helicopter

Radar and electronics: Hollandse Signaalapparaten LW 02 air surveillance, M20 gun fire-control and M44 Seacat fire-control radars
Sonar:
Powerplant: 1 Bristol Siddeley Olympus gas turbine, delivering 19,500 shp, and 1 Crossley/Pielstick diesel, delivering 3,850 bhp, to two shafts
Speed: 26 knots with gas turbine; 16 knots on diesel alone
Range: 6,000 miles (9,655 km) at 16 knots
Crew: 140
Used only by: Malaysia
Notes: *Rahmat* was built by Yarrow Shipbuilders between 1966 and 1967, and commissioned in 1971. She has many automatic systems, this helping to save manpower.

Yarrow type frigate (1)

Class: one ship, ex-British *Mermaid* (F76)
Displacement: 2,300 tons (2,337 tonnes) standard; 2,530 tons (2,560 tonnes) full load
Dimensions: Length 339 ft 4 in (103.5 m)
Beam 40 ft (12.2 m)
Draught 12 ft (3.7 m)
Armament:
Guns 2 4-in (102-mm) in a twin turret
2 40-mm Bofors in single mountings
Missile systems
none
A/S weapons
1 3-barrel Limbo
Torpedo tubes
none
Aircraft
none
Radar and electronics:
Sonar:
Powerplant: 8 diesels, delivering 14,400 hp to two shafts
Speed: 24 knots

Range: 4,800 miles (7,725 km) at 15 knots
Crew:
Used only by: Malaysia
Notes: This frigate was originally built for Ghana by Yarrow Shipbuilders between 1965 and 1966, as a development of the 'Salisbury' and 'Leopard' classes. Ghana refused the vessel after the fall of President Nkrumah, and she was bought by the Royal Navy in 1972, commissioning in 1973. She was transferred to Malaysia in 1977.

'Jerong' class fast attack craft (gun) (6)

Class: *Jerong* (3505), *Todak* (3506), *Paus* (3507), *Yu* (3508), *Baung* (3509), *Pari* (3510)
Displacement: 254 tons (258.1 tonnes) full load
Dimensions: Length 147 ft 3½ in (44.9 m)
Beam 23 ft (7.0 m)
Draught 12 ft 9 in (3.9 m)
Armament:
Guns 1 57-mm
1 40-mm Bofors
Missile systems
none
A/S weapons
none
Torpedo tubes
none
Aircraft
none
Radar and electronics:
Sonar:
Powerplant: 3 Maybach Mercedes-Benz diesels, delivering 3,300 bhp to three shafts
Speed: 32 knots
Range: 2,000 miles (4,830 km) at 15 knots
Crew:
Used only by: Malaysia
Notes: All six craft were built by Hong-Leong-Lürssen at Butterworth in Malaysia, to a basic Lürssen design, and commissioned in 1976 and 1977.

'Spica-M' class fast attack craft (missile) (4)

Class: four craft building
Displacement: 240 tons (243.8 tonnes)
Dimensions: Length 143 ft (43.6 m)
Beam 23 ft 2½ in (7.1 m)
Draught 7 ft 10½ in (2.4 m)
Armament:
Guns 1 57-mm
1 40-mm
Missile systems
4 MM 38 Exocet SSM launchers
1 Blowpipe SAM launcher
A/S weapons
none
Torpedo tubes
none
Aircraft
none
Radar and electronics:
Sonar:
Powerplant: 3 MTU diesels, delivering 10,800 hp to three shafts
Speed: 34½ knots
Range: 1,850 miles (2,977 km) at 14 knots
Crew:
Used only by: Malaysia
Notes: Basically similar to the Swedish 'Spica T131' class, the four craft of the Malaysian class are building at Karlskrona shipyards for delivery in 1979.

'Perdana' class fast attack craft (missile) (4)

Class: *Perdana* (P3501), *Serang* (P3502), *Ganas* (P5303), *Ganyang* (P5304)
Displacement: 234 tons (237.7 tonnes) standard; 265 tons (269.2 tonnes) full load
Dimensions: Length 154 ft 2½ in (47.0 m)
Beam 23 ft 1 in (7.0 m)
Draught 12 ft 10 in (3.9 m)
Armament:
Guns 1 57-mm Bofors
1 40-mm Bofors
Missile systems
2 MM38 Exocet SSM launchers

A/S weapons
none
Torpedo tubes
none
Aircraft
none
Radar and electronics: Thomson-CSF Triton surface-search and Pollux fire-control radars (Vega system)
Sonar:
Powerplant: 4 MTU diesels, delivering 14,000 bhp to four shafts
Speed: 36½ knots
Range: 800 miles (1,290 km) at 25 knots
Crew:
Used only by: Malaysia

Notes: The 'Perdana' class are of the same basic design as the 'La Combattante II' class, and were all built by Constructions Mécaniques de Normandie for commissioning in late 1972 and 1973.

'Perkasa' class fast attack craft (missile) (4)

Class: *Perkasa* (P150), *Handalan* (P151), *Gempita* (P152), *Pendekar* (P153)
Displacement: 95 tons (96.5 tonnes) standard; 114 tons (115.8 tonnes) full load
Dimensions: Length 99 ft (30.2 m)
Beam 25 ft 6 in (7.8 m)
Draught 7 ft (2.1 m)
Armament:
Guns 1 40-mm Bofors
1 20-mm

Missile systems
2 quadruple SS.12(M) SSM launchers
A/S weapons
none
Torpedo tubes
none
Aircraft
none
Radar and electronics:
Sonar:
Powerplant: 3 Rolls-Royce Proteus gas turbines, delivering 12,750 bhp, and 2 General Motors Corporation diesels, delivering power to three shafts

Speed: 54 knots on gas turbines; 10 knots on two wing shafts and diesel power alone
Range:
Crew:
Used only by: Malaysia
Notes: The four craft were built as torpedo boats (4 21-in/533-mm tubes) by Vosper at Portsmouth, commissioning in 1967. The craft combine the hull form of the 'Brave' class, with the construction of the 'Ferocity' class. The missiles replaced the torpedo tubes in 1971. Now deleted.

Maldives

Patrol Forces:
3 trawlers (PC)
1 Fairey coastal PC
4 landing craft
2 launches

Mali

50 men

Patrol Forces:
3 river PC

Malta

A coastguard force of the Maltese Regiment

Patrol Forces:
2 Swift coastal PC
8 coastal PC

Mauritania

300 men

Light Forces:
2 Barcelo FAC(G)

Patrol Forces:
2 Mirny PC
4 large PC
2 coastal PC

Mauritius

Patrol Forces:
1 Abhay PC

Mexico

19,000 men including 350 naval air force and 2,000 marines

Destroyers:
2 Fletcher

Frigates:
1 Edsall (training ship)
1 Durango
4 Charles Lawrence and Crossley

Corvettes:
18 Auk
16 Admirable

Patrol Forces:
22 Azteca PC (+9)
2 Azueta coastal PC
4 Polimar coastal PC
8 river PC

Auxiliaries:
1 survey vessel
1 transport
2 LST 511-1152
1 patrol forces tender
2 harbour tankers
17 others

Naval Air Force:
10 HU-16
1 Learjet 24D
4 C-45
3 DC-3
1 Beech Baron
3 Beech Bonanza
4 Cessna 150
4 Alouette II
3 Bell 47
5 Hughes 269A

Marine Force:
19 security coys

'Fletcher' class destroyer (2)

Class: *Cuauthemoc* (IE01, ex-F1), ex-US *Harrison* (DD573); *Cuitlahuac* (IE02, ex-F2), ex-US *John Rodgers* (DD574)
Displacement: 2,100 tons (2,134 tonnes) standard; 3,050 tons (3,099 tonnes) full load
Dimensions: Length 376 ft 6 in (114.7 m)
Beam 39 ft 6 in (12.0 m)
Draught 18 ft (5.5 m)
Armament:
Guns 5 5-in (127-mm) in single turrets
10 40-mm in twin mountings
Missile systems
none
A/S weapons
none
Torpedo tubes
1 quintuple 21-in (533-mm)
Aircraft
none

Radar and electronics: SC and SG1 search, and Mark 12 (Mark 37 director system) gun fire-control radars
Sonar:
Powerplant: 4 boilers supplying steam to 2 General Electric geared turbines, delivering 60,000 shp to two shafts
Speed: 36 knots
Range: 5,000 miles (8,047 km) at 14 knots
Crew: 197
Used also by: Argentina, Brazil, Chile, Greece, Italy, Peru, South Korea, Spain, Taiwan, Turkey, West Germany
Notes: Both ships were built by Consolidated Steel at Orange, Texas, between 1941 and 1942, being commissioned into US service in 1943. They were transferred to Mexico in 1970.

'Edsall' class frigate (1)

Class: *Como Manuel Azueta* (A06), ex-US *Hurst* (DE250)
Displacement: 1,200 tons (1,219 tonnes) standard; 1,850 tons (1,880 tonnes) full load

Dimensions: Length 306 ft (93.3 m)
Beam 36 ft 9 in (11.2 m)
Draught 13 ft (4.0 m)
Armament:
Guns 3 3-in (76-mm) in single mountings
Missile systems
none

A/S weapons
none
Torpedo tubes
none
Aircraft
none

Radar and electronics: Kelvin Hughes Types 14 and 17
Sonar: QCS-1
Powerplant: 4 diesels, delivering 6,000 shp to two shafts
Speed: 20 knots
Range: 13,000 miles (20,922 km) at 12 knots
Crew: 15 + 201

Used only by: Mexico
Notes: *Hurst* was built between 1942 and 1943 as a destroyer escort by Brown Shipbuilding of Houston, Texas, and commissioned into US service in 1943. She was transferred to Mexico in 1973, and is used as a training ship.

'Durango' class frigate (1)

Class: *Durango* (B-01, ex-128)
Displacement: 1,600 tons (1,626 tonnes) standard; 2,000 tons (2,032 tonnes) full load
Dimensions: Length 256 ft 6 in (78.2 m)
Beam 36 ft 7 in (11.2 m)
Draught 10 ft 6 in (3.1 m)
Armament:
Guns 2 4-in (102-mm) in single mountings
2 57-mm in single mountings
4 20-mm in single mountings
Missile systems
none
A/S weapons
none
Torpedo tubes
none
Aircraft
none

Radar and electronics:
Sonar:
Powerplant: 2 Enterprise DMR-38 diesel-electric drives, delivering 5,000 bhp to two shafts
Speed: 18 knots
Range: 3,000 miles (4,830 km) at 12 knots
Crew: 24+125

Used only by: Mexico
Notes: *Durango* was built as an armed transport between 1934 and 1935 by Union Naval de Levante at Valencia, and commissioned in 1936. At that time she had a conventional geared turbine propulsion of British manufacture.

'Azteca' class large patrol craft (22)

Class: *Andres Quintana Roos* (P01), *Matias de Cordova* (P02), *Miguel Ramos Arizpe* (P03), *Jose Maria Izazgu* (P04), *Juan Bautista Morales* (P05), *Ignacio Lopez Rayon* (P06), *Manuel Crecencio Rejon* (P07), *Antonio de la Fuente* (P08), *Leon Guzman* (P09), *Ignacio Ramirez* (P10), *Ignacio Mariscal* (P11), *Heriberto Jara Corona* (P12), *Jose Maria Maja* (P13), *Felix Romero* (P14), *Fernando Lizardi* (P15), *Francisco J. Mujica* (P16), *Pastor Rouaix* (P17), *Jose Maria del Castillo Velasco* (P18), *Luis Manuel Rojas* (P19), *Jose Natividad Macias* (P20), *Esteban Baca Calderon* (P21), *Ignacio Zaragosa* (P22)
Displacement: 130 tons (132.1 tonnes)
Dimensions: Length 111 ft 9 in (34.1 m)
Beam 28 ft 2 in (8.6 m)
Draught 6 ft 9 in (2.0 m)
Armament:
Guns 1 40-mm
1 20-mm
Missile systems
none

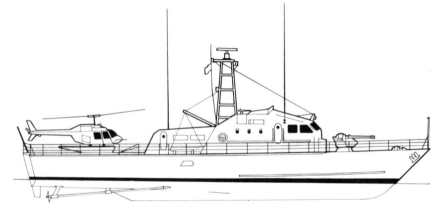

A/S weapons
none
Torpedo tubes
none
Aircraft
none
Radar and electronics:
Sonar:

Powerplant: 2 Paxman Ventura diesels, delivering 3,600 bhp to two shafts
Speed: 24 knots
Range: 2,500 miles (4,025 km) at 12 knots
Crew: 24
Used only by: Mexico
Notes: Of British design, some 22 of this class are already in service with the Mexican Navy, and another nine are on order. The craft are built by a number of yards.

Montserrat

Coastguard element of the Montserrat
Police Force

Patrol Forces:
1 Brooke 12-m type coastal PC

Morocco

2,000 men including 600 marines

Frigates:
(1 + 4 Modified Descubierta)

Patrol Forces:
2 PR 72 type PC (+2)
3 large PC
12 P32 type coastal PC
3 Arcor 31 coastal PC
(4 Modified Lazaga FAC(G))

Mine Warfare Forces:
1 Sirius coastal minesweeper

Amphibious Forces:
3 Batral type landing ships logistic
1 EDIC type LCT

Marine Force:
1 naval infantry bn

Large patrol craft (1)

Class: *Al Bachir* (22, ex-12)
Displacement: 125 tons (127 tonnes) light;
154 tons (156.5 tonnes) full load
Dimensions: Length 133 ft 2½ in (40.6 m)
Beam 21 ft (6.4 m)
Draught 4 ft 8 in (1.4 m)
Armament:
Guns 2 40-mm in single mountings
2 machine-guns
Missile systems
none
A/S weapons
none
Torpedo tubes
none
Aircraft
none
Radar and electronics:
Sonar:
Powerplant: 2 SEMT-Pielstick diesels, deliv-
ering 3,600 bhp to two shafts
Speed: 25 knots
Range: 2,000 miles (3,220 km) at 15 knots
Crew: 23
Used only by: Morocco
Notes: *Al Bachir* was built at Cherbourg be-
tween 1965 and 1967 by Constructions
Mécaniques de Normandie, and com-
missioned in 1967.

Modified 'Le Fougueux' class large patrol craft (1)

Class: *Lieutenant Riffi* (32)
Displacement: 311 tons (316 tonnes) stan-
dard; 374 tons (380 tonnes) full load
Dimensions: Length 174 ft (53.0 m)
Beam 23 ft (7.0 m)
Draught 4 ft 8½ in (1.4 m)
Armament:
Guns 1 76-mm
2 40-mm
Missile systems
none
A/S weapons
2 A/S mortars
Torpedo tubes
none
Aircraft
none
Radar and electronics:
Sonar:
Powerplant: 2 SEMT-Pielstick diesels, deliver-
ing 3,600 bhp to two propellers
Speed: 19 knots
Range: 3,000 miles (4,830 km) at 12 knots
Crew: 49
Used only by: Morocco
Notes: *Lieutenant Riffi* was built at Cherbourg
by Constructions Mécaniques de Nor-
mandie and commissioned in 1964.

'PR 72' class fast attack craft (2)

Class: *Okba, Triki*
Displacement: 375 tons (381 tonnes) stan-
dard; 445 tons (452.1 tonnes) full load
Dimensions: Length 188 ft 7¾ in (57.5 m)
Beam 25 ft (7.6 m)
Draught 7 ft 1 in (2.1 m)
Armament:
Guns 1 76-mm OTO Melara
1 40-mm Breda
Missile systems
none
A/S weapons
none
Torpedo tubes
none
Aircraft
none
Radar and electronics: Thomson-CSF Vega
system radars
Sonar:
Powerplant: 4 AGO V16 diesels, delivering
11,040 hp to four shafts
Speed: 28 knots
Range: 2,500 miles (4,025 km) at 16 knots
Crew: 5+48
Used only by: Morocco
Notes: Both craft were built by the Société
Française de Construction Navale, and
commissioned in 1976 and 1977 respecti-
vely. Another pair are on order. All four craft
can be fitted with the MM38 Exocet SSM.

Mozambique

700 men

Patrol Forces:
1 Poluchat PC
1 Antares PC
3 Jupiter PC
2 Bellatrix PC

Amphibious Forces:
1 Alfange LCT

Netherlands

The Royal Netherlands Navy
The Netherlands are in a position similar to that of Belgium, with limited overseas obligations, but an important coastline and port facilities to protect against maritime attack, and vital economic sealanes to guard against enemy intervention. Thus the Netherlands' naval requirements are double: ocean-going warships for the protection of trade and as a contribution to NATO's main surface forces, and coastal vessels for the protection of ports and the coast itself. For this purpose the Royal Netherlands Navy has six submarines and 19 major surface ships, manned by some of the 17,000 men in the navy. This represents some 15.5 per cent of the total manpower strength of the armed forces, whose budget is some 4 per cent of the gross national product.

The main elements of the Dutch fleet are the two versatile ships of the 'Tromp' class, classified as guided-missile light cruisers or destroyers. These are fitted as flagships, have the latest air search radar, and are armed with one Tartar SAM launcher, Sea Sparrow short-range SAMs, and Harpoon SSMs, as well as guns and A/S weapons. General support is provided by the eight 'Friesland' and one 'Holland' class conventional destroyers, though these are to be replaced by the ships of the new 'Kortenaer' frigate class, intended to number 12 by the later 1980s. The first of these commissioned in 1978 and the second in 1979. Designed as general-purpose frigates, the ships of the 'Kortenaer' class have an A/S helicopter, two triple torpedo tube mountings for A/S torpedoes, Harpoon SSMs, Sea Sparrow SAMs, guns, and gas turbine propulsion, as well as advanced electronics and radar. The 'Kortenaer' class ships will be partnered by the 'Van Speijk' class frigates, the six of which are being modernised to include Harpoon SAMs, triple A/S tubes and more advanced sensors and electronics.

Confident that long-range operations provide the best defence, Holland has not invested in FAC types, coastal defence being entrusted to the six corvettes of the elderly 'Wolf' class, and the five large patrol craft of the equally elderly 'Balder' class. Great store is set on mine countermeasures, though, and to complement the 15 new Improved 'Circe' class minehunters to be built shortly, the Netherlands have four 'Onversaagd' class MCM support ships, 18 'Dokkum' class coastal minesweepers/minehunters, and 16 'Van Straelen' class inshore minesweepers.

Fleet support is provided by a number of modern ships, which ensure that the Dutch long-range forces are well supplied. They also receive adequate air support from the naval air arm's two maritime reconnaissance squadrons, equipped with Atlantic and Neptune aircraft, and two ASW helicopter squadrons, equipped with Lynx and Wasp helicopters.

The big question mark over the Dutch navy seems to lie in the belief that such a force can do without light forces and their FAC types, either missile- or torpedo-armed.

17,000 men (2,000 conscripts) including 1,900 naval air arm and 2,900 marines

Cruisers (DLG):
2 Tromp

Destroyers:
8 Friesland
1 Holland

Frigates (FFG):
2 Kortenaer (+10)

Frigates (FF):
6 Van Speijk

SS:
2 Zwaardvis
2 Potvis
2 Dolfijn

Corvettes:
6 Wolf

Patrol Forces:
5 Balder PC

Mine Warfare Forces:
4 Onversaagd mine countermeasures support ships
18 Dokkum class coastal minesweepers and minehunters
16 Van Straelen inshore minesweepers (15 Improved Circe or Alkmaar)

Amphibious Forces:
11 LCA type

Auxiliaries:
3 survey ships
2 fast combat support ships
2 training ships
others

Naval Air Arm:
(2 MR sqns) 8 Atlantic 15 P-2 Neptune
(2 ASW helicopter sqns) 6 Lynx, 12 Wasp
(18 Lynx)

Marine Force:
2 amphibious combat groups
1 mountain/arctic coy

'Tromp' class guided missile destroyer (2)

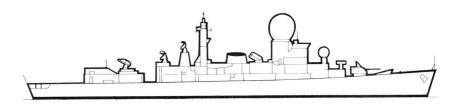

Class: *Tromp* (F801) and *De Ruyter* (F806)
Displacement: 4,300 tons (4,369 tonnes) standard; 5,400 tons (5,486 tonnes) full load
Dimensions: Length 454 ft 0¾ in (138.4 m)
Beam 48 ft 7 in (14.8 m)
Draught 15 ft 1 in (4.6 m)
Armament:
Guns 2 4.7-in (120-mm) in a twin turret
Missile systems
  1 Tartar SAM launcher
  1 Sea Sparrow Basic Point Missile Defence System
  2 quadruple Harpoon SSM launchers
A/S weapons
  2 triple 12.75-in (324-mm) Mark 32 tubes
Torpedo tubes
  none

Aircraft
  1 helicopter
Radar and electronics: Hollandse Signaalapparaten 3D search, HSA WM 25 Sea Sparrow and gun fire-control, SPG-51 Tartar fire-control and Decca navigation radars; 2 Knebworth Corvus chaff dispensers; SEWACO I automated action data automation and command and control system
Sonar: CWE 610

Powerplant: 2 Rolls-Royce Olympus gas turbines, delivering 50,000 hp, and 2 Rolls-Royce Tyne gas turbines, delivering 8,000 hp to two shafts
Speed: 30 knots
Range:
Crew: 306
Used only by: Netherlands
Notes: The two ships were built at Vlissingen between 1971 and 1974 by Koninklijke Maatschappij de Schelde, and commissioned in 1975 and 1976 respectively.

'Friesland' class destroyer (8)

Class: *Friesland* (D812), *Groningen* (D813), *Limburg* (D814), *Overijssel* (D815), *Drenthe* (D816), *Utrecht* (D817), *Rotterdam* (D818), *Amsterdam* (D819)
Displacement: 2,497 tons (2,537 tonnes) standard; 3,070 tons (3,119 tonnes) full load
Dimensions: Length 380 ft 6 in (116.0 m)
Beam 38 ft 6 in (11.7 m)
Draught 17 ft (5.2 m)
Armament:
Guns 4 4.7-in (120-mm) in twin turrets
  4 40-mm in single mountings
Missile systems
  none
A/S weapons
  2 4-barrel 375-mm Bofors rocket-launchers
  2 DC racks

Torpedo tubes
  none
Aircraft
  none
Radar and electronics: Hollandse Signaalap-
  paraten LW 03 search, DA 05 tactical,
  M45 main armament fire-control, and
  separate 40-mm and Bofors fire-control
  radars
Sonar:
Powerplant: 4 Babcock boilers supplying
  steam to 2 Werkspoor geared turbines, de-
  livering 60,000 shp to two shafts
Speed: 36 knots
Range:
Crew: 284

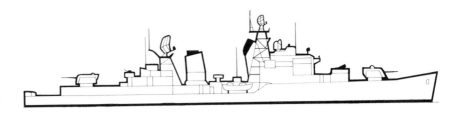

Used only by: Netherlands
Notes: The eight ships of the class were built
  by four yards in the period between 1951
  and 1956, and commissioned between
  1956 and 1958. They have deck and side
  armour.

'Holland' class destroyer (1)

Class: Zeeland (D809)
Displacement: 2,215 tons (2,250 tonnes)
  standard; 2,765 tons (2,809 tonnes) full
  load
Dimensions: Length 371 ft 1 in (113.1 m)
            Beam 37 ft 6 in (11.4 m)
            Draught 16 ft 10 in (5.1 m)
Armament:
Guns 4 4.7-in (120-mm) in twin turrets
  1 40-mm
Missile systems
  none
A/S weapons
  2 4-barrel 375-mm Bofors rocket-
    launchers
  2 DC racks
Torpedo tubes
  none
Aircraft
  none
Radar and electronics: Hollandse Signaalap-
  paraten LW 03 search, DA 02 tactical,
  M45 main armament fire-control, and
  separate A/S fire-control radars
Sonar:

Powerplant: 4 Babcock boilers supplying
  steam to 2 Werkspoor Parsons geared tur-
  bines, delivering 45,000 shp to two shafts
Speed: 32 knots
Range:
Crew: 247
Used also by: Peru

Notes: Holland was built between 1950 and
  1953 by Rotterdamse Droogdok Mij, and
  sold to Peru in 1978; Zeeland was built
  between 1951 and 1953 by Koninklijke
  Maatschappij de Schelde at Vlissingen, and
  commissioned in 1955. Two sisterships
  were built: Gelderland is now a training
  hulk, and Noord Brabant was written off in
  an accident in 1974.

'Kortenaer' class frigate (8)

Class: Kortenaer (F807), Callenburgh (F808),
  Van Kinsbergen (F809), Banckert (F810),
  Piet Heyn (F811), Pieter Florisz (F812),
  Witte de With (F813), Abraham Crijnssen
  (F814)
Displacement: 3,500 tons (3,556 tonnes)
Dimensions: Length 419 ft 10 in (128.0 m)
            Beam 47 ft 2½ in (14.4 m)
            Draught 14 ft 3 in (4.4 m)

Radar and electronics: Hollandse Signaalap-
  paraten search, tactical and fire-control
  radars
Sonar: SQS-505
Powerplant: 2 Rolls-Royce Olympus gas tur-
  bines, delivering 50,000 shp, and 2 Rolls-
  Royce Tyne gas turbines, delivering 8,000
  shp, to two shafts
Speed: 30
Range: 4,000 miles (6,440 km) on Tynes
Crew: 176
Used only by: Netherlands

Armament:
Guns 2 76-mm OTO Melara
Missile systems
  1 NATO Sea Sparrow Point Defence Mis-
    sile System
  8 Harpoon SSM launchers
A/S weapons
  2 triple 12.75-in (324-mm) Mark 32 tubes
Torpedo tubes
  none
Aircraft
  1 helicopter

Radar and electronics: Hollandse Signaalapparaten search, tactical and fire-control
radars
Sonar: SQS-505
Powerplant: 2 Rolls-Royce Olympus gas turbines, delivering 50,000 shp, and 2 Rolls-
Royce Tyne gas turbines, delivering 8,000
shp, to two shafts
Speed: 30 knots

Range: 4,000 miles (6,440 km) on Tynes
Crew: 176
Used only by: Netherlands
Notes: All vessels are to be built in the Vliss-
ingen yards of Koninklijke Maatschappij de
Schelde, between 1975 and 1980, for
commissioning between 1978 and 1984.
Another four will then be built, two by the
present builders and two by Wilton-

Fijenoord. The aft 76-mm gun will be
replaced by a twin 35-mm mounting when
this is available.

'Van Speijk' class frigate (6)

Class: *Van Speijk* (F802), *Van Galen* (F803),
Tjerk Hiddes (F804), *Van Nes* (F805), *Isaac
Sweers* (F814), *Evertsen* (F815)
Displacement: 2,200 tons (2,235 tonnes)
standard; 2,850 tons (2,896 tonnes) full
load
Dimensions: Length 372 ft (113.4 m)
Beam 41 ft (12.5 m)
Draught 18 ft (5.5 m)
Armament:
Guns 2 4.5-in (114-mm) in a twin turret
Missile systems
2 quadruple Seacat SAM launchers
A/S weapons
1 3-barrel Limbo A/S mortar
Torpedo tubes
none
Aircraft
1 small helicopter
Radar and electronics: Hollandse Signaalap-
paraten LW-02 search, DA 05 target indi-
cator, M45 main armament fire-control,
M44 Seacat fire-control and Kelvin-
Hughes surface warning/navigation radars
Sonar: hull-mounted and variable-depth
Powerplant: 2 Babcock & Wilcox boilers
supplying steam to 2 double-reduction
geared turbines, delivering 30,000 shp to
two shafts
Speed: 30 knots
Range:
Crew: 254
Used only by: Netherlands
Notes: The ships were built in two groups of
three, at Vlissingen by Koninklijke Maatschappij de Schelde and at Amsterdam by
Nederlandse Dok en Scheepsbouw Mij.
The ships were laid down between 1963
and 1965, launched between 1965 and
1967, and commissioned between 1967
and 1967. The design is based on that of
the British 'Leander' class frigates. The
class is being modernised, a 76-mm OTO

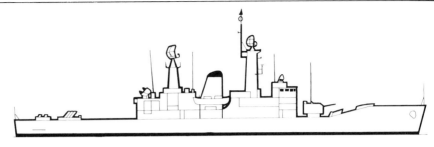

Melara replacing the twin 4.5-in, the Limbo
being replaced by 2 triple Mark 32 tubes as
A/S armament, and 2 quadruple Harpoon
SSM launchers being added.

'Zwaardvis' class submarine (2)

Class: *Zwaardvis* (S806), *Tijgerhaai* (S807)
Displacement: 2,350 tons (2,388 tonnes)
surfaced; 2,640 tons (2,682 tonnes) dived
Dimensions: Length 217 ft 2½ in (66.2 m)
Beam 33 ft 10 in (10.3 m)
Draught 23 ft 3 in (7.1 m)
Armament:
Guns none
Missile systems
none
A/S weapons
none
Torpedo tubes
6 533-mm (21-in)
Aircraft
none
Radar and electronics: Type 1001
Sonar:
Powerplant: 3 diesel generators, delivering
power to one shaft
Speed: 13 knots (surfaced); 20 knots (dived)

Range:
Crew: 67
Used only by: Netherlands

Notes: The two boats were built between
1966 and 1971 in Rotterdam by Rotterdamse Droogdok Mij, and commissioned in
1972.

'Potvis' and 'Dolfijn' class submarine (4)

Class: *Potvis* (S804), *Tonijn* (S805), *Dolfijn* (S808), *Zeehond* (S809)
Displacement: 1,140 tons (1,158 tonnes) standard; 1,494 tons (1,518 tonnes) surfaced; 1,826 tons (1,855 tonnes) dived
Dimensions: Length 260 ft 10 in (79.5 m)
Beam 25 ft 10 in (7.8 m)
Draught 15 ft 10 in (4.8 m)
Armament:
Guns none

Missile systems
none
A/S weapons
none
Torpedo tubes
8 533-mm (21-in)
Aircraft
none
Radar and electronics: Type 1001 radar
Sonar:
Powerplant: 2 MAN diesels, delivering 3,100 bhp, and electric motors delivering 4,200 hp to two shafts
Speed: 14½ knots (surfaced); 17 knots (dived)

Range:
Crew: 64
Used only by: Netherlands
Notes: S804 and S805, the two 'Potvis' class boats, were built in Schiedam by Wilton-Fijenoord between 1962 and 1965, for commissioning in 1965 and 1966; the two 'Dolfijn' class boats were built at Rotterdam by Rotterdamse Droogdok Mij between 1954 and 1960, for commissioning in 1960 and 1961. The boats were voted for at the same time, but the 'Potvis' class was considerably delayed. Triple-hull construction gives a diving depth of 984 ft (300 m).

'Wolf' class corvette (6)

Class: *Wolf* (F817), ex-US *PCE1607*; *Fret* (F818), ex-US *PCE1604*; *Hermelijn* (F819), ex-US *PCE1605*; *Vos* (F820), ex-US *PCE1616*; *Panter* (F821), ex-US *PCE1608*; *Jaguar* (F822), ex-US *PCE1608*
Displacement: 870 tons (833.1 tonnes) standard; 975 tons (990.6 tonnes) full load
Dimensions: Length 184 ft 6 in (56.2 m)
Beam 33 ft (10.0 m)
Draught 14 ft 6 in (4.4 m)
Armament:
Guns 1 3-in (76-mm)
6 40-mm in all except *Panter* and *Jaguar*: 4 40-mm
Missile systems
none
A/S weapons
1 Hedgehog
2 (4 in *Panter* and *Jaguar*) DCTs
2 DC racks
Torpedo tubes
none
Aircraft
none
Radar and electronics: Kelvin-Hughes navigation radar
Sonar: hull-mounted
Powerplant: 2 General Motors Corporation diesels, delivering 1,800 bhp to two shafts
Speed: 15 knots
Range: 4,300 miles (6,920 km) at 10 knots
Crew: 96
Used only by: Netherlands
Notes: The six vessels were commissioned into service in 1954.

'Balder' class large patrol craft (5)

Class: *Balder* (P802), *Bulgia* (P803), *Freyr* (P804), *Hadda* (P805), *Hefring* (P806)
Displacement: 169 tons (171.7 tonnes) standard; 225 tons (228.6 tonnes) full load
Dimensions: Length 119 ft 1 in (36.3 m)
Beam 20 ft 2½ in (6.2 m)
Draught 5 ft 11 in (1.8 m)
Armament:
Guns 1 40-mm
3 20-mm
Missile systems
none
A/S weapons
1 Mousetrap
Torpedo tubes
none
Aircraft
none
Radar and electronics: Decca navigation radar
Sonar: hull-mounted
Powerplant: diesels, delivering 1,300 shp to two shafts
Speed: 15½ knots
Range: 1,000 miles (1,610 km) at 10 knots

Crew: 27
Used only by: Netherlands
Notes: All five craft were built with US finance at Rijkswerf Willemsoord, and commissioned in 1954 and 1955.

New Zealand

2,750 men and 325 reservists

Frigates:
1 Leander
1 Broad-beamed Leander
2 Whitby

Patrol Forces:
4 Lake PC
4 HDML type coastal PC

Auxiliaries:
1 survey ship
2 HDML type
1 research vessel
2 tugs

'Leander' and 'Broad-Beamed Leander' class frigate (2)

Class: *Waikato* (F55), *Canterbury* (F421)
Displacement: 2,450 tons (2,489 tonnes) standard and 2,860 tons (2,906 tonnes) full load for *Waikato*; 2,470 tons (2,510 tonnes) standard and 2,990 tons (3,038 tonnes) full load for *Canterbury*
Dimensions: Length 372 ft (113.4 m)
Beam 41 ft (12.5 m) for *Waikato*; 43 ft (13.1 m) for *Canterbury*
Draught 18 ft (5.5 m)
Armament:
Guns 2 4.5-in (114-mm) in a twin turret
2 20-mm
Missile systems
1 quadruple Seacat launcher
A/S weapons
1 Limbo 3-barrel DC mortar in *Waikato*
2 Mark 32 Model 5 A/S tubes in *Canterbury*

Torpedo tubes
none
Aircraft
1 small helicopter
Radar and electronics: Type 965 search, Type 993 tactical, and I-band (in MRS 3 system) fire-control radars
Sonar: hull-mounted
Powerplant: 2 Babcock & Wilcox boilers supplying steam to 2 double-reduction geared turbines, delivering 30,000 shp to two shafts
Speed: 30 knots (*Waikato*); 28 knots (*Canterbury*)
Range:
Crew: 14+234 in *Waikato*; 14+229 in *Canterbury*
Used also by: Chile, India, UK
Notes: *Waikato* was built by Harland & Wolff in Belfast between 1964 and 1965, and commissioned in 1966; *Canterbury* was built by Yarrow on the Clyde between 1969 and 1970, and commissioned in 1971.

'Whitby' class frigate (2)

Class: *Otago* (F111), ex-British *Hastings*; *Taranaki* (F148)
Displacement: 2,144 tons (2,178 tonnes) standard; 2,557 tons (2,598 tonnes) full load
Dimensions: Length 370 ft (112.8 m)
Beam 41 ft (12.5 m)
Draught 17 ft 4 in (5.3 m)
Armament:
Guns 2 4.5-in (114-mm) in a twin turret
2 20-mm in *Taranaki* only
Missile systems
1 quadruple Seacat SAM launcher

A/S weapons
2 triple 12.75-in (324-mm) Mark 32 Model 5 tubes
Torpedo tubes
none
Aircraft
none
Radar and electronics: Types 993 and 277 search, and I-band fire-control radars
Sonar: hull-mounted
Powerplant: 2 Babcock & Wilcox boilers supplying steam to 2 double-reduction geared turbines, delivering 30,000 shp to two shafts
Speed: 30 knots

Range:
Crew: 13+227
Used also by: India, UK
Notes: *Otago* was built by Thornycroft at Woolston between 1957 and 1958, and commissioned into NZ service in 1960; *Taranaki* was built by J. Samuel White in the Isle of Wight between 1958 and 1959, and commissioned in 1961. Both vessels have the alterations found on the 'Rothesay' class. The original 12 21-in (533-mm) torpedo tubes have been removed.

'Lake' class large patrol craft (4)

Class: *Pukaki* (P3568), *Rotoiti* (P3569), *Taupo* (P3570), *Hawea* (P3571)
Displacement: 105 tons (106.7 tonnes) standard; 134 tons (136.1 tonnes) full load
Dimensions: Length 107 ft (32.8 m)
Beam 20 ft (6.1 m)
Draught 11 ft 10 in (3.6 m)

Armament:
Guns 2 0.5-in (12.7-mm) machine-guns
1 81-mm mortar/0.5-in (12.7-mm) machine-gun combination
Missile systems
none
A/S weapons
none
Torpedo tubes
none

Aircraft
none
Radar and electronics:
Sonar:
Powerplant: 2 Paxman 12YJCM diesels, delivering 3,000 bhp to two shafts
Speed: 25 knots
Range:
Crew: 3+18
Used only by: New Zealand

Nicaragua

200 men

Patrol Forces:
10 patrol craft

Nigeria

4,500 men

Frigates:
1 Nigeria
(1 ?)

Corvettes:
2 Vosper Thornycroft Mark 3
(2 Vosper Thornycroft Mark 9)

Light Forces:
(3 Lürssen S-143 FAC(M))
(3 La Combattante IIIB FAC(M))

Patrol Forces:
4 Brooke 32.6-m PC
4 Ford PC
4 Abeking and Rasmussen type PC

Auxiliaries:
2 survey vessels
1 LCT(4) transport
1 supply ship
1 training ship
others

Vosper Thornycroft Mark 3 corvette (2)

Class: Dorina (F81), Otobo (F82)
Displacement: 500 tons (508 tonnes) standard; 650 tons (660.4 tonnes) full load
Dimensions: Length 202 ft (61.6 m)
    Beam 31 ft (9.5 m)
    Draught 11 ft 4 in (3.5 m)
Armament:
Guns 2 4-in (102-mm) in a twin turret
  2 40-mm Bofors in single mountings
  2 20-mm
Missile systems
  none
A/S weapons
  none

Torpedo tubes
  none
Aircraft
  none
Radar and electronics: Plessey AWS-1 air search, Hollandse Signaalapparaten M20 fire-control, and Decca TM626 navigation radars
Sonar:
Powerplant: 2 MAN diesels
Speed: 23 knots
Range: 3,500 miles (5,635 km) at 14 knots
Crew: 7+59
Used only by: Nigeria
Notes: Both ships were built by Vosper Thornycroft and commissioned in 1972.

129

'Nigeria' class frigate (1)

Class: *Nigeria* (F87)
Displacement: 1,724 tons (1,752 tonnes) standard; 2,000 tons (2,032 tonnes) full load
Dimensions: Length 360 ft 2½ in (109.8 m)
Beam 37 ft (11.3 m)
Draught 11 ft 6 in (3.5 m)

Armament:
Guns 2 4-in (102-mm) in a twin turret
3 40-mm in single mountings
Missile systems
none
A/S weapons
1 Squid 3-barrel A/S mortar
Torpedo tubes
none
Aircraft
facilities for 1 helicopter

Radar and electronics: Type 293/AWS-4
Sonar: none
Powerplant: 4 MAN diesels, delivering 16,000 bhp to two shafts
Speed: 26 knots
Range: 3,500 miles (5,635 km) at 15 knots
Crew: 216
Used only by: Nigeria
Notes: *Nigeria* was built by Wilton-Fijenoord in the Netherlands between 1964 and 1965, and commissioned in 1965.

Vosper Thornycroft Mark 9 corvette (2)

Class: *Erin'mi, Enyimiri*
Displacement: 820 tons (833.1 tonnes)
Dimensions: Length 226 ft 4½ in (69.0 m)
Beam 34 ft 5½ in (10.5 m)
Draught 11 ft 9¾ in (3.6 m)
Armament:
Guns 1 76-mm OTO Melara
1 40-mm
2 20-mm

Missile systems
1 Seacat SAM launcher
A/S weapons
1 Bofors A/S rocket-launcher
Torpedo tubes
none
Aircraft
none
Radar and electronics: Plessey AWS-2 search radar
Sonar:
Powerplant: 4 MTU-20V 956 TB92 diesels, delivering 19,740 shp

Speed: 29 knots
Range: 4,100 miles (6,599 km) at 14 knots
Crew: 90
Used only by: Nigeria
Notes: Both ships are built by Vosper Thornycroft, for commissioning in 1978 and 1979.

North Korea

27,000 men

Frigates:
3 Najin (+1)

SS:
11 Romeo
4 Whiskey

Light Forces:
8 Osa I FAC(M)
10 Komar I FAC(M)
8 Shanghai FAC(G)
8 Swatow FAC(G)
4 Chodo FAC(G)

4 K-48 FAC(G)
20 MO IV FAC(G)
60 Chako FAC(G)
30 Chong-jin FAC(G)
4 Shershen FAC(T)
62 P-6 FAC(T)
12 P-4 FAC(T)
15 Iwon FAC(T)
6 Au Ju FAC(T)
60 Sin Hung and Kosong FAC(T)

Patrol Forces:
2 Tral PC
3 Sariwan PC
4 Hainan PC

15 SO I PC
1 or 2 Artillerist PC
10 KM-4 coastal PC
20 small gunboats

Amphibious Forces:
c 90 LCM type

Auxiliaries:
5–10 small trawlers and cargo vessels
100 support/patrol craft

'Najin' class frigate (3)

Class: *3025, 3026, 3027*
Displacement: 1,500 tons (1,524 tonnes)
Dimensions: Length 328 ft (100.0 m)
Beam 32 ft 10 in (10.0 m)
Draught 8 ft 10 in (2.7 m)
Armament:
Guns 2 100-mm in single mountings
4 57-mm in twin mountings
4 25-mm in twin mountings
8 14.5-mm
Missile systems
none
A/S weapons
3 launchers, 2 racks, 2 mortars
Torpedo tubes
3 533-mm (21-in)
Aircraft
none
Radar and electronics: 'Skin Head' and 'Pot Head' surface-search radar; 'Ski Pole' IFF
Sonar:
Powerplant: 2 diesels, delivering 15,000 bhp to two shafts
Speed: about 25 knots
Range: 4,000 miles (6,438 km) at 14 knots
Crew: 180
Used only by: North Korea
Notes: Built in North Korean yards, the first ship was commissioned in 1973, the second in 1975. A third was laid down in 1976 and a fourth should be commissioned in 1978.

'Romeo' class submarine (11)

Class: eleven ex-Chinese boats
Displacement: 1,000 tons (1,016 tonnes) surfaced; 1,600 tons (1,626 tonnes) dived
Dimensions: Length 249 ft 4 in (76.0 m)
Beam 24 ft (7.3 m)
Draught 14 ft 6 in (4.4 m)
Armament:
Guns none
Missile systems
none
A/S weapons
none
Torpedo tubes
6 533-mm (21-in) with 18 torpedoes
Aircraft
none
Radar and electronics:
Sonar:
Powerplant: 2 diesels, delivering 4,000 bhp, and 2 electric motors, delivering 4,000 hp, to two shafts
Speed: 17 knots (surfaced); 14 knots (dived)
Range: 16,000 miles (25,750 km) at 10 knots surfaced
Crew: 65
Used also by: Bulgaria, China, Egypt, USSR
Notes: Two boats were transferred by China in 1973, two more in 1974, and three in 1975. The North Koreans themselves built two additional boats in 1976, and others with altered specifications continue to be built in North Korea.

'Whiskey' class submarine (4)

Class: four ex-Russian boats
Displacement: 1,030 tons (1,046 tonnes) surfaced; 1,350 tons (1,372 tonnes) dived
Dimensions: Length 249 ft 4 in (76.0 m)
Beam 22 ft (6.7 m)
Draught 15 ft (4.6 m)
Armament:
Guns none
Missile systems
none
A/S weapons
none
Torpedo tubes
6 533-mm (21-in) with 18 torpedoes or 40 mines
Aircraft
none
Radar and electronics: 'Snoop Plate' surface-search radar
Sonar: 'Tamir'
Powerplant: 2 diesels, delivering 4,000 bhp, and 2 electric motors, delivering 2,500 hp to two shafts
Speed: 17 knots (surfaced); 15 knots (dived)
Range: 13,000 miles (20,925 km) at 8 knots
Crew: 60
Used also by: Albania, Bulgaria, China, Egypt, Indonesia, Poland, USSR
Notes:

'Chodo' class fast attack craft (gun) (4)

Class: four craft
Displacement: about 130 tons (132.1 tonnes)
Dimensions: Length 140 ft (42.7 m)
Beam 19 ft (5.8 m)
Draught 8 ft 6 in (2.6 m)
Armament:
Guns 4 37-mm in single mountings
4 25-mm in twin mountings
Missile systems
none
A/S weapons
none
Torpedo tubes
none
Aircraft
none
Radar and electronics: 'Skin Head' surface search radar
Sonar:
Powerplant: diesels, delivering 6,000 bhp to two shafts
Speed: about 24 knots
Range:
Crew: about 40
Used only by: North Korea
Notes: All four craft were built in North Korean yards during the mid-1960s.

'K-48' class fast attack craft (gun) (4)

Class: four craft
Displacement: about 110 tons (111.8 tonnes)
Dimensions: Length 125 ft (38.1 m)
Beam 18 ft (5.5 m)
Draught 5 ft (1.5 m)
Armament:
Guns 1 76-mm
3 37-mm in single mountings
4 or 6 14.5-mm machine-guns in twin mountings
Missile systems
none
A/S weapons
none
Torpedo tubes
none
Aircraft
none
Radar and electronics: 'Skin Head' surface search radar
Sonar:
Powerplant: diesels, delivering up to 5,000 bhp to two shafts
Speed: about 24 knots
Range:
Crew:
Used only by: North Korea
Notes: The four craft were probably built in North Korean yards during the mid-1950s.

'Tral' class large patrol craft (2)

Class: two ex-Russian craft
Displacement: 475 tons (482.6 tonnes)
Dimensions: Length 203 ft 6 in (62.0 m)
Beam 23 ft 10 in (7.2 m)
Draught 7 ft 9 in (2.4 m)
Armament:
Guns 1 100-mm
3 37-mm in single mountings
4 12.7-mm machine-guns
Missile systems
none
A/S weapons
2 DC racks
Torpedo tubes
none
Aircraft
none
Radar and electronics: 'Skin Head' surface search radar; 'Yard Rake' IFF
Sonar:
Powerplant: 2 diesels, delivering 2,800 hp to two shafts
Speed: 18 knots
Range:
Crew: 55
Used only by: North Korea
Notes: Designed as fleet minesweepers, the ships of the 'Tral' class are no longer used by the USSR, but some four or five were transferred to North Korea as patrol craft in the mid-1950s, and one or possibly two still survive. The craft can carry 40 mines.

'Sariwan' class large patrol craft (3)

Class: 725, 726, 727(?)
Displacement: 475 tons (482.6 tonnes)
Dimensions: Length 203 ft 6 in (62.1 m)
Beam 24 ft (7.3 m)
Draught 7 ft 9 in (2.4 m)
Armament:
Guns 1 85-mm
2 57-mm in a twin mounting
12 or 16 14.5-mm machine-guns
Missile systems
none
A/S weapons
none
Torpedo tubes
none
Aircraft
none
Radar and electronics: 'Skin Head' surface search; 'Ski Pole' or 'Yard Pole' IFF
Sonar:
Powerplant: 2 diesels, delivering 3,000 bhp to two shafts
Speed: about 21 knots
Range:
Crew: about 70
Used only by: North Korea
Notes: The three craft were built by North Korean yards in the mid-1960s, and each craft can carry 30 mines.

North Yemen

500 men

Light Forces:
4 P-4 FAC(T)

Patrol Forces:
4 Poluchat PC
c 12 coastal PC

Auxiliaries:
2 small landing craft

Norway

The Norwegian Navy

Norway's navy is intended primarily for the defence of Norway's long coastline, and the importance attached to this task may well be gauged by the fact that the navy's 9,000 men constitute 23 per cent of the country's 39,000 servicemen, an unusually high percentage for what is normally a *matériel*-rather than a manpower-intensive service. Norway, it should be noted, spends some 3.6 per cent of her gross national product on defence.

The major elements in Norway's maritime defence are the five frigates of the 'Oslo' class, and two corvettes of the 'Sleipner' class. The former are general-purpose ships with a strong A/S armament, Penguin SSMs and Sea Sparrow SAMs, while the latter are principally A/S ships.

Coastal submarines are also reckoned to be of great importance, as proved by the fact that Norway has 15 Type 207 submarines, developed from the successful West German Type 205. It is expected that, during the 1980s, the West German Type 205 and the Norwegian Type 207 boats will be replaced by the new Type 210 coastal submarine currently under consideration.

The main strength of Norway's maritime defences lies with missile-armed FAC types, however. So important does Norway consider the naval surface-to-surface missile, indeed, that she has developed her own such missile to meet the stringent requirements of the navy. This is the Penguin, which is currently being developed for air launching, and its SSM version is the primary armament of the 40 FAC(M) built or building in Norway: four in each of the 14 'Hauk' class building, four in each of the six 'Snögg' class in service, and six in each of the 20 'Storm' class in service. The torpedo also has an important part in

Norwegian plans, and there are 19 FAC(T) of the 'Tjeld' class so armed.

Mine warfare is also a strategic prospect for Norway, especially for the offensive defence of territorial waters. Mines can be laid by three coastal minelayers, and there are also a number of minesweepers: 10 of the 'Falcon' coastal type, and one of the inshore 'Gässten' type.

Amphibious warfare forces consist of seven LCTs, and the whole offensive force is supported by a number of depot and support ships.

9,000 (6,000 conscripts) including 1,600 coast artillery, plus 22,000 reservists

Frigates:
5 Oslo

Corvettes:
2 Sleipner

SS:
15 Type 207

Light Forces:
1 Hauk FAC(M) (+13)
6 Snögg FAC(M)
20 Storm FAC(M)
19 Tjeld FAC(T)

Mine Warfare Forces:
2 coastal minelayers
1 controlled minelayer
10 Falcon coastal minesweepers
1 Gässten inshore minesweeper

Amphibious Forces:
2 Kvalsund LCT
5 Reinoysund LCT

Auxiliaries:
(1 submarine/light forces depot ship)
1 light forces depot ship
2 diving tenders
1 yacht
1 research ship

Coast Artillery:
36 coast arty btys

There is also a coastguard service with six fishery/oil rig protection ships (+ seven) and (1 support ship).

'Oslo' class frigate (5)

Class: *Oslo* (F300), *Bergen* (F301), *Trondheim* (F302), *Stavanger* (F303), *Narvik* (F304)
Displacement: 1,450 tons (1,473 tonnes) standard; 1,745 tons (1,773 tonnes) full load
Dimensions: Length 317 ft (96.6 m)
 Beam 36 ft 8 in (11.2 m)
 Draught 17 ft 5 in (5.3 m)
Armament:
Guns 4 76-mm in twin turrets
Missile systems
 6 Penguin SSM launchers
 1 octuple NATO Sea Sparrow Point Defence Missile System
A/S weapons
 1 Terne A/S system
 2 triple 12.75-in (324-mm) Mark 32 tubes
Torpedo tubes
 none
Aircraft
 none
Radar and electronics: DRBV 22 search, and Hollandse Signaalapparaten M24 tactical and fire-control system radars
Sonar: Terne III Mark 3 and AN/SQS-36
Powerplant: 2 Babcock & Wilcox boilers supplying steam to 1 De Laval Ljungstrom double-reduction geared turbine, delivering 20,000 shp to one shaft
Speed: 25 knots
Range:
Crew: 11+140
Used only by: Norway
Notes: All five ships were built at Horten by Marinens Hovedverft between 1963 and 1965, and commissioned in 1966 and 1967. Half the financial burden for the class was borne by the USA. The basic design of the class is that of the 'Dealey' class of US destroyers, with alterations to suit Norwegian operation requirements.

'Sleipner' class corvette (2)

Class: *Sleipner* (F310), *Aeger* (F311)
Displacement: 600 tons (609.6 tonnes) standard; 780 tons (792.5 tonnes) full load
Dimensions: Length 226 ft 4½ in (69.0 m)
 Beam 26 ft 3 in (8.0 m)
 Draught 8 ft 3 in (2.4 m)
Armament:
Guns 1 76-mm
 1 40-mm Bofors
Missile systems
 none
A/S weapons
 1 Terne ASW system
 2 triple 12.75-in (324-mm) Mark 32 tubes
Torpedo tubes
 none
Aircraft
 none
Radar and electronics: Mark 34 radar as part of the Mark 63 gun fire-control system
Sonar: Terne III Mark 3 and AN/SQS-36
Powerplant: 4 MTU diesels, delivering 9,000 bhp to two shafts
Speed: 20+ knots
Range:
Crew: 62
Used only by: Norway
Notes: The two ships were built between 1963 and 1965, for commissioning in 1965 and 1967, by Nylands Verksted (*Sleipner*) and Akers (*Aeger*). Five of the class were initially planned, and the two built are now used mainly as training ships.

Type 207 submarine (15)

Class: *Ula* (S300), *Utsira* (S301), *Utstein* (S302), *Utvaer* (S303), *Uthaug* (S304), *Sklinna* (S305), *Skolpen* (S306), *Stadt* (S307), *Stord* (S308), *Svenner* (S309), *Kaura* (S315), *Kinn* (S316), *Kya* (S317), *Kobben* (S318), *Kunna* (S319)
Displacement: 370 tons (375.9 tonnes) standard; 435 tons (442 tonnes) dived
Dimensions: Length 149 ft (45.2 m)
Beam 15 ft (4.6 m)
Draught 14 ft (4.3 m)
Armament:
Guns none
Missile systems
none
A/S weapons
none
Torpedo tubes
8 533-mm (21-in)
Aircraft
none
Radar and electronics:
Sonar:
Powerplant: 2 Maybach Mercedes-Benz MB 820 diesels, delivering 1,200 bhp, and 1

electric motor, delivering 1,200 hp to one shaft
Speed: 10 knots (surfaced); 17 knots (dived)
Range:
Crew: 5 + 13
Used only by: Norway

Notes: The Type 207 is a development of the Ingenieurkontor Lübeck (IKL) Type 205 with increased diving depth. All boats were built by Rheinstahl-Nordseewerke of Emden in West Germany between 1960 and 1967, and commissioned between 1964 and 1967. Half the cost of the class was borne by the USA.

'Hauk' class fast attack craft (missile) (14)

Class: *P986 (Hauk)* to *P999*
Displacement: 120 tons (121.9 tonnes) standard; 150 tons (154 tonnes) full load
Dimensions: Length 119 ft 9 in (36.5 m)
Beam 20 ft 4 in (6.2 m)
Draught 5 ft 6 in (1.6 m)
Armament:
Guns 1 40-mm Bofors
Missile systems
6 Penguin SSM launchers
A/S weapons
none
Torpedo tubes
4 533-mm (21-in)
Aircraft
none
Radar and electronics: Kongsberg Vappenfabrikk MSI-80S fire-control system

Sonar:
Powerplant: 2 MTU diesels, delivering 7,000 hp to two shafts
Speed: 34 knots
Range: 440 miles (710 km) at 34 knots
Crew: 22

Used only by: Norway
Notes: Based on the 'Snögg' class craft, the boats of the 'Hauk' class are coming into service during 1978. Ten boats are being produced by Bergens Mek. Verksteder at Lakeseväg, and four by Westermöen at Alta.

'Snögg' class fast attack craft (missile) (6)

Class: *Snögg*, ex-*Lyr* (P980), *Rapp* (P981), *Snar* (P982), *Rask* (P983), *Kvikk* (P984), *Kjapp* (P985)
Displacement: 100 tons (101.6 tonnes) standard; 125 tons (127 tonnes) full load
Dimensions: Length 119 ft 9 in (36.5 m)
Beam 20 ft 6 in (6.2 m)
Draught 5 ft (1.3 m)
Armament:
Guns 1 40-mm Bofors
Missile systems
4 Penguin SSM launchers
A/S weapons
none
Torpedo tubes
4 533-mm (21-in)
Aircraft
none
Radar and electronics:
Sonar:
Powerplant: 2 MTU diesels, delivering 7,200 bhp to two shafts
Speed: 32 knots
Range:

Crew: 18
Used only by: Norway
Notes: All the craft were commissioned in 1970 and 1971 after building in the Mandal yards of Båtservis Verft. The hull is based on that of the 'Storm' class gunboat.

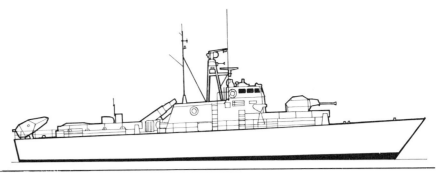

'Storm' class fast attack craft (missile) (20)

Class: *Storm* (P960), *Blink* (P961), *Glimt* (P962), *Skjold* (P963), *Trygg* (P964), *Kjekk* (P965), *Djerv* (P966), *Skudd* (P967), *Arg* (P968), *Steil* (P969), *Brann* (P970), *Tross* (P971), *Hvass* (P972), *Traust* (P973), *Brott* (P974), *Odd* (P975), *Pil* (P976), *Brask* (P977), *Rokk* (P978), *Gnist* (P979)
Displacement: 100 tons (101.6 tonnes) standard; 125 tons (127 tonnes) full load
Dimensions: Length 119 ft 9 in (36.5 m)
    Beam 20 ft 4 in (6.2 m)
    Draught 5 ft (1.5 m)
Armament:
Guns 1 76-mm
    1 40-mm Bofors
Missile systems
    6 Penguin SSM launchers
A/S weapons
    none
Torpedo tubes
    none
Aircraft
    none
Radar and electronics:
Sonar:
Powerplant: 2 MTU diesels, delivering 7,200 bhp to two shafts
Speed: 32 knots

Range:
Crew:
Used only by: Norway
Notes: Fourteen of the craft were built by Bergens MV, and the other six by Westermöen at Mandal. The commissioning dates of the class run from 1965 to 1968. The original *Storm* has been scrapped, and a new *Storm* is being produced as the last of the class.

Kongsberg Penguin

Type: naval surface-to-surface tactical guided missile
Guidance: inertial, plus infra-red terminal homing
Dimensions: Span 55$\frac{1}{10}$ in (1.4 m)
    Body diameter 11 in (28.0 cm)
    Length 10 ft (3.05 m)
Booster: solid-propellant rocket
Sustainer: solid-propellant rocket
Warhead: 265-lb (120-kg) semi-armour piercing high explosive
Weights: Launch 728 lb (330 kg)
    Burnt out
Performance: speed Mach 0.8; range 11$\frac{1}{2}$ miles (18.5 km)
Used also by: Greece, Sweden, Turkey
Notes: Launched in the direction of the target from a fixed container-launcher, the Penguin cruises at Mach 0.8 under inertial control until the passive infra-red seeker head picks up the target and homes the missile onto it. The possibility of an active infra-red seeker head is being considered. An air-to-surface Mark 2 version is under development. This will have a range of 17 miles (27 km).

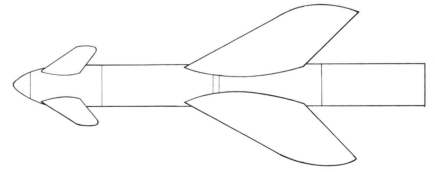

Oman

900 men

Corvettes:
1 Al Said
2 Wildervank

Patrol Forces:
7 Brooke 37.5-m PC
4 Vosper Thornycroft 22.9-m PC
3 Cheverton 8.2-m coastal PC

Amphibious Forces:
2 Cheverton 18.3-m Loadmaster
1 Cheverton 13.7-m Loadmaster
(1 LCL)

Auxiliaries:
1 transport
1 training ship
1 launch

'Al Said' class corvette (1)

Class: Al Said
Displacement: 900 tons (914.4 tonnes)
Dimensions: Length 203 ft 5 in (62.0 m)
Beam 35 ft 1 in (10.7 m)
Draught 9 ft 10 in (3.0 m)
Armament:
Guns 1 40-mm Bofors
Missile systems
none
A/S weapons
none
Torpedo tubes
none
Aircraft
none
Radar and electronics: Decca TM626 navigation radar
Sonar:
Powerplant: 2 Paxman Ventura diesels, delivering 2,740 bhp to two shafts
Speed:
Range:
Crew: 32 + 7 staff + 32 troops
Used only by: Oman
Notes: Al Said was built at Lowestoft by Brooke Marine, and commissioned in 1971 as the sultan's yacht. The gun was fitted later.

Brooke Marine 37.5-m fast attack craft (missile) (7)

Class: Al Bushra (B1), Al Mansur (B2), Al Nejah (B3), Al Wafi (B4), Al Fulk (B5), Al Aul (B6), Al Jabbar (B7)
Displacement: 135 tons (137.1 tonnes) standard; 153 tons (155.4 tonnes) full load
Dimensions: Length 123 ft (37.5 m)
Beam 22 ft 6 in (6.9 m)
Draught 5 ft 6 in (1.7 m)
Armament:
Guns 1 76-mm OTO Melara Compact (B4-7)
2 40-mm Bofors (B1-3)
1 20-mm (B4-7)
Missile systems
2 MM38 Exocet SSM launchers
A/S weapons
none
Torpedo tubes
none
Aircraft
none
Radar and electronics: Decca TM916 radar
Sonar:
Powerplant: 2 Paxman Ventura diesels, delivering 4,800 bhp to two shafts
Speed: 29 knots
Range: 3,300 miles (5,310 km) at 15 knots
Crew: 25
Used also by: Kenya
Notes: All craft have been built by Brooke Marine at Lowestoft, the first group of three commissioning in 1977, and the remaining four in 1977.

Pakistan

11,000 men

Cruiser:
1 Modified Dido (training ship)

Destroyers:
2 Gearing FRAM 1
1 Battle
1 CH
2 CR

Frigates:
2 Type 16

SS:
4 Daphné
6 SX404

Light Forces:
12 Shanghai II FAC(G)
4 Hu Chwan FAC(G)

Patrol Forces:
2 Hainan PC(+3)
1 Town PC
(? 50.6-m coastal PC)

Mine Warfare Forces:
7 MSC type coastal minesweepers

Auxiliaries:
1 survey ship
2 tankers
1 rescue ship
3 tugs
3 others

Aircraft:
SAR unit with 4 Alouette III, 6 Sea
King

Modified 'Dido' class cruiser (1)

Class: *Babur* (C84), ex-British *Diadem*
Displacement: 5,900 tons (5,994 tonnes) standard; 7,560 tons (7,681 tonnes) full load
Dimensions: Length 512 ft (156.1 m)
Beam 52 ft (15.8 m)
Draught 18 ft 6 in (5.6 m)
Armament:
Guns 8 5.25-in (133-mm) in twin turrets
14 40-mm Bofors
Missile systems
none
A/S weapons
none
Torpedo tubes
2 triple 21-in (533-mm)
Aircraft
none
Radar and electronics: Types 960 and 293 search, and Types 284 and 285 fire-control radars

Sonar:
Powerplant: 4 Admiralty boilers supplying steam to Parsons geared turbines, delivering 62,000 shp to four shafts
Speed: 20 knots
Range: 4,000 miles (6,440 km) at 18 knots
Crew: 588
Used only by: Pakistan
Notes: *Diadem* was built at Hebburn-on-Tyne by R. & W. Hawthorn Leslie between 1939 and 1942, and commissioned into British service in 1944. She was sold to Pakistan in 1956, and commissioned into Pakistani service in 1957. She was converted into a cadet training ship in 1961, although she retains an operational capability. Her sides are armoured to 3 in (76 mm), and her decks and turrets to 2 in (51 mm).

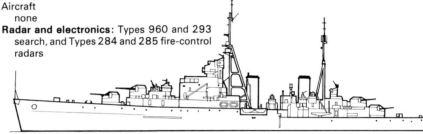

'Gearing FRAM I' class destroyer (2)

Class: *Tariq* (D165), ex-US *Wiltsie* (DD716); T Taimur (D166), ex-US *Epperson* (DD719)

Displacement: 2,425 tons (2,464 tonnes) standard; 3,500 tons (3,556 tonnes) full load
Dimensions: Length 390 ft 6 in (119.0 m)
Beam 40 ft 10 in (12.4 m)
Draught 19 ft (5.8 m)
Armament:
Guns 4 5-in (127-mm) in twin turrets
Missile systems
none
A/S weapons
2 triple 12.75-in (324-mm) Mark 32 tubes
Torpedo tubes
none

Aircraft
1 small ASW helicopter
Radar and electronics: SPS-10 surface search and SPS-40 air search radars
Sonar: SQS-23
Powerplant: 4 Babcock & Wilcox boilers supplying steam to 2 geared turbines, delivering 60,000 shp to two shafts
Speed: 30 knots
Range:
Crew: 274
Used also by: Brazil, Greece, South Korea, Spain, Taiwan, Turkey, USA
Notes: The ships were built by Federal Shipbuilding and Todd Pacific Shipyards in 1944 and 1945, being commissioned into US service in 1946 and 1945 respectively. They were sold to Pakistan in 1977.

'Battle' class destroyer (1)

Class: *Badr* (D161), ex-British *Gabbard*
Displacement: 2,325 tons (2,362 tonnes) standard; 3,361 tons (3,415 tonnes) full load
Dimensions: Length 379 ft (115.5 m)
Beam 40 ft 3 in (12.3 m)
Draught 17 ft (5.2 m)
Armament:
Guns 4 4.5-in (114-mm) in single turrets

7 40-mm Bofors in 2 twin and 3 single mountings
Missile systems
none
A/S weapons
1 Squid 3-barrel A/S mortar
Torpedo tubes
2 quadruple 21-in (533-mm)
Aircraft
none
Radar and electronics: Type 293 search and Type 275 fire-control

Sonar:
Powerplant: 2 Admiralty boilers supplying steam to Parsons geared turbines, delivering 50,000 shp to two shafts
Speed: 35¾ knots
Range: 6,000 miles (9,655 km) at 20 knots
Crew: 270
Used also by: Iran

Notes: *Gabbard* was built at Wallsend-on-Tyne by Swan, Hunter & Wigham Richardson between 1944 and 1945, and was commissioned into British service in 1946. She was sold to Pakistan in 1956, refitted with US funds and commissioned in Pakistani service in 1957. Her sistership *Khaibar*, ex-British *Cadiz*, was sunk in the Indo-Pakistan War of 1971.

'CH' class destroyer (1)

Class: *Shah Jahan* (D164), ex-British *Charity*
Displacement: 1,710 tons (1,737 tonnes) standard; 2,545 tons (2,586 tonnes) full load
Dimensions: Length 362 ft 8 in (110.5 m)
Beam 35 ft 8 in (10.9 m)
Draught 17 ft (5.2 m)
Armament:
Guns 3 4.5-in (114-mm) in single turrets
6 40-mm Bofors
Missile systems
none
A/S weapons
2 Squid 3-barrel DC mortars
Torpedo tubes
1 quadruple 21-in (533-mm)
Aircraft
none
Radar and electronics: Type 293 search and Type 275 fire-control radars
Sonar:
Powerplant: 2 Admiralty boilers supplying steam to Parsons geared turbines, delivering 40,000 shp to two shafts
Speed: 36¾ knots
Range: 5,600 miles (9,010 km) at 20 knots
Crew: 200
Used only by: Pakistan
Notes: *Charity* was built at Woolston by John I. Thornycroft between 1943 and 1944, and commissioned into British service in 1945. She was bought for Pakistan by the USA in 1958, at the same time as her sistership *Chivalrous*, which became *Taimur* and was scrapped in 1960.

'CR' class destroyer (2)

Class: *Alamgir* (D160), ex-British *Creole*; *Jahangir* (D162), ex-British *Crispin*, ex-*Craccher*
Displacement: 1,730 tons (1,758 tonnes) standard; 2,560 tons (2,601 tonnes) full load
Dimensions: Length 362 ft 9 in (110.5 m)
Beam 35 ft 8 in (10.9 m)
Draught 17 ft (5.2 m)
Armament:
Guns 3 4.5-in (114-mm) in single turrets
6 40-mm Bofors
Missile systems
none
A/S weapons
2 Squid 3-barrel DC mortars
Torpedo tubes
1 quadruple 21-in (533-mm)
Aircraft
none
Radar and electronics: Type 293 search, and Type 275 fire-control radars
Sonar: Types 170 and 174
Powerplant: 2 Admiralty boilers supplying steam to Parsons geared turbines, delivering 40,000 shp to two shafts
Speed: 36¾ knots
Range: 5,600 miles (9,010 km) at 20 knots
Crew: 200
Used only by: Pakistan
Notes: Both ships were built in the Isle of Wight by J. Samuel White of Cowes, in the period between 1944 and 1945, for commissioning into British service in 1946. The two were bought by Pakistan in 1956 and commissioned in 1958 after extensive refits. Funding was provided by the USA.

Type 16 frigate (1)

Class: *Tippu Sultan* (F260), ex-British *Onslow*, ex-*Pakenham*
Displacement: 1,800 tons (1,829 tonnes) standard; 2,300 tons (2,337 tonnes) full load
Dimensions: Length 345 ft (107.2 m)
Beam 35 ft (10.7 m)
Draught 15 ft 8 in (4.8 m)
Armament:
Guns 2 4-in (102-mm) in a twin mounting
5 40-mm Bofors
Missile systems
none
A/S weapons
2 Squid 3-barrel DC mortars
Torpedo tubes
4 21-in (533-mm)
Aircraft
none
Radar and electronics: Type 293 search radar
Sonar:
Powerplant: 2 Admiralty boilers supplying steam to Parsons geared turbines, delivering 40,000 shp to two shafts
Speed: 34 knots
Range:
Crew: 170
Used only by: Pakistan
Notes: The ship was built as an 'O' class destroyer in 1940 and 1941 and entered British service in 1941. She was bought with her sisterships *Tughril*, ex-British *Onslaught*, and *Tariq*, ex-British *Offa*, by Pakistan in 1949 and 1951. In 1957 *Tippu Sultan* and *Tughril* were converted into A/S frigates with US funding, and in 1959 *Tariq* was scrapped. *Tughril* was deleted in 1977.

'Daphné' class submarine (4)

Class: *Hangor* (S131), *Shushuk* (S132), *Mangro* (S133), *Ghazi* (S134), ex-Portuguese *Cachalote*
Displacement: 700 tons (711.2 tonnes) standard; 869 tons (882.9 tonnes) surfaced; 1,043 tons (1,060 tonnes) dived
Dimensions: Length 189 ft 7 in (57.8 m)
Beam 22 ft 4 in (6.8 m)
Draught 15 ft 1 in (4.6 m)
Armament:
Guns none
Missile systems
none
A/S weapons
none
Torpedo tubes
12 550-mm (21.7-in)
Aircraft
none
Radar and electronics:
Sonar:

Powerplant: diesel-electric propulsion, with 1,300 bhp on the surface and 1,600 bhp dived, with two shafts
Speed: 13 knots (surfaced); 15½ knots (dived)
Range:
Crew: 45
Used also by: France, Libya, Portugal, South Africa, Spain

Notes: S131 was built by the Arsenal de Brest, the next two by C. N. Ciotat at Le Trait, and the last by Dubigeon in Cherbourg. The boats were built between 1967 and 1970, and commissioned in 1970 (*Cachalote* in 1969). The Portuguese boat was bought by Pakistan in 1975.

'SX 404' class submarine (6)

Class: six boats
Displacement: 40 tons (40.6 tonnes)
Dimensions: Length 52 ft 6 in (16.0 m)
Beam 6 ft 7 in (2.0 m)
Draught
Armament:
Guns none
Missile systems
none
A/S weapons
none
Torpedo tubes
none
Aircraft
none
Radar and electronics:
Sonar:
Powerplant:
Speed: 11 knots (surfaced); 6½ knots (dived)
Range: 1,200 miles (1,930 km) on the surface; 60 miles (95 km) submerged
Crew: 4
Used only by: Pakistan
Notes: Built by Cosmos of Livorno, these boats are intended for clandestine operations, and can carry 12 passengers. The diving depth is only 328 ft (100 m).

'Town' class large patrol craft (1)

Class: *Rajshahi* (P140)
Displacement: 115 tons (116.8 tonnes) standard; 143 tons (145.3 tonnes) full load
Dimensions: Length 107 ft (32.6 m)
Beam 20 ft (6.1 m)
Draught 11 ft (3.4 m)
Armament:
Guns 2 40-mm Bofors in single mountings
Missile systems
none
A/S weapons
none
Torpedo tubes
none
Aircraft
none
Radar and electronics:
Sonar:
Powerplant: 2 MTU 12V 538 diesels, delivering 3,400 bhp to two shafts

Speed: 24 knots
Range:
Crew: 19
Used only by: Pakistan
Notes: *Rajshahi* is one of four 'Town' class craft built by Brooke Marine at Lowestoft in 1965, the other three having been sunk.

Panama

About 300 men of the coastguard service

Patrol Forces:
2 Vosper 31.4-m PC
2 AVR coastal PC
2 CG Utility type coastal PC

Auxiliaries:
1 Elk River LCM
3 LCM8

Papua-New Guinea

Marine part of the Papua–New Guinea Defence Force

Patrol Forces:
5 Attack PC

Amphibious Forces:
2 LCH

Paraguay

2,000, including naval air arm and 500 marines

River Defence Vessels:
2 Humaita

Corvettes:
3 Bouchard

Patrol Forces:
1 large PC
2 CG type coastal PC
6 701 coastal PC

Auxiliaries:
1 tender
3 tugs
1 transport/training ship
6 others

Aircraft:
4 Cessna U-206
2 Cessna 150
2 Bell 47G helicopters

'Humaita' class river defence vessel (2)

Class: *Paraguay* (C1), ex-*Commodor Meza*; *Humaita* (C2), ex-*Capitan Cabral*
Displacement: 636 tons (646.2 tonnes) standard; 865 tons (878.8 tonnes) full load
Dimensions: Length 231 ft (70.0 m)
Beam 35 ft (10.7 m)
Draught 5 ft 4 in (1.7 m)
Armament:
Guns 4 120-mmm
3 76-mm
2 40-mm
Missile systems

A/S weapons
  none
Torpedo tubes
  none
Aircraft
  none
Radar and electronics:
Sonar:

Powerplant: 2 boilers supplying steam to Parsons geared turbines, delivering 3,800 shp to two shafts
Speed: 17 knots
Range: 1,700 miles (2,735 km) at 16 knots
Crew: 86
Used only by: Paraguay
Notes: The two ships were built by Odero of Genoa, and commissioned in 1931.

'Bouchard' class corvette (3)

Class: *Nanawa* (M1), ex-Argentinian *Bouchard*; *Capitan Meza* (M2), ex-Argentinian *Parker*; *Teniente Farina* (M3), ex-Argentinian *Py*
Displacement: 450 tons (457.2 tonnes) standard; 650 tons (660.4 tonnes) full load
Dimensions: Length 197 ft (60.0 m)
          Beam 24 ft (7.3 m)
          Draught 8 ft 6 in (2.6 m)

Armament:
Guns 4 40-mm Bofors
  2 machine-guns
Missile systems
  none
A/S weapons
  none
Torpedo tubes
  none
Aircraft
  none
Radar and electronics:

Sonar:
Powerplant: 2 MAN diesels, delivering 2,000 bhp to two shafts
Speed: 16 knots
Range: 6,000 miles (9,655 km) at 12 knots
Crew: 70
Used also by: Argentina
Notes: These are ex-Argentinian minesweepers, and were commissioned into Argentinian service in 1937 and 1938. Four of the class were sold to Paraguay: 1964 (two) and 1967 (two). The type can carry mines.

Peru

14,000 men including naval air arm and 1,000 marines

Cruisers:
2 De Ruyter
2 Ceylon

Destroyers:
2 Daring
2 Fletcher

Frigates (FFG):
2 modified Lupo (+2)

Frigates (FF):
2 Cannon

SS:
2 Type 209 (+4)
2 Guppy 1A
4 Abtao

Light Forces:
(6 PR-72P FAC(M))

Patrol Forces:
2 Maranon river gunboats
2 Loreto river gunboats
1 river gunboat
3 river PC
4 coastal PC
4 lake PC

Amphibious Forces:
1 LST1
1 LST511-1152
2 LSM1

Auxiliaries:
(1 oceanographic ship)
2 survey vessels
1 research vessel
1 transport
4 replenishment tankers
3 support tankers
14 others

Naval Air Arm:
9 S-2A ASW
6 C-47 transports
2 F-27 transports
1 Piper Aztec transport
6 AB 212ASW helicopters
5 Bell 47G helicopters
10 Bell 206 helicopters
6 UH-1D/H helicopters
2 Alouette III helicopters
8 T-34 trainers

Marine Force:
1 bn

'De Ruyter' class guided missile cruiser (2)

Class: *Almirante Grau* (CL81), ex-Dutch *De Ruyter*; *Aguirre* (CL84), ex-Dutch *De Zeven Provincien*
Displacement: 9,529 tons (9,681 tonnes) standard; 11,850 tons (12,040 tonnes) full load
Dimensions: Length 615 ft 6 in (187.6 m)
          Beam 56 ft 9 in (17.3 m)
          Draught 22 ft (6.7 m)
Armament:
Guns 8 152-mm in twin turrets
  8 57-mm in twin mountings
  8 40-mm
Missile systems
  4 MM38 Exocet SSM launchers
A/S weapons
  none
Torpedo tubes
  none
Aircraft
  3 ASW helicopters
Radar and electronics: Hollandse Signaalapparaten LWO 1 search, SGR 104 height finder, DA 02 tactical, M20 main armament fire-control, and M45 secondary armament fire-control radars
Sonar:
Powerplant: 4 Werkspoor-Yarrow boilers supplying steam to 2 De Schelde-Parsons geared turbines, delivering 85,000 shp to two shafts
Speed: 32 knots
Range:
Crew: 49 + 904
Used only by: Peru
Notes: *De Ruyter* was built between 1939 and 1944 by Wilton-Fijenoord at Schiedam, and commissioned in 1953; *De Zeven Provincien* was built between 1939 and 1950 by Rotterdamse Droogdok Maatschappij, and commissioned in 1953. *De Ruyter* was bought by Peru in 1973, and *De Zeven Provincien* in 1976.

'Ceylon' class cruiser (2)

Class: *Coronel Bolognesi* (CL82), ex-British *Ceylon*; *Capitan Quiñones* (CL83), ex-British *Newfoundland*
Displacement: 8,781 tons (8,921 tonnes) standard, and 11,110 tons (11,288 tonnes) full load for *Coronel Bolognesi*; 8,800 tons (8,941 tonnes) standard, and 11,090 tons (11,267 tonnes) full load for *Capitan Quiñones*
Dimensions: Length 555 ft 6 in (169.3 m)
Beam 63 ft 7 in (19.4 m)
Draught 20 ft 6 in (6.2 m)
Armament:
Guns 9 6-in (152-mm) in triple turrets
8 4-in (102-mm) in twin turrets
18 (*Bolognesi*) or 12 (*Quiñones*) 40-mm
Missile systems
none
A/S weapons
none
Torpedo tubes
none
Aircraft
none

Radar and electronics: Types 960, 277 and 293 search, E-band main armament fire-control and I-band secondary armament fire-control radars
Sonar:
Powerplant: 4 Admiralty boilers supplying steam to Parsons geared turbines, delivering 72,500 shp to four shafts
Speed: 31½ knots
Range: 6,000 miles (9,655 km) at 13 knots
Crew: 766 (*Bolognesi*); 743 (*Quiñones*)
Used only by: Peru

Notes: *Ceylon* was built between 1939 and 1942 by Alexander Stephen & Sons at Govan, and commissioned into British service in 1943; *Newfoundland* was built between 1939 and 1941 by Swan, Hunter & Wigham Richardson at Wallsend-on-Tyne, and commissioned into British service in 1942. *Newfoundland* became the Peruvian *Almirante Grau* in 1959, and was renamed *Capitan Quiñones* in 1973; *Ceylon* became the Peruvian *Coronel Bolognesi* in 1960.

'Daring' class guided missile destroyer (2)

Class: *Palacios* (DD73), ex-British *Diana*; *Ferré* (DD74), ex-British *Decoy*
Displacement: 2,800 tons (2,845 tonnes) standard; 3,600 tons (3,658 tonnes) full load
Dimensions: Length 390 ft (118.9 m)
Beam 43 ft (13.1 m)
Draught 18 ft (5.5 m)
Armament:
Guns 4 4.5-in (114-mm) in twin turrets
2 40-mm
Missile systems
8 MM38 Exocet SSM launchers
A/S weapons
none
Torpedo tubes
none
Aircraft
provision for 1 helicopter
Radar and electronics: Plessey AWS-1 search and TSF fire-control radars
Sonar:

Powerplant: 2 Foster Wheeler boilers supplying steam to English Electric double-reduction geared turbines, delivering power to two shafts
Speed: 34 knots
Range: 3,000 miles (4,830 km) at 20 knots
Crew: 297

Used also by: Australia
Notes: Both ships were built at Scotstoun by Yarrow between 1946 and 1952, for commissioning into British service in 1954 and 1953 respectively. They were bought by Peru in 1969, and have since undergone two major reconstructions.

'Fletcher' class destroyer (2)

Class: *Villar* (DD71), ex-US *Benham* (DD796); *Guise* (DD72), ex-US *Isherwood* (DD520)
Displacement: 2,120 tons (2,154 tonnes) standard; 3,050 tons (3,099 tonnes) full load
Dimensions: Length 376 ft 3 in (114.7 m)
Beam 39 ft 9 in (12.1 m)
Draught 18 ft (5.5 m)
Armament:
Guns 4 (*Villar*) or 5 (*Guise*) 5-in (127-mm) in single turrets
6 3-in (76-mm) in twin turrets
Missile systems
none
A/S weapons
2 Hedgehogs
2 side-launching racks for A/S torpedoes
Torpedo tubes
1 quintuple 21-in (533-mm)
Aircraft
facilities for 1 helicopter
Radar and electronics: SPS 6 and SPS 10 search, GFCS 68 fire-control forward, and GFCS 56 aft radars

Sonar:
Powerplant: 4 Babcock & Wilcox boilers supplying steam to 2 General Electric geared turbines, delivering 60,000 shp to two shafts
Speed: 34 knots
Range: 5,000 miles (8,047 km) at 15 knots
Crew: 15+230
Used also by: Argentina, Brazil, Chile, Greece, Italy, Mexico, South Korea, Spain, Taiwan,
Turkey, West Germany
Notes: Both ships were built on Staten Island by the Bethlehem Steel Corporation in 1943 and 1942 respectively, for commissioning into US service in 1943. They were transferred to Peru in 1960 and 1961. Peru also has ex-US *La Vallette* (DD448) and ex-US *Terry* (DD513) for spares.

Modified 'Lupo' class guided missile frigate (4)

Class: *Meliton Carvajal, Manuel Villavicencio* and two others
Displacement: 2,208 tons (2,243 tonnes) standard; 2,500 tons (2,540 tonnes) full load
Dimensions: Length 347 ft 9 in (116.0 m)
Beam 39 ft 6 in (12.0 m)
Draught 12 ft (3.7 m)
Armament:
Guns 1 127-mm OTO Melara
4 40-mm Breda in twin turrets
Missile systems
2 twin Otomat SSM launchers
1 octuple Albatros SAM system
A/S weapons
2 105-mm Breda/Elsag 20-barrel rocket-launchers
2 triple 12.75-in (324-mm) Mark 32 tubes
Torpedo tubes
none
Aircraft
1 helicopter
Radar and electronics:
Sonar:
Powerplant: CODOG arrangement, with 2 General Electric/Fiat LM 2500 gas turbines, delivering 50,000 hp, and 2 Fiat A 230 diesels, delivering 7,800 hp, to two shafts
Speed: 35 knots
Range:
Crew:
Used only by: Peru
Notes: The first two ships are building at Riva Trigosa in the yards of CNR for commissioning in 1978 and 1979. The second pair will be commissioned in 1979 and 1980 after building at SIM's yards at Callao. The main difference between the Peruvian and Italian 'Lupo' class vessels is the inclusion of a helicopter and its facilities at the expense of 4 Otomat launchers in the Peruvian vessels.

Type 209 submarine (4)

Class: *Islay* (S45), *Arica* (S46) and two others (S47 and S48)
Displacement: 990 tons (1,006 tonnes) surfaced; 1,290 tons (1,311 tonnes) dived
Dimensions: Length 177 ft 2 in (54.0 m)
Beam 20 ft 4 in (6.2 m)
Draught
Armament:
Guns none
Missile systems
none
A/S weapons
none
Torpedo tubes
8 533-mm (21-in)
Aircraft
none
Radar and electronics:
Sonar: active and passive
Powerplant: diesel-electric, with 4 MTU Siemens diesel-generators and 1 Siemens

electric motor, delivering power to one shaft
Speed: 10 knots (surfaced); 22 knots (dived)
Range: 50 days' endurance
Crew: 31
Used also by: Argentina, Colombia, Ecuador, Iran, Turkey, Uruguay, Venezuela
Notes: The Type 209 boats are an Ingenieurkontor Lübeck (IKL) design, built by Howaldtswerke of Kiel. The two current boats were built between 1971 and 1974, and were commissioned in 1974 and 1975. Another two boats were ordered in 1976, and a further two in 1977.

'Guppy 1A' class submarine (2)

Class: *La Pedrera* (S49), ex-*Pabellon de Pica*, ex-US *Sea Poacher* (SS406); *Pacocha* (S50), ex-US *Atule* (SS403)
Displacement: 1,870 tons (1,900 tonnes) standard; 2,440 tons (2,479 tonnes) dived
Dimensions: Length 308 ft (93.8 m)
　　　　　　　Beam 27 ft (8.2 m)
　　　　　　　Draught 17 ft (5.2 m)
Armament:
Guns none

Missile systems
　none
A/S weapons
　none
Torpedo tubes
　10 21-in (533-mm)
Aircraft
　none
Radar and electronics:
Sonar:
Powerplant: 3 diesels, delivering 4,800 hp, and 2 electric motors, delivering 5,400 shp to two shafts

Speed: 18 knots (surfaced); 15 knots (dived)
Range:
Crew: 85
Used also by: Argentina, Turkey
Notes: Both boats were built in Portsmouth Navy Yard between 1943 and 1944, and were commissioned in US service in 1944. They were modernised in 1951, and sold to Peru in 1974. Peru also has ex-*Tench* (SS417) for spares.

'Abtao' class submarine (4)

Class: *Dos de Mayo* (S41), ex-*Lobo*; *Abtao* (S42), ex-*Tiburon*; *Angamos* (S43), ex-*Atun*; *Iquique* (S44), ex-*Merlin*
Displacement: 825 tons (838.2 tonnes) standard; 1,400 tons (1,422 tonnes) dived
Dimensions: Length 243 ft (74.1 m)
　　　　　　　Beam 22 ft (6.7 m)
　　　　　　　Draught 14 ft (4.3 m)
Armament:
Guns 1 5-in (127-mm) in *Dos de Mayo* and *Abtao*

Missile systems
　none
A/S weapons
　none
Torpedo tubes
　6 21-in (533-mm)
Aircraft
　none
Radar and electronics:
Sonar:
Powerplant: 2 General Motors Corporation 278A diesels, delivering 2,400 bhp, and electric motors delivering power to two shafts

Speed: 16 knots (surfaced); 10 knots (dived)
Range: 5,000 miles (8,047 km) at 10 knots surfaced
Crew: 40
Used only by: Peru
Notes: All four boats were built by the Electric Boat Division of General Dynamics at Groton in Connecticut, the first pair between 1952 and 1954, for commissioning in 1957. The design is based on that of the US 'Mackerel' class.

Philippines

20,000 men including 7,000 marines and naval engineers

Frigates:
1 Savage
4 Casco
3 Cannon

Corvettes:
2 Auk
8 PCE 827
1 Admirable

Patrol Forces:
6 Hamelin type PC (+14?)
4 PC461 PC
5 PGM PC
2 hydrofoil PC
2 PT32 hydrofoil PC
31 de Havilland type coastal PC (+49?)
15 Swift Marks 1 and 2 coastal PC
13 Improved Swift coastal PC
2 coastal PC

Mine Warfare Forces:
2 MSC coastal minesweepers

Amphibious Forces:
27 LST
4 LSM1
4 LSSL1
4 LSIL
11 LSM8
50 LCM6
7 LCVP
3 LCU

Auxiliaries:
3 repair ships
2 presidential yachts
6 tankers
4 survey vessels
others

Aircraft:
10 Islander (1 SAR sqn)
3 BO 105 helicopters

Marine Force:
6 marine bns (1 bde)

'Savage' class frigate (1)

Class: *Rajah Lakandula* (PS4), ex-South Vietnamese *Tran Hung Dao*, ex-US *Camp* (DER251)
Displacement: 1,590 tons (1,615 tonnes) standard; 1,850 tons (1,880 tonnes) full load
Dimensions: Length 306 ft (93.3 m)
　　　　　　　Beam 36 ft 7 in (11.2 m)
　　　　　　　Draught 14 ft (4.3 m)
Armament:
Guns 2 3-in (76-mm) in single turrets
Missile systems
　none
A/S weapons
　1 Mark 15 Hedgehog
　1 DC rack
　2 triple 12.75-in (324-mm) Mark 32 tubes
Torpedo tubes
　none
Aircraft
　none
Radar and electronics: SPS-28 and SPS-10 search, and SPG-34 fire-control radars
Sonar: SQS-31

Powerplant: Fairbanks Morse diesels, delivering 6,000 bhp to two shafts
Speed: 19 knots
Range:
Crew: about 170
Used also by: Tunisia

Notes: Built in Houston, Texas, by Brown Shipbuilding, *Camp* was commissioned as an escort vessel in 1943. During the Vietnamese War she was used for coastal patrol and interdiction by the US and South Vietnamese Navies before her acquisition by the Philippines in 1975.

'Casco' class frigate (4)

Class: *Andres Bonifacio* (PS7), ex-South Vietnamese *Ly Thoung Kiet*, ex-US *Chincoteague* (WHEC375); *Gregorio de Pilar* (PS8), ex-South Vietnamese *Ngo Kuyen*, ex-US *McCulloch* (WHEC386); *Diego Silang* (PS9), ex-South Vietnamese *Tran Quang Hai*, ex-US *Bering Strait* (WHEC382); *Francisco Dagahoy* (PS10), ex-South Vietnamese *Tran Binh Trong*, ex-US *Castle Rock* (WHEC383); and two others, ex-South Vietnamese *Tran Nhat Duat*, ex-US *Yukutat* (WHEC380) and ex-South Vietnamese *Tran Quoc Toan*, ex-US *Cook Inlet* (WHEC 384)
Displacement: 1,766 tons (1,794 tonnes) standard; 2,800 tons (2,845 tonnes) full load

Dimensions: Length 310 ft 9 in (94.7 m)
Beam 41 ft 1 in (12.5 m)
Draught 13 ft 6 in (4.1 m)
Armament:
Guns 1 5-in (127-mm)
1 or 2 81-mm mortars
2 or 3 40-mm
Missile systems
none
A/S weapons
none
Torpedo tubes
none
Aircraft
none
Radar and electronics: SPN-21 and SPS-29 search, and Mark 26 (as part of Mark 52 GFCS) fire-control radars
Sonar:

Powerplant: Fairbanks Morse diesels, delivering 6,080 bhp to two shafts
Speed: about 18 knots
Range:
Crew: about 200
Used also by: US Coast Guard
Notes: All but WHEC380 (Associated Shipbuilders) were built between 1942 and 1944 by Lake Washington Shipyard, and commissioned in 1943 and 1944 as US Navy seaplane tenders of the AVP type ('Barnegat' class). In 1946–8 they were transferred to the US Coast Guard as cutters. They were transferred to South Vietnam in 1971–2, and to the Philippines in 1975–6.

'PC 461' class large patrol craft (4)

Class: *Batangas* (PS24), ex-US *PC1134*; *Capiz* (PS27), ex-US *PC1564*; *Negros Oriental* (PS29), ex-US *PC1171*; *Nueva Viscaya* (PS80), ex-US *PC568*
Displacement: 280 tons (284.5 tonnes) standard; 450 tons (457.2 tonnes) full load
Dimensions: Length 173 ft 8 in (56.9 m)
Beam 23 ft (7.5 m)
Draught 10 ft 10 in (3.5 m)

Armament:
Guns 1 3-in (76-mm)
1 40-mm
20-mm (several, in single or twin mountings)
Missile systems
none
A/S weapons
DCs (except *Negros Oriental*)
Torpedo tubes
none
Aircraft
none
Radar and electronics:

Sonar:
Powerplant: General Motors Corporation diesels, delivering 2,800 bhp to two shafts
Speed: 20 knots
Range:
Crew: about 70
Used also by: Indonesia
Notes: Commissioned between 1942 and 1944, these vessels were used as patrol craft by the USA. *Nueva Viscaya* was formerly the USAF *Altus*, and *Negros Oriental* the French *L'Inconstant* and Cambodian *P636*.

PGM type large patrol craft (5)

Class: *Basilan* (PG60), ex-South Vietnamese *Hon Troc*; *Agusan* (PG61); *Catanduanes* (PG62); *Romlbon* (PG63); *Palawan* (PG64)
Displacement: 122 tons (124 tonnes) full load
Dimensions: Length 100 ft 4 in (32.9 m)
Beam 21 ft 1 in (6.9 m)
Draught 6 ft 11 in (2.3 m)
Armament:
Guns 1 40-mm
4 20-mm in twin mountings

2 or 4 0.5-in (12.7-mm) machine-guns
Missile systems
none
A/S weapons
none
Torpedo tubes
none
Aircraft
none
Radar and electronics:
Sonar:
Powerplant: 2 Mercedes-Benz diesels, delivering 1,900 bhp to two shafts

Speed: 17 knots
Range:
Crew: about 15
Used also by: Dominican Republic, Burma, Ethiopia, Turkey
Notes: PG61-64 were built by Tacoma Boatbuilding of Washington and commissioned into Philippine service in 1960. PG60 was built by Petersen Builders of Wisconsin and transferred to South Vietnam in 1967, and from there to the Philippines in 1975. The design is basically a lengthened version of the US Coast Guard 85-ft 'Cape' class.

Poland

22,500 (6,000 conscripts) including marines, plus 45,000 reservists

Destroyers (DDG):
1 SAM Kotlin

SS:
4 Whiskey

Light Forces:
12 Osa FAC(M)
15 Wisla FAC(T)
6 P-6 FAC(T)

Patrol Forces:
5 Obluze PC
8 Modified Obluze PC

Mine Warfare Forces:
12 Krogulec ocean minesweepers
12 T-43 ocean minesweepers
20 K-48 minesweeping boats

Amphibious Forces:
23 Polnocny LCT
15 LCP (+?)

Auxiliaries:
1 surveying vessel
1 intelligence vessel
6 training ships
1 training ship (sail)
3 tankers
2 salvage ships
others

Naval Aviation Regiment:
1 bomber/recce sqn with 10 Il-28
4 fighter sqns with 12 MiG-15, 38 MiG-17
2 helicopter sqns with c 25 Mi-1/2/4

There is also a coastguard service with nine large and three coastal PC

'SAM Kotlin' class guided missile destroyer (1)

Class: *Warszawa* (275), ex-Russian *Spravedlivy*
Displacement: 2,850 tons (2,896 tonnes) standard; 3,885 tons (3,947 tonnes) full load
Dimensions: Length 415 ft (126.5 m)
Beam 42 ft 4 in (12.9 m)
Draught 16 ft 1 in (4.9 m)
Armament:
Guns 2 130-mm in a twin turret
4 45-mm in a quadruple mounting
Missile systems
1 twin SA-N-1 'Goa' SAM launcher
A/S weapons
2 16-barrel MBU launchers
Torpedo tubes
1 quintuple 533-mm (21-in)
Aircraft
none
Radar and electronics: 'Head Net A' air search, 'Peel Group' SAM fire-control, 'Wasp Head' and 'Sun Visor B' gun fire-control and 'Hawk Screech' gun fire-control radars; 'High Pole B' IFF
Sonar: 'Hercules'
Powerplant: boilers supplying steam to geared turbines, delivering 72,000 shp to two shafts
Speed: 36 knots
Range: 5,500 miles (8,850 km) at 16 knots
Crew: 285
Used also by: USSR
Notes: The first 'Kotlin' class destroyer was laid down in 1954, and commissioned in 1955. The first missile-armed example, designated 'SAM Kotlin' by NATO, was seen in 1962. This vessel was transferred to Poland in 1970.

'Whiskey' class submarine (4)

Class: *Orzel* (292), *Sokol* (293), *Kondor* (294), *Bielik* (295), all ex-Russian boats
Displacement: 1,030 tons (1,046 tonnes) surfaced; 1,350 tons (1,372 tonnes) dived
Dimensions: Length 249 ft 4 in (76.0 m)
Beam 22 ft (6.7 m)
Draught 15 ft 1 in (4.6 m)
Armament:
Guns none
Missile systems
none
A/S weapons
none
Torpedo tubes
6 533-mm (21-in) with 12 torpedoes
Aircraft
none
Radar and electronics: 'Snoop Plate' surveillance radar; 'Stop Light' passive ECM fit
Sonar: 'Tamir'
Powerplant: diesel-electric, with 2 diesels, delivering 4,000 hp, and 2 electric motors, delivering 2,500 hp, to two shafts
Speed: 17 knots (surfaced); 15 knots (dived)
Range: 13,000 miles (20,925 km) at 8 knots surfaced
Crew: 60
Used also by: Albania, Bulgaria, China, Egypt, Indonesia, North Korea, USSR
Notes: The first of the class were laid down in 1950 and commissioned in 1951.

'Obluze' class large patrol craft (5)

Class: Nos 349, 350, 351, 352, 353
Displacement: 170 tons (172.7 tonnes)
Dimensions: Length 137 ft 9½ in (42.0 m)
Beam 19 ft 8 in (6.0 m)
Draught 6 ft 10½ in (2.1 m)
Armament:
Guns 4 30-mm in twin mountings
Missile systems
none
A/S weapons
2 DC racks
Torpedo tubes
none
Aircraft
none
Radar and electronics: 'Drum Tilt' fire-control radar
Sonar: Tamirio RN 231
Powerplant: 2 diesels, delivering power to two shafts
Speed: 20 knots
Range:
Crew:
Used only by: Poland
Notes: All five craft were built by Oksywie Shipyard and commissioned in 1965 and 1966.

Modified 'Obluze' class large patrol craft (8)

Class: Nos 301, 302, 303, 304, 305, 306, 307, 308
Displacement: 150 tons (152.4 tonnes)
Dimensions: Length 134 ft 6 in (41.0 m)
Beam 16 ft 8 in (6.0 m)
Draught 6 ft 6¾ in (2.0 m)
Armament:
Guns 4 30-mm in twin mountings
Missile systems
none
A/S weapons
2 DC racks
Torpedo tubes
none
Aircraft
none
Radar and electronics: 'Drum Tilt' fire-control radar
Sonar: Tamirio RN 231
Powerplant: 2 diesels, delivering power to two shafts
Speed: 20 knots
Range:
Crew:
Used only by: Poland
Notes: The Modified 'Obluze' class craft are slightly smaller than the original craft, and were built in the late 1960s.

'Oksywie' class large patrol craft (4)

Class: Nos 336, 337, 338, 339
Displacement: 170 tons (172.7 tonnes) standard
Dimensions: Length 134 ft 6 in (41.0 m)
Beam 19 ft 8 in (6.0 m)
Draught 6 ft 6¾ in (2.0 m)
Armament:
Guns 2 37-mm in single mountings
4 12.7-mm machine-guns
Missile systems
none
A/S weapons
2 DC racks
Torpedo tubes
none
Aircraft
none
Radar and electronics:
Sonar: 'Tamir'
Powerplant: diesels, delivering power to two shafts
Speed: 20 knots
Range:
Crew:
Used only by: Poland
Notes: The craft were built between 1962 and 1964, and are based on the hull design of German World War II 'R' craft.

'Krogulec' class ocean mine-sweeper (12)

Class: *Orlik* (643), *Krogulec* (644), *Jastrab* (645), *Kormoran* (646), *Czapla* (647), *Albatros* (648), *Pelikan* (649), *Tukan* (650), *Kania* (651), *Jaskolka* (652), *Zuraw* (653), *Czalpa* (654)
Displacement: 500 tons (508 tonnes)

Dimensions: Length 190 ft 3½ in (58.0 m)
Beam 27 ft 6½ in (8.4 m)
Draught 8 ft 2½ in (2.5 m)
Armament:
Guns 6 25-mm in twin mountings
Missile systems
    none
A/S weapons
    none
Torpedo tubes
    none
Aircraft
    none

Radar and electronics:
Sonar:
Powerplant: diesels, delivering power to two shafts
Speed: 16 knots
Range:
Crew:
Used only by: Poland
Notes: All 12 ships were built at Gdynia by the Stocznia Yard, and commissioned between 1963 and 1967.

Portugal

14,000 men including 2,500 marines

Frigates:
4 Comandante João Belo
3 Almirante Pereira da Silva
10 João Coutinho

SS:
3 Daphné

Patrol Forces:
10 Cacine PC
2 Dom Aleixo coastal PC
5 Albatroz coastal PC
1 coastal PC

Mine Warfare Forces:
4 Sao Roque coastal minesweepers

Amphibious Forces:
1 Bombarda LCT
9 LDM400 LCM
3 LDM100 LCM
1 LDP200 LCA

Auxiliaries:
(1 oceanographic vessel)
1 surveying vessel
1 replenishment tanker
1 training ship (sail)
4 others

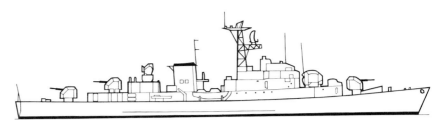

'Comandante João Belo' class frigate (4)

Class: *Comandante João Belo* (F480), *Comandante Hermenegildo Capelo* (F481), *Comandante Roberto Ivens* (F482), *Comandante Sacadura Cabral* (F483)
Displacement: 1,990 tons (2,022 tonnes) standard; 2,230 tons (2,266 tonnes) full load
Dimensions: Length 337 ft 11 in (103.0 m)
Beam 37 ft 8¾ in (11.5 m)
Draught 14 ft 6 in (4.42 m)
Armament:
Guns 3 100-mm in single mountings
2 40-mm in single mountings
Missile systems
none
A/S weapons
1 305-mm 4-barrel A/S mortar
Torpedo tubes
2 triple 550-mm (21.7-in) tubes
Aircraft
none
Radar and electronics: Thomson-CSF DRBV 22A search, DRBV 50 tactical, DRBC 31D fire-control, and Decca RM 316 navigation radars
Sonar: SQS-17A search, and DUBA-3A attack
Powerplant: SEMT-Pielstick diesels, delivering 18,760 bhp to two shafts
Speed: 25 knots
Range: 4,500 miles (7,240 km) at 15 knots; 2,300 miles (3,700 km) at 25 knots
Crew: 14+186
Used only by: Portugal
Notes: The four ships were built between 1965 and 1968 by Ateliers et Chantiers de Nantes, and commissioned between 1967 and 1969. The design is modelled closely on that of the French 'Commandant Rivière' class.

'Almirante Pereira da Silva' class frigate (3)

Class: *Almirante Pereira da Silva* (F472), ex-US *DE1039*; *Almirante Gago Countinho* (F473), ex-US *DE1042*; *Almirante Magalhães Correa* (F474), ex-US *DE1046*
Displacement: 1,450 tons (1,473 tonnes) standard; 1,914 tons (1,945 tonnes) full load
Dimensions: Length 314 ft 7 in (95.9 m)
Beam 36 ft 8 in (11.18 m)
Draught 17 ft 6 in (5.33 m)
Armament:
Guns 4 3-in (76-mm) in twin mountings
Missile systems
none
A/S weapons
2 375-mm Bofors 4-barrel A/S rocket-launchers
2 triple 12.75-in (324-mm) Mark 32 tubes
Torpedo tubes
none

Aircraft
none
Radar and electronics: MLA-1b search, Type 978 tactical, AN/SPG-34 main armament fire-control, and Decca RM 316P navigation radars
Sonar: A/SQS-30/32A search, AN/SQA-10A variable-depth, and DUBA-3A attack
Powerplant: 2 Foster Wheeler boilers supplying steam to De Laval double-reduction geared turbines, delivering 20,000 shp to one shaft
Speed: 27 knots
Range: 3,220 miles (5,180 km) at 15 knots
Crew: 12+154
Used only by: Portugal
Notes: The ships of this class were built at Estaleiros Navais in Lisbon (F472 and F473), and at Estaleiros Navais de Viana do Castelo, between 1962 and 1966, with commissioning dates in 1966, 1967, and 1968. The design is based on that of the 'Dealey' class of US destroyer escorts.

'Joao Coutinho' class frigate (10)

Class: *Antonio Enes* (F471), *Joao Countinho* (F475), *Jacinto Candido* (F476), *General Pereira d'Eca* (F477), *Augusto de Castilho* (F484), *Honorio Barreto* (F485), *Baptista de Andrade* (F486), *Joao Roby* (F487), *Alfonso Cerqueira* (F488), *Oliveira E. Carmo* (F489)

Displacement: 1,203 tons (1,222 tonnes) standard; 1,380 tons (1,402 tonnes) full load

Dimensions: Length 277 ft 6½ in (84.6 m)
Beam 33 ft 9½ in (10.3 m)
Draught 11 ft 9½ in (3.6 m)

Armament:
Guns 2 76-mm in a twin turret (first six)
2 40-mm (first six)
Missile systems
none
A/S weapons
1 Hedgehog
2 DC racks
2 DCTs
Torpedo tubes
none
Aircraft
none

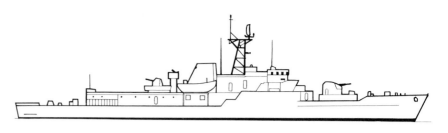

Radar and electronics: MLA-1b air search, AN/SPG-34 gun fire-control, and Decca TM 626 navigation radars
Sonar:
Powerplant: 2 Pielstick OEW diesels, delivering 10,560 bhp to two shafts
Speed: 24½ knots

Range: 5,900 miles (9,495 km) at 18 knots
Crew: 9+91
Used only by: Portugal
Notes: Three of the class were built by Empresa Nacional Bazan, in Spain, and 475, 476 and 477 by Blohm und Voss of Hamburg. The class was built between 1968 and 1974, with commissioning dates between 1970 and 1975.

'Daphné' class submarine (3)

Class: *Albacora* (S163), *Barracuda* (S164), *Delfin* (S166)

Displacement: 700 tons (711.2 tonnes) standard; 869 tons (882.9 tonnes) surfaced; 1,043 tons (1,060 tonnes) dived

Dimensions: Length 189 ft 7½ in (57.8 m)
Beam 22 ft 3½ in (6.8 m)
Draught 15 ft 1 in (4.6 m)

Armament:
Guns none
Missile systems
none

A/S weapons
none
Torpedo tubes
12 550-mm (21.7-in)
Aircraft
none
Radar and electronics:
Sonar:
Powerplant: SEMT-Pielstick diesels, delivering 1,300 bhp, and electric motors delivering 1,600 hp to two shafts
Speed: 13¼ knots (surfaced); 16 knots (dived)

Range: 2,710 miles (4,360 km) at 12½ knots surfaced; 2,130 miles (3,430 km) at 10 knots snorting
Crew: 5+45
Used also by: France, Libya, Pakistan, South Africa, Spain
Notes: The three boats were built by Dubigeon-Normandie between 1965 and 1968, and commissioned into Portuguese service in 1967, 1968 and 1969. Their sistership *Cachalote* was sold to Pakistan in 1975.

'Cacine' class large patrol craft (10)

Class: *Cacine* (P1140), *Cunene* (P1141), *Mandovi* (P1142), *Rovuma* (P1143), *Cuanza* (P1144), *Geba* (P1145), *Zaire* (P1146), *Zambeze* (P1147), *Limpopo* (P1160), *Sava* (P1161)

Displacement: 292.5 tons (297.2 tonnes) standard; 310 tons (315 tonnes) full load

Dimensions: Length 144 ft 4 in (44.0 m)
Beam 25 ft 3 in (7.7 m)
Draught 7 ft 2½ in (2.2 m)

Armament:
Guns 2 40-mm in single mountings
Missile systems
1 37-mm 32-barrel rocket-launcher
A/S weapons
none
Torpedo tubes
none
Aircraft
none

Radar and electronics: KH 975 radar
Sonar:
Powerplant: 2 MTU 12V 538 diesels, delivering 4,000 bhp to two shafts
Speed: 20 knots

Range: 4,400 miles (7,080 km) at 12 knots
Crew: 3+30
Used only by: Portugal

Notes: Six of the craft were built by the Arsenal do Alfeite, and the other four (1144, 1145, 1146, 1147) by Estaleiros Navais do Mendogo. The craft were commissioned between 1969 and 1973.

Qatar

400 men of the Marine Police Division of the Qatar Police Force

Patrol Forces:
6 Vosper Thornycroft 33.4-m PC
2 22.5-m coastal PC
2 Keith Nelson 13.5-m coastal PC
25 Fairey Spear coastal PC
2 Fairey Interceptor rescue craft

Vosper Thornycroft 33.4-m type large patrol craft (6)

Class: *Barzan* (Q11), *Hwar* (Q12), *That Assuari* (Q13), *Al Wusaail* (Q14), *Fateh-al-Khair* (Q15), *Tariq* (Q16)
Displacement: 120 tons (121.9 tonnes)
Dimensions: Length 109 ft 8 in (33.4 m)
Beam 21 ft (6.4 m)
Draught 5 ft 6 in (1.7 m)
Armament:
Guns 2 20-mm in single mountings
Missile systems
none
A/S weapons
none
Torpedo tubes
none
Aircraft
none
Radar and electronics:
Sonar:
Powerplant: 2 diesels, delivering 4,000 hp to two shafts
Speed: 27 knots
Range:
Crew: 25
Used only by: Qatar
Notes: All five craft were built by Vosper Thornycroft and commissioned in 1975 and 1976.

Romania

10,500 men (5,000 conscripts) plus 20,500 reservists

Corvettes:
3 Poti

Light Forces:
18 Shanghai FAC(G)
5 Osa FAC(M)
10 Hu Chwan FAC(T)
13 P-4 FAC(T)

Patrol Forces:
3 Kronshtadt PC
9 river PC
10 VG coastal PC
9 SM165 coastal PC

Mine Warfare Forces:
4 M40 coastal minesweepers
10 T-301 inshore minesweepers
8 TR-40 minesweeping boats

Auxiliaries:
2 tugs
1 training ship (sail)
others

Aircraft:
4 Mi-4 helicopters

Sabah

Patrol Forces:
4 coastal PC

Auxiliaries:
1 yacht

St Kitts

Marine detachment of police force

Patrol Forces:
1 Fairey Spear coastal PC

St Lucia

Patrol Forces:
1 Brooke coastal PC

St Vincent

Marine detachment of police force

Patrol Forces:
1 Brooke coastal PC

Saudi Arabia

1,500 men

Corvettes (missile):
(9 720-ton)

Light Forces:
(4 FAC(M))
3 Jaguar FAC(T)

Patrol Forces:
1 USCG type PC
8 P32 type coastal PC
12 Rapier coastal PC
2 12.2-m coastal PC
43 C-80 coastal PC
10 Fairey Huntress coastal PC
20 6.1-m coastal PC
8 SRN-6 hovercraft

Mine Warfare Forces:
4 MSC322 coastal minesweepers

Auxiliaries:
4 LCU
3 others
(4 landing craft)

Fast attack craft (missile) (4)

Class: *Badr* (612), *Al Yarmuk* (614), *Hitteen* (616), *Tabuk* (618)
Displacement: 320 tons (325 tonnes)
Dimensions: Length 184 ft 5 in (56.2 m)
　　　　　　 Beam 25 ft (7.6 m)
　　　　　　 Draught 5 ft 9 in (1.8 m)
Armament:
Guns 1 76-mm OTO Melara
　　 1 81-mm mortar
　　 2 40-mm mortar
　　 2 20-mm
Missile systems
　　 2 twin Harpoon SSM launchers
A/S weapons
　　 none
Torpedo tubes
　　 none
Aircraft
　　 none
Radar and electronics: AN/SPS-60 surface warning, AN/SPS-40B air warning, and Mark 92 fire-control radars
Sonar:
Powerplant: CODOG arrangement, with 1 General Electric gas turbine, delivering 16,500 hp, and 2 diesels, delivering 1,500 hp

Speed: 38 knots (gas turbine); 18 knots (diesels)
Range:
Crew: 35
Used only by: Saudi Arabia
Notes: The craft are building in the USA and are expected in service in 1980 and 1981.

Senegal

350 men

Patrol Forces:
3 P48 PC
2 VC type coastal PC
12 Vosper 13.7-m coastal PC
1 Fairey Lance coastal PC
1 Fairey Spear coastal PC
2 Fairey Huntress coastal PC
1 trawler type PC

Amphibious Forces:
1 EDIC LCT
2 LCM6

Auxiliaries:
1 tender

'P 48' class large patrol craft (3)

Class: *Saint Louis, Popenguine, Podor*
Displacement: 250 tons (254 tonnes) full load
Dimensions: Length 155 ft 10 in (47.5 m)
　　　　　　 Beam 23 ft 3½ in (7.1 m)
　　　　　　 Draught 8 ft 2½ in (2.5 m)
Armament:
Guns 2 40-mm in single mountings
Missile systems
　　 none
A/S weapons
　　 none
Torpedo tubes
　　 none
Aircraft
　　 none
Radar and electronics:

Sonar:
Powerplant: 2 MGO diesels, delivering 2,400 bhp to one shaft
Speed: 18½ knots
Range: 2,000 miles (3,220 km) at 18 knots
Crew: 25
Used also by: Cameroon, Ivory Coast, Malagasy Republic, Tunisia
Notes: *Saint Louis* was built by Chantiers Navales Franco-Belges and commissioned in 1971. The other two were built by the Société Français de Constructions Navales and commissioned in 1974 and 1977 respectively.

Sierra Leone

150 men

Light Forces:
3 Shanghai II FAC(G)

Singapore

3,000 men

Light Forces:
6 Lürssen TNC-48 FAC(M)
3 Vosper Thornycroft Type A FAC(G)
3 Vosper Thornycroft Type B FAC(G)

Patrol Forces:
1 Ford PC
1 large PC

Mine Warfare Forces:
2 Redwing coastal minesweepers

Amphibious Forces:
6 LST511-1152
6 landing craft

There is also a marine police force with four coastal PC

'TNC 48' class fast attack craft (missile) (6)

Class: *Sea Wolf* (P76), *Sea Lion* (P77), *Sea Dragon* (P78), *Sea Tiger* (P79), *Sea Hawk* (P80), *Sea Scorpion* (P81)
Displacement: 230 tons (233.7 tonnes)
Dimensions: Length 157 ft 6 in (48.0 m)
Beam 23 ft (7.0 m)
Draught 7 ft 6½ in (2.3 m)
Armament:
Guns 1 57-mm
1 40-mm
Missile systems
5 Gabriel SSM launchers
A/S weapons
none
Torpedo tubes
none
Aircraft
none
Radar and electronics:
Sonar:
Powerplant: 4 MTU diesels, delivering 14,400 hp to four shafts
Speed: 34 knots
Range:
Crew: 40
Used also by: Thailand, Turkey
Notes: The designers, Lürssen Werft of Vegesack, built the first pair, and the other four were built by Singapore Shipbuilding & Engineering. The first pair were commissioned in 1972, the second pair in 1974 and the third pair in 1975.

Vosper Thornycroft 'Type A' fast attack craft (gun) (3)

Class: *Independence* (P69), *Freedom* (P70), *Justice* (P72)
Displacement: 100 tons (101.6 tonnes) standard
Dimensions: Length 109 ft 8 in (33.5 m)
Beam 21 ft (6.4 m)
Draught 5 ft 7 in (1.8 m)
Armament:
Guns 1 40-mm
1 20-mm
Missile systems
none
A/S weapons
none
Torpedo tubes
none
Aircraft
none
Radar and electronics:
Sonar:
Powerplant: 2 MTU 16V 538 diesels, delivering 7,200 bhp
Speed: 32 knots
Range: 1,100 miles (1,770 km) at 15 knots
Crew: 19 to 22
Used only by: Singapore
Notes: The lead craft was built by the designers, Vosper Thornycroft, and the other two by Vosper Thornycroft Private Ltd of Singapore. The first craft was commissioned in 1970, the other two in 1971.

Vosper Thornycroft 'Type B' fast attack craft (gun) (3)

Class: *Sovereignty* (P71), *Daring* (P73), *Dauntless* (P74)
Displacement: 100 tons (101.6 tonnes) standard; 130 tons (132.1 tonnes) full load
Dimensions: Length 109 ft 8 in (33.5 m)
Beam 21 ft (6.4 m)
Draught 5 ft 7 in (1.8 m)
Armament:
Guns 1 76-mm Bofors
1 20-mm
Missile systems
none
A/S weapons
none
Torpedo tubes
none
Aircraft
none
Radar and electronics:
Sonar:
Powerplant: 2 MTU 16V 538 diesels, delivering 7,200 bhp
Speed: 32 knots
Range: 1,100 miles (1,770 km) at 15 knots
Crew: 3+16
Used only by: Singapore
Notes: The lead craft was built by the designers, Vosper Thornycroft, and the other two by Vosper Thornycroft Private Ltd of Singapore. All three craft were commissioned in 1971.

Somali Republic

500 men

Light Forces:
3 Osa II FAC(M)
4 P-6 FAC(T)

Patrol Forces:
4 Mol PC
6 Poluchat PC

Amphibious Forces:
1 Polnocny LCT
4 T-4 LCM

South Africa

5,500 men (1,400 conscripts)

Destroyer:
1 W

Frigates:
3 President

SS:
3 Daphné

Light Forces:
6 Reshef

Patrol Forces:
5 Ford PC

Mine Warfare Forces:
10 Ton coastal minesweepers

Auxiliaries:
2 surveying vessels
1 fleet replenishment ship
10 others

'W' class destroyer (1)

Class: *Jan van Riebeeck* (D378), ex-British *Wessex*, ex-British *Zenith*
Displacement: 2,205 tons (2,240 tonnes) standard; 2,850 tons (2,896 tonnes) full load
Dimensions: Length 362 ft 9 in (110.6 m)
Beam 35 ft 8 in (10.9 m)
Draught 17 ft 1 in (5.2 m)
Armament:
Guns 4 4-in (102-mm) in twin turrets
2 40-mm in single mountings
Missile systems
none
A/S weapons
2 DCTs
2 DC racks
2 triple 12.75-in (324-mm) Mark 32 tubes
Torpedo tubes
none
Aircraft
2 small helicopters
Radar and electronics: Type 293 search and I-band (NSG NA 9 system) fire-control radars
Sonar:
Powerplant: 2 Admiralty boilers supplying steam to 2 Parsons geared turbines, delivering 40,000 shp to two shafts
Speed: 36 knots
Range: 3,260 miles (5,245 km) at 14 knots
Crew: 11+181
Used only by: South Africa
Notes: *Wessex* was built between 1942 and 1943 by Fairfield Shipbuilding & Engineering at Govan on the Clyde, and commissioned into British service in 1944. She was bought by South Africa in 1950, and was extensively modernised in 1964–6.

'President' class frigate (3)

Class: *President Pretorius* (F145), *President Steyn* (F147), *President Kruger* (F150)
Displacement: 2,250 tons (2,286 tonnes) standard; 2,800 tons (2,849 tonnes) full load
Dimensions: Length 370 ft (112.8 m)
Beam 41 ft 1 in (12.5 m)
Draught 17 ft 1 in (5.2 m)
Armament:
Guns 2 4.5-in (114-mm) in a twin turret
2 40-mm Bofors in single mountings
Missile systems
none
A/S weapons
1 Limbo 3-barrel mortar
2 triple 12.75-in (324-mm) Mark 32 tubes
Torpedo tubes
none
Aircraft
1 small helicopter
Radar and electronics: Thomson-CSF Jupiter surveillance, Type 293 air and surface search, and Elsag NA 9C fire-control radars
Sonar:
Powerplant: 2 Babcock & Wilcox boilers supplying steam to 2 double-reduction geared turbines, delivering 30,000 shp to two shafts
Speed: 30 knots
Range: 4,500 miles (7,240 km) at 12 knots
Crew: 13+190
Used only by: South Africa
Notes: The three ships were originally built as 'Rothesay' class frigates, the first and last by Yarrow at Scotstoun, and the second by Alex Stephen & Sons at Yarrow, in the period between 1959 and 1962. The ships were commissioned in 1962, 1963 and 1964. They have been quite extensively modernised in South African yards.

'A69' class frigate (2)

Class: two ships, ex-French *Lieutenant de Vaisseau Le Hénaff* and ex-French *Commandant de l'Herminier*
Displacement: 950 tons (965.2 tonnes) standard; 1,170 tons (1,189 tonnes) full load
Dimensions: Length 262 ft 5½ in (80.0 m)
Beam 33 ft 9½ in (10.3 m)
Draught 9 ft 10 in (3.0 m)
Armament:
Guns 1 100-mm
2 20-mm
Missile systems
2 MM38 Exocet SSM launchers
A/S weapons
1 375-mm Mark 54 rocket-launcher
4 533-mm (21-in) tubes for L3 or L5 torpedoes
Torpedo tubes
none
Aircraft
none
Radar and electronics:
Sonar:
Powerplant: 2 SEMT-Pielstick PC2V diesels, delivering 11,000 bhp to two shafts
Speed: 24 knots
Range: 4,500 miles (7,240 km) at 15 knots
Crew: 5+70
Used also by: France
Notes: Both ships were built by Lorient Naval Dockyard between 1976 and 1977, and sold to South Africa whilst still under construction. They are due to enter service in 1978, and there are reports that South Africa has ordered another two of the same class. A UN embargo on arms sales to South Africa has prevented delivery.

'Daphné' class submarine (3)

Class: *Maria van Riebeeck* (S97), *Emily Hobhouse* (S98), *Johanna van der Merve* (S99)
Displacement: 850 tons (863.6 tonnes) surfaced; 1,040 tons (1,057 tonnes) dived
Dimensions: Length 190 ft 3 in (58.0 m)
Beam 22 ft 2½ in (6.8 m)
Draught 15 ft 5 in (4.7 m)
Armament:
Guns none
Missile systems
none
A/S weapons
none
Torpedo tubes
12 550-mm (21.7-in)
Aircraft
none
Radar and electronics:
Sonar:
Powerplant: SEMT-Pielstick diesel-electric, with diesels delivering 1,300 bhp and electric motors 1,600 hp to two shafts
Speed: 16 knots (surfaced and dived)
Range: 4,500 miles (7,240 km) at 5 knots snorting
Crew: 6+41
Used also by: France, Libya, Pakistan, Portugal, Spain
Notes: The three boats were built by Dubigeon-Normandie at Nantes between 1968 and 1970, and were commissioned in 1970 and 1971.

'Agosta' class submarine (2)

Class: two boats
Displacement: 1,470 tons (1,494 tonnes) surfaced; 1,790 tons (1,819 tonnes) dived
Dimensions: Length 222 ft 9 in (67.9 m)
Beam 22 ft 2½ in (6.8 m)
Draught 17 ft 0½ in (5.2 m)
Armament:
Guns none
Missile systems
none
A/S weapons
none
Torpedo tubes
4 550-mm (21.7-in) with 20 torpedoes
Aircraft
none
Radar and electronics:
Sonar:
Powerplant: diesel-electric, with 2 SEMT-Pielstick diesels, developing 3,600 bhp, and 1 main electric motor, delivering 4,600 bhp to one shaft

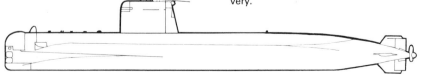

Speed: 12 knots (surfaced); 20 knots (dived)
Range: 9,000 miles (14,485 km) at 9 knots surfaced; 350 miles (565 km) at 3½ knots dived
Crew: 50
Used also by: France, Spain
Notes: The two boats are on order from Dubigeon-Normandie of Nantes, for delivery in 1978 and 1979. A UN embargo on arms sales to South Africa has prevented delivery.

South Korea

32,000 men, plus 25,000 reservists

Destroyers:
2 Gearing FRAM 1
2 Gearing FRAM II
2 Allen M. Sumner FRAM II
3 Fletcher

Frigates:
1 Rudderow
6 Charles Lawrence and Crossley
(1 + 3 1,600-ton)

Corvettes:
3 Auk
3 PCE827

Light Forces:
7 Tacoma PSMM 5 FAC(M)
1 Asheville FAC(M) (+4)

Patrol Forces:
5 CPIC type FAC(P)
8 Cape PC
2 32.7-mm PC
10 Schoolboy coastal PC
9 Sewart 21.3-m coastal PC
4 Sewart 13.1-m coastal PC

Mine Warfare Forces:
8 MSC268 and 294 coastal minesweepers
1 MSB minesweeping boat

Amphibious Forces:
3 LST1-510
5 LST511-1152
1 Elk River LSMR
11 LSM1
1 LCU501

Auxiliaries:
1 repair ship
6 supply ships
1 tanker
3 harbour tankers
others

There is also a coastguard service
operating about 25 vessels

'Gearing FRAM I' and 'Gearing FRAM II' class destroyer (4)

Class: *Kwang Ju* (DD90), ex-US *Richard E. Kraus* (DD849); *Chung Buk* (DD95), ex-US *Chevalier* (DD805); *Jeong Buk* (DD96), ex-US *Everett F. Larson* (DD830); *Taejon* (DD99), ex-US *New* (DD818)
Displacement: 2,425 tons (2,464 tonnes) standard; about 3,500 tons (3,556 tonnes) full load
Dimensions: Length 390 ft 6 in (119.0 m)
Beam 40 ft 10 in (12.4 m)
Draught 19 ft (5.8 m)
Armament:
Guns 6 5-in (127-mm) in twin turrets
  1 20-mm Vulcan rotary cannon (DDs 95 and 96)
  2 30-mm Emerlec in a twin mounting in *Jeong Buk*
Missile systems
  none
A/S weapons
  2 Mark 11 Hedgehogs
  2 triple 12.75-in (324-mm) Mark 32 tubes
Torpedo tubes
  none

Aircraft
  1 small helicopter
Radar and electronics: SPS-10 search and SPS-40 air search radars
Sonar: SQS-29 series
Powerplant: 4 Babcock & Wilcox boilers supplying steam to 2 General Electric geared turbines, delivering 60,000 shp to two shafts
Speed: 34 knots
Range:
Crew: about 275
Used also by: Argentina, Brazil, Greece, Pakistan, Spain, Taiwan, Turkey, USA
Notes: Three of the ships were built by Bath Iron Works, of Bath (Maine), and the last by Consolidated Steel Corporation, in the period between 1943 and 1946, for commissioning into US service in 1945 and 1946. In 1949 they were modified into radar picket destroyers, and in the 1950s the first two were modernised to FRAM II standard, and the second two to FRAM I standard. The first pair were transferred in 1972, and the second pair in 1977.

'Allen M. Sumner FRAM II' class destroyer (2)

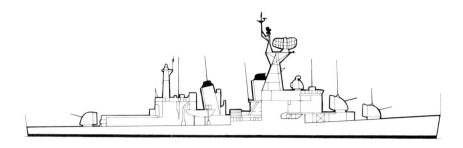

Class: *Dae Gu* (DD95), ex-US *Wallace L. Lind* (DD703); *In Cheon* (DD98), ex-US *De Haven* (DD727)
Displacement: 2,200 tons (2,235 tonnes) standard; 3,320 tons (3,373 tonnes) full load
Dimensions: Length 376 ft 6 in (114.8 m)
Beam 40 ft 10 in (12.4 m)
Draught 19 ft (5.8 m)
Armament:
Guns 6 5-in (127-mm) in twin turrets
1 20-mm Vulcan rotary cannon
Missile systems
none
A/S weapons
2 Mark 11 Hedgehogs
2 triple 12.75-in (324-mm) Mark 32 tubes
Torpedo tubes
none
Aircraft
1 small helicopter

Radar and electronics: SPS-10 surface search and SPS-40 air search (*Dae Gu*) or SPS-37 air search (*In Cheon*) radars
Sonar: hull-mounted SQS-29 and variable-depth SQA-10
Powerplant: 4 Babcock & Wilcox boilers supplying steam to 2 General Electric geared turbines, delivering 60,000 shp to two shafts
Speed: 34 knots
Range:

Crew: about 275
Used also by: Brazil, Chile, Colombia, Iran, Turkey, Venezuela
Notes: The ships were built between 1943 and 1944 by Bath Iron Works of Bath (Maine) and by Federal Shipbuilding & Drydock of Kearney (New Jersey), and commissioned into US service in 1944. They both received FRAM II modification during the 1950s, and were transferred to South Korea in 1973.

'Fletcher' class destroyer (3)

Class: *Chung Mu* (DD91), ex-US *Erben* (DD631); *Seoul* (DD92), ex-US *Halsey Powell* (DD686); *Pusan* (DD93), ex-US *Hickox* (DD673)
Displacement: 2,050 tons (2,083 tonnes) standard; 3,050 tons (3,099 tonnes) full load
Dimensions: Length 376 ft 6 in (114.8 m)
Beam 39 ft 7 in (12.0 m)
Draught 18 ft (5.5 m)
Armament:
Guns 5 5-in (127-mm) in single turrets
10 40-mm in 1 twin and 2 quadruple mountings (not in *Seoul*)

Missile systems
none
A/S weapons
2 Mark 11 Hedgehogs
DCs
2 triple 12.75-in (324-mm) Mark 32 tubes
Torpedo tubes
none
Aircraft
none
Radar and electronics: SPS-6 search and SPS-10 surface search radars
Sonar:

Powerplant: 4 Babcock & Wilcox boilers supplying steam to General Electric geared turbines, delivering 60,000 shp to two shafts
Speed: 35 knots
Range:
Crew: about 250
Used also by: Argentina, Brazil, Chile, Greece, Italy, Mexico, Peru, Spain, Taiwan, Turkey, West Germany
Notes: The three ships were built between 1942 and 1943 by Bath Iron Works of Bath (Maine), Bethlehem Steel of Staten Island (New York) and Federal Shipbuilding of Kearney (New Jersey), and commissioned into US service in 1943. *Erben* was transferred in 1963, and the other two in 1968.

'Rudderow' class frigate (1)

Class: *Chung Nam* (DE73), ex-US *Holt* (DE706)
Displacement: 1,450 tons (1,473 tonnes) standard; 1,890 tons (1,920 tonnes) full load
Dimensions: Length 306 ft (83.2 m)
Beam 37 ft (11.3 m)
Draught 14 ft (4.3 m)
Armament:
Guns 2 5-in (127-mm) in single turrets
4 40-mm in twin mountings

Missile systems
none
A/S weapons
1 Hedgehog
DCs
2 triple 12.75-in (324-mm) Mark 32 tubes
Torpedo tubes
none
Aircraft
none
Radar and electronics: SPS-5 surface surveillance and SPS-6 search radars

Sonar:
Powerplant: 2 Combustion Engineering boilers supplying steam to General Electric geared turbines (turbo-electric drive), delivering 12,000 shp to two shafts
Speed: 24 knots
Range:
Crew: about 210
Used also by: Taiwan
Notes: *Holt* was built by Defoe Shipbuilding of Bay City (Michigan) in 1943, and commissioned in 1944. She was transferred to South Korea in 1963.

'Auk' class corvette (3)

Class: *Shin Song* (PCE1001), ex-US *Ptarmigan* (MSF376); *Sunchon* (PCE1002), ex-US *Speed* (MSF116); *Koje* (PCE1003), ex-US *Dextrous* (MSF341)
Displacement: 890 tons (904.25 tonnes) standard; 1,250 tons (1,270 tonnes) full load
Dimensions: Length 221 ft 3 in (63.2 m)
Beam 32 ft 3 in (9.2 m)
Draught 10 ft 10 in (3.0 m)
Armament:
Guns 2 3-in (76-mm) in single mountings
4 40-mm in twin mountings
2 20-mm in single mountings

Missile systems
none
A/S weapons
1 Hedgehog
DCs
1 triple 12.75-in (324-mm) Mark 32 tubes
Torpedo tubes
none
Aircraft
none
Radar and electronics:
Sonar:

Powerplant: General Motors Corporation diesels as part of a diesel-electric drive delivering 3,532 bhp to two shafts
Speed: 18 knots
Range:
Crew: about 110
Used also by: Mexico, Norway, Philippines, Taiwan, Uruguay
Notes: The three ships were built between 1942 and 1944 as minesweepers of the AM type. The first ship was transferred to South Korea in 1963, and the other two in 1967. Transfer arrangements included the removal of the sweeping gear and the addition of the second 3-in (76-mm) gun.

Tacoma PSMM 5 type fast attack craft (missile) (7)

Class: *Paek Ku 12* (102), *Paek Ku 13* (103), *Paek Ku 15* (105), *Paek Ku 16* (106), *Paek Ku 17* (107), *Paek Ku 18* (108), *Paek Ku 19* (109)
Displacement: about 250 tons (254 tonnes) full load
Dimensions: Length 165 ft (50.3 m)
Beam 24 ft (7.3 m)
Draught 9 ft 6 in (2.9 m)
Armament:

Guns 1 3-in (76-mm)
1 40-mm (possibly removed)
2 0.5-in (12.7-mm) machine-guns
Missile systems
4 Standard SAM launchers with eight missiles
A/S weapons
none
Torpedo tubes
none
Aircraft
none
Radar and electronics:
Sonar:

Powerplant: 6 Avco Lycoming TF35 gas turbines, delivering 16,800 hp to two shafts
Speed: 40+ knots
Range:
Crew: 5+27
Used only by: South Korea
Notes: Designed by Tacoma Boatbuilding of Tacoma (Washington), the PSMM is a multi-mission patrol ship based in design on the US Navy 'Asheville' class. Tacoma built the first three craft, which were commissioned in 1975 and 1976, and the remaining four craft of the class were built in South Korea, commissioning in 1976 and 1977.

South Yemen

600 men under army control

Light Forces:
2 P-6 FAC(T)

Patrol Forces:
2 SO I PC

1 Poluchat PC
3 Fairey Spear coastal PC
1 Fairey Interceptor coastal PC
2 Zhuk FAC(P)

Mine Warfare Forces:
3 Ham inshore minesweepers

Amphibious Forces:
2 Polnocny LCT
3 T-4 LCVP

Auxiliaries:
1 lighter

Spain

The Spanish Navy
Spain is not a member of the NATO alliance, but inevitably her fortunes are bound up with those of the rest of Europe. Therefore, because she has long coastlines on both the Atlantic and the Mediterranean, as well as extensive overseas trade, Spain requires strong armed forces, especially a strong navy. Naval personnel amount to 40,000, some 12.7 per cent of the total Spanish armed forces, whose budget is about 1.9 per cent of the gross national product.

Spain's maritime defence policy is based on a twofold notion of long-range offensive action by powerful surface strike forces and submarines, and short-range coastal defence by smaller units. The ocean strike force is built round the light carrier *Dédalo* and its AV-8A Matador VTOL strike aircraft, while defence of the strike force against submarine attack is greatly strengthened by the *Dédalo*'s ability to operate, in addition to the AV-8As, some 20 ASW helicopters. It should be noted, though, that *Dédalo* can also be used in support of assault landings, the ASW helicopters being replaced by HueyCobra helicopter gunships and/or Bell 204 and 212 assault transport helicopters.

Dédalo will be supported by units from Spain's destroyer force: five 'D60/ Gearing FRAM 1', two 'Roger de Lauria', one 'Oquendo' and five 'D20/Fletcher' class. Although the number of destroyers appears adequate, their modernity does not, and the real utility of these somewhat elderly ships is open to doubt, the more so as none have been modernised to include any type of missile armament, and only seven carry a light ASW helicopter.

Spain is better provided with frigates. A new class of such ships, similar to the US 'Oliver Hazard Perry' class, is under construction. But in the meantime Spain has the 'F30' class, with four building for commissioning by 1979, another four approved, and possibly another three to be approved. The ships will have a Sea Sparrow short-range SAM defence, and Harpoon SSMs. There are also the five 'F70/Baleares' class ships, with a single Tartar/Standard SAM launcher, and the other nine frigates of the 'Audaz', 'Alava', Modernised 'Pizarro' and 'F60/Atrevida' classes, all of them conventional ships but useful for escort and general-purpose duties.

The Spanish submarine arm is well provided for, with two 'S70/Agosta' class boats building and two ordered, four 'S60/Daphné' class boats in service, as well as three 'S30/Guppy 11A'.

For long-range patrol work, Spain relies on the available six 'P-00/ Lazaga' and the six 'P-10/Barcelo' class large patrol craft, though these are of limited combat value. There are also a number of coastal and river patrol craft, more useful for policing than for military duties. Spain needs missile- and torpedo-armed FAC types, but future plans indicate that construction of this type will consist of six small patrol ships and six large patrol craft.

Amphibious warfare plays a major part in Spanish defence thinking, as indicated by the existence of one attack transport, one attack freighter, one LSD, three LSTs, eight LCTs, two LCUs and six LCMs. Mine warfare also features prominently: there are four 'Aggressive' class ocean minesweepers, with another four to be delivered, 12 'Nalon' class coastal minesweepers, and four 'Guadiaro' class units, which are now used mainly for patrol, but could be used for their intended role of coastal minesweeper if necessary.

Service and auxiliary forces are well catered for, and so the most important criticism of the Spanish navy must be that although it has enough types, these are not of the right kind. For the most part Spain's major surface vessels are obsolescent, and both they and the light forces need bolstering with missile-armed units. Matters will be partially rectified if the proposed additional four corvettes are built to supplement the four already under construction. Approval is also being sought for one sea control ship, three frigates, and another two corvettes, all of which will help the Spanish navy modernise itself in an age of rapid, but totally necessary, technological innovation.

44,800 men (32,000 conscripts) plus 10,600 marines and 200,000 reservists

CV:
1 Independence (CVL)

Destroyers:
5 D60/Gearing FRAM1
2 Roger de Lauria
1 Oquendo
5 D20/Fletcher

Frigates (FFG):
(3 FFG7)
4 F30 (+4)
5 F70/Baleares

Frigates (FF):
1 Audaz
2 Alava
2 Modernised Pizarro
4 F60/Atrevida

SS:
(4 Agosta)
4 S60/Daphné
3 S30/Guppy IIA

Patrol Forces:
6 Lazaga PC
6 Barcelo PC
4 Guadiaro PC
5 LP1 coastal PC
3 USCG 25.4-m coastal PC
1 fishery protection vessel
1 patrol vessel
13 coastal/river patrol launches

Amphibious Forces:
1 Haskell attack transport
1 Andromeda attack freighter
1 Cabildo LSD
3 Terrebonne Parish LST
2 LCT(4)
3 Spanish LCT
3 EDIC LCT
2 LCU
6 LCM8

Mine Warfare Forces:
4 Aggressive ocean minesweepers (+4)
12 Nalon/MSC coastal minesweepers

Auxiliaries:
4 survey ships
2 oceanographic ships
1 transport
1 replenishment tanker
13 harbour tankers
1 training ship (sail)
1 royal yacht
others

Naval Air Service:
1 FGA sqn with 5AV-8A, 2 TAV-8A
4 Piper Commanche (1 communication sqn)
(5 helicopter sqns) 10 SH-3D, 11 AB 204/212 ASW, 12 Bell 47G, 12 Hughes 500HM, 6 AH-1G
(5 AV-8A)
(5 AB 212)
(6 SH-3D)

Marine Force:
4 light inf regts
2 independent groups

'Independence' class light air-craft-carrier (1)

Class: *Dédalo* (PH01), ex-US *Cabot* (AVT3), ex-US *Cabot* (CVL28)
Displacement: 13,000 tons (13,208 tonnes) standard; 16,416 tons (16,679 tonnes) full load
Dimensions: Length 623 ft (189.9 m)
  Beam (hull) 71 ft 6 in (21.8 m)
  Draught 26 ft (7.9 m)
Armament:
Guns 26 40-mm in 2 quadruple and 9 twin mountings
Missile systems
  none
A/S weapons
  none
Torpedo tubes
  none
Aircraft
  7 aircraft and 20 helicopters
Radar and electronics: SPS-6 search, SPS-40 search, SPS-52B 3D surveillance, AN/WLR-1 height-finder, SPS-10 tactical, and 4 fire-control radars
Sonar:
Powerplant: 4 Babcock & Wilcox boilers supplying steam to General Electric geared turbines, delivering 100,000 shp to four shafts

Speed: 32 knots
Range: 7,200 miles (11,590 km) at 15 knots
Crew: 1,112 without air groups
Used only by: Spain
Notes: *Cabot* was laid down in 1942 by New York Shipbuilding as CL79, a light cruiser of the 'Cleveland' class. She was converted on the stocks into an aircraft-carrier, and launched in 1943, also being commissioned into US service in 1943. She was later modernised to incorporate better protection and additional electronic gear, with a flight deck measuring 545 ft by 108 ft (166.1 m by 32.9 m). She was loaned to Spain in 1967, and sold to her in 1973.

'D60' ('Gearing FRAM I') class destroyer (5)

Class: *Churruca* (D61), ex-US *Eugene A. Greene* (DD711); *Gravina* (D62), ex-US *Furse* (DD882); *Mendez Nuñez* (D63), ex-US *O'Hare* (DD889); *Langaria* (D64), ex-US *Leary* (DD879); *Blas de Lezo* (D65), ex-US *Noa* (DD841)
Displacement: 2,425 tons (2,464 tonnes) standard; 3,480 tons (3,536 tonnes) full load
Dimensions: Length 390 ft 6 in (119.0 m)
  Beam 40 ft 9 in (12.4 m)
  Draught 19 ft (5.8 m)

Armament:
Guns 4 5-in (127-mm) in twin turrets
Missile systems
  none
A/S weapons
  1 ASROC launcher
  2 triple 12.75-in (324-mm) Mark 32 tubes
Torpedo tubes
  none
Aircraft
  1 small helicopter
Radar and electronics: SPS-40 air search (D61, D62), SPS-37 air search (others), SPS-10 surface search, and Mark 37 fire-control radars
Sonar: SQS-23

Powerplant: 4 Babcock & Wilcox boilers supplying steam to 2 General Electric or Westinghouse geared turbines, delivering 60,000 shp to two shafts
Speed: 34 knots
Range: 4,800 miles (7,725 km) at 15 knots
Crew: 17+257
Used also by: Brazil, Greece, Pakistan, South Korea, Taiwan, Turkey, USA
Notes: The five ships were built between 1944 and 1945, the first by Federal Shipbuilding & Drydocking, the next three by Consolidated Steel Corporation, and the last by Bath Iron Works. All five were commissioned into US service in 1945. The first two were transferred in 1972, and the other three in 1973, all five being bought in 1975.

'Roger de Lauria' class destroyer (2)

Class: *Roger de Lauria* (D42), *Marqués de la Ensenada* (D43)
Displacement: 3,012 tons (3,060 tonnes) standard; 3,785 tons (3,846 tonnes) full load
Dimensions: Length 391 ft 6 in (119.3 m)
  Beam 42 ft 8 in (13.0 m)
  Draught 18 ft 5 in (5.6 m)
Armament:
Guns 6 5-in (127-mm) in twin turrets
Missile systems
  none
A/S weapons
  2 triple 12.75-in (324-mm) Mark 32 tubes
Torpedo tubes
  2 21-in (533-mm)
Aircraft
  1 small helicopter
Radar and electronics: SPS-40 search, SPS-10 tactical, Mark 25 (Mark 37 director) and Mark 35 (Mark 56 director) radars
Sonar: SQS-32C hull-mounted and SQA-10 variable-depth

Powerplant: 3 boilers supplying steam to 2 Rateau-Bretagne geared turbines, delivering 60,000 shp to two shafts
Speed: 28 knots
Range: 4,500 miles (7,245 km) at 15 knots
Crew: 20+298
Used only by: Spain

Notes: Both ships were built at the Ferrol yards, being laid down in 1951 to the same specification as the 'Oquendo' class. They were launched in 1958 and 1959, and then towed to Cartagena for modification. Armament and electronics are identical to those of 'Gearing FRAM II' class destroyers. D42 was finally commissioned in 1969, and D43 in 1970.

'Oquendo' class destroyer (1)

Class: *Oquendo* (D41)
Displacement: 2,342 tons (2,379 tonnes) standard; 3,005 tons (3,053 tonnes) full load
Dimensions: Length 382 ft (116.4 m)
Beam 36 ft 6 in (11.1 m)
Draught 12 ft 6 in (3.8 m)
Armament:
Guns 4 120-mm in twin turrets
6 40-mm in single mountings
Missile systems
none
A/S weapons
2 Mark 11 Hedgehogs
2 Mark 4 side-launchers with 3 Mark 32 torpedoes each
Torpedo tubes
none
Aircraft
none
Radar and electronics: Type 293 search, Marconi SNW 10 air search, and Type 275 and Type 262 fire-control radars
Sonar: QHB a
Powerplant: 3 boilers supplying steam to 2 Rateau-Bretagne geared turbines, delivering 60,000 shp to two shafts

Speed: 32½ knots
Range: 5,000 miles (8,047 km) at 15 knots
Crew: 17+233
Used only by: Spain

Notes: *Oquendo* was built at the Ferrol yards between 1951 and 1956, and commissioned in 1960. Designed as a fleet destroyer, *Oquendo* was modified during construction into an anti-submarine destroyer.

'D20' ('Fletcher') class destroyer (5)

Class: *Lepanto* (D21), ex-US *Capps* (DD550); *Almirante Ferrandiz* (D22), ex-US *David W. Taylor* (DD551); *Almirante Valdes* (D23), ex-US *Converse* (DD509); *Alcala Galiano* (D24), ex-US *Jarvis* (DD799); *Jorge Juan* (D25), ex-US *McGowan* (DD678)
Displacement: 2,080 tons (2,113 tonnes) standard; 3,050 tons (3,099 tonnes) full load
Dimensions: Length 376 ft 6 in (114.8 m)
Beam 39 ft 6 in (12.0 m)
Draught 18 ft (5.5 m)
Armament:
Guns 5 (D21, D22) or 4 (others) 5-in (127-mm) in single turrets

6 3-in (76-mm) in twin turrets (D23, D24, D25)
6 40-mm in twin mountings (D21, D22)
6 20-mm in single mountings (D21, D22)
Missile systems
none
A/S weapons
2 Mark 11 Hedgehogs
6 (D21, D22) or 4 (others) DCTs
2 (D21, D22) or 1 (others) DC racks
2 side-launching Mark 4 racks, each with 3 Mark 32 A/S torpedoes
Torpedo tubes
3 21-in (533-mm) in D23, D24, D25
Aircraft
none
Radar and electronics: SPS-6C search, SPS-10 tactical, Mark 37 (D21, D22) fire-control, and Marks 37, 56 and 63 (others) fire-control radars

Sonar: SQS-4 or SQS-29
Powerplant: 4 Babcock & Wilcox boilers supplying steam to Westinghouse (D21, D22) or General Electric (others) geared turbines, delivering 60,000 shp to two shafts
Speed: 35 knots
Range: 5,000 miles (8,047 km) at 15 knots
Crew: 17+273
Used also by: Argentina, Brazil, Chile, Greece, Italy, Mexico, Peru, South Korea, Taiwan, Turkey, West Germany
Notes: The five ships were built between 1941 and 1943, for commissioning into US service in 1943 and 1944. The first two were transferred to Spain in 1957, the third in 1959, and the last two in 1960. Spain bought all five ships in 1972.

'Baleares' or 'F70' class guided missile frigate (5)

Class: *Baleares* (F71), *Andalucia* (F72), *Cataluña* (F73), *Asturias* (F74), *Extremadura* (F75)
Displacement: 3,015 tons (3,063 tonnes) standard; 4,177 tons (4,244 tonnes) full load
Dimensions: Length 438 ft (133.6 m)
Beam 46 ft 11 in (14.3 m)
Draught 15 ft 5 in (4.7 m)
Armament:
Guns 1 5-in (127-mm)
Missile systems
1 Mark 22 Tartar/Standard SAM launcher with 16 missiles

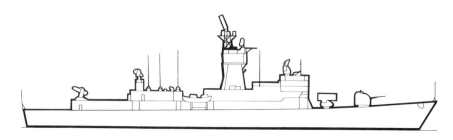

A/S weapons
1 octuple ASROC launcher with 8 reloads
4 Mark 32 tubes for Mark 46 torpedoes
2 Mark 25 tubes for Mark 37 torpedoes
Torpedo tubes
none

Aircraft
none
Radar and electronics: SPS-52A 3D search, SPS-10 tactical, SPG-51C missile fire-

control, and SPG-53B gun fire-control radars

Sonar: SQS-23 hull-mounted and SQS-35V variable-depth

Powerplant: 2 V2M boilers supplying steam to 1 Westinghouse geared turbine, delivering 35,000 shp to one shaft

Speed: 28 knots

Range: 4,500 miles (7,240 km) at 15 knots

Crew: 15+241

Used only by: Spain

Notes: All five ships were built by Bazán at Ferrol between 1968 and 1972, for commissioning between 1973 and 1976. The class was ordered to replace the 'Leander' class frigates ordered from UK, but cancelled in 1962 as a result of British insults to Spain. The design is based on that of the US 'Knox' class, and Spain enjoyed full US co-operation in the design of the class.

'F30' class guided missile frigate (8)

Class: *Descubierta* (F31), *Diana* (F32), *Infanta Elena* (F33), *Infanta Cristina* (F34), and four others (F35, F36, F37, F38)

Displacement: 1,200 tons (1,219 tonnes) standard; 1,497 tons (1,521 tonnes) full load

Dimensions: Length 291 ft 4 in (88.8 m)
Beam 34 ft (10.5 m)
Draught 11 ft 6 in (3.5 m)

Armament:
Guns 1 76-mm OTO Melara
2 40-mm in single mountings
1 or 2 20-mm Meroka 12-barrel AA weapons
Missile systems
1 octuple Sea Sparrow SAM launcher with 16 reloads
2 quadruple MM39 Exocet or Harpoon SSM launchers
A/S weapons
1 375-mm Bofors twin-barrel launcher
2 triple 12.75-in (324-mm) Mark 32 tubes

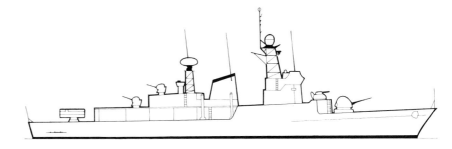

Torpedo tubes
none
Aircraft
none

Radar and electronics: Hollandse Signaalapparaten DA 05/2 combined search, 2W-06 navigation and helicopter control and WM 22/41 fire-control system radars; Elettronica 'Beta' ECM fit

Sonar: 1 Raytheon 1160B

Powerplant: 4 MTU-Bazán 16V 956 TB 91 diesels, delivering up to 18,000 bhp to two shafts

Speed: 26 knots

Range: 4,000 miles (6,440 km)

Crew: about 100

Used only by: Spain

Notes: The first four of the class were built by Bazán at Cartagena between 1974 and 1976, for commissioning between 1977 and 1979. The second four are being built by Bazán at Ferrol, for commissioning in the early 1980s. The design is similar to that of the Portuguese 'João Coutinho' class, but with new engines and armament. It seems likely that another four of the class will eventually be built.

'Audaz' class frigate (1)

Class: *Intrepido* (D38)

Displacement: 1,227 tons (1,247 tonnes) standard; 1,550 tons (1,575 tonnes) full load

Dimensions: Length 308 ft 5 in (94.0 m)
Beam 30 ft 6 in (9.3 m)
Draught 17 ft 1 in (5.2 m)

Armament:
Guns 2 3-in (76-mm)
2 40-mm
Missile systems
none

A/S weapons
2 Mark 11 Hedgehogs
8 DC mortars
2 DC racks
2 side-launching racks for A/S torpedoes
Torpedo tubes

Aircraft
 none
Radar and electronics: SPS-5B surface
 search, MLA-1B air search, and Mark 63
 fire-control radars
Sonar: QHBa

Powerplant: 3 La Seine boilers supplying
 steam to 2 Rateau-Bretagne geared tur-
 bines, delivering 28,000 shp to two shafts
Speed: 28 knots
Range: 3,800 miles (6,115 km) at 14 knots
Crew: 13+186

Used only by: Spain
Notes: The ship was built between 1945 and
 1961 at the Ferrol yards, and commissioned in 1965. She is modelled on the
 French 'Le Fier' design.

'Alava' class frigate (2)

Class: *Liniers* (D51, ex-21), *Alava* (D52, ex-
 23)
Displacement: 1,842 tons (1,871 tonnes)
 standard; 2,287 tons (2,324 tonnes) full
 load
Dimensions: Length 336 ft 3½ in (102.5 m)
 Beam 31 ft 6 in (9.6 m)
 Draught 19 ft 8 in (6.0 m)
Armament:
Guns 3 3-in (76-mm) in single mountings
 3 40-mm
Missile systems
 none

A/S weapons
 2 Hedgehogs
 8 DC mortars
 2 DC racks
 2 side-launching racks for A/S torpedoes
Torpedo tubes
 none
Aircraft
 none
Radar and electronics: MLA-1B air search,
 SG-6B surface search, and Decca TM 626
 navigation radars
Sonar: SQS-30A
Powerplant: 4 Yarrow boilers supplying
 steam to Parsons geared turbines, delivering 31,500 shp to two shafts

Speed: 29 knots
Range: 4,100 miles (6,600 km) at 15 knots
Crew: 15+207
Used only by: Spain
Notes: Both ships were built by Bazán at Car-
 tagena between 1944 and 1947, for com-
 missioning in 1951 and 1950 respectively.
 The ships were ordered in 1936 but
 delayed by the start of the Spanish Civil
 War, started again in 1940, but again
 delayed by the problems occasioned by
 World War II, and finally built from 1944
 onwards. They are the last survivors of the
 18-strong 'Churruca' class.

Modernised 'Pizarro' class frigate (2)

Class: *Vicente Yañez Pinzon* (F41), *Legazpi*
 (F42)
Displacement: 1,924 tons (1,955 tonnes)
 standard; 2,228 tons (2,264 tonnes) full
 load
Dimensions: Length 312 ft 6 in (95.3 m)
 Beam 39 ft 6 in (12.0 m)
 Draught 17 ft 9 in (5.4 m)
Armament:
Guns 2 5-in (127-mm) in single turrets
 4 40-mm

Missile systems
 none
A/S weapons
 2 Hedgehogs
 8 DC mortars
 2 DC racks
 2 side-launching racks for A/S torpedoes
Torpedo tubes
 none
Aircraft
 none
Radar and electronics: SPS-5B surface

search, MLA-1B air search, and Decca TM
 626 navigation radars
Sonar:
Powerplant: 2 Yarrow boilers supplying
 steam to 2 Parsons geared turbines, deliver-
 ing 6,000 shp to two shafts
Speed: 18½ knots
Range: 3,000 miles (4,830 km) at 15 knots
Crew: 16+239
Used only by: Spain
Notes: Both ships were built at Ferrol be-
 tween 1943 and 1945, and commissioned
 in 1949 and 1951 respectively. Both were
 modernised in 1949 and 1950.

'Atrevida' or 'F60' class frigate (4)

Class: *Atrevida* (F61), *Princesa* (F62), *Nau-
 tilus* (F64), *Villa de Bilbao* (F65)
Displacement: 1,031 tons (1,047 tonnes)
 standard; 1,135 tons (1,153 tonnes) full
 load
Dimensions: Length 247 ft 8½ in (75.5 m)
 Beam 33 ft 6 in (10.2 m)
 Draught 9 ft 10 in (3.0 m)
Armament:
Guns 1 3-in (76-mm)
 3 40-mm in single mountings
Missile systems
 none
A/S weapons
 2 Hedgehogs
 8 DC mortars
 2 DC racks
Torpedo tubes
 none
Aircraft
 none
Radar and electronics: Modified SPS-5B air/
 surface search radar
Sonar: QHBa
Powerplant: Sulzer diesels, delivering 3,000
 bhp to two shafts
Speed: 18½ knots

Range: 8,000 miles (12,875 km) at 10 knots
Crew: 9+123
Used only by: Spain
Notes: The ships were all built by Bazán, the
 first two at Cartagena, the second pair at

Cadiz. They were built between 1950 and
 1958, and commissioned between 1954
 and 1960. They can carry 20 mines. The
 class has the unusual feature of no funnels,
 the diesels exhausting on the starboard
 side just above the waterline.

'S70' ('Agosta') class submarine (4)

Class: S71, S72, S73, S74
Displacement: 1,450 tons (1,473 tonnes)
 surfaced; 1,725 tons (1,753 tonnes) dived

Dimensions: Length 221 ft 9½ in (67.6 m)
 Beam 22 ft 4 in (6.8 m)
 Draught 17 ft 9 in (5.4 m)
Armament:
Guns none
Missile systems
 none

A/S weapons
 none
Torpedo tubes
 4 550-mm (21.7-in) with 20 torpedoes
Aircraft

Radar and electronics: Thomson-CSF
Calypso surveillance and navigation radar
Sonar: DUUA active, and DSUV passive
Powerplant: diesel-electric, with 2 diesels,
delivering 3,600 hp, and 1 electric motor,

delivering 6,400 hp, to one shaft
Speed: 12 knots (surfaced); 20 knots (dived)
Range: 9,000 miles (14,485 km) at 9 knots
snorting; 350 miles (565 km) at 3½ knots
dived

Crew: 50
Used also by: France
Notes: The boats are building in the Bazán
yards at Cartagena, with the first two craft
to be commissioned in 1980 and 1981.

'S60' ('Daphné') class submarine (4)

Class: *Delfin* (S61), *Tonina* (S62), *Marsopa*
(S63), *Narval* (S64)
Displacement: 870 tons (883.8 tonnes) surfaced; 1,040 tons (1,057 tonnes) dived
Dimensions: Length 189 ft 7½ in (57.8 m)
Beam 22 ft 4 in (6.8 m)
Draught 15 ft 1 in (4.6 m)
Armament:
Guns none
Missile systems
none

A/S weapons
none
Torpedo tubes
12 550-mm (21.7-in) with 12 torpedoes
Aircraft
none
Radar and electronics: Thomson-CSF
DRUA-31 radar; ECM fit
Sonar: DUUA-1 active, DSUV passive, and
DUUG-1
Powerplant: SEMT-Pielstick diesel-electric,
with diesels delivering 2,600 bhp, and
electric motor delivering 2,700 hp, to two
shafts

Speed: 13¼ knots (surfaced); 15½ knots
(dived)
Range: 4,500 miles (7,245 km) at 5 knots
snorting; 2,710 miles (4,360 km) at 12¼
knots surfaced
Crew: 6+41
Used also by: France, Libya, Pakistan, Portugal, South Africa
Notes: The four boats were built by Bazán at
Cartagena in two pairs, the first between
1968 and 1972, commissioning in 1973,
and the second pair between 1971 and
1974, commissioning in 1975.

'S30' ('Guppy IIA') class submarine (3)

Class: *Isaac Peral* (S32), ex-US *Ronquil*
(SS396); *Cosme Garcia* (S34), ex-US *Bang*
(SS385); S35, ex-US *Jallao* (SS368)
Displacement: 1,840 tons (1,869 tonnes)
surfaced; 2,445 tons (2,484 tonnes) dived
Dimensions: Length 306 ft (93.3 m)
Beam 27 ft (8.2 m)
Draught 17 ft (5.2 m)
Armament:
Guns none
Missile systems
none
A/S weapons
none
Torpedo tubes
10 21-in (533-mm)
Aircraft
none
Radar and electronics: SS 2 radar
Sonar: BQS and BQR
Powerplant: 3 Fairbanks-Morse diesels, delivering 4,800 bhp, and 2 Elliot electric
motors, delivering 5,400 shp to two shafts
Speed: 18 knots (surfaced); 14 knots (dived)
Range: 12,000 miles (19,313 km) at 10
knots surfaced

Crew: 74
Used also by: Greece, Turkey
Notes: The first two boats were built by
Portsmouth Navy Yard, the last by Manitowoc Shipbuilding, between 1943 and
1944, for commissioning in 1943 and

1944. The boats were transferred in 1971,
1972 and 1974.

'Lazaga (P-00)' class large patrol craft (6)

Class: *Lazaga* (P01), *Alsedo* (P02), *Cadarso*
(P03), *Villamil* (P04), *Bonifaz* (P05),
Recalde (P06)
Displacement: 275 tons (279.4 tonnes)
standard; 400 tons (406.4 tonnes) full load
Dimensions: Length 190 ft 3 in (58.0 m)
Beam 24 ft 11 in (7.6 m)
Draught 8 ft 6 in (2.6 m)
Armament:

Guns 1 76-mm OTO Melara
1 40-mm Breda-Bofors
2 20-mm Oerlikon
Missile systems
provision for 4 MM38 Exocet, or 8 MM39
or Harpoon SSM launchers
A/S weapons
2 DC racks
provision for 2 triple 12.75-in (324-mm)
Mark 32 tubes
Torpedo tubes
none
Aircraft
none
Radar and electronics: Hollandse Signaalapparaten M29 series surface search and
target indicator and Decca TM626 navigation radar

Sonar: ELAC (?)
Powerplant: 2 MTU-Bazán MA15 TB91 diesels, delivering 8,000 bhp
Speed: 28 knots
Range: 6,100 miles (9,815 km) at 17 knots
Crew: 3+27
Used only by: Spain
Notes: The class was designed by Lürssen of
Vegesack, who built the first craft for commissioning in 1975. The rest were built by
Bazán at La Carraca, for commissioning in
1976 and 1977. The hull is based on that
of the Israeli 'Reshef' class.

'Barcelo (P10)' class large patrol craft (6)

Class: *Barceló* (P11), *Laya* (P12), *Xavier Quiroga* (P13), *Ordoñez* (P14), *Acevedo* (P15), *Candido Perez* (P16)
Displacement: 139 tons (141.2 tonnes)
Dimensions: Length 118 ft 9 in (36.2 m)
   Beam 19 ft (5.8 m)
   Draught 8 ft 3 in (2.5 m)
Armament:
Guns 1 40-mm Breda-Bofors
   2 20-mm Oerlikon
   2 12.7-mm machine-guns
Missile systems
   provision for 2 or 4 SSMs
A/S weapons
   none
Torpedo tubes
   provision for 2 533-mm (21-in) tubes
Aircraft
   none
Radar and electronics:
Sonar:
Powerplant: 2 MTU-Bazán MD-16V TB90 diesels, delivering 6,000 bhp to two shafts
Speed: 34 knots
Range: 1,200 miles (1,930 km) at 17 knots

Crew: 19
Used only by: Spain
Notes: The first craft was built by the designers, Lürssen of Vegesack, and the other five by Bazán at La Carraca. The first two were commissioned in 1976, the next three in 1977, and the last in 1978.

Sri Lanka

2,400 men

Frigate:
1 Canadian River

Light Forces:
5 Sooraya/Shanghai II FAC(G)
1 Mol FAC(G)

Patrol Forces:
20 Thornycroft 14.9-m coastal PC
10 coastal PC (+1)

Auxiliaries:
4 survey craft

Canadian 'River' class frigate (1)

Class: *Gajabahu* (F232), ex-Israeli *Misnak*, ex-Canadian *Hallowell*
Displacement: 1,445 tons (1,468 tonnes) standard; 2,360 tons (2,398 tonnes) full load
Dimensions: Length 310 ft 6 in (91.9 m)
   Beam 36 ft 6 in (11.1 m)
   Draught 13 ft 9 in (4.2 m)
Armament:
Guns 1 4-in (102-mm)
   3 40-mm
Missile systems
   none
A/S weapons
   none
Torpedo tubes
   none
Aircraft
   none
Radar and electronics:
Sonar:
Powerplant: 2 boilers supplying steam to triple-expansion engines, delivering 5,500 ihp to two shafts
Speed: 20 knots
Range: 4,200 miles (6,760 km) at 12 knots
Crew: 190
Used also by: Australia, Burma, Dominican Republic
Notes: *Hallowell* was built in 1944, and commissioned into Canadian service in 1945 after completion by Canadian Vickers of Montreal. She was bought by Israel in 1950, and by Sri Lanka in 1959. Up to 1965 her armament consisted of 3 4.7-in (119-mm) and 8 20-mm.

'Mol' class fast attack craft (gun) (1)

Class: *Samudra Devi*
Displacement: 205 tons (208.3 tonnes) standard; 245 tons (248.9 tonnes) full load
Dimensions: Length 126 ft 7½ in (38.6 m)
   Beam 25 ft 7 in (7.8 m)
   Draught 9 ft 6 in (2.9 m)
Armament:
Guns 4 30-mm in twin mountings
Missile systems
   none
A/S weapons
   none
Torpedo tubes
   none
Aircraft
   none
Radar and electronics: 'Don' navigation radar; 'High Pole' IFF
Sonar:
Powerplant: 3 M504 diesels, delivering 15,500 bhp to two shafts
Speed: 40 knots
Range:
Crew: 25
Used only by: Sri Lanka
Notes: *Samudra Devi* was built in Russia and commissioned in 1975. The hull is basically that of an 'Osa' class craft.

Sudan

600 men

Light Forces:
6 101 FAC(G)

Patrol Forces:
2 Kraljevica PC
4 PBR type PC
3 coastal PC

Amphibious Forces:
2 DTK221 LCT
1 LCU

Auxiliaries:
1 survey ship
1 support tanker
1 water boat

PBR type large patrol craft (4)

Class: *Gihad* (PB1), *Horriya* (PB2), *Istiqlal* (PB3), *Shaab* (PB4)
Displacement: 100 tons (101.6 tonnes)
Dimensions: Length 114 ft 10 in (35.0 m)
Beam 16 ft 5 in (5.0 m)
Draught 5 ft 7 in (1.7 m)
Armament:
Guns 1 40-mm
1 20-mm
2 7.62-mm machine-guns
Missile systems
none
A/S weapons
none
Torpedo tubes
none
Aircraft
none
Radar and electronics:
Sonar:
Powerplant: MTU 12V 493 diesels, delivering 1,800 bhp to two shafts
Speed: 20 knots
Range: 1,400 miles (2,255 km) at 12 knots
Crew: 20
Used only by: Sudan
Notes: The four craft were built by the Mosor yard of Trogir in Yugoslavia, the first pair being commissioned into Sudanese service in 1961, and the second pair in 1962.

Surinam

Patrol Forces:
3 large PC
7 coastal PC

Sweden

The Swedish Navy
The defence problems facing Sweden are similar to those facing Norway, with the principal difference that Sweden's coastline is in the Baltic, and that Swedish warships must face a greater threat of air attack by land-based Russian aircraft than do their Norwegian counterparts. Sweden's navy has a manpower strength of 11,800, some 18 per cent of the total unmobilised strength of the country's armed forces, which have a budget of about 3.55 per cent of the nation's gross national product.

The main striking force of the Royal Swedish Navy is found by the four destroyers of the 'Södermanland' class and the two destroyers of the 'Halland' class. Basically conventional ships, these have been modernised in recent years, the former now having a Seacat SAM air defence system, and the latter an RB08A SSM launcher. Both ships can also lay mines, as can the two frigates of the 'Öland' class. Sweden's last four major warships, the four 'Visby' class frigates, have no special equipment and are to be disposed of in the near future.

Again like Norway, Sweden feels that submarines can play a major part in the defence of the country; accordingly, the 20 submarines available ('Näcken', 'Sjöormen', 'Draken' and 'Hajen' classes) have key tasks. In these they are aided by good underwater manoeuvrability and speed, combined with an adequate torpedo armament and quiet running.

Like the other Scandinavian countries, Sweden feels that fast attack craft, armed with missiles or torpedoes, stand the best chance of defeating enemy naval forces in her territorial waters. The FAC types can operate from concealed bases, reach the scene of action quickly, strike devastatingly from a distance, and then retire to safety again. To co-ordinate the activities of such craft, three corvette-type flotilla leaders are to be built, but the weight of action will fall on the three Hugin class FAC(M), with another 14 on order, armed with six Penguin SSMs, and the 32 FAC(T) types of the 'Spica T131', 'Spica T121', 'Plejad' and 'T42' classes. It is hoped, moreover, that minefields laid by the four minelayers, nine coastal minelayers and 37 small minelayers will take their toll of attackers, and channel the survivors into areas of advantage to the Swedish attack forces.

Swedish naval forces will be protected from enemy mines, it is hoped, by the efforts of the nine new minehunters which are to be built, and the 18 coastal and 18 inshore minesweepers already in service.

11,800 men (6,950 conscripts), plus 10,000 reservists

Destroyers:
4 Södermanland
2 Halland

Frigates:
2 Oland
4 Visby

SS:
3 Näcken
5 Sjöormen
6 Draken
6 Häjen

Light Forces:
3 Hugin FAC(M) (+14)
12 Spica T131 FAC(T)
6 Spica T121 FAC(T)
3 Plejad FAC(T)
11 T-42 FAC(T)

Patrol Forces:
1 large PC
26 coastal PC

Mine Warfare Forces:
2 Alvsborg minelayers
1 minelayer/training ship
9 coastal minelayers
36 small minelayers
6 Hanö coastal minesweepers
12 Arkö coastal minesweepers
3 M47 inshore minesweepers
3 M31 inshore minesweepers
4 M44 inshore minesweepers
8 M15 inshore minesweepers
2 mine transports

Amphibious Forces:
3 36-m LCM
2 35-m LCM
4 Ane LCM
19 256 LCU (+5)

14 242 LCU
41 201 LCU
5 L51 LCU
54 LCA

Auxiliaries:
5 survey vessels (+1)
1 supply ship
1 support tanker
1 salvage ship
2 training ships (sail)
others

Aircraft:
5 Alouette II
3 Vertol 107
7 KV-107/II
10 Bell Jet Ranger

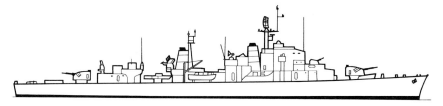

'Södermanland' class destroyer (4)

Class: *Östergötland* (J20), *Södermanland* (J21), *Gästrikland* (J22), *Hälsingland* (J23)
Displacement: 2,150 tons (2,184 tonnes) standard; 2,600 tons (2,642 tonnes) full load
Dimensions: Length 367 ft 6 in (112.0 m)
Beam 36 ft 9 in (11.2 m)
Draught 12 ft (3.7 m)
Armament:
Guns 4 120-mm in twin turrets
4 40-mm Bofors in single mountings
Missile systems
1 quadruple Seacat SAM launcher
1 RB08A SSM launcher
A/S weapons
1 3-barrel Squid mortar
Torpedo tubes
1 sextuple 533-mm (21-in)

Aircraft
none
Radar and electronics: Thomson-CSF Saturn search and target designator, Hollandse Signaalapparaten M45 gun fire control, and Hollandse Signaalapparaten M44 missile fire-control radars
Sonar:
Powerplant: 2 Babcock & Wilcox boilers supplying steam to De Laval geared turbines, delivering 47,000 bhp to two shafts
Speed: 35 knots
Range: 2,200 miles (3,540 km) at 20 knots
Crew: 18+226
Used only by: Sweden
Notes: The four ships were built between 1955 and 1957 by Götaverken of Göteborg, Eriksberg Mekaniska Verkstad, Götaverken, and Kockums Mek Verkstads, the first pair being commissioned in 1958, the second pair in 1959. The class was extensively modernised between 1965 and 1969.

'Halland' class destroyer (2)

Class: *Halland* (J18), *Smäland* (J19)
Displacement: 2,800 tons (2,845 tonnes) standard; 3,400 tons (3,454 tonnes) full load
Dimensions: Length 397 ft (121.0 m)
　　　　　Beam 41 ft 4 in (12.6 m)
　　　　　Draught 14 ft 9 in (4.5 m)
Armament:
Guns 4 120-mm in twin turrets
　2 57-mm in a twin mounting
　6 40-mm Bofors
Missile systems
　1 RB08A SSM launcher
A/S weapons
　2 4-barrel Bofors rocket-launchers
Torpedo tubes
　2 quadruple 533-mm (21-in)
Aircraft
　none
Radar and electronics: Thomson-CSF Saturn search and target designator, Hollandse Signaalapparaten LW-02/03 air warning, and Hollandse Signaalapparaten M22 fire-control radars; ECM fit
Sonar:
Powerplant: 2 Penhöet boilers supplying steam to De Laval double-reduction geared

turbines, delivering 58,000 bhp to two shafts
Speed: 35 knots
Range: 3,000 miles (4,830 km) at 20 knots
Crew: 18+272
Used also by: Colombia

Notes: The ships were built between 1951 and 1952 by Götaverken of Göteborg and Eriksberg Mekaniska Verstad of Göteborg, and commissioned into Swedish service in 1955 and 1956. Both were fully modernised in 1962.

'Oland' class frigate (2)

Class: *Öland* (F16), *Uppland* (F17)
Displacement: 2,000 tons (2,032 tonnes) standard; 2,400 tons (2,438 tonnes) full load
Dimensions: Length 367 ft 5½ in (112.0 m)
　　　　　Beam 36 ft 9 in (11.2 m)
　　　　　Draught 11 ft 1½ in (3.4 m)
Armament:
Guns 4 120-mm in twin turrets
　6 40-mm Bofors in single mountings

Missile systems
　none
A/S weapons
　1 3-barrel Squid mortar
Torpedo tubes
　2 triple 533-mm (21-in)
Aircraft
　facilities for 1 helicopter (*Uppland*)
Radar and electronics: Thomson-CSF Saturn search and target designator, and Hollandse Signaalapparaten M45 fire-control radars
Sonar:

Powerplant: 2 Penhöet boilers supplying steam to De Laval geared turbines, delivering 44,000 bhp to two shafts
Speed: 35 knots
Range: 2,500 miles (4,025 km) at 20 knots
Crew: 210
Used only by: Sweden
Notes: The two ships were built between 1943 and 1946 by Kockums Mek Verstads of Malmö and Karlskrona Dockyard, being commissioned in 1947 and 1949 respectively. *Öland* was modernised in 1960 and 1969, and *Uppland* in 1963. Both vessels have a mine capacity of 60.

'Visby' class frigate (4)

Class: *Visby* (F11), *Sundsvall* (F12), *Hälsingborg* (F13), *Kalmar* (F14)
Displacement: 1,150 tons (1,168 tonnes) standard; 1,320 tons (1,341 tonnes) full load
Dimensions: Length 321 ft 6 in (98.0 m)
Beam 30 ft (9.1 m)
Draught 12 ft 6 in (3.5 m)
Armament:
Guns 3 120-mm
2 57-mm
3 40-mm
Missile systems
none
A/S weapons
1 375-mm Bofors 4-barrel rocket-launcher
Torpedo tubes
none
Aircraft
facilities for 1 helicopter
Radar and electronics: Thomson-CSF Saturn search and target designator, Hollandse Signaalapparaten M24 fire-control radars

Sonar:
Powerplant: 3 boilers supplying steam to De Laval geared turbines, delivering 36,000 shp to two shafts
Speed: 39 knots
Range: 1,600 miles (2,575 km) at 20 knots
Crew: 140
Used only by: Sweden
Notes: The four ships were built between 1941 and 1943, for commissioning in 1943 and 1944. All are due for disposal.

'Näcken' class submarine (3)

Class: *Näcken* (NÄC), *Najad* (NAJ), *Neptun* (NP)
Displacement: 980 tons (995.7 tonnes) surfaced; 1,125 tons (1,143 tonnes) dived
Dimensions: Length 134 ft 6 in (41.0 m)
Beam 20 ft (6.1 m)
Draught 16 ft 9 in (5.1 m)
Armament:
Guns none
Missile systems
none
A/S weapons
none
Torpedo tubes
4 533-mm (21-in) with 12 torpedoes
Aircraft
none
Radar and electronics:
Sonar:
Powerplant: diesels and electric motors, delivering power to one shaft
Speed: 20 knots (surfaced and dived)
Range:
Crew: 25
Used only by: Sweden
Notes: The three boats were built between 1972 and 1976 by Kockums Mek Verkstads of Malmö, Karlskrona Dockyard, and

Kockums Mek Verstads of Malmö, for commissioning in 1977, 1978 and 1979. The boats have a high beam to length ratio to ensure high underwater speeds.

'Sjöormen' class submarine (5)

Class: *Sjöormen* (SOR), *Sjölejonet* (SLE), *Sjöhunden* (SHU), *Sjöbjörnen* (SBJ), *Sjöhästen* (SHÄ)
Displacement: 1,125 tons (1,143 tonnes) standard; 1,400 tons (1,422 tonnes) dived
Dimensions: Length 165 ft 8 in (50.5 m)
Beam 20 ft (6.1 m)
Draught 16 ft 9 in (5.1 m)
Armament:
Guns none
Missile systems
none
A/S weapons
2 A/S torpedo tubes
Torpedo tubes
4 533-mm (21-in)
Aircraft
none

Radar and electronics:
Sonar:
Powerplant: 2 Pielstick diesels, delivering 2,200 bhp, and 1 electric motor, delivering power to one shaft
Speed: 15 knots (surfaced); 20 knots (dived)
Range:
Crew: 23
Used only by: Sweden
Notes: The first three boats were built by Kockums Mek Verstads at Malmö between 1965 and 1968, for commissioning in 1967 and 1968; the last two by Karlskrona Dockyard between 1966 and 1968 for commissioning in 1968. The class have high beam to length ratios, and a diving depth of 492 ft (150 m).

'Draken' class submarine (6)

Class: *Delfinen* (DEL), *Draken* (DRA), *Gripen* (GRI), *Nordkaparen* (NOR), *Springaren* (SPR), *Vargen* (VGN)
Displacement: 770 tons (782.3 tonnes) standard; 835 tons (848.4 tonnes) surfaced; 1,110 tons (1,128 tonnes) dived
Dimensions: Length 226 ft 4½ in (69.0 m)
Beam 16 ft 9 in (5.1 m)
Draught 17 ft 4½ in (5.3 m)
Armament:
Guns none
Missile systems
none
A/S weapons
none
Torpedo tubes
4 533-mm (21-in)
Aircraft
none
Radar and electronics:
Sonar:
Powerplant: 2 Pielstick diesels, delivering 1,660 bhp, and 1 electric motor, delivering power to one shaft
Speed: 17 knots (surfaced); 20 knots (dived)
Range:
Crew: 36
Used only by: Sweden
Notes: The first and third boats were built by Karlskrona Dockyard, the other boats by Kockums Mek Verkstads of Malmö, between 1958 and 1961, for commissioning in 1961 and 1962.

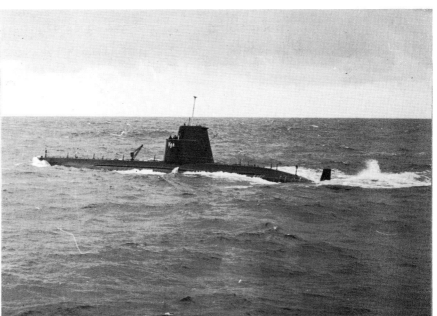

'Häjen' class submarine (6)

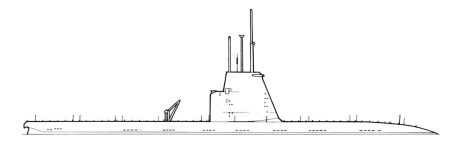

Class: *Bävern* (BAV), *Häjen* (HAJ), *Illern*
(ILN), *Sälen* (SAL), *Uttern* (UTN), *Valen*
(VA)
Displacement: 720 tons (731.5 tonnes)
standard; 785 tons (797.7 tonnes) sur-
faced; 1,000 tons (1,016 tonnes) dived
Dimensions: Length 216 ft 6$\frac{1}{2}$ in (66.0 m)
Beam 16 ft 9 in (5.1 m)
Draught 16 ft 5 in (5.0 m)
Armament:
Guns none
Missile systems
none
A/S weapons
none
Torpedo tubes
4 533-mm (21-in) with 8 torpedoes
Aircraft
none

Radar and electronics:
Sonar:
Powerplant: 2 SEMT – Pielstick diesels, de-
livering 1,660 bhp, and 2 electric motors,
delivering power to two shafts
Speed: 16 knots (surfaced); 17 knots (dived)
Range:

Crew: 44
Used only by: Sweden
Notes: All but the last boat were built by
Kockums Mek Verstads of Malmö, *Valen*
being built by Karlskrona Dockyard. The
boats were built between 1953 and 1958,
for commissioning between 1957 and
1960.

'Hugin' class fast attack craft (missile) (17)

Class: *Jägaren* (P150), *Hugin* (P151) and
15 others (P152–P166)
Displacement: 140 tons (142.25 tonnes)
Dimensions: Length 118 ft 1 in (36.0 m)
Beam 20 ft 4 in (6.2 m)
Draught 4 ft 11 in (1.5 m)
Armament:
Guns 1 57-mm Bofors
Missile systems
6 Penguin Mark 2 SSM launchers
A/S weapons
none
Torpedo tubes
provision for 4 533-mm (21-in)
Aircraft
none
Radar and electronics:
Sonar:
Powerplant: 2 MTU MB20V 672 TY90 die-
sels, delivering 7,000 bhp to two shafts
Speed: 35 knots

Range:
Crew: 19
Used only by: Sweden
Notes: The design is similar to that of the Norwegian 'Hauk' class, and all 17 craft will be built in Norway, the first 12 by Bergens Mekaniske Verksted, and the remaining five by Westermöen. *Jägaren* was commissioned in 1972, the next two in 1977, and the rest will follow in the late 1970s and early 1980s.

'Spica T131' class fast attack craft (torpedo) (12)

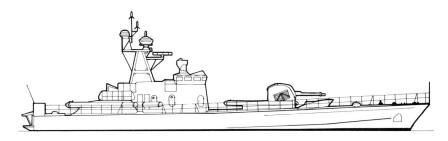

Class: *Norrköping* (T131), *Nynäshamn* (T132), *Norrtälje* (T133), *Varberg* (T134), *Västeräs* (T135), *Västervik* (T136), *Umeä* (T137), *Pitea* (T138), *Lulea* (T139), *Halmstad* (T140), *Stromstäd* (T141), *Ystad* (T142)
Displacement: 230 tons (233.7 tonnes) standard
Dimensions: Length 134 ft 6 in (41.0 m)
Beam 23 ft 3½ in (7.1 m)
Draught 5 ft 3 in (1.6 m)
Armament:
Guns 1 57-mm Bofors
Missile systems
none
A/S weapons
none
Torpedo tubes
6 533-mm (21-in)
Aircraft
none
Radar and electronics: Philips Teleindustrie 9 LV 200 air and surface search radar
Sonar:
Powerplant: 3 Rolls-Royce Proteus gas turbines, delivering 12,900 bhp to three shafts
Speed: 40½ knots
Range:
Crew: 27
Used only by: Sweden
Notes: The craft were all built by Karlskronavarvet, and commissioned between 1973 and 1976. Some craft are to be fitted with 2 twin SSM launchers in the near future.

'Spica T121' class fast attack craft (torpedo) (6)

Class: *Spica* (T121), *Sirius* (T122), *Capella* (T123), *Castor* (T124), *Vega* (T125), *Virgo* (T126)
Displacement: 200 tons (203.2 tonnes) standard; 230 tons (233.7 tonnes) full load
Dimensions: Length 134 ft 6 in (41.0 m)
Beam 23 ft 3½ in (7.1 m)
Draught 5 ft 3 in (1.6 m)

Armament:
Guns 1 57-mm Bofors
Missile systems
none
A/S weapons
none
Torpedo tubes
6 533-mm (21-in)
Aircraft
none
Radar and electronics: Hollandse Signaalapparaten M22 fire-control radar
Sonar:

Powerplant: 3 Bristol Siddeley Proteus gas turbines, delivering 12,720 shp to three shafts
Speed: 40 knots
Range:
Crew: 7+21
Used only by: Sweden
Notes: The first three craft were built by Götaverken of Göteborg, the other three by Karlskronavarvet, the commissioning dates being 1966 and 1967 respectively.

'Plejad' class fast attack craft (torpedo) (3)

Class: *Aldebaran* (T107), *Arcturus* (T110), *Astrea* (T112)
Displacement: 155 tons (157.5 tonnes) standard; 170 tons (172.7 tonnes) full load
Dimensions: Length 147 ft 7½ in (45.0 m)
Beam 19 ft (5.8 m)
Draught 5 ft 3 in (1.6 m)
Armament:
Guns 2 40-mm Bofors in single turrets
Missile systems
none
A/S weapons
none
Torpedo tubes
6 533-mm (21-in)
Aircraft
none

Radar and electronics:
Sonar:
Powerplant: 3 MTY 20V 672 diesels, delivering 9,000 bhp to three shafts
Speed: 37½ knots
Range: 600 miles (965 km) at 30 knots

Crew: 33
Used only by: Sweden
Notes: The craft were all built by Lürssen of Vegesack, and commissioned between 1955 and 1957. Only three of the original 11 are still in service.

Saab-Scania RB08A

Type: naval surface-to-surface tactical cruise missile
Guidance: autopilot, plus (probably) active radar terminal homing
Dimensions: Span 9 ft 10½ in (3.01 m)
Length 18 ft 9 1/10 in (5.72 m)
Height 4 ft 4⅔ in (1.33 m)
Booster: solid-propellant rocket
Sustainer: Turboméca Marboré IID turbojet, rated at 882-lb (400-kg) static thrust
Warhead: high explosive
Weights: Launch 2,679 lb (1,215 kg)
Burnt out
Performance: speed and range classified
Used only by: Sweden
Notes: Fired from a variety of launchers, the RB08A climbs to cruising altitude and speed after launch, and then flies in the direction of the target until the radar homing head guides the missile into the attack. The booster, which weighs 694 lb (315 kg), drops away after expenditure.

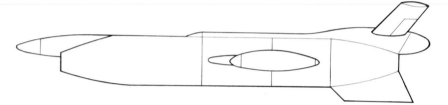

TP41

Type: ship- and submarine-launched torpedo
Guidance: passive homing sonar
Launch method: tube
Dimensions: Length 8 ft (2.44 m)
Diameter 15.75 in (400 mm)
Weight: 551 lb (250 kg)
Engine: electric
Speed:
Range:
Warhead: high explosive
Used only by: Sweden
Notes: This weapon is intended for use in conditions of considerable acoustic difficulty, such as shallow water and the like. The torpedo can be used against surface and submarine targets, and both impact and proximity fuses are standard fittings.

TP42

Type: ship-, submarine- and helicopter-launched torpedo
Guidance: passive sonar homing or optional wire-guidance
Launch method: tube or air-drop
Dimensions: Length 8 ft (2.44 m), plus 7.1 in (18 cm) for wire-guidance casket
Diameter 15.75 in (400 mm)
Weight: 551 lb (250 kg) in basic form
Engine: electric
Speed:
Range:
Warhead: high explosive
Used only by: Sweden
Notes: Developed from the TP41, the TP42 has the same capabilities for operation in acoustically difficult conditions, plus the ability to be air-dropped from helicopters and optional wire-guidance for use in conditions of counter-measures. Impact and proximity fuses are fitted.

TP61

Type: ship- and submarine-launched torpedo
Guidance: wire-guidance from launch vessel
Launch method: tube
Dimensions: Length 23 ft 0⅜ in (7.025 m)
Diameter 21 in (533 mm)
Weight: 3,891 lb (1,765 kg)
Engine: thermal
Speed:
Range:
Warhead: 551 lb (250 kg) high explosive
Used also by: Denmark, Norway
Notes: Intended for use against surface targets, the TP61 is a highly effective and reliable weapon, its thermal engine, using hydrogen peroxide as its oxidiser, ensuring high speed without wake and very long range (some three to five times that of electrically driven torpedoes). Impact and proximity fuses are fitted.

Switzerland

Maritime detachment of the army

Patrol Forces:
10 lake PC

Syria

2,500 men, plus 2,500 reservists

Frigates:
2 Petya I

Light Forces:
6 Osa I FAC(M)
6 Komar FAC(M)
8 P-4 FAC(T)

Patrol Forces:
3 CH type PC

Mine Warfare Forces:
1 T-43 ocean minesweeper
2 Vanya coastal minesweepers

Auxiliaries:
1 diving tender

'Petya I' class frigate (2)

Class: two ex-Russian ships
Displacement: 950 tons (965.2 tonnes) standard; 1,150 tons (1,168 tonnes) full load
Dimensions: Length 270 ft (82.3 m)
Beam 29 ft 11 in (9.1 m)
Draught 10 ft 6 in (3.2 m)
Armament:
Guns 4 76-mm in twin turrets
Missile systems
none
A/S weapons
4 16-barrel MBU 2500 launchers
Torpedo tubes
3 533-mm (21-in)
Aircraft
none
Radar and electronics: 'Slim Net' surface target, 'Neptune' navigation, 'Hawk Screech' gun fire-control radars; 'High Pole' IFF
Sonar: 'Hercules'
Powerplant: 1 diesel, delivering 6,000 hp, and 2 gas turbines, delivering 30,000 hp, to three shafts
Speed: 30 knots
Range: 5,200 miles (8,370 km) at 20 knots
Crew: 100
Used also by: USSR
Notes: The ships were transferred in 1975.

Taiwan

35,000 men, plus 45,000 reservists

Destroyers:
3 Gearing FRAM 1
6 Gearing FRAM II
1 Gearing FRAM II radar picket
8 Allen M. Sumner
4 Fletcher

Frigates:
10 APD 37 and 87
1 Rudderow

Corvettes:
3 Auk

SS:
2 Guppy II

Light Forces:
1 PSMM Mark 5 FAC(M) (+1)
2 25.9-m FAC(T)
2 23.3-m FAC(T)
2 22.6-m FAC(T)

Patrol Forces:
14 coastal PC

Mine Warfare Forces:
14 Adjutant coastal minesweepers
1 minesweeping boat
7 minesweeping launches

Amphibious Forces:
1 Ashland LSD
1 Casa Grande LSD
3 LST1-510

19 LST511-1152
1 LST511-1152 flagship
4 LSM1
22 LCU501 and 1466

Auxiliaries:
4 survey ships
1 repair ship
2 transports
7 support tankers
others

'Gearing FRAM I' and 'Gearing FRAM II' class guided missile destroyer (9)

Class: *Dang Yang* (DD11), ex-US *Lloyd Thomas* (DD764); *Chien Yang* (DD12), ex-US *James E. Kyes* (DD787); *Han Yang* (DD15), ex-US *Herbert J. Thomas* (DD833); *Lao Yang* (DD20), ex-US *Shelton* (DD790); *Liao Yang* (DD21), ex-US *Hanson* (DD832); *Kai Yang*, ex-US *Richard B. Anderson* (DD786); *Te Yang*, ex-US *Sarsfield* (DD837); *Shen Yang*, ex-US *Power* (DD839); and one other, ex-US *Leonard F. Mason* (DD852)
Displacement: 2,425 tons (2,464 tonnes) standard; about 3,500 tons (3,556 tonnes) full load
Dimensions: Length 390 ft 6 in (119.0 m)
Beam 40 ft 10 in (12.4 m)
Draught 19 ft (5.8 m)
Armament:
Guns 4 5-in (127-mm) in twin turrets
4 40-mm in twin mountings (*Han Yang* only)
Missile systems
3 Gabriel SSM launchers (*Dang Yang* only)
A/S weapons
1 octuple ASROC launcher (except DD11, ex-DD786 and ex-DD782)
1 Mark 15 Hedgehog (DD11)
2 triple 12.75-in (324-mm) Mark 32 tubes
Torpedo tubes
none
Aircraft
1 helicopter
Radar and electronics: SPS-37 and SPS-10 search radar (except *Dang Yang*: SPS-6 and SPS-10; and *Chien Yang*: SPS-40 and SPS-10)

Sonar: SQS-23 (except *Dang Yang*: SQS-29)
Powerplant: 4 boilers supplying steam to 2 General Electric geared turbines, delivering 60,000 shp to two shafts
Speed: 34 knots

Range:
Crew: about 275
Used also by: Argentina, Brazil, Greece, Pakistan, South Korea, Spain, Turkey, USA
Notes: The ships were built between 1944 and 1945, and commissioned into US ser-

vice in 1945, 1946 and 1947. *Dang Yang* is the FRAM II vessel, and the ships were transferred as follows: DD11 in 1972; DD12, DD20, DD21 in 1973; DD15 in 1974; ex-DD786, ex-DD837 and ex-DD839 in 1977; and ex-DD852 in 1978.

'Gearing FRAM II' radar-picket guided missile destroyer (1)

Class: *Fu Yang* (DD7), ex-US *Ernest G. Small* (DD838)
Displacement: 2,425 tons (2,464 tonnes) standard; about 3,500 tons (3,556 tonnes) full load
Dimensions: Length 390 ft 6 in (119.0 m)
Beam 40 ft 10 in (12.4 m)
Draught 19 ft (5.8 m)
Armament:
Guns 6 5-in (127-mm) in twin turrets

8 40-mm in twin mountings
4 0.5-in (12.7-mm) in single mountings
Missile systems
3 Gabriel SSM launchers
A/S weapons
2 Hedgehogs
2 triple 12.75-in (324-mm) Mark 32 tubes
Torpedo tubes
none
Aircraft
none
Radar and electronics: SPS-37 and SPS-10 search radars
Sonar: SQS-29 hull-mounted and SQS-10 variable-depth

Powerplant: 4 Babcock & Wilcox boilers supplying steam to 2 General Electric geared turbines, delivering 60,000 shp to two shafts
Speed: 34
Range:
Crew: about 275
Used also by: Argentina, Greece, South Korea, Turkey
Notes: *Small* was built by Bath Iron Works in 1945, and commissioned into US service in 1945. She was converted into a radar picket (DDR) during 1952 and then brought up to FRAM II standards. Transferred in 1971.

'Allen M. Sumner' class guided missile destroyer (8)

Class: *Hsiang Yang* (DD1), ex-US *Brush* (DD745); *Heng Yang* (DD2), ex-US *Samuel N. Moore* (DD747); *Hua Yang* (DD3), ex-US *Bristol* (DD857); *Yuen Yang* (DD5), ex-US *Haynsworth* (DD700); *Huei Yang* (DD6), ex-US *English* (DD696); *Po Yang* (DD10), ex-US *Maddox* (DD731); *Lo Yang* (DD14), ex-US *Taussig* (DD746); *Nan Yang* (DD17), ex-US *John W. Thomason* (DD760)

Displacement: 2,200 tons (2,235 tonnes) standard; 3,320 tons (3,373 tonnes) full load

Dimensions: Length 376 ft 6 in (114.8 m)
Beam 40 ft 11 in (12.4 m)
Draught 19 ft (5.8 m)

Armament:
Guns 6 5-in (127-mm) in twin turrets
4 3-in (76-mm) in twin turrets
8 40-mm in 1 quadruple and 2 twin mountings in some ships
Missile systems
1 triple and 2 twin Gabriel SSM launchers in DD1, DD3 and DD5
A/S weapons
2 Hedgehogs
DCs in some ships
2 triple 12.75-in (324-mm) Mark 32 tubes
Torpedo tubes
none
Aircraft
none

Radar and electronics: SPS-6 and SPS-10 search radars (except *Po Yang*: SPS-10 and SPS-40; and *Nan Yang*: SPS-10 and SPS-37; and *Lo Yang*: SPS-10 and SPS-29)
Sonar:

Powerplant: 4 Babcock & Wilcox boilers supplying steam to 2 General Electric or Westinghouse geared turbines, delivering 60,000 shp to two shafts
Speed: 34 knots
Range:
Crew: about 275
Used also by: Argentina, Brazil, Colombia, Greece, Venezuela
Notes: All except DD5 and DD6 were built by Bethlehem Steel at three yards, while DD5 and DD6 were built by Federal Shipbuilding & Dry Dock, in the period between 1943 and 1944, commissioning into US service in 1944 and 1945. None of the ships received FRAM modernisation. DD1 and DD3 were transferred in 1969; DD2, DD5, DD6 in 1970; DD10 in 1972; and DD14, DD17 in 1974.

'Fletcher' class destroyer (4)

Class: *Kwei Yang* (DD8), ex-US *Twining* (DD540); *Chiang Yang* (DD9), ex-US *Mullany* (DD528); *An Yang* (DD18), ex-US *Kimberly* (DD521); *Kuen Yang* (DD19), ex-US *Yarnall* (DD541)

Displacement: 2,100 tons (2,134 tonnes) standard; 3,050 tons (3,099 tonnes) full load

Dimensions: Length 376 ft 6 in (114.7 m)
Beam 35 ft 11 in (11.9 m)
Draught 18 ft (5.5 m)

Armament:
Guns 4 (*Chiang Yang*) or 5 (others) 5-in (127-mm) in twin turrets
4 3-in (76-mm) in twin turrets in *Kwei Yang* and *Chiang Yang*
Missile systems
1 Sea Chaparral SAM launcher
A/S weapons
2 Hedgehogs in some ships
DCs in some ships
2 triple 12.75-in (324-mm) Mark 32 tubes in *Kwei Yang* and *Chiang Yang*

Torpedo tubes
1 quintuple 21-in (533-mm) in *Kuen Yang*
Aircraft
none
Radar and electronics: SPS-6 and SPS-10 (DDs 8, 9, 19); SPS-10 and SPS-12 (DD18)
Sonar:
Powerplant: 4 Babcock & Wilcox boilers supplying steam to Allis Chalmers (*Kuen Yang*), General Electric (*An Yang*) or Westinghouse (others) geared turbines, delivering 60,000 shp to two shafts
Speed: 36 knots
Range:
Crew: about 250
Used also by: Argentina, Brazil, Chile, Greece, Italy, Mexico, Peru, South Korea, Spain, Turkey, West Germany
Notes: All four ships were built by Bethlehem Steel at two yards between 1942 and 1943, commissioning in US service in 1943. DD8 was transferred in 1971, DD9 in 1971, DD18 in 1967, and DD19 in 1968.

'APD 37' and 'APD 87' class frigate (10)

Class: *Yu Shan* (PF32), ex-US *Kinzer* (APD91); *Hwa Shan* (PF33), ex-US *Donald W. Wolf* (APD129); *Wen Shan* (PF34), ex-US *Gantner* (APD42); *Fu Shan* (PF35), ex-US *Truxton* (APD98); *Lu Shan* (PF36), ex-US *Bull* (APD78); *Shoa Shan* (PF37), ex-US *Kline* (APD120); *Tai Shan* (PF38) ex-US *Register* (APD92); *Kang Shan* (PF42), ex-US *G. W. Ingram* (APD43); *Chung Shang* (PF43), ex-US *Blessman* (APD48); *Tien Shan* (APD215), ex-US *Kleinsman* (APD134)
Displacement: 1,400 tons (1,422 tonnes) standard; 2,130 tons (2,164 tonnes) full load
Dimensions: Length 306 ft (93.3 m)
Beam 37 ft (11.3 m)
Draught 12 ft 7 in (3.2 m)
Armament:
Guns 2 5-in (127-mm) in single turrets
6 40-mm in twin mountings
4 or 8 (*Hwa Shan*) 20-mm in twin mountings
Missile systems
none
A/S weapons
2 Hedgehogs in some DCs
2 triple 12.75-in (324-mm) Mark 32 tubes
Torpedo tubes
none
Aircraft
none
Radar and electronics: SPS-5 and Decca 707 in most
Sonar:
Powerplant: 2 Foster Wheeler boilers supplying steam to General Electric geared turbines, for a turbo-electric drive delivering 12,000 shp to two shafts
Speed: 23⅔ knots
Range:
Crew: about 200
Used only by: Taiwan
Notes: These ships were laid down between 1942 and 1944 as destroyer escorts, but were converted on the stocks into high-speed transports for up to 160 men. The ships were completed between 1943 and 1945, and commissioned between 1943 and 1945. The 'APD 37' class has a high bridge, while that of the 'APD 87' class is low. The ships were transferred between 1962 and 1967.

'Guppy II' class submarine (2)

Class: *Hai Shih* (SS91), ex-US *Cutlass* (SS478); *Hai Pao* (SS92), ex-US *Tusk* (SS426)
Displacement: 1,870 tons (1,900 tonnes) standard; 2,420 tons (2,459 tonnes) dived
Dimensions: Length 307 ft 6 in (93.6 m)
Beam 27 ft 3 in (8.3 m)
Draught 18 ft (5.5 m)
Armament:
Guns none
Missile systems
none
A/S weapons
none
Torpedo tubes
10 21-in (533-mm)
Aircraft
none
Radar and electronics:
Sonar:
Powerplant: 3 Fairbanks Morse diesels, delivering 4,800 bhp, and 2 Elliot electric motors, delivering 5,400 shp to two shafts
Speed: 18 knots (surfaced); 15 knots (dived)
Range:
Crew: 11+70
Used also by: Argentina, Brazil, Venezuela
Notes: The two boats were built by Portsmouth Navy Yard and Federal Shipbuilding & Dry Dock, and entered service with the US Navy in 1945 and 1946. Originally of the 'Tench' class, they were modernised under the GUPPY II programme, and transferred to Taiwan in 1973.

Tanzania

700 men

Light Forces:
7 Shanghai FAC(G)
4 Hu Chwan FAH(T)
3 P-6 FAC(G)
4 P-4 FAC(T)

Patrol Forces:
1 Poluchat PC
2 Schwalbe coastal PC
2 24-m coastal PC
4 Yu Lin coastal PC
4 22.9-m coastal PC

Auxiliaries:
2 LCM

Thailand

28,000, including 8,000 marines

Frigates:
1 Yarrow
2 PF103
1 Cannon
2 Tacoma

Light Forces:
3 Lürssen 45-m FAC(M)
(3 Breda BMB30 FAC(M))

Patrol Forces:
4 Trad PC
7 Liulom PC
1 Klongyai PC
10 PGM71 PC
1 SC type PC
4 Cape PC
21 coastal PC (+1)

Mine Warfare Forces:
2 Bangrachan coastal minesweepers
4 Bluebird coastal minesweepers
1 MCM support ship
10 minesweeping boats

Amphibious Forces:
1 LST1-510
4 LST511-1152
3 LSM1
1 LSG type
2 LSIL
26 LCM6
6 LCU
6 LCVP
?LCA

Auxiliaries:
3 training ships
1 survey ship
3 oceanographic craft
2 support tankers
2 harbour tankers

2 transports
others

Air Arm:
1 MR sqn with 10 S-2F, 2 HU-16
(2 CL-215)

Marine Force:
1 marine bde with 3 inf bns, 1 arty bn

Yarrow type frigate (1)

Class: *Makut Rajakumarn*
Displacement: 1,650 tons (1,676 tonnes) standard; 1,900 tons (1,930 tonnes) full load
Dimensions: Length 320 ft (97.6 m)
        Beam 36 ft (11.0 m)
        Draught 18 ft 1 in (5.5 m)
Armament:
Guns 2 4.5-in (114-mm) in single turrets
    2 40-mm Bofors in single mountings
Missile systems
    1 quadruple Seacat SAM launcher

A/S weapons
    1 3-barrel Limbo mortar
    2 DCTs
    1 DC rack
Torpedo tubes
    none
Aircraft
    none
Radar and electronics: Hollandse Signaalapparaten LW-04 surveillance, M20 fire-control, M44 SAM fire-control and Decca TM 626 navigation radars; HSA combat information centre system
Sonar: Type 170 and Plessey Type MS 27

Powerplant: 1 Rolls-Royce Olympus gas turbine, delivering 23,125 shp, and 1 Crossley-Pielstick 12 PC2V diesel, delivering 6,000 bhp, to two shafts
Speed: 26 knots on gas turbine; 18 knots on diesel
Range: 5,000 miles (8,047 km) on diesel
Crew: 16+124
Used only by: Thailand
Notes: The ship was built by Yarrow at Scotstoun between 1970 and 1971, and commissioned into Thai service in 1973. The use of many automatic systems helps to keep the crew small.

'Trad' class large patrol craft (4)

Class: *Pattani* (13), *Surasdra* (21), *Chandhaburi* (22), *Rayong* (23)
Displacement: 318 tons (323.1 tonnes) atandard; 470 tons (477.5 tonnes) full load
Dimensions: Length 223 ft (68.0 m)
        Beam 21 ft (6.4 m)
        Draught 7 ft (2.1 m)
Armament:
Guns 2 3-in (76-mm) in single mountings

    1 40-mm
    2 20-mm
Missile systems
    none
A/S weapons
    none
Torpedo tubes
    2 twin 18-in (457-mm)
Aircraft
    none
Radar and electronics:

Sonar:
Powerplant: 2 Yarrow boilers supplying steam to Parsons geared turbines, delivering 9,000 hp to two shafts
Speed: 31 knots
Range: 1,700 miles (2,735 km) at 15 knots
Crew: 70
Used only by: Thailand
Notes: These four are the survivors of a class of seven, built in the second half of the 1930s by Cantieri Riuniti dell'Adriatico at Monfalcone.

Togo

200 men

Patrol Forces:
2 coastal PC

Tonga

Patrol Forces:
2 coastal PC

Trinidad and Tobago

286 men of the coastguard service

Patrol Forces:
2 Vosper 31.5-m PC
2 Vosper 31.4-m PC
3 coastal PC

Vosper 31.5-m large patrol craft (2)

Class: *Chaguaramus* (CG3), *Bucco Reef* (CG4)
Displacement: 100 tons (101.6 tonnes) standard; 125 tons (127 tonnes) full load
Dimensions: Length 103 ft (31.5 m)
Beam 19 ft 9 in (5.9 m)
Draught 5 ft 9 in (1.6 m)
Armament:
Guns 1 20-mm Hispano-Suiza
Missile systems
none
A/S weapons
none
Torpedo tubes
none
Aircraft
none
Radar and electronics:
Sonar:
Powerplant: 2 Paxman Ventura diesels, delivering 2,900 bhp to two shafts
Speed: 24 knots
Range: 2,000 miles (3,220 km) at 13 knots
Crew: 3+16
Used only by: Trinidad and Tobago
Notes: Both craft were built by Vosper at Portsmouth, and commissioned in 1972.

Tunisia

2,500 men (500 conscripts)

Frigate:
1 Savage

Patrol Forces:
1 Le Fougueux PC
3 P48 PC
2 Vosper 31.4-m PC
4 32-m coastal PC
6 25-m coastal PC

Mine Warfare Forces:
2 Acacia coastal minesweepers

Auxiliaries:
3 tugs

'Savage' class frigate (1)

Class: *President Bourguiba* (E7), ex-US *Thomas J. Gary* (DER326)
Displacement: 1,590 tons (1,615 tonnes) standard; 2,100 tons (2,134 tonnes) full load
Dimensions: Length 306 ft (93.3 m)
Beam 36 ft 7 in (11.1 m)
Draught 14 ft (4.3 m)
Armament:
Guns 2 3-in (76-mm) in single turrets
2 20-mm
Missile systems
none
A/S weapons
2 triple 12.75-in (324-mm) Mark 32 tubes
Torpedo tubes
none
Aircraft
none
Radar and electronics: SPS-10 surface search and SPS-29 air surveillance radars
Sonar:
Powerplant: 4 diesels, delivering 6,000 bhp to two shafts
Speed: 19 knots
Range: 11,500 miles (18,510 km) at 11 knots
Crew: 169
Used only by: Tunisia
Notes: *Thomas J. Gary* was laid down by Consolidated Steel as an 'Edsall' class destroyer escort, and commissioned into US service as such in 1943. In 1958 she was converted into a 'Savage' class radar picket, and transferred to Tunisia in 1973.

Turkey

45,000 men (31,000 conscripts) plus
25,000 reservists

Destroyers:
3 Gearing FRAM 1
2 Gearing FRAM II
1 Robert H. Smith (minelayer)
1 Allen M. Sumner FRAM II
5 Fletcher

Frigates:
2 Berk

SS:
2 Type 209 (+ 2)
2 Guppy III
7 Guppy IIA

Light Forces:
4 Lürssen FAC(M)
4 Kartal FAC(M)
5 Kartal FAC(T)
7 Jaguar FAC(T)
1 Nasty FAC(T)

Patrol Forces:
2 Asheville PC
6 PC 1638 PC
10 large PC
4 PGM PC
19 J type PC
(14 SAR33 type PC)
4 25.3-m coastal PC

Mine Warfare Forces:
1 77-m minelayer
5 LSM coastal minelayers
1 YMP type coastal minelayer
12 MSC coastal minesweepers
4 MCB coastal minesweepers
5 Vegesack coastal minesweepers
4 inshore minesweepers
9 minehunting boats

Amphibious Forces:
2 Terrebonne Parish LST
2 LST511-1152
5 British LCT
12 LCT
12 LCU
4 LCU501
20 LCM8 type

Auxiliaries:
2 survey ships
1 depot ship
1 support ship
3 support tankers
3 repair ships
others

Air Arm:
(2 ASW sqns) 8 S-2A, 12 S-2E, 2 TS-2A
3 AB 204B helicopters
6 AB 212 ASW helicopters
(10 AB212 ASW helicopters)

'Gearing FRAM I' and 'Gearing FRAM II' class destroyer (5)

Class: *M. Fevzi Çakmak* (D351), ex-US *Charles H. Roan* (DD853); *Gayret* (D352), ex-US *Eversole* (DD789); *Adatepe* (D353), ex-US *Forrest Royal* (DD872); *Kocatepe* (D354), ex-US *Norris* (DD859); *Tinaztepe* (D355), ex-US *Keppler* (DD765)
Displacement: 2,425 tons (2,464 tonnes) standard; 3,500 tons (3,556 tonnes) full load
Dimensions: Length 390 ft 6 in (119.0 m)
Beam 40 ft 11 in (12.5 m)
Draught 19 ft (5.8 m)
Armament:
Guns 4 5-in (127-mm) in twin turrets
Missile systems
none
A/S weapons (FRAM I)
1 octuple ASROC launcher
2 triple 12.75-in (324-mm) Mark 32 tubes
A/S weapons (FRAM II)
1 Hedgehog
2 triple 12.75-in (324-mm) Mark 32 tubes
Torpedo tubes
none

Aircraft
1 helicopter
Radar and electronics: SPS-40 (FRAM I) or SPS-6 (FRAM II) long-range air-search, SPS-10 surface search, and Mark 25 (GFCS Mark 37) fire-control radars
Sonar: SQS-23 (FRAM I) or SQS-29 (FRAM II)
Powerplant: 4 Babcock & Wilcox boilers supplying steam to 2 geared turbines, delivering 60,000 shp to two shafts
Speed: 34 knots
Range: 4,800 miles (7,725 km) at 15 knots
Crew: 15+260
Used also by: Argentina, Brazil, Greece, Pakistan, South Korea, Spain, Taiwan, USA
Notes: With the exception of *Eversole*, which was built by Todd Pacific Shipyard, the ships were produced by Bethlehem Steel, in four different yards. The ships were commissioned into US service in 1945, 1946 and 1947. *Adatepe*, *Gayret* and *Çakmak* are FRAM I modernisations, the others FRAM II. They were transferred to Turkey between 1972 and 1975.

'Robert H. Smith' class destroyer (1)

Class: *Muavenet* (D357), ex-US *Gwin* (DD772)
Displacement: 2,250 tons (2,286 tonnes) standard; 3,375 tons (3,429 tonnes) full load
Dimensions: Length 376 ft 6 in (114.8 m)
Beam 41 ft (12.5 m)
Draught 19 ft (5.8 m)
Armament:
Guns 6 5-in (127-mm) in twin turrets
12 40-mm in 2 quadruple and 2 twin mountings
11 20-mm
Missile systems
none
A/S weapons
none
Torpedo tubes
none

Aircraft
none
Radar and electronics: SPS-6 air search, SPS-10 surface search, Mark 28 (GFCS Mark 37) main armament fire-control, and Mark 34 (GFCS Mark 51) 40-mm quad fire-control radars
Sonar: QCU or QHB
Powerplant: 4 Babcock & Wilcox boilers supplying steam to 2 geared turbines, delivering 60,000 shp to two shafts
Speed: 34
Range: 4,600 miles (7,400 km) at 15 knots
Crew: 274
Used only by: Turkey
Notes: Built at Bethlehem Steel's San Pedro yard between 1943 and 1944, *Gwin* was altered on the stocks from an 'Allen M. Sumner' class fleet destroyer into a minelaying destroyer (MMD), and commissioned as such in 1944. She has a capacity of 80 mines. She was transferred to Turkey in 1971.

'Allen M. Sumner FRAM II' class destroyer (1)

Class: *Zafer* (D356), ex-US *Hugh Purvis* (DD709)
Displacement: 2,200 tons (2,235 tonnes) standard; 3,320 tons (3,373 tonnes) full load
Dimensions: Length 376 ft 6 in (114.8 m)
Beam 40 ft 11 in (12.5 m)
Draught 19 ft (5.8 m)

Armament:
Guns 6 5-in (127-mm) in twin turrets
Missile systems
none
A/S weapons
2 Hedgehogs
2 triple 12.75-in (324-mm) Mark 32 tubes
Torpedo tubes
none
Aircraft
provision for 1 helicopter
Radar and electronics: SPS-40 air search and SPS-10 surface search radars
Sonar: SQS-29

Powerplant: 4 Babcock & Wilcox boilers supplying steam to 2 geared turbines, delivering 60,000 shp to two shafts
Speed: 34 knots
Range: 4,600 miles (7,400 km) at 15 knots
Crew: 15+260
Used also by: Brazil, Chile, Colombia, Iran, South Korea, Venezuela
Notes: *Hugh Purvis* was built in 1944 by Federal Shipbuilding & Dry Dock, and commissioned into US service in 1945. She was transferred to Turkey in 1972.

'Fletcher' class destroyer (5)

Class: *Istanbul* (D340), ex-US *Clarence K. Bronson* (DD668); *Izmir* (D341), ex-US *Van Valkenburgh* (DD656); *Izmit* (D342), ex-US *Cogswell* (DD651); *Iskenderun* (D343), ex-US *Boyd* (DD544); *Içel* (D344), ex-US *Preston* (DD795)
Displacement: 2,050 tons (2,083 tonnes) standard; 3,000 tons (3,048 tonnes) full load
Dimensions: Length 376 ft 6 in (114.8 m)
Beam 39 ft 6 in (12.1 m)
Draught 18 ft (5.5 m)
Armament:
Guns 4 5-in (127-mm) in single turrets
6 3-in (76-mm)
Missile systems
none
A/S weapons
2 Hedgehogs
Torpedo tubes
1 quintuple 21-in (533-mm)
Aircraft
none
Radar and electronics: SPS-6 air search, SPS-10 surface search, Mark 25 (GFCS Mark 37) fire-control, Mark 35 (GFCS Mark 56) fire-control, and Mark 34 (GFCS Mark 51) fire-control radars
Sonar:
Powerplant: 4 Babcock & Wilcox boilers supplying steam to 2 General Electric

geared turbines, delivering 60,000 shp to two shafts
Speed: 34 knots
Range: 5,000 miles (8,047 km) at 15 knots
Crew: 250
Used also by: Argentina, Brazil, Chile, Greece, Italy, Mexico, Peru, South Korea, Spain, Taiwan, West Germany

Notes: The ships were built by Federal Shipbuilding & Dry Dock, Gulf Shipbuilding, Bath Iron Works, and Bethlehem Steel between 1942 and 1943, for commissioning into US service in 1943 and 1944. The first two were transferred to Turkey in 1967, the other three in 1969.

'Berk' class frigate (2)

Class: *Berk* (D358), *Peyk* (D359)
Displacement: 1,450 tons (1,473 tonnes) standard; 1,950 tons (1,981 tonnes) full load
Dimensions: Length 311 ft 5½ in (95.0 m)
Beam 38 ft 8½ in (11.8 m)
Draught 18 ft 1 in (5.5 m)
Armament:
Guns 4 3-in (76-mm) in twin turrets
Missile systems
none
A/S weapons
1 DC rack
2 triple 12.75-in (324-mm) Mark 32 32 tubes
Torpedo tubes
none
Aircraft
1 helicopter
Radar and electronics: SPG-34 fire-control, SPS-40 air search, and SPS-10 surface search radars
Sonar:
Powerplant: 4 Fiat diesels, delivering 24,000 bhp to two shafts
Speed: 25 knots
Range:
Crew:

Used only by: Turkey
Notes: The two ships were built by Gölcük Navy Yard between 1967 and 1972, for commissioning into Turkish service in 1972 and 1975. The design is based on that of the US 'Claud Jones' class.

Type 209 submarine (4)

Class: *Atilay* (S347), *Saldiray* (S348), *Batiray* (S349), *Yildiray* (S350)
Displacement: 990 tons (1,006 tonnes) surfaced; 1,290 tons (1,311 tonnes) dived
Dimensions: Length 183 ft 8¾ in (56.0 m)
Beam 20 ft 4 in (6.2 m)
Draught
Armament:
Guns none
Missile systems
none
A/S weapons
none
Torpedo tubes
8 533-mm (21-in)
Aircraft
none
Radar and electronics:
Sonar: active and passive
Powerplant: diesel-electric, with 4 MTU-Siemens diesel generators, and 1 Siemens electric motor, delivering power to one shaft

Speed: 10 knots (surfaced); 22 knots (dived)
Range: 50 days endurance
Crew: 31
Used also by: Argentina, Colombia, Ecuador, Iran, Peru, Uruguay, Venezuela

Notes: The Type 209 is an Ingenieurkontor of Lübeck design, built by Howaldtswerke of Kiel between 1972 and 1977, for commissioning into Turkish service in 1975 and 1977 (first two). Two more of the class are to be built by Gölcük Navy Yard.

'Guppy III' class submarine (2)

Class: *Ikinci Inonü* (S333), ex-US *Corporal* (SS346); *Çanakkale* (S341), ex-US *Cobbler* (SS344)
Displacement: 1,975 tons (2,007 tonnes) standard; 2,540 tons (2,581 tonnes) dived
Dimensions: Length 326 ft 6 in (99.4 m)
Beam 27 ft (8.2 m)
Draught 17 ft (5.2 m)
Armament:
Guns none
Missile systems
none

A/S weapons
none
Torpedo tubes
10 21-in (533-mm)
Aircraft
none
Radar and electronics:
Sonar:

Powerplant: 4 General Motors Corporation 278A diesels, delivering 6,400 shp, and 2 General Electric electric motors, delivering 5,400 bhp to two shafts
Speed: 20 knots (surfaced); 15 knots (dived)
Range:
Crew: 86
Used also by: Brazil, Greece, Italy
Notes: Both boats were built by the Electric Boat Company and commissioned into the US Navy in 1945. They are of the basic 'Balao' class, modernised under the GUPPY III programme. They were transferred in 1975, and it seems likely that another two, *Clamagore* and *Tiru*, will have been transferred by 1979.

'Guppy 1A' class submarine (1)

Class: *Dumlupinar* (S339), ex-US *Caiman* (SS323)
Displacement: 1,840 tons (1,869 tonnes) standard; 2,445 tons (2,484 tonnes) dived
Dimensions: Length 306 ft (93.2 m)
Beam 27 ft (8.2 m)
Draught 17 ft (5.2 m)
Armament:
Guns none
Missile systems
none
A/S weapons
none
Torpedo tubes
10 21-in (533-mm) with 24 torpedoes

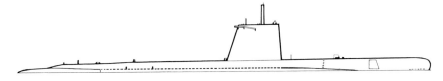

Aircraft
none
Radar and electronics:
Sonar:
Powerplant: 3 General Motors Corporation diesels, delivering 4,800 hp, and 2 electric motors, delivering 5,400 hp to two shafts
Speed: 17 knots (surfaced); 15 knots (dived)
Range: 12,000 miles (19,313 km) at 10 knots surfaced

Crew: 85
Used also by: Argentina, Peru
Notes: *Caiman* was built by the Electric Boat Company and commissioned into US service in 1944. She was transferred to Turkey in 1972, and has been deleted as a result of damage.

'Guppy IIA' class submarine (7)

Class: *Burak Reis* (S335), ex-US *Seafox* (SS402); *Murat Reis* (S336), ex-US *Razorback* (SS394); *Oruc Reis* (S337), ex-US *Pomfret* (SS391); *Uluç Ali Reis* (S338), ex-US *Thornback* (SS418); *Çerbe* (S340), ex-US *Trutta* (SS421); *Preveze* (S345), ex-US *Entemedor* (SS340); *Birinci Inönü* (S346), ex-US *Threadfin* (SS410)
Displacement: 1,840 tons (1,869 tonnes) standard; 2,445 tons (2,484 tonnes) dived
Dimensions: Length 306 ft (93.2 m)
Beam 27 ft (8.2 m)
Draught 17 ft (5.2 m)

Armament:
Guns none
Missile systems
none
A/S weapons
none
Torpedo tubes
10 21-in (533-mm) with 24 torpedoes
Aircraft
none
Radar and electronics:
Sonar:

Powerplant: 3 General Motors Corporation diesels, delivering 4,800 hp, and 2 electric motors, delivering 5,400 hp to two shafts
Speed: 17 knots (surfaced); 15 knots (dived)
Range: 12,000 miles (19,313 km) at 10 knots surfaced
Crew: 85
Used also by: Greece, Spain
Notes: With the exception of *Entemedor*, which was built by Electric Boat, these boats were built by Portsmouth Navy Yard and commissioned into US service in 1944 and 1945. The first pair were transferred in 1970, the second pair in 1972, and the last three in 1973.

Modified 'Balao' class submarine (2)

Class: *Turgut Reis* (S342), ex-US *Bergall* (SS320); *Hizir Reis* (S344), ex-US *Mero* (SS378)
Displacement: 1,562 tons (1,587 tonnes) standard; 2,424 tons (2,463 tonnes) dived
Dimensions: Length 311 ft 9 in (95.0 m)
Beam 27 ft 3 in (8.3 m)
Draught 13 ft 9 in (4.2 m)

Armament:
Guns none
Missile systems
none
A/S weapons
none
Torpedo tubes
10 21-in (533-mm) with 24 torpedoes
Aircraft
none
Radar and electronics:
Sonar:
Powerplant: 4 General Motors Corporation diesels, delivering 6,400 shp, and 2 electric motors, delivering 5,400 shp to two shafts

Speed: 20 knots (surfaced); 10 knots (dived)
Range: 12,000 miles (19,313 km) at 10 knots surfaced
Crew: 85
Used also by: Chile, Greece, Italy, Venezuela
Notes: The boats were built by Electric Boat and Manitowic Shipbuilding between 1943 and 1945, and commissioned into US service in 1944 and 1945 respectively. They were transferred in 1958 and 1960, and bought by Turkey in 1973. Both have now been deleted.

Lürssen type fast attack craft (missile) (4)

Class: *Dogan* (P340), *Marti* (P341), *Tayfun* (P342), *Volkan* (P343)
Displacement: 410 tons (416.6 tonnes)
Dimensions: Length 190 ft 7 in (58.1 m)
Beam 24 ft 11 in (7.6 m)
Draught 7 ft 2½ in (2.2 m)
Armament:

Guns 1 76-mm OTO Melara
2 35-mm in a twin mounting
Missile systems
8 Harpoon SSM launchers
A/S weapons
none
Torpedo tubes
none
Aircraft
none
Radar and electronics: Hollandse Signaalapparaten WM 27 missile fire-control radar

Sonar:
Powerplant: 4 MTU diesels, delivering 18,000 hp
Speed: 38 knots
Range: 700 miles (1,125 km) at 35 knots
Crew:
Used also by: Ecuador
Notes: The lead craft was built by the designers, Lürssen of Vegesack, and the other three by Taskizak Yard of Istanbul. *Dogan* was commissioned in 1976, *Marti* and *Tayfun* in 1977, and *Volkan* in 1978.

'Kartal' class fast attack craft (torpedo/missile) (9)

Class: *Denizkusu* (P321), *Atmaca* (P322), *Sahin* (P323), *Kartal* (P324), *Meltem* (P325), *Pelikan* (P326), *Albatros* (P327), *Şimşek* (P328), *Kasirga* (P329)
Displacement: 160 tons (162.6 tonnes) standard; 180 tons (182.9 tonnes) full load
Dimensions: Length 140 ft 5 in (42.8 m)
Beam 23 ft 3½ in (7.1 m)
Draught 7 ft 2½ in (2.2 m)
Armament:
Guns 2 40-mm in single mountings
Missile systems
Harpoon SSM launchers in *Meltem*, *Pelikan*, *Albatros* and *Simsek*
A/S weapons
none

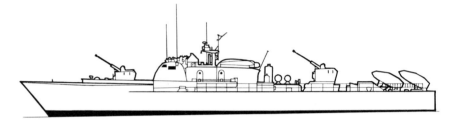

Torpedo tubes
4 533-mm (21-in)
Aircraft
none
Radar and electronics:
Sonar:
Powerplant: 4 MTU 16V 538 diesels, delivering 12,000 bhp to four shafts

Speed: 42 knots
Range:
Crew: 39
Used only by: Turkey
Notes: All the class were built by Lürssen of Vegesack, and commissioned between 1967 and 1968. They are closely related to the German 'Jaguar' class.

Uganda

Lake service being formed

Union of Soviet Socialist Republics

The Navy of the USSR

One of the more misleading generalisations currently in use is the statement that 'The Russian is a land animal.' This is misleading on two counts: firstly 'Russian' refers to only a little over half the population of the USSR; secondly the Empire of the Czars had a long history of naval operations and exploration. These two facts are significant.

At the end of the nineteenth century the Czar's navy ranked fourth in world strengths but it was poorly led, of inferior material quality and widely dispersed. In the Russo-Japanese War of 1904–5 its main strength was destroyed and although sensible and practical plans were produced for its rehabilitation these were frustrated by the stifling effects of court bureaucracy. Thus by 1914 when war was joined with Germany the rebuilding programme was years behind schedule and the showing of the Czar's ships was, to say the least, undistinguished. It was due only to the support given by the sailors to the October Revolution of 1917 that the navy became more widely recognised so that by 1921 the 10th Party Congress decided 'to take measures towards the revival and strengthening of the Red Navy'.

Despite this statement the attitude of the Party, the state of the shipyards and the condition of the economy prevented any new construction for another five years. Then, under the First Five Year Plan of 1928–32, there began a rapid acceleration of new construction which increased as Stalin recognised his maritime incapacity during the Spanish Civil War. By the time of the German invasion in June 1941 the USSR had some 275 ships and submarines in commission with another 220 on the building-ways – a powerful force which did little to distinguish itself in the ensuing four years other than in a variety of amphibious operations and river patrols.

When, in July 1945, Stalin called for the building of a fleet 'still stronger and more powerful' the background was not encouraging. Over half the Soviet surface ships and a high proportion of their submarines had been lost. The western building yards had been destroyed. The tatty, ill-assorted groups of surviving ships were manned by men lacking in both leadership and experience. Within ten years the situation had changed dramatically.

In 1953 the first prototype marine nuclear reactor was put in hand and five years after that the first Soviet nuclear submarine was commissioned. In September 1955 came the launching of the first submarine-oriented ballistic missile, pre-dating the first American Polaris launch.

By 1955 the first Soviet ship-borne cruise missile was under test, being incorporated in the 'Krupny' class destroyer design from 1958. Although the US Navy introduced the Regulus cruise-missile before this time it was a design which was dropped, leaving the Soviet navy alone in its possession of shipboard cruise-missiles until Exocet was introduced by France, and Sea Killer by Italy, in the late 1960s. Since then the adoption of Harpoon by the USN in the mid 1970s with the possible arrival of the Tomahawk long-range cruise missile means that the American fleet is slowly catching up with Soviet armament. In the interim the USSR has produced five new ballistic missiles, extending the range from 370 miles to 5,200; five new cruise-missiles including one type for dived launch from a submarine; five various surface-to-air missiles; three forms of anti-submarine missiles as well as six variants of the air-to-surface missile.

The last of these are carried by the aircraft of the Soviet Naval Air Force which reached a peak of 4,000 machines in 1955 before it passed the fighter protection of naval bases to the Soviet Air Force. Today its fleet of bomber reconnaissance aircraft, amphibians and helicopters numbers some 1,500, including the Mach 2.5 'Backfire' bomber. This considerable force was originally able to cover only the northern areas of the Atlantic and Pacific but now with bases in Cuba, West Africa, East Africa and Aden, the whole Atlantic and Indian Ocean theatres can be subjected to aerial surveillance and, if necessary, attack.

One of the main sea-going bases for helicopters is the 'Kiev' class of aircraft-carrier. In 1967 the first of two helicopter cruisers joined the Soviet fleet carrying eighteen of the then new Hormone helicopters. The reason for the unusually small number of this class became apparent in July 1976 when *Kiev* herself emerged from the Black Sea. Prolonged arguments had taken place over the years in the Soviet navy as to the advisability of building aircraft-carriers – under Stalin two had been ordered, only to be cancelled in 1940. In the post-war plan there was no sign of any ship specifically designed to carry aircraft of any type until the helicopter-cruisers of 1967–8 appeared. But in the same year a new aircraft appeared also – the Yakovlev Freehand vertical/short-take-off (V/STOL) machine. With this future capability the cruiser design was discarded in favour of a carrier capable of carrying both V/STOL and helicopters. The eventual result, a 43,000 ton ship with an angled flight

deck, eight surface-to-surface missile launchers as well as an anti-aircraft and anti-submarine capability, was a radical departure from all previous Soviet ships. Her size gives her accommodation for a fleet staff, her communications the ability for area command and control and her endurance a world-wide operating capability. *Kiev* means that, when supported by the other two ships of her class, the USSR will have the nucleus of powerful task-forces in peacetime and a potent anti-submarine group in war.

As other constituents of such task forces, the Soviet navy has produced a variety of classes of ocean-going cruisers and destroyers as well as providing support in the shape of considerable mine-warfare, amphibious and supply groups. All the modern major surface ships are provided with surface-to-air missiles, some anti-surface ship missiles, some A/S missiles. None is lacking in speed comparable if not superior to Western ships, most of the newer classes relying on the flexibility and acceleration of gas turbines, a not surprising fact when it is recalled that the Soviet navy introduced the world's first all gas-turbine warship – the 'Kashin' class of 1962.

It is not only in their major surface ships that the ingenuity and inventiveness of Soviet designers has been evidenced. Their early attempts with nuclear-propelled submarines and ballistic missiles has already been mentioned. Over the twenty years since their first nuclear boat was built great advances have been made in propulsion, hull form and armament until today they possess over ninety nuclear powered attack and cruise missile submarines in addition to seventy nuclear submarines carrying ballistic missiles as well as 150 diesel boats, with another 100 in reserve. This, the largest submarine fleet in the world, practises operations in all parts of the world's oceans.

Another world 'first' was achieved in 1959 when the first Soviet fast attack craft armed with missiles were commissioned. This trend has been reflected in most of the world's major navies and now provides a very powerful striking force in coastal waters for a comparatively small outlay. High speed operations are also possible with the rapidly increasing number of hydrofoils and hovercraft now being provided. While no more than fifty may be today's total, these multi-purpose craft will probably expand in both size and quantity in the very near future.

World-wide commitments are currently supported by the extensive use of both naval and mercantile tankers and store-ships, and recuperative visits are now possible in many ports where Marxist governments make the Soviet ships welcome. Knowledge of the oceans and what floats upon them is available from the very large numbers of survey, research, mercantile and fishery ships which cover all navigable areas and which are centrally controlled by ministries of the Moscow government.

From the foregoing it is clear that the Soviet Union has a fleet of great potential which has altered out of all recognition from the coast-defence navy of twenty-five years ago. It is powerful, well-armed and widely deployed but, to see it in proportion to other navies, the weaknesses must be borne in mind. The state of the personnel is of prime importance. The officers are highly trained technicians who are, in many cases, constrained by their background. Command does not come as naturally to them as to many Western counterparts because of this and the rigid control exercised from the top. All junior ratings are conscripts with the training and abilities which might be expected when a sailor is on a three-year term. They come from a vast area with a multitude of languages and, as the urban birth rate falls steadily, a higher proportion will appear outlandish to the true Russians. Behind all the 433,000 people of the fleet, however, stand the political officers led by Admiral Grishanov providing motivation and education for all; an education which lacks one very important factor – only the more senior members of the Soviet navy have ever seen action under war conditions. How the remainder would react under fire and in moments of great stress we hope never to discover. Materially the fleet is good, its organisation is efficient. How the man behind the missile, the instrument, the gun would prove himself is the great unknown but he seems to be the possible weak link in the whole impressive chain.

433,000 including 59,000 Naval Air Force, 12,000 Naval Infantry and 8,000 Coast Artillery and Rocket Troops.

SSBN:
6 Delta III (+3)
5 Delta II (+3)
15 Delta I
34 Yankee
1 Hotel III
7 Hotel II

SSB:
13 Golf II
9 Golf I

SSGN:
2 Papa
3 Charlie II
12 Charlie I
29 Echo II

SSG:
16 Juliett
7 Whiskey Long-Bin
3 Whiskey Twin-Cylinder

SSN:
2 Alfa
5 Victor II
16 Victor I
13 November
5 Echo I
(plus 2 in reserve)

SS:
7 Tango
4 Bravo
60 Foxtrot
19 Zulu IV
10 Romeo
50 Whiskey
4 Whiskey Canvas Bag
20 Quebec
(plus 115 in reserve)

CV:
3 Kiev

Helicopter Cruisers:
2 Moskva

Cruisers (CG):
6 Kara (+2)
10 Kresta II
4 Kresta I
4 Kynda
1 Sverdlov

Cruisers (CA):
7 Sverdlov
(plus 4 in reserve)
1 Chapaev

Destroyers (DDG):
4 Krivak II (+?)
15 Krivak I
5 Modified Kashin
14 Kashin
4 Kildin
8 Kanin
3 SAM Kotlin II
5 SAM Kotlin I

Destroyers (DD):
19 Kotlin
36 Skory

Frigates (FF):
1 Koni (+?)
20 Mirka I and II
26 Petya II
9 Modified Petya I
13 Petya I
37 Riga
3 Kola

Corvettes:
8 Grisha III (+?)
4 Grisha II
18 Grisha I
17 Nanuchka (+?)
64 Poti

Light Forces:
50 Osa II FAC(M)
70 Osa I FAC(M)
62 Stenka FAC(P) (+?)
30 Turya FAH(P) (+?)
3 Sarancha FAH (P) (+?)
50 Shershen FAC(T)
20 P-6 FAC(T)

Patrol Forces:
60 SO I PC
15 MO VI FAC(P)
20 Pchela FAH(P)
25 Zhuk coastal PC
80 Shmel river PC
20 BK3 river PC
10 BK2 river PC
20 BKL4 river PC

Mine Warfare Forces:
3 Alesha minelayers
24 Natya ocean minesweepers
47 Yurka ocean minesweepers
20 T-58 ocean minesweepers
84 T-43 ocean minesweepers
5 T-43/AGR radar pickets
12 Sonya coastal minesweepers
3 Zenya coastal minesweepers
73 Vanya coastal minesweepers
40 Sasha coastal minesweepers
8 Evgenya inshore minesweepers
4 Ilyusha inshore minesweepers
20 TR-40 inshore minesweepers
70 K8 minesweeping boats

Amphibious Warfare Forces:
14 Alligator LST
10 Ropucha LST (+?)
60 Polnocny LCT
35 Vydra LCU
2 MP 2 LCU
20 MP 4 LCU
10 MP 10 LCU
40 SMB1 LCU
100 T 4 LCM
25 Gus hovercraft
5 Aist hovercraft

Auxiliaries:
9 submarine depot ships
12 submarine support ships
8 missile support ships
27 repair ships
5 submarine tenders
54 intelligence ships
74 survey ships (plus 24 civilian +2)
11 research ships (+1) (plus 24 civilian)
14 space associated ships (plus 8 civilian)
6 fleet replenishment ships
6 replenishment tankers
37 support tankers
20 salvage ships
15 submarine rescue ships
41 icebreakers
others

Naval Air Force:
280 Tu-16 Badger medium bombers
30 Tu-26(?) Backfire B medium bombers
40 Tu-22 Blinder medium bombers
c 30 Yak-36 FGA
30 Su-17 Fitter C FGA

40 Tu-16 Badger E/F recce
30 Tu-16 Badger ECM
45 Tu-95 Bear D MR
25 Tu-95 Bear F MR
50 Il-38 May MR
90 Be-12 Mail MR
80 Tu-16 tankers
220 Mi-4 Hound, Mi-14 Haze, Ka-25
   Hormone A/B ASW
280 transport and training aircraft

Naval Infantry:
5 naval inf reqts with 15 inf bns, 5 tank
   bns

'Delta II' class nuclear ballistic missile submarine (8)

Class: five boats, plus three building
Displacement: 9,000 tons (9,144 tonnes)
   surfaced; 11,000 tons (11,176 tonnes)
   dived
Dimensions: Length 500 ft (152.5 m)
   Beam 39 ft 4⅓ in (12.0 m)
   Draught 29 ft 6⅓ in (9.0 m)
Armament:
Guns none
Missile systems
   16 SS-N-8 SLBM launch tubes
A/S weapons
   none
Torpedo tubes
   6 533-mm (21-in)

Aircraft
   none
Radar and electronics:
Sonar:
Powerplant: 1 pressurised water-cooled
   nuclear reactor supplying steam to 2 tur-
   bines, delivering 40,000 shp to two shafts
Speed: possibly 25 knots (dived)
Range: limited only by food capacity and
   crew efficiency
Crew: 110
Used only by: USSR
Notes: The boats of this class are building at
   Severodvinsk and Komsomolsk, and first
   came to the notice of western observers in
   1973. Also built at the same yards are six
   'Delta III' boats, with a further three build-
   ing, with a missile armament of 16 SS-N-18
   SLBMs.

'Delta I' class nuclear ballistic missile submarine (15)

Class: 15 boats
Displacement: 8,500 tons (8,636 tonnes)
   surfaced; 10,500 tons (10,668 tonnes)
   dived
Dimensions: Length 442 ft 10½ in (135.0 m)
   Beam 39 ft 4⅔ in (12.0 m)
   Draught 29 ft 6⅓ in (9.0 m)
Armament:
Guns none
Missile systems
   12 SS-N-8 SLBM launch tubes
A/S weapons
   none
Torpedo tubes
   6 533-mm (21-in) with 18 torpedoes or 36
   mines

Aircraft
   none
Radar and electronics:
Sonar:
Powerplant: 1 pressurised water-cooled
   nuclear reactor supplying steam to 2 tur-
   bines, delivering about 40,000 shp to two
   shafts
Speed: 20 knots (surfaced); 26 knots (dived)
Range: limited only by food capacity and
   crew efficiency
Crew: 100
Used only by: USSR
Notes: The class is built at Severdvinsk, and it
   seems that half the USSR's output of 12
   submarines per year is of the 'Delta I' and
   'Delta II' classes. The first boats came to
   the notice of western observers in 1972.

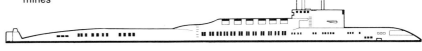

'Yankee' class nuclear ballistic missile submarine (34)

Class: 34 boats
Displacement: 8,500 tons (8,636 tonnes)
   surfaced; 10,000 tons (10,160 tonnes)
   dived
Dimensions: Length 426 ft 6 in (130.0 m)
   Beam 36 ft (11.0 m)
   Draught 27 ft 10⅓ in (8.5 m)
Armament:
Guns none
Missile systems
   16 SS-N-6 SLBM launch tubes
A/S weapons
   none
Torpedo tubes
   8 533-mm (21-in) with 18 torpedoes or 36
   mines
Aircraft
   none

Radar and electronics:
Sonar:
Powerplant: 2 pressurised water-cooled reactors supplying steam to 2 turbines, delivering 40,000 shp to two shafts
Speed: 20 knots (surfaced); 25 knots (dived)
Range: limited only by food capacity and crew efficiency
Crew: 100
Used only by: USSR

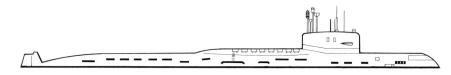

Notes: The boats of this class were built at Severodvinsk and Komsomolsk, and were delivered from 1967 to 1975. They incorporate features from the 'Golf' and 'Hotel' class boats. *Leninets* is the only name known.

'Hotel II' and 'Hotel III' class nuclear ballistic missile submarine (8)

Class: one boat ('Hotel III') and seven boats ('Hotel II')
Displacement: 5,000 tons (5,080 tonnes) surfaced; 6,000 tons (6,096 tonnes) dived
Dimensions: Length 377 ft 3 in (115.2 m)
　　Beam 29 ft 6¼ in (9.0 m)
　　Draught 25 ft (7.6 m)
Armament:
Guns none
Missile systems
　3 SS-N-5 SLBM launch tubes
A/S weapons
　none
Torpedo tubes
　6 533-mm (21-in)
　4 406-mm (16-in)
Aircraft
　none
Radar and electronics: 'Snoop Tray' surface search radar; 'Stop Light' passive ECM
Sonar: 'Hercules' and 'Feniks'
Poerplant: 2 pressurised water-cooled reactors supplying steam to 2 turbines, delivering 30,000 shp to two shafts
Speed: 20 knots (surfaced); 22 knots (dived)
Range: limited only by food capacity and crew efficiency

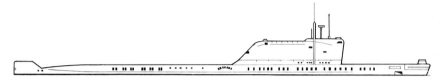

Crew: 90
Used only by: USSR
Notes: The boats were all built between 1958 and 1962 at Severodvinsk, and will probably be placed in reserve or scrapped. The 'Hotel III' boat is an experimental craft with an armament of 6 SS-N-8 SLBM launch tubes. The original 'Hotel I' boats were provided with 3 SS-N-4 SLBM launch tubes. The only known name is *Krasnogvardits*.

'Golf I' and 'Golf II' class ballistic missile submarine (22)

Class: nine ('Golf I') and 13 ('Golf II') boats
Displacement: 2,350 tons (2,388 tonnes) surfaced; 2,800 tons (2,845 tonnes) dived
Dimensions: Length 321 ft 6⅛ in (98.0 m)
　　Beam 27 ft 10½ in (8.5 m)
　　Draught 19 ft 8¼ in (6.0 m)
Armament:
Guns none
Missile systems
　3 SS-N-4 SLBM launch tubes ('Golf I')
　3 SS-N-5 SLBM launch tubes ('Golf I')
A/S weapons
　none
Torpedo tubes
　10 533-mm (21-in) with some 22 torpedoes or 44 mines
Aircraft
　none
Radar and electronics: 'Snoop Plate' surface search radar; 'Stop Light' passive ECM
Sonar: 'Hercules' and 'Feniks'
Powerplant: 3 diesels, delivering 6,000 hp, and 3 electric motors, delivering 6,000 hp, to three shafts
Speed: 17⅔ knots (surfaced); 17 knots (dived)
Range: 22,700 miles (36,535 km) on the surface
Crew: 12+74
Used only by: USSR
Notes: The boats were built at Severodvinsk, the first being laid down in 1957 and completed in 1961, with the last of the class completed in 1962. The boats were

planned as large attack craft, but were converted into intermediate-type missile boats in the mid-1950s.

'Papa' class nuclear cruise missile submarine (2)

Class: two boats
Displacement: 5,500 tons (5,588 tonnes) surfaced; 6,500 tons (6,604 tonnes) dived
Dimensions: Length 328 ft (100.0 m)
Beam 39 ft 4½ in (12.0 m)
Draught 26 ft 3 in (8.0 m)
Armament:
Guns none
Missile systems
10 SS-N-7 SLCM launchers

A/S weapons
none
Torpedo tubes
6 533-mm (21-in)
Aircraft
none
Radar and electronics:
Sonar:
Powerplant: 1 nuclear reactor supplying steam to 2(?) turbines, delivering about

40,000 shp to one shaft
Speed: 20 knots (surfaced); 28 knots (dived)
Range: limited only by food capacity and crew efficiency
Crew: 89
Used only by: USSR
Notes: This was probably conceived as an experimental craft, and only two were built, between 1968 and 1970, probably at Severodvinsk.

'Charlie I' and 'Charlie II' class nuclear cruise missile submarine (15)

Class: 12 ('Charlie I') and three ('Charlie II') boats
Displacement: 4,000 tons (4,064 tonnes) surfaced; 5,100 tons (5,182 tonnes) dived
Dimensions: Length 288 ft 8⅔ in (90.0 m)
Beam 32 ft 9 in (10.0 m)
Draught 24 ft 7 in (7.5 m)
Armament:
Guns none
Missile systems
8 SS-N-7 SLCM launchers
A/S weapons
none
Torpedo tubes
6 533-mm (21-in)
Aircraft
none
Radar and electronics:
Sonar:

Powerplant: 1 pressurised water-cooled reactor supplying steam to 2 turbines, delivering about 30,000 shp to two shafts
Speed: 20 knots (surfaced); 30+ knots (dived)
Range: limited only by food capacity and crew efficiency
Crew: 80

Used only by: USSR
Notes: The first of the boats, replacements for the 'Echo II' class, was laid down in 1967, at the Krasnoye Sormovo yard at Gorkii. The three 'Charlie II' boats are some 29 ft 6⅓ in (9.0 m) longer than the 'Charlie I' class boats • and possibly carry torpedo tube-launched SS-N-15 missiles.

'Echo II' class nuclear cruise missile submarine (29)

Class: 29 boats
Displacement: 4,800 tons (4,877 tonnes) surfaced; 6,000 tons (6,096 tonnes) dived
Dimensions: Length 390 ft 5 in (119.0 m)
Beam 31 ft 2 in (9.5 m)
Draught 25 ft 11 in (7.9 m)
Armament:
Guns none
Missile systems
8 SS-N-3 SLCM launchers
A/S weapons
none
Torpedo tubes
6 533-mm (21-in)
4 406-mm (16-in)
Aircraft
none
Radar and electronics: 'Snoop Plate' or 'Snoop Slab' surface search, 'Front Piece' target acquisition radars; 'Stop Light' passive ECM
Sonar: 'Hercules' and 'Feniks'
Powerplant: 1 pressurised water-cooled reactor supplying steam to 2 turbines, delivering 22,500 shp to two shafts

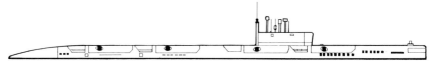

Speed: 20 knots (surfaced); 22 knots (dived)
Range: limited only by food capacity and crew efficiency
Crew: 92
Used only by: USSR
Notes: The 'Echo II' class was derived from

the 'Echo I' class by a lengthening of the hull to accommodate another pair of SLCM launchers. The first boat was laid down in 1963, and the class was built at Severodvinsk and Komsomolsk. The only named boat known is *Frunze*.

'Juliett' class cruise missile submarine (16)

Class: 16 boats
Displacement: 3,200 tons (3,251 tonnes) surfaced; 3,600 tons (3,658 tonnes) dived

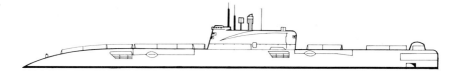

Dimensions: Length 285 ft 5 in (87.0 m)
Beam 32 ft 9⅔ in (10.0 m)
Draught 19 ft 8¼ in (6.0 m)
Armament:
Guns none
Missile systems
4 SS-N-3 SLCM launchers
A/S weapons
none
Torpedo tubes
6 533-mm (21-in)
Aircraft
none
Radar and electronics: 'Snoop Slab' surface
search radar; 'Stop Light' passive ECM
Sonar: 'Hercules' and 'Feniks'
Powerplant: 3 diesel engines, delivering
7,000 bhp, and 3 electric motors, delivering
5,000 hp
Speed: 16 knots (surfaced and dived)

Range: 15,000 miles (24,140 km) on the surface
Crew: 90
Used only by: USSR
Notes: The 'Juliett' class boats were built in Leningrad, the first boat being laid down in

1961, and the last completed in 1967. The missiles can only be fired when the boat is on the surface. There are indications that some of the class have been modified to launch the SS-N-12 missile.

'Whiskey Long-Bin' class cruise missile submarine (7)

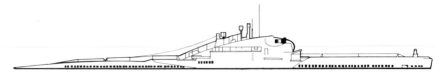

Class: seven boats
Displacement: 1,200 tons (1,219 tonnes) surfaced; 1,600 tons (1,626 tonnes) dived
Dimensions: Length 275 ft 7 in (84.0 m)
Beam 23 ft 11 in (7.3 m)
Draught 16 ft 5 in (5.0 m)
Armament:
Guns none
Missile systems
4 SS-N-3 SLCM launchers
A/S weapons
none
Torpedo tubes
6 533-mm (21-in)
Aircraft
none

Radar and electronics: 'Snoop Plate' surface search radar; 'Stop Light' passive ECM
Sonar: 'Hercules' and 'Feniks'
Powerplant: 2 diesel engines, delivering 4,000 bhp, and 2 electric motors, delivering 2,500 hp to two shafts
Speed: 16 knots (surfaced); 14 knots (dived)
Range: 13,000 miles (20,925 km) on the surface

Crew: 75
Used only by: USSR
Notes: The 'Whiskey Long-Bin' class represents a more successful adaptation of the 'Whiskey' class patrol boat to carry cruise missiles than the earlier 'Whiskey Twin-Cylinder' class. The lack of on-board guidance means that long-range missile accuracy is dependent on mid-course correction by aircraft or other ships. Compared with the 'Whiskey Twin-Cylinder' class, the 'Whiskey Long-Bin' class is some 32 ft 10 in (10.0 m) longer.

'Whiskey Twin-Cylinder' class cruise missile submarine (3)

Class: three boats
Displacement: 1,100 tons (1,118 tonnes) surfaced; 1,400 tons (1,422 tonnes) dived
Dimensions: Length 246 ft (75.0 m)
Beam 23 ft 11 in (7.3 m)
Draught 16 ft 5 in (5.0 m)
Armament:
Guns none
Missile systems
2 SS-N-3 SLCM launchers
A/S weapons
none
Torpedo tubes
4 533-mm (21-in) with 18 torpedoes or 24 mines
Aircraft
none
Radar and electronics: 'Snoop Plate' surface search radar; 'Stop Light' passive ECM
Sonar: 'Hercules' and 'Feniks'

Powerplant: 2 diesels, delivering 4,000 bhp, and 2 electric motors, delivering 2,500 hp to two shafts
Speed: 17 knots (surfaced); 15 knots (dived)
Range: 13,000 miles (20,925 km) on the surface
Crew: 70
Used only by: USSR

Notes: The conversion of these boats was undertaken between 1958 and 1961, and provided a temporary means of getting Russian SLCMs to sea. The whole system is inefficient, and very noisy under the water. For firing, the submarine must be surfaced, and the two cylinders elevated into the firing angle of about 20°.

'Alfa' class nuclear attack submarine (2)

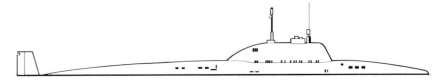

Class: two boats
Displacement: 2,500 tons (2,540 tonnes) surfaced; 3,000 tons (3,048 tonnes) dived
Dimensions: Length 255 ft 11 in (78.0 m)
Beam 32 ft 10 in (10.0 m)
Draught 26 ft 3 in (8.0 m)
Armament:
Guns none

Missile systems
none
A/S weapons
none

Torpedo tubes
6 533-mm (21-in)
Aircraft

Radar and electronics:
Sonar:
Powerplant: 1 reactor supplying steam to 1 geared turbine, delivering 25,000 shp to one shaft
Speed: 16 knots (surfaced); 28 knots (dived)

Range: limited only by food capacity and crew efficiency
Crew:
Used only by: USSR
Notes: These boats were probably unsuccessful prototypes for a new class of attack submarine, or experimental craft, for no more have been built. The original boat was built by the Sudomekh Yard in Leningrad between 1968 and 1970. The two are the world's smallest nuclear submarines.

'Victor I' and 'Victor II' class attack submarine (21)

Class: 16 ('Victor I') and five ('Victor II') boats
Displacement: 4,000 tons (4,064 tonnes) surfaced and 5,200 tons (5,283 tonnes) dived for 'Victor I'; 4,700 tons (4,775 tonnes) surfaced and 6,000 tons (6,096 tonnes) dived for 'Victor II'
Dimensions: Length 285 ft 5 in (87.0 m) for 'Victor I'; 308 ft 4¾ in (94.0 m) for 'Victor II'
Beam 32 ft 10 in (10.0 m)
Draught 26 ft 3 in (8.0 m)
Armament:
Guns none
Missile systems
none
A/S weapons
none
Torpedo tubes
8 533-mm (21-in)
Aircraft
none
Radar and electronics:
Sonar:
Powerplant: 1 pressurised water-cooled reactor supplying steam to turbines, delivering 30,000 shp to two shafts
Speed: 26 knots (surfaced); 30+ knots (dived) for 'Victor I' and 33 knots for 'Victor II'
Range: limited only by food capacity and crew efficiency

Crew: 90 ('Victor I'); 85 ('Victor II')
Used only by: USSR
Notes: The 'Victor' was the first Russian submarine class to feature a tear-drop shape to their hulls. The first boat was laid down in 1965 at the Admiralty Yard in Leningrad, and completed in 1968. The boats can carry up to 64 mines. The only known named boat is Letya SSR, the building rate is two boats per year, and the type is reputedly the fastest submarine in the world. The 'Victor II' class appeared in 1971, its extra length necessary for the tube-launched SS-N-15.

'November' class nuclear attack submarine (13)

Class: 13 boats
Displacement: 4,200 tons (4,267 tonnes) surfaced; 5,000 tons (5,080 tonnes) dived
Dimensions: Length 357 ft 7⅓ in (109.0 m)
Beam 32 ft 1 in (9.8 m)
Draught 24 ft 4 in (7.4 m)
Armament:
Guns none
Missile systems
none
A/S weapons
none
Torpedo tubes
6 533-mm (21-in) with 32 torpedoes or 64 mines
4 406-mm (16-in)
Aircraft
none
Radar and electronics: 'Snoop Tray' surface search radar; 'Stop Light' passive ECM
Sonar: 'Hercules' and 'Feniks'
Powerplant: 2 pressurised water-cooled reactors supplying steam to 2 turbines, delivering 32,500 shp to two shafts
Speed: 20 knots (surfaced); 25 knots (dived)
Range: limited only by food capacity and crew efficiency .
Crew: 88
Used only by: USSR
Notes: This was the first series-built Russian nuclear-powered submarine class, the first boat being laid down in 1958 and completed in 1961, probably at Severodvinsk. Both the hull and the powerplant are noisy, but the boats are fast and have a deep diving depth.

'Echo I' class nuclear attack submarine (5)

Class: five boats
Displacement: 4,300 tons (4,369 tonnes) surfaced; 5,500 tons (5,588 tonnes) dived
Dimensions: Length 367 ft 5½ in (112.0 m)
Beam 31 ft 3 in (9.5 m)
Draught 25 ft 11 in (7.9 m)
Armament:
Guns none
Missile systems
none
A/S weapons
none
Torpedo tubes
6 533-mm (21-in)
Aircraft
none
Radar and electronics: 'Snoop Tray' or 'Snoop Plate' surface search radar; 'Stop Light' passive ECM
Sonar: 'Hercules' and 'Feniks'
Powerplant: 1 pressurised water-cooled reactor supplying steam to 2 turbines, delivering 30,000 shp to 2 shafts
Speed: 20 knots (surfaced); 25 knots (dived)
Range: limited only by food capacity and crew efficiency
Crew: 12+80
Used only by: USSR
Notes: The first boat was laid down in 1961 and completed in 1962. The boats of the class were built up to 1963 at Severod-

vinsk and, probably, Komsomolsk. Based on experience with the 'Hotel' and 'November' class boats, the 'Echo I' class boats were produced at the same time as the 'Juliett' class cruise missile submarines, and like them at first had six (instead of four) launchers for SS-N-3 mis-

siles. The class was probably intended to pioneer nuclear-powered cruise missile boats, but does not appear to have been very successful. Indeed, during 1973 and 1974 the boats were converted into attack submarines with the removal of the SLCMs.

'Tango' class patrol submarine (7)

Class: seven boats
Displacement: 3,000 tons (3,048 tonnes) surfaced; 3,500 tons (3,556 tonnes) dived
Dimensions: 298 ft 6⅔ in (91.0 m)
Beam 30 ft (9.1 m)
Draught 19 ft 8¼ in (6.0 m)
Armament:
Guns none
Missile systems
none
A/S weapons
none
Torpedo tubes
6 (?) 533-mm (21-in)
Aircraft
none
Radar and electronics:
Sonar:
Powerplant: 3 diesels, delivering 6,000 hp, and 3 electric motors, delivering 6,000 shp to three shafts
Speed: 16 knots (surfaced); 20 knots (dived)
Range:

Crew: 62
Used only by: USSR
Notes: The 'Tango' class of conventional attack submarine became known to western observers in 1973, and a building pro-

gramme of two boats per year has been instituted, possibly with a view to replacing older diesel-powered boats or providing Russia's allies with modern conventional boats.

'Bravo' class patrol submarine (4)

Class: four boats
Displacement: 2,300 tons (2,337 tonnes) surfaced; 2,800 tons (2,845 tonnes) dived
Dimensions: Length 219 ft 9¾ in (67.0 m)
Beam 30 ft (9.1 m)
Draught 23 ft (7.0 m)
Armament:
Guns none
Missile systems
none
A/S weapons
none
Torpedo tubes
6 533-mm (21-in)

Aircraft
none
Radar and electronics:
Sonar:
Powerplant: 2 diesels, delivering 5,000 hp, and 2 electric motors, delivering 5,000 bhp to two shafts
Speed: 14 knots (surfaced); 16 knots (dived)
Range:
Crew: 60
Used only by: USSR

Notes: The first of these boats appeared in 1966, and only four have been built. The type may have been experimental, to judge by the low length:beam ratio, in an effort to gain access to greater underwater speeds. Alternatively, the fact that one of these boats is attached to each of the major Russian fleets may indicate that the boats' extra beam is 'padding', and that the boats are used as targets for torpedo and A/S firings.

'Kiev' class aircraft-carrier (3)

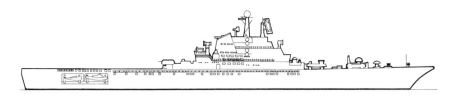

Class: *Kiev, Minsk, Komsomolec*
Displacement: about 43,000 tons (43,688 tonnes) full load
Dimensions: Length 898 ft 10⅜ in (274.0 m)
Beam (hull) 135 ft (41.2 m)
Draught
Armament:
Guns 4 76-mm in twin turrets
8 6-barrel 23-mm AA mountings
Missile systems
4 twin SS-N-12 SSM launchers
2 twin SA-N-3 SAM launchers
2 SA-N-4 SAM launchers
1 SUWN-1 A/S launcher, probably for SS-N-14 or FRAS-1
A/S weapons
2 12-barrel MBU 2500A launchers
Torpedo tubes
2 quintuple 533-mm (21-in)
Aircraft
30–35 helicopters and V/STOL aircraft
Radar and electronics: 'Top Sail' 3D long-range air search, 'Head Net' air search, 'Head Light' SA-N-3 fire-control, 'Pop Group' SA-N-4 fire-control, 'Owl Screech' 76-mm fire-control, plus other radars; a full fit of ECM equipment, including 'Side Globe'
Sonar: probably hull-mounted and variable-depth
Powerplant: geared steam turbines or gas turbines, delivering power to four shafts
Speed: 30+ knots
Range: 13,000 miles (20,922 km) at 18 knots
Crew:
Used only by: USSR

Notes: The three ships are of Nikolayev South construction, being laid down in 1971, 1972, and 1973, for launching in 1973, 1974 and 1976, and commissioning in 1976, 1977 and 1979. Originally known as the 'Kuril' class, these ships have flight decks 68 ft (20.7 m) wide, and armaments of great versatility. It is assumed that catapults may be fitted to allow the embarcation of aircraft other than VTOL types. The Russians designate the ships Anti-Submarine Cruisers.

'Moskva' class helicopter cruiser (2)

Class: *Moskva* and *Leningrad*
Displacement: 14,500 tons (14,732 tonnes) standard; 19,200 tons (19,507 tonnes) full load
Dimensions: Length 644 ft 9 in (196.6 m)
Beam 111 ft 6 in (34.0 m)
Draught 24 ft 11 in (7.6 m)
Armament:
Guns 4 57-mm in twin turrets
Missile systems
2 twin SA-N-3 SAM launchers with 180 missiles
A/S weapons
1 twin SUWN-1 A/S missile launcher
2 12-barrel MBU 2500A launchers
Torpedo tubes
2 quintuple 533-mm (21-in)
Aircraft
18 ASW helicopters
Radar and electronics: 'Top Sail' 3D long-range air search, 'Head Net-C' 3D air warning, 'Don-2' navigation, 'Head Light' SA-N-3 target tracking, 'Muff Cob' 57-mm fire-control radars; 'High Pole' IFF and 'Side Globe' ECM
Sonar: 'Tamir' or 'Hercules' hull-mounted, plus variable-depth
Powerplant: 4 boilers supplying steam to geared turbines, delivering 100,000 shp to two shafts
Speed: 30 knots
Range: 8,000 miles (12,875 km) at 15 knots
Crew: 800
Used only by: USSR
Notes: The two ships were built between 1962 and 1968 at Nikolayev South, and commissioned in 1968 and 1969. They are indications of a new Russian approach to sea power, being the first Russian ships to

mount aircraft (or rather helicopters) as their primary armament. The Russian classification for the ships (Anti-Submarine Cruiser) is probably accurate. The flight deck is located aft of the superstructure, and measures 295 ft 4 in (90.0 m) by 115 ft (35.0 m).

'Kara' class guided missile cruiser (8)

Class: *Azov, Kerch, Nikolayev, Ochakov, Petropavlovsk* and one other, plus two building
Displacement: 8,200 tons (8,331 tonnes) standard; 10,000 tons (10,160 tonnes) full load
Dimensions: Length 570 ft (173.8 m)
Beam 60 ft (18.3 m)
Draught 20 ft (6.2 m)
Armament:
Guns 4 76-mm in twin turrets
4 6-barrel 23-mm mountings
Missile systems
2 quadruple SS-N-14 SSM launchers
2 twin SA-N-4 SAM launchers
2 twin SA-N-3 SAM launchers
A/S weapons
2 12-barrel MBU 2500A launchers
2 6-barrel DCTs
Torpedo tubes
2 quintuple 533-mm (21-in)
Aircraft
1 ASW helicopter
Radar and electronics: 'Top Sail' 3D long-range air search, 'Head Net-C' 3D air warning, 'Head Light' SA-N-3 control, 'Pop Group' SA-N-4 control, 'Owl Screech' 76-mm fire-control, 'Bass Tilt' 23-mm fire-control, 'Don' navigation, 'Sheet Curve' search radars; 'Side Globe' ECM; 'High Pole' IFF

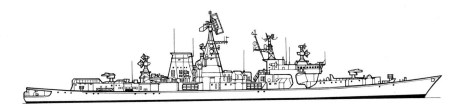

Sonar: bow-mounted and variable-depth
Powerplant: gas turbines, delivering 120,000 hp to two shafts
Speed: about 34 knots
Range:
Crew: about 500
Used only by: USSR

Notes: The ships are of Nosenko Yard, Nikola-yev, construction, and the first was laid down in 1969. They are formidable warships with a comprehensive armament, and are classified by the Russians as Large Anti-Submarine Ships, which slightly belies their powerful AA armaments.

'Kresta II' class guided missile cruiser (10)

Class: *Admiral Isachenkov, Admiral Isakov, Admiral Makarov, Admiral Nakhimov, Admiral Oktyabrsky, Admiral Yumaschev, Kronshtadt, Marshal Timoshenko, Marshal Voroshilov, Vasili Chapaev*, plus two others building
Displacement: 6,000 tons (6,096 tonnes) standard; 8,000 tons (8,128 tonnes) full load
Dimensions: Length 520 ft (158.5 m)
Beam 55 ft 1 in (16.8 m)
Draught 19 ft 8 in (6.0 m)
Armament:
Guns 4 57-mm in twin turrets
4 6-barrel 23-mm mountings
Missile systems
2 quadruple SS-N-14 launchers
2 twin SA-N-3 launchers
A/S weapons
2 12-barrel MBU 2500A launchers
2 6-barrel DCTs
Torpedo tubes
2 quintuple 533-mm (21-in)
Radar and electronics: 'Top Sail' 3D long-range air search, 'Head Net-C' 3D air-warning, 'Head Light' SA-N-3 control, 'Muff Cob' 57-mm fire-control, 'Bass Tilt' 23-mm fire-control, 'Don-Kay' surface search radars; 'Side Globe' ECM; 'High Pole' IFF
Sonar: bow-mounted
Powerplant: 4 boilers supplying steam to 2

geared turbines, delivering 100,000 shp to two shafts
Speed: 35 knots
Range: 5,500 miles (8,850 km) at 18 knots
Crew: 500
Used only by: USSR
Notes: The first ship was laid down in 1967 at the Zhdanov Yard in Leningrad, and com-

pleted in 1970. The design is clearly an updating of that of the 'Kresta I' class, with the addition of more modern equipment and anti-submarine missiles, compared with the 'Kresta I' class armament of SAM missiles. The Russian classification is Large Anti-Submarine Ship.

'Kresta I' class guided missile cruiser (4)

Class: *Admiral Zozulya, Sevastopol, Vice-Admiral Drozd, Vladivostok*
Displacement: 6,140 tons (6,238 tonnes) standard; 8,000 tons (8,128 tonnes) full load

Dimensions: Length 510 ft (155.5 m)
Beam 55 ft 9¼ in (17.0 m)
Draught 19 ft 8¼ in (6.0 m)
Armament:
Guns 4 57-mm in twin turrets
4 6-barrel 23-mm mountings (*Drozd*)
Missile systems
2 twin SS-N-3 with no reloads
2 SA-N-1 launchers

A/S weapons
2 12-barrel MBU 2500A launchers
2 6-barrel DCTs
Torpedo tubes
2 quintuple 533-mm (21-in)
Aircraft
1 ASW helicopter

Radar and electronics: 'Head Net-C' 3D air-warning, 'Big Net' long-range air-warning, 'Plinth Net' medium-range target designator, 'Scoop Pair' SS-N-3 control, 'Peel Group' SA-N-1 control, 'Muff Cob' 57-mm fire-control, 'Bass Tilt' 23-mm fire-control (*Drozd* only), and 'Don' navigation radars; 'Side Globe' ECM; 'High Pole' IFF

Sonar: 'Hercules'

Powerplant: 4 boilers supplying steam to 2 geared turbines, delivering 100,000 shp to two shafts

Speed: 35 knots

Range: 5,500 miles (8,850 km) at 18 knots

Used only by: USSR

Notes: The four ships were built by the Zhdanov Yard in Leningrad, the first unit being laid down in 1964 and completed in 1966. The last of the four was completed in

1968. Although somewhat limited in their armament (by Russian standards), the 'Kresta I' class ships are powerful units capable of detached operations. The Russian classification is Large Anti-Submarine Ship.

'Kynda' class guided missile cruiser (4)

Class: *Admiral Fokin, Admiral Golovko, Grozny, Varyag*

Displacement: 4,800 tons (4,877 tonnes) standard; 5,700 tons (5,791 tonnes) full load

Dimensions: Length 465 ft 9 in (142.0 m)
Beam 51 ft 9 in (15.8 m)
Draught 17 ft 5 in (5.3 m)

Armament:
Guns 4 76-mm in twin turrets
Missile systems
   2 quadruple SS-N-3 launchers
   1 twin SA-N-1 launcher with 32 missiles
A/S weapons
   2 12-barrel MBU 2500A launchers
Torpedo tubes
   2 triple 533-mm (21-in)
Aircraft
   facilities for 1 helicopter

Radar and electronics: 'Head Net-A' long-range air search, 'Scoop Pair' SS-N-3 control, 'Peel Group' SA-N-1 control, 'Owl Screech' 76-mm fire-control, 'Don' navigation radars; 'High Pole' IFF; 'Watch Dog' passive ECM

Sonar: 'Hercules'

Powerplant: 4 boilers supplying steam to 2

geared turbines, delivering 100,000 shp to two shafts

Speed: 35 knots

Range: 7,000 miles (7,112 km) at 15 knots

Used only by: USSR

Notes: The four ships were built by the Zhdanov Yard in Leningrad, the first being laid down in 1960 and completed in 1962.

The last was completed in 1965. The class was the first surface type to carry the SS-N-3 missile, although control of this is dependent on mid-course guidance from other sources, as the 'Kynda' class ships carry no helicopter as standard. The Russian designation is Large Rocket Cruiser.

'Sverdlov' class guided missile cruiser, command cruiser and cruiser (12)

Class: *Dzerzhinski* (1), *Admiral Senyavin* and *Zhdanov* (2), and *Admiral Lazarev, Admiral Ushakov, Aleksandr Nevski, Aleksandr Suvorov, Dmitri Pozharski, Mikhail Kutusov, Murmansk, Octyabrskaya Revolutsiya, Sverdlov* (9)

Displacement: 16,000 tons (16,256 tonnes) standard; 17,500 tons (17,780 tonnes) full load

Dimensions: Length 689 ft (210.0 m)
Beam 72 ft 3 in (22.0 m)
Draught 24 ft 6 in (7.5 m)

Armament:
Guns 12 152-mm in triple turrets (except *Dzerzhinski* and *Zhdanov*: 9 152-mm in triple turrets, and *Senyavin* 6 152-mm in triple turrets)
   12 100-mm in twin turrets
   8 30-mm in twin turrets (*Zhdanov*)
   16 30-mm in twin turrets (*Senyavin*)
   8 6-barrel 23-mm cannon (*Octyabrskaya Revolutsiya*)
Missile systems
   1 twin SA-N-2 launcher (*Dzerzhinski*)
   1 twin SA-N-4 launchers (*Zhdanov* and *Senyavin*)

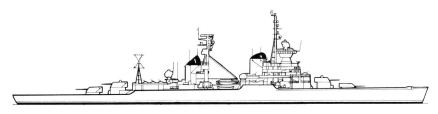

A/S weapons
  none
Torpedo tubes
  none
Aircraft
  facilities for 1 helicopter (*Zhdanov*)
  1 helicopter (*Senyavin*)
Radar and electronics: (unmodified ships) 'Big Net' or 'Knife Rest' or 'Top Trough' or 'Hair/Slim Net' air search, 'Low Sieve' or 'High Sieve' surface search, 'Half Bow' target indicator, 'Top Bow' 152-mm tracker, 'Egg Cup-A' 152-mm fire-control, 'Sun Visor' 100-mm fire-control, and 'Don' navigation radars; 'High Pole' IFF, 'Square Head' IFF; 'Watch Dog' passive ECM
Radar and electronics: (*Dzerzhinski*) 'Big Net' and 'Slim Net' air search, 'Low Sieve' surface search, 'Fan Song-E' missile control, 'High Lane' height-finder, fire-control as in unmodified ships, and 'Neptune' navi-

gation radars; 'High Pole' IFF, 'Square Head' IFF; 'Watch Dog' passive ECM
Radar and electronics: (*Senyavin* and *Zhdanov*) 'Top Trough' air search, surface search, fire-control and navigation as in *Dzerzhinski*, 'Pop Group' SA-N-4 control, and 'Drum Tilt' 30-mm fire-control radars; 'High Pole' IFF; 'Watch Dog' passive ECM
Sonar: 'Tamir'
Powerplant: 6 boilers supplying steam to geared turbines, delivering 110,000 shp to two shafts
Speed: 30 knots
Range: 8,700 miles (14,000 km) at 18 knots
Crew: about 1,000
Used only by: USSR
Notes: These were the last conventional cruisers built by the Russians. Some 24 of the class were projected, 20 were laid down, 17 were launched from 1951 onwards, and

14 were eventually completed by 1956. *Dzerzhinski* was built by the Nosenko Yard, Nikolayev; *Zhdanov* by Nosenko Yard, Nikolayev; *Admiral Senyavin* by Amur Yard, Komsomolsk; and the others at the Baltic Yard, Leningrad, the Marti Yard, Leningrad, Yard 402, Severodvinsk, the Nosenko Yard, Nikolayev, and the Amur Yard, Komsomolsk. *Dzerzhinski* has her twin SA-N-2 launcher in place of X turret; *Admiral Senyavin* has neither X nor Y turrets, the former being replaced by a helicopter hangar with 4 twin 30-mm turrets and a twin SA-N-4 launcher on top, and the latter by a helicopter pad; and *Zhdanov* has a twin SA-N-4 launcher replacing her X turret. *Admiral Senyavin* is flagship of the Pacific Fleet, and *Zhdanov* of the Black Sea Fleet. All except these two can carry 150 mines.

'Chapaev' class cruiser (1)

Class: *Komsomolets* (ex-*Chkalov*)
Displacement: 11,300 tons (11,481 tonnes) standard; 15,000 tons (15,240 tonnes) full load
Dimensions: Length 665 ft (202.8 m)
  Beam 62 ft (18.9 m)
  Draught 24 ft (7.3 m)
Armament:
Guns 12 152-mm in triple turrets
  8 100-mm in twin turrets
  24 37-mm in twin mountings
Missile systems
  none

A/S weapons
  none
Torpedo tubes
  none
Aircraft
  none
Radar and electronics: 'Slim Net' air search, 'Low Sieve' surface search, 'Top Bow' 152-mm fire-control, 'Egg Cup' 152-mm tracking, 'Sun Visor' 100-mm fire-control, 'Neptune' navigation radars; 'High Pole' and 'Square Head' IFF
Sonar: 'Tamir'
Powerplant: 6 boilers supplying steam to

geared turbines, delivering 110,000 shp to four shafts, and diesels for cruising
Speed: 30 knots
Range: 7,000 miles (11,265 km) at 20 knots
Crew: 900
Used only by: Russia
Notes: Some nine of the class were planned, six were laid down, and only five were completed. The class was heavily influenced by German and Italian cruiser design in the late 1930s. *Chkalov* was built by the Marti Yard at Nikolayev between 1939 and 1950. *Komsomolets* is now used as a training cruiser. She has the capability of carrying 200 mines.

'Krivak' class guided missile destroyer (19)

Class: *Bditelny, Bodry, Deiatelny, Doblestny, Dostoyny, Drozny, Razumny, Razyashchy, Razytelny, Retivy, Rezky, Rezvy, Silny, Storozhevoy, Svirepy, Zharki* and three others
Displacement: 3,300 tons (3,353 tonnes) standard; 3,600 tons (3,658 tonnes) and 3,700 tons (3,759 tonnes) full load for 'Krivak I' and 'Krivak II' respectively
Dimensions: Length 404 ft 9 in (123.4 m) for 'Krivak I'; 418 ft (127.4 m) for 'Krivak II'
  Beam 45 ft 11 in (14.0 m)
  Draught 16 ft 5 in (5.0 m)
Armament:
Guns 4 76-mm in twin turrets ('Krivak I')
  2 100-mm in single turrets ('Krivak II')
Missile systems
  1 quadruple SS-N-14 launcher with 4 missiles
  2 twin SA-N-4 launchers with 36 missiles

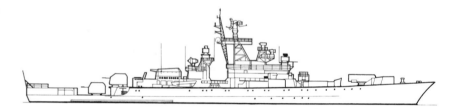

A/S weapons
  2 12-barrel MBU 2500A launchers
Torpedo tubes
  2 quadruple 533-mm (21-in)
Aircraft
  none
Radar and electronics: 'Head Net-C' 3D air-warning, 'Eye Bowl' SS-N-14 control, 'Pop Group' SA-N-4 control, 'Owl Screech' ('Krivak II') or 'Kite Screech' ('Krivak I') gun fire-control and 'Low Trough' ('Krivak II') or 'Don' navigation radars; 'High Pole' IFF
Sonar: bow-mounted and variable-depth

Powerplant: 4 gas turbines, delivering 80,000 shp to two shafts
Speed: 32 knots
Range:
Crew: 250
Used only by: USSR
Notes: The ships of the class have been built since 1971, and continue at the rate of about four per year. The first 12 ships may be designated 'Krivak I', and the subsequent 100-mm gunned ships 'Krivak II'. These vessels are described as Large Anti-Submarine Ships by the Russians.

'Kashin' and Modified 'Kashin' class guided missile destroyer (19)

Class: *Komsomolets Ukrainy, Krasny-Kavkaz, Krasny-Krim, Obraztsovy, Odarenny, Provorny, Skory, Reshitelny, Smetlivy, Soobrazitelny, Sposobny, Sterogushchy, Strogy* and *Stroyny* ('Kashin'); *Ognevoy, Sderzhanny, Slavny, Smely Smyshleny* (Modified 'Kashin')
Displacement: 3,750 tons (3,810 tonnes) standard; 4,500 tons (4,572 tonnes) full load for 'Kashin'; 4,700 tons (4,775 tonnes) full load for Modified 'Kashin'

Dimensions: Length 470 ft 11 in (143.3 m) for 'Kashin'; 481 ft (146.5 m) for Modified 'Kashin'
  Beam 52 ft 6 in (15.9 m)
  Draught 15 ft 5 in (4.7 m)

Armament:
Guns 4 76-mm in twin turrets
  4 30-mm in single mountings (Modified 'Kashin' class only)

Missile systems
    2 twin SA-N-1 launchers with 44 missiles
    4 SS-N-2 (modified) launchers with four
        missiles (Modified 'Kashin' class only)
A/S weapons
    2 12-barrel MBU 2500A launchers
    2 6-barrel DCTs
Torpedo tubes
    1 quintuple 533-mm (21-in)
Aircraft
    provision for 1 helicopter
Radar and electronics: 'Head Net-C' 3D air-
    warning, 'Big Net' long-range air-warning,
    'Peel Group' SA-N-1 control, 'Owl Screech'
    gun fire-control, 'Bass Tilt' 30-mm fire-
    control (Modified 'Kashin' only), and 'Don'
    navigation radars; 'High Pole' IFF
Sonar: 'Hercules', and variable-depth in mod-
    ernised ships
Powerplant: 4 gas turbines, delivering
    96,000 shp to two shafts
Speed: 35 knots
Range: 4,000 miles (6,440 km) at 18 knots
Crew: 300
Used also by: India
Notes: The 'Kashin' class destroyers were the
    world's first series-built warships to rely ex-
    clusively on gas-turbine propulsion. The

ships were built by the Zhdanov Yard in Leningrad and the Nosenko Yard in Nikolayev. The first ship was laid down in 1960, for completion in 1962. The basic role for the ships seems to be AA and A/S protection of 'Kynda' class cruisers, each cruiser being escorted by three or four 'Kashin' class ships. A modernisation programme initiated in 1974 has led to the Modified 'Kashin' class, some 10 feet longer than the originals, and mounting 4 30-mm AA guns, 4 SS-N-2 launchers, and variable-depth sonar, at the expense of the two 6-barrel DCTs.

'Kildin' class guided missile destroyer (4)

Class: *Bedovy, Neudersimy, Neulovimy, Prozorlivy*
Displacement: 3,000 tons (3,048 tonnes)
    standard; 3,600 tons (3,658 tonnes) full
    load
Dimensions: Length 414 ft 11 in (126.5 m)
    Beam 42 ft 7 in (13.0 m)
    Draught 16 ft 1 in (4.9 m)
Armament:
Guns 4 76-mm in twin turrets (after modern-
    isation)
    16 45-mm in quadruple mountings (after
    modernisation)
    16 57-mm in quadruple mountings (before
    modernisation)
Missile systems
    1 SS-N-1 launcher with 4 missiles (before
        modernisation)
    4 SS-N-2 (Modified) with 4 missiles (after
        modernisation)
A/S weapons
    2 16-barrel MBU 2500 launcher
Torpedo tubes
    2 twin 533-mm (21-in)
Aircraft
    none

Radar and electronics: (before modern-
    isation) 'Slim Net' air search, 'Top Bow' SS-
    N-1 control, 'Hawk Screech' 57-mm gun
    fire-control, and 'Neptune' navigation
    radars; 'High Pole and 'Square Head' IFF;
    'Watch Dog' passive ECM
Radar and electronics: (after modernisation)
    'Head Net-C' 3D air-warning, 'Owl
    Screech' 76-mm gun fire-control, 'Hawk
    Screech' 45-mm gun fire-control, and
    'Neptune' navigation radars; 'High Pole'
    and 'Square Head' IFF; 'Watch Dog' pass-
    ive ECM
Sonar: 'Hercules'
Powerplant: 4 boilers supplying steam to
    geared turbines, delivering 72,000 shp to
    two shafts
Speed: 35 knots
Range: 4,000 miles (6,440 km) at 16 knots

Crew: 300
Used only by: USSR
Notes: The four ships were built by the
    Zhdanov Yard in Leningrad the Nosenko
    Yard in Nikolayev, the first being laid down
    in 1958 and completed in 1960. The class
    comprised the world's first guided missile
    destroyers, and is an adaptation of the
    'Kotlin' class, *Bedovy* actually being laid
    down as a 'Kotlin' class ship. The class is
    being modernised by the removal of the
    SS-N-1 launcher from the quarter-deck,
    where 2 76-mm guns are to be fitted, the
    addition of new radar, and the adding of 2
    SS-N-2 (Modified) (otherwise SS-N-11)
    launchers on each side of the rear funnel.
    So far, only *Neudersimy* has not received
    this modernisation. The Russian designation
    is Large Anti-Submarine Ship.

'Kanin' class guided missile destroyer (8)

Class: *Boyky, Derzky, Gnevny, Gordy, Grem-
    yashchyi, Uporny, Zhguchy, Zorky*
Displacement: 3,700 tons (3,759 tonnes)
    standard; 4,700 tons (4,775 tonnes) full
    load
Dimensions: Length 456 ft (139.0 m)
    Beam 48 ft 3 in (14.7 m)
    Draught 16 ft 5 in (5.0 m)
Armament:
Guns 8 57-mm in quadruple mountings
    8 30-mm in twin mountings
Missile systems
    1 twin SA-N-1 launcher with 22 missiles
A/S weapons
    3 12-barrel MBU 2500A launchers
Torpedo tubes
    2 quintuple 533-mm (21-in)

Aircraft
    facilities for 1 helicopter
Radar and electronics: 'Head Net-C' 3D air-
    warning, 'Peel Group' SA-N-1 control,
    'Hawk Screech' 57-mm gun fire-control,
    'Drum Tilt' 30-mm gun fire-control, and
    'Don' navigation radars; 'High Pole' IFF
Sonar: 'Hercules'

Powerplant: 4 boilers supplying steam to 2
    geared turbines, delivering 84,000 shp to
    two shafts
Speed: 34 knots
Range: 4,500 miles (7,240 km) at 16 knots
Crew: 350
Used only by: USSR

Notes: The 'Kanin' class are all converted
    'Krupny' class ships, with their SSM arma-
    ment replaced by SAM missile systems, and
    other detail improvements. The conversion
    was carried out from 1967 by the Zhdanov
    Yard in Leningrad. The Russians designate
    the class Large Anti-Submarine Ships.

'SAM Kotlin I' and 'SAM Kotlin II' class guided missile destroyer (8)

Class: *Bravy, Nakhodchivy, Nastoychivy, Skromny, Vozbuzhdenny; Nesokrushimy, Skrytny, Soznatelny*
Displacement: 2,850 tons (2,896 tonnes) standard; 3,600 tons (3,658 tonnes) full load
Dimensions: Length 414 ft 11 in (126.5 m)
    Beam 42 ft 7 in (13.0 m)
    Draught 16 ft 1 in (4.9 m)
Armament:
Guns 2 130-mm in a twin turret
    4 45-mm in 1 quadruple or 2 twin mountings
    12 45-mm in *Bravy*
    8 30-mm in twin mountings ('SAM Kotlin II' class)
Missile systems
    1 twin SA-N-1 launcher with about 20 missiles
A/S weapons
    2 12-barrel MBU 2500A launchers

2 16-barrel MBU 2500 launchers (*Bravy* and 'SAM Kotlin II' class only)
Torpedo tubes
    1 quintuple 533-mm (21-in) (not in *Bravy*)
Aircraft
    none
Radar and electronics: 'Head Net-C' or 'Head Net-A' 3D air-warning or long-range air search, 'Peel Group' SA-N-1 control, 'Sun Visor' 130-mm gun fire-control, 'Egg Cup-B' 130-mm turret control, 'Hawk Screech' 45-mm gun fire-control, 'Drum Tilt' 30-mm gun fire-control ('SAM Kotlin II' class only), and 'Don' navigation radars; 'Watch Dog' passive ECM

Sonar: 'Hercules'
Powerplant: 4 boilers supplying steam to turbines, delivering 72,000 shp to two shafts
Speed: 36 knots
Range: 4,000 miles (6,440 km) at 16 knots
Crew: 360
Used also by: Poland
Notes: These are converted 'Kotlin' class destroyers, the first being converted in 1962, and the others since 1962. The last three have 30-mm guns, and are designated 'SAM Kotlin II' class ships. The Russians classify the class as Destroyers.

'Kotlin' class destroyer (19)

Class: *Bessledny, Blagorodny, Blestyashchy, Burlivy, Byvaly, Naporisty, Plamenny, Spleshny, Dalnevostochny Komsomolets, Moskovsky Komsomolets, Spokojny, Svedujschy, Svetly, Vdokhnovenny, Vesky, Vlijatelny, Vozmushchenny, Vyderzhanny, Vyzyvajuschy*
Displacement: 2,850 tons (2,896 tonnes) standard; 3,600 tons (3,658 tonnes) full load
Dimensions: Length 414 ft 11 in (126.5 m)
    Beam 42 ft 7 in (13.0 m)
    Draught 16 ft 1 in (4.9 m)
Armament:
Guns 4 130-mm in twin turrets
    16 45-mm in quadruple mountings
    8 25-mm in twin mountings (modified ships only)
    4 25-mm (unmodified ships only)
Missile systems
    none
A/S weapons
    4 MBU launchers (various types)
    6 DCTs (except *Svetly*)
Torpedo tubes
    1 or 2 quintuple 533-mm (21-in)

Aircraft
    facilities for 1 helicopter (*Svetly* only)
Radar and electronics: 'Slim Net' long-range air/surface search, 'Sun Visor' 130-mm gun fire-control, 'Egg Cup-B' 130-mm turret control, 'Hawk Screech' 45-mm gun fire-control, 'Post Lamp' target designation, and 'Don' navigation radars; 'High Pole' and 'Square Head' IFF; 'Watch Dog' passive ECM
Sonar: 'Tamir'
Powerplant: 4 boilers supplying steam to geared turbines, delivering 72,000 shp to two shafts

Speed: 36 knots
Range: 4,000 miles (6,440 km) at 16 knots
Crew: 285
Used also by: Poland
Notes: The first ship of the class was laid down in 1954, and the type has been built at Leningrad, Nikolayev and Komsomolsk. The design has its origins in the 'Tallinn' class. The ships were the world's last 'conventional' destroyers to be built as such.

'Skory' class destroyer (36)

Class: *Besnervny, Bessmenny, Bessmertny, Bezupretchny, Bezukoriznenny, Ognenny, Ostervenely, Ostorozny, Ostroglazy, Otchayanny, Otretovenny, Otvetstvenny, Ozhestochenny, Ozzhivlenny, Serdity, Seriozny, Smotryashchy, Sokrushitelny, Solidny, Sovershenny, Statny, Stepenny, Stojky, Stremitelny, Surovy, Svobodny, Vazhny, Vdumchivy, Verduschchy, Verny, Vidny, Vikhrevoy, Vnesapny, Vnimatelny,*

Volevoy, Vrazumitelny
Displacement: 2,300 tons (2,337 tonnes) standard; 3,100 tons (3,150 tonnes) full load
Dimensions: Length 395 ft 3 in (120.5 m)
    Beam 38 ft 10 in (11.8 m)
    Draught 15 ft 1 in (4.6 m)
Armament:
Guns 4 130-mm in twin turrets
    2 85-mm in a twin turret
    8 37-mm in twin mountings

Missile systems
    none
A/S weapons
    4 DCTs
Torpedo tubes
    2 quintuple 533-mm (21-in)
Aircraft
    none
Radar and electronics: 'Slim Net' long-range air/surface search, 'Hawk Screech' 57-mm gun fire-control, and 'Don' navigation

radars (on modified ships); 'Knife Rest-B' very long-range air-warning and 'Cross Bird' long-range air warning radars (on unmodified ships); 'High Pole' and 'Square Head' IFF; 'Watch Dog' passive ECM (on modified ships)

Sonar: 'Tamir'

Powerplant: 4 boilers supplying steam to

geared turbines, delivering 60,000 shp to two shafts

Speed: 33 knots

Range: 3,900 miles (6,275 km) at 13 knots

Crew: 280

Used also by: Egypt

Notes: The first of the class was laid down in 1949, and the ships were built in the Black

Sea, White Sea, Baltic and Far East. From 1959 onwards some of the class were modernised, with new radar and electronics, 5 single 57-mm guns instead of the 85- and 37-mm guns, only one quintuple torpedo tube mounting, and 2 16-barrel MBU 2500 A/S launchers.

'Mirka I' and 'Mirka II' class frigate (20)

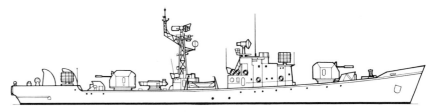

Class: 20 ships

Displacement: 1,050 tons (1,067 tonnes) standard; 1,100 tons (1,118 tonnes) full load

Dimensions: Length 269 ft (82.0 m)
Beam 29 ft 11 in (9.1 m)
Draught 9 ft 10 in (3.0 m)

Armament:
Guns 4 76-mm in twin turrets
Missile systems
none
A/S weapons
4 12-barrel MBU 2500A launchers ('Mirka I')
2 12-barrel MBU 2500A launchers ('Mirka II')
Torpedo tubes
1 quintuple 406-mm (16-in) ('Mirka I')

2 quintuple 406-mm (16-in) ('Mirka II')
Aircraft
none

Radar and electronics: 'Strut Curve' or 'Slim Net' long-range air search, 'Hawk Screech' 76-mm gun fire-control, and 'Don' navigation radars; 'High Pole' and 'Square Head' IFF; 'Watch Dog' passive ECM

Sonar: 'Hercules'

Powerplant: CODOG (COmbined Diesel Or Gas turbine) arrangement, with 2 gas turbines, delivering 30,000 hp, and 2 diesels, delivering 12,000 hp, to two shafts

Speed: 28 knots (gas turbines); 20 knots (diesels)

Range: 5,000 miles (8,047 km) at 10 knots

Crew: 100

Used only by: USSR

Notes: The ships were built between 1964 and 1969 in Leningrad and Kaliningrad, and are derived from the 'Petya' class. The Russian designation is Small Anti-Submarine Ship.

'Petya I', Modified 'Petya I' and 'Petya II' class frigate (48)

Class: 13 ships ('Petya I'), nine ships (Modified 'Petya I'), 26 ships ('Petya II')

Displacement: 950 tons (965.2 tonnes) standard; 1,100 tons (1,118 tonnes) full load

Dimensions: Length 269 ft (82.0 m)
Beam 29 ft 11 in (9.1 m)
Draught 10 ft 6 in (3.2 m)

Armament:
Guns 4 (2 in Modified 'Petya I') 76-mm in twin turrets
Missile systems
none

A/S weapons
4 (2 in 'Petya II') 12-barrel MBU 2500A launchers
Torpedo tubes
1 (2 in 'Petya II') quintuple 406-mm (16-in)
Aircraft
none

Radar and electronics: 'Strut Curve' air search, 'Hawk Screech' 76-mm gun fire-control, and 'Neptune' or 'Don' navigation radars; 'High Pole' and 'Square Head' IFF; 'Watch Dog' passive ECM

Sonar: 'Hercules', plus variable-depth in some ships, now known as Modified 'Petya I' and earlier as 'Petya III'

Powerplant: CODOG (COmbined Diesel Or Gas turbine) arrangement, with 2 gas turbines, delivering 36,000 hp, and 2 diesels, delivering 4,000 hp, to two shafts

Speed: 30 knots (gas turbines); 18 knots (diesels)

Range: 5,000 miles (8,047 km) at 10 knots

Crew: 100

Used also by: India, Syria

Notes: The 'Petya I' class was built between 1960 and 1964 at Kaliningrad and probably at Nikolayev, before being superseded by the 'Petya II' class, which has an extra quintuple torpedo tube mounting in place of the after MBU launchers. The Russian designation is Small Anti-Submarine Ship.

'Riga' class frigate (37)

Class: *Barsuk, Bujvol, Byk, Gepard, Giena, Kobchik, Lisa, Medved, Pantera, Sakal, Turman, Volk* and 25 others

Displacement: 1,200 tons (1,219 tonnes) standard; 1,300 tons (1,321 tonnes) full load

Dimensions: Length 298 ft 9 in (91.0 m)
Beam 31 ft 3 in (9.5 m)
Draught 11 ft (3.4 m)

Armament:
Guns 3 100-mm in single turrets
4 37-mm in twin mountings

4 25-mm in twin mountings (only some ships)
Missile systems
none
A/S weapons
2 MBU 1800, 2500, 2500A or 900 launchers (only some ships)
Torpedo tubes
2 or 3 533-mm (21-in) (only some ships)
Aircraft
none

Radar and electronics: 'Slim Net' air search, 'Sun Visor' 100-mm gun fire-control, and 'Don' navigation radars; 'High Pole' and 'Square Head' IFF; 'Watch Dog' passive ECM

Sonar: 'Tamir' or 'Hercules'

Powerplant: 2 boilers supplying steam to turbines, delivering 20,000 shp to two shafts

Speed: 28 knots

Range: 2,000 miles (3,220 km) at 10 knots

Crew: 150

Used also by: Bulgaria, China, East Germany, Finland, Indonesia

Notes: The 'Riga' class escorts were built at Kaliningrad and Nikolayev between 1952 and 1959, as successors to the 'Kola' class. The types can carry 50 mines, and are classified by the Russians as Escort Ships. The class may be about to be replaced by the new 'Koni' class of frigate.

'Kola' class frigate (3)

Class: *Sovietsky Azerbaidjan, Sovietsky Dagestan, Sovietsky Turkmenistan*

Displacement: 1,200 tons (1,219 tonnes) standard; 1,600 tons (1,626 tonnes) full load

Dimensions: Length 321 ft 5 in (98.0 m)
Beam 31 ft 3 in (9.5 m)
Draught 10 ft 7 in (3.2 m)

Armament:
Guns 4 100-mm in single turrets
4 37-mm in twin mountings
Missile systems
none
A/S weapons
4 DC rails
Torpedo tubes
3 533-mm (21-in)
Aircraft
none

Radar and electronics: 'Ball Gun' surface search, 'Cross Bird' air search, 'Sun Visor' 100-mm gun fire-control radars; 'High Pole' and 'Square Head' IFF

Sonar: 'Tamir'

Powerplant: 2 boilers supplying steam to geared turbines, delivering 25,000 shp to two shafts

Speed: 30 knots

Range: 3,500 miles (5,635 km) at 12 knots

Crew: 190
Used only by: USSR
Notes: The ships were built at Kalingrad and on the Black Sea between 1950 and 1952.

They display a German influence in design and are highly visible from the air. They are classified as Escort Ships by the Russians.

'Grisha I', 'Grisha II' and 'Grisha III' class corvette (30)

Class: 18 ships ('Grisha I'), four ships ('Grisha II'), eight ships ('Grisha III')
Displacement: 900 tons (914.4 tonnes) standard; 1,000 tons (1,016 tonnes) full load
Dimensions: Length 236 ft 2⅔ in (72.0 m)
Beam 32 ft 9 in (10.0 m)
Draught 11 ft (3.6 m)
Armament:
Guns 2 (4 in 'Grisha II') 57-mm in twin turrets
1 6-barrel 23-mm mounting ('Grisha III' only)
Missile systems
1 twin SA-N-4 launcher with 18 missiles ('Grisha I' only)
A/S weapons
2 12-barrel MBU 2500A launchers
DCs
Torpedo tubes
2 twin 533-mm (21-in)
Aircraft
none

Radar and electronics: 'Strut Curve' air search, 'Pop Group' SA-N-4 control ('Grisha I' only), 'Muff Cob' 57-mm gun fire-control, and 'Don' navigation radars; 'High Pole' IFF
Sonar: hull-mounted, plus variable-depth in some ships
Powerplant: CODAG (COmbined Diesel And Gas turbine) arrangement, with 1 gas turbine, delivering 12,000 shp, and 2 diesels, delivering 18,000 shp, to three shafts

Speed: 30 knots
Range: 4,600 miles (7,400 km) at 12 knots
Crew: 80
Used only by: USSR
Notes: The class entered production in 1969 at various Black Sea yards, and is being built at the rate of three or four ships per year. It is a useful multi-purpose type, with good sea-keeping qualities. The type is classified as a Small Anti-Submarine Ship by the Russians.

'Nanuchka' class guided missile corvette (17)

Class: 17 ships
Displacement: 800 tons (812.8 tonnes) standard; 950 tons (965.2 tonnes) full load
Dimensions: Length 193 ft 6¾ in (59.0 m)
Beam 39 ft 5 in (12.0 m)
Draught 9 ft 10 in (3.0 m)
Armament:
Guns 2 57-mm in a twin turret
Missile systems
2 triple SS-N-9 launchers with six missiles
1 twin SA-N-4 launcher with 18 missiles
A/S weapons
none
Torpedo tubes
none
Aircraft
none
Radar and electronics: 'Band Stand' search, 'Pop Group' SA-N-4 control, 'Muff Cob'

57-mm gun fire-control, and 'Don' navigation radars
Sonar:
Powerplant: 6 diesels, delivering 28,000 shp to three shafts
Speed: 32 knots
Range:
Crew: 70
Used also by: India

Notes: The 'Nanuchka' class ships entered production in 1969 at the Petrovsky Yard in Leningrad, and are being built at the rate of three ships per year. Designed for coastal operations, the class packs maximum 'punch' onto minimum hull, and poses a formidable threat to surface ships and aircraft.

'Poti' class corvette (64)

Class: 64 ships
Displacement: 400 tons (406.4 tonnes) standard; 600 tons (609.6 tonnes) full load
Dimensions: Length 193 ft 6¾ in (59.0 m)
Beam 26 ft 3 in (8.0 m)
Draught 8 ft (2.4 m)
Armament:
Guns 2 57-mm in a twin turret
Missile systems
none

A/S weapons
2 12-barrel MBU 2500A launchers
Torpedo tubes
4 406-mm (16-in)
Aircraft·
none
Radar and electronics: 'Strut Curve' air search, 'Muff Cob' 57-mm gun fire-control, and 'Don' navigation radars; 'Watch Dog' passive ECM
Sonar: 'Hercules'
Powerplant: CODAG (COmbined Diesel And

Gas turbine) arrangement, with 2 gas turbines, delivering 24,000 shp, and 2 diesels, delivering 8,000 shp, to two shafts
Speed: 34 knots
Range: 6,900 miles (11,100 km) at 10 knots
Crew: 50
Used also by: Bulgaria, Romania
Notes: The ships of the 'Poti' class were built between 1961 and 1968, and are classified by the Russians as Small Anti-Submarine Ships.

'Natya' class ocean minesweeper (24)

Class: 24 ships
Displacement: 650 tons (660.4 tonnes) full load
Dimensions: Length 190 ft 3 in (58.0 m)
Beam 29 ft 6 in (9.0 m)
Draught 7 ft 3 in (2.2 m)
Armament:
Guns 4 30-mm in twin turrets

Missile systems
none
A/S weapons
2 5-barrel MBU 1800
Torpedo tubes
none
Aircraft
none
Radar and electronics: 'Drum Tilt' 30-mm gun fire-control, and 'Don' navigation radars; 'High Pole' and 'Square Head' IFF

Sonar: 'Tamir'
Powerplant: 2 diesels, delivering 4,800 bhp to two shafts
Speed: 18 knots
Range:
Crew: 50
Used only by: USSR
Notes: The class is designed to succeed the 'Yurka' class, and has been building at the rate of three ships per year since 1971.

'T-58' class ocean minesweeper (20)

Class: 20 ships
Displacement: 790 tons (802.6 tonnes) standard; 900 tons (914.4 tonnes) full load
Dimensions: Length 229 ft 11 in (70.1 m)
Beam 29 ft 6 in (9.0 m)
Draught 7 ft 10 in (2.4 m)
Armament:
Guns 4 57-mm in twin turrets

Missile systems
none
A/S weapons
2 5-barrel MBU 1800 launchers
2 DCTs
Torpedo tubes
none
Aircraft
none
Radar and electronics: 'Muff Cob' 57-mm gun fire-control, and 'Neptune' navigation radars; 'High Pole' and 'Square Head' IFF;

'Watch Dog' passive ECM
Sonar:
Powerplant: 2 diesels, delivering 4,000 bhp to two shafts
Speed: 18 knots
Range:
Crew: 82
Used also by: India
Notes: The class was built between 1957 and 1964.

'T-43' class ocean minesweeper (84)

Class: 84 ships
Displacement: 500 tons (508 tonnes) standard; 570 tons (579 tonnes) full load
Dimensions: Length 190 ft 3 in (58.0 m) in older ships; 198 ft (60.3 m) in newer ships
Beam 28 ft 3 in (8.6 m)
Draught 6 ft 10 in (2.1 m)
Armament:
Guns 2 45-mm in single turrets
4 25-mm in twin mountings (in newer boats only)
Missile systems
none
A/S weapons
none
Torpedo tubes
none
Aircraft
none
Radar and electronics: 'Ball Gun' surface search, and 'Don' navigation radars; 'High Pole' and 'Square Head' IFF
Sonar:
Powerplant: 2 diesels, delivering 4,000 bhp to two shafts
Speed: 17 knots
Range: 1,600 miles (2,575 km) at 10 knots
Crew: 40
Used also by: Albania, Algeria, Bulgaria, China, Egypt, Indonesia, Iraq, Poland, Syria
Notes: The class was built by yards in many parts of Russia between 1947 and 1956.

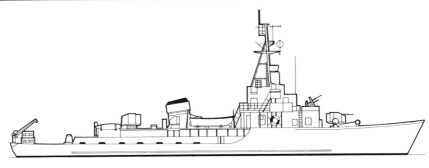

'T-43/AGR' class radar picket (5)

Class: five ships
Displacement: 500 tons (508 tonnes) standard; 570 tons (579 tonnes) full load
Dimensions: Length 190 ft 3 in (58.0 m)
Beam 28 ft 3 in (8.6 m)
Draught 6 ft 10 in (2.1 m)
Armament:
Guns 4 37-mm in twin mountings
2 25-mm in a twin mounting
Missile systems
none

A/S weapons
none
Torpedo tubes
none
Aircraft
none
Radar and electronics: 'Big Net' long-range air-warning or 'Knife Rest' early air-warning, and 'Neptune' navigation radars; 'Watch Dog' passive ECM; 'High Pole', 'Fish Net' and 'Score Board' IFF
Sonar:
Powerplant: 2 diesels, delivering 2,000 bhp to two shafts
Speed: 17 knots

Range: 1,600 miles (2,575 km) at 10 knots
Crew: 60
Used only by: USSR
Notes: The 'T-43/AGR' class is a conversion of the 'T43' ocean minesweeper into a radar picket by the addition of early warning radar: in the first series, 'Knife Rests' were fitted, one forward and one aft; and in later series, a 'Big Net' radar was fitted on a large four-leg mast added towards the stern of the ship. The first conversion was made about 1958.

SS-N-4 'Sark'

Type: submarine-launched ballistic missile
Guidance: inertial
Dimensions: Body diameter 5 ft 10$\frac{9}{16}$ in (1.8 m)
Length 49 ft 2 $\frac{1}{2}$ in (15.0 m)
Booster: solid-propellant rocket
Sustainer: solid-propellant rocket
Warhead: nuclear
Weights: Launch 18.75 tons (19.05 tonnes)
Burnt out

Performance: range 404 miles (650 km)
Used only by: USSR
Notes: Russia's first submarine-launched ballistic missile. Introduced in 1958, and may no longer be operational.

SS-N-5 'Serb'

Type: submarine-launched ballistic missile
Guidance: inertial
Dimensions: Diameter 4 ft 7$\frac{9}{10}$ in (1.42 m) maximum
Length 42 ft 3$\frac{9}{10}$ in (12.9 m) approximately
Booster: solid-propellant rocket
Sustainer: solid-propellant rocket
Warhead: nuclear, in the megaton range
Weights: Launch 18 tons (18.29 tonnes) approximately
Burnt out
Performance: range estimates vary from 746 miles (1,200 km) to 1,491 miles (2,400 km); throw-weight 1,500 lb (680 kg); CEP 2.3 miles (3.71 km)
Used only by: USSR
Notes: Russian 2nd-generation SLBM. Introduced in 1963.

SS-N-6 'Sawfly'

Type: submarine-launched ballistic missile
Guidance: inertial
Dimensions: Body diameter 5 ft 5 in (1.65 m) approximately
Length 31 ft 7$\frac{9}{10}$ in (9.65 m) approximately
Booster: liquid-propellant rocket
Sustainer: liquid-propellant rocket
Warhead: Model 1 and 2 nuclear, 1-2 megatons
Model 3 nuclear, 3xl-kiloton MRV
Weights: Launch 18.75 tons (19.05 tonnes)
Burnt out
Performance: range 1,491 miles (2,400 km) for Model 1; range 1,864 miles (3,000 km) for Models 2 and 3; throw-weight 1,500 lb (680 kg); CEP 1.2 miles (1.93 km)
Used only by: USSR
Notes: Russian 3rd-generation SLBM. Model 1 introduced in 1968, Models 2 and 3 in 1973-4.

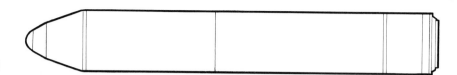

SS-N-7

Type: naval underwater-to-surface tactical cruise missile
Guidance: autopilot, plus radar terminal homing
Dimensions: Span
Body diameter
Length about 22 ft (6.7 m)
Booster:
Sustainer:
Warhead:
Weights: Launch
Burnt out
Performance: speed about Mach 1.5; range in the region of 28 to 34 miles (45 to 55 km)
Used only by: USSR
Notes: Carried in an octuple launcher by Soviet 'Charlie' class nuclear submarines, SS-N-7 missiles began to enter service in 1969 or 1970. Virtually nothing is known about them, but it is presumed that the missile is a surface skimmer in the terminal homing phase of its attack.

SS-N-8

Type: submarine-launched ballistic missile
Guidance: inertial
Dimensions: Body diameter 5 ft 5 in (1.65 m) approximately
Length 42 ft 5$\frac{4}{5}$ in (12.95 m) approximately
Booster: liquid-propellant rocket
Sustainer: liquid-propellant rocket
Warhead: nuclear, 1-2 megatons
Weights: Launch 20.08 tons (20.41 tonnes)
Burnt out
Performance: range 4,850 miles (7,800 km); throw-weight 2-3,000 lb (907-1,361 kg); CEP 0.25 mile (0.4 km)
Used only by: USSR
Notes: Introduced in 1972. Incorporates stellar correction programme as part of the inertial navigation system.

SS-N-11 (or SS-N-2 Modified)

Type: naval surface-to-surface tactical missile
Guidance: autopilot or radio command, plus terminal homing
Dimensions: Span
Body diameter
Length 21 ft (6.4 m)
Booster: solid-propellant jettisonable rocket
Sustainer: rocket
Warhead: high explosive
Weights: Launch
Burnt out
Performance: speed Mach 0.9; range 31 miles (50 km)
Used only by: USSR
Notes: Deployed on 'Osa II' class missile boats in 1968, and then on 'Kildin' and 'Kashin' class destroyers, the SS-N-11 is believed to be derived from the SS-N-2 'Styx'. The terminal homing system is probably active radar.

SS-N-17

Type: submarine launched ballistic missile
Guidance: presumed inertial
Dimensions: Body diameter 5 ft 5 in (1.65 m) approximately
Length 36 ft 3$\frac{2}{5}$ in (11.06 m) approximately
Booster: solid-propellant rocket
Sustainer: solid-propellant rocket
Warhead: nuclear, 1 megaton
Weights: Launch
Burnt out
Performance: range 3,000+ miles (4,800+ km); throw-weight 3,000+ lb (1,361+ kg); CEP 0.33 mile (0.54 km)
Used only by: USSR
Notes: First Russian SLBM to use solid propellant and to be fitted with a post-boost vehicle, suggesting a MIRV capability.

SS-N-18

Type: submarine-launched ballistic missile
Guidance: presumed inertial
Dimensions: Body diameter 5 ft 10$\frac{9}{10}$ in (1.8 m) approximately
Length 46 ft 3$\frac{1}{10}$ in (14.1 m) approximately
Booster: liquid-propellant rocket
Sustainer: liquid-propellant rocket
Warhead: nuclear, 3 x 1 or 2-megaton MIRV
Weights: Launch
Burnt out
Performance: range 5,000+ miles (8,000+ km); throw-weight 5,000+ lb (2,268+ kg)
Used only by: USSR
Notes: Similar to, but larger than, the SS-N-8, with larger volume, advanced guidance and a post-boost vehicle.

SS-N-1 'Scrubber'

Type: naval surface-to-surface tactical cruise missile
Guidance: probably infra-red terminal homing
Dimensions: Span about 15 ft 1 in (4.6 m)
Body diameter about $39\frac{2}{5}$ in (1.0 m)
Length about 24 ft $11\frac{1}{5}$ in (7.6 m)
Booster: solid-propellant rocket
Sustainer: probably ramjet
Warhead: probably high explosive
Weights: Launch 9,000 lb (4,080 kg)
Burnt out
Performance: speed subsonic; range possibly up to 115 miles (185 km)

Used only by: USSR
Notes: Little is known of this first Russian anti-ship missile, which is probably no longer operational. Designed in the form of an aircraft, the 'Scrubber' is launched from a trainable ramp some 55 ft 9 in (17.0 m) in length. The 'Scrubber' entered service in 1958 on board 'Kildin' and 'Krupny' class destroyers.

SS-N-3 'Shaddock'

Type: naval surface-to-surface tactical cruise missile
Guidance: radio command, plus infra-red terminal homing
Dimensions: Span 6 ft $10\frac{3}{4}$ in (2.1 m)
Body diameter $39\frac{2}{5}$ in (1.0 m)
Length 45 ft $3\frac{1}{4}$ in (13.8 m)
Booster: twin JATO units
Sustainer: turbojet
Warhead: nuclear (1 kiloton) or high explosive
Weights: Launch (Shaddock) 26,000 lb (11,790 kg) approximately
Burnt out
Performance: speed Mach 1.5; range 280

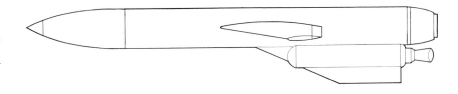

miles (450 km)
Used only by: USSR
Notes: The naval version of the SSC-1 'Shaddock', the SS-N-3 'Shaddock' is the largest Russian maritime cruise missile, and has the configuration of an aircraft. The type entered service in 1962. Estimates of the

SS-N-3's performance and dimensions are difficult, as there are apparently several versions in service on board Russian surface vessels and submarines. Once launched from surface vessels, SS-N-3 missiles are tracked by 'Scoop Pair' radar, and are then controlled by radio command.

SS-N-2 'Styx'

Type: naval surface-to-surface tactical cruise missile
Guidance: probably autopilot or radio command for the cruise phase, and command, active radar or infra-red terminal homing
Dimensions: Span about 9 ft (2.75 m)
Body diameter about $29\frac{1}{2}$ in (75.0 cm)
Length about 20 ft 6 in (6.25 m)
Booster: jettisonable solid-propellant rocket
Sustainer: rocket
Warhead: 794-lb (360-kg) high explosive
Weights: Launch 5,500 lb (2,495 kg)
Burnt out

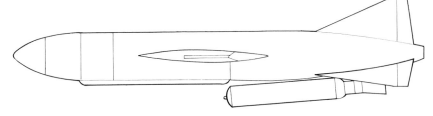

Performance: Speed Mach 0.9; range 25 miles (40 km)
Used also by: Algeria, Bulgaria, China, Cuba, East Germany, Egypt, Finland, India, Indonesia, Iraq, North Korea, Poland, Romania, Somalia, Syria, Vietnam, Yugoslavia

Notes: Introduced into service in 1959 or 1960, the 'Styx' has proved a successful weapon, and has probably been used with a number of guidance methods during its lifetime. All performance and dimension figures are approximate.

SS-N-9

Type: naval surface-to-surface tactical cruise missile
Guidance: autopilot, with optional radio command for mid-course correction by helicopter or aircraft, plus terminal homing
Dimensions: Span
Body diameter
Length about 29 ft $10\frac{1}{4}$ in (9.1 m)
Booster:
Sustainer:
Warhead: high explosive
Weights: Launch
Burnt out
Performance: speed about Mach 1.4; range $46\frac{1}{2}$ miles (75 km) normally, or about 170 miles (285 km) with mid-course guidance
Used only by: USSR
Notes: Deployed only in triple launchers aboard 'Nanuchka' class corvettes, the SS-N-9 entered service in 1968 or 1969. The terminal homing system may be active radar.

SS-N-14

Type: naval surface-to-surface tactical cruise missile
Guidance: autopilot, with possible mid-course radio command correction from a helicopter or aircraft, plus terminal homing
Dimensions: Span
Body diameter
Length about 24 ft $11\frac{1}{4}$ in (7.6 m)
Booster:
Sustainer:
Warhead: high explosive, and possibly nuclear
Weights: Launch about 6,000 lb (2,720 kg)
Burnt out
Performance: speed about Mach 1.2; range about 34 miles (55 km) without mid-course correction
Used only by: USSR
Notes: Deployed aboard 'Kresta II' class cruisers and 'Krivak' class destroyers, SS-N-10 missiles are probably intended for the anti-shipping, and possibly for the anti-submarine, role. It is likely that the terminal homing system is active radar, with optional anti-radiation homing. The SS-N-14 became operational in 1968.

SA-N-1 'Goa'

Type: naval surface-to-air tactical guided missile
Guidance: radio command, plus (probably) radar terminal homing
Dimensions: Span 3 ft 11¼ in (1.2 m)
Body diameter (booster) 23⅜ in (60.0 cm); (second stage) 17¾ in (45.0 cm)
Length 22 ft (6.7 m)
Booster: solid-propellant rocket
Sustainer: solid-propellant rocket
Warhead: high explosive
Weights: Launch 882 lb (400 kg)
Burnt out
Performance: speed Mach 2; slant range about 9 miles (15 km); ceiling 39,370 ft (12,000 m)

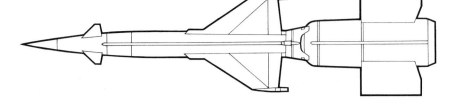

Used also by: Poland
Notes: The SA-3 and SA-N-1 missiles are probably identical, but the radars associated with the land and naval systems are totally different, the naval system being used in conjunction with the 'Peel Group'

compound radar complex. The launcher is a twin one, the arms rotating to the vertical position for reloading through deck hatches.

SA-N-2 'Guideline'

Type: naval surface-to-air tactical guided missile
Guidance: radio command
Dimensions: Span 5 ft 6⁹⁄₁₆ in (1.7 m)
Body diameter (booster) 27⅜ in (70.0 cm); (second stage) 19⁷⁄₁₀ in (50.0 cm)
Length 35 ft 1¼ in (10.7 m)
Booster: solid-propellant rocket
Sustainer: liquid-propellant rocket
Warhead: 287-lb (130-kg) high explosive
Weights: Launch about 5,071 lb (2,300 kg)
Burnt out
Performance: speed Mach 3.5; slant range about 25 miles (40 km); ceiling 59,055 ft (18,000 m)
Used only by: USSR
Notes: Derived from the land-based SA-2 'Guideline, the SA-N-2 is used only on the cruiser *Dzerzhinski*, perhaps because of the difficulty of installing the necessary 'Fan Song' radar in smaller vessels.

SA-N-3 'Goblet'

Type: naval surface-to-air tactical guided missile
Guidance: radio command, plus semi-active radar terminal homing
Dimensions: Span 4 ft 0⅘ in (1.24 m)
Body diameter 13⅛ in (33.5 cm)
Length 29 ft 4⁷⁄₁₀ in (6.2 m) with tail cone
Booster: solid-propellant rocket
Sustainer: ramjet, using the same combustion chamber as the booster
Warhead: 88-lb (40-kg) high explosive
Weights: Launch about 1,213 lb (550 kg)
Burnt out
Performance: speed Mach 2.8; range about 37 miles (60 km) at high altitude, 18½ miles (30 km) at low altitude; minimum range about 2½ miles (4 km); ceiling 59,055 ft (18,000 m)
Used only by: USSR
Notes: First seen on 'Kresta II' class cruisers and the helicopter-carrier *Moskva*, the SA-N-3 system is only conjectured to be the naval equivalent of the land-based SA-6 'Gainful' missile, whose specifications are quoted above. The radar associated with the SA-N-3 is 'Head Lights'. The system is also used on the 'Kara' class and the aircraft-carrier *Kiev*.

SA-N-4

Type: naval surface-to-air tactical guided missile
Guidance: radio command
Dimensions: Span about 23⅜ in (60.0 cm)
Body diameter about 8¼ in (21.0 cm)
Length about 10 ft 6 in (3.2 m)
Booster: probably solid-propellant rocket
Sustainer: probably solid-propellant rocket
Warhead: high explosive
Weights: Launch
Burnt out
Performance: speed possibly Mach 2; range between 5 and 10 miles (8 and 16 km); operating altitude between 164 and 19,685 ft (50 and 6,000 m)
Used only by: USSR
Notes: Although widely used, virtually nothing is known of this naval missile system, and the only reason to conjecture that it is similar to the land SA-8 'Gecko' (to which the details given above relate) is the coincidence of various aspects of the naval 'Pop Group' and land radars. The naval missile, on a twin launcher, is located in wells under the deck, and 'pops up' before launching.

21-in torpedo

Type: ship-, submarine- and aircraft-launched torpedo
Guidance:
Launch method: tube
Dimensions: Length possibly 27 ft 0¾ in (8.25 m)
Diameter 21 in (533 mm)

Weight:
Engine: thermal
Speed:
Range:
Warhead: high explosive, or in rare cases nuclear
Used only by: Russian-built warships

Notes: Very little is known of Russian torpedoes, but it is assumed that they have followed Western practice in following up the development of German World War II torpedoes. It is also reported that there are two other types of torpedo: a 457-mm (18-in) weapon used by aircraft, and a 16-in (406-mm) weapon for use in light destroyers and submarine chasers.

United Arab Emirates

(Abu Dhabi, Ajman, Dubai, Fujairah, Ras al Khaimah, Sharjah and Umm al Qaiwan)

600 men

Patrol Forces:
6 Vosper Thornycroft 33.5-m PC
3 Keith Nelson 17.4-m coastal PC
6 Dhafeer coastal PC
2 Cheverton 27-ft coastal PC

The police force operates five Fairey Spear coastal PC

United Kingdom

The Royal Navy
It is particularly difficult to assess the current state of the Royal Navy: since World War II Britain has withdrawn from any real pretensions of world power, at least so far as worldwide commitments are concerned, and the defence forces are still in a relative state of turmoil, adapting themselves to their new role as members of the NATO alliance armed forces. However, Britain still relies enormously on overseas trade, and the need to protect these vital trade lanes, or rather the shipping using them, seems to be less and less in the forefront of defence planning. The Royal Navy has four primary missions (contribution to NATO's main surface forces, trade protection, coastal defence and the protection of offshore interests such as the North Sea oilfields, combined with the need to protect dwindling overseas commitments), neither of which seems to have been fully met. For its tasks, the Royal Navy has 67,770 personnel, some 21.6 per cent of the total armed forces, who have a budget of 4.95 per cent of the gross national product.

What may be considered the Royal Navy's fifth major mission, the provision of Britain's strategic nuclear deterrent force in the form of SLBMs carried in four nuclear-powered submarines, is in a sense divorced from the other missions. Even so, although the deterrent force is still just about effective, it will not remain so for much longer, for the Polaris missiles embarked are rapidly approaching the stage of obsolescence, and the defence planners must before long decide on a replacement or alternative to this costly system.

NATO commitments and trade protection require similar ships, and here Britain is reasonably well placed. Although argument still continues about the desirability of abandoning aircraft-carriers entirely, the situation is partially remedied by the construction of new anti-submarine cruisers able to operate VTOL aircraft and helicopters. Unfortunately, there will be a gap in the Royal Navy's ranks until the first of these, *Invincible*, is commissioned possibly in 1980. Another unit of the type is building, and it seems that a third may also be ordered. For the rest, the Royal Navy's most important major surface warships are the two helicopter cruisers of the 'Tiger' class, the one Type 82 cruiser, the seven 'County' class cruisers, the six Type 42 'Sheffield' class destroyers (with four more to follow), and frigates. The helicopter cruisers each embark four A/S helicopters, but must surely be near the ends of their effective lives. Superficially, the cruisers and destroyers appear effective units, but

suffer from two grave deficiencies: firstly, none is equipped to carry more than one A/S helicopter and, secondly, although most are adequately provided with SAM launchers, and some with SSM launchers, missiles of all types are totally insufficient in numbers as a result of financial restrictions.

Much the same applies to the frigates of the Type 21 'Amazon', Type 22 'Broadsword', 'Leander', 'Broad-beamed Leander', Type 81 'Tribal', Modified Type 12 'Rothesay' and Type 61 'Salisbury' classes. All are adequate ships, but limited in helicopter and missile armament. Many of these ships have only obsolescent A/S equipment as well.

It is in coastal defence and offshore protection that the Royal Navy is most deficient, however. And it is on these forces that the main burden of local defence would fall in the event of a crisis calling the major surface ships away into the North Atlantic. Offshore protection is the province of the five 'Island' and four 'Bird' class craft, which are slow, and have no armament worthy of note. In a crisis they could be supported by a number of other small craft, but again none of these has any powerful armament, even torpedoes. In coastal waters moreover, it is reckoned that the cutback in MCM forces means that the British have the means to clear only three major ports of mines at any one time, a situation boding ill for any prospects of worthwhile reinforcements reaching British shores or being transshipped to continental destinations. It is clear, therefore, that the Royal Navy is in urgent need of substantial numbers of FAC types, with missile and torpedo armament, as well as quantities of missile-armed hovercraft for offshore protection. Only thus can coastal and offshore protection be ensured.

Of the major forces this leaves the submarine arm and the Fleet Air Arm. Submarines are adequately provided for, the Royal Navy having nine nuclear and 17 diesel attack submarines, although thought will have to be given in the near future to the replacement of the diesel-powered boats by more modern craft with high underwater speed, great manoeuvrability, and quiet running characteristics. The Fleet Air Arm has been heaviest hit by governmental monetary restrictions, strategic indecisions, and the decision finally to phase out the Royal Navy's aircraft-carriers. This leaves the Fleet Air Arm with one attack squadron of Phantom aircraft, one strike squadron of Buccaneer aircraft, one AEW squadron with Gannet aircraft, and seven helicopter squadrons with a miscellany of types, plus various training and transport units, and SAR

helicopter flights.

The lesson is clear: the Royal Navy is well equipped with major surface ships and service/support forces, but needs a clear politico-military decision on where it is to go from here. Modern weapons such as missiles are urgently needed, and high-speed patrol and attack forces are vitally necessary, especially given the political ambitions entertained from British North Sea oilfields. The mine warfare forces, although adequate in quality, are desperately short of the latest equipment and enough vessels.

67,770 men including Fleet Air Arm and Royal Marines, plus 29,100 regular and 6,500 volunteer reservists

SSBN:
4 Resolution

SSN:
4 Swiftsure (+2)
5 Valiant
1 Dreadnought
(1 Trafalgar + ?)

SS:
13 Oberon
4 Porpoise

V/STOL Carrier:
(1 Hermes being reactivated)

Helicopter Carrier:
1 Hermes

Anti-Submarine Cruisers:
(2 Invincible)

Helicopter Cruisers:
2 Tiger

Light Cruisers:
1 Type 82
7 County

Destroyers (DDG):
6 Type 42/Sheffield (+4)

Frigates (FFG):
8 Type 21/Amazon
(1 Type 22/Broadsword + 3)

Frigates (FF):
16 Leander
10 Broad-beamed Leander
7 Type 81/Tribal
9 Modified Type 12/Rothesay
2 Type 61/Salisbury
1 Type 41/Leopard
1 Type 12/Whitby
1 Type 14/Blackwood

Amphibious Warfare Forces:
2 assault ships (LPD)
*6 logistic landing ships
14 LCM(9)
†2 logistic landing craft

2 LCM(7)
†11 LCM
3 LCP(L)(3)
26 LCVP (1), (2) and (3)
†3 LCT(8) type
*1 LST(3)

* = manned by Royal Fleet Auxiliary
† = manned by Royal Corps of Transport

Mine Warfare Forces:
1 training minelayer
(2 Hunt coastal minehunters)
1 Wilton coastal minehunter
15 Ton minehunters
18 Ton minesweepers
3 Ham inshore minesweepers
2 Ley inshore minehunters

Auxiliaries:
1 helicopter support ship
1 maintenance ship
1 escort maintenance ship
1 royal yacht (hospital ship)
1 submarine depot ship
1 ice patrol ship
4 hovercraft
1 diving ship
13 survey ships and craft
6 fleet tankers
4 support tankers
4 fleet replenishment ships
Others

Patrol Forces:
5 Island offshore PC (+2)
4 Bird PC
3 fast training craft
1 Vosper FAC(P)
5 Modified Ton PC
2 Ford PC

Fleet Air Arm:
1 strike sqn with 14 Buccaneer S2
1 FGA sqn with 14 Phantom FG1
1 AEW sqn with 11 Gannet
5 ASW sqns with 29 Sea King
1 ASW sqn with 39 Wasp
1 ASW sqn with 6 Wessex, 4 Lynx
1 cdo assault sqn with 16 Wessex
SAR flights and training with various helicopters
(35 Sea Harrier)
(21 Sea King)
(60 Lynx)

'Resolution' class nuclear ballistic missile submarine (4)

Class: *Resolution* (S22), *Repulse* (S23), *Renown* (S26), *Revenge* (S27)
Displacement: 7,500 tons (7,620 tonnes) surfaced; 8,400 tons (8,534 tonnes) dived
Dimensions: Length 425 ft (129.5 m)
Beam 33 ft (10.1 m)
Draught 30 ft (9.1 m)
Armament:
Guns none
Missile systems
16 Polaris A-3 SLBM launchers
A/S weapons
none
Torpedo tubes
6 21-in (533-mm)
Aircraft
none
Radar and electronics: I-band search radar
Sonar: Types 2001 and 2007
Powerplant: 1 pressurised water-cooled reactor, supplying steam to geared turbines, delivering power to one shaft
Speed: 20 knots (surfaced); 25 knots (dived)
Range: limited only by food capacity and crew efficiency
Crew: 13+130 (two crews)
Used only by: UK
Notes: The first pair were built between 1964 and 1967 by Vickers (Shipbuilding) at Barrow-in-Furness, being commissioned in 1967 and 1968; the second pair were built between 1964 and 1968 by Cammell Laird at Birkenhead, being commissioned in 1968 and 1969. The boats each have two crews to ensure maximum sea time.

'Swiftsure' class nuclear attack submarine (6)

Class: *Sceptre* (S104), *Sovereign* (S108), *Superb* (S109), *Spartan* (S111), *Severn* (S112), *Swiftsure* (S126)
Displacement: 4,200 tons (4,267 tonnes) standard; 4,500 tons (4,572 tonnes) dived
Dimensions: Length 272 ft (82.9 m)
Beam 32 ft 4 in (9.8 m)
Draught 27 ft (8.2 m)
Armament:
Guns none
Missile systems
none
A/S weapons
none
Torpedo tubes
5 21-in (533-mm) with 25 torpedoes
Aircraft
none
Radar and electronics: Type 1003 search radar
Sonar: Type 2001, Type 2007, Type 197 and Type 183
Powerplant: 1 pressurised water-cooled reactor supplying steam to English Electric geared turbines, delivering power to one shaft
Speed: 30 knots (dived)
Range: limited only by food capacity and crew efficiency
Crew: 12+85
Used only by: UK
Notes: All the boats of this class are of Vickers (Shipbuilding) construction at Barrow-in-Furness. The first boat, *Swiftsure,* was laid down in 1969, and the last, *Severn,* in 1976. *Swiftsure* was commissioned in 1973, *Sovereign* in 1974, *Superb* in 1976, and *Sceptre* in 1978. *Spartan* and *Severn* will probably be commissioned in 1980 and 1981.

'Valiant' class nuclear attack submarine (5)

Class: *Churchill* (S46), *Conqueror* (S48), *Courageous* (S50), *Valiant* (S102), *Warspite* (S103)
Displacement: 4,400 tons (4,470 tonnes) standard; 4,900 tons (4,978 tonnes) full load
Dimensions: Length 285 ft (86.9 m)
Beam 33 ft 3 in (10.1 m)
Draught 27 ft (8.2 m)
Armament:
Guns none
Missile systems
none
A/S weapons
none
Torpedo tubes
6 21-in (533-mm) with 32 torpedoes
Aircraft
none
Radar and electronics: Type 1003 search radar
Sonar: Type 2001, Type 2007, Type 197 and Type 183
Powerplant: 1 pressurised water-cooled reactor supplying steam to English Electric geared turbines, delivering power to one shaft
Speed: 28 knots (dived)
Range: limited only by food capacity and crew efficiency
Crew: 13+90
Used only by: UK
Notes: *Conqueror* was built by Cammell Laird at Birkenhead, the others by Vickers (Shipbuilding) at Barrow-in-Furness. The first boat, *Valiant,* was laid down in 1962, launched in 1963, and commissioned in 1966; the last boat, *Courageous,* in 1968, 1970, and 1971.

'Dreadnought' class nuclear attack submarine (1)

Class: *Dreadnought* (S101)
Displacement: 3,000 tons (3,048 tonnes) standard; 3,500 tons (3,556 tonnes) surfaced; 4,000 tons (4,064 tonnes) dived
Dimensions: Length 265 ft 9 in (81.0 m)
Beam 32 ft 3 in (9.8 m)
Draught 26 ft (7.9 m)
Armament:
Guns none
Missile systems
none
A/S weapons
none
Torpedo tubes
6 21-in (533-mm)
Aircraft
none
Radar and electronics: I-band search radar
Sonar: Type 2001 and Type 2007
Powerplant: 1 Westinghouse S5W pressurised water-cooled reactor, supplying steam to geared turbines, delivering power to one shaft
Speed: 28 knots (dived)
Range: limited only by food capacity and crew efficiency
Crew: 11+77
Used only by: UK
Notes: *Dreadnought* was the UK's first nuclear-powered submarine, and was built between 1959 and 1960 by Vickers-Armstrong at Barrow-in-Furness. She was commissioned in 1963.

'Oberon' and 'Porpoise' class submarine (17)

Class: *Porpoise* (S01), *Finwhale* (S05), *Sealion* (S07), *Walrus* (S08), *Oberon* (S09), *Odin* (S10), *Orpheus* (S11), *Olympus* (S12), *Osiris* (S13), *Onslaught* (S14), *Otter* (S15), *Oracle* (S16), *Ocelot* (S17), *Otus* (S18), *Opossum* (S19), *Opportune* (S20), *Onyx* (S21)
Displacement: 1,610 tons (1,636 tonnes) standard; 2,030 tons (2,062 tonnes) surfaced; 2,410 tons (2,449 tonnes) dived
Dimensions: Length 295 ft 3 in (90.0 m)
Beam 26 ft 6 in (8.1 m)
Draught 18 ft (5.5 m)
Armament:
Guns none

Missile systems
  none
A/S weapons
  none
Torpedo tubes
  8 21-in (533-mm) with 24 torpedoes
Aircraft
  none
Radar and electronics: I-band search radar
Sonar: Types 186 and 187

Powerplant: 2 Admiralty Standard Range diesels, delivering 3,680 bhp, and 2 electric motors, delivering 6,000 shp to two shafts
Speed: 12 knots (surfaced); 17 knots (dived)
Range:
Crew: 6+65 in 'Porpoise' class; 6+62 in 'Oberon' class
Used also by: Australia, Brazil, Canada, Chile

Notes: The four boats of the 'Porpoise' class and 13 boats of the 'Oberon' class were built by a number of yards, the 'Porpoise' class being built between 1954 and 1958, commissioning between 1958 and 1961, and the 'Oberon' class being built between 1957 and 1964, commissioning between 1961 and 1967.

'Hermes' class helicopter/VTOL carrier (1)

Class: *Hermes* (R12)
Displacement: 23,900 tons (24,282 tonnes) standard; 28,700 tons (29,159 tonnes) full load
Dimensions: Length 744 ft 4 in (226.7 m)
  Beam (hull) 90 ft (27.4 m)
  Draught 29 ft (8.8 m)
Armament:
Guns none
Missile systems
  2 quadruple Seacat SAM launchers
A/S weapons
  none
Torpedo tubes
  none
Aircraft
  13 helicopters
Radar and electronics: Type 965 surveillance, Type 993 search, Type 975 navigation, and GWS 22 fire-control radars
Sonar:
Powerplant: 4 Admiralty boilers supplying steam to Parsons geared turbines, delivering 76,000 shp to two shafts
Speed: 28 knots
Range:
Crew: 980
Used only by: UK
Notes: *Hermes* was built between 1944 and 1953 by Vickers-Armstrong at Barrow-in-Furness, and commissioned in 1959. She

was modernised between 1964 and 1966, and converted into a commando carrier between 1971 and 1973. In 1976 and 1977 she was again converted, this time into an anti-submarine carrier with commando capability. The carrier *Bulwark* (R08), recommissioned in 1979 as a replacement for *Ark Royal*, is a sistership of *Hermes*.

'Invincible' class anti-submarine cruiser (2)

Class: *Invincible* (CAH1), *Illustrious* (CAH2)
Displacement: 16,000 tons (16,256 tonnes) standard; 19,500 tons (19,812 tonnes) full load
Dimensions: Length 677 ft (206.6 m)
  Beam (deck) 104 ft 7 in (31.9 m)
  Draught 24 ft (7.3 m) (?)
Armament:
Guns none
Missile systems
  1 twin Sea Dart SAM launcher
  4 MM38 Exocet SSM launchers (possibly)
A/S weapons
  none
Torpedo tubes
  none

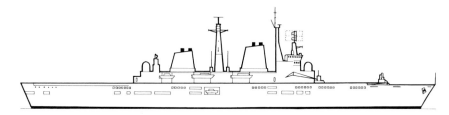

Aircraft
  10 helicopters and 5 aircraft
Radar and electronics: Type 965 surveillance, Type 992R search, Type 909 fire-control, and Type 1006 navigation radars
Sonar: Type 184
Powerplant: 4 Rolls-Royce Olympus gas turbines, delivering 112,000 shp to two shafts
Speed: 28 knots
Range: 5,000 miles (8,047 km) at 18 knots

Crew: 31+869 (excluding aircrew)
Used by: building for UK
Notes: *Invincible* was built by Vickers at Barrow-in-Furness between 1973 and 1977, and is scheduled for commissioning in 1979. *Illustrious* was laid down in 1976 at the Wallsend-on-Tyne yard of Swan Hunter. There are indications that a third ship of the class may be ordered.

'Tiger' class helicopter cruiser (2)

Class: *Tiger* (C20), ex-*Bellerophon; Blake* (C99), ex-*Tiger,* ex-*Blake*
Displacement: 9,500 tons (9,652 tonnes) standard; 12,080 tons (12,273 tonnes) full load

Dimensions: Length 566 ft 6 in (172.8 m)
  Beam 64 ft (19.5 m)
  Draught 23 ft (7.0 m)
Armament:
Guns 2 6-in (152-mm) in a twin turret
  2 3-in (76-mm) in a twin turret
Missile systems
  2 quadruple Seacat SAM launchers

A/S weapons
  none
Torpedo tubes
  none
Aircraft
  4 helicopters
Radar and electronics: Types 965 and 993 search, Type 277 or 278 height-finder,

MRS 3 fire-control, and Type 975 navigation radars
Sonar:
Powerplant: 4 Admiralty boilers supplying steam to 4 Parsons geared turbines, delivering 80,000 shp to four shafts
Speed: 30 knots

Range: 4,000 miles (6,440 km) at 20 knots
Crew: 85+800
Used only by: UK
Notes: *Tiger* was built between 1941 and 1945 by John Brown on Clydebank, and commissioned in 1959; *Blake* was built between 1942 and 1945 by Fairfield Shipbuilding & Engineering at Govan, and commissioned in 1961. Designed and laid down as conventional cruisers, the ships were suspended in construction in 1946, and restarted in 1954, when work was further delayed by redesign.

Type 82 light cruiser (1)

Class: *Bristol* (D23)
Displacement: 6,100 tons (6,198 tonnes) standard; 7,100 tons (7,214 tonnes) full load
Dimensions: Length 507 ft (154.5 m)
Beam 55 ft (16.8 m)
Draught 23 ft (7.0 m) to bottom of sonar dome
Armament:
Guns 1 4.5-in (114-mm)
Missile systems
1 twin Sea Dart SAM launcher
A/S weapons
1 Ikara launcher

1 3-barrel Limbo mortar
Torpedo tubes
none
Aircraft
facilities for 1 small helicopter
Radar and electronics: Type 965 surveillance, Type 992 search, Type 909 fire-control, and Types 1006 and 978 navigation radars; Action Data Automation Weapon System
Sonar: Types 162, 170, 182, 184, 185 and 189
Powerplant: COSAG (COmbined Steam And Gas turbine) arrangement with 2 boilers supplying steam to 2 Standard Range geared turbines, delivering 30,000 shp,

and 2 Bristol Siddeley Marine Olympus TMIA gas turbines delivering 56,000 shp to two shafts
Speed: 30 knots
Range: 5,000 miles (8,047 km) at 18 knots
Crew: 29+378
Used only by: UK
Notes: *Bristol* was built between 1967 and 1969 by Swan Hunter & Tyne Shipbuilders, and commissioned in 1973. She is officially rated as a destroyer, with some justification.

'County' class light cruiser (7)

Class: *Devonshire* (D02), *Kent* (D12), *London* (D16), *Antrim* (D18), *Glamorgan* (D19), *Fife* (D20), *Norfolk* (D21)
Displacement: 5,440 tons (5,527 tonnes) standard; 6,200 tons (6,299 tonnes) full load
Dimensions: Length 520 ft 6 in (158.7 m)
Beam 54 ft (16.5 m)
Draught 20 ft (6.1 m)
Armament:
Guns 4 (*Devonshire, Kent* and *London*) or 2 (others) 4.5-in (114-mm) in twin turrets
2 20-mm in single mountings
Missile systems
4 MM38 Exocet SSM launchers in *Antrim, Glamorgan, Fife* and *Norfolk*
1 twin Seaslug SAM launcher
2 quadruple Seacat SAM launchers
A/S weapons
none
Torpedo tubes
none
Aircraft
1 helicopter
Radar and electronics: Type 965 air search, Type 992 surveillance, Type 277 height-finder, Type 901 Seaslug fire-control, MRS 3 gun fire-control, GWS 21 (*Devonshire* and *London*) or GWS 22 (others) Seacat fire-control radars

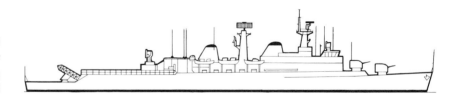

Sonar:
Powerplant: COSAG (COmbined Steam And Gas turbine) arrangement, with 2 Babcock & Wilcox boilers supplying steam to 2 geared turbines, delivering 30,000 shp, and 4 G.6 gas turbines, delivering 30,000 shp to two shafts

Speed: 30 knots
Range:
Crew: 33+438
Used only by: UK
Notes: The ships were built by five yards in the period between 1959 and 1967, and commissioned between 1962 and 1970. Their sistership *Hampshire* has been paid off for financial reasons. The vessels are officially described as destroyers.

Type 42 ('Sheffield' class) destroyer (10)

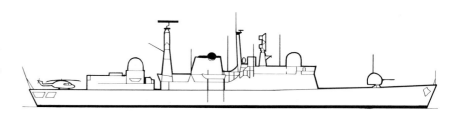

Class: *Sheffield* (D80), *Birmingham* (D86), *Newcastle* (D87), *Glasgow* (D88), *Cardiff* (D108), *Coventry* (D118), *Exeter, Southampton, Nottingham*, and one other
Displacement: 3,150 tons (3,200 tonnes) standard; 4,100 tons (4,166 tonnes) full load
Dimensions: Length 410 ft (125.0 m)
Beam 46 ft (14.0 m)
Draught 14 ft (4.3 m)
Armament:
Guns 1 4.5-in (114-mm)
2 20-mm
Missile systems
1 twin Sea Dart SAM launcher
A/S weapons
2 triple 12.75-in (324-mm) tubes
Torpedo tubes
none
Aircraft
1 ASW helicopter

Radar and electronics: Type 965 search, Type 992Q surveillance and target indicator, Type 909 SAM fire-control, and Type 1006 navigation radars; ADAWS 4 action data automation and weapons system
Sonar: Types 184 and 162
Powerplant: COGOG (COmbined Gas turbines Or Gas turbine) arrangement, with 2 Rolls-Royce Olympus gas turbines, delivering 50,000 shp, and 2 Rolls-Royce Tyne gas turbines, delivering 8,000 shp to two shafts
Speed: 30 knots
Range: 4,500 miles (7,245 km) at 18 knots
Crew: 26+273

Used also by: Argentina
Notes: The ships have been built by several yards in the period between 1970 and 1976, the first six ships being commissioned in the period from 1975 to 1978. *Exeter* and *Southampton* are building in the yards of Swan Hunter at Wallsend-on-Tyne and Vosper Thornycroft, and *Nottingham* has been ordered from the Vosper Thornycroft yard, and a tenth unit from Cammell Laird, Birkenhead.

Type 21 ('Amazon' class) guided missile frigate (8)

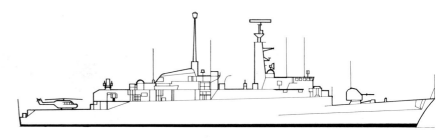

Class: *Amazon* (F169), *Antelope* (F170), *Active* (F171), *Ambuscade* (F172), *Arrow* (F173), *Alacrity* (F174), *Ardent* (F175), *Avenger* (F185)
Displacement: 2,750 tons (2,794 tonnes) standard; 3,250 tons (3,302 tonnes) full load
Dimensions: Length 384 ft (117.0 m)
Beam 41 ft 9 in (12.7 m)
Draught 14 ft 6 in (4.4 m)
Armament:
Guns 1 4.5-in (114-mm)
2 20-mm in single mountings

Missile systems
1 quadruple Seacat SAM launcher (Seawolf to be retrofitted)
4 MM38 Exocet SSM launchers
A/S weapons
2 triple 12.75-in (324-mm) tubes to be fitted

Torpedo tubes
none
Aircraft
1 ASW helicopter
Radar and electronics: Type 992Q surveillance and target indicator, GWS 24 SAM fire-control, Orion RTN-10X WSA 4 gun

fire-control, and Type 978 navigation radars; CAAIS
Sonar: Type 184M and Type 162M
Powerplant: COGOG (COmbined Gas turbine Or Gas turbine) arrangement, with 2 Rolls-Royce Olympus gas turbines, delivering 56,000 shp, and 2 Rolls-Royce Tyne gas turbines, delivering 8,500 shp to two shafts
Speed: 32 knots
Range: 3,500 miles (5,635 km) at 18 knots
Crew: 13+164
Used only by: UK

Notes: The class was designed by Vosper Thornycroft, and built by them (first three) and by Yarrow at Glasgow (last five), in the period between 1969 and 1975, with commissioning in the period between 1974 and 1978.

Type 22 ('Broadsword' class) guided missile frigate (4)

Class: *Broadsword* (F88), *Battleaxe, Brilliant, Boxer*
Displacement: 3,500 tons (3,556 tonnes) standard; 4,000 tons (4,064 tonnes) full load
Dimensions: Length 430 ft (131.2 m)
Beam 48 ft 6 in (14.8 m)
Draught 14 ft (4.3 m)
Armament:
Guns 2 40-mm
Missile systems
2 Sea Wolf SAM launchers
1 quadruple MM38 Exocet SSM launcher

A/S weapons
2 triple 12.75-in (324-mm) Mark 32 tubes
Torpedo tubes
none
Aircraft
2 ASW helicopters
Radar and electronics: Type 967/8 surveillance and Type 1006 navigation radars
Sonar: Type 2016
Powerplant: COGOG (COmbined Gas turbine Or Gas turbine) arrangement, with 2 Rolls-Royce Olympus gas turbines, delivering 56,000 bhp, and 2 Rolls-Royce Tyne gas turbines, delivering 8,500 bhp to two shafts
Speed: 30+ knots
Range: 4,500 miles (7,245 km) at 18 knots on Tynes
Crew: about 250
Used by: building for UK
Notes: The 'Broadsword' class, of which some 14 ships are planned, is to be the successor to the 'Leander' class. The four present ships are of Yarrow construction, with *Broadsword* entering service in 1979. Intended mainly for A/S operations, the class is notable for its lack of gun armament except for a pair of 40-mm AA weapons

'Leander' and 'Broad-beamed Leander' class frigate (26)

Class: *Aurora* (F10), *Euryalus* (F15), *Galatea* (F18), *Cleopatra* (F28), *Arethusa* (F38), *Naiad* (F39), *Sirius* (F40), *Phoebe* (F42), *Minerva* (F45), *Danae* (F47), *Juno* (F52), *Argonaut* (F56), *Dido* (F104), *Leander* (F109), *Ajax* (F114), *Penelope* (F127); *Achilles* (F12), *Diomede* (F16), *Andromeda* (F57), *Hermione* (F58), *Jupiter* (F60), *Bacchante* (F69), *Apollo* (F70), *Scylla* (F71), *Ariadne* (F72), *Charybdis* (F75)
Displacement: 2,450 tons (2,489 tonnes) standard and 2,860 tons (2,906 tonnes) full load for 'Leander'; 2,500 tons (2,540 tonnes) standard and 2,962 tons (3,009 tonnes) full load for 'Broad-beamed Leander'
Dimensions: Length 373 ft (113.4 m)
Beam 41 ft (12.5 m) for 'Leander'; 43 ft (13.1 m) for 'Broad-beamed Leander'
Draught 18 ft (5.5 m)
Armament:
Guns 2 4.5-in (114-mm) in a twin turret
2 40-mm (generally)
2 20-mm (in ships fitted with Seacat)
Missile systems
4 MM38 Exocet SSM launchers (in place of 4.5-in/114-mm guns) in 'Broad-beamed Leanders', *Cleopatra, Sirius, Phoebe, Minerva, Juno, Argonaut, Dido, Danae*
1 quadruple Seacat SAM launcher, except Ikara ships (2 quadruple Seacat SAM launchers) and Exocet ships (3 quadruple Seacat SAM launchers)
A/S weapons
1 Ikara launcher (in place of 4.5-in/114-mm guns) in *Leander, Ajax, Galatea, Naiad, Euryalus, Aurora, Arethusa, Penelope*
1 3-barrel Limbo mortar (not Exocet ships)
2 triple 12.75-in (324-mm) Mark 32 tubes (Exocet ships only)
Torpedo tubes
none
Aircraft
1 small helicopter
Radar and electronics: Type 965 surveillance (not Ikara ships), Type 993 combined air/surface warning, MRS 3/GWS 22 fire-control, and Type 975 navigation radars
Sonar: Type 199 variable-depth in Ikara ships
Powerplant: 2 boilers supplying steam to 2 double-reduction geared turbines, delivering 30,000 shp to two shafts

Speed: 30 knots
Range:
Crew: 251 ('Leander'); 260 ('Broad-beamed Leander')
Used also by: Chile, India, New Zealand
Notes: The 'Leander' class was developed from the 'Rothesay' class, and its ships were built in a number of yards from 1959 to 1971. The first unit, *Leander*, was commissioned in March 1963, and the last, *Ariadne*, in February 1973. There are 16 of the original 'Leander' class, and 10 of the improved 'Broad-beamed Leander' class.

Type 81 ('Tribal' class) frigate (7)

Class: *Ashanti* (F117), *Eskimo* (F118), *Gurka* (F122), *Zulu* (F124), *Mohawk* (F125), *Nubian* (F131), *Tartar* (F133)
Displacement: 2,300 tons (2,337 tonnes) standard; 2,700 tons (2,743 tonnes) full load
Dimensions: Length 360 ft (109.7 m)
Beam 42 ft 4 in (12.9 m)
Draught 17 ft 6 in (5.3 m)
Armament:
Guns 2 4.5-in (114-mm) in single turrets
2 20-mm
Missile systems
2 quadruple Seacat SAM launchers
A/S weapons
1 3-barrel Limbo mortar
Torpedo tubes
none
Aircraft
1 small helicopter
Radar and electronics: Type 965 search, Type 293 combined air/surface warning, MRS 3 gun fire-control, GWS 21 SAM fire-control, and Type 975 navigation radars

Sonar: Types 177, 170 and 162, plus Type 199 variable-depth in *Ashanti* and *Gurkha*
Powerplant: COSAG (COmbined Steam And Gas turbine) arrangement, with 2 Babcock & Wilcox boilers supplying steam to 1 Metrovick turbine, delivering 12,500 shp, and 1 Metrovick gas turbine, delivering 7,500 shp to one shaft
Speed: 28 knots
Range:

Crew: 13+240
Used only by: UK
Notes: The seven ships of the 'Tribal' class were designed for distant operations, in which a fair measure of self-sufficiency and great range would be needed. The ships were built by seven different yards between 1958 and 1962, being commissioned between 1961 and 1964.

Modified Type 12 ('Rothesay' class) frigate (9)

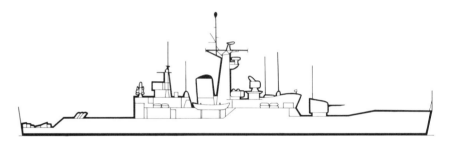

Class: *Yarmouth* (F101), *Lowestoft* (F103), *Brighton* (F106), *Rothesay* (F107), *Londonderry* (F108), *Falmouth* (F113), *Berwick* (F115), *Plymouth* (F126), *Rhyl* (F129)
Displacement: 2,380 tons (2,418 tonnes) standard; 2,800 tons (2,845 tonnes) full load
Dimensions: Length 370 ft (112.8 m)
Beam 41 ft (12.5 m)
Draught 17 ft 4 in (5.3 m)
Armament:
Guns 2 4.5-in (114-mm) in a twin turret
2 20-mm in single mountings
Missile systems
1 quadruple Seacat SAM launcher
A/S weapons
1 3-barrel Limbo mortar
Torpedo tubes
none

Aircraft
1 small helicopter
Radar and electronics: Type 993 search, MRS 3 fire-control, and Type 975 navigation radars
Sonar:
Powerplant: 2 Babcock & Wilcox boilers supplying steam to 2 Admiralty Standard Range double-reduction geared turbines, delivering 30,000 shp to two shafts

Speed: 30 knots
Range:
Crew: 15+220
Used only by: UK
Notes: The nine ships of the class were built in eight yards in the period between 1956 and 1960, being commissioned in 1960 and 1961. The design was based on that of the 'Whitby' class.

Type 61 ('Salisbury' class) frigate (2)

Class: *Salisbury* (F32), *Lincoln* (F99)
Displacement: 2,170 tons (2,205 tonnes) standard; 2,408 tons (2,447 tonnes) full load
Dimensions: Length 339 ft 9 in (103.6 m)
Beam 40 ft (12.2 m)
Draught 15 ft 6 in (4.7 m)
Armament:
Guns 2 4.5-in (114-mm) in a twin turret
2 20-mm
Missile systems
1 quadruple Seacat SAM launcher
A/S weapons
1 3-barrel Squid mortar
Torpedo tubes
none
Aircraft
none
Radar and electronics: Type 965 long-range surveillance. Type 993 combined air/surface warning, Type 277Q height-finder. Type 982 target indicator. Type 275 (Mark 6M director) fire-control, and Type 975 navi-

gation radars; Knebworth Corvus chaff dispensers
Sonar: Types 174 and 170B
Powerplant: 8 Admiralty Standard Range diesels, delivering 14,400 bhp to two shafts
Speed: 24 knots
Range: 7,500 miles (12,070 km) at 16 knots
Crew: 14+223
Used also by: Bangladesh

Notes: *Salisbury* was built by Devonport Dockyard, *Lincoln* by Fairfield Shipbuilding & Engineering at Govan, between 1955 and 1959, for commissioning in 1960. The class is intended primarily to provide direction for strike aircraft. Their sistership *Llandaff* was transferred to Bangladesh in 1976.

Type 12 ('Whitby' class) frigate (1)

Class: *Torquay* (F43)
Displacement: 2,150 tons (2,184 tonnes) standard; 2,560 tons (2,601 tonnes) full load
Dimensions: Length 369 ft 9 in (112.7 m)
Beam 41 ft (12.5 m)
Draught 17 ft (5.2 m)
Armament:
Guns 2 4.5-in (114-mm) in a twin turret
Missile systems
none
A/S weapons
13-barrel Limbo mortar
Torpedo tubes
none
Aircraft
none
Radar and electronics: Type 993 search, Type 275 fire-control, and Type 1006 navigation radars
Sonar: Types 174, 170 and 162
Powerplant: 2 Babcock & Wilcox boilers supplying steam to 2 double-reduction geared turbines, delivering 30,430 shp to two shafts
Speed: 31 knots
Range:
Crew: 12+213
Used also by: Bangladesh, India, New Zealand
Notes: *Torquay* was built between 1953 and 1954 by Harland & Wolff at Belfast, for commissioning in 1956. She is now used as a navigation/direction trials and training ship.

Type 14 ('Blackwood' class) frigate (1)

Class: *Hardy* (F54)
Displacement: 1,180 tons (1,199 tonnes) standard; 1,456 tons (1,479 tonnes) full load
Dimensions: Length 310 ft (94.5 m)
Beam 33 ft (10.1 m)
Draught 15 ft 6 in (4.7 m)
Armament:
Guns 2 40-mm Bofors
Missile systems
none
A/S weapons
2 3-barrel Limbo mortars
Torpedo tubes
none
Aircraft
none
Radar and electronics: Type 278 search radar
Sonar: Types 174, 170 and 162
Powerplant: 2 Babcock & Wilcox boilers supplying steam to 1 geared turbine, delivering 15,000 shp to one shaft
Speed: 26 knots
Range: 4,000 miles (6,440 km) at 12 knots
Crew: 8+132
Used also by: India
Notes: The single survivor of the class was built by Yarrow in 1953 for commissioning in 1955. Her sisterships *Duncan* (F80) and *Russell* (F97) are used for harbour training work.

Assault ship (2)

Class: *Fearless* (L10), *Intrepid* (L11)
Displacement: 11,060 tons (11,237 tonnes) standard; 12,120 tons (12,314 tonnes) full load
Dimensions: Length 520 ft (158.5 m)
Beam 80 ft (24.4 m)
Draught 20 ft 6 in (6.2 m)
Armament:
Guns 2 40-mm Bofors
Missile systems
4 quadruple Seacat SAM launchers
A/S weapons
none
Torpedo tubes
none
Aircraft
facilities for 5 helicopters
Radar and electronics: Type 993 air/surface search and Type 975 navigation radars; Computer Assisted Action Information System (CAAIS); Knebworth Corvus chaff dispensers
Sonar:
Powerplant: 2 Babcock & Wilcox boilers supplying steam to 2 English Electric turbines, delivering 22,000 shp to two shafts
Speed: 21 knots
Range: 5,000 miles (8,047 km) at 20 knots
Crew: 580
Used only by: UK
Notes: The ships were built by Harland & Wolff in Belfast and John Brown on Clydebank, between 1962 and 1964, for commissioning in 1965 and 1967. Each ship can carry up to 700 troops, 15 tanks and up to 30 other vehicles, landed by the ship's four LCM(9)s in the dock and four LCVPs at the davits. The dock at the rear of the ship is flooded by flooding down the stern to a draught of 32 ft (9.8 m). Only one ship is kept in commission at any one time.

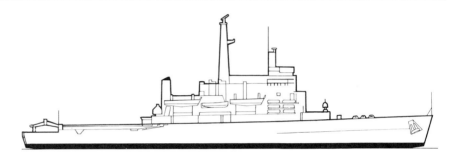

'Ton' class minehunter and minesweeper (33)

Class: *Bildeston* (M1110), *Brereton* (M1113), *Brinton* (M1114), *Bronington* (M1140), *Hubberston* (M1147), *Iveston* (M1151), *Kedleston* (M1153), *Kellington* (M1154), *Kirkliston* (M1157), *Maxton* (M1165), *Nurton* (M1166), *Sheraton* (M1181) and *Shoulton* (M1182); *Alfriston* (M1103), *Bickington* (M1109), *Crichton* (M1124), *Cuxton* (M1125), *Glasserton* (M1141), *Hodgeston* (M1146), *Laleston* (M1158), *Repton* (M1167), *Pollington* (M1173), *Shavington* (M1180), *Upton* (M1187), *Walkerton* (M1188), *Wotton* (M1195), *Soberton* (M1200), *Stubbington* (M1204), *Wiston* (M1205), *Lewiston* (M1208) and *Crofton* (M1216)
Displacement: 360 tons (365.8 tonnes) standard; 425 tons (431.8 tonnes) full load
Dimensions: Length 153 ft (46.3 m)
Beam 28 ft 9 in (8.8 m)
Draught 8 ft 3 in (2.5 m)
Armament:
Guns very varied, most minehunters having 1 or 2 40-mm and 2 20-mm, and minesweepers 0 or 1 40-mm
Missile systems
none
A/S weapons
none
Torpedo tubes
none

Aircraft
none
Radar and electronics: Type 975
Sonar: Type 193 in minehunters
Powerplant: 2 JVSS 12 Mirlees diesels, delivering 2,500 bhp, or 2 Napier 18A-7A Deltic diesels, delivering 3,000 bhp to two shafts
Speed: 15 knots
Range: 2,300 miles (3,700 km) at 13 knots
Crew: 29 (minesweeper); 5+33 (minehunter)

Used also by: Argentina, Eire, Ghana, India, Malaysia, South Africa
Notes: Some 118 of these craft were originally built between 1953 and 1960, by a number of yards under the directorship of John I. Thornycroft of Southampton. The first 15 ships above are minehunters, the remaining 17 minesweepers. *Kedleston, Kellington, Hodgeston, Repton, Upton* and *Crofton* are used as Royal Naval Reserve training ships.

'Island' class offshore patrol craft (5)

Class: *Jersey* (P295), *Guernsey* (P297), *Shetland* (P298), *Orkney* (P299), *Lindisfarne* (P300)
Displacement: 925 tons (939.8 tonnes) standard; 1,250 tons (1,270 tonnes) full load
Dimensions: Length 195 ft 4 in (59.6 m)
Beam 35 ft 9 in (10.9 m)
Draught 14 ft (4.3 m)

Armament:
Guns 1 40-mm
Missile systems
none
A/S weapons
none
Torpedo tubes
none
Aircraft
none

Radar and electronics:
Sonar:
Powerplant: 2 diesels, delivering 4,380 hp to one shaft
Speed: 16 knots
Range: 7,000 miles (11,265 km) at 15 knots
Crew: 34
Used only by: UK
Notes: All five craft were built by Hall Russell & Co. *Jersey* was commissioned in 1976 and the others in 1977–78. Two more units were ordered in 1977.

'Bird' class large patrol craft (4)

Class: *Kingfisher* (P260), *Cygnet* (P261), *Peterel* (P262), *Sandpiper* (P263)
Displacement: 190 tons (193 tonnes)
Dimensions: Length 120 ft (36.6 m)
Beam 23 ft (7.0 m)
Draught 6 ft 6 in (2.0 m)
Armament:
Guns 1 40-mm
2 machine-guns
Missile systems
none
A/S weapons
none
Torpedo tubes
none
Aircraft
none
Radar and electronics:
Sonar:
Powerplant: 2 Paxman 16YJ diesels, delivering 4,800 bhp

Speed: 18 knots
Range:
Crew: 24
Used only by: UK
Notes: All four craft were built by R. Dunston Ltd at Hessle, the first craft being commissioned in 1975, the next two in 1976, and the last in 1977. The design is based on that of the RAF's 'Seal' class rescue craft, with modifications to improve seakeeping qualities.

British Aerospace (BAC) Seawolf

Type: naval short-range surface-to-air missile
Guidance: line-of-sight by means of radio command

Dimensions: Span about 24 in (61.0 cm)
Body diameter about 7 in (17.75 cm)
Length about 6 ft 6¾ in (2.0 m)
Booster: solid-propellant rocket
Sustainer: none

Warhead: high explosive
Weights: Launch
Burnt out
Performance: speed in excess of Mach 2
Used by: under development for UK
Notes: The Seawolf is the missile component

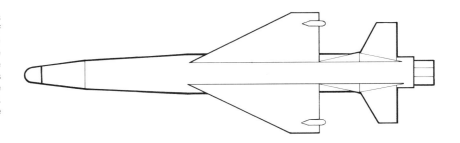

of the Guided Weapon System 25, and is designed for the close-range air defence of ships displacing 2,000 tons (2032 tonnes) or more. It is used in conjunction with the Types 967 and 968 air and low-altitude surveillance, Type 910 tracker radars, plus a variety of TV and other installations. The missile is fired from a six-round launcher. Various other models of the missile are under development.

British Aerospace (HSD) Sea Dart

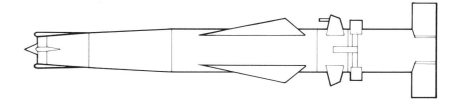

Type: naval surface-to-air tactical guided missile
Guidance: radar guidance with semi-active radar terminal homing
Dimensions: Span 36 in (91.4 cm)
Body diameter $16\frac{1}{2}$ in (41.9 cm)
Length 14 ft $3\frac{3}{4}$ (4.36 m)
Booster: solid-propellant rocket
Sustainer: Rolls-Royce Odin ramjet
Warhead: probably high explosive
Weights: Launch 1,213 lb (550 kg)
Burnt out
Performance: range at least $18\frac{1}{2}$ miles (30 km)
Used also by: Argentina
Notes: The Sea Dart system is highly flexible, and provides its parent vessels with protection against aircraft attack from anywhere between very high and very low levels. The system can also be used against missiles and other ships. Sea Dart is used with Type 919 target tracking and illuminating radar. The system is currently being updated to improve its immunity to ECM.

British Aerospace (HSD) Seaslug

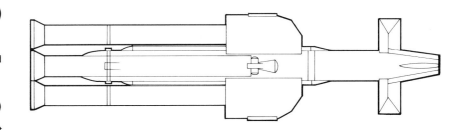

Type: naval surface-to-air tactical guided missile, with surface-to-surface capability
Guidance: beam-riding
Dimensions: Span 4 ft $8\frac{1}{2}$ in (1.435 m)
Body diameter 16 in (40.64 cm)
Length 19 ft 8 in (6.0 m)
Booster: four jettisonable solid-propellant rockets
Sustainer: solid-propellant rocket
Warhead: high explosive
Weights: Launch
Burnt out
Performance: range more than 28 miles (45 km); ceiling more than 49,200 ft (15,000 m)

Used only by: UK
notes: Designed as a long-range guided missile, the Seaslug is used with Type 901M radar for guidance, Type 965 long-range surveillance radar, Type 277 height-finding radar, and Type 901 tracking and illuminating radar. The Seaslug is fired from a twin launcher, and became operational in 1961. The system is now obsolescent.

Short Brothers Seacat

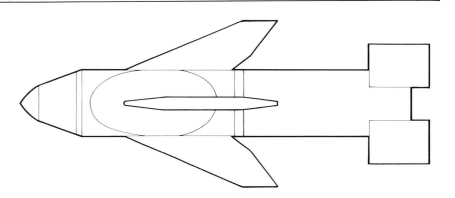

Type: naval surface-to-air tactical guided missile
Guidance: radio command
Dimensions: Span $25\frac{1}{2}$ in (64.77 cm)
Body diameter $7\frac{1}{2}$ in (19.05 cm)
Length 4 ft 10 in (1.48 m)
Booster: solid-propellant rocket
Sustainer: solid-propellant rocket
Warhead: high explosive
Weights: Launch about 139 lb (63 kg)
Burnt out
Performance: range 5,200 yards (4,755 m)
Used also by: Argentina, Australia, Brazil, Chile, India, Iran, Libya, Malaysia, Netherlands, New Zealand, Sweden, Thailand, Venezuela, West Germany

Notes: Designed as a close-range ship-borne missile system, the Seacat was at first provided with optical sighting arrangements, in which the operator gathered the missile into his field of vision and then guided it onto the target with his thumb control. Later versions, however, have been combined with a number of naval fire-control systems.

Mark 8 torpedo

Type: submarine-launched anti-ship torpedo
Guidance: preset angle, course and depth
Launch method: tube
Dimensions: Length 22 ft (6.7 m)
Diameter 21 in (533 mm)
Weight: 3,384 lb (1,350 kg)
Engine: compressed air
Speed: 45 knots
Range: 4,921 yards (4,500 m)
Warhead: high explosive
Used also by: other navies
Notes: Although obsolescent, this torpedo has given good service since its introduction in the mid-1930s. It is capable of operating up to 59 ft (18 m) down.

Mark 20 (Improved) torpedo

Type: submarine-launched anti-ship and anti-submarine torpedo
Guidance: preset angle, course and depth, with passive sonar homing
Launch method: tube
Dimensions: Length 13 ft 6 in (4.11 m)
Diameter 21 in (533 mm)
Weight: about 1,810 lb (821 kg)
Engine: electric
Speed:
Range: 12,030 yards (11,000 m) at 20 knots
Warhead: 200 lb (91 kg) high explosive
Used only by: UK
Notes: Designed principally as an anti-submarine weapon, running at depths up to 210 ft (64 m) and homing on the propeller cavitation noise of submarines at depths of up to 800 ft (244 m). Problems with the initial guidance system have made the type none too successful.

Mark 23 torpedo

Type: submarine-launched anti-ship and anti-submarine torpedo
Guidance: wire-guidance from launch vessel, plus passive sonar homing
Launch method: tube
Dimensions: Length
Diameter 21 in (533 mm)
Weight:
Engine: electric
Speed:
Range: about 8,800 yards (8,047 m)
Warhead: 200 lb (91 kg) high explosive
Used only by: UK
Notes: Britain's first wire-guided torpedo, essentially a Mark 20 weapon with an extra section inserted for the wire casket. Intended as an interim and training weapon pending the introduction of the Mark 24, the Mark 23 is still in service as a result of delays with the Mark 24 programme.

Mark 24 'Tigerfish' torpedo

Type: submarine-launched anti-submarine torpedo
Guidance: wire-guidance from launch vessel, plus active/passive acoustic homing
Launch method: tube
Dimensions: Length 21 ft 2½ in (6.464 m)
Diameter 21 in (533 mm)
Weight: 3,417 lb (1,550 kg)
Engine: electric
Speed: high or low speeds
Range: probably at least 20 miles (32 km)
Warhead: high explosive
Used also by: other navies
Notes: Sophisticated anti-submarine weapon, with onboard computer, roll stabilisation by means of retractable stub wings, and wire dispensed from both torpedo and launch submarine.

United States of America

The United States Navy

In the twenty years between the end of the Civil War, in which the Union Navy played a considerable part in obtaining a victory, and the mid-1880s, the navy of the USA grew steadily more moribund. Political jobbery, graft, inefficiency and a proportion of one officer to every four enlisted men were among the factors which assisted in this state of affairs. From 1883 onwards building programmes were authorised which gave a tentative, if inadequate, start to the modernisation of the fleet and its support. This construction continued to accelerate until, at the outbreak of war with Spain in April 1898 the total of modern warships stood at 53 with 16,452 personnel. Even so a considerable augmentation of this force was thought necessary and 123 ships ranging from tugs to auxiliary cruisers were taken up from trade or other services in addition to the purchase of half-a-dozen foreign warships.

These facts, apparently irrelevant to modern affairs, have been included as a symptom of a truth which afflicts the navy of any democracy after a bloody war and a prolonged peace – there are never enough ships when hostilities once again erupt. Despite the enthusiasm and activities of President Theodore Roosevelt and some of his successors, an objective assessment of the state of the USN a year after the outbreak of World War I in August 1914 listed fifteen major deficiencies including a 40 per cent shortage of officers, lack of fast major war-vessels, minewarfare ships, aircraft and gunnery practices. From 1914 onwards a rapidly expanding programme allowed for the construction of large numbers of all types of warships from battleships to auxiliaries. Once again the fleet had been proved inadequate for its wartime task.

When the Japanese attacked Pearl Harbour on 7 December 1941 they found an unprepared area in which they wreaked major havoc. This was hardly surprising in view of the fact that warnings from Washington had not resulted in any genuine apprehension amongst the local commanders. This attitude, however, was not true of that in the White House. Shortly after his election, in June 1933, President Franklin D. Roosevelt set aside a large slice of the funds of the National Industrial Recovery Act to stimulate ship building and the resurgence of the USN. Two years later, almost to the day, the Senate Committee on the Munitions Industry commented that 'The Navy has become big business' . . . 'The need for many ships in 1933 was the main cause for the increase in prices charged by

private shipbuilders', and, looking over their shoulders, 'The record of present shipbuilding companies during the (1917–18) war . . . was little short of being disgraceful. They made very considerable profits – on Treasury audits they showed up to 90%.'

It was in the face of this profiteering and the Congressional methods of patronage that Franklin D. Roosevelt built up his navy to a state where it not only sustained the disaster of Pearl Harbour but gave better than it had received at Midway, in the Coral Sea and throughout the Pacific island campaigns. These operations, combined with the war in the Atlantic, called for an astonishing shipbuilding effort which produced nigh on 1,400 major warships and submarines as well as a host of minor war vessels and the majority of allied merchant ships. Again numbers had been too few in 1941 but it was a fitting tribute that the final surrender should have been signed in an American battleship in Tokyo Bay on 3 September 1945.

By this time the USN had a pre-eminent capability in carrier warfare, had a deep knowledge of amphibious operations and had achieved a submarine success rate of astonishing dimensions. It was these three abilities which were to be of great value in the post-war years. Less than five years after the Tokyo Bay surrender, US naval forces were once again engaged, this time off Korea in the war which began on 25 June 1950. Carrier operations supported the land forces and the amphibious landings at Inchon in September 1950 were of immense importance. At no time was the superiority of the United Nations' fleets challenged – by the ceasefire in July 1953 no major allied ship had been sunk yet their activities had contributed greatly to the outcome.

In August 1964, in the wake of the 'Tonkin Gulf incident' the USN was once more involved in a foreign war; for the next eleven years the reinforced Seventh Fleet was continually in action of one sort or another off Vietnam. This period was to have a profound and long-lasting effect on the navy. In 1961 the new president, John F. Kennedy, had appointed Robert McNamara as Secretary of Defense, a business man who introduced theories of cost-effectiveness into service planning which were to cause much bitterness and opposition. In that year three carriers, two of the 'Kitty Hawk' class and the first nuclear propelled carrier, *Enterprise*, joined the fleet. In February 1963 McNamara instructed the Navy Department to justify the retention of fifteen attack carriers in addition to plans for new construction. If the latter had been totally cancelled

only ten attack carriers would be in service now. Despite the mathematicians' attempts, however, a continued carrier building programme enabled the USN to retain on 1 February 1978 a force of thirteen active ships, with one nuclear ship building and five elderly oil-fired ships in reserve. The arguments advanced in the McNamara era have been resurrected by President Carter's advisers. This time the arguments for the retention of a strong carrier force are being assailed with a theory that the use of shore-bases on friendly territory would provide an equally efficient deployment of aircraft. This does not appear to take full account of the political problems which affect such operations – the instability in Portugal and the Azores, problems in Italy and reactions from some quarters in Spain, the continued frictions in the Eastern Mediterranean, objections to foreign bases in the Indian Ocean, the USA's own attitude to South Africa, difficulties in South America, the Norwegian refusal to have foreign forces based on their territory, and uncertainties over Icelandic reactions are only some of these. If the USN is to retain its capacity for world-wide operations a strong carrier force is essential.

In the period 1941–5 American submarines achieved spectacular success. Since then an imaginative and highly profitable series of research and development projects have provided the basis for the nuclear submarine building programme from which has stemmed the ballistic-missile submarine force. By February 1978 there were 41 of these large craft available with 7 of the huge 'Ohio' class ordered or proposed. Behind this major contribution to the strategic deterrent, 70 attack submarines with nuclear propulsion plus a further 28 ordered or building provide a highly efficient force with particular capabilities for the detection and destruction of enemy submarines.

The inroads made by the costs of eleven years of war in Vietnam were greatest in the replacement programmes of surface ships other than carriers and into the provision of up-to-date weaponry for those that were built. Great numbers of World War II ships were retained in service after 1964 and the running costs of this huge force absorbed vast amounts of finance. Thus when the decision was made in the early 1970s to delete the over-age ships, the total of major surface combatants dropped dramatically from 960 to 480 – a figure well below the 600-ship navy considered necessary to carry out peacetime operations of surveillance, presence and support for threatened allies, the latter comprising a very extensive list throughout the world. If hostilities should develop, this figure of 600 would need reinforcement similar to that provided in the five major wars in which the USN has been involved in the last eighty years. However, the current US administration has recommended cuts in the proposed five-year programme which will make the attainment of a 600-ship fleet out of the question. The resulting arguments in Congress and the Pentagon are effectively delaying the implementation of vital building plans.

Similar delays, caused partly in Washington and partly by the Vietnam situation, has retarded the introduction of modern surface-to-surface missiles in the USN. It is only now that the fitting of the 50-mile Harpoon is providing the USN with a capability possessed by the Soviet navy for the last twenty years. At the same time the future of the Tomahawk cruise-missile remains uncertain, a possible bargaining counter whose cancellation would deprive the USN of a most potent weapon of deterrence.

In the midst of political indecision and the refusal by the top management to accept the truths of history, the USN does the best it can with what it is allowed to have. And allied to these problems is that of retention of experienced enlisted men. But, despite these recurrent dilemmas, the fleet has two great advantages: it is manned by volunteers of good education and sound training and this training is founded on eighteen years of combat experience during the last thirty-seven, a situation unique amongst the world's navies.

532,300, including 21,600 women, plus 94,100 reservists

SSBN:
(4+9 Ohio)
31 Benjamin Franklin and Lafayette
5 Ethan Allen
5 George Washington

SSN:
13 Los Angeles (+27)
1 Glenard P. Lipscomb
1 Narwhal
37 Sturgeon
13 Thresher
1 Tullibee
5 Skipjack
4 Skate
1 Seawolf
1 Nautilus
(+2 in reserve)

SS:
3 Barbel
1 Grayback LPSS
1 Darter
1 Sailfish
4 Tang
(+3 in reserve)

CVN:
2 Nimitz (+1)
1 Enterprise

CV:
4 Kitty Hawk and John F. Kennedy
4 Forrestal
2 Midway
1 Hancock
(+4 in reserve)

CGN:
3 Virginia (+1)
2 California
1 Truxtun
1 Bainbridge
1 Long Beach

CG:
9 Belknap
9 Leahy
2 Albany
1 Converted Cleveland

CA:
3 Des Moines
1 Baltimore
1 Canberra
(all 5 in reserve)

DDG:
10 Coontz
2 Mitscher
4 Converted Forrest Sherman
23 Charles F. Adams

DD:
18 Spruance (+12)
14 Forrest Sherman and Hull
28 Gearing FRAM 1
2 Carpenter FRAM 1

FFG:
1 Oliver Hazard Perry (+17+56)
6 Brooke

FF:
46 Knox
10 Garcia
2 Bronstein

Amphibious Warfare Forces:
2 Blue Ridge LCC
2 Tarawa LHA (+3)
7 Iwo Jima LPH
12 Austin LPD
2 Raleigh LPD
5 Anchorage LSD
8 Thomaston LSD
(plus 7 Casa Grande LSD in reserve)
20 Newport LST
(plus 3 De Soto County LST in reserve)
5 Charleston LKA
1 Tulare LKA
2 Paul Revere LPA
60 LCU 1610 series
24 LCU 1466 series
21 LCU 501 series
? LCM8
? LCM6
? LCVP

Command Ships:
1 Converted Raleigh AGF
(plus 2 CC in reserve)

Patrol Forces:
1 Pegasus PCH(M) (+5)
2 Asheville PG
1 High Point PCH
4 PTF23

Mine Warfare Forces:
2 Acme ocean minesweepers
23 Aggressive and Dash ocean mine-sweepers
8 minesweeping boats

Auxiliaries:
15 destroyer tenders (+5)
13 ammunition ships
7 combat store ships
14 oilers (+14)
4 fast combat support ships (+1)
7 replenishment oilers
7 repair ships
4 landing craft repair ships
14 salvage ships
13 submarine tenders (+3)
8 submarine rescue ships

Naval Aviation:
168 F-14A (14 fighter sqns)
144 F-4 (12 fighter sqns)
110 A-6E (11 attack sqns)
300 A-7E (25 attack sqns)
30 RA-5C and RF-8 (10 recce sqns)
280 P-3B/C (24 MR sqns)
130 S-3A (13 ASW sqns)
52 E-2B/C (13 AEW sqns)
96 SH-3A/D/G/H (12 ASW sqns)
17 support sqns with 12 C-130, 7 C-118, 12 C-9B, 12 CT-39, 13 C-131, 6 C-117, 20 C-1, 15 C-2, 36 EA-6
30 RH-53D, CH-46, SH-3 and SH-2
13 F-5E/F (1 aggressor training sqn)
19 training sqns with 11 aircraft and 3 helicopter types
(There are some 41 squadrons in reserve)

Marine Aviation:
144 F-4N/S (12 FGA sqns)
80 AV-8A (3 FGA sqns)
60 A-4F/M (5 FGA sqns)
60 A-6A/E (5 FGA sqns)
10 RF-4B (1 recce sqn)
10 EA-6B (1 ECM sqn)
36 OV-10A (2 observation sqns)
36 KC-130F (3 tanker sqns)
54 AH-1J (3 attack helicopter sqns)
96 UH-1E/N (4 light helicopter sqns)
162 CH-46F (9 medium helicopter sqns)
126 CH-53D (6 heavy helicopter sqns)
(There are 16 squadrons in reserve)

The US Coast Guard has 37,500 men, and operates (on the active list):
18 high-endurance cutters, 22 medium-endurance cutters (+2), 7 icebreakers, 1 patrol hydrofoil, 75 patrol craft, 3 training cutters, 2 oceanographic cutters.
Other vessels, as well as the following aircraft:
34 HC-130, 18 HU-16, 12 Gulfstream, 38 HH-3F, 79 HH-2A.

'Ohio' class nuclear ballistic missile submarine (13)

Class: *Ohio* (SSBN726), *Michigan* (SSNB727) and 11 others (SSBN728 to SSBN738)
Displacement: 16,600 tons (16,865 tonnes) surfaced; 18,700 tons (18,999 tonnes) dived
Dimensions: Length 560 ft (170.7 m)
Beam 42 ft (12.8 m)
Draught 35 ft 6 in (10.8 m)
Armament:
Guns none
Missile systems
24 Trident I SLBM launch tubes
A/S weapons
none
Torpedo tubes
4 21-in (533-mm)
Aircraft
none
Radar and electronics:
Sonar: BQQ-5 passive
Powerplant: 1 General Electric S8G pressurised water-cooled reactor supplying steam

to geared turbines, delivering power to one shaft
Speed: classified
Range: limited only by food capacity and crew efficiency
Crew: 16+117
Used by: building for USA
Notes: Planned as the USA's main deterrent force for the 1980s and 1990s, the boats

of the 'Ohio' class are the largest submarines yet designed. The only two yards capable of building such craft are Newport News Shipbuilding & Dry Dock, and the Electric Boat Division of General Dynamics. The latter is building the first five boats, scheduled for commissioning between 1979 and 1982. The rest have not yet been laid down.

'Benjamin Franklin' and 'Lafayette' class nuclear ballistic missile submarine (31)

Class: *Lafayette* (SSBN616), *Alexander Hamilton* (SSBN617), *Andrew Jackson* (SSBN619), *John Adams* (SSBN620), *James Munroe* (SSBN622), *Nathan Hale* (SSBN623), *Woodrow Wilson* (SSBN624), *Henry Clay* (SSBN625), *Daniel Webster* (SSBN626), *James Madison* (SSBN627), *Tecumseh* (SSBN628), *Daniel Boone* (SSBN629), *John C. Calhoun* (SSBN630), *Ulysses S. Grant* (SSBN631), *Von Steuben* (SSBN632), *Casimir Pulaski* (SSBN633), *Stonewall Jackson* (SSBN634), *Sam Rayburn* (SSBN635), *Nathaniel Greene* (SSBN636), *Benjamin Franklin* (SSBN640), *Simon Bolivar* (SSBN641), *Kamehameha* (SSBN642), *George Bancroft* (SSBN643), *Lewis and Clark* (SSBN644), *James K. Polk* (SSBN645), *George C. Marshall* (SSBN654), *Henry L. Stimson* (SSBN655), *George Washington Carver* (SSBN656), *Francis Scott Key* (SSBN657), *Mariano G. Vallejo* (SSBN658), *Will Rogers* (SSBN659)

Displacement: 7,250 tons (7,366 tonnes) standard surfaced; 8,250 tons (8,382 tonnes) dived
Dimensions: Length 425 ft (129.5 m)
Beam 33 ft (10.1 m)
Draught 31 ft 6 in (9.6 m)
Armament:
Guns none
Missile systems
16 Poseidon C-3 SLBM launch tubes
A/S weapons
none
Torpedo tubes
4 21-in (533-mm)
Aircraft
none
Radar and electronics:
Sonar:
Powerplant: 1 Westinghouse S5W pressurised water-cooled reactor supplying steam

to 2 geared turbines, delivering 15,000 shp to one shaft
Speed: 20 knots (surfaced); about 30 knots (dived)
Range: limited only by food capacity and crew efficiency
Crew: 20+148 (two crews) from SSBN640; 14+126 in others
Used only by: USA
Notes: The 31 boats of these two classes, which have only minimal differences, were built between 1961 and 1966 by the Electric Boat Division of General Dynamics, Mare Island Naval Shipyard, Portsmouth Naval Shipyard, and Newport News Shipbuilding & Dry Dock. The boats were commissioned between 1963 and 1967, and form the backbone of the US nuclear deterrent force. Each boat has two crews for maximum sea time.

'Ethan Allen' class nuclear ballistic missile submarine (5)

Class: *Ethan Allen* (SSBN608), *Sam Houston* (SSBN609), *Thomas A. Edison* (SSBN610), *John Marshall* (SSBN611), *Thomas Jefferson* (SSBN618)
Displacement: 6,955 tons (7,066 tonnes) surfaced; 7,880 tons (8,006 tonnes) dived
Dimensions: Length 410 ft (125.0 m)
Beam 33 ft (10.1 m)
Draught 32 ft (9.8 m)
Armament:
Guns none
Missile systems
16 Polaris A-3 SLBM launch tubes
A/S weapons
none
Torpedo tubes
4 21-in (533-mm)
Aircraft
none
Radar and electronics:
Sonar:
Powerplant: 1 Westinghouse S5W pressurised water-cooled reactor supplying steam to 2 General Electric geared turbiness, delivering 15,000 shp to one shaft
Speed: 20 knots (surfaced); about 30 knots (dived)
Range: limited only by food capacity and crew efficiency
Crew: 15+127

Used only by: USA
Notes: The first and third boats were built by the Electric Boat Division of General Dynamics, and the other three by Newport News Shipbuilding & Dry Dock, between 1959 and 1962, for commissioning between 1961 and 1963. The boats are of an improved 'George Washington' design, but built with better steel to improve the diving depth. They are not to be converted to fire Poseidon missiles, as were the boats of the 'Benjamin Franklin' and 'Lafayette' classes.

'George Washington' class nuclear ballistic missile submarine (5)

Class: *George Washington* (SSBN598), *Patrick Henry* (SSBN599), *Theodore Roosevelt* (SSBN600), *Robert E. Lee* (SSBN601), *Abraham Lincoln* (SSBN602)
Displacement: 6,019 tons (6,115 tonnes) standard surfaced; 6,888 tons (6,998 tonnes) dived
Dimensions: Length 381 ft 8 in (116.3 m)
Beam 33 ft (10.1 m)
Draught 29 ft (8.8 m)
Armament:
Guns none
Missile systems
16 Polaris A-3 SLBM launch tubes
A/S weapons
none
Torpedo tubes
6 21-in (533-mm)
Aircraft
none
Radar and electronics:
Sonar:
Powerplant: 1 Westinghouse S5W pressurised water-cooled reactor supplying steam to 2 General Electric geared turbines, delivering 15,000 shp to one shaft
Speed: 20 knots (surfaced); about 30 knots (dived)
Range: limited only by food capacity and crew efficiency

Crew: 12+100
Used only by: USA
Notes: These boats were the first ballistic missile-armed submarines in US service, and were built by four yards between 1957 and 1960, for commissioning between 1959 and 1961.

'Los Angeles' class nuclear attack submarine (40)

Class: *Los Angeles* (SSN688), *Baton Rouge* (SSN689), *Philadelphia* (SSN690), *Memphis* (SSN691), *Omaha* (SSN692), *Cincinatti* (SSN693), *Groton* (SSN694), *Birmingham* (SSN695), *New York City* (SSN696), *Indianapolis* (SSN697), *Bremerton* (SSN698), *Jacksonville* (SSN699), *Dallas* (SSN700), *La Jolla* (SSN701), *Phoenix* (SSN702), *Boston* (SSN703), *Baltimore* (SSN704), 16 others (SSN705 to SSN720), and seven others (unnumbered as yet)
Displacement: 6,000 tons (6,096 tonnes) standard; 6,900 tons (7,010 tonnes) dived
Dimensions: Length 360 ft (109.7 m)
Beam 33 ft (10.1 m)
Draught 33 ft (10.1 m)
Armament:
Guns none

Missile systems
   tube-launched Harpoon SSM from 1978
A/S weapons
   SUBROC
Torpedo tubes
   4 21-in (533-mm)
Aircraft
   none
Radar and electronics: BPS-15 search and navigation radar
Sonar: BQQ-5 long-range acquisition and BQS-15 close-range

Powerplant: 1 General Electric S6G pressurised water-cooled reactor supplying steam to 2 geared turbines, delivering power to one shaft
Speed: 30+ knots (dived)
Range: limited only by food capacity and crew efficiency

Crew: 12+115
Used only by: USA
Notes: The boats are being built by Newport News Shipbuilding & Dry Dock, and the Electric Boat Division of General Dynamics. The first 18 boats are to be built between 1972 and 1980, for commissioning between 1976 and 1980, with the other 22 following during the 1980s. Particular attention has been paid to making the boats as quiet as possible.

'Glenard P. Lipscomb' class nuclear attack submarine (1)

Class: *Glenard P. Lipscomb* (SSN685)
Displacement: 5,813 tons (6,906 tonnes) standard; 6,480 tons (6,584 tonnes) dived
Dimensions: Length 365 ft (111.3 m)
          Beam 31 ft 9 in (9.7 m)
          Draught
Armament:
Guns none
Missile systems
   none
A/S weapons
   SUBROC
Torpedo tubes
   4 21-in (533-mm)
Aircraft
   none
Radar and electronics:
Sonar:
Powerplant: 1 Westinghouse S5Wa pressurised water-cooled reactor supplying steam to 1 General Electric turbo-electric drive, delivering power to one shaft
Speed: about 25+ knots (dived)

Range: limited only by food capacity and crew efficiency
Crew: 12+108
Used only by: USA
Notes: The only boat of its class, this was produced to test the efficiency of various quietening measures, subsequently adopted in the 'Los Angeles' class. The boat was built by the Electric Boat Division of General Dynamics between 1971 and 1973, and commissioned in 1974.

'Narwhal' class nuclear attack submarine (1)

Class: *Narwhal* (SSN671)
Displacement: 4,450 tons (4,521 tonnes) standard; 5,350 tons (5,436 tonnes) dived
Dimensions: Length 314 ft 7 in (95.9 m)
          Beam 43 ft (13.1 m)
          Draught 27 ft (8.2 m)
Armament:
Guns none
Missile systems
   none
A/S weapons
   SUBROC
Torpedo tubes
   4 21-in (533-mm)
Aircraft
   none

Radar and electronics:
Sonar: BQS-8 upward-looking, BQQ-2 system (with BQS-6 active and BQS-7 passive)
Powerplant: 1 General Electric S5G pressurised water-cooled reactor supplying steam to two turbines, delivering 17,000 shp to one shaft

Speed: 20+ knots (surfaced); 30+ knots (dived)
Range: limited only by food capacity and crew efficiency
Crew: 12+95
Used only by: USA
Notes: *Narwhal* was built by the Electric Boat Division of General Dynamics between 1966 and 1967, and commissioned in 1969. Although based on the design of the 'Sturgeon' class, the *Narwhal* is fitted with a special natural circulation reactor, which is simpler and quieter than the reactors that rely on mechanically circulated coolant.

'Sturgeon' class nuclear attack submarine (37)

Class: *Sturgeon* (SSN637), *Whale* (SSN638), *Tautog* (SSN639), *Grayling* (SSN646), *Pogy* (SSN647), *Aspro* (SSN648), *Sunfish* (SSN649), *Pargo* (SSN650), *Queenfish* (SSN651), *Puffer* (SSN652), *Ray* (SSN653), *Sand Lance* (SSN660), *Lapon* (SSN661), *Gurnard* (SSN662), *Hammerhead* (SSN663), *Sea Devil* (SSN664), *Guitarro* (SSN665), *Hawkbill* (SSN666), *Bergall* (SSN667), *Spadefish* (SSN668), *Seahorse* (SSN669), *Finback* (SSN670), *Pintado* (SSN672), *Flying Fish* (SSN673), *Trepang* (SSN674), *Bluefish* (SSN675), *Billfish* (SSN676), *Drum* (SSN677), *Archerfish* (SSN678), *Sil-*

versides (SSN679), *William H. Bates* (SSN680), *Batfish* (SSN681), *Tunny* (SSN682), *Parche* (SSN683), *Cavalla* (SSN684), *L. Mendel Rivers* (SSN686) *Richard B. Russell* (SSN687)
Displacement: 3,640 tons (3,698 tonnes) standard; 4,640 tons (4,714 tonnes) dived
Dimensions: Length 292 ft 3 in (89.0 m)
          Beam 31 ft 8 in (9.5 m)
          Draught 26 ft (7.9 m)

Armament:
Guns none
Missile systems
   none
A/S weapons
   SUBROC
Torpedo tubes
   4 21-in (533-mm)
Aircraft

Radar and electronics: BPS-14 search radar

Sonar: BQQ-2 system, with BQS-6 active and BQS-7 passive sonars, plus BQS-8 upward-looking and BQS-12 (first 16) or BQS-13 (others) active/passive sonars

Powerplant: 1 Westinghouse S5W pressurised water-cooled reactor supplying steam to 2 turbines, delivering 15,000 shp to one shaft

Speed: 20+ knots (surfaced); 30+ knots (dived)

Range: limited only by food capacity and crew efficiency

Crew: 12+95

Used only by: USA

Notes: The 'Sturgeon' class is a development of the 'Thresher' class, with the same propulsion, but slightly larger and probably slightly slower. The 37 boats were built by a number of yards between 1963 and 1974, and were commissioned between 1967 and 1975.

'Thresher' class nuclear attack submarine (13)

Class: *Permit* (SSN594), *Plunger* (SSN595), *Barb* (SSN596), *Pollack* (SSN603), *Haddo* (SSN604), *Jack* (SSN605), *Tinosa* (SSN606), *Dace* (SSN607), *Guardfish* (SSN612), *Flasher* (SSN613), *Greenling* (SSN614), *Gato* (SSN615), *Haddock* (SSN621)

Displacement: 3,750 tons (3,810 tonnes) standard and 4,300 tons (4,369 tonnes) dived for all except *Flasher, Greenling* and *Gato*: 3,800 tons (3,861 tonnes) and 4,470 tons (4,542 tonnes)

Dimensions: Length 278 ft 6 in (84.9 m)
Beam 31 ft 8 in (9.6 m)
Draught 28 ft 5 in (8.7 m)

Armament:
Guns none
Missile systems
none
A/S weapons
SUBROC
Torpedo tubes
4 21-in (533-mm)
Aircraft
none

Radar and electronics:
Sonar: BQQ-2 system with BQS-6 active and BQS-7 passive sonars

Powerplant: 1 Westinghouse S5W pressurised water-cooled reactor supplying steam to 2 turbines, delivering 15,000 shp to one shaft

Speed: 20+ knots (surfaced); 30+ knots (dived)

Range: limited only by food capacity and crew efficiency

Crew: 12+91

Used only by: USA

Notes: The name boat of the class, *Thresher* (SSN593), was lost at sea in 1963. The 14 boats of the class were built by various yards between 1959 and 1966, for commissioning between 1962 and 1967. *Jack, Flasher, Greenling* and *Gato* are longer than the other boats, at 297 ft 5 in (90.7 m) for *Jack*, which has different propulsion characteristics, and 292 ft 3 in (89.1 m) for the others.

'Tullibee' class nuclear attack submarine (1)

Class: *Tullibee* (SSN597)

Displacement: 2,317 tons (2,354 tonnes) standard; 2,640 tons (2,682 tonnes) dived

Dimensions: Length 273 ft (83.2 m)
Beam 23 ft 4 in (7.1 m)
Draught 21 ft (6.4 m)

Armament:
Guns none
Missile systems
none
A/S weapons
none

Torpedo tubes
4 21-in (533-mm)
Aircraft
none

Radar and electronics:
Sonar: BQQ-2 system, with BQS-6 active and BQS-7 passive sonars, and BQG-4 PUFFS (Passive Underwater Fire-control Feasibility System)

Powerplant: 1 Combustion Engineering S2C pressurised water-cooled reactor supplying steam to 1 Westinghouse turbo-electric drive, delivering 2,500 shp to one shaft

Speed: 15 knots (surfaced); 20+ knots (dived)

Range: limited only by food capacity and crew efficiency

Crew: 6+50

Used only by: USA

Notes: *Tullibee* was built by the Electric Boat Division of General Dynamics between 1958 and 1960 to test the turbo-electric drive propulsion and other advanced attack submarine features incorporated on later attack boats. She was commissioned in 1960. She is intended for anti-submarine operations.

'Skipjack' class nuclear attack submarine (5)

Class: *Skipjack* (SSN585), *Scamp* (SSN588), *Sculpin* (SSN590), *Shark* (SSN591), *Snook* (SSN592)
Displacement: 3,075 tons (3,124 tonnes) surfaced; 3,513 tons (3,569 tonnes) dived
Dimensions: Length 251 ft 8 in (76.7 m)
Beam 31 ft 6 in (9.6 m)
Draught 29 ft 5 in (8.9 m)
Armament:
Guns none
Missile systems
none
A/S weapons
none
Torpedo tubes
6 21-in (533-mm)

Aircraft
none
Radar and electronics:
Sonar: Modified BQS-4
Powerplant: 1 Westinghouse S5W pressurised water-cooled reactor supplying steam to 2 Westinghouse (*Skipjack*) or General Electric (others) turbines, delivering 15,000 shp to one shaft
Speed: 16 knots (surfaced); 30+ knots (dived)

Range: limited only by food capacity and crew efficiency
Crew: 8+85
Used only by: USA
Notes: The boats were built in four yards between 1956 and 1960, and commissioned in the period from 1959 to 1961. Their sistership *Scorpion* (SSN589) was lost at sea in 1968. The class introduced the teardrop hull design, the Westinghouse S5W reactor and single-screw propulsion, all features of later attack boats.

'Skate' class nuclear attack submarine (4)

Class: *Skate* (SSN578), *Swordfish* (SSN579), *Sargo* (SSN583), *Seadragon* (SSN584)
Displacement: 2,570 tons (2,611 tonnes) standard; 2,861 tons (2,907 tonnes) dived
Dimensions: Length 267 ft 8 in (81.5 m)
Beam 25 ft (7.6 m)
Draught 22 ft (6.7 m)
Armament:
Guns none
Missile systems
none
A/S weapons
none
Torpedo tubes
8 21-in (533-mm)

Aircraft
none
Radar and electronics:
Sonar: BQS-4
Powerplant: 1 Westinghouse S3W (*Skate* and *Sargo*) or Westinghouse S4W (*Swordfish* and *Seadragon*) pressurised water-cooled reactor supplying steam to Westinghouse turbines, delivering 6,600 shp to two shafts

Speed: 20+ knots (surfaced); 25+ knots (dived)
Range: limited only by food capacity and crew efficiency
Crew: 8+87
Used only by: USA
Notes: The 'Skate' class boats were the world's first production-line nuclear-powered submarines; their design is essentially a scaled-down version of the *Nautilus'* design.

'Seawolf' class nuclear attack submarine (1)

Class: *Seawolf* (SSN575)
Displacement: 3,765 tons (3,825 tonnes) standard; 4,200 tons (4,267 tonnes) dived
Dimensions: Length 337 ft 6 in (102.9 m)
Beam 27 ft 8 in (8.4 m)
Draught 23 ft (7.0 m)
Armament:
Guns none
Missile systems
none
A/S weapons
none
Torpedo tubes
6 21-in (533-mm)
Aircraft
none
Radar and electronics:
Sonar: BQS-4
Powerplant: 1 Westinghouse S2Wa pressurised water-cooled reactor supplying steam to 2 General Electric turbines, delivering 15,000 shp to two shafts
Speed: 20+ knots (surfaced and dived)
Range: limited only by food capacity and crew efficiency
Crew: 11+90
Used only by: USA
Notes: *Seawolf* has a hull design based on that of the 'Guppy' type conventional submarines, and was produced as a test vehicle for the Knolls Atomic Power Laboratory/General Electric Submarine Intermediate Reactor (SIR) II/S2G liquid-metal reactor, to evaluate its performance in comparison with the pressurised water-cooled reactor (S2W) used in the *Nautilus*.

The boat is now used mainly for experimental work, with a Westinghouse reactor in place of the General Electric unit.

'Nautilus' class nuclear attack submarine (1)

Class: *Nautilus* (SSN571)
Displacement: 3,764 tons (3,824 tonnes) surfaced; 4,040 tons (4,105 tonnes) dived
Dimensions: Length 319 ft 5 in (97.4 m)
Beam 27 ft 7 in (8.4 m)
Draught 22 ft (6.7 m)
Armament:
Guns none
Missile systems
none
A/S weapons
none
Torpedo tubes
6 21-in (533-mm)
Aircraft
none
Radar and electronics:
Sonar: BQS-4
Powerplant: 1 Westinghouse G2W pressurised water-cooled reactor supplying steam to 2 Westinghouse turbines, delivering 15,000 shp to two shafts
Speed: 20+ knots (surfaced and dived)

Range: limited only by food capacity and crew efficiency
Crew: 13+92
Used only by: USA
Notes: *Nautilus* was the world's first nuclear-powered submarine, having been built between 1952 and 1954 by the Electric Boat Division of General Dynamics, and commissioned in 1954. She is used mainly for experimental work. The pressurised water-cooled reactor, the type that was to become standard in US Navy boats, was developed as the Submarine Thermal Reactor (STR) by the Bettis Atomic Power Laboratory and Westinghouse, after initial research by the Argonne National Laboratory.

'Barbel' class submarine (3)

Class: *Barbel* (SS580), *Blueback* (SS581), *Bonefish* (SS582)
Displacement: 2,146 tons (2,180 tonnes) surfaced; 2,894 tons (2,940 tonnes) dived
Dimensions: Length 219 ft 6 in (66.8 m)
Beam 29 ft (8.8 m)
Draught 28 ft (8.5 m)
Armament:
Guns none
Missile systems
none
A/S weapons
none
Torpedo tubes
6 21-in (533-mm)
Aircraft
none
Radar and electronics:
Sonar: BQS-4
Powerplant: 3 Fairbanks Morse diesels, delivering 4,800 bhp, and 2 General Electric electric motors, delivering 3,150 shp to one shaft
Speed: 15 knots (surfaced) 21 knots (dived)

Range:
Crew: 8+69
Used only by: USA
Notes: The boats were built between 1956 and 1958 by Portsmouth Naval Shipyard, Ingalls Shipbuilding and New York Shipbuilding, for commissioning in 1959. The boats have a teardrop-shaped hull, and an attack centre for all essential controls and crew, features used in all later US submarines.

'Nimitz' class nuclear aircraft-carrier (3)

Class: *Nimitz* (CVN68), *Dwight D. Eisenhower* (CVN69), *Carl Vinson* (CVN70)
Displacement: 81,600 tons (82,906 tonnes) standard; 91,400 tons (92,862 tonnes) full load
Dimensions: Length 1,092 ft (332.0 m)
Beam (hull) 134 ft (40.8 m)
Draught 37 ft (11.3 m)
Armament:
Guns none
Missile systems
3 Sea Sparrow Basic Point Defense Missile Systems
A/S weapons
none
Torpedo tubes
none
Aircraft
90+
Radar and electronics: SPS-48 3D air search, SPS-43A air search, SPS-10 surface search, and SPS-42, 43 and 44 navigation radars; NTDS (Naval Tactical Data System)
Sonar: none
Powerplant: 2 pressurised water-cooled reactors (A4W/A1G) supplying steam to geared turbines, delivering 280,000 shp to four shafts
Speed: 30+ knots
Range: between 800,000 and 1,000,000 miles (1,287,500 and 1,609,400 km)
Crew: 3,300 (ship) + 3,000 (air group)
Used only by: USA

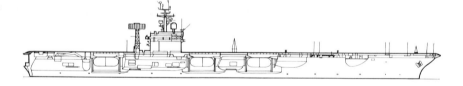

Notes: Newport Shipbuilding & Dry Dock are building all three ships in the period between 1968 and 1979, for commissioning in 1975, 1977 and 1981. The ships are the largest warships in the world, and have flight decks some 252 ft (76.8 m) in width.

'Enterprise' class nuclear air-craft-carrier (1)

Class: *Enterprise* (CVN65)
Displacement: 75,700 tons (76,911 tonnes) standard; 89,600 tons (91,034 tonnes) full load
Dimensions: Length 1,102 ft (335.9 m)
Beam (hull) 133 ft (40.5 m)
Draught 35 ft 9 in (10.8 m)
Armament:
Guns none
Missile systems
2 Sea Sparrow Basic Point Defense Missile Systems
A/S weapons
none
Torpedo tubes
none
Aircraft
84

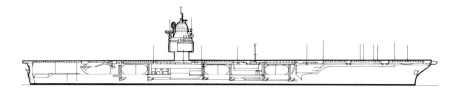

Radar and electronics: SPS-32 3D air/surface search, SPS-33 3D target-tracker, SPS-58 low-level air search, SPS-10 and 12 search, and various navigation radars; NTDS (Naval Tactical Data System)
Sonar: none
Powerplant: 8 Westinghouse A2W pressurised water-cooled reactors supplying steam to 4 Westinghouse geared turbines, delivering about 280,000 shp to four shafts
Speed: about 35 knots
Range: some 10 to 13 years of steaming

Crew: 162+2,940 (ship) + 2,400 (air group)
Used only by: USA
Notes: *Enterprise* was built between 1958 and 1960 by Newport News Shipbuilding & Dry Dock, and commissioned into US service in 1961. She was at first classified as an attack carrier (CVAN), but reclassified as an aircraft-carrier (CVN) in 1975. The hull is derived from that of the 'Forrestal' class aircraft-carriers, with a prominent rectangular 'island' covered with electronic sensors and radar antennae.

'Kitty Hawk' and 'John F. Kennedy' class aircraft-carrier (4)

Class: *Kitty Hawk* (CV63), *Constellation* (CV64), *America* (CV66), *John F. Kennedy* (CV67)
Displacement: 60,100 tons (61,062 tonnes) and 80,800 tons (82,093 tonnes) full load for *Kitty Hawk* and *Constellation*; 60,300 tons (61,265 tonnes) standard and 78,500 tons (79,756 tonnes) full load for *America*; 61,000 tons (61,976 tonnes) standard and 82,000 tons (83,312 tonnes) full load for *John F. Kennedy*
Dimensions: Length 1,046 ft (318.8 m) for *Kitty Hawk* and *Constellation*; 1,047 ft 6 in (319.3 m) for *America*; 1,052 ft (320.7 m) for *John F. Kennedy*
Beam (hull) 130 ft (39.6 m)
Draught 35 ft 10 in (10.9 m) for *John F. Kennedy*; 37 ft (11.3 m) for others
Armament:
Guns none
Missile systems
2 twin Terrier SAM launchers in *Constellation* and *America*
3 Sea Sparrow Basic Point Defense Missile Systems in *John F. Kennedy* and *Kitty-hawk*

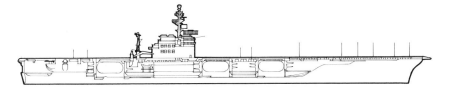

A/S weapons
 none
Torpedo tubes
 none
Aircraft
 about 85
Radar and electronics: SPS-52 3D surveillance (all except *John F. Kennedy*), SPS-48 and 58 search (*John F. Kennedy* only), SPS-43 air search, and SPS-30 long-range height-finder (except *John F. Kennedy*) radars; NTDS (Naval Tactical Data System)

Sonar: SQS-23 (*America* only)
Powerplant: 8 Foster Wheeler boilers supplying steam to 4 Westinghouse geared turbines, delivering 280,000 shp to four shafts
Speed: 30+ knots
Range:
Crew: 150+2,650 (ship) + 2,150 (air group)
Used only by: USA

Notes: The first two ships were built by New York Shipbuilding and New York Naval Shipyard, the other two by Newport News Shipbuilding & Dry Dock, in the period between 1956 and 1967. The ships were commissioned in 1961, 1961, 1965, and 1968, with the classification of attack carriers (CVA). They were reclassified as aircraft-carriers (CV) in 1973, 1975, 1975 and 1974.

'Forrestal' class aircraft-carrier (4)

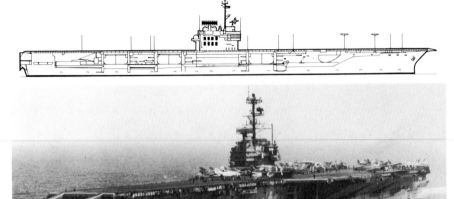

Class: *Forrestal* (CV59), *Saratoga* (CV60), *Ranger* (CV61), *Independence* (CV62)
Displacement: 59,060 tons (60,005 tonnes) standard and 75,900 tons (77,114 tonnes) full load for *Forrestal* and *Saratoga*; 60,000 tons (60,960 tonnes) standard and 79,300 tons (80,569 tonnes) full load for *Ranger* and *Independence*
Dimensions: Length 1,086 ft (331.0 m) for *Forrestal*; 1,063 ft (324.0 m) for *Saratoga*; 1,071 ft (326.4 m) for *Ranger*; 1,070 ft (326.1 m) for *Independence*
Beam (hull) 129 ft 6 in (38.5 m)
Draught 37 ft (11.3 m)
Armament:
Guns 2 5-in (127-mm) in single turrets (*Ranger* only)
Missile systems
 2 Sea Sparrow Basic Point Defense Missile Systems (except *Ranger*)
A/S weapons
 none
Torpedo tubes
 none
Aircraft
 about 70
Radar and electronics: SPS-43 air search, SPS-30 height-finder, SPS-58 low-level air search, and SPN-10 navigation radars; NTDS (Naval Tactical Data System)
Sonar: none
Powerplant: 8 Babcock & Wilcox boilers supplying steam to 4 Westinghouse geared turbines, delivering 260,000 shp (*Forrestal*) or 280,000 shp (others) to four shafts
Speed: 33 knots (*Forrestal*); 34 knots (others)
Range:
Crew: 145+2,645 (ship) + 2,150 (air group)
Used only by: USA
Notes: The ships were built in alternate pairs by Newport News Shipbuilding & Dry Dock and by New York Naval Shipyard, between 1952 and 1958, for commissioning in 1955, 1956, 1957 and 1959. At first classified as large aircraft-carriers (CVB), they were reclassified as attack carriers (CVA) in 1952, and as aircraft-carriers (CV) in 1975, 1972, 1975 and 1973. *Ranger* is to have 3 BPDMS Sea Sparrow systems in 1978–79.

'Midway' class aircraft-carrier (2)

Class: *Midway* (CV41), *Coral Sea* (CV43)
Displacement: 51,000 tons (51,816 tonnes) standard for *Midway*. 52,500 tons (53,340 tonnes) standard for *Coral Sea*; about 64,000 tons (65,024 tonnes) full load for all
Dimensions: Length 979 ft (298.4 m)
Beam (hull) 121 ft (36.9 m)
Draught 35 ft 3 in (10.8 m)
Armament:
Guns 3 5-in (127-mm) in single turrets
Missile systems
 2 Sea Sparrow Basic Point Defense Missile Systems (*Midway* only)
A/S weapons
 none
Torpedo tubes
 none
Aircraft
 about 75
Radar and electronics: SPS-10 surface search, SPS-43 air search, SPS-30 height-finder, SPS-58 low-level air search, and SPS-6 and 10 navigation radars; NTDS (Naval Tactical Data System)

Sonar: none
Powerplant: 12 Babcock & Wilcox boilers supplying steam to 4 Westinghouse geared turbines, delivering 212,000 shp to four shafts
Speed: 30+ knots
Range:

Crew: 140+2,475 (Midway) or 165+2,545 (Coral Sea) + 1,800 (air group)
Notes: The ships were built by Newport News Shipbuilding & Dry Dock, between 1943 and 1946, for commissioning in 1945 and 1947. Initially classified as large

aircraft-carriers (CVB), they were reclassified as attack carriers (CVA) in 1952, and as aircraft-carriers (CV) in 1975. Both have been very considerably modernised, with angled decks, new lifts, improved electronics, and steam catapults.

'Hancock' and 'Intrepid' class aircraft-carrier (5)

Class: Intrepid (CVS11), Lexington (CVT16), Bonne Homme Richard (CVA31), Oriskany (CV34), Shangri-La (CVS38)
Displacement: 41,900 tons (42,570 tonnes) full load (except Oriskany: 40,600 tons/ 41,250 tonnes)
Dimensions: Length 899 ft (274.0 m), except Lexington, Oriskany and Shangri-La: 889 ft (270.9 m)
Beam 103 ft (30.8 m), except Oriskany: 106 ft 6 in (32.5 m)
Draught 31 ft (9.4 m)
Armament:
Guns 4 or 2 (Oriskany) 5-in (127-mm) in single mountings, except Lexington, which has no guns
Missile systems
none

A/S weapons
none
Torpedo tubes
none
Aircraft
80 for CVA/CV; 45 for CVS; none for CVT
Radar and electronics: SPS-10, SPS-30 and SPS-43 search, and SPN-10 navigation radars, except Lexington, which has SPS-12 instead of SPS-30 search radar
Sonar: none
Powerplant: 8 Babcock & Wilcox boilers supplying steam to 4 Westinghouse geared

turbines, delivering 150,000 shp to four shafts
Speed: 30+ knots
Range:
Crew: CVA/CV 110+1,980; CVS 115+1,500; and CVT 75+1,365
Used only by: USA
Notes: The ships were built as 'Hancock' class aircraft-carriers between 1941 and 1945, and commissioned in 1943, 1943, 1944, 1950, and 1944. Only Lexington is now in commission, as a training carrier.

'Virginia' class nuclear guided missile cruiser (4)

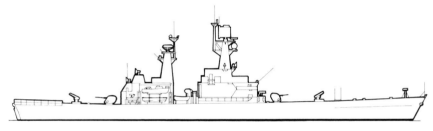

Class: Virginia (CGN38), Texas (CGN39), Mississippi (CGN40), Arkansas (CGN41)
Displacement: 10,000 tons (10,160 tonnes) full load
Dimensions: Length 585 ft (177.3 m)
Beam 63 ft (18.9 m)
Draught 29 ft 6 in (9.0 m)
Armament:
Guns 2 5-in (127-mm) in single turrets
Missile systems
2 Mark 26 twin ASROC/Tartar-D launchers for Standard SAMs
A/S weapons
ASROC (see above)
2 triple 12.75-in (324-mm) Mark 32 tubes
Torpedo tubes
none
Aircraft
2 helicopters

Radar and electronics: SPS-48A 3D search, SPS-40B air search, and SPS-55 surface search radars; NTDS (Naval Tactical Data System)
Sonar: SQS-53A
Powerplant: 2 General Electric D2G pressurised water-cooled reactors supplying steam to 2 geared turbines, delivering power to two shafts
Speed: 30+ knots
Range: virtually unlimited

Crew: 27+415
Used only by: USA
Notes: All four ships will have been built by Newport News Shipbuilding & Dry Dock between 1972 and 1979, with commissioning in 1976, 1977, 1978 and 1980. Harpoon SSM launchers are to be fitted in the near future. The 'Virginia' class is very similar to the 'California' class, but with better AA facilities, ECM equipment and ASW control systems.

'California' class nuclear guided missile cruiser (2)

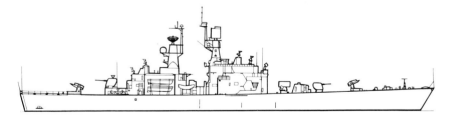

Class: California (CGN36), South Carolina (CGN37)
Displacement: 9,561 tons (9,714 tonnes) full load
Dimensions: Length 596 ft (181.7 m)
Beam 61 ft (18.6 m)
Draught 31 ft 6 in (9.6 m)
Armament:
Guns 2 5-in (127-mm) in single turrets
Missile systems
2 Mark 13 single Tartar-D launchers for 80 Standard MR SAMs
A/S weapons
1 octuple ASROC launcher
4 12.75-in (324-mm) Mark 32 tubes
Torpedo tubes
none
Aircraft
none
Radar and electronics: SPS-48 3D air search and target acquisition, SPS-10 and

40 search, and SPG-51D, SPG-60 and SPQ-9A fire-control radars; NTDS (Naval Tactical Data System)
Sonar: SQS-26CX
Powerplant: 2 General Electric D2G pressurised water-cooled reactors supplying steam to 2 geared turbines, delivering power to two shafts
Speed: 30+ knots
Range: about 700,000 miles (1,126,600 km)
Crew: 28+512
Used only by: USA

Notes: Both ships were built by Newport News Shipbuilding & Dry Dock between 1970 and 1972, for commissioning in 1974 and 1975. The type was at first classified as a guided-missile frigate (DLGN) type. Two 20-mm Phalanx Close-In Weapons Systems (CIWS) are to be fitted, and Mark 36 Chaffroc Rapid Bloom Overhead Chaff (RBOC) is standard. Harpoon SSM capability is to be added.

'Truxtun' class nuclear guided missile cruiser (1)

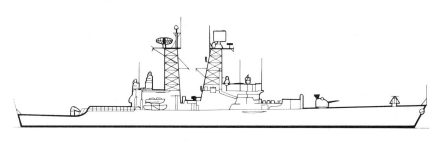

Class: *Truxtun* (CGN35)
Displacement: 8,200 tons (8,331 tonnes) standard; 9,127 tons (9,273 tonnes) full load
Dimensions: Length 564 ft (117.9 m)
Beam 58 ft (17.7 m)
Draught 31 ft (9.4 m)
Armament:
Guns 1 5-in (127-mm)
2 3-in (76-mm) in single mountings
Missile systems
1 Mark 10 twin ASROC/Standard ER launcher
A/S weapons
ASROC (see above)
4 12.75-in (324-mm) Mark 32 tubes
Torpedo tubes
none
Aircraft
facilities for 1 helicopter
Radar and electronics: SPS-48 3D search, SPS-10 surface search, and SPS-40 air search radars; NTDS (Naval Tactical Data System); Mark 36 Chaffroc (RBOC); fire-control is by SPG-53A and SPG-55B radars
Sonar: SQS-26
Powerplant: 2 General Electric D2G pressurised water-cooled reactors supplying steam to 2 geared turbines, delivering 60,000 shp to two shafts
Speed: 30+ knots
Range:
Crew: 36+456
Used only by: USA
Notes: *Truxtun* was built by New York Shipbuilding between 1963 and 1964, and

commissioned into US service in 1967. Her classification was altered from guided-missile frigate (DLGN) to guided-missile cruiser (CGN) in 1975. Two 20-mm Phalanx Close-In Weapons Systems (CIWS) are to be fitted in the near future.

'Belknap' class guided missile cruiser (9)

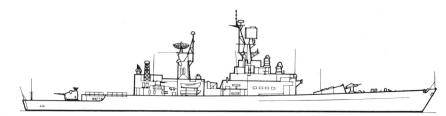

Class: *Belknap* (CG26), *Josephus Daniels* (CG27), *Wainwright* (CG28), *Jouett* (CG29), *Horne* (CG30), *Sterett* (CG31), *William H. Standley* (CG32), *Fox* (CG33), *Biddle* (CG34)
Displacement: 6,570 tons (6,675 tonnes) standard; 7,930 tons (8,057 tonnes) full load
Dimensions: Length 547 ft (166.7 m)
Beam 54 ft 9 in (16.7 m)
Draught 28 ft 9 in (8.7 m)
Armament:
Guns 1 5-in (127-mm)
2 3-in (76-mm) in single mountings
Missile systems
1 Mark 10 twin ASROC/Standard ER launcher with 60 missiles (including up to 20 ASROCs)
A/S weapons
ASROC
2 triple 12.75-in (324-mm) Mark 32 tubes
Torpedo tubes
none

Aircraft
1 helicopter
Radar and electronics: SPS-48 3D air search, SPS-10 surface search, SPS-37 (*Belknap, Daniels, Wainwright*) or SPS-40 (others) airsearch, SPG-53A and SPG-55B weapon control radars; NTDS (Naval Tactical Data System); Mark 36 Chaffroc RBOC
Sonar: SQS-26
Powerplant: 4 Babcock & Wilcox (*Belknap, Daniels, Wainwright*) or Combustion Engineering (others) boilers supplying steam to 2 General Electric (*Belknap, Daniels, Wainwright*) or De Laval (others) geared turbines, delivering 85,000 shp to two shafts

Speed: 34 knots
Range:
Crew: 31+387
Used only by: USA
Notes: The ships were built by four yards in the period between 1962 and 1965, for commissioning between 1964 and 1967. Originally classified as guided-missile frigates (DLG), they were reclassified as guided-missile cruisers (CG) in 1975. All vessels will receive the Harpoon SSM system and 20-mm Phalanx Close-In Weapons System (CIWS). *Belknap* is currently out of service after a collision in 1975.

'Leahy' class guided missile cruiser (9)

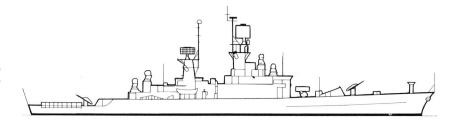

Class: *Leahy* (CG16), *Harry E. Yarnell* (CG17), *Worden* (CG18), *Dale* (CG19), *Richmond K. Turner* (CG20), *Gridley* (CG21), *England* (CG22), *Halsey* (CG23), *Reeves* (CG24)
Displacement: 5,670 tons (5,760 tonnes) standard; 7,800 tons (7,925 tonnes) full load

Dimensions: Length 533 ft (162.5 m)
Beam 54 ft 11 in (16.6 m)
Draught 26 ft (7.9 m)
Armament:
Guns 4 3-in (76-mm) in twin turrets
Missile systems
2 twin Standard ER SAM launchers with 80 missiles
A/S weapons
1 octuple ASROC launcher
2 triple 12.75-in (324-mm) Mark 32 tubes
Torpedo tubes
none
Aircraft
facilities for 1 helicopter
Radar and electronics: SPS-48 3D search and target acquisition, SPS-10 surface

search, SPS-37 air search, SPG-50 and SPG-55 weapons control radars; NTDS (Naval Tactical Data System); Mark 36 Chaffroc RBOC
Sonar: SQS-23
Powerplant: 4 Babcock & Wilcox (CG16 to CG20) or Foster Wheeler (others) boilers supplying steam to General Electric (CG16 to CG18), De Laval (CG19 to CG22) or Allis-Chalmers (CG23 and CG24) geared turbines, delivering 85,000 shp to two shafts
Speed: 34 knots

Range:
Crew: 18+359 (CG16, 17, 21, 23); 32+381 (others)
Used only by: USA
Notes: The ships were built by five yards between 1959 and 1962, and commissioned between 1962 and 1964. They were originally classified as guide-missile frigates (DLG), being reclassified as guided-missile cruisers (CG) in 1975. They are designed for the AA and A/S protection of carrier task forces. Each ship is to be fitted with Harpoon SSMs and two 20-mm Phalanx Close-In Weapon Systems (CIWS).

'Bainbridge' class nuclear guided missile cruiser (1)

Class: *Bainbridge* (CGN25)
Displacement: 7,600 tons (7,722 tonnes) standard; 8,580 tons (8,717 tonnes) full load
Dimensions: Length 565 ft (172.5 m)
Beam 57 ft 11 in (17.6 m)
Draught 31 ft (9.5 m)
Armament:
Guns 4 3-in (76-mm) in twin turrets
Missile systems
2 Mark 10 twin Terrier/Standard ER SAM launchers with 80 missiles

A/S weapons
1 octuple ASROC launcher
2 triple 12.75-in (324-mm) Mark 32 tubes
Torpedo tubes
none
Aircraft
facilities for 1 helicopter
Radar and electronics: SPS-52 3D surveillance, SPS-10 surface search, SPS-37 air search, SPG-50 and SPG-55A weapons control radars; NTDS (Naval Tactical Data System); Mark 36 Chaffroc RBOC

Sonar: SQS-23
Powerplant: 2 General Electric D2G pressurised water-cooled reactors supplying steam to 2 geared turbines, delivering 60,000 shp to two shafts
Speed: 30+ knots
Range:
Crew: 34+436
Used only by: USA
Notes: *Bainbridge* is similar to the 'Leahy' class except for the provision of nuclear power. She was built by Bethlehem Steel at Quincy, Massachusetts between 1959 and 1961, and commissioned in 1962. Harpoon SSMs are to be fitted.

'Long Beach' class nuclear guided missile cruiser (1)

Class: *Long Beach* (CGN9)
Displacement: 14,200 tons (14,427 tonnes) standard; 17,100 tons (17,374 tonnes) full load
Dimensions: Length 721 ft 3 in (219.8 m)
Beam 73 ft 3 in (22.3 m)
Draught 31 ft (9.5 m)
Armament:
Guns 2 5-in (127-mm) in single turrets
Missile systems
1 Mark 12 twin Talos SAM launcher with 46 missiles
2 Mark 10 twin Terrier/Standard ER SAM launchers with 120 Terrier missiles
A/S weapons
1 octuple ASROC launcher
2 triple 12.75-in (324-mm) Mark 32 tubes
Torpedo tubes
none

Aircraft
facilities for 1 helicopter
Radar and electronics: SPS-32 long-range search, SPS-33 long-range tracking, SPS-10 surface search, SPS-12 long-range surveillance, and SPG-49B and SPG-55A weapons control radars; NTDS (Naval Tactical Data System); Mark 36 Chaffroc RBOC
Sonar: SQS-23
Powerplant: 2 Westinghouse C1W pressurised water-cooled reactors supplying steam to 2 General Electric geared turbines, delivering about 80,000 shp to two shafts
Speed: 30 knots
Range:
Crew: 79+1,081
Used only by: USA

Notes: *Long Beach* was the first nuclear-powered surface warship in the world, and the first to have missiles as its primary armament. The ship was built between 1957 and 1959 by Bethlehem Steel at Quincy, Massachusetts, and was commissioned in 1961. Harpoon SSMs are to be fitted, as are two 20-mm Phalanx Close-In Weapons Systems (CIWS).

'Albany' class guided missile cruiser (2)

Class: *Albany* (CG10), *Chicago* (CG11)
Displacement: 13,700 tons (13,919 tonnes) standard; 17,500 tons (17,780 tonnes) full load
Dimensions: Length 674 ft (205.4 m)
Beam 71 ft (21.6 m)
Draught 30 ft (9.1 m)
Armament:
Guns 2 5-in (127-mm) in single turrets
Missile systems
2 Mark 12 twin Talos SAM launchers with 92 missiles
2 Mark 11 Tartar SAM launchers with 80 missiles
A/S weapons
1 octuple ASROC launcher
2 triple 12.75-in (324-mm) Mark 32 tubes
Torpedo tubes
none
Aircraft
facilities for helicopters
Radar and electronics: SPS-48 long-range search and target acquisition, SPS-10 surface search, SPS-30 height-finder, SPS-43 air search radars (*Albany*); SPS-10 surface search, SPS-30 height-finder, SPS-43 air search, and SPS-52 3D surveillance radars (*Chicago*), plus SPG-49B and SPG-51C fire-control radars; NTDS (Naval Tactical Data System) in *Albany*; Mark 28 Chaffroc
Sonar: SQS-23
Powerplant: 4 Babcock & Wilcox boilers

supplying steam to 4 General Electric geared turbines, delivering 120,000 shp to four shafts
Speed: 32 knots
Range:
Crew: 72+1,150
Used only by: USA
Notes: The two were originally 'Oregon City' and 'Baltimore' class heavy cruisers respectively, being built between 1943 and 1945 by Bethlehem Steel on the Fore River, and Philadelphia Navy Yard, for commissioning in 1946 and 1945. The two were converted to missile cruisers between 1959 and 1964, with completely new superstructures. *Albany* received Anti-Air Warfare (AAW) modernisation between 1967 and 1969, but *Chicago* will not be so updated. Harpoon SSMs are to be fitted, as is the 20-mm Phalanx Close-In Weapons System (CIWS).

Converted 'Cleveland' class guided missile cruiser (1)

Class: *Oklahoma City* (CG5)
Displacement: 10,670 tons (10,841 tonnes) standard; 14,400 tons (14,630 tonnes) full load
Dimensions: Length 610 ft (185.9 m)
Beam 66 ft 4 in (20.2 m)
Draught 25 ft (7.6 m)
Armament:
Guns 3 6-in (152-mm) in a triple turret
2 5-in (127-mm) in a twin turret
Missile systems
1 Mark 7 twin Talos SAM launcher with 46 missiles
A/S weapons
none
Torpedo tubes
none
Aircraft
facilities for 1 helicopter
Radar and electronics: SPS-10 surface search, SPS-30 long-range height-finder, and SPS-43 air search radars, plus SPG-49A weapons control radar
Sonar: none
Powerplant: 4 Babcock & Wilcox boilers supplying steam to 4 General Electric geared turbines, delivering 100,000 shp to four shafts
Speed: 31 knots
Range:
Crew: 89+1,245
Used only by: USA
Notes: The ship was originally CL91, a light cruiser of the 'Cleveland' class, built by Cramp Shipbuilding in Philadelphia between 1942 and 1944, for commissioning in 1944. *Oklahoma City* was recommissioned as a guided-missile light cruiser (CLG) in 1960, and was reclassified as a guided-missile cruiser (CG) in 1975. Two 20-mm Phalanx Close-In Weapons Systems are to be fitted. Her sisterships

Providence (CG6) and *Springfield* (CG7), with twin Terrier SAM launchers and 120 missiles, are in reserve.

'Coontz' class guided missile destroyer (10)

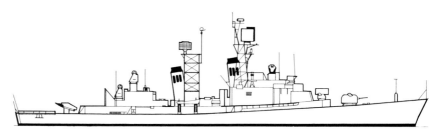

Class: *Farragut* (DDG37), *Luce* (DDG38), *MacDonough* (DDG39), *Coontz* (DDG40), *King* (DDG41), *Mahan* (DDG42), *Dahlgren* (DDG43), *William V. Pratt* (DDG44), *Dewey* (DDG45), *Preble* (DDG46)
Displacement: 4,700 tons (4,775 tonnes) standard; 5,800 tons (5,893 tonnes) full load
Dimensions: Length 512 ft 6 in (156.2 m)
Beam 52 ft 6 in (15.9 m)
Draught 25 ft (7.6 m)
Armament:
Guns 1 5-in (127-mm)
1 20-mm Phalanx CIWS (*King*)
Missile systems
1 Mark 10 twin Terrier/Standard ER SAM launcher with 40 missiles
A/S weapons
1 octuple ASROC launcher
2 triple 12.75-in (324-mm) Mark 32 tubes
Torpedo tubes
none
Aircraft
facilities for 1 helicopter
Radar and electronics: SPS-48 3D long-range search and target acquisition (SPS-52 in *King* and *Pratt*), SPS-10 surface search, and SPS-37 air search radars, plus SPG-53A and SPG-55B weapons control radars; NTDS (Naval Tactical Data System); Mark 36 Chaffroc
Sonar: SQS-23
Powerplant: 4 Foster Wheeler (DDG37 to DDG39) or Babcock & Wilcox (DDG40 to DDG46) boilers supplying steam to 2 De Laval (DDG37 to DDG39) or Allis-Chalmers (DDG40 to DDG46) geared turbines delivering 85,000 shp to two shafts
Speed: 34 knots
Range:
Crew: 21+356
Used only by: USA
Notes: The ships were built by five yards in the period between 1957 and 1960, and were commissioned between 1959 and 1961. Original armament in the initial frigate classification was 4 3-in (76-mm) in twin turrets. The ships then became guided-missile frigates (DLG), in 1956, and finally guided-missile destroyers (DDG) in 1975. All vessels will have the 20-mm Phalanx CIWS and Harpoon SSMs.

'Mitscher' class guided missile destroyer (2)

Class: *Mitscher* (DDG35), *John S. McCain* (DDG36)
Displacement: 5,200 tons (5,283 tonnes) full load
Dimensions: Length 493 ft (150.3 m)
Beam 50 ft (15.2 m)
Draught 21 ft (6.7 m)
Armament:
Guns 2 5-in (127-mm) in single turrets
Missile systems
1 Mark 13 single Tartar SAM launcher with 40 missiles
A/S weapons
1 octuple ASROC launcher
2 triple 12.75-in (324-mm) Mark 32 tubes
Torpedo tubes
none
Aircraft
facilities for 1 helicopter
Radar and electronics: SPS-48 3D long-range search and target acquisition, SPS-10 surface search, and SPS-37 air search radars, plus SPG-51C weapons control radar; Mark 36 Chaffroc RBOC
Sonar: SQS-23
Powerplant: 4 Foster Wheeler boilers supplying steam to 2 General Electric geared turbines, delivering 80,000 shp to two shafts
Speed: 33 knots
Range:
Crew: 28+349
Used only by: USA
Notes: The two ships were built by Bath Iron Works between 1949 and 1952 as fleet destroyers (DD927 and DD928). They were reclassified as destroyer leaders (DL) in 1951, and commissioned as such in 1953. In 1955 DL became the designation for frigates, but the two became guided-missile destroyers (DDG) during missile conversion in 1967.

Converted 'Forrest Sherman' class guided missile destroyer (4)

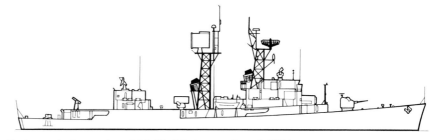

Class: *Decatur* (DDG31), *John Paul Jones* (DDG32), *Parsons* (DDG33), *Somers* (DDG34)
Displacement: 4,150 tons (4,216 tonnes) full load
Dimensions: Length 418 ft 5 in (127.5 m)
Beam 44 ft (13.4 m)
Draught 20 ft (6.1 m)
Armament:
Guns 1 5-in (127-mm)
Missile systems
1 Mark 13 single Tartar SAM launcher with 40 missiles
A/S weapons
1 octuple ASROC launcher
2 triple 12.75-in (324-mm) Mark 32 tubes
Torpedo tubes
none
Aircraft
none
Radar and electronics: SPS-48 3D long-range search and target acquisition, SPS-10 surface search, and SPS-37 (SPS-40 in *Somers*) air search radars, plus SPG-51C and SPG-53B weapons control radars; Mark 36 Chaffroc
Sonar: SQS-23
Powerplant: 4 Babcock & Wilcox (Foster Wheeler in *Decatur*) boilers supplying steam to 2 General Electric (*Parsons* and *Somers*) or Westinghouse (others) geared turbines, delivering 70,000 shp to two shafts
Speed: 32½ knots
Range:
Crew: 22+315 (*Decatur* and *John Paul Jones*); 25+339 (*Parsons* and *Somers*)
Used only by: USA
Notes: The ships were built by three yards between 1954 and 1958 as fleet destroyers (DD936, DD932, DD949, DD947) and were commissioned as such, the first pair in 1956, the second in 1959. They were converted into guided-missile destroyers (DDG) in 1965 (three ships) and 1967 (one ship), being recommissioned in 1967 (three ships) and 1968 (one ship).

'Charles F. Adams' class guided missile destroyer (23)

Class: *Charles F. Adams* (DDG2), *John King* (DDG3), *Lawrence* (DDG4), *Claude V. Ricketts* (DDG5), *Barney* (DDG6), *Henry B. Wilson* (DDG7), *Lynde McCormick* (DDG8), *Towers* (DDG9), *Sampson* (DDG10), *Sellers* (DDG11), *Robison* (DDG12), *Hoel* (DDG13), *Buchanan* (DDG14), *Berkeley* (DDG15), *Joseph Strauss* (DDG16), *Conyngham* (DDG17), *Semmes* (DDG18), *Tattnall* (DDG19), *Goldsborough* (DDG20), *Cochrane* (DDG21), *Benjamin Stoddart* (DDG22), *Richard E. Byrd* (DDG23), *Waddell* (DDG24)
Displacement: 3,370 tons (3,424 tonnes) standard; 4,500 tons (4,572 tonnes) full load
Dimensions: Length 437 ft (113.2 m)
Beam 47 ft (14.3 m)
Draught 20 ft (6.1 m)
Armament:
Guns 2 5-in (127-mm) in single turrets
Missile systems (DDG2 to DDG14)
 1 Mark 11 twin Tartar SAM launcher with 42 missiles
Missile systems (DDG15 to DDG24)
 1 Mark 13 single Tartar SAM launcher with 40 missiles
A/S weapons
 1 octuple ASROC launcher
 2 triple 12.75-in (324-mm) Mark 32 tubes
Torpedo tubes
 none
Aircraft
 none
Radar and electronics: SPS-52 3D surveillance, SPS-10 surface search, SPS-37 (DDG2 to DDG14) or SPS-40 (DDG15 to DDG24) air search, and SPS-39 3D air target search radars, plus SPG-51C and SPG-53A weapon control radars; Mark 36 Chaffroc
Sonar: SQS-23
Powerplant: 4 Babcock & Wilcox (DDGs 2, 3, 7, 8, 10–13, 20–22), Foster Wheeler (DDGs 4–6, 9, 14) or Combustion Engineering (DDGs 15–19) boilers supplying steam to 2 General Electric (DDGs 2, 3, 7, 8, 10–13, 15–22) or Westinghouse (DDGs 4–6, 9, 14, 23, 24) geared turbines, delivering 70,000 shp to two shafts
Speed: 31+ knots
Range:
Crew: 24+330
Used also by: West Germany
Notes: The ships were built by a number of yards between 1959 and 1963, for commissioning between 1960 and 1964. The design is basically an improvement of the 'Forrest Sherman' class, and the first eight were built as fleet destroyers (DD952 to DD959). All the ships are being fitted with provision to fire Standard SAMs, and Harpoon SSMs will be fitted in the near future.

'Spruance' class destroyer (30)

Class: *Spruance* (DD963), *Paul F. Foster* (DD964), *Kinkaid* (DD965), *Hewitt* (DD966), *Elliott* (DD967), *Arthur W. Radford* (DD968), *Peterson* (DD969), *Caron* (DD970), *David R. Ray* (DD971), *Oldendorf*. (DD972), *John Young* (DD973), *Comte de Grasse* (DD974), *O'Brien* (DD975), *Merrill* (DD976), *Briscoe* (DD977), *Stump* (DD978), *Conolly* (DD979), *Moosburgger* (DD980), *John Hancock* (DD981), *Nicholson* (DD982), *John Rodgers* (DD983), *Leftwich* (DD984), *Cushing* (DD985), *Harry W. Hill* (DD986), *O'Bannon* (DD987), *Thorn* (DD988), *Deyo* (DD989), *Ingersoll* (DD990), *Fife* (DD991), *Fletcher* (DD992)
Displacement: 7,300 tons (7,417 tonnes) full load
Dimensions: Length 563 ft 4 in (171.1 m)
Beam 55 ft (17.6 m)
Draught 29 ft (8.8 m)
Armament:
Guns 2 5-in (127-mm) in single turrets
Missile systems
 none
A/S weapons
 1 octuple ASROC launcher
 2 triple 12.75-in (324-mm) Mark 32 tubes
Torpedo tubes
 none

Aircraft
 1 ASW helicopter
Radar and electronics: SPS-40 air search, plus SPG-60 and SPQ-9 weapons control radars; Mark 36 Chaffroc RBOC
Sonar: SQS-53
Powerplant: 4 General Electric LM2500 gas turbines, delivering 80,000 shp to two shafts
Speed: 30+ knots
Range: 6,000 miles (9,655 km) at 20 knots
Crew: 24+272
Used also by: Iran

Notes: The ships of the 'Spruance' class, which is designed primarily for A/S warfare, are all being built by the Ingalls Shipbuilding Corporation of Litton Industries at Pascagoula, Mississippi, between 1972 and 1978, with commissioning dates between 1975 and 1980. It is planned to fit two 20-mm Phalanx Close-In Weapons Systems (CIWS) and a NATO Sea Sparrow multiple SAM launcher. Some 18 of the class were in service by the end of 1978.

'Forrest Sherman' and 'Hull' class destroyer (14)

Class: *Forrest Sherman* (DD931), *Bigelow* (DD942), *Mullinnix* (DD944), *Hull* (DD945), *Edson* (DD946), *Turner Joy* (DD951), *Barry* (DD933), *Davis* (DD937), *Jonas Ingram* (DD938), *Manley* (DD940), *Du Pont* (DD941), *Blandy* (DD943), *Morton* (DD948), *Richard S. Edwards* (DD950)
Displacement: 2,800–3,000 tons (2,845–3,048 tonnes) standard; 3,960–4,200 tons (4,023–4,267 tonnes) full load
Dimensions: Length 418 ft (127.4 m)
Beam 45 ft (13.7 m)
Draught 20 ft (6.1 m)
Armament:
Guns 3 5-in (127-mm) in single turrets, and 2 3-in (76-mm) in single turrets, except A/S group (DD933 to DD950): 2 5-in (127-mm) in single turrets; and *Hull*: 1 8-in (203-mm), 2 5-in (127-mm) and 2 3-in (76-mm) in single mountings
Missile systems
 none
A/S weapons
 1 octuple ASROC launcher in A/S group (DD933 to DD950)
 2 triple 12.75-in (324-mm) Mark 32 tubes
Torpedo tubes
 none
Aircraft
 none
Radar and electronics: SPS-10 surface search and SPS-37 or SPS-40 air search radars
Sonar: SQS-23, and variable-depth in A/S group (DD933 to DD950)
Powerplant: 4 Babcock & Wilcox (DDs 931, 933, 940–942, 945, 946, 950, 951) or Foster Wheeler (others) boilers supplying steam to 2 Westinghouse (DDs 931, 933, 938) or General Electric (others) geared turbines, delivering 70,000 shp to two shafts
Speed: 32½ knots
Range:
Crew: 17+275 (unmodified ships); 17+287 (A/S group)
Used only by: USA
Notes: The ships were built by a number of yards between 1953 and 1958, for commissioning between 1955 and 1959. The eight A/S modified ships were adapted in the period from 1967 to 1971.

'Gearing FRAM I' class destroyer (28)

Class: *William R. Rush* (DD714), *Hamner* (DD718), *Southerland* (DD743), *William C. Lawe* (DD763), *McKean* (DD784), *Henderson* (DD785), *Hollister* (DD788), *Higbee* (DD806), *Corry* (DD817), *Johnston* (DD821), *Robert H. McHard* (DD822), *Agerholm* (DD826), *Myles C. Fox* (DD829), *Charles P. Cecil* (DD835), *Fiske* (DD842), *Bausell* (DD845), *Vogelgesang* (DD862), *Steinaker* (DD863), *Harold J. Ellison* (DD864), *Cone* (DD866), *Damato* (DD871), *Hawkins* (DD873), *Rogers* (DD876), *Dyess* (DD880), *Newman K. Perry* (DD883), *John R. Craig* (DD885), *Orleck* (DD886), *Meredith* (DD890)
Displacement: 2,425 tons (2,464 tonnes) standard; 3,480 to 3,530 tons (3,536 to 3,586 tonnes) full load
Dimensions: Length 390 ft 6 in (119.0 m)
Beam 40 ft 11 in (12.4 m)
Draught 19 ft (5.8 m)
Armament:
Guns 4 5-in (127-mm) in twin turrets
Missile systems
none
A/S weapons
1 octuple ASROC launcher
2 triple 12.75-in (324-mm) Mark 32 tubes
Torpedo tubes
none

Aircraft
none
Radar and electronics: SPS-10 surface search, and SPS-37 or SPS-40 air search radars
Sonar: SQS-23
Powerplant: 4 Babcock & Wilcox or Babcock & Wilcox and Foster Wheeler boilers supplying steam to 2 General Electric or Westinghouse geared turbines, delivering 60,000 shp to two shafts
Speed: 34 knots

Range: 5,800 miles (9,335 km) at 15 knots
Crew: 14+260 (USN); 19+288 (USNRF)
Used also by: Brazil, Greece, Pakistan, South Korea, Spain, Taiwan, Turkey
Notes: These ships were built between 1944 and 1946, and commissioned into US service between 1944 and 1947. They were updated in the Fleet Modernisation and Rehabilitation (FRAM) I programme between 1961 and 1965, and 26 of the 28 now serve with the Naval Reserve Force.

'Oliver Hazard Perry' class guided missile frigate (74)

Class: *Oliver Hazard Perry* (FFG7), FFG8 to FFG16, FFG19 to FFG26, and possibly 56 others
Displacement: 3,605 tons (3,663 tonnes) full load
Dimensions: Length 445 ft (135.6 m)
Beam 45 ft (13.7 m)
Draught 24 ft 6 in (7.5 m)
Armament:
Guns 1 76-mm OTO Melara
1 20-mm Phalanx CIWS
Missile systems
1 Mark 13 single launcher for Standard MR SAMs and Harpoon SSMs
A/S weapons
2 LAMPS helicopters
2 triple 12.75-in (324-mm) Mark 32 tubes
Torpedo tubes
none

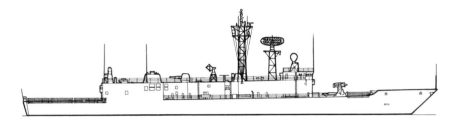

Aircraft
2 helicopters (see above)
Radar and electronics: SPS-49 long-range air search, SPS-55 surface search and navigation, and STIR (modified SPG-60) weapon control radars
Sonar: SQS-56 hull-mounted, and TACTAS towed passive array
Powerplant: 2 General Electric LM 2500 gas

turbines, delivering 41,000 shp to one shaft
Speed: 30 knots
Range: 4,500 miles (7,240 km) at 20 knots
Crew: 11+152
Used also by: Australia, Spain
Notes: The first 8 ships of the class are being built by Bath Iron Works of Bath, Maine, and Todd Shipyards of San Pedro, Calforia, between 1975 and 1981, for commissioning between 1977 and 1982.

'Brooke' class guided missile frigate (6)

Class: *Brooke* (FFG1), *Ramsey* (FFG2), *Schofield* (FFG3), *Talbot* (FFG4), *Richard L. Page* (FFG5), *Julius A. Furer* (FFG6)
Displacement: 2,640 tons (2,682 tonnes) standard; 3,426 tons (3,481 tonnes) full load
Dimensions: Length 414 ft 6 in (126.3 m)
Beam 44 ft 3 in (13.5 m)
Draught 24 ft (7.3 m)
Armament:
Guns 1 5-in (127-mm)
Missile systems
1 Mark 22 single Tartar/Standard MR SAM launcher with 16 missiles

A/S weapons
1 octuple ASROC launcher
2 triple 12.75-in (324-mm) Mark 32 tubes
Torpedo tubes
none
Aircraft
1 LAMPS helicopter
Radar and electronics: SPS-52 3D long-range surveillance, SPS-10 surface search, and SPG-51C weapons control radars
Sonar: SQS-26AX
Powerplant: 2 Foster Wheeler boilers supplying steam to 1 Westinghouse (first three) or General Electric (last three) geared turbines, delivering 35,000 shp to one shaft
Speed: 27¼ knots
Range:
Crew: 17+231

Used only by: USA
Notes: The first three ships were built by Lockheed Shipbuilding & Construction, and the second three by Bath Iron Works between 1962 and 1966, for commissioning between 1966 and 1968. The design is identical with that of the 'Garcia' class frigate except for the substitution of the missile launcher in place of the second 5-in (127-mm) gun. They were originally classified as missile ocean escorts (DEG), but reclassified in 1975.

'Knox' class frigate (46)

Class: *Knox* (FF1052), *Roark* (FF1053), *Gray* (FF1054), *Hepburn* (FF1055), *Connole* (FF1056), *Rathburne* (FF1057), *Meyerkord* (FF1058), *W. S. Sims* (FF1059), *Lang* (FF1060), *Patterson* (FF1061), *Whipple* (FF1062), *Reasoner* (FF1063), *Lockwood* (FF1064), *Stein* (FF1065), *Marvin Shields* (FF1066), *Francis Hammond* (FF1067), *Vreeland* (FF1068), *Bagley* (FF1069), *Downes* (FF1070), *Badger* (FF1071), *Blakely* (FF1072), *Robert E. Peary* (FF1073), *Harold E. Holt* (FF1074), *Trippe* (FF1075), *Fanning* (FF1076), *Quellet* (FF1077), *Joseph Hewes* (FF1078), *Bowen* (FF1079), *Paul* (FF1080), *Aylwin* (FF1081), *Elmer Montgomery* (FF1082), *Cook* (FF1083), *McCandless* (FF1084), *Donald B. Beary* (FF1085), *Brewton* (FF1086), *Kirk* (FF1087), *Barbey* (FF1088), *Jesse L. Brown* (FF1089), *Ainsworth* (FF1090), *Miller* (FF1091), *Thomas C. Hart* (FF1092), *Capodanno* (FF1093), *Pharris* (FF1094), *Truett* (FF1095), *Valdez* (FF1096), *Moinester* (FF1097)
Displacement: 3,011 tons (3,059 tonnes) standard; 3,877 tons (3,939 tonnes) full load for FF1052 to FF1077; 3,963 tons (4,026 tonnes) full load for FF1078 to FF1097
Dimensions: Length 438 ft (133.5 m)
Beam 46 ft 9 in (14.25 m)
Draught 24 ft 9 in (7.55 m)

Armament:
Guns 1 5-in (127-mm)
Missile systems
1 Sea Sparrow Basic Point Defense Missile System (FF1052 to FF1069 and FF1071 to FF1083)
1 NATO Sea Sparrow launcher in *Downes*
Harpoon SSMs in *Thomas C. Hart* and *Ainsworth*, and soon in all others
A/S weapons
1 octuple ASROC launcher (also capable of firing Standard SAM)
4 12.75-in (324-mm) Mark 32 tubes
Torpedo tubes
none
Aircraft
1 LAMPS helicopter (except *Patterson* and *Downes*)
Radar and electronics: SPS-10 surface search, SPS-40 air search, and (*Downes* only) SPS-58 threat detection radar as part of the Improved Point Defense/Target

Acquisition System (IPD/TAS), plus SPG-53A weapons control radar; Mark 36 Chaffroc RBOC
Sonar: SQS-26CX bow-mounted, and SQS-35 variable-depth (except FF1053–55, 1057–62, 1072, 1077)
Powerplant: 2 boilers supplying steam to 1 Westinghouse geared turbine, delivering 35,000 shp to one shaft
Speed: 27+ knots
Range:
Crew: 17+228, or 22+261 for ships with BPDMS and LAMPS helicopter
Used only by: USA
Notes: The ships were built between 1965 and 1973 by Todd Shipyards and Avondale Shipyards, for commissioning between 1969 and 1974. They were originally classified as ocean escorts (DE). In design, the class is similar to the preceding 'Brooke' and 'Garcia' class frigates.

'Garcia' class frigate (10)

Class: *Garcia* (FF1040), *Bradley* (FF1041), *Edward McDonnell* (FF1043), *Brumby* (FF1044), *Davidson* (FF1045), *Voge* (FF1047), *Sample* (FF1048), *Koelsch* (FF1049), *Albert David* (FF1050), *O'Callaghan* (FF1051)
Displacement: 2,620 tons (2,662 tonnes) standard; 3,403 tons (3,457 tonnes) full load
Dimensions: Length 414 ft 6 in (126.3 m)
Beam 44 ft 3 in (13.5 m)
Draught 24 ft (7.3 m)
Armament:
Guns 2 5-in (127-mm) in single turrets
Missile systems
none
A/S weapons
1 octuple ASROC launcher
2 triple 12.75-in (324-mm) Mark 32 tubes
Torpedo tubes
none
Aircraft
1 LAMPS helicopter (except *Sample* and *Albert David*)

Sonar: SQS-26AXR (FF1040–41, 1043–45), or SQS-26BR (FF1047–51)
Powerplant: 2 Foster Wheeler boilers supplying steam to 1 Westinghouse (FF1040, 1041, 1043, 1043–45) or General Electric (others) geared turbine, delivering 35,000 shp to one shaft
Radar and electronics: SPS-10 surface search and SPS-40 air search radars; ASW NTDS (Naval Tactical Data System) in *Voge* and *Koelsch*

Speed: 27 knots
Range:
Crew: 13+226 (FF1040, 1041 and 1043–45); 16+231 in others
Used only by: USA
Notes: The ships were built by four yards between 1962 and 1965, for commissioning between 1964 and 1968. They were at first classified as ocean escorts (DE), being reclassified in 1975.

'Bronstein' class frigate (2)

Class: *Bronstein* (FF1037), *McCloy* (FF1038)
Displacement: 2,360 tons (2,398 tonnes) standard; 2,650 tons (2,692 tonnes) full load
Dimensions: Length 371 ft 6 in (113.2 m)
Beam 40 ft 6 in (12.3 m)
Draught 23 ft (7.0 m)
Armament:
Guns 2 3-in (76-mm) in a twin turret
Missile systems
none

A/S weapons
1 octuple ASROC launcher
2 triple 12.75-in (324-mm) Mark 32 tubes
Torpedo tubes
none
Aircraft
facilities for 1 helicopter
Radar and electronics: SPS-10 surface search and SPS-40 air search radars
Sonar: SQS-26 bow-mounted, and TASS (Towed Array Surveillance System)
Powerplant: 2 Foster Wheeler boilers supplying steam to 1 De Laval geared turbine, delivering 20,000 shp to one shaft

Speed: 26 knots
Range:
Crew: 16+180
Used only by: USA
Notes: Both ships were built by Avondale Shipyards at Westwego, Louisiana, between 1961 and 1962, for commissioning in 1963. They are intermediate vessels, and proved a number of features incorporated in later frigate classes. They were at first classified as ocean escorts (DE), but reclassified as frigates (FF) in 1975.

'Blue Ridge' class amphibious command ship (2)

Class: *Blue Ridge* (LCC19), *Mount Whitney* (LCC20)
Displacement: 17,100 tons (17,374 tonnes) full load
Dimensions: Length 620 ft (188.5 m)
Beam 82 ft (25.3 m)
Draught 27 ft (8.2 m)
Armament:
Guns 4 3-in (76-mm) in twin turrets
Missile systems
2 Sea Sparrow Basic Point Defense Missile Systems
A/S weapons
none
Torpedo tubes
none
Aircraft
facilities for 1 helicopter
Radar and electronics: SPS-48 3D long-range surveillance, SPS-10 surface search, and SPS-40 air search radars; NTDS (Naval Tactical Data System), ACIS (Amphibious Command Information System), and NIPS (Naval Information Processing System)

Sonar: none
Powerplant: 2 Foster Wheeler boilers supplying steam to 1 General Electric geared turbine, delivering 22,000 shp to one shaft
Speed: 20 knots
Range:
Crew: 40+680 (ship) + 200+500 (flag staff)
Used only by: USA
Notes: The ships were built by Philadelphia Naval Shipyard and Newport News Shipbuilding & Dry Dock between 1967 and 1970, for commissioning in 1970 and 1971. Their hulls are similar to those of the 'Iwo Jima' class assault ships.

'Tarawa' class amphibious assault ship (5)

Class: *Tarawa* (LHA1), *Saipan* (LHA2), *Belleau Wood* (LHA3), *Nassau* (LHA4), *Da Nang* (LHA5)
Displacement: 39,300 tons (39,929 tonnes) full load
Dimensions: Length 820 ft (250.0 m)
Beam 106 ft (32.3 m)
Draught 27 ft 6 in (8.5 m)
Armament:
Guns 3 5-in (127-mm) in single turrets
6 20-mm in single mountings
Missile systems
2 Sea Sparrow Basic Point Defense Missile Systems
A/S weapons
none
Torpedo tubes
none
Aircraft
26 helicopters, or VTOL aircraft in place of some helicopters
Radar and electronics: SPS-52 3D surveillance, SPS-10 surface search, SPS-40 air search, and SPS-35 air/navigation radars, plus SPG-60 and SPG-9A weapons control radars; TAWDS (Tactical Amphibious Warfare Data System)
Sonar: none
Powerplant: 2 Combustion Engineering boilers supplying steam to 2 Westinghouse geared turbines, delivering 140,000 shp to two shafts

Speed: about 24 knots
Range:
Crew: 90+812 (ship) plus 172+1,731 (troops)
Used only by: USA
Notes: The ships are being built by Ingalls Shipbuilding of Litton Industries at Pascagoula, Mississippi, between 1971 and 1980, for commissioning between 1976 and 1981. They are capable of assault-landing a full regimental combat team with all its vehicles and equipment, by means of helicopters and LCUs, the latter operating from an internal dock 268 ft (81.7 m) by 78 ft (23.8 m) capable of accommodating 4 LCUs at a time.

'Iwo Jima' class amphibious assault ship (7)

Class: *Iwo Jima* (LPH2), *Okinawa* (LPH3), *Guadalcanal* (LPH7), *Guam* (LPH9), *Tripoli* (LPH10), *New Orleans* (LPH11), *Inchon* (LPH12)
Displacement: 18,000 tons (18,288 tonnes) full load for *Iwo Jima, Okinawa, Guadalcanal*; 18,300 tons (18,593 tonnes) full load for *Guam, Tripoli*; 17,706 tons (17,989 tonnes) full load for *New Orleans*; 17,515 tons (17,795 tonnes) full load for *Inchon*
Dimensions: Length 592 ft (180.0 m)
Beam (hull) 84 ft (25.6 m)
Draught 26 ft (7.9 m)
Armament:
Guns 4 3-in (76-mm) in twin turrets
Missile systems
2 Sea Sparrow Basic Point Defense Missile Systems
A/S weapons
none
Torpedo tubes

none
Aircraft
up to 24 helicopters
Radar and electronics: SPS-10 surface search, SPS-40 air search, and SPN-10 navigation radars, plus SPG-50 weapon control radar
Sonar: none
Powerplant: 2 Combustion Engineering (Babcock & Wilcox in *Guam*) boilers supplying steam to 1 De Laval (*Tripoli*), General Electric (*Inchon*) or Westinghouse (others) geared turbine, delivering 22,000 shp to one shaft
Speed: 23 knots

Range:
Crew: 47+605 (ship) plus 143+1,581 (troops)
Used only by: USA
Notes: The ships were built between 1959 and 1969 by Philadelphia Naval Shipyard and Ingalls Shipbuilding Corporation of Pascagoula, Mississippi, and commissioned between 1961 and 1970. Each ship is designed to carry and land a US Marine Corps battalion combat team with all its vehicles and support equipment. The helicopter deck is 104 ft (31.9 m) wide, and can handle up to seven helicopters at a time.

ASROC (RUR-5A)

Type: ship-launched anti-submarine ballistic missile
Guidance: unguided in flight; acoustic homing if Mark 46 torpedo is carried
Launch method: 8-cell launcher, Mark 46 launching system, or Mark 10 Terrier launcher
Dimensions: Length (missile) 15 ft (4.6 m)
Diameter (missile) $12\frac{3}{4}$ in (32.5 cm)
Span (missile) $33\frac{1}{4}$ in (84.5 cm)
Weight: (missile) about 960 lb (435 kg)
Engine: Naval Propellant Plant solid-fuel tandem-boost rocket
Speed: transonic
Range: estimated from 2,187 to 10,936 yards (2,000 to 10,000 m)
Warhead: nuclear depth charge or 100 lb (45.4 kg) high explosive in Mark 46
Used also by: Canada, Italy, Japan, West Germany

Notes: ASROC consists of a ballistic missile, with a Mark 46 torpedo or nuclear depth charge as warhead. The missile is aimed and fired by a computer acting on the information supplied by the ship's sonar. After launch, the missile follows a ballistic trajectory to a predetermined point, where it releases its warhead. If this is a torpedo, it is lowered into the water by parachute, and then homes conventionally. ASROC is made by Honeywell

Bendix RIM-8 Talos

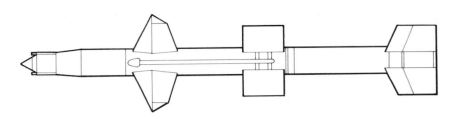

Type: naval surface-to-air tactical guided missile
Guidance: beam-riding, plus semi-active radar terminal homing
Dimensions: Span 9 ft 6 in (2.89 m)
Body diameter 2 ft 6 in (76.2 cm)
Length (with booster) 31 ft 3 in (9.525 m); (without booster) 21 ft (6.4 m)
Booster: Allegheny Ballistics solid-fuel tandem rocket
Sustainer: ramjet, rated at 20,000-lb (9,070-kg) static thrust
Warhead: nuclear or high explosive
Weights: Launch (with booster) 7,000 lb (3,175 kg)
Burnt out
Performance: speed Mach 2.5; ceiling more

than 86,940 ft (26,500 m); range more than 75 miles (120 km)
Used only by: USA
Notes: The Talos missile is the US Navy's most powerful anti-aircraft missile, and was designed for long-range fleet defence, based on cruisers; but later models have a surface-to-surface capability. US Navy designations run from RIM-8A to RIM-8J, the three latest models being:

1. RIM-8G high-altitude interceptor, with provision for mid-course beam-riding guidance and continuous-wave interferometer terminal homing
2. RGM-8H surface-to-surface anti-radiation homing head version
3. RIM-8J adaptation of the RIM-8G but with improved terminal homing.
Talos is normally used with AN/SPG-49 target illuminating radar, and AN/SPG-56 tracking and guidance radar.

General Dynamics BGM-109 Tomahawk

Type: sea-launched cruise missile
Guidance: TAINS (Terrain Contour Matching-Aided Inertial Navigation System) for land attack; McDonnell Douglas inertial plus active radar homing for anti-ship operations
Dimensions: Span 100 in (2.54 m)
Body diameter 21 in (0.53 m)
Length 18 ft 3 in (5.56 m) without booster; 20 ft 6 in (6.25 m) with booster

Booster: Atlantic Research solid-fuel rocket, delivering 7,000-lb (3,175-kg) thrust
Sustainer: Williams Research F107-WR-400 turbofan, rated at 600-lb (272-kg) thrust
Warhead: nuclear, W80, up to 200 kilotons for land attack; high explosive, Bullpup B of 1,000 lb (454 kg), for anti-shipping role
Weights: Launch 4,000 lb (1,814 kg) for land-attack model
Burnt out

Performance: cruising speed 550 mph (885 kph) for land-attack model; range 1,990 miles (3,200 km) for land-attack model; more than 300 miles (480 km) for anti-shipping model; CEP no more than 100 ft (30.5 m) with NAVstar homing
Used by: under development for the US Navy
Notes: Designed for launching from a submarine's torpedo tubes. Aerodynamic surfaces and engine intake deploy after the missile has left the water. Cruise to the target area is at very low level and at high subsonic speed.

General Dynamics RIM-2 Terrier

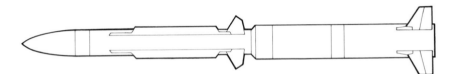

Type: naval surface-to-air tactical guided missile
Guidance: beam-riding, plus semi-active radar terminal homing
Dimensions: Span 20 in (50.8 cm)
Body diameter 11⅘ in (30.0 cm)
Length (with booster) 26 ft 3 in (8.0 m); (without booster) 15 ft (4.6 m)
Booster: solid-propellant rocket
Sustainer: solid-propellant rocket
Warhead: high explosive (nuclear in RIM-2D)
Weights: Launch about 3,085 lb (1,400 kg)
Burnt out

Performance: speed Mach 2.5; ceiling more than 65,620 ft (20,000 m); range about 21¾ miles (35 km)
Used also by: Italy, Netherlands
Notes: The Terrier missile provides aircraft-carriers, cruisers and frigates with a powerful AA weapon, twin launchers being fed from automatic magazines. US Navy designations for the Terrier run from RIM-2A to RIM-2F, the last being known as the

Advanced Terrier. Like the Tartar, the Terrier is being upgraded in the CG/SM-2 (ER) programme. Associated equipment includes AN/SPG-44 continuous-wave target illuminating radar, AN/SPG-49 guidance radar, AN/SPG-55 fire-control radar, and AN/SPG-5A long-range tracking and guidance radar. The Terrier has limited surface-to-surface capability.

General Dynamics RIM-24 Tartar

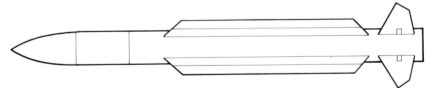

Type: naval surface-to-air tactical guided missile
Guidance: semi-active radar homing
Dimensions: Span 20 in (50.8 cm)
Body diameter 11⅘ in (30.0 cm)
Length 15 ft (4.6 m)
Booster: dual-thrust solid-propellant rocket
Sustainer: as above
Warhead: high explosive
Weights: Launch 1,500 lb (680 kg)
Burnt out
Performance: speed Mach 2; ceiling more

than 39,370 ft (12,000 m); range more than 10 miles (16 km)
Used also by: Australia, France, Iran, Italy, Japan, Netherlands, Spain, West Germany
Notes: Designed as a medium-range air defence weapon, the Tartar is deployed as the primary AA weapon of destroyers, and the secondary AA weapon of cruisers. Associated equipment includes the Mark 73/

74 gun and guided missile director, and the AN/SPG-51 guidance radar. The Tartar is currently being updated by the improvement of launch vessels' radar in readiness for Standard SM-2 adoption. The programme, known as CG/SM-2 (ER), involves the fitting of AN/SPS-52 3-dimensional radar, AN/SPS-65 radar, and improved plotting equipment.

General Dynamics RIM-66 and RIM-67 Standard

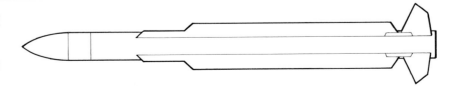

Type: naval surface-to-air tactical guided missile, with surface-to-surface capability
Guidance: semi-active radar homing

Dimensions: Span (M2) 42 in (107 cm);
(ER) 62 in (157 cm)
Body diameter 12 in (30.5 cm)
Length (MR) 15 ft (4.57 m);
(ER) 27 ft (8.23 m)
Booster: (MR) Aerojet/Hercules Mark 56
Model 0 rocket; (ER) Atlantic Research
Mark 30 Model 2 solid-propellant rocket
Sustainer: (MR) as above; (ER) Naval Pro-
pellant Plant Mark 12 Model 1 solid-
propellant rocket
Warhead: high explosive
Weights: Launch (MR) about 1,300 lb (590
kg); (ER) about 2,335 lb (1,060 kg)
Burnt out
Performance: (MR) speed more than Mach 2,
ceiling more than 65,620 ft (20,000 m),
range more than 11 miles (18 km); (ER)

speed more than Mach 2.5, ceiling more
than 65,620 ft (20,000 m); range more
than 34 miles (55 km)
Used only by: USA
Notes: The RIM-66A is a medium-range
(MR) model, and the RIM-67A the ex-
tended-range (ER) model, with a longer
body, more fuel and an improved engine.
There are various versions:
1. RIM-66A Standard basic model
2. RIM-66B Standard improved model
but with an improved motor
3. RIM-66C Standard (MR) adaptation
of the RIM-66B for use with the
Aegis anti-cruise missile defence
system currently under development
4. RGM-66D Standard (ARM) adaptation of the RIM-66B intended for the

surface-to-surface anti-radiation missile (ARM) role
5. RTM-66D Standard (ARM) training
version of the RGM-66D
6. RGM-66E (ARM) adaptation of the
RGM-66D for use with an ASROC
launcher
7. RIM-67A Standard (ER), with a new
booster to give greater range.
The above missiles are all versions of the
Standard 1. There is also a Standard 2
under development for use with the Aegis
system, which is expected to become operational in 1982. The Standard 2, which will
also be available in MR and ER versions,
has improved electronics, making possible
a far more economical trajectory.

Lockheed UGM-27C Polaris A-3

Type: submarine-launched ballistic missile
Guidance: inertial
Dimensions: Body diameter 4 ft 6 in (1.37 m)
Length 31 ft 6 in (9.6 m)
Booster (1st stage): Aerojet solid-propellant
rocket
Sustainer (2nd stage): Hercules liquid-
injection rocket
Warhead: nuclear, 3 200-kiloton MRV (ear-
lier models had a single warhead of about 1
megaton)

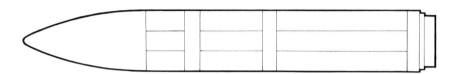

Weights: Launch 15.625 tons (15.85 tonnes)
approximately
Burnt out
Performance: range 2,875 miles (4,630 km);
speed Mach 10 at burn-out; throw-weight
1,000 lb (454 kg) CEP 0.6 mile (0.97 km)

Used also by: UK
Notes: Final development of the Polaris
SLBM, with reduced structure weight and
improved propellant to improve range by a
considerable margin over the Polaris A-2
(range 1,725 miles/2,780 km).

Lockheed UGM-73A Poseidon C-3

Type: submarine-launched ballistic missile
Guidance: inertial
Dimensions: Body diameter 6 ft 2 in (1.88
cm)
Length 34 ft 0 in (10.36 m)
Booster (1st stage): Thiokol/Hercules solid-
propellant rocket
Sustainer (2nd stage): Hercules solid-pro-
pellant rocket
Warhead: thermonuclear, 10 50-kiloton
MIRV

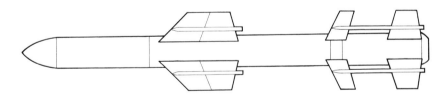

Weights: Launch 29.0 tons (29.48 tonnes)
Burnt out
Performance: range 2,875 miles (4,630 km);
throw-weight 2–3,000 lb (907–1,361
kg); CEP 0.33 mile (0.54 km)

Used only by: USA
Notes: Successor to the Polaris, with the
same range but double the weight and
greatly superior offensive capabilities. Can
be launched from the same tubes as Polaris
missiles.

McDonnell Douglas RGM-84A Harpoon

Type: naval surface-to-surface tactical guided
missile
Guidance: preprogrammed attitude allied to
a radio altimeter, plus active radar terminal
homing
Dimensions: Span 36 in (91.4 cm)
Body diameter 13$\frac{1}{2}$ in (34.0 cm)
Length 15 ft (4.57 m) with
booster
Booster: Aerojet MX(TBD) B446-2 tandem
solid-propellant rocket
Sustainer: Teledyne CAE J402 turbojet,
rated at 660-lb (299-kg) static thrust
Warhead: 500-lb (227-kg) high explosive
Weights: Launch (AGM) 1,160 lb (526 kg);

(RGM) 1,460 lb to 1,530 lb (662
kg to 694 kg)
Burnt out
Performance: speed Mach 0.85; range 70
miles (113 km)
Used also by: Australia, Denmark, Iran,
Israel, Japan, Netherlands, Saudi Arabia,
South Korea, Turkey, UK, West Germany
Notes: The Harpoon is an anti-ship missile

with high subsonic speed, and can also be
launched from aircraft, in which mode the
solid-propellant booster is omitted, reduc-
ing length to 12 ft 7 in (3.84 m). One of the
Harpoon's most important adjuncts is its
excellent electronic counter-countermeasures
(ECCM) capability, especially in the terminal
phase. The HE warhead is of the penetrating-
blast type.

Raytheon Sea Sparrow Point Defense Missile System

Type: naval surface-to-air tactical guided
missile defence system
Guidance: semi-active radar homing
Dimensions: Span 3 ft 4 in (1.02 m)
Body diameter 8 in (20.32 cm)

Length 12 ft (3.66 m)
Booster: Aerojet Mark 53 Model 2 or Hercules
Mark 58 dual-thrust solid-propellant rocket
Sustainer: same as above
Warhead: 66-lb (30-kg) high explosive
Weights: Launch 500 lb (227 kg)
Burnt out
Performance: speed Mach 3.5+; range 8
miles (13 km)

Used also by: Belgium, Denmark, Italy,
Netherlands, Norway, West Germany
Notes: The Sea Sparrow missile, derived from
the air-to-air AIM-7 Sparrow III, is used in
two basic naval defence systems, the US
Navy's Basic Point Defense Missile
System, and the NATO Sea Sparrow Point
Defence Missile System Mark 57. The US
BPMDS uses the modified AIM-7E Spar-

row III, fired from a modified octuple ASROC launcher on an adapted 3-in (76.2-mm) automatic gun carriage. The target is illuminated by a Mark 51 director and illuminator, and the missile fired by the manual Mark 115 fire-control system, with target data coming from the ship's combat information centre. The NATO system uses the RIM-7H, the naval version of the AIM-7E, in an eight-cell launcher, and using computerised launch techniques. The data above refer to the AIM-7F, soon to be adapted for naval use.

SUBROC (UUM-44A)

Type: submarine-launched anti-submarine missile
Guidance: computer-generated programme plus an inertial platform
Launch method: tube
Dimensions: Length 20 ft 6 in (6.25 m)
Diameter 21 in (533 mm)
Weight: about 4,085 lb (1,853 kg)

Engine: Thiokol TE-260G tandem-boost solid-propellant rocket
Speed: supersonic
Range: about 35 miles (56.3 km)
Warhead: nuclear
Used only by: USA
Notes: SUBROC is an advanced anti-submarine weapon system for use by US nuclear-powered attack submarines. Once

an enemy submarine has been detected by sonar, the weapon control system calculates the necessary trajectory for the SUBROC missile. This is then fired from a torpedo tube, moves through the water before emerging into the air for the main part of the flight. At a predetermined point the warhead separates from the missile and follows a ballistic trajectory until it lands in the water. The warhead then sinks towards the enemy submarine and detonates. SUBROC is made by Goodyear.

Freedom Torpedo

Type: ship- or submarine-launched anti-ship torpedo
Guidance: wire-guidance from launch vessel with programmed terminal phase, or wire-guidance with homing

Launch method: tube or rack
Dimensions: Length 18 ft 9 in (5.72 m)
Diameter 19 in (482.6 mm)
with runners for 21-in tubes
Weight: 2,557 lb (1,160 kg)

Engine: electric
Speed: 40 knots
Range: up to 15,310 yards (14,000 m)
Warhead: 650 lb (295 kg) high explosive
Used by:
Notes: Private venture torpedo by Westinghouse.

Mark 14 Model 5 torpedo

Type: submarine-launched torpedo
Guidance: preset course and depth
Launch method: tube

Dimensions: Length 17 ft 2¾ in (5.25 m)
Diameter 21 in (533 mm)
Weight: 3,925 lb (1,780 kg)
Engine: thermal/compressed air
Speed: 32–46 knots
Range: 5,000 to 10,000 yards (4,572 to 9,144 m)
Warhead: 500 lb (227 kg) high explosive

Used also by: other navies
Notes: An effective conventional torpedo, introduced in the mid-1930s. There were teething problems with the contact and proximity fuses, but these were solved swiftly during World War II.

Mark 37 Models 0 and 3 torpedo

Type: submarine-launched anti-submarine torpedo
Guidance: preset course and depth, plus active/passive sonar homing
Launch method: tube
Dimensions: Length 11 ft 6¾ in (3.52 m)
Diameter 19 in (482.6 mm)
with guides to fit 21-in tubes
Weight: 1,422 lb (645 kg)
Engine: electric
Speed: 24 knots
Range:
Warhead: 330 lb (150 kg) high explosive
Used only by: USA
Notes: This is the world's first high-performance submarine-launched anti-submarine torpedo, but can also be launched from surface vessels. After launch, the torpedo maintains its preset course until after a certain distance the missile is armed and freed to follow the selected homing mode. The Model 3 is basically similar to the Model 0, but incorporates the results of experience with the earlier model. The Model 0 went into service in 1957.

Mark 37 Model 1 and 2 torpedo

Type: submarine-launched anti-submarine torpedo
Guidance: wire-guidance from launch vessel
Launch method: tube
Dimensions: Length 13 ft 5 in (4.09 m)
Diameter 19 in (482.6 mm)
with guides to fit 21-in tubes
Weight: 1,690 lb (766 kg)
Engine: electric
Speed: 24 knots
Range:
Warhead: 330 lb (150 kg) high explosive
Used only by: USA
Notes: These two torpedoes are wire-guided developments of the Mark 37 Models 0 and 3, the Model 2 having the same relationship to the Model 1 as the Model 3 to the Model 0. The extra length of the Models 1 and 2 are needed for the wire-guidance casket.

Mark 45 ASTOR torpedo

Type: submarine-launched anti-submarine torpedo
Guidance: wire-guidance from launch vessel
Launch method: tube
Dimensions: Length about 18 ft 10¾ in (5.76 m)
Diameter 19 in (482.6 mm)
Weight: about 2,888 lb (1,310 kg)
Engine:
Speed:
Range: about 12,000 yards (10,973 m)
Warhead: nuclear or high explosive
Used only by: USA
Notes: The Anti-Submarine Torpedo Ordnance Rocket (ASTOR) is a powerful, long-range high-speed anti-submarine weapon for use in American attack submarines. It can also be used against surface targets.

Mark 46 torpedo

Type: ship- and aircraft-launched light-weight anti-submarine torpedo
Guidance: active/passive acoustic homing
Launch method: Mark 32 tube, aircraft, helicopter, or ASROC
Dimensions: Length (Model 0) 8 ft 9 in (2.67 m); (Model 1) 8 ft 6 in (2.59 m)
Diameter 12.75 in (324 mm)
Weight: (Model 0) about 570 lb (259 kg);

(Model 1) 507 lb (230 kg)
Engine: (Model 0) solid-fuel motor; (Model 1) mono-propellant Otto
Speed:
Range:
Warhead: 100 lb (45.4 kg) high explosive
Used by: various navies
Notes: Developed as a Mark 44 replacement under the Research Torpedo Configuration

(RETORC) programme. The Mark 46 torpedo is deep-diving and fast, and is capable of repeated attacks. The Model 0 was the first US torpedo to use a solid-fuel motor.

Mark 48 torpedo

Type: submarine-launched anti-submarine and anti-ship torpedo
Guidance: active/passive acoustic homing, with or without wire-guidance
Launch method: tube

Dimensions: Length 19 ft (5.8 m)
Diameter 21 in (533 mm)
Weight: about 3,525 lb (1,599 kg)
Engine: mono-propellant Otto driving pump-jet propulsors
Speed: 50 knots
Range: 28½ miles (56 km)
Warhead: high explosive

Used only by: USA
Notes: Primary armament of US submarines, and developed under the Research Torpedo Configuration (RETORC) programme. The Mark 48 is very complex, but highly versatile, being capable of repeated attacks until a target is hit, and can operate up to a depth of 3,000 ft (914 m).

NT-37 torpedo

Type: submarine- and ship-launched anti-submarine and anti-ship torpedo
Guidance: preset course and depth, with sonar homing, or wire-guidance
Launch method: tube
Dimensions: Length as for Mark 37 Models 2 and 3
Diameter as for Mark 37 Models 2 and 3
Weight:
Engine: liquid mono-propellant (Otto engine)
Speed: 40 per cent greater than Mark 37
Range: 150 per cent greater than Mark 37
Warhead: 330 lb (150 kg) high explosive
Used also by: other navies
Notes: Basically a conversion package developed by Northrop for the Mark 37 Models 2 and 3 torpedoes, and an Otto engine instead of the electric motor. There are three attack modes:

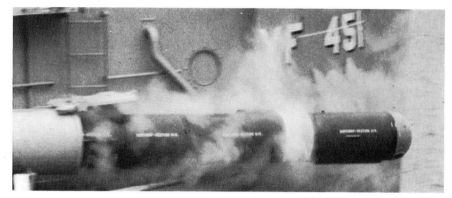

Mode A for anti-ship attack, with all homing and search modes cut out
Mode B for anti-ship attack, with all homing and search modes cut out for a preset distance, after which the target is presumed missed and sonar

homing combined with a search pattern is activated
Mode C standard anti-submarine attack, but with the improvements provided by more modern systems.

Uruguay

4,000 men including naval air arm, marines and coastguard

Frigates:
1 Dealey
2 Cannon

Corvettes:
1 Auk
1 Aggressive

SS:
(2 Type 209)

Patrol Forces:
1 Adjutant PC
6 coastal PC

Amphibious Forces:
2 LCM6

Auxiliaries:
2 survey ships
1 salvage vessel
2 tankers
others

Naval Air Arm:
2 S-2A MR
3 C-45 transports
1 T-34B trainer
4 SNJ-4 trainers
4 T-6 trainers
2 Bell 47G
2 SH-34J

'Dealey' class frigate (1)

Class: *18 de Julio* (DE3), ex-US *Dealey* (DE1006)
Displacement: 1,450 tons (1,473 tonnes) standard; 1,900 tons (1,930 tonnes) full load
Dimensions: Length 314 ft 6 in (95.9 m)
Beam 36 ft 9 in (11.2 m)
Draught 13 ft 7 in (4.2 m)
Armament:
Guns 4 3-in (76-mm) in twin turrets
Missile systems
none
A/S weapons
2 triple 12.75-in (324-mm) Mark 32 tubes
Torpedo tubes
none

Aircraft
none
Radar and electronics: SPS-6 search, SPS-10 surface search, and SPG-34 fire-control radars
Sonar:
Powerplant: 2 Foster Wheeler boilers supplying steam to 1 De Laval geared turbine, delivering 20,000 shp to one shaft
Speed: 25 knots
Range:
Crew: 165
Used only by: Uruguay
Notes: *Dealey* was built by the Bath Iron Works between 1952 and 1953, for entry into US service in 1954. She was bought by Uruguay in 1972.

Venezuela

8,000 men including 4,000 marines

Destroyers:
2 Aragua
1 Allen M. Sumner FRAM II
1 Allen M. Sumner

Frigates (FFG):
(6 Lupo)

Frigates (FF):
4 Almirante Clemente

SS:
2 Type 209 (+2)
2 Guppy II

Light Forces:
3 Vosper Thornycroft 36.9-m FAC(M)
3 Vosper Thornycroft 36.9-m FAC(G)
(10 FAC(M))

Patrol Forces:
10 Rio Orinoco coastal PC (+11)

Amphibious Forces:
1 Terrebonne Parish LST
4 LSM
1 ARL (transport)

Auxiliaries:
3 transports
1 survey ship
2 survey launches
others

Naval Air Arm:
2 S-2E MR
4 HU-16 SAR
3 C-47 transports
2 Bell 47J
(6 AB 212ASW)

Marine Force:
3 bns

'Aragua' class destroyer (2)

Class: *Nueva Esparta* (D11), *Zulia* (D12)
Displacement: 2,600 tons (2,642 tonnes) standard; 3,670 tons (3,729 tonnes) full load
Dimensions: Length 402 ft (122.5 m)
Beam 43 ft (13.1 m)
Draught 19 ft (5.8 m)
Armament:
Guns 6 4.5-in (114-mm) in twin turrets
16 (4 in *Nueva Esparta*) 40-mm in twin mountings
Missile systems
2 quadruple Seacat SAM launchers (*Nueva Esparta* only)
A/S weapons
2 Squids
2 DCTs
2 DC racks
Torpedo tubes
none
Aircraft
none
Radar and electronics: AWS 2 (*Nueva Esparta*) or SPS-6 (*Zulia*) search, SPS-12 medium and long-range surveillance, and I-band fire-control radars
Sonar:
Powerplant: 2 Yarrow boilers supplying steam to Parsons geared turbines, delivering 50,000 shp to two shafts
Speed: 34 knots
Range: 5,000 miles (8,047 km) at 10 knots
Crew: 20+236
Used only by: Venezuela
Notes: Both ships were built by Vickers at Barrow-in-Furness between 1951 and 1953, and commissioned in 1953 and 1954. They have subsequently been modernised, especially in their A/S and AA particulars.

'Allen M. Sumner FRAM II' class destroyer (1)

Class: *Fálcon* (D22), ex-US *Robert K. Huntingdon* (DD781)
Displacement: 2,200 tons (2,235 tonnes) standard; 3,320 tons (3,373 tonnes) full load
Dimensions: Length 376 ft 6 in (114.8 m)
Beam 40 ft 11 in (12.4 m)
Draught 19 ft (5.8 m)
Armament:
Guns 6 5-in (127-mm) in twin turrets
Missile systems
none
A/S weapons
2 Hedgehogs
2 triple 12.75-in (324-mm) Mark 32 tubes
Torpedo tubes
none
Aircraft
facilities for 1 small ASW helicopter
Radar and electronics: SPS-10 surface search and SPS-40 air search radars
Sonar: SQS-29 hull mounted, plus variable-depth
Powerplant: 4 boilers supplying steam to 2 geared turbines, delivering 60,000 shp to two shafts
Speed: 34 knots
Range: 4,600 miles (7,400 km) at 15 knots
Crew: 274
Used also by: Brazil, Chile, Colombia, Iran, South Korea, Turkey
Notes: *Huntingdon* was built in 1944 by Todd Pacific Shipyards, and commissioned into US service in 1945. She was bought by Venezuela in 1973.

'Allen M. Sumner' class destroyer (1)

Class: *Carabobo* (D21), ex-US *Beatty* (DD756)
Displacement: 2,200 tons (2,235 tonnes) standard; 3,320 tons (3,373 tonnes) full load
Dimensions: Length 376 ft 6 in (114.8 m)
Beam 40 ft 11 in (12.8 m)
Draught 19 ft (5.8 m)
Armament:
Guns 6 5-in (127-mm) in twin turrets
Missile systems
none
A/S weapons
2 Hedgehogs
2 triple 12.75-in (324-mm) Mark 32 tubes
DCs
Torpedo tubes
none
Aircraft
none
Radar and electronics: SPS-6 search, SPS-10 surface search, and Mark 25 (Mark 37 GFCS) gun fire-control radars
Sonar:
Powerplant: 4 boilers supplying steam to 2 geared turbines, delivering 60,000 shp to two shafts
Speed: 34 knots
Range: 4,600 miles (7,400 km) at 15 knots
Crew: 274
Used also by: Argentina, Brazil, Colombia, Greece, Taiwan
Notes: *Beatty* was built in 1944 by Bethlehem Steel at Staten Island, and commissioned into US service in 1945. She was transferred in 1972.

'Almirante Clemente' class frigate (4)

Class: *Almirante Clemente* (F11), *General José Trinidad Moran* (F12), *Almirante Brion* (F13), *Almirante José Garcia* (F14)
Displacement: 1,300 tons (1,321 tonnes) standard; 1,500 tons (1,524 tonnes) full load
Dimensions: Length 325 ft 11 in (99.1 m)
Beam 35 ft 6 in (10.8 m)
Draught 12 ft 3 in (3.7 m)
Armament:
Guns 4 4-in (102-mm) in twin turrets (F13 and F14)
2 76-mm OTO Melara (F11 and F12)
4 40-mm
8 20-mm (not F14)
Missile systems
none
A/S weapons (F11, F12 and F13)
2 Hedgehogs
4 DCTs
DC racks
A/S weapons (F14)
1 A/S mortar
4 DCTs
2 DC racks
Torpedo tubes
1 triple 533-mm (21-in) (F13)
Aircraft
none
Radar and electronics: MLA-1 or Plessey AWS-1 search, and I-band fire-control radars
Sonar:
Powerplant: 2 Foster Wheeler boilers supplying steam to 2 geared turbines, delivering 24,000 shp to two shafts
Speed: 32 knots
Range: 3,500 miles (5,635 km) at 15 knots
Crew: 12+150
Used only by: Venezuela
Notes: These four ships, and another two since deleted, were built between 1954 and 1956 by Ansaldo at Livorno, and commissioned in 1956 and 1957. F14 was modernised in 1962 and 1963 to improve her A/S capabilities.

Type 209 submarine (2)

Class: *Sabalo* (S31), *Caribe* (S32)
Displacement: 990 tons (1,006 tonnes) surfaced; 1,350 tons (1,372 tonnes) dived
Dimensions: Length 177 ft 1 in (54.0 m)
Beam 20 ft 4 in (6.2 m)
Draught 18 ft (5.5 m)
Armament:
Guns none
Missile systems
none
A/S weapons
none
Torpedo tubes
8 533-mm (21-in)
Aircraft
none
Radar and electronics:
Sonar: active and passive

Powerplant: diesel-electric, with 4 MTU-Siemens diesel generators and 1 Siemens electric motor, delivering 5,000 hp to one shaft
Speed: 10 knots (surfaced); 22 knots (dived)
Range: 50 days endurance
Crew: 31
Used also by: Argentina, Colombia, Ecuador, Iran, Peru, Turkey, Uruguay
Used also by: various nations
Notes: The boats were designed by Ingenieurkontor of Lübeck (IKL) and built by Howaldtswerke of Kiel between 1973 and 1975. They were commissioned into Venezuelan service in 1976 and 1977. Another two are on order.

'Guppy II' class submarine (2)

Class: *Tiburon* (S21), ex-US *Cubera* (SS347); *Picuda* (S22), ex-US *Grenadier* (SS525)
Displacement: 1,870 tons (1,900 tonnes) surfaced; 2,420 tons (2,459 tonnes) dived
Dimensions: Length 307 ft 6 in (93.8 m)
Beam 27 ft (8.2 m)
Draught 18 ft (5.5 m)
Armament:
Guns none
Missile systems
none
A/S weapons
none
Torpedo tubes
10 21-in (533-mm)
Aircraft
none
Radar and electronics:
Sonar:
Powerplant: 3 diesels, delivering 4,800 shp, and 2 electric motors, delivering 5,400 shp to two shafts
Speed: 18 knots (surfaced); 15 knots (dived)
Range: 12,000 miles (19,313 km) at 10 knots surfaced
Crew: 80
Used also by: Argentina, Brazil, Taiwan
Notes: The boats were built by the Electric Boat Company and Boston Navy Yard in 1944 and 1945, and commissioned into US service in 1945 and 1951. They were transferred in 1972 and 1973.

Vosper Thornycroft 36.9-m fast attack craft (missile/gun) (6)

Class: *Constitucion* (P11), *Federacion* (P12), *Independencia* (P13), *Libertad* (P14), *Patria* (P15), *Victoria* (P16)
Displacement: 150 tons (152.4 tonnes)
Dimensions: Length 121 ft (36.9 m)
　　　　　　　Beam 23 ft 4 in (7.6 m)
　　　　　　　Draught 5 ft 7 in (1.7 m)
Armament:
Guns 1 76-mm OTO Melara (P11, P13, P15)
　　　1 40-mm (P12, P14, P16)
Missile systems
　　2 Otomat SSM launchers (P12, P14, P16)
A/S weapons
　　none
Torpedo tubes
　　none
Aircraft
　　none
Radar and electronics: SPQ-2D radar
Sonar:

Powerplant: 2 MTU diesels, delivering 7,200 hp to two shafts
Speed: 27 knots
Range: 1,350 miles (2,175 km) at 16 knots
Crew: 18
Used only by: Venezuela

Notes: The craft were built by Vosper Thornycroft between 1973 and 1974, and commissioned in 1974 and 1975. Another 10 missile-armed craft will probably be ordered.

Vietnam

3,000 men

Light Forces:
2 Komar FAC(M)
8 Shanghai FAC(G)
14 Swatow FAC(G)
2 P-6 FAC(T)
2 P-4 FAC(T)

Patrol Forces:
3 SO I PC
c 30 coastal PC

Amphibious Forces:
c 20 landing craft

Aircraft:
10 Mi-4 SAR

Virgin Islands

Police force

Patrol Forces:
1 Brooke 13.1-m coastal PC

West Germany

The West German Navy
West Germany has only a relatively short coastline, but it is one that is vital to the security of NATO: it provides a means of entry into the North German plain, where it is likely that major military operations will occur in the event of hostilities between the forces of the Warsaw Treaty Organisation, and also forms an important link in the allied communications with the northern flank of NATO in Norway. The West German Navy or *Bundesmarine* has a manpower strength of 36,500, some 7.45 per cent of the total armed forces, whose annual budget amounts to about 3.4 per cent of the gross national product.

For operations in the North Sea, the West German Navy relies on submarines and surface vessels. For long-range operations the most

important boats are the 18 Type 206 craft, which have a good torpedo armament and adequate dived speed. Additionally, the boats are relatively quiet, a vital factor in modern underwater warfare. For surface operations, Germany has three of the first-class 'Charles F. Adams' class guided-missile destroyers, four 'Hamburg' class conventional destroyers (recently upgraded by the addition of Exocet SSM launchers in place of one gun turret), and four somewhat elderly 'Fletcher' class destroyers. However, the survival of even the most modern missile-armed ships in an area within easy range of Russian land-based aircraft is at best problematical.

Germany is building six new Type 122 guided-missile frigates, based on the Dutch 'Kortenaer' class, with the

first to commission in 1981, followed by others to make a total of 12 Type 122 ships. These will have Harpoon SSMs, Sea Sparrow SAMs and Stinger SAMs, a powerful A/S armament of torpedoes and up to two helicopters. The new ships will complement the six 'Köln' class frigates, which are useful general-purpose ships (they can carry mines), but possibly lack the armament to be truly effective in modern conditions.

West Germany naturally worries about the security of her North Sea coast, a fact reflected in the strength of her coastal forces, based on six Type 205 coastal submarines for longer-range defence, and five 'Thetis' class corvettes to co-ordinate and co-operate with a number of missile- and torpedo-armed FACs. At present these consist primarily of the 10 Type 143 craft armed with four Exocet launchers, the

20 Type 148 craft with four Exocet launchers each, and the 10 'Zobel' class craft with two wire-guided torpedoes each. In the 1980s the missile-armed boats will be supplemented by Improved Type 143 FAC(M)s to replace the 'Zobel' class craft.

Mine warfare will also play an important part in German operations, it is believed, and Germany deploys 18 Type 320 or 'Lindau' class coastal minesweepers/hunters, 22 Type 340-341 or 'Schütze' class fast coastal minesweepers, 10 Type 394 or 'Frauenlob' class inshore minesweepers, eight Type 393 or 'Ariadne' class inshore minesweepers, and two 'Niobe' class inshore minesweepers. These and the other coastal forces have the support of no less than 11 'Rhein' class depot ships, which can also double as frigates by reason of their two 100-mm guns. German minehunting capabilities are to be improved by the building of 12 new minehunters.

Vitally important to Germany's maritime effort is the naval air arm, which has 6,000 men and 134 combat aircraft. Some 85 of these are F-104G fighter-bombers, equipping three squadrons, and providing the navy with a first-class strike capability with Kormoran air-to-surface anti-shipping missiles. To supplement and then replace these F-104Gs, the naval air arm has on order 110 Panavia Tornado aircraft. Information on communist maritime movements is clearly of great importance, and the Germans deploy 19 Atlantic aircraft in two squadrons for the purpose. The possibility of replacing the Atlantic with S-3 Viking aircraft is under consideration.

The *Bundesmarine* is well provided with service and auxiliary ships, and has a forward-looking building programme. Coastal protection seems well cared for, and it is only in the matter of North Sea operations by surface vessels that the German situation seems parlous. However, the existence of the F-104G/Tornado force may well rectify matters in this sphere.

36,500 men (11,000 conscripts) including naval air arm

Destroyers (DDG):
3 Charles F. Adams
4 Hamburg

Destroyers (DD):
4 Fletcher

Frigates (FFG):
(6 Type 122)

Frigates:
6 Köln

Corvettes:
5 Thetis

SS:
18 Type 206
6 Type 205
1 Converted Type XXI (trials)

Light Forces:
10 Type 143 FAC(M)
20 Type 148 FAC(M)
10 Type 142/Zobel FAC(T)
(10 Type 143A FAC(M))

Amphibious Forces:
22 Type 520 LCU
19 Type 521 LCM

Mine Warfare Forces:
18 Type 320/Lindau coastal minesweepers/hunters
22 Type 340-341/Schütze fast coastal minesweepers
10 Type 394/Frauenlob inshore minesweepers
8 Type 393/Ariadne inshore minesweepers
2 Niobe inshore minesweepers
1 trials minesweeper
(12 ? minehunters)

Auxiliaries:
11 depot ships
2 repair ships
6 replenishment tankers
5 support tankers
8 support ships
2 ammunition transports
2 mine transports
others

'Charles F. Adams' class guided missile destroyer (3)

Class: *Lütjens* (D185), ex-US *DDG 28*; *Mölders* (D186), ex-US *DDG 29*; *Rommel* (D186), ex-US *DDG 30*
Displacement: 3,370 tons (3,424 tonnes) standard; 4,500 tons (4,572 tonnes) full load
Dimensions: Length 440 ft (134.1 m)
 Beam 47 ft (14.3 m)
 Draught 20 ft (6.1 m)
Armament:
Guns 2 5-in (127-mm) in single mountings
Missile systems
 1 Tartar launcher
A/S weapons
 1 ASROC launcher
 1 DCT
Torpedo tubes
 2 triple 12.75-in (324-mm) Mark 32
Aircraft
 none
Radar and electronics: SPS 52 3D air-search and target designator, SPS 40 air-surveillance, two SPG 51 Tartar fire-control, SPS 10 surface-warning, and GFCS 68 gunfire-control radars; SATIR I data automation system and TACAN
Sonar: SQS 23
Powerplant: 4 Combustion Engineering boi-

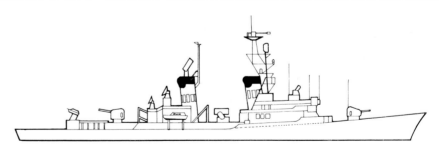

lers supplying steam to geared turbines, delivering 70,000 shp to two shafts
Speed: 35 knots
Range: 4,500 miles (7,242 km) at 20 knots
Crew: 21+319
Used also by: USA
Notes: All three were built to West German requirements by Bath Iron Works. The three ships were laid down in March 1966, April 1966, August 1967; launched in August 1967, April 1968, February 1969; and commissioned in March 1969, September 1969, April 1970.

'Hamburg' class guided missile destroyer (4)

Class: *Hamburg* (D181), *Schleswig-Holstein* (D182), *Bayern* (D183), *Hessen* (D184)
Displacement: 3,400 tons (3,455 tonnes) standard; 4,400 tons (4,471 tonnes) full load
Dimensions: Length 439 ft 7½ in (134.0 m)
Beam 44 ft (13.4 m)
Draught 17 ft 1 in (5.2 m)
Armament:
Guns 4 100-mm (3.9-in) in single mountings
8 40-mm in twin mountings
Missile systems
4 MM38 Exocet
A/S weapons
2 quadruple Bofors DC mortars
1 DCT
Torpedo tubes
4 21-in (533-mm) A/S
Aircraft
none
Radar and electronics: LW 02/3 air-warning, DAO 2 target-designator, two M45 100-mm fire-control, two M45 40-mm fire-control and navigation/air-warning radars, all made by Hollandse Signaalapparaten; FCS for A/S weapons: ECM fit
Sonar: hull-mounted ELAC 1 BV
Powerplant: 4 Wahodag boilers supplying steam to 2 Wahodag double-reduction geared turbines, delivering 68,000 shp to two shafts
Speed: 35¾ knots
Range: 6,000 miles (9,656 km) at 13 knots; 920 miles (1,481 km) at 35 knots
Crew: 17+263

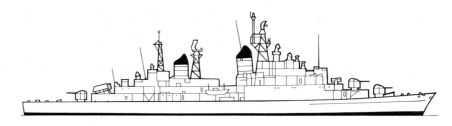

Used only by: West Germany
Notes: All built by H. C. Stülcken Sohn of Hamburg between 1959 and 1963, being commissioned in May 1964, October 1964, July 1965 and October 1968 respectively.

'Fletcher' class destroyer (4)

Class: *Z2* (D171), ex-US *Ringgold* (DD500); *Z3* (D172), ex-US *Wadsworth* (DD516); *Z4* (D178), ex-US *Claxton* (DD571); *Z5* (D179), ex-US *Dyson* (DD572)
Displacement: 2,100 tons (2,134 tonnes) standard; 2,750 tons (2,794 tonnes) full load
Dimensions: Length 376 ft 6 in (114.8 m)
Beam 39 ft 6 in (12.0 m)
Draught 18 ft (5.5 m)
Armament:
Guns 4 5-in (127-mm) in single mountings
6 3-in (76-mm) in twin mountings

Missile systems
none
A/S weapons
2 Hedgehog
1 DC rack
2 torpedo-tubes
Torpedo tubes
1 quintuple 21-in (533-mm)
Aircraft
none
Radar and electronics: SPS 6 search, SPS 10 surface surveillance, and GFCS 56 and 68 fire-control radars
Sonar: SQS 29
Powerplant: 4 Babcock & Wilcox boilers supplying steam to 2 Westinghouse geared

turbines, delivering 60,000 shp to two shafts
Speed: 32 knots
Range: 6,000 miles (9,656 km) at 15 knots
Crew: 250
Used also by: Argentina, Brazil, Chile, Greece, Italy, Mexico, Peru, South Korea, Spain, Taiwan, Turkey
Notes: These vessels were built by Federal Shipbuilding, Bath Iron Works, Consolidated Steel Corporation and Consolidated Steel Corporation, between 1941 and 1943, being commissioned into US service in 1942 and 1943. They were originally lent to Germany for five years in 1958, the period having been extended ever since.

'Köln' class frigate (6)

Class: *Köln* (F220), *Emden* (F221), *Augsburg* (F222), *Karlruhe* (F223), *Lübeck* (F224), *Braunschweig* (F225)
Displacement: 2,100 tons (2,134 tonnes) standard; 2,550 tons (2,591 tonnes) full load
Dimensions: Length 360 ft 11 in (110.0 m)
Beam 36 ft 1 in (11.0 m)
Draught 11 ft 2 in (3.4 m)
Armament:
Guns 2 100-mm (3.9-in) in single mountings
6 40-mm in 2 twin and 2 single mountings
Missile systems
none
A/S weapons
2 quadruple Bofors DC mortars
Torpedo tubes
4 21-in (533-mm) A/S
Aircraft
none
Radar and electronics: DA 02 target designator, two M45 100-mm fire-control,

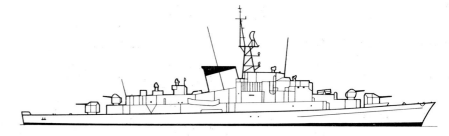

two M45 40-mm fire-control, and navigation/surface-search radars, all built by Hollandse Signaalapparaten; FCS for Bofors A/S
Sonar: PAE/CWE
Powerplant: (CODAG) 4 MAN diesels, delivering 12,000 bhp, and 2 Brown Boveri gas turbines, delivering 24,000 shp, to two shafts
Speed: 32 knots
Range: 920 miles (1,481 km) at 32 knots
Crew: 200
Used only by: West Germany

Notes: All built by H.C. Stülcken Sohn of Hamburg between 1957 and 1960, and commissioned between 1961 and 1964.

242

Type 206 submarine (18)

Class: *U 13* (S192), *U 14* (S193), *U 15* (S194), *U 16* (S195), *U 17* (S196), *U 18* (S197), *U 19* (S198), *U 20* (S199), *U 21* (S170), *U 22* (S171), *U 23* (S172), *U 24* (S173), *U 25* (S174), *U 26* (S175), *U 27* (S176), *U 28* (S177), *U 29* (S178), *U 30* (S179)
Displacement: 400 tons (406.4 tonnes) surfaced; 600 tons (609.6 tonnes) dived
Dimensions: Length 159 ft 5 in (48.6 m)
Beam 15 ft 5 in (4.7 m)
Draught 13 ft 1 in (4.0 m)
Armament:
Guns none
Missile systems
none
A/S weapons
none
Torpedo tubes
8 21-in (533-mm)
Aircraft
none

Radar and electronics:
Sonar:
Powerplant: MTU diesel-electric, delivering 1,800 hp to one shaft
Speed: 10 knots surfaced; 17 knots dived

Range: 4,500 miles (7,242 km) at 5 knots surfaced
Crew: 22
Used also by: Israel
Notes: Nine boats each built by Howaldtswerke of Kiel and Reinstahl Nordseewerke of Emden. The boats were laid down between 1969 and 1972, launched between 1971 and 1974, and commissioned between 1973 and 1975.

Type 205 submarine (6)

Class: *U 1* (S180), *U 2* (S181), *U 9* (S188), *U 10* (S189), *U 11* (S190), *U 12* (S191)
Displacement: 370 tons (375.9 tonnes) surfaced; 450 tons (457.2 tonnes) dived
Dimensions: Length 142 ft 8 in (43.5 m)
Beam 15 ft 1 in (4.6 m)
Draught 12 ft 10 in (3.8 m)
Armament:
Guns none
Missile systems
none

A/S weapons
none
Torpedo tubes
8 21-in (533-mm)
Aircraft
none
Radar and electronics: Thomson-CSF Calypso attack and navigation radar
Sonar:
Powerplant: (diesel-electric) 2 MTU diesels, delivering 1,200 shp, and 2 Siemens elec-

tric motors, delivering 1,700 bhp to one shaft
Speed: 10 knots (surfaced); 17 knots (dived)
Range:
Crew: 21
Used only by: West Germany
Notes: All built by Howaldtswerke of Kiel and commissioned between 1962 and 1969. The first German-designed submarines since World War II. Torpedoes are loaded into the bow tubes after the stern has been trimmed down.

'Thetis' class corvette (5)

Class: *Thetis* (P6052), *Hermes* (P6053), *Najade* (P6054), *Triton* (P6055), *Theseus* (P6056)
Displacement: 564 tons (573 tonnes) standard; 650 tons (660.4 tonnes) full load
Dimensions: Length 229 ft 8 in (70.0 m)
Beam 27 ft (8.5 m)
Draught 14 ft (4.2 m)

Armament:
Guns 2 40-mm Breda L70 in twin mounting (to be replaced by 1 76-mm OTO-Melara)
Missile systems
none
A/S weapons
1 quadruple Bofors A/S mortar
Torpedo tubes
4 21-in (533-mm)
Aircraft
none
Radar and electronics: KH14 navigation and

surface-warning radar
Sonar: ELAC 1BV
Powerplant: 2 MAN diesels, delivering 6,800 bhp to two shafts
Speed: 24 knots
Range:
Crew: 48
Used only by: West Germany
Notes: All built by Rolandwerft of Bremen, and commissioned between 1961 and 1963.

Type 143 fast attack craft (missile) (10)

Class: *S 61* (P6111), *S 62* (P6112), *S 63* (P6113), *S 64* (P6114), *S 65* (P6115), *S 66* (P6116), *S 67* (P6117), *S 68* (P6118), *S 69* (P6119), *S 70* (P6120)
Displacement: 378 tons (384 tonnes) full load
Dimensions: Length 187 ft (57.0 m)
Beam 25 ft 7 in (7.8 m)
Draught 8 ft 6 in (2.4 m)
Armament:
Guns 2 76-mm (3-in) OTO-Melara
Missile systems
4 MM38 Exocet launchers
A/S weapons
none
Torpedo tubes
2 21-in (533-mm)
Aircraft
none
Radar and electronics: Hollandse Signaalapparaten WM 27 gun-, missile- and torpedo-control radar; probably AGIS data

automatation system to allow Type 143 craft to be used as controls for Type 148 craft operations
Sonar:
Powerplant: 4 MTU diesels, delivering 16,000 hp to four shafts
Speed: 38 knots

Range: 1,300 miles (2,092 km) at 30 knots
Crew: 40
Used only by: West Germany
Notes: Built by Lürssen of Vegesack and Kröger of Rendsburg, and commissioned in 1976 and 1977. Intended as replacements for the 'Jaguar' class craft.

Type 148 fast attack craft (missile) (20)

Class: *S 41* (P6141) to *S 60* (P6160)
Displacement: 234 tons (237.75 tonnes) standard; 265 tons (269.25 tonnes) full load
Dimensions: Length 154 ft 2 in (47.0 m)
Beam 23 ft (7.0 m)
Draught 6 ft 7 in (2.0 m)
Armament:
Guns 1 76-mm (3-in) OTO-Melara
1 40-mm Bofors
Missile systems
4 MM38 Exocet launchers
A/S weapons
none
Torpedo tubes
none
Aircraft
none
Radar and electronics: RM 20 navigation, Triton air- and surface-search/target designator and Pollux tracking radars; Thomson-CSF Vega-Pollux PCET gun- and missile-control system
Sonar:
Powerplant: 4 MTU diesels, delivering 12,000 bhp to four shafts
Speed: 35½ knots
Range: 600 miles (965 km) at 30 knots
Crew: 4+26
Used only by: West Germany
Notes: All built or completed by Constructions Mécaniques de Normandie of Cherbourg as replacements for the first 20 craft of the 'Jaguar' class. Commissioned between 1972 and 1975.

'Zobel' class fast attack craft (torpedo) (10)

Class: *Zobel* (P6092), *Wiesel* (P6093), *Dachs* (P6094), *Hermelin* (P6095), *Nerz* (P6096), *Puma* (P6097), *Gepard* (P6098), *Hyane* (P6099), *Frettchen* (P6100), *Ozelot* (P6101)
Displacement: 225 tons (228.6 tonnes) full load
Dimensions: Length 139 ft 5 in (42.5 m)
Beam 23 ft 5 in (7.2 m)
Draught 7 ft 11 in (2.4 m)
Armament:
Guns 2 40-mm Bofors L70 in single mountings
Missile systems
none
A/S weapons
none
Torpedo tubes
2 21-in (533-mm) for wire-guided Seal torpedoes
Aircraft
none
Radar and electronics: two M20 fire-control radars

Sonar:
Powerplant: 4 MTU diesels, delivering 12,000 bhp to four shafts
Speed: 40½ knots
Range:
Crew: 39
Used only by: West Germany
Notes: Commissioned between 1961 and 1963 as units of the 'Jaguar' class, after construction by Lürssen of Vegesack and Kröger of Rendsburg. Became 'Zobel' class after conversion to torpedo boats.

Sea Eel

Type: ship- and submarine-launched anti-submarine torpedo
Guidance: wire-guidance from launch vessel, plus active/passive sonar homing
Launch method: tube
Dimensions: Length 13 ft 1½ in (4.0 m) with guidance-wire casket
Diameter 21 in (533 mm)
Weight:
Engine: electric
Speed: 23 to 35 knots
Range:
Warhead: 220 lb (100 kg) high explosive
Used only by: West Germany
Notes: Generally similar to the Seal, but with only half the battery capacity, a smaller warhead, and three-dimensional sonar in the homing head.

Seal

Type: ship- or submarine-launched anti-surface vessel torpedo
Guidance: wire-guidance from launch ship, plus active/passive sonar homing
Launch method: tube
Dimensions: Length 20 ft 11½ in (6.39 m) with guidance-wire casket
Diameter 21 in (533 mm)
Weight: 3,020 lb (1,370 kg)
Engine: electric
Speed: 23 to 35 knots
Range: 8.1 to 17.4 miles (13 to 28 km) depending on speed
Warhead: 573 lb (260 kg) high explosive
Used only by: West Germany
Notes: The Seal sets off on a programmed course if the wire breaks or control signal ceases for some other reason. There are contact and proximity fuses, the torpedo can operate in deep or shallow water, and the homing is three-dimensional.

SST 4

Type: ship- and submarine-launched anti-surface vessel torpedo
Guidance: wire-guidance from launch vessel, plus active/passive sonar homing
Launch method: tube
Dimensions: Length 21 ft (6.4 m)
Diameter 21 in (533 mm)
Weight:
Engine: electric
Speed:
Range:
Warhead: 573 lb (260 kg) high explosive
Used also by: seven NATO and South American countries
Notes: The SST 4 is similar to the Seal, and has contact and magnetic proximity fuses. It is used on Type 209 submarines, 'Combattante II', 'Combattante III' and 'Jaguar' class attack craft.

SUT (Surface and Underwater Target)

Type: ship-launched anti-ship and anti-submarine torpedo
Guidance: wire-guidance from launch vessel, plus active/passive sonar homing
Launch method: tube
Dimensions: Length 21 ft 11¾ in (6.7 m) with guidance-wire casket
Diameter 21 in (533 mm)
Weight:
Engine: electric
Speed:
Range:
Warhead: high explosive
Used only by: West Germany
Notes: The SUT is a development of the SST 4 with features of the Seal and Sea Eel. A feed-back circuit allows the launch vessel to control the torpedo even in the terminal homing phase of the run if necessary. The torpedo can be used to the maximum depth attainable by conventional submarines. Long ranges are available, and at low, medium and high speeds the torpedo is relatively noiseless.

Yugoslavia

27,000 (8,000 conscripts) including marines

Destroyer:
1 Split

Corvettes:
2 Mornar
1 Le Fougeux
(1 ?)

SS:
(2 Improved Heroj)
3 Heroj
2 Sutjeska
1 Mala

Light Forces:
1 Rade Koncar Type 211 FAC(M/G)
   +9)
10 Osa FAC(M)
14 Shershen FAC(T)
6 158 FAC(G)

Patrol Forces:
10 Type 131 PC
13 Kraljevica PC

Mine Warfare Forces:
4 Vukovklanac coastal minesweepers
6 M117 inshore minesweepers
4 Ham inshore minesweepers
14 M301 river minesweepers

Amphibious Forces:
(2 ? LST)
25 DTK 221/DTM230 type LCT
2 MZ type LCT
1 LCU
? LCA

Auxiliaries:
1 training ship
1 presidential yacht
1 survey ship
others

Aircraft:
? Mi-8
? Ka-25
? Gazelle

Marine Force:
1 marine bde

'Split' class destroyer (1)

Class: *Split* (R11), ex-*Spalato*
Displacement: 2,400 tons (2,438 tonnes) standard; 3,000 tons (3,048 tonnes) full load
Dimensions: Length 393 ft 8 in (120.0 m)
Beam 36 ft 6 in (11.1 m)
Draught 12 ft 3 in (3.8 m)
Armament:
Guns 4 127-mm in single turrets
12 40-mm
Missile systems
none
A/S weapons
2 Hedgehogs
6 DCTs
2 DC racks
Torpedo tubes
5 533-mm (21-in)
Aircraft
none
Radar and electronics: SC and SG1 radars, plus Marks 12 and 22 (Mark 37 GFCS) gun fire-control radars
Sonar:
Powerplant: 2 boilers supplying steam to geared turbines, delivering 50,000 shp to two shafts
Speed: 31½ knots
Range:
Crew: 240
Used only by: Yugoslavia
Notes: The ship was built at Rijeka between 1939 and 1940, but completed only in 1958 and commissioned in 1959.

'Mornar' class corvette (2)

Class: *Mornar* (551), *Borac* (552)
Displacement: 330 tons (335.3 tonnes) standard; 430 tons (436.9 tonnes) full load
Dimensions: Length 174 ft 9 in (53.3 m)
Beam 23 ft (7.0 m)
Draught 6 ft 7 in (2.0 m)
Armament:
Guns 1 76-mm
2 40-mm in single mountings
4 20-mm in quadruple mounting
Missile systems
none
A/S weapons
4 MBU 1200 launchers
2 DCTs
2 DC racks
Torpedo tubes
none
Aircraft
none
Radar and electronics:
Sonar:
Powerplant: 4 SEMT-Pielstick diesels, delivering 3,240 bhp to two shafts
Speed: 20 knots
Range: 3,000 miles (4,830 km) at 12 knots
Crew: 60
Used only by: Yugoslavia
Notes: The two ships were built in Yugoslavia between 1957 and 1958, for commissioning in 1959, and between 1964 and 1965, for commissioning in 1965.

'Heroj' class submarine (3)

Class: *Heroj* (821), *Junak* (822), *Uskok* (823)
Displacement: 1,068 tons (1,085 tonnes) dived
Dimensions: Length 210 ft (64.0 m)
Beam 23 ft 7 in (7.2 m)
Draught 16 ft 5 in (5.0 m)
Armament:
Guns none
Missile systems
none
A/S weapons
none
Torpedo tubes
6 533-mm (21-in)
Aircraft
none
Radar and electronics:
Sonar:
Powerplant: diesels and electric motors, delivering 2,400 hp
Speed: 16 knots (surfaced); 10 knots (dived)
Range:
Crew: 55
Used only by: Yugoslavia
Notes: All three boats were built by the Uljanik Shipyard at Pula between 1964 and 1969, and commissioned into Yugoslav service in 1968, 1969 and 1970.

'Sutjeska' class submarine (2)

Class: *Sutjeska* (811), *Neretva* (812)
Displacement: 820 tons (833.1 tonnes) surfaced; 945 tons (960.1 tonnes) dived
Dimensions: Length 196 ft 9 in (60.0 m)
Beam 22 ft 3 in (6.8 m)
Draught 16 ft 1 in (4.9 m)
Armament:
Guns none
Missile systems
none
A/S weapons
none
Torpedo tubes
6 533-mm (21-in)
Aircraft
none
Radar and electronics:
Sonar:
Powerplant: diesels and electric motors, delivering 1,800 hp
Speed: 14 knots (surfaced); 9 knots (dived)
Range: 4,800 miles (7,725 km) at 8 knots surfaced
Crew: 38
Used only by: Yugoslavia
Notes: Both boats were built by the Uljanik Shipyard at Pula between 1957 and 1959, and commissioned into Yugoslav service in 1962 and 1960 respectively.

Zaire

400 men

Light Forces:
3 P-4 FAC(T)

Patrol Forces:
15 coastal PC (+12)

List of Abbreviations

AA	anti-aircraft		FRAM	fleet rehabilitation and modernisation
AGSS	auxiliary submarine		GUPPY	greater underwater propulsion project
ASROC	anti-submarine rocket		LAMPS	light airborne multi-purpose system
ASW	anti-submarine warfare		LCA	landing craft, assault
bde	brigade		LCC	amphibious command ship
bn	battalion		LCT	landing craft, tank
BPDMS	basic point defence missile system		LHA	amphibious assault ship
CA	heavy cruiser		LPD	amphibious transport dock
CC	command ship		LPSS	amphibious transport submarine
CEP	circular error probable		LSM	landing ship, medium
CG	guided missile cruiser		LST	landing ship, tank
CGN	nuclear guided missile cruiser		MARV	manoeuvrable re-entry vehicle
CIWS	close-in weapons system		MCS	mine-countermeasures ship
CL	light cruiser		MIRV	multiple independently-targetable re-entry vehicles
CODAG	combined diesel and gas turbine		MRV	multiple re-entry vehicles
CODOG	combined diesel or gas turbine		MSC	non-magnetic coastal minesweeper
COGOG	combined gas turbine or gas turbine		MSO	ocean minesweeper
COSAG	combined steam turbine and gas turbine		NTDS	naval tactical data system
CV	aircraft-carrier		PC	patrol craft
CVA	attack aircraft-carrier		PSE	patrol escort
CVL	light aircraft-carrier		PG	patrol combatant
CVN	nuclear aircraft-carrier		PSMM	patrol ship multi-mission
CVS	anti-submarine aircraft-carrier		PUFFS	passive underwater fire feasibility system
CVT	transport aircraft-carrier		RBOC	rapid bloom overhead chaff
DC	depth charge		RV	re-entry vehicle
DCT	depth charge thrower		SAM	surface-to-air missile
DD	destroyer		SAR	search and rescue
DDG	guided missile destroyer		SLBM	submarine-launched ballistic missile
DE	ocean escort		SLCM	submarine-/ship-launched cruise missile
ECM	electronic countermeasures		sqn	squadron
EW	early warning		SS	attack submarine
FAC(G)	fast attack craft (gun)		SSBN	nuclear ballistic missile submarine
FAC(M)	fast attack craft (missile)		SSG	guided missile submarine
FAC(P)	fast attack craft (patrol)		SSM	surface-to-surface missile
FAC(T)	fast attack craft (torpedo)		SSN	nuclear attack submarine
FAH(M)	fast attack hydrofoil (missile)		STOL	short take-off and landing
FAH(T)	fast attack hydrofoil (torpedo)		SUBROC	submarine rocket
FF	frigate		VDS	variable-depth sonar
FFG	guided missile frigate		VTOL	vertical take-off and landing
flt	flight			

Index

Illustration Credits

Picture Editor: Jonathan Moore

Many organisations and archives kindly helped with photographic material during the preparation of this volume. We would wish particularly to thank the following for their invaluable assistance:

Australian Department of Defence, Canberra; Bundesmarine, Wilhelmshaven; Cdr. Aldo Fraccaroli, Switzerland; Hellenic General Naval Staff, Athens; Japanese Defence Agency, Tokyo; Kongsberg Vapenfabrikk, Norway; E. Speakman and S. Reed and staff of the Press Photographs Department, Ministry of Defence, London; Netherlands Ministry of Defence, Gravenhage; Service d'Information et des Relations Publiques de la Marine, Paris; C & S Taylor, Eastbourne; Robert A. Carlisle, Head of the US Navy's Photojournalism Branch, Washington DC, and staff; and Wright & Logan Limited, Southsea.

All artworks in this volume were produced by The County Studio, Leicestershire.

Unless otherwise indicated, all photographs were supplied through Military Archive & Research Services (MARS), London.

Key to picture positions: (T) = top, (C) = centre, (B) = bottom, (UC) = upper centre, (LC) = lower centre.

13 *Pegaso* (P362), Portuguese Argos-class large patrol boat now of the Angolan Navy (*Portuguese Navy, Lisbon*)

14 *Hercules* (D28) British Type 42 destroyer of the Argentine Navy; 1977 (*Vickers Shipbuilding Group*)

15 *Rosales* (D-22) ex-US Fletcher-class destroyer of the Argentine Navy underway during joint US-South American manoeuvres UNITAS XIV in the Atlantic Ocean; November 1973 (*US Navy*)

18 HMAS *Perth* (38) Perth-class guided missile destroyer of the Royal Australian Navy during manoeuvres (*Defence PR, Canberra*)

19 HMAS *Stuart* (48) River-class frigate of the Royal Australian Navy (*Defence PR, Canberra*)

20(T) HMAS *Oxley* (57) Oxley-class submarine of the Royal Australian Navy, built to the same design as British Oberon-class submarines (*Defence PR, Canberra*)

(B) HMAS *Curlew* (1121) modified British Ton-class minehunter, of the Royal Australian Navy (*Defence PR, Canberra*)

21(T) HMAS *Adroit* (82) Attack-class large patrol craft of the Royal Australian Navy (*Defence PR, Canberra*)

(B) Ikara long-range shipborne anti-submarine system on the foredeck of HMS *Bristol* (*Hawker Siddeley Dynamics, Herts, UK*)

24(T) *Minas Gerais* (A11) ex-British Colossus-class aircraft carrier of the Brazilian Navy during joint US-South American fleet manoeuvres; September 1972 (*US Navy*)

(B) *Niteroi* (F40) Niteroi-class destroyer of the Brazilian Navy during trials; October 1976 (*Vosper Thornycroft, Portsmouth*)

25 *Paraiba* (D28) ex-US Fletcher-class destroyer of the Brazilian Navy underway during joint US-South American manoeuvres Operation Unitas XIV in the Atlantic; November 1973 (*US Navy*)

26(T) *Mariz E Barros* (D26) ex-US Gearing FRAM I-class destroyer of the Brazilian Navy entering San Juan harbour, Puerto Rico, July 1968 (*US Navy*)

(B) *Humaita* (S20) British Oberon-class submarine of the Brazilian Navy (*Vickers Shipbuilding Group*)

27 *Bahia* (S12) ex-US Guppy II-class submarine of the Brazilian Navy arrives alongside the quay at Salvador, Brazil, October 1973 (*US Navy*)

31(T) HMCS *Huron* (281) Tribal-class anti-submarine destroyer of the Canadian Armed Forces; 1974 (*Canadian Armed Forces*)

(B) HMCS *Annapolis* (265) Annapolis-class frigate of the Canadian Armed Forces; 1972 (*Canadian Armed Forces*)

32(T) HMCS *Saskatchewan* (262) Mackenzie-class frigate of the Canadian Armed Forces (*Canadian Armed Forces*)

(B) HMCS *Chaudière* (235) Restigouche-class frigate of the Canadian Armed Forces (*Canadian Armed Forces*)

33(T) HMCS *Gatineau* (236) Improved Restigouche-class frigate of the Canadian Armed Forces; 1972 (*Canadian Armed Forces*)

(B) HMCS *Assiniboine* (234) St Laurent-class frigate of the Canadian Armed Forces, recovering a Sea King helicopter (*Canadian Armed Forces*)

34(T) HMCS *Okanagan* (74) Oberon-class submarine of the Canadian Armed Forces (*Canadian Armed Forces*)

(B) *Latorre* (04) ex-Swedish Göta Lejon-class cruiser of the Chilean Navy; 1973 (*Chilean Navy*)

35(T) *Prat* (03) ex-US Brooklyn-class cruiser of the Chilean Navy; 1975 (*Chilean Navy*)

(B) *Almirante Riveros* (18) Almirante-class destroyer of the Chilean Navy; 1975 (*Chilean Navy*)

36(T) *Blanco Encalada* (14) ex-US Fletcher-class destroyer of the Chilean Navy (*Chilean Navy*)

(C) *Ministro Zenteno* (16) ex-US Allen M Sumner FRAM II-class destroyer of the Chilean Navy; 1976 (*Chilean Navy*)

(B) *Condell* (06) Leander-class frigate of the Chilean Navy; 1976 (*Chilean Navy*)

37(T) *Serrano* (26) ex-US Charles Lawrence-class frigate of the Chilean Navy (*Chilean Navy*)

(UC) *Hyatt* (23) Oberon-class submarine of the Chilean Navy; 1976 (*Chilean Navy*)

(LC) *Simpson* (SS21) ex-US Balao-class submarine of the Chilean Navy; 1972 (*Chilean Navy*)

(B) *Lautaro* (62) ex-US Sotoyomo-class corvette of the Chilean Navy (*Chilean Navy*)

38(T) *Papudo* (37) PC-1638-class large patrol craft of the Chilean Navy; 1976 (*Chilean Navy*)

(B) Lürssen-type fast torpedo attack craft *Quidora*, *Tequalda*, *Guacolda* and *Fresia* of the Chilean Navy; 1976 (*Chilean Navy*)

41(T) Golf I-class ballistic missile submarine of the Soviet Navy. Three vertical launch tubes for SS-N-4 missiles are fitted in the fin; August 1961 (*US Navy*)

(B) Whiskey-class submarine (*Novosti Press Agency*)

43 USS *Keith* (DD-775) Allen M Sumner-class destroyer of the US Navy; December 1959 (*US Navy*)

44 USS *Hartley* (DE-1029) Courtney-class frigate of the US Navy; August 1957. Now *Boyaca*, a frigate of the Colombian Navy (*US Navy*)

45 *Pijao* (SS28) Type 209 submarine of the Colombian Navy during trials; 1975 (*Howaldtswerke, Kiel*)

46 *Peder Skram* (F352) Peder Skram-class frigate of the Royal Danish Navy (*Wright & Logan, Southsea*)

47 *Bellona* (F344) Triton-class corvette of the Royal Danish Navy (*Wright & Logan, Southsea*)

49 *Moen* (N82) Falster-class minelayer of the Royal Danish Navy (*C & S Taylor, Eastbourne*)

51 *Huancavilca* Type 209 submarine of the Ecuadorian Navy during trials; 1977 (*Howaldtswerke, Kiel*)

53(T) Whiskey-class patrol submarine; 1974 (*Crown Copyright, MOD RN, London*)

(B) *Deidre* (P20) corvette of the Republic of Ireland Navy (*Irish Army Air Corps*)

54 *Karjala* Turunmaa-class corvette of the Finnish Navy; 1977 (*Finnish Navy, Helsinki*)

55(T) *Tuuli* Tuima-class missile-armed fast attack craft of the Finnish Navy based on the Soviet Osa-class vessels; 1977 (*Finnish Navy, Helsinki*)

(C) *Isku* the Finnish Navy's experimental missile craft fitted with four SS-N-2 missile launchers; 1974 (*Finnish Navy, Helsinki*)

(B) *Raisio* (4) Ruissalo-class large patrol craft of the Finnish Navy; 1974 (*Finnish Navy, Helsinki*)

56(T) *Rihtniemi* Rihtniemi-class large patrol craft of the Finnish Navy; 1969 (*Finnish Navy, Helsinki*)

(B) *Keihassalmi*, Improved Ruotsinsalmi-class minelayer of the Finnish Navy; 1976 (*Finnish Navy, Helsinki*)

57 The first three nuclear-powered ballistic missile submarines of the French Navy: in the foreground is the class leader *Le Redoutable* (S611) with *Le Terrible* (S612) and *Le Foudroyant* (S610) behind; 1973 (*ECP/Armées, Ivry-sur-Seine, France*)

58(T) *Agosta* (S620) Agosta-class diesel-electric submarine of the French Navy; 1976 (*ECP/Armées, France*)

(C) *Daphné* (S641) Daphné-class diesel-electric submarine of the French Navy; 1968 (*ECP/Armées, France*)

(B) *Aréthuse* (S635) Aréthuse-class diesel-electric submarine of the French Navy; 1976 (*Marine Nationale, France*)

59(T) *Narval* (S631) Narval-class diesel-electric submarine of the French Navy; 1971 (*Marine Nationale, France*)

(B) *Clemenceau* (R98) fleet aircraft-carrier of the French Navy, about to recover an Etendard IV; November 1975 (*ECP/Armées, France*)

60(T) *Jeanne d'Arc* (R97) anti-submarine warfare helicopter cruiser of the French Navy. Beyond is the *Alphée* (Y696) a small transport of the French Navy; 1975 (*ECP/Armées, France*)

(B) *Colbert* (C611) guided missile cruiser of the French Navy 1976 (*ECP/Armées, France*)

61(T) *Georges Leygues* (D640) C70 Type destroyer fitting out for the French Navy; 1978 (*Marine Nationale, Paris*)

(B) *Suffren* (D602) Suffren-class destroyer of the French Navy; July 1976 (*ECP/Armées, France*)

62(T) *Tourville* (D610) Type F67 destroyer of the French Navy; July 1976 (*ECP/Armées, France*)

(C) *La Galissonnière* (D638) Type T56 destroyer of the French Navy; 1976 (*ECP/Armées, France*)

(B) *Duperré* (D633) Type T53 Modified anti-submarine warfare destroyer of the French Navy; 1975 (*Marine Nationale, France*)

63(T) *Dupetit Thouars* (D625) Type T47 guided missile destroyer of the French Navy; 1975 (*ECP/Armées, France*)

(B) *D'Estrées* (D629) Type T47 anti-submarine destroyer of the French Navy; 1976 (*ECP/Armées, France*)

64(T) *Aconit* (D609) Type C65 destroyer of the French Navy; 1977 (*ECP/Armées, France*)

(C) *Commandant Rivière* (F733) Commandant Rivière-class escort frigate of the French Navy, before fitting with Exocet; 1975 (*Marine Nationale, France*)

(B) *L'Alsacien* (F776) Type E52 frigate of the French Navy; 1974 (*ECP/Armées, France*)

65 *Détroyat* (F784) Type A69 anti-submarine warfare frigate of the French Navy; 1977 (*ECP/Armées, France*)

66(T) *La Combattante* (P730) La Combattante I-type fast missile attack craft of the French Navy (*Marine Nationale, France*)

(C) *L'Ardent* (P635) Le Fougueux-class large patrol craft of the French Navy; 1976 (*ECP/Armées, France*)

(B) *La Lorientaise* (P652) La Dunkerquoise class large patrol craft of the French Navy (*Marine Nationale, France*)

67(T) *Circé* (M715) Circé-class minehunter of the French Navy; 1977 (*Marine Nationale, Paris*)

(B) *Vinh Long* (M619) Aggressive-class minesweeper of the French Navy (*Copyright of and print from Marius Bar, Toulon*)

68(T) MM38 Exocet surface-to-surface missile being fired from the guided-missile destroyer HMS *Norfolk* (D21); 1974 (*Crown Copyright, MOD RN, London*)

68(UC) MM38 Exocet surface-to-surface ship-borne tactical missile being launched (*Aérospatiale, Paris*)

(LC) Royal Navy frigate *Undaunted* after being struck by an Exocet surface-to-surface missile fired by the guided-missile destroyer HMS *Norfolk*; 1973 (*Crown Copyright, MOD RN, London*)

(B) Crotale naval mount for a shipborne area defence system against airborne targets (*Thomson-CSF/Thierry Scart*)

69(T) Malafon 233 anti-submarine missile (*Latecoère, Paris, France*)

(B) Loading an MSBS M-20 missile into the launch tubes on a French nuclear-powered ballistic missile submarine (*Aérospatiale, Paris*)

70 Launch of a MSBS M-20 ballistic missile from a submerged French Navy submarine (*Aérospatiale, Paris*)

71 *Keta* (F18) Vosper Mk 1 corvette of the Ghanaian Navy (*Wright & Logan, Southsea*)

73(T) HS *Themistokles* (210) ex-US Gearing FRAM II-class destroyer of the Hellenic Navy; 1972 (*Hellenic Navy, Athens*)

(C) HS *Miaoulis* (211) ex-US Allen M Sumner-class destroyer of the Hellenic Navy; 1973 (*Hellenic Navy, Athens*)

(B) HS *Thyella* (28) ex-US Fletcher-class destroyer of the Hellenic Navy (*Hellenic Navy, Athens*)

74(T) HS *Leon* (54) ex-US Cannon-class frigate of the Hellenic Navy (*Hellenic Navy, Athens*)

(B) HS *Glavkos* (S110) Type 209 submarine of the Hellenic Navy (*Hellenic Navy, Athens*)

75(T) HS *Katsonis* (S115) ex-US Guppy III-class submarine of the Hellenic Navy (*Hellenic Navy, Athens*)

(C) HS *Papanikolis* (S114) ex-US Guppy IIA-class submarine of the Hellenic Navy; 1973 (*Hellenic Navy, Athens*)

(B) HS *Triaina* (S86) ex-US Balao-class submarine of the Hellenic Navy (*Hellenic Navy, Athens*)

76(T) HS *Ipoploiarhos Mikonios* (P53) La Combattante III-class fast missile attack craft of the Hellenic Navy (*Hellenic Navy, Athens*)

(B) HS *Ipoploiarhos Konidis* (P57) La Combattante II-class fast missile attack craft of the Hellenic Navy (*Hellenic Navy, Athens*)

77(T) HS *Kelefstis Stamou* (P28) fast attack craft of the Hellenic Navy (*Hellenic Navy, Athens*)

(C) HS *Tyfon* (P230) ex-FDR Jaguar-class fast attack craft of the Hellenic Navy (*Hellenic Navy, Athens*)

(B) HS *Astrapi* (P20) Vosper Brave-class fast attack craft of the Hellenic Navy (*Hellenic Navy, Athens*)

78 HS *Ploiarhos Arslanoglou* (P14) ex-US PGM-9-class large patrol craft of the Hellenic Navy (*Hellenic Navy, Athens*)

80 *Mysore* (C60) Fiji-class cruiser of the Indian Navy (*Wright & Logan, Southsea*)

81(T) *Udaygiri* (F35) Leander-class frigate of the Indian Navy (*C & S Taylor, Eastbourne*)

(B) *Betwa* (F139) Leopard-class frigate of the Indian Navy (*Wright & Logan, Southsea*)

83 USS *McMorris* (DE 1036) Claud Jones-class frigate of the US Navy at sea in the Pacific; June 1969. Now *Ngurah Rai* frigate of the Indonesian Navy (*US Navy*)

84 Whiskey-class patrol submarine of the Soviet Navy; November 1970 (*US Navy*)

85 IIS *Zaal* (72, though shown here with old pennant number) Saam-class frigate of the Imperial Iranian Navy (*Vickers Shipbuilding Group*)

88(T) *Dolphin* (77) ex-British T-class patrol submarine of the Israeli Navy (*Israeli Navy, Tel Aviv*)

(B) Saar-class fast missile attack craft of the Israeli Navy (*Israeli Navy, Tel Aviv*)

89 Gabriel ship-to-ship missile (*Israel Aircraft Industries, Lod, Israel*)

91 *Vittorio Veneto* (C550) helicopter cruiser of the Italian Navy (*Italian Navy, Rome*)

92(T) *Caio Duilio* (C554) Andrea Doria-class frigate of the Italian Navy (*Italian Navy, Rome*)

(B) *Audace* (D551) Audace-class guided missile destroyer of the Italian Navy; 1975 (*Italian Navy, Rome*)

93(T) *Impavido* (D570) Impavido-class guided missile destroyer of the Italian Navy; 1976 (*Italian Navy, Rome*)

(B) *San Giorgio* (D562) destroyer/training ship of the Italian Navy (*Italian Navy, Rome*)

94 *Impetuoso* (D558) Impetuoso-class destroyer of the Italian Navy (*Italian Navy, Rome*)

95(T) *Lupo* (D564) Lupo-class frigate of the Italian Navy (*Italian Navy, Rome*)

(B) *Alpino* (F580) Alpino-class frigate of the Italian Navy (*Italian Navy, Rome*)

96(T) *Carlo Bergamini* (F593) Bergamini-class frigate of the Italian Navy (*Italian Navy, Rome*)

(B) *Centauro* (F554) Centauro-class frigate of the Italian Navy (*Italian Navy, Rome*)

97(T) *Pietro de Cristofaro* (F540) de Cristofaro-class corvette of the Italian Navy (*Italian Navy, Rome*)

(C) *Albatros* (F543) Albatros-class corvette of the Italian Navy (*Italian Navy, Rome*)

(B) *Nazario Sauro* Sauro-class submarine of the Italian Navy; 1977 (*Italian Navy, Rome*)

98(T) *Enrico Toti* (S506) Toti-class submarine of the Italian Navy (*Italian Navy, Rome*)

(B) *Romeo Romei* (S516) ex-US Tang-class submarine of the Italian Navy (*Italian Navy, Rome*)

99(T) *Gianfranco Gazzana Priaroggia* (S502) ex-US Guppy III-class submarine of the Italian Navy (*Italian Navy, Rome*)

(C) *Alfredo Cappellini* (S507) ex-US Balao-class submarine of the Italian Navy (*Italian Navy, Rome*)

(B) *Sparviero* (P420) Sparviero-class missile-armed hydrofoil of the Italian Navy. The Otomat ship-to-ship missile launchers can be seen at the stern (*Italian Navy, Rome*)

100(T) *Freccia* (P493) Freccia-class fast attack craft of the Italian Navy; 1974 (*Italian Navy, Rome*)

(B) *Lampo* (P491) Lampo-class fast attack craft of the Italian Navy (*Italian Navy, Rome*)

101(T) Albatros shipborne anti-aircraft and anti-missile system being fired from a ship of the Italian Navy. The missile used is the naval Sparrow III (designated Sea Sparrow RIM-7H) (*Selenia Spa, Rome, Italy*)

(B) Otomat anti-ship missile in flight (*OTO Melara, Italy*)

104(T) *Tachikaze* (DD168) Tachikaze-class destroyer of the Japanese Navy (*Japanese Maritime Self-Defence Force*)

(B) *Hiei* (DD142) Haruna-class destroyer of the Japanese Navy (*Japanese Maritime Self-Defence Force*)

105(T) *Kikuzuki* (DD165) Takatsuki-class destroyer of the Japanese Navy (*Japanese Maritime Self-Defence Force*)

(B) *Akigumo* (DD120) Yamagumo-class destroyer of the Japanese Navy (*Japanese Maritime Self-Defence Force*)

106(T) *Natsugumo* (DD117) Minegumo-class destroyer of the Japanese Navy (*Japanese Maritime Self-Defence Force*)

(B) *Amatsukaze* (DD163) Amatsukaze-class destroyer of the Japanese Navy (*Japanese Maritime Self-Defence Force*)

107(T) *Akizuki* (DD161) Akizuki-class destroyer of the Japanese Navy (*Japanese Maritime Self-Defence Force*)

(C) *Murasame* (DD107) Murasame-class destroyer of the Japanese Navy (*Japanese Maritime Self-Defence Force*)

(B) *Takanami* (DD110) Ayanami-class destroyer of the Japanese Navy (*Japanese Maritime Self-Defence Force*)

108(T) *Chikugo* (DE215) Chikugo-class frigate of the Japanese Navy (*Japanese Maritime Self-Defence Force*)

(B) *Ooi* (DE214) Isuzu-class frigate of the Japanese Navy (*Japanese Maritime Self-Defence Force*)

109(T) *Yamadori* (312) Mizutori-class corvette of the Japanese Navy (*Japanese Maritime Self-Defence Force*)

(B) Uzushio-class submarine of the Japanese Navy (*Japanese Maritime Self-Defence Force*)

110(T) *Asashio* (SS562) Ooshio-class submarine of the Japanese Navy (*Japanese Maritime Self-Defence Force*)

(B) PT11 (811) fast torpedo attack craft of the Japanese Navy (*Japanese Maritime Self-Defence Force*)

111 *Madaraka* (P3121), *Harambee* (P3123) and *Jamhuri* (P3122) Brooke Marine 37.5 metre-class large patrol craft of the Kenyan Navy (*Brooke Marine, Lowestoft*)

112 *Mamba* (P3100) Brooke Marine 32.6 metre-class large patrol craft of the Kenyan Navy; January 1974 (*Brooke Marine, Lowestoft*)

113 *Dat Assawari* (F01) Vosper Thornycroft Mk 7 type frigate of the Libyan Navy (*Vosper Thornycroft, Portsmouth*)

114 *Wadi M 'Ragh* corvette of the Libyan Navy under sea trials off Genoa, May 1978 (*Commander Aldo Fraccaroli, Switzerland*)

115(T) *Susa* Susa-class fast missile attack craft of the Libyan Navy firing SS. 12M missile (*Vosper Thornycroft, Portsmouth*)

(B) *Garian* Garian-class large patrol craft of the Libyan Navy (*Brooke Marine, Lowestoft*)

116(T) *Homs* Vosper Thornycroft type large patrol craft of the Libyan Navy (*Vosper Thornycroft, Portsmouth*)

(B) *Rahmat* Yarrow type frigate of the Malaysian Navy (*Wright & Logan, Southsea*)

117 *Hang Tuah* Yarrow type frigate of the Malaysian Navy (*Wright & Logan, Southsea*)

118 *Perkasa* (P150) Perkasa-class fast missile attack craft of the Malaysian Navy (*Vosper Thornycroft, Portsmouth*)

119(T) *Cuitlahuac* (IE 02) ex-US Fletcher-class destroyer of the Mexican Navy (*Mexican Navy*)

(B) *Como Manuel Azueta* (A06) ex-US Edsall-class frigate of the Mexican Navy (*Mexican Navy*)

120(T) *Durango* (B-01) Durango-class frigate of the Mexican Navy (*Mexican Navy*)

(B) *Jose Maria Izazgu* (P-04) Azteca-class large patrol craft of the Mexican Navy (*Mexican Navy*)

121 *Al Bachir* (22) large patrol craft of the Moroccan Navy (*Print from and copyright of Marius Bar, Toulon*)

123(T) *De Ruyter* (F806) Tromp-class destroyer of the Royal Netherlands Navy; 1976 (*Royal Netherlands Navy, Den Haag*)

(B) *Drenthe* (D816) Friesland-class destroyer of the Royal Netherlands Navy; 1973 (*Royal Netherlands Navy, Den Haag*)

124(T) *Zeeland* (D809) Holland-class destroyer of the Royal Netherlands Navy; 1976 (*Royal Netherlands Navy, Den Haag*)

(B) *Kortenaer* (F807) Kortenaer-class frigate of the Royal Netherlands Navy; 1978 (*Royal Netherlands Navy, Den Haag*)

125(T) *Van Speijk* (F802) Van Speijk-class frigate of the Royal Netherlands Navy; 1976 (*Royal Netherlands Navy, Den Haag*)

(B) *Zwaardvis* (S806) Zwaardvis-class submarine of the Royal Netherlands Navy; 1974 (*Royal Netherlands Navy, Den Haag*)

126(T) *Dolfijn* (S808) Dolfijn-class submarine of the Royal Netherlands Navy; 1973 (*Royal Netherlands Navy, Den Haag*)

(B) *Fret* (F818) Wolf-class corvette of the Royal Netherlands Navy; 1978 (*Royal Netherlands Navy, Den Haag*)

127(T) *Balder* (P802) Balder-class large patrol craft of the Royal Netherlands Navy; 1971 (*Royal Netherlands Navy, Den Haag*)

(B) HMNZS *Canterbury* (F421) Leander-class frigate of the Royal New Zealand Navy (*Royal New Zealand Navy, Wellington*)

128 HMNZS *Taranaki* (F148) Whitby-class frigate of the Royal New Zealand Navy (*Royal New Zealand Navy, Wellington*)

129(T) HMNZS *Rotoiti* (P3569) Lake-class large patrol craft of the Royal New Zealand Navy (*Royal New Zealand Navy, Wellington*)

(B) NNS *Otobo* (F82) Vosper Thornycroft Mark 3 corvette of the Nigerian Navy (*C & S Taylor, Eastbourne*)

130 NNS *Otobo* (F82) Mk 3 Vosper Thornycroft type corvette of the Nigerian Navy (*Vosper Thornycroft, Portsmouth*)

131 Whiskey-class patrol submarine; 1974 (*Crown Copyright, MOD RN, London*)

133(T) *Bergen* Oslo-class frigate of the Royal Norwegian Navy (*Wright & Logan, Southsea*)

(B) *Sleipner* (F310) Sleipner-class corvette of the Royal Norwegian Navy (*Royal Norwegian Navy, Oslo*)

134(T) *Utstein* (S302) Type 207 submarine of the Royal Norwegian Navy (*Royal Norwegian Navy, Oslo*)

(C) P986 Hauk-class fast missile attack craft of the Royal Norwegian Navy (*Royal Norwegian Navy, Oslo*)

(B) *Rapp* (P981) Snögg-class fast missile attack craft of the Royal Norwegian Navy (*AS Kongsberg Vapenfabrikk, Norway*)

135(T) *Traust* (P973) Storm-class fast missile attack craft of the Royal Norwegian Navy (*AS Kongsberg Vapenfabrikk, Norway*)

(B) *Skudd* (P967) Storm-class fast missile craft of the Royal Norwegian Navy firing a Penguin missile (*AS Kongsberg Vapenfabrikk, Norway*)

136(T) SNV *Al Said* corvette of the Oman Navy (*Brooke Marine, Lowestoft*)

(B) SNV *Al Jabbar* (B7) large patrol craft of the Sultanate of Oman Navy; September 1977 (*Brooke Marine, Lowestoft*)

137 *Babur* (C84) Modified Dido-class cruiser of the Pakistani Navy (*Wright & Logan, Southsea*)

138 *Ghazi* (S134) Daphné-class submarine of the Pakistani Navy (*Print from and copyright of Marius Bar, Toulon*)

139 *Jessore* (P141) Town-class large patrol boat of the Pakistan Navy. This vessel was sunk during the Indo-Pakistan War, December 1971 (*Brooke Marine, Lowestoft*)

141(T) *Capitan Quiñones* (83) ex-British Ceylon-class cruiser of the Peruvian Navy; 1975 (*Peruvian Navy, Lima*)

(C) *Palacios* (DD73) ex-British Daring-class destroyer of the Peruvian Navy; 1976 (*Peruvian Navy, Lima*)

(B) *Villar* (DD71) ex-US Fletcher-class destroyer of the Peruvian Navy; 1976 (*Peruvian Navy, Lima*)

142(T) *Islay* (S45) Type 209 submarine of the Peruvian Navy; 1975 (*Peruvian Navy, Lima*)

(B) *Arica* (S46) Type 209 submarine of the Peruvian Navy leaving Kiel after building; 1974 (*Howaldtswerke, Kiel*)

143 *Iquique* (S44) Abtao-class submarine of the Peruvian Navy; 1974 (*Peruvian Navy, Lima*)

145 *Warszawa* (275) SAM Kotlin-class guided missile destroyer of the Polish Navy (*Wright & Logan, Southsea*)

146 *Pelikan* (here shown under old pennant number, 619) Krogulec-class ocean mine-
(T & B) sweeper of the Polish Navy (*Wright & Logan, Southsea; C & S Taylor, Eastbourne*)

147(T) *Comandante João Belo* (F480) Comandante João Belo-class frigate of the Portuguese Navy (*Portuguese Navy, Lisbon*)

(B) *Almirante Pereira da Silva* (F472) Almirante Pereira da Silva-class frigate of the Portuguese Navy (*Portuguese Navy, Lisbon*)

148(T) *João Coutinho* (F475) class-name frigate of the Portuguese Navy (*Portuguese Navy, Lisbon*)

(B) *Cacine* (P1140) Cacine-class large patrol craft of the Portuguese Navy (*Portuguese Navy, Lisbon*)

149 *Al Wusaail* (Q14) Vosper Thornycroft 33.4-m type large patrol craft of the Qatar Navy (*C & S Taylor, Eastbourne*)

151 RSS *Independence* (P69) Type A fast attack craft of the Singapore Navy (*Vosper Thornycroft, Portsmouth*)

152 RSS *Sovereignty* (P71) Type B fast attack craft of the Singapore Navy (*Vosper Thornycroft, Portsmouth*)

153 *President Kruger* (F150) President-class frigate of the South African Navy (*South African Navy*)

154 *Emily Hobhouse* (S98) Daphné-class submarine of the South African Navy (*South African Navy*)

155 USS *New* (DD-818) Gearing FRAM I destroyer of the US Navy at sea; April 1968. Now in service with the South Korean Navy (*US Navy*)

156 USS *Wallace L Lind* (DD-703) Allen M Sumner FRAM II-class destroyer of the US Navy; May 1966. Now *Dae Gu*, destroyer of the South Korean Navy (*US Navy*)

159(T) *Dédalo* (PH01) ex-US Independence-class helicopter carrier of the Spanish Navy (*Spanish Navy, Madrid*)

(B) *Roger de Lauria* (D42) Roger de Lauria-class destroyer of the Spanish Navy (*Spanish Navy, Madrid*)

160 *Oquendo* (D41) Oquendo-class destroyer of the Spanish Navy (*Spanish Navy, Madrid*)

161 *Baleares* (F71) Baleares-class frigate of the Spanish Navy (*Spanish Navy, Madrid*)

162 *Atrevida* (F61) Atrevida F60-class frigate of the Spanish Navy (*Spanish Navy, Madrid*)

163 *Isaac Peral* (S32) S30-class submarine of the Spanish Navy (*Spanish Navy, Madrid*)

164 *Laya* (P12) Barcelo-class large patrol craft of the Spanish Navy (*Spanish Navy, Madrid*)

166 *Östergötland* (J20) Södermanland-class destroyer of the Royal Swedish Navy (*Royal Swedish Navy*)

167(T) *Halland* (J18) Halland-class destroyer of the Royal Swedish Navy (*Royal Swedish Navy*)

(B) *Öland* (F16, shown here under old pennant number) Oland-class frigate of the Royal Swedish Navy (*Kockums, Sweden*)

168(T) *Visby* (F11) Royal Swedish Navy Visby-class frigate (*Royal Swedish Navy*)

(B) *Neptun* (Np) Royal Swedish Navy Näcken-class (A14) submarine (*Kockums, Sweden*)

169(TL) *Sjöormen* (Sor) Royal Swedish Navy Sjöormen-class submarine (*Royal Swedish Navy*)

(TR) *Sjöhästen* (Sha) Royal Swedish Navy Sjöormen-class submarine (*Kockums, Sweden*)

(B) *Vargen* (Vgn) Royal Swedish Navy Draken-class submarine (*Kockums, Sweden*)

170(T) *Valen* (Va) Royal Swedish Navy Hajen-class submarine (*Kockums, Sweden*)

(B) *Hugin* (P151) Hugin-class fast missile attack craft of the Royal Swedish Navy (*AS Kongsberg Vapenfabrikk, Norway*)

171(T) Spica T131-class torpedo-armed fast attack craft at speed: in the foreground is the *Nynäshamn* (T132), with *Västerås* (T135) and *Norrtälje* (T133) beyond (*Karlskronavaret AB, Sweden*)

(B) *Castor* (T124) Royal Swedish Navy Spica T121-class torpedo-armed fast attack craft (*Karlskronavaret AB, Sweden*)

172(T) *Plejad* (T102) Royal Swedish Navy Plejad-class torpedo-armed fast attack craft (*Royal Swedish Navy*)

(B) RB 08 coastal defence weapon of the Royal Swedish Navy being test fired (*Saab-Scania, Sweden*)

174(T) USS *Hanson* (DD-832) FRAM I destroyer of the US Navy off the coast of Oahu, Hawaii; February 1971. Now *Liao Yang*, a destroyer of the Taiwan Navy (*US Navy*)

(B) USS *Ernest G Small* (DD-838) Gearing FRAM II-class radar picket of the US Navy underway in the Gulf of Tonkin; June 1970. Now *Fu Yang* of the Taiwan Navy (*US Navy*)

175 USS *John W Thomason* (DD-760) Allen M Sumner-class destroyer of the US Navy in the Gulf of Tonkin; October 1969. Now *Nan Yang* destroyer of the Taiwan Navy (*US Navy*)

177 *Makut Rajakumarn* Yarrow type frigate of the Thai Navy (*Wright & Logan, Southsea*)

178 *Chaguaramus* (CG3) Later Vosper type large patrol craft of the Trinidad & Tobago Coast Guard (*Vosper Thornycroft, Portsmouth*)

179 *Gayret* (D352) ex-US Gearing FRAM I-class destroyer of the Turkish Navy (*Wright & Logan, Southsea*)

180(T) USS *Preston* (D-795) Fletcher-class destroyer of the US Navy. Now *Icel* destroyer of the Turkish Navy (*US Navy*)

(B) *Berk* (D358) Berk-class frigate of the Turkish Navy (*C & S Taylor, Eastbourne*)

181 *Atilay* (S347) Type 209 submarine of the Turkish Navy during trials; 1975 (*Howaldtswerke, Kiel*)

185(T) Delta I-class ballistic missile submarine of the Soviet Navy. This class of ship is fitted with 12 SS-N-8 missiles in vertical launch tubes aft of the fin; 1975 (*Crown Copyright, MOD RN, London*)

(B) Yankee-class ballistic missile submarine of the Soviet Navy. This class of ship is fitted with 16 SS-N-6 missile launch tubes aft of the fin; August 1976 (*US Navy*)

186(T) Hotel II-class ballistic missile submarine of the Soviet Navy in difficulties 600 miles north-east of Newfoundland as located by a US Navy P-3 patrol aircraft. This vessel carries three SS-N-5 missiles in vertical tubes within the fin. 29 February 1972 (*US Navy*)

(B) Golf II-class ballistic missile submarine of the Soviet Navy in the North Atlantic en route to Cuba. Three vertical launch tubes for SS-N-5 missiles are fitted in the fin; May 1974 (*US Navy*)

187(T) Charlie-class nuclear cruise missile submarine of the Soviet Navy (*Novosti Press Agency*)

(B) Echo II-class cruise missile submarine of the Soviet Navy. These vessels are fitted with eight launchers for SS-N-3 missiles; July 1973 (*US Navy*)

188(T) Juliett-class cruise missile submarine of the Soviet Navy. This vessel is armed with four SS-N-3 missiles fired from tubes fore and aft of the fin; November 1970 (*US Navy*)

(B) Whiskey Twin Cylinder-class cruise missile submarine of the Soviet Navy (*Novosti Press Agency*)

189(T) Victor-class nuclear powered fleet submarine of the Soviet Navy in the South China Sea; April 1974 (*US Navy*)

(B) November-class nuclear powered fleet submarine of the Soviet Navy, in trouble in the Atlantic; April 1970 (*Crown Copyright MOD RN, London*)

190(T) Echo I-class nuclear powered fleet submarine of the Soviet Navy; September 1975 (*US Navy*)

(B) Tango-class patrol submarine of the Soviet Navy during a naval review. In front of this ship can be seen a Whiskey Twin Cylinder-class cruise missile submarine; 1975 (*US Navy*)

191(T) The Soviet aircraft carrier *Kiev* viewed from the Wasp helicopter of HMS *Danae* which can be seen shadowing the Russian ship as she passes through the Shetland-Faroes gap in the North Atlantic; August 1976 (*Crown Copyright, MOD RN, London*)

(B) *Moskva* Moskva-class helicopter cruiser of the Soviet Navy (*Novosti Press Agency*)

192(T) *Ochakov* (539) Kara-class cruiser of the Soviet Navy during exercises in the Mediterranean as seen from an RAF Nimrod operating from St Mawgan, Cornwall; February 1976 (*Crown Copyright, MOD RAF, London*)

(B) *Admiral Oktyabrsky* (225) Kresta II-class cruiser of the Soviet Navy passing through the English Channel; May 1974 (*Crown Copyright, MOD RN, London*)

193(T) Kresta I-class guided missile cruiser of the Soviet Navy photographed from a Nimrod operating from RAF Kinloss; March 1975 (*Crown Copyright, MOD RAF, London*)

(C) *Admiral Golovko* Kynda-class guided missile cruiser at anchor in the Mediterranean. Clearly visible are the two sets of quadruple SS-N-3 fore and aft and the SA-N-1 twin launcher on the foredeck; Summer 1974 (*US Navy*)

(B) *Sverdlov* unconverted Sverdlov-class cruiser of the Soviet Navy viewed from a Sea King helicopter operating from HMS *Blake* in the North Sea; July 1976 (*Crown Copyright, MOD RN, London*)

195(T) A Soviet Kashin-class destroyer in the North Sea as seen from a Sea King helicopter operating from HMS Blake; July 1976 (*Crown Copyright, MOD RN, London*)

(B) The British commando carrier HMS *Hermes* being shadowed by a Soviet Kanin-class destroyer. October 1973 (*Crown Copyright, MOD RN, London*)

196 *Svetly* (490) Kotlin-class destroyer of the Soviet Navy as seen from a Sea King helicopter operating from HMS *Blake* in the North Sea; July 1976 (*Crown Copyright, MOD RN, London*)

199 T-43-class ocean minesweeper of the Soviet Navy; August 1965 (*US Navy*)

200 SS-N-6 'Sawfly' type submarine-launched ballistic missile on view at the May Day parade in Moscow, 1968 (*Novosti Press Agency*)

204(T) HMS *Resolution* (S22) nuclear-powered ballistic missile submarine of the Royal Navy. *Resolution* is fitted with 16 tubes for the Polaris A-3 missile. (*Crown Copyright, MOD RN, London*)

(B) HMS *Superb* (S109) Swiftsure-class nuclear-powered fleet submarine of the Royal Navy, seen during contractor's trials in the Clyde Estuary with a Sea King helicopter overhead; June 1976 (*Crown Copyright, MOD RN, London*)

205(T) HMS *Churchill* (S46) Valiant-class nuclear powered fleet submarine of the Royal Navy with HMS *Renown* (SSBN) off the Scottish coast; October 1970 (*Crown Copyright, MOD RN, London*)

(B) HMS *Orpheus* (S11) Oberon-class patrol submarine of the Royal Navy in the Clyde Estuary; January 1978 (*Crown Copyright, MOD RN, London*)

206 HMS *Hermes* (R12) anti-submarine carrier of the Royal Navy entering the Grand Harbour at Malta; April 1977 (*Crown Copyright, MOD RN, London*)

207(T) HMS *Tiger* (C20) Tiger-class helicopter cruiser of the Royal Navy enters Rotterdam harbour during a visit to Holland. Behind is HMS *Hermes*; September 1974 (*Crown Copyright, MOD RN, London*)

(B) HMS *Kent* (D12) County-class guided-missile destroyer of the Royal Navy off Gibraltar; 1978 (*Crown Copyright, MOD RN, London*)

208 HMS *Newcastle* (D87) Type 42 guided-missile destroyer of the Royal Navy; March 1978 (*Crown Copyright, MOD RN, London*)

209(T) HMS *Ariadne* (F72) Broad-beamed Leander-class frigate of the Royal Navy; August 1977 (*Crown Copyright, MOD RN, London*)

(B) HMS *Jupiter* (F60) Broad-beamed Leander-class frigate of the Royal Navy (*Crown Copyright, MOD RN, London*)

210(T) HMS *Ashanti* (F117) Tribal-class frigate of the Royal Navy 1973 (*Crown Copyright, MOD RN, London*)

(B) HMS *Salisbury* (F32) Salisbury (Type 61) class frigate of the Royal Navy; December 1974 (*Crown Copyright, MOD RN, London*)

211 HMS *Fearless* (L10) LPD assault ship showing her stern door lowered and landing craft operating from the dock between the two hulls; 1973 (*Crown Copyright, MOD RN, London*)

212(T) HMS *Cuxton* (M1125) Ton-class coastal minesweeper of the Royal Navy leaves Faslane, Dumbartonshire, at the end of Clyde Week; July 1977 (*Crown Copyright, MOD RN, London*)

(B) HMS *Kingfisher* (P260) Bird-class large patrol craft of the Royal Navy leaving Rosyth; October 1975 (*Crown Copyright, MOD RN, London*)

213 Hawker Siddeley Sea Dart missiles on the Royal Navy Type 82 destroyer HMS *Bristol*; May 1975 (*Hawker Siddeley Dynamics, Herts*)

214(T) Seacat, a short-range ship-to-air defence system, capable of being deployed on even small craft (*Shorts, Belfast*)

(B) Final tests of a Tigerfish Mk 24 Mod 0 torpedo (*Crown Copyright, MOD, London*)

217(T) An artist's impression of the US Navy's Ohio-class nuclear ballistic missile submarine (*US Navy*)

(B) USS *Stonewall Jackson* (SSBN 634) Lafayette-class nuclear powered ballistic missile submarine of the US Navy during trials in 1964 (US Navy)

218(T) USS *George Washington* (SSBN 598) The US Navy's first nuclear powered fleet ballistic missile submarine (*General Dynamics, Electric Boat Div, Connecticut, USA*)

(B) USS *Los Angeles* (SSN 688) Los Angeles-class nuclear submarine of the US Navy during sea trials; September 1976 (*US Navy*)

219 USS *Glenard P Lipscomb* (SSN 685) Glenard P Lipscomb-class nuclear-powered submarine of the US Navy; November 1974 (*US Navy*)

220(T) USS *Flying Fish* (SSN 673) Sturgeon-class nuclear-powered fleet attack submarine of the US Navy, seen here on her first sea trials (*General Dynamics, Electric Boat Div, Connecticut, USA*)

(B) USS *Thresher* (SSN 593) Thresher-class nuclear-powered submarine of the US Navy; July 1961 (*US Navy*)

221 USS *Seawolf* (SSN 575) Seawolf-class nuclear-powered submarine of the US Navy cruising off Groton, Connecticut, USA; March 1957 (*US Navy*)

222(T) USS *Nautilus* (SSN 571), Nautilus-class, the world's first nuclear-powered submarine; 1975 (*US Navy*)

(B) USS *Nimitz* (CVN 68) Nimitz-class nuclear powered aircraft of the US Navy underway in the Atlantic during NATO exercises; August 1975 (*US Navy*)

223(T) USS *Enterprise* (CVN 65) Enterprise-class nuclear powered aircraft-carrier of the US Navy underway off Point Loma, California, USA; 21 June 1976 (*US Navy*)

(B) USS *John F Kennedy* (CVA 67) John F Kennedy-class aircraft-carrier of the US Navy underway in the Atlantic during manoeuvers; March 1969 (*US Navy*)

224(T) USS *Forrestal* (CV 59) Forrestal-class aircraft-carrier of the US Navy underway in the Mediterranean; August 1975 (*US Navy*)

(B) USS *Coral Sea* (CV 43) Midway-class aircraft carrier underway in the Gulf of Tonkin; May 1970 (*US Navy*)

226 USS *Truxtun* (CGN 35) Truxtun-class nuclear-powered guided missile cruiser of the US Navy underway off the coast of Oahu, Hawaii; July 1970 (*US Navy*)

227 USS *Bainbridge* (CGN 25) Bainbridge-class nuclear powered guided missile cruiser of the US Navy underway in the Pacific Ocean; 23 March 1971 (*US Navy*)

228(T) USS *Chicago* (CG 11) Albany-class guided missile cruiser of the US Navy underway in the Pacific Ocean; March 1971 (*US Navy*)

(B) USS *Oklahoma City* (CG 5) Converted Cleveland-class guided missile cruiser of the US Navy at sea; January 1976 (*US Navy*)

229 USS *Mitscher* (DDG 35) Mitscher-class guided missile destroyer of the US Navy underway off the coast of Guantanamo Bay, Cuba; 13 January 1975 (*US Navy*)

230 USS *Peterson* (DD 969) Spruance-class destroyer of the US Navy off Pascagoula, Mississippi, USA; July 1977 (*US Navy*)

231 *William R Rush* (DD 714) Gearing-class (FRAM I) destroyer of the US Navy underway in Narragansett Bay, Rhode Island, USA; March 1970 (*US Navy*)

232(T) USS *Brewton* (FF 1086) Knox-class frigate of the US Navy underway in the South China Sea; July 1975 (*US Navy*)

(B) USS *Garcia* (FF 1040) Garcia-class frigate underway; August 1972 (*US Navy*)

237(T) Deck-launch for a Northrop NT-37C torpedo during trials at the US Naval Torpedo Station, Keyport, Washington (*Northrop—Ventura Div., USA*)

(B) *18 de Julio* (DE 3) ex-US Dealey-class frigate of the Uruguayan Navy during joint US-South American manoeuvres Operation Unitas XIV in the Atlantic Ocean; November 1973 (*US Navy*)

238 Warships manoeuvring during joint US-Venezuelan exercises: the nearest vessel is the Venezuelan destroyer *Nueva Esparta* (D-11); September 1965 (*US Navy*)

239 *Congrio* (S22) Type 209 submarine of the Venezuelan Navy during trials off the German coast; 1976 (*Howaldtswerke, Kiel*)

240 *Federacion* (P-12) Vosper Thornycroft 121 ft-class fast missile attack craft of the Venezuelan Navy armed with two Otomat and one 40mm gun (*Vosper Thornycroft, Portsmouth*)

242 *Hessen* (D184) Hamburg-class destroyer of the Federal German Navy (*Federal German Navy, Wilhelmshaven*)

243(T) U 29 (S 178) Type 206 submarine of the Federal German Navy during trials; 1974 (*Howaldtswerke, Kiel*)

(B) S 62 (P 6112) Type 143 fast missile attack craft of the Federal German Navy (*Federal German Navy, Wilhelmshaven*)

244 *Frettchen* (P 6100) Zobel-class fast attack craft of the Federal German Navy (*Federal German Navy, Wilhelmshaven*)